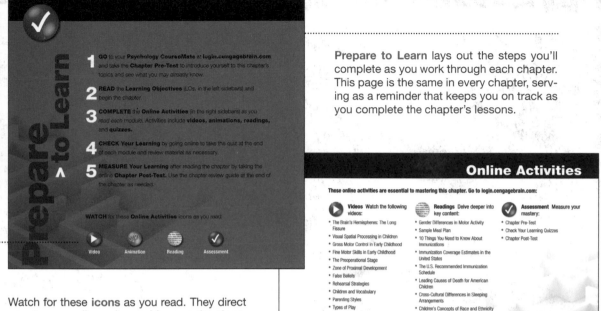

Prepare to Learn

1 **GO** to your **Psychology CourseMate** at login.cengagebrain.com and take the **Chapter Pre-Test** to introduce yourself to this chapter's topics and see what you may already know.

2 **READ** the **Learning Objectives** (LOs, in the left sidebars) and begin the chapter.

3 **COMPLETE** the **Online Activities** (in the right sidebars) as you read each module. Activities include **videos, animations, readings, and quizzes.**

4 **CHECK Your Learning** by going online to take the quiz at the end of each module and review material as necessary.

5 **MEASURE Your Learning** after reading the chapter by taking the online **Chapter Post-Test**. Use the chapter review guide at the end of the chapter as needed.

WATCH for these **Online Activities** icons as you read:

Video   Animation   Reading   Assessment

Prepare to Learn lays out the steps you'll complete as you work through each chapter. This page is the same in every chapter, serving as a reminder that keeps you on track as you complete the chapter's lessons.

Online Activities

These online activities are essential to mastering this chapter. Go to login.cengagebrain.com:

Videos Watch the following videos:
- The Brain's Hemispheres: The Long Fissure
- Visual Spatial Processing in Children
- Gross Motor Control in Early Childhood
- Fine Motor Skills in Early Childhood
- The Preoperational Stage
- Zone of Proximal Development
- False Beliefs
- Rehearsal Strategies
- Children and Vocabulary
- Parenting Styles
- Types of Play
- Gender Roles
- Relational Aggression

Animations Interact with and visualize important

Readings Delve deeper into key content:
- Gender Differences in Motor Activity
- Sample Meal Plan
- 10 Things You Need to Know About Immunizations
- Immunization Coverage Estimates in the United States
- The U.S. Recommended Immunization Schedule
- Leading Causes of Death for American Children
- Cross-Cultural Differences in Sleeping Arrangements
- Children's Concepts of Race and Ethnicity
- Highlights of the Preoperational Stage
- Research on Scaffolding
- Mixed-Aged Classrooms
- Helping Children Wisely Choose TV Programming

Assessment Measure your mastery:
- Chapter Pre-Test
- Check Your Learning Quizzes
- Chapter Post-Test

Watch for these **icons** as you read. They direct you to go online where videos, animations, additional reading, and quizzes illuminate the text discussion at hand. You'll be quizzed on information covered in these online activities when you take the chapter test, so be sure to complete them.

On the page next to **Prepare to Learn**, check out the resources you'll interact with online. In the chapter shown here, you'll see a video about types of play, interact with an animation about preoperational thought, explore gender stereotypes, and more.

PREPARE

TO LEARN

QUIZ SUMMARY

| CORRECT | 7 | INCORRECT | 18 | TOTAL ANSWERED | 25 | SCORE | 28% |

1. _____ is a condition that destroys cells in the brain, resulting in significant memory loss. ✔

2. The cause of Alzheimer's disease is: ✔

3. The result of fertilization of the mother's egg by the father's sperm is a(n) _____. ✔

4. What will happen when a recessive gene is paired with a dominant gene? ✔

5. The theory of evolution was postulated by which author of Origin of Species? ✔

6. Accidental errors in genetic instructions that produce changes are called _____. ✘

Accidental errors in genetic instructions that produce changes are called _____.

- a. genetic misprints
- ✖ b. adaptations ✖
- c. mutations
- d. polymorphisms

Incorrect. Adaptations are common features of a species that provide it with improved function.

7. Of the 1 trillion cells that make up your brain, approximately 900 billion of them are _____. ✔

8. A(n) _____ is a brain cell with two specialized extensions. ✔

9. The neuron's genetic instructions are contained in the _____ of the cell body ✘

Screenshots are for illustrative purposes only; content may be from other courses.

Step 1 when you begin a new chapter is to go to **Psychology CourseMate** at **login.cengagebrain.com** and take the **Chapter Pre-Test** to introduce yourself to the chapter's topics. Seeing your correct and incorrect answers will help you identify topics to pay particular attention to in the chapter—and those that may not require as much attention. You may already know more than you think you do!

Each chapter is divided into several brief learning modules. **Learning Objectives (LOs)** appear in the upper left sidebar throughout each module. They keep you focused by highlighting what you are expected to learn in the pages that immediately follow. Study each objective, and then read the accompanying narrative.

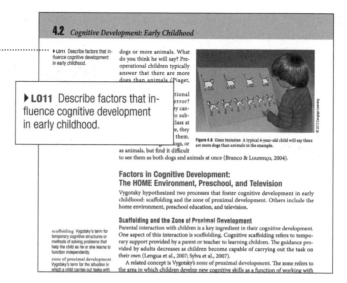

▶ LO11 Describe factors that influence cognitive development in early childhood.

dogs or more animals. What do you think he will say? Preoperational children typically answer that there are more dogs than animals (Piaget,

▶ **LO11** Describe factors that influence cognitive development in early childhood.

tional error? ey can- o sub- class at e, they them. ogs, or as animals, but find it difficult to see them as both dogs and animals at once (Branco & Lourenço, 2004).

Figure 4.8 Class Inclusion A typical 4-year-old child will say there are more dogs than animals in the example.

Factors in Cognitive Development: The HOME Environment, Preschool, and Television

Vygotsky hypothesized two processes that foster cognitive development in early childhood: scaffolding and the zone of proximal development. Others include the home environment, preschool education, and television.

Scaffolding and the Zone of Proximal Development

scaffolding Vygotsky's term for temporary cognitive structures or methods of solving problems that help the child as he or she learns to function independently.

zone of proximal development Vygotsky's term for the situation in which a child carries out tasks with

Parental interaction with children is a key ingredient in their cognitive development. One aspect of this interaction is scaffolding. Cognitive scaffolding refers to temporary support provided by a parent or teacher to learning children. The guidance provided by adults decreases as children become capable of carrying out the task on their own (Lengua et al., 2007; Sylva et al., 2007).

A related concept is Vygotsky's zone of proximal development. The zone refers to the area in which children develop new cognitive skills as a function of working with

WANT TO READ ONLINE? READ THE EBOOK!

Psychology CourseMate gives you access to an electronic version of this text. You can read the text, take notes, get one-click access to all of the online resources—and do your homework wherever there's a computer.

2

FOCUS ON

THE TEXT

③ INTERACT

ONLINE

For example, girls perceive other girls as nicer, more hardworking, and less selfish than boys. Boys, on the other hand, think that they are nicer, more hardworking, and less selfish than girls (Matlin, 2008; C. F. Miller et al., 2006).

Gender Differences

Clearly, females and males are anatomically different. And according to gender-role stereotypes, people believe that females and males also differ in their behaviors, personality characteristics, and abilities (Amanatullah & Morris, 2010; Lippa, 2010). Gender differences in infancy are small and rather inconsistent. Preschoolers display some

Gender Stereotypes
Explore a world view of gender stereotypes.

Gender Roles and Children
Watch and learn more about how children view gender.

Remember the icons on the **Prepare to Learn** page? They always appear in the lower right sidebars throughout each module, prompting you to go online to enhance your understanding of text discussions through videos, animations, and readings.

▶ Video: Gender Roles and Children

Module 4.4: LO26: Discuss the development of gender roles

You'll view and interact with online resources many times as you work through each chapter. You may find them so interesting that you won't even know you're studying.

Fears: The Horrors of Early Childhood

Children's fears change as they move from infancy into the preschool years. The number of fears seems to peak between 2½ and 4 years and then tapers off (S. M. Miller et al., 1990). The preschool period is marked by a decline in fears of loud noises, falling, sudden movement, and strangers. In Erikson's view, fear of violating parental prohibitions can be a powerful force in the life of a young child, but preschoolers are most likely to fear animals, imaginary creatures, the dark, and personal danger, not social disapproval (A. P. Field, 2006; Muris et al., 2003). The fantasies of young children frequently involve stories they are told and media imagery. Although fears taper off after the age of 4, many preschoolers are reluctant to have the lights turned off at night for fear that imaginary creatures may assault them. Real objects and situations also cause many preschoolers to fear for their safety—lightning, thunder, other loud noises, high places, sharp objects, blood, unfamiliar people, and stinging and crawling insects.

During middle childhood, children become less fearful of imaginary creatures, but fears of bodily harm and injury remain common. Children grow more fearful of failure and criticism in school and in social relationships (Ollendick & King, 1991).

This **Check Your Learning Quiz** icon signifies that you've reached the end of a module.

✓
Check Your Learning Quiz 4.3
Go to **login.cengagebrain.com**
and take the online quiz.

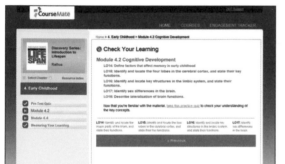

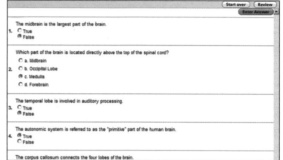

Go online and take this self-study quiz to make sure you "get it" (in other words, that you can demonstrate your understanding of the module's learning objectives).

For the questions you miss, go back and review the text and related online materials before you move on. Reviewing is also a great way to ensure that what you've just learned "sinks in."

CHECK
YOUR LEARNING

4

⑤ MEASURE

After reading each chapter, find out how well you've absorbed the material in all of the modules by taking the online **Chapter Post-Test.** Results go to your instructor's gradebook, so take your time and answer carefully. Your results, tied to **Learning Objectives**, will also help you identify areas that require further review so you can overcome weak areas and prepare more effectively for course exams.

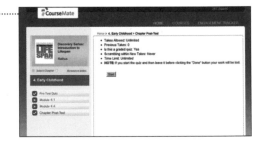

GO to your Psychology CourseMate at login.cengagebrain.com and take the Chapter Post-Test to see which Learning Objectives you've mastered and which need more review. Use the chapter review guide below and the online activities—including flashcards to review key terms—to measure your learning.

Module		Learning Objectives
4.1 Physical Development: Early Childhood 192		
Growth Patterns	LO1	Describe physical changes during early childhood.
	LO2	Explain what it means to be left-brained or right-brained.
	LO3	Discuss plasticity of the brain.
Motor Development	LO4	Describe the development of motor skills in early childhood.
	LO5	Discuss handedness.
Nutrition	LO6	Describe nutritional needs in early childhood.
Health and Illness	LO7	Describe health problems during early childhood.
Sleep	LO8	Discuss sleep during early childhood.
Elimination Disorders	LO9	Discuss elimination problems.

The **Measure Your Learning** chart simplifies study and review by providing an at-a-glance summary of **Learning Objectives**, key terms, important online media resources, and page references to discussions of key topics.

4.1 Physical Development: Early Childhood 192		
Growth Patterns	LO1	Describe physical changes during early childhood.
	LO2	Explain what it means to be left-brained or right-brained.

Let's say your **Post-Test** indicates that you should review the material on growth patterns. In a snap, you can see the text page on which the discussion begins. If you aced the **Post-Test**, you're done with the chapter.

GET STARTED FOR REAL

Now that you've got the hang of how *Discovery Series: Introduction to Lifespan* works, it's time to get started for real. Use the printed card on the inside front cover of this text to register at **login.cengagebrain.com**. Good luck!

Author Spencer A. Rathus would like to extend his appreciation to the focus group participants and to the reviewers of this project for their time, opinions, and helpful suggestions.

Reviewers

Nancy Ashton, *Richard Stockton College of New Jersey*
Marisa Beeble, *The Sage Colleges*
Bruce Caine, *Belmont University*
Drew Curtis, *Lonestar Community College*
Loretta Duncan, *Lord Fairfax Community College*
Mark Evans, *Tarrant County College*
Gabriel Feldmar, *Nassau Community College*
Lara Fields, *Salt Lake Community College*
Jenny Fredricks, *Connecticut College*
Shawn Haake, *Iowa Central Community College*
John S. Klein, *Carleton State College*
Jeremy Long, *Brevard Community College*
Donna Mantooth, *Georgia Highlands College*
Rajni Nair, *Arizona State University*
Ian Payton, *Bethune Cookman University*
Kelly Spillman, *Gwinnett Technical College*
Courtney Stein, *Colby-Sawyer College*
Kathy Trotter, *Chattanooga State Community College*

Focus Group Participants

Kenneth Foster, *Texas Woman's University*
David Giles, *Tarrant County College*
Lois Herrin, *Brookhaven College*
Regina Hughes, *Collin College*
Franz Klutschkowski, *North Central Texas College*
Tracy Meyer, *Collin College*
Cynthia Reed, *Tarrant County College*
Karl Robinson, *Tarrant County College*

About the Author

Spencer A. Rathus, who received his Ph.D. from the University at Albany, is on the faculty of The College of New Jersey. His research interests include treatment of obesity and eating disorders, smoking cessation, human growth and development, methods of therapy, and sexual dysfunctions. He is the author of the widely used Rathus Assertiveness Schedule and has written several college textbooks, including *Psychology: Concepts and Connections, AIDS: What Every Student Needs to Know, Human Sexuality in a World of Diversity,* and *Childhood and Adolescence: Voyages in Development.*

DISCOVERY SERIES

INTRODUCTION TO
LIFE SPAN

Spencer A. Rathus
The College of New Jersey

WADSWORTH
CENGAGE Learning·

Australia • Brazil • Japan • Korea • Mexico • Singapore • Spain • United Kingdom • United States

WADSWORTH
CENGAGE Learning®

Discovery Series:
Introduction to Lifespan
Spencer A. Rathus

Publisher: Jon-David Hague

Executive Psychology Editor: Jaime Perkins

Developmental Editor: Tangelique Williams

Sr. Editorial Assistant: Jessica Alderman

Assistant Editor: Lauren Moody

Media Editor: Lauren Keyes

Marketing Manager: Christine Sosa

Marketing Communications Manager:
    Laura Localio

Sr. Content Project Manager: Rita Jaramillo

Design Director: Rob Hugel

Art Director: Vernon Boes

Print Buyer: Karen Hunt

Rights Acquisitions Specialist:
    Dean Dauphinais

Production Service: Graphic World Inc.

Text Designer: Irene Morris

Photo Researcher: Bill Smith Group

Text Researcher: Ashley Liening

Copy Editor: Graphic World Inc.

Illustrator: Graphic World Inc.

Cover Designer: Irene Morris

Compositor: Graphic World Inc.

For product information and technology assistance, contact us at
Cengage Learning Customer & Sales Support, 1-800-354-9706.

For permission to use material from this text or product,
submit all requests online at **www.cengage.com/permissions.**
Further permissions questions can be e-mailed to
permissionrequest@cengage.com.

Library of Congress Control Number: 2012931273

ISBN-13: 978-0-8400-3006-1

ISBN-10: 0-8400-3006-1

Wadsworth
20 Davis Drive
Belmont, CA 94002-3098
USA

Cengage Learning is a leading provider of customized learning solutions with office locations around the globe, including Singapore, the United Kingdom, Australia, Mexico, Brazil, and Japan. Locate your local office at **www.cengage.com/global.**

Cengage Learning products are represented in Canada by Nelson Education, Ltd.

To learn more about Wadsworth, visit **www.cengage.com/Wadsworth**

Purchase any of our products at your local college store or at our preferred online store **www.CengageBrain.com.**

Printed in the United States of America
1 2 3 4 5 6 7 16 15 14 13 12

Brief Contents

Contents

What Is Life-Span Development? 1

2 *Beginnings* 38

4 *Early Childhood* 188

6 *Adolescence* 340

 Prepare to Learn   342

Measure Your Learning   400

7 *Early Adulthood* 404

 Prepare to Learn 470

 Measure Your Learning 522

9 *Late Adulthood* 526

What Is Life-Span Development?

1

Chapter Outline and Learning Objectives

Prepare ^ to Learn

1 **GO** to your **Psychology CourseMate** at **login.cengagebrain.com** and take the **Chapter Pre-Test** to introduce yourself to this chapter's topics and see what you may already know.

2 **READ** the **Learning Objectives** (LOs, in the left sidebars) and begin the chapter.

3 **COMPLETE** the **Online Activities** (in the right sidebars) *as you read each module.* Activities include **videos, animations, readings,** and **quizzes.**

4 **CHECK Your Learning** by going online to take the quiz at the end of each module and review material as necessary.

5 **MEASURE Your Learning** after reading the chapter by taking the online **Chapter Post-Test.** Use the chapter review guide at the end of the chapter as needed.

WATCH for these **Online Activities** icons as you read:

Video   Animation   Reading   Assessment

These online activities are essential to mastering this chapter. Go to login.cengagebrain.com:

Videos Watch the following videos:

- A Tour of the Skinner Box
- Current Views of the Skinner Box
- "Little Albert"

Animations Interact with and visualize important processes, timelines, and concepts:

- Schematic Representation of Classical Conditioning
- Positive versus Negative Reinforcers
- Negative Reinforcers versus Punishments
- The Experiential Method

Readings Delve deeper into key content:

- The Bell-and-Pad Method for Treating Bed-Wetting
- Operant Conditioning of Vocalizations in Infants
- Influence of the Macrosystem on the Development of Independence
- Perspectives on Development
- The Conditioning of "Little Albert": A Case Study in Ethics

Assessment Measure your mastery:

- Chapter Pre-Test
- Check Your Learning Quizzes
- Chapter Post-Test

Did you know that—

- During the Middle Ages, children were often treated as miniature adults?
- Although some mental abilities decline as we age, others can grow for a lifetime?
- Sigmund Freud believed that nail biting and cigarette smoking are signs of conflict experienced during early childhood?
- Many developmental experts argue that children should not be punished?
- Jean Piaget believed that small children who squish their food and laugh enthusiastically are acting as budding scientists?
- Birds raised in isolation from other birds build nests during the mating season even though they have never seen a nest or seen another bird building one?

▼

This book has a story to tell. An important story. A remarkable story. It is your story. It is about the amazing journey you have already taken through childhood. It is about the unfolding of your adult life. Billions of people have made this journey before. You have much in common with them. Yet you are unique in your personal genetic heritage, your experiences, and your outlook on life—and things will happen to you, and because of you, that have never happened before.

The Development of the Study of Development

Scientific inquiry into human development has existed for little more than a century. In ancient times and in the Middle Ages, children often were viewed as innately evil and discipline was harsh. Legally, medieval children were treated as property and servants. They could be sent to the monastery, married without consultation, and convicted of crimes. Children were nurtured until they were 7 years old, which was considered the "age of reason"; then they were expected to work alongside adults in the home and in the field.

The Study of Child and Adolescent Development

The transition to modern thinking about children is marked by the writings of philosophers such as John Locke and Jean-Jacques Rousseau. Locke (1632–1704), an

Englishman, believed that the child came into the world as a *tabula rasa*—a "blank tablet" or clean slate—that was written on by experience. He did not believe that inborn predispositions toward good or evil play an important role in the conduct of the child. Instead, he focused on the roles of the environment and of experience. Locke believed that social approval and disapproval are powerful shapers of behavior. But Rousseau (1712–1778), a Swiss-French philosopher, argued that children are inherently good and that, if allowed to express their natural impulses, they will develop into generous and moral individuals.

During the Industrial Revolution—a period from the latter eighteenth through the nineteenth centuries when machine-based production replaced much manual labor—family came to be defined in terms of the nuclear unit of mother, father, and children rather than the extended family. Children became more visible, fostering awareness of childhood as a special time of life. Still, children often labored in factories from dawn to dusk through the early years of the twentieth century.

In the twentieth century, laws were passed to protect children from strenuous labor, to require that they attend school until a certain age, and to prevent them from getting married or being sexually exploited. Whereas children were once considered the property of parents, laws now protect them from abuse by parents and other adults. In addition, juvenile courts see that children who break the law receive treatment in the criminal justice system.

Pioneers in the Study of Child Development

Various thoughts about child development coalesced into a field of scientific study in the nineteenth and early twentieth centuries. G. Stanley Hall (1844–1924) is credited with founding child development as an academic discipline and bringing scientific attention to focus on the period of adolescence. By the start of the twentieth century, child development had emerged as a scientific field of study. Soon major theories of the developing child were proposed by theorists such as Arnold Gesell, Sigmund Freud, John B. Watson, and Jean Piaget.

Fuse/Getty Images

1.1 *Theories of Development*

▶ **LO2** Discuss Freud's theory of psychosexual development.

The Study of Adult Development

Developmental psychology is the discipline that studies the physical, cognitive, social, and emotional development of humans. It focuses on the many influences on behavior, including the effects of the person's physical, social, and cultural environment, and how these factors interact to influence the developments that occur over time. The traditional focus of developmental psychologists was on childhood and adolescence because of the dramatic physical and cognitive changes that occur during those years. But in the twentieth century, psychologists began to take on a **life-span perspective**, in which they studied the biological, cognitive, social, and emotional changes across the entire life span.

William Perry and Gisela Labouvie-Vief, for example, have studied the development of cognitive complexity from adolescence to late adulthood. K. W Schaie and others have studied trends in various mental abilities throughout middle and late adulthood, showing that some abilities decline in middle and late adulthood but that others represent the accumulation of decades of knowledge and can advance into late adulthood. Though young adulthood is the time of peak physical development, people perform at their best on some of the most complex intellectual tasks during midlife, and many people are most well-adjusted during late adulthood.

Theories of Development

Give me a dozen healthy infants, well-formed, and my own specified world to bring them up in, and I'll guarantee to train them to become any type of specialist I might suggest—doctor, lawyer, merchant, chief, and, yes, even beggar and thief, regardless of their talents, penchants, tendencies, abilities, vocations, and the race of their ancestors.
—John B. Watson, 1924, p. 82

Theories are formulations of apparent relationships among observed events. They allow us to derive explanations and predictions. Many psychological theories combine statements about behavior (such as reflexes), mental processes (such as whether infants intend to engage in reflexes), and biological processes (such as maturation of the nervous system). A satisfactory theory allows us to predict behavior. For example, a theory about a reflex should allow us to predict the age at which it will drop out or be replaced by intentional behavior. John B. Watson (1878–1958), the founder of American **behaviorism**, viewed development in terms of learning theory. He generally agreed with Locke that children's ideas, preferences, and skills are shaped by

developmental psychology The discipline that studies the physical, cognitive, social, and emotional development of humans.

life-span perspective The perspective in which psychologists study the biological, cognitive, social, and emotional changes across the life span.

behaviorism Watson's view that science must study observable behavior only and investigate relationships between stimuli and responses.

maturation The unfolding of genetically determined traits, structures, and functions.

psychosexual development The process by which libidinal energy is expressed through different erogenous zones during different stages of development.

stage theory A theory of development characterized by distinct periods of life.

experience. There has been a long-standing nature–nurture debate in the study of children—that is, developmentalists have argued whether one's genetic heritage (nature) or one's experiences (nurture), including nourishment and education, have a greater influence on children. In his theoretical approach to understanding children, Watson came down on the side of nurture—the importance of the physical and social environments—as found, for example, in parental training and approval.

Arnold Gesell expressed the opposing idea that biological **maturation** is the main principle of development: "All things considered, the inevitability and surety of maturation are the most impressive characteristics of early development. It is the hereditary ballast which conserves and stabilizes growth of each individual infant" (Gesell, 1928, p. 378). Watson was talking about the behavior patterns that children develop, whereas Gesell was focusing mainly on physical aspects of growth and development.

Theories such as behavioral theory and maturational theory help developmentalists explain, predict, and influence the events they study. Let's consider theories that are popular among developmentalists today. They fall within broad perspectives on development.

The Psychoanalytic Perspective

A number of theories of development fall within the psychoanalytic perspective. Each owes its origin to Sigmund Freud and views children—and adults—as caught in conflict. Early in development, the conflict is between the child and the world outside. The expression of basic drives, such as sex and aggression, conflicts with parental expectations, social rules, moral codes, even laws. But the external limits—parental demands and social rules—are brought inside or *internalized*. Once internalization occurs, the conflict takes place between opposing *inner* forces. The child's observable behavior, thoughts, and feelings reflect the outcomes of these hidden battles.

Let's consider Freud's theory of **psychosexual development** and Erik Erikson's theory of psychosocial development. Each is a **stage theory** that sees children as developing through distinct periods of life. Each suggests that experiences during early stages affect the child's emotional and social life at the time and later on.

Sigmund Freud's Theory of Psychosexual Development

Sigmund Freud's (1856–1939) theory of psychosexual development focused on emotional and social development and on the origins of psychological traits such as dependence, obsessive neatness, and vanity. Freud theorized three parts of the personality: the *id, ego,* and *superego.* The id is present at birth and *unconscious.* It represents biological drives and demands instant gratification, as suggested by a baby's wailing. The ego, or the conscious sense of self, begins to develop when children learn to obtain gratification consciously, without screaming or crying. The ego curbs the appetites of the id and makes plans that are in keeping with social conventions so that a person can find gratification but avoid social disapproval. The superego blossoms throughout infancy and early childhood, although people have the capacity for conscience to develop throughout a lifetime. It brings inward the wishes and morals of the child's caregivers and other members of the community. Throughout the remainder of the child's life, the superego will monitor the intentions and behavior of the ego, hand down judgments of right and wrong, and attempt to influence behavior through flooding the person with feelings of guilt and shame when the judgment is in the negative.

According to Freud, there are five stages of psychosexual development: *oral, anal, phallic, latency,* and *genital.* If a child receives too little or too much gratification during a stage, the child can become *fixated* in that stage. For example, during the first year of life, which Freud termed the *oral stage,* "oral" activities such as sucking and biting bring pleasure and gratification. If the child is weaned early or breast-fed too long, the child may become fixated on oral activities such as nail biting or smoking, or may even show a "biting wit."

In the second, or *anal,* stage, gratification is obtained through control and elimination of waste products. Excessively strict or permissive toilet training can lead to the development of anal-retentive traits, such as perfectionism and neatness, or anal-expulsive traits, such as sloppiness and carelessness. In the third stage, the *phallic stage,* parent–child conflict may develop over masturbation, which many parents treat with punishment and threats. It is also normal during the phallic stage for children to develop a strong sexual attachment to the parent of the opposite sex and to begin to view the parent of the same sex as a rival.

By age 5 or 6, Freud believed, children enter a *latency stage* during which sexual feelings remain unconscious and children turn to schoolwork and typically prefer playmates of their own gender. The final stage of psychosexual development, the *genital stage,* begins with the biological changes that usher in adolescence. Adolescents generally desire sexual gratification through intercourse with a member of the other gender. Freud believed that oral or anal stimulation, masturbation, and male–

psychosocial development
Erikson's theory emphasizing the importance of social relationships and conscious choice throughout eight stages of development.

life crisis An internal conflict that attends each stage of psychosocial development.

male or female–female sexual activity are immature forms of sexual conduct that reflect fixations at early stages of development.

Evaluation Freud's views about the anal stage have influenced child-care workers to recommend that toilet training not be started too early or handled punitively. His emphasis on the emotional needs of children has influenced educators to be more sensitive to the possible emotional reasons behind a child's misbehavior. Freud's work has also been criticized. For one thing, Freud developed his theory on the basis of contacts with adult patients (mostly women) (D. P. Schultz & Schultz, 2008), rather than observing children directly. Freud may also have inadvertently guided patients into expressing ideas that confirmed

Sigmund Freud

his views. Psychology is a science, and, as we will see, the rules of evidence require that researchers collect information in an unbiased manner.

Some of Freud's own disciples, including Erik Erikson, believed that Freud placed too much emphasis on basic instincts and unconscious motives. Erikson argued that people are motivated not only by drives such as sex and aggression but also by social relationships and conscious desires to achieve, to have aesthetic experiences, and to help others.

Erik Erikson's Theory of Psychosocial Development

Erik Erikson (1902–1994) modified Freud's theory and extended it through the adult years (see Table 1.1). Erikson's theory, like Freud's, focuses on the development of the emotional life and psychological traits, but Erikson focused on social relationships rather than sexual or aggressive instincts. Therefore, Erikson spoke of **psychosocial development** rather than of *psychosexual development*. Furthermore, Erikson placed greater emphasis on the ego, or the sense of self. Erikson (1963) extended Freud's five stages to eight to include the concerns of adulthood. Rather than label his stages after parts of the body, Erikson labeled them after the **life crisis** that people might encounter during that stage.

Erikson proposed that social relationships and physical maturation give each stage its character. For example, the parent–child relationship and the infant's dependence and helplessness are responsible for the nature of the earliest stages of development.

Early experiences affect future developments. With parental support, most children resolve early life crises productively. Successful resolution of each crisis bolsters their sense of identity—of who they are and what they stand for—and their expectation of future success.

Erikson's views, like Freud's, have influenced child rearing, early childhood education, and child therapy. For example, Erikson's views about an adolescent **identity crisis** have entered the popular culture and have affected the way many parents and teachers deal with teenagers. Some schools help students master the crisis by means of life-adjustment courses and study units on self-understanding in social studies and literature classes.

Erik Erikson

Ted Streshinsky/Time Life Pictures/Getty Images

Evaluation Erikson's views are appealing in that they emphasize the importance of human consciousness and choice. They are also appealing in that they portray us as prosocial and helpful, whereas Freud portrayed us as selfish and needing to be compelled to comply with social rules. There is also some empirical support for Erikson's view that positive outcomes of early life crises help put us on the path to positive development (Hoegh & Bourgeois, 2002).

The Learning Perspective

Psychologists derived an ingenious method for helping 5- and 6-year-old children overcome bed-wetting from the behavioral perspective. Most children at this age wake up and go to the bathroom when their bladders are full. Bed-wetters, though, sleep through bladder tension and reflexively urinate in bed. With this method, the psychologists placed a special pad beneath the sleeping child. Wetness in the pad closed an electrical circuit, causing a bell to ring and wake the sleeping child. After several repetitions, most children learned to wake up before they wet the pad. How? They learned through a technique called *classical conditioning*, which is explained in this section.

identity crisis According to Erikson, a period of inner conflict during which one examines one's values and makes decisions about one's life roles.

Table 1.1
Comparison of Freud's and Erikson's Stages of Development

Age	Freud's Stages of Psychosexual Development	Erikson's Stages of Psychosocial Development
Birth to 1 year	**Oral stage.** Gratification derives from oral activities, such as sucking. Fixation leads to development of oral traits such as dependence, depression, and gullibility.	**Trust vs. mistrust.** The developmental task is to come to trust the key caregivers, primarily the mother, and the environment. It is desirable for the infant to connect its environment with inner feelings of satisfaction and contentment.
About 1 to 3 years	**Anal stage.** Gratification derives from anal activities involving elimination. Fixation leads to development of anal-retentive traits (e.g., excessive neatness) or anal-expulsive traits (e.g., sloppiness).	**Autonomy vs. shame and doubt.** The developmental task is to develop the desire to make choices and the self-control to regulate one's behavior so that choices can be actualized.
About 3 to 6 years	**Phallic stage.** Gratification derives from stimulation of the genital region. Oedipus and Electra complexes emerge and are resolved. Fixation leads to development of phallic traits, such as vanity.	**Initiative vs. guilt.** The developmental task is to add initiative—planning and attacking—to choice. The preschooler is on the move and becomes proactive.
About 6 to 12 years	**Latency stage.** Sexual impulses are suppressed, allowing the child to focus on development of social and technological skills.	**Industry vs. inferiority.** The developmental task is to become absorbed in the development and implementation of skills, to master the basics of technology, and to become productive.

Continued

▶ **LO3** Discuss the behaviorist perspective on development.

Age	Freud's Stages of Psychosexual Development	Erikson's Stages of Psychosocial Development
Adolescence	**Genital stage.** Reappearance of sexual impulses, with gratification sought through sexual relations with an adult of the other sex.	**Identity vs. role diffusion.** The developmental task is to associate one's skills and social roles with the development of career goals. More broadly, the development of identity refers to a sense of who one is and what one believes in.
Young adulthood	**Genital stage continues…**	**Intimacy vs. isolation.** The developmental task is to commit oneself to another person, to engage in a mature sexual love.
Middle adulthood		**Generativity vs. stagnation.** The developmental task is to appreciate the opportunity to "give back." Not only are generative people creative, but they also give encouragement and guidance to the younger generation, which may include their own children.
Late adulthood		**Ego integrity vs. despair.** The developmental task is to achieve wisdom and dignity in the face of declining physical abilities. Ego integrity also means accepting the time and place of one's own life cycle.

classical conditioning A simple form of learning in which one stimulus comes to bring forth the response usually brought forth by a second stimulus by being paired repeatedly with the second stimulus.

operant conditioning A simple form of learning in which an organism learns to engage in behavior that is reinforced.

reinforcement The process of providing stimuli following responses to increase the frequency of the responses.

The so-called bell-and-pad method for overcoming bed-wetting is an exotic example of the application of learning theory in human development. Most applications of learning theory to development are found in everyday events, however. In this section, we consider two theories of learning: behaviorism and social cognitive theory.

Behaviorism

John B. Watson argued that a scientific approach to development must focus only on observable behavior and not on things like thoughts, fantasies, and other mental images.

Classical conditioning is a simple form of learning in which an originally neutral stimulus comes to bring forth, or elicit, the response usually brought forth by a second stimulus as a result of being paired repeatedly with the second stimulus. In the bell-and-pad method for eliminating bed-wetting, psychologists repeatedly pair tension in the children's bladders with a stimulus that awakens them (the bell). The children learn to respond to the bladder tension as if it were a bell; that is, they wake up (see Figure 1.1).

Behaviorists argue that much emotional learning is acquired through classical conditioning. In **operant conditioning** (a different kind of conditioning), children learn to do something because of its effects. B. F. Skinner introduced the key concept of **reinforcement**. Reinforcers are stimuli that increase the frequency of the behavior they follow. Most children learn to adjust their behavior to conform to social codes and rules to earn reinforcers such as the attention and approval of their parents and teachers. Other children, ironically, may learn to misbehave because misbehavior also draws attention.

© Bettmann/Corbis

John B. Watson

Nina Leen/Time Life Pictures/Getty Images

B. F. Skinner

The Bell-and-Pad Method

Explore research on treating bed-wetting with the bell-and-pad method.

Classical Conditioning

Explore an interactive version of Figure 1.1.

Positive vs. Negative Reinforcers

Explore an interactive version of Figure 1.2 to see how positive and negative reinforcers impact behavior.

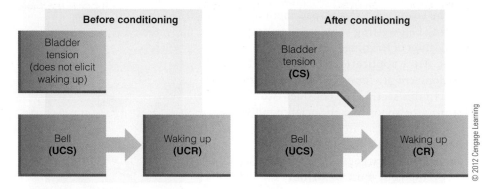

Figure 1.1 Schematic Representation of Classical Conditioning Before conditioning, the bell is an unlearned or unconditioned stimulus that elicits waking up, which is an unlearned or unconditioned response. Bladder tension does not elicit waking up, which is the problem. During the conditioning procedure, bladder tension repeatedly precedes urination, which in turn causes the bell to ring. After several repetitions, bladder tension has become associated with the bell, making bladder tension into a learned or conditioned stimulus that causes the child to awaken. Awakening in response to bladder tension is a learned or conditioned response.

Any stimulus that increases the frequency of the responses preceding it serves as a reinforcer. Skinner distinguished between positive and negative reinforcers. **Positive reinforcers** increase the frequency of behaviors when they are *applied*. Food and approval usually serve as positive reinforcers. **Negative reinforcers** increase the frequency of behaviors when they are *removed*. Fear acts as a negative reinforcer in that its removal increases the frequency of the behaviors preceding it. Figure 1.2 compares positive and negative reinforcers.

Extinction results from repeated performance of operant behavior without reinforcement. After a number of trials, the operant behavior no longer occurs. Children's temper tantrums and crying at bedtime can often be extinguished by parents' remaining out of the bedroom after the children have been put to bed. Punishments are aversive events that suppress or *decrease* the frequency of the behavior they follow. (Figure 1.3 compares negative reinforcers with punishments.) Many learning theorists agree that punishment is undesirable in rearing children because punishment does not in itself suggest an alternative acceptable form of behavior; punishment tends to suppress behavior only when its delivery is guaranteed; and punishment can create feelings of anger and hostility.

positive reinforcer A reinforcer that, when applied, increases the frequency of a response.

negative reinforcer A reinforcer that, when removed, increases the frequency of a response.

extinction The cessation of a response that is performed in the absence of reinforcement.

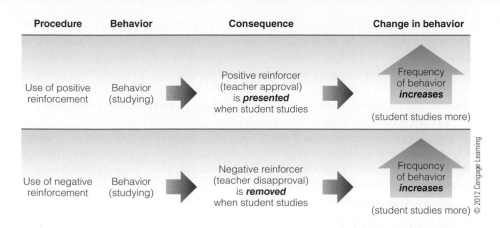

Figure 1.2 Positive Versus Negative Reinforcers All reinforcers *increase* the frequency of behavior. In these examples, teacher approval functions as a positive reinforcer when students study harder because of it. Teacher *disapproval* functions as a negative reinforcer when its *removal* increases the frequency of studying.

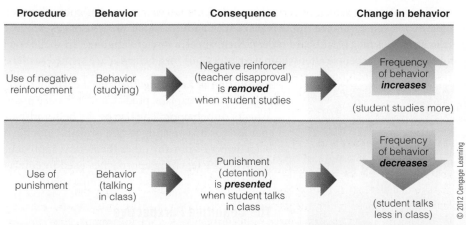

Figure 1.3 Negative Reinforcers Versus Punishments Both negative reinforcers and punishments tend to be aversive stimuli. Reinforcers, however, *increase* the frequency of the behavior—in the case of negative reinforcers, when they are *removed*. Punishments *decrease* the frequency of the behavior.

The Skinner Box

Tour a Skinner box and learn more about operant conditioning.

Current Views of the Skinner Box

Watch and learn more about the operant chamber.

Vocalizations in Infants

Explore research on the operant conditioning of vocalizations in infants.

Negative Reinforcers

Observe the differences between negative reinforcers and punishments in an interactive version of Figure 1.3.

▶ **LO4** Discuss the social cognitive perspective on development.

▶ **LO5** Discuss Piaget's concepts and his stages of cognitive development.

Research suggests that when teachers praise and attend to appropriate behavior and ignore misbehavior, studying and classroom behavior improve while disruptive and aggressive behaviors decrease (McIlvane & Dube, 2003; M. Takahashi & Sugiyama, 2003). By ignoring misbehavior or by using *time-out* from positive reinforcement, we can avoid reinforcing misbehavior in children. In time-out, children are placed in drab, restrictive environments for a specified time period, such as 10 minutes, when they behave disruptively.

Operant conditioning is used every day in the *socialization* of young children. Parents and peers influence children to acquire gender-appropriate behaviors through the elaborate use of rewards and punishments. Thus, boys may ignore other boys when they play with dolls and housekeeping toys but play with boys when they use transportation toys.

Social Cognitive Theory

social cognitive theory A cognitively oriented learning theory that emphasizes observational learning.

cognitive-developmental theory The stage theory that holds that the child's abilities to mentally represent the world and solve problems unfold as a result of the interaction of experience and the maturation of neurological structures.

scheme An action pattern or mental structure that is involved in the acquisition and organization of knowledge.

adaptation The interaction between the organism and the environment, consisting of assimilation and accommodation.

assimilation The incorporation of new events or knowledge into existing schemes.

accommodation The modification of existing schemes to permit the incorporation of new events or knowledge.

Behaviorists tend to limit their view of learning to conditioning. **Social cognitive theorists,** such as Albert Bandura (1986, 2006a, 2006b), have shown that much learning also occurs through observing other people, reading, and viewing characters in the media. People may need practice to refine their skills, but they can acquire the basic know-how through observation.

Observational learning occurs when children observe how parents cook, clean, or repair a broken appliance. It takes place when adults watch supervisors sketch out sales strategies on a blackboard or hear them speak a foreign language. In social cognitive theory, the people after whom we pattern our own behavior are termed *models*.

Jon Brenneis/Life Magazine/Time & Life Pictures/Getty Images

Albert Bandura

Evaluation of Learning Theories Learning theories allow us to explain, predict, and influence many aspects of behavior. The use of the bell-and-pad method for bed-wetting would probably not have been derived from any other theoretical approach. Many of the teaching approaches used in educational TV shows are based on learning theory.

The Cognitive Perspective

Cognitive theorists focus on people's mental processes. They investigate the ways in which children perceive and mentally represent the world, how they develop thinking, logic, and problem-solving ability. **Cognitive-developmental theory**, originated by Swiss biologist Jean Piaget (1896–1980), is the best-known cognitive perspective on development.

Cognitive-Developmental Theory

Early in his career, Jean Piaget obtained a job at the Binet Institute in Paris, where research on intelligence tests was being conducted. Through his studies, Piaget realized that when children answered questions incorrectly, their wrong answers still often reflected consistent—although illogical—mental processes. Piaget regarded children as natural physicists who actively intend to learn about and take intellectual charge of their worlds. In the Piagetian view, children who squish their food and laugh enthusiastically are often acting as budding scientists. They are studying both the texture and consistency of their food, as well as their parents' response.

© Farrell Grehan/Corbis

Jean Piaget

Piaget used concepts such as *schemes, adaptation, assimilation, accommodation*, and *equilibration* to describe and explain cognitive development. Piaget defined a **scheme** as a pattern of action or a mental structure that is involved in acquiring or organizing knowledge. For example, newborn babies might be said to have a sucking scheme (others call this a *reflex*), responding to things put in their mouths as "things I can suck" versus "things I can't suck."

Adaptation refers to the development of schemes that enable the organism to cope with its environment. According to Piaget, all organisms adapt to their environment. Adaptation consists of assimilation and accommodation, which occur throughout life. Cognitive **assimilation** is the process by which someone responds to new objects or events according to existing schemes or ways of organizing knowledge. Two-year-olds who refer to horses as "doggies" can be said to be assimilating horses into the dog scheme. Sometimes a novel object or event cannot be made to fit into an existing scheme. In that case, the scheme may be changed or a new scheme may be created to incorporate the new event. This process is called **accommodation**. Consider the sucking reflex. Infants accommodate by rejecting objects that are too large, that taste bad, or that are of the wrong texture or temperature. During their second year, infants may first assume that all four-legged creatures are "doggies," but later they accommodate to new information by recognizing that some four-legged animals are cats, horses, and so on.

Piaget theorized that when children can assimilate new events to existing schemes, they are in a state of cognitive harmony, or equilibrium. When something happens that does not fit, their state of equilibrium is disturbed and they may try to accommodate. The process of restoring equilibrium is termed **equilibration**. Piaget believed that the attempt to restore equilibrium lies at the heart of the natural curiosity of the child.

Piaget's Stages of Cognitive Development Piaget (1963) hypothesized that children's cognitive processes develop in an orderly sequence, or series, of stages. Piaget identified four major stages of cognitive development: *sensorimotor*, *preoperational*, *concrete operational*, and *formal operational* (see Table 1.2). These stages are discussed in subsequent chapters.

Because Piaget's theory focuses on cognitive development, its applications are primarily in educational settings. Teachers following Piaget's views actively engage the child in solving problems. They gear instruction to the child's developmental level and offer activities that challenge the child to advance to the next level.

Piaget's theory ends with formal operational thought. Life-span theorists such as William Perry, on the other hand, note that college students' views on what they know and how they get to know what they know become more complex as they are exposed to the complexities of college thought. Gisela Labouvie-Vief noted that the "cognitively healthy" adult is more willing than the egocentric adolescent to compromise and cope within the world as it is, not the world as she or he would like it to be.

Evaluation Many researchers, using a variety of methods, have found that Piaget may have underestimated the ages when children are capable of doing certain things. It also appears that many cognitive skills may develop gradually and not in distinct stages. Nevertheless, Piaget has provided a strong theoretical foundation for researchers concerned with sequences in cognitive development. He published nearly 100 articles and books, and his work has been cited thousands of times (Buela-Casal et al., 2011).

The Biological Perspective

equilibration The creation of an equilibrium, or balance, between assimilation and accommodation.

ethology The study of behaviors that are specific to a species.

The biological perspective directly relates to physical development—gains in height and weight; development of the brain; and developments connected with hormones, reproduction, and heredity. Here we consider two biologically oriented theories of development: evolutionary psychology and ethology.

Table 1.2
Jean Piaget's Stages of Cognitive Development

Stage	Approximate Age	Comments	
Sensorimotor	Birth–2 years	At first, the child lacks language and does not use symbols or mental representations of objects. In time, reflexive responding ends, and intentional behavior—as in making interesting stimulation last—begins. The child develops the object concept and acquires the basics of language.	
Preoperational	2–7 years	The child begins to represent the world mentally, but thought is egocentric. The child does not focus on two aspects of a situation at once and therefore lacks conservation. The child shows animism, artificialism, and objective responsibility for wrongdoing.	
Concrete operational	7–12 years	Logical mental actions—called operations—begin. The child develops conservation concepts, can adopt the viewpoint of others, can classify objects in series, and shows comprehension of basic relational concepts (such as one object being larger or heavier than another).	
Formal operational	12 years and older	Mature, adult thought emerges. Thinking is characterized by deductive logic, consideration of various possibilities (mental trial and error), abstract thought, and the formation and testing of hypotheses.	

© 2012 Cengage Learning

Evolutionary Psychology and Ethology: "Doing What Comes Naturally"

Evolutionary psychology and ethology were heavily influenced by the nineteenth-century work of Charles Darwin and by the work of twentieth-century ethologists Konrad Lorenz and Nikolaas Tinbergen. **Ethology** is concerned with instinctive, or inborn, behavior patterns that have evolved as species have developed. According to

1.1 *Theories of Development*

▶ **LO6** Discuss Bronfenbrenner's ecological perspective on development.

evolutionary psychology The branch of psychology that deals with the ways in which the history of human adaptation to the environment influences behavior and mental processes, with special focus on aggressive behavior and mating strategies.

fixed action pattern A stereotyped pattern of behavior that is evoked by a "releasing stimulus"; an instinct.

ecology The branch of biology that deals with the relationships between living organisms and their environment.

ecological systems theory The view that explains child development in terms of the reciprocal influences between children and environmental settings.

microsystem The immediate settings with which the child interacts, such as the home, the school, and peers.

mesosystem The interlocking settings that influence the child, such as the interaction of the school and the larger community.

exosystem Community institutions and settings that indirectly influence the child, such as the school board and the parents' workplaces.

macrosystem The basic institutions and ideologies that influence the child.

the theory of evolution, there is a struggle for survival as various species and individuals compete for a limited quantity of resources. The combined genetic instructions from parents lead to variations among individuals. There are also sharper differences from parents, caused by sudden changes in genetic material called *mutations*. Those individuals whose traits are better adapted to their environments are more likely to survive (that is, to be "naturally selected"). Survival permits them to reach sexual maturity, select mates, and reproduce, thereby transmitting their features or traits to the next generation. What began as a minor variation or a mutation becomes embedded in more and more individuals over the generations—if it fosters survival.

The field called **evolutionary psychology** studies the ways in which adaptation and natural selection are connected with mental processes and behavior. One of the concepts of evolutionary psychology is that not only physical traits but also patterns of behavior, including social behavior, evolve and are transmitted genetically from generation to generation. In other words, behavior patterns that help an organism to survive and reproduce are likely to be transmitted to the next generation. Such behaviors are believed to include aggression, strategies of mate selection, even altruism—that is, self-sacrifice of the individual to help perpetuate the family group. The behavior patterns are termed *instinctive* or *species-specific*, because they evolved within certain species.

The nervous systems of most, and perhaps all, animals are "prewired" to respond to some situations in specific ways. For example, birds raised in isolation from other birds build nests during the mating season even if they have never seen a nest or seen another bird building one. Nest building could not have been learned. Birds raised in isolation also sing the songs typical of their species. These behaviors are "built in," or instinctive. They are also referred to as inborn **fixed action patterns**.

Most theorists also believe that in many species, including humans, sex hormones can "masculinize" or "feminize" the embryonic brain by creating tendencies to behave in stereotypical masculine or feminine ways. Testosterone, the male sex hormone, seems to be connected with feelings of self-confidence, high activity levels, and—the negative side—aggressiveness (J. Archer, 2006; S. R. Davis et al., 2005; Geary, 2006).

Research into the biological perspective suggests that instinct may play a role in human behavior. Two questions that ethological research seeks to answer are: What areas of human behavior and development, if any, involve instincts? How powerful are instincts in people?

The Ecological Perspective

Ecology is the branch of biology that deals with the relationships between living organisms and their environment. The **ecological systems theory** of development addresses aspects of psychological, social, and emotional development as well as aspects of biological development. Ecological systems theorists explain development in terms of the interaction between people and the settings in which they live (Bronfenbrenner & Morris, 2006).

According to Urie Bronfenbrenner (1917–2005), for example, we need to focus on the two-way interactions between the child and the parents, not just maturational forces (nature) or child-rearing practices (nurture). Bronfenbrenner (Bronfenbrenner & Morris, 2006) suggested that we can view the setting or contexts of human development as consisting of multiple systems, each embedded within the next larger context. From narrowest to widest, these systems are the microsystem, mesosystem, exosystem, macrosystem, and chronosystem (Figure 1.4).

The **microsystem** involves the interactions of the child and other people in the immediate setting, such as the home, the school, or the peer group. Initially, the microsystem is small, involving caregiving interactions with the parents or others, usually at home. As children get older, they do more, with more people, in more places.

The **mesosystem** involves the interactions among the various settings within the microsystem. For instance, the home and the school interact during parent–teacher conferences. The school and the larger community interact when children are taken on field trips. The ecological systems approach addresses the joint effect of two or more settings on the child.

The **exosystem** involves the institutions in which the child does not directly participate but that exert an indirect influence on the child. For example, the school board is part of the child's exosystem because board members put together programs for the child's education, determine what textbooks will be acceptable, and so forth. In similar fashion, the parents' workplaces and economic situations determine the hours during which they will be available to the child, and so on (Kaminski & Stormshak, 2007). As a result, children may misbehave at home and in school.

The **macrosystem** involves the interaction of children with the beliefs, values, expectations, and lifestyles of their cultural settings. Cross-cultural studies examine children's interactions with their macrosystem. Macrosystems exist within a particular culture. In the United States, the dual-earner family, the low-income single-parent household, and the family with the father as sole breadwinner are

▶ **LO7** Discuss Vygotsky's theory of sociocultural development.

▶ **LO8** Discuss controversies in development.

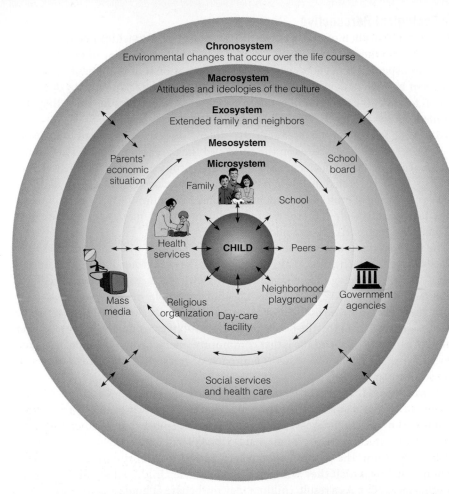

Figure 1.4 The Contexts of Human Development According to ecological systems theory, the systems within which children develop are embedded within larger systems. Children and these systems reciprocally influence each other.

chronosystem The environmental changes that occur over time and have an effect on the child.

zone of proximal development Vygotsky's term for the situation in which a child carries out tasks with the help of someone who is more skilled.

© 2012 Cengage Learning

three different macrosystems. Each has its own lifestyle, set of values, and expectations (Bronfenbrenner & Morris, 2006; Silbereisen, 2006).

The **chronosystem** considers the changes that occur over time. For example, the effects of divorce peak about a year after the event, and then children begin to recover. The breakup has more of an effect on boys than on girls. The ecological approach broadens the strategies for intervention in problems such as prevention of teenage pregnancy, child abuse, and juvenile offending, including substance abuse (Khurana et al., 2011; H. W. Wilson & Widom, 2010).

The Sociocultural Perspective

The sociocultural perspective teaches that people are social beings who are affected by the cultures in which they live. Developmentalists use the term *sociocultural* in a couple of different ways. One refers quite specifically to the *sociocultural theory* of Russian psychologist Lev Semenovich Vygotsky (1896–1934). The other addresses the effect of human diversity on people, including such factors as ethnicity and gender. Here we focus on Vygotsky's views.

Vygotsky's Sociocultural Theory

Whereas genetics is concerned with the biological transmission of traits from generation to generation, Vygotsky's (1978) theory is concerned with the transmission of information and cognitive skills from generation to generation. The transmission of skills involves teaching and learning, but Vygotsky did not view learning in terms of conditioning. Rather, he focused on how the child's social interaction with adults, largely in the home, organizes a child's learning experiences in such a way that the child can obtain cognitive skills—such as computation or reading skills—and use them to acquire information. Like Piaget, Vygotsky saw the child's functioning as adaptive (Kanevsky & Geake, 2004), and the child as adapting to his or her social and cultural interactions.

Key concepts in Vygotsky's theory include the *zone of proximal development* and *scaffolding*. The **zone of proximal development** refers to a range of tasks that a child can carry out with the help of someone who is more skilled, as in an apprenticeship. When learning with other people, children internalize—or bring

© RIA Novosti/Alamy

Lev Vygotsky

The Macrosystem and Independence

How does the macrosystem influence the development of independence?

inward—the conversations and explanations that help them gain the necessary skills (Ash, 2004; Umek et al., 2005; Vygotsky, 1962).

A *scaffold* is a temporary skeletal structure that enables workers to fabricate a building or other more permanent structure. In Vygotsky's theory, teachers and parents provide children with problem-solving methods that serve as cognitive **scaffolding** while the child gains the ability to function independently. For example, children may be offered scaffolding that enables them to use their fingers or their toes to do simple calculations. Eventually, the scaffolding is removed and the cognitive structures stand alone.

Controversies in Development

The discussion of theories of development reveals that developmentalists can see things in very different ways. Let us consider how they react to three of the key issues in the field.

Nature and Nurture

Researchers are continually trying to sort out the extent to which human behavior is the result of **nature** (heredity) and of **nurture** (environmental influences). What aspects of behavior originate in our genes and are biologically programmed to unfold as time goes on, as long as minimal nutrition and social experience are provided? What aspects of behavior can be traced largely to such environmental influences as nutrition and learning?

Scientists seek the natural causes of development in children's genetic heritage, in the functioning of the nervous system, and in maturation. They seek the environmental causes of development in children's nutrition, cultural and family backgrounds, and opportunities to learn about the world, including cognitive stimulation during early childhood and formal education.

Some theorists (e.g., cognitive-developmental and biological theorists) lean heavily toward natural explanations of development, whereas others (e.g., learning theorists) lean more heavily toward environmental explanations. Today, though, nearly all researchers agree that nature and nurture play important roles in nearly every area of development. Consider the development of language. Language is based in structures found in certain areas of the brain. Thus, biology (nature) plays a vital role. Children also come to speak the languages spoken by their caretakers. Parent–child similarities in accent and vocabulary provide additional evidence for the role of learning (nurture) in language development.

scaffolding Vygotsky's term for temporary cognitive structures or methods of solving problems that help the child as he or she learns to function independently.

nature The processes within an organism that guide it to develop according to its genetic code.

nurture Environmental factors that influence development.

Continuity and Discontinuity

Some developmentalists view human development as a continuous process in which the effects of learning mount gradually, with no major sudden qualitative changes. In contrast, other theorists believe that a number of rapid qualitative changes usher in new stages of development. Maturational theorists point out that the environment, even when enriched, profits us little until we are ready, or mature enough, to develop in a certain way. For example, newborn babies will not imitate their parents' speech, even when parents speak clearly and deliberately. Nor does aided practice in "walking" during the first few months after birth significantly accelerate the emergence of independent walking. Infants are not ready to do these things.

Stage theorists such as Sigmund Freud and Jean Piaget saw development as discontinuous. They saw biological changes as providing the potential for psychological changes. Freud focused on the ways in which biological developments might provide the basis for personality development. Piaget believed maturation of the nervous system allowed cognitive development.

Certain aspects of physical development do occur in stages. For example, from the age of 2 years to the onset of puberty, children continuously and gradually grow larger. Then the adolescent growth spurt occurs, and rushes of hormones cause rapid and discontinuous biological changes in structure and function (as in the development of the sex organs) and in size. Psychologists disagree on whether developments in cognition occur in stages.

Activity and Passivity

Historical views of children as willful and unruly suggest that people have generally seen children as active, even if mischievous (at best) or evil (at worst). John Locke introduced a view of children as passive beings (blank tablets); experience "wrote" features of personality and moral virtue on them.

At one extreme, educators who view children as passive may assume that they must be motivated to learn by their instructors. Such educators are likely to provide a rigorous traditional curriculum with a powerful system of rewards and punishments to promote absorption of the subject matter. At the other extreme, educators who view children as active may assume that they have a natural love of learning. Such educators are likely to argue for open education and encourage children to explore and pursue their unique likes and talents.

Perspectives of Development

Review the theories of child development.

Check Your Learning Quiz 1.1

Go to **login.cengagebrain.com** and take the online quiz.

▶ **LO9** Describe the naturalistic-observation method.

▶ **LO10** Describe the case study.

▶ **LO11** Discuss the correlational method.

Did you know that—

- Research with monkeys has helped psychologists understand the formation of attachment in humans?
- There is a "negative" relationship between an adolescent's grades in school and his or her participation in delinquent acts?
- Although it has been shown that children in divorced families tend to show more behavioral problems than children in intact families, it has not been shown that divorce *causes* the behavioral problems?
- To learn how a person develops over a lifetime, researchers have tracked some individuals for more than 50 years?
- Human participants in research—or their parents or guardians—must be informed of the purposes and methods used in research?

▼

naturalistic observation A scientific method in which organisms are observed in their natural environments.

case study A carefully drawn biography of the life of an individual.

standardized test A test in which an individual's score is compared to the scores of a group of similar individuals.

correlation coefficient A number ranging from +1.00 to −1.00 that expresses the direction (positive or negative) and strength of the relationship between two variables.

positive correlation A relationship between two variables in which one variable increases as the other increases.

negative correlation A relationship between two variables in which one variable increases as the other decreases.

What is the relationship between intelligence and achievement? What are the effects of maternal use of aspirin and alcohol on the fetus? What are the effects of parental divorce on children? What are the effects of early retirement? We may have expressed opinions on such questions at one time or another, but scientists insist that such questions be answered by research. Strong arguments and reference to authority figures are not evidence. Scientific evidence is obtained only by gathering sound information and conducting research.

Gathering Information

Researchers use various methods to gather information. For example, they may ask teachers or parents to report on the behavior of children, use interviews or questionnaires with adults, or study statistics compiled by the government or the United Nations. They also directly observe children in the laboratory, the playground, or the classroom. Let us discuss two ways of gathering information: the naturalistic-observation method and the case-study method.

Naturalistic Observation

Naturalistic-observation studies are conducted "in the field," that is, in the natural, or real-life, settings in which they happen. In field studies, investigators observe the natural behavior of children in settings such as homes, playgrounds, and classrooms and try not to interfere with it. Researchers may try to "blend into the wood-work" by sitting quietly in the back of a classroom or by observing the class through a one-way mirror.

Naturalistic-observation studies have been done with children of different cultures. For example, researchers have observed the motor behavior of Native American Hopi children who are strapped to cradle boards during their first year. You can read more about this in Module 3.2.

The Case Study

A **case study** is a carefully drawn account of the behavior of an individual. Parents who keep diaries of their children's activities are involved in informal case studies. Case studies themselves often use a number of different kinds of information. In addition to direct observation, case studies may include questionnaires, **standardized tests**, and interviews. Information gleaned from public records may be included. Scientists who use the case-study method try to record all relevant factors in a person's behavior, and they are cautious in drawing conclusions about what leads to what.

Correlation: Putting Things Together

Researchers use the correlational method to determine whether one behavior or trait being studied is related to, or correlated with, another. Consider intelligence and achievement. These variables are assigned numbers such as intelligence test scores and grade-point averages. Then the numbers or scores are mathematically related and expressed as a **correlation coefficient**—a number that varies between +1.00 and −1.00.

In general, the higher people score on intelligence tests, the better their academic performance (or income) is likely to be. The scores attained on intelligence tests have a **positive correlation** (about +0.60 to +0.70) with overall academic achievement (and income). There is a **negative correlation** between adolescents' grades and delinquent acts. The higher an adolescents' grades, the less likely he or she is to engage in criminal behavior. Figure 1.5 illustrates positive and negative correlations.

Limitations of Correlational Information

Correlational information can reveal relationships between variables, but it does not show cause and effect. It may seem logical to assume that exposure to violent media makes people more aggressive, but it may also be that more aggressive people *choose* violent media. This research bias is termed a *selection factor*.

▶ **L012** Define *hypothesis*.

▶ **L013** Discuss the experimental method.

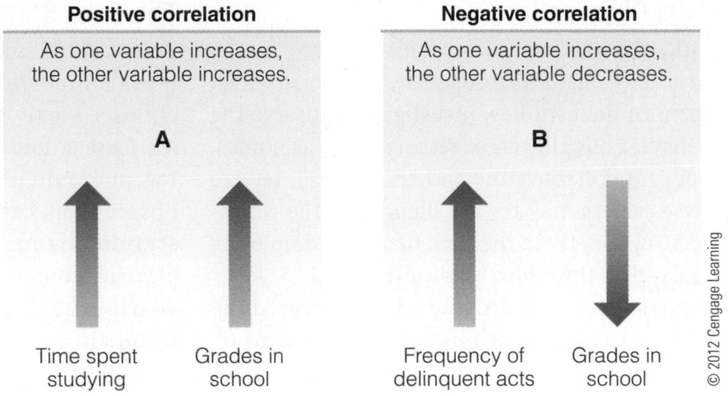

Figure 1.5 Examples of Positive and Negative Correlations When two variables are positively correlated, one increases as the other increases. There is a positive correlation between the amount of time spent studying and grades, as shown in part A. When two variables are negatively correlated, one increases as the other decreases. There is a negative correlation between the frequency of a child's delinquent acts and his or her grades, as shown in part B. As delinquent behavior increases, grades tend to decline.

experiment A method of scientific investigation that seeks to discover cause-and-effect relationships by introducing independent variables and observing their effects on dependent variables.

hypothesis A proposition to be tested.

independent variable A condition in a scientific study that is manipulated so that its effects can be observed.

dependent variable A measure of an assumed effect of an independent variable.

experimental group A group made up of participants who receive a treatment in an experiment.

control group A group made up of participants in an experiment who do not receive the treatment but for whom all other conditions are comparable to those of participants in the experimental group.

Similarly, studies have reported that children (especially boys) in divorced families tend to show more behavioral problems than children in intact families (S. M. Greene et al., 2006; Lansford et al., 2006). These studies, however, did not show that divorce causes these adjustment problems; it could be that the factors that led to divorce—such as parental conflict—also led to adjustment problems among the children (Hetherington, 2006). To investigate cause and effect, researchers turn to the experimental method.

The Experiment: Trying Things Out

The experiment is the preferred method for investigating questions of cause and effect. In an **experiment**, a group of subjects receives a treatment and another group does not. The subjects are then observed to determine whether the treatment changes their behavior. Experiments are usually undertaken to test a **hypothesis**. For example, a researcher might hypothesize that TV violence will cause aggressive behavior in children.

Independent and Dependent Variables

In an experiment to determine whether TV violence causes aggressive behavior, subjects in the experimental group would be shown a TV program containing violence, and its effects on their behavior would be measured. TV violence would be considered an **independent variable**, a variable whose presence is manipulated by the experimenters so that its effects can be determined. The measured result—in this case, the child's behavior—is called a **dependent variable**. Its presence or level presumably depends on the independent variable.

Experimental and Control Groups

Experiments use experimental and control groups. Subjects in the **experimental group** receive the treatment, whereas subjects in the **control group** do not. All other conditions are held constant for both groups. Thus, we can have confidence that experimental outcomes reflect the treatments and not chance factors.

Random Assignment

Subjects should be assigned to experimental or control groups on a chance or random basis. We could not conclude much from an experiment on the effects of TV violence if the children were allowed to choose whether they would be in a group that watched TV violence or in a group that did not. A *selection factor* rather than the treatment might then be responsible for the results of the experiment.

Ethical and practical considerations also prevent researchers from doing experiments on the effects of many life circumstances, such as divorce or different patterns of child rearing. We cannot randomly assign some families to divorce or conflict and assign other families to bliss. Nor can we randomly assign parents to rear their children in an authoritarian or permissive manner. In some areas of investigation, we must settle for correlational evidence.

When experiments cannot ethically be performed on humans, researchers sometimes carry them out with animals and try to generalize the findings to humans. No researcher would separate human infants from their parents to study the effects of isolation on development, yet experimenters have deprived monkeys of early social experience. Such research with monkeys has helped psychologists investigate the formation of parent–child bonds of attachment.

The Experiential Method

Learn more about conducting research, the scientific method, independent and dependent variables and more.

Longitudinal Research: Studying Development Over Time

The processes of development occur over time, and researchers have devised different strategies for comparing children of one age with children or adults of other ages. In **longitudinal research**, the same people are observed repeatedly over time, and changes in development, such as gains in height or changes in mental abilities, are recorded. In **cross-sectional research**, children of different ages are observed and compared. It is assumed that when a large number of children are chosen at random, the differences found in the older age groups are a reflection of how the younger children will develop, given time.

Longitudinal Studies

The Terman Studies of Genius, begun in the 1920s, tracked children with high IQ scores for more than 50 years. Male subjects, but not female subjects, went on to high achievements in the professional world. Why? Recent studies of women show that women can generally match the vocational achievements of men; women, in fact, may be somewhat more persistent than men, although a bit less competitive (van der Sluis et al., 2010). In later chapters we will see that women in large numbers are entering "STEM" fields (science, technology, engineering, and mathematics)— which were once the preserve of men.

Most longitudinal studies span months or a few years, not decades. For example, briefer longitudinal studies have found that the children of divorced parents undergo the most severe adjustment problems within a few months of the divorce, peaking at about a year. By 2 or 3 years afterward, many children regain their equilibrium, as indicated by improved academic performance and social behavior (Hetherington et al., 1992).

Longitudinal studies have drawbacks. For example, it can be difficult to enlist volunteers to participate in a study that will last a lifetime. Many subjects fall out of touch as the years pass; others die. The researchers must be patient or arrange to enlist future generations of researchers.

longitudinal research The study of developmental processes by taking repeated measures of the same group of participants at various stages of development.

cross-sectional research The study of developmental processes by taking measures of participants of different age groups at the same time.

cohort effect Similarities in behavior among a group of peers that stem from the fact that group members were born at the same time in history.

cross-sequential research An approach that combines the longitudinal and cross-sectional methods by following individuals of different ages for abbreviated periods of time.

time lag The study of developmental processes by taking measures of participants of the same age group at different times.

Cross-Sectional Research

Because of the drawbacks of longitudinal studies, most research that compares children of different ages is cross-sectional. In other words, most investigators gather data on what the "typical" 6-month-old is doing by finding children who are

6 months old today. When they expand their research to the behavior of typical 12-month-olds, they seek another group of children, and so on.

A major challenge to cross-sectional research is the **cohort effect**. A cohort is a group of people born at about the same time. As a result, they experience cultural and other events unique to their age group. In other words, children and adults of different ages are not likely to have shared similar cultural backgrounds. People who are 80 years old today, for example, grew up without TV. Today's children are growing up taking iPods and the Internet for granted.

Children of past generations also grew up with different expectations about gender roles and appropriate social behavior. Women in the Terman study generally chose motherhood over careers because of the times. Today's girls are growing up with female role models who are astronauts and government officials.

In longitudinal studies, we know that we have the same individuals as they have developed over 5, 25, even 50 years or more. In cross-sectional research, we can only hope that they will be comparable.

Cross-Sequential Research

Cross-sequential research combines the longitudinal and cross-sectional methods so that many of their individual drawbacks are overcome. In a cross-sequential study, the full span of the ideal longitudinal study is broken up into convenient segments (see Figure 1.6). Assume that we wish to follow the attitudes of children toward gender roles from the age of 4 through the age of 12. The typical longitudinal study would take 8 years. We can, however, divide this 8-year span in half by attaining two samples of children (a cross-section) instead of one: 4-year-olds and 8-year-olds. We would then interview, test, and observe each group at the beginning of the study (2012) and 4 years later (2016).

An obvious advantage to this collapsed method is that the study is completed in 4 years rather than 8 years. Still, the testing and retesting of samples provides some of the continuity of the longitudinal study. By observing both samples at the age of 8 (a **time-lag** comparison), we can also determine whether they are, in fact, comparable or whether the 4-year difference in their birth date is associated with a cohort effect.

▶ **LO16** Discuss ethical issues in developmental research.

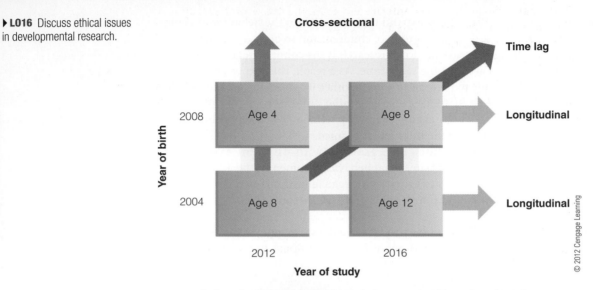

Figure 1.6 **An Example of Cross-Sequential Research** Cross-sequential research combines three methods: cross-sectional, longitudinal, and time lag. The child's age at the time of testing appears in the boxes. Columns represent cross-sectional comparisons. Rows represent longitudinal comparisons. Diagonals represent time-lag comparisons.

Ethical Considerations

Researchers adhere to ethical standards that are intended to promote the dignity of the individual, foster human welfare, and maintain scientific integrity. These standards also ensure that researchers do not use methods or treatments that harm subjects:

- Researchers are not to use methods that may do physical or psychological harm.
- Participants (and parents, if participants are minors) must be informed of the purposes of the research and of the research methods.
- Participants must provide voluntary consent to participate in the study.
- Participants may withdraw from the study at any time, for any reason.

- Participants should be offered information about the results of the study.
- The identities of the participants are to remain confidential.
- Researchers should present their research plans to a committee of their colleagues and gain the committee's approval before proceeding.

These guidelines present researchers with a number of hurdles to overcome before and during research, but because they protect the welfare of participants, the guidelines are valuable.

This infant is being prepared for a psychological study to determine if he recognizes his mother's face. Is the psychologist proceeding in an ethical manner?

Ethics and Conditioning
Little Albert

Read about an 11-month old baby conditioned to fear rats.

Little Albert's Conditioning

Watch the classic film clip of "Little Albert" being conditioned as a baby.

Check Your Learning Quiz 1.2

Go to **login.cengagebrain.com** and take the online quiz.

GO to your Psychology CourseMate at login.cengagebrain.com and take the Chapter Post-Test to see which Learning Objectives you've mastered and which need more review. Use the chapter review guide below and the online activities—including flashcards to review key terms—to measure your learning.

Measure ^**Your Learning**

Module	Learning Objectives
1.1 The Theories of Development 4	
The Development of the Study of Development	**LO1** Relate the history of the study of human development.
Theories of Development	**LO2** Discuss Freud's theory of psychosexual development.
	LO3 Discuss the behaviorist perspective on development.
	LO4 Discuss the social cognitive perspective on development.
	LO5 Discuss Piaget's concepts and his stages of cognitive development.
	LO6 Discuss Bronfenbrenner's ecological perspective on development.
	LO7 Discuss Vygotsky's theory of sociocultural development.
Controversies in Development	**LO8** Discuss controversies in development.

Online Activities

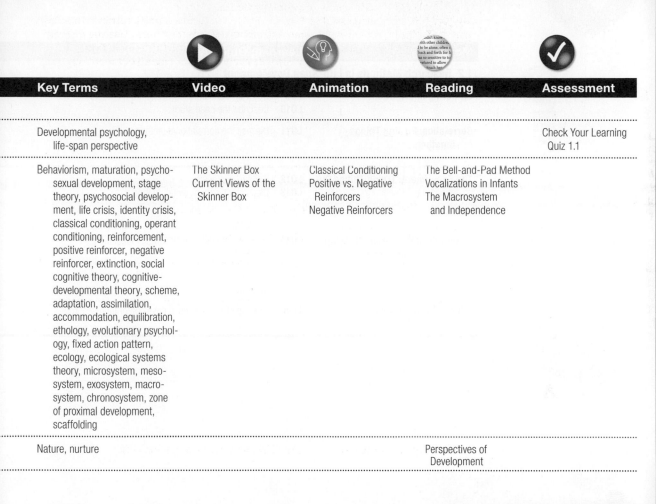

Key Terms	Video	Animation	Reading	Assessment

Key Terms	Video	Animation	Reading	Assessment
Developmental psychology, life-span perspective				Check Your Learning Quiz 1.1
Behaviorism, maturation, psychosexual development, stage theory, psychosocial development, life crisis, identity crisis, classical conditioning, operant conditioning, reinforcement, positive reinforcer, negative reinforcer, extinction, social cognitive theory, cognitive-developmental theory, scheme, adaptation, assimilation, accommodation, equilibration, ethology, evolutionary psychology, fixed action pattern, ecology, ecological systems theory, microsystem, mesosystem, exosystem, macrosystem, chronosystem, zone of proximal development, scaffolding	The Skinner Box Current Views of the Skinner Box	Classical Conditioning Positive vs. Negative Reinforcers Negative Reinforcers	The Bell-and-Pad Method Vocalizations in Infants The Macrosystem and Independence	
Nature, nurture			Perspectives of Development	

Measure ^Your Learning

Online Activities

Key Terms	Video	Animation	Reading	Assessment

Key Terms	Video	Animation	Reading	Assessment
Naturalistic observation, case study, standardized test				Check Your Learning Quiz 1.2
Correlation coefficient, positive correlation, negative correlation				
Experiment, hypothesis, independent variable, dependent variable, experimental group, control group		The Experiential Method		
Longitudinal research, cross-sectional research				
Cohort effect, cross-sequential research, time lag				
	Little Albert's Conditioning		Ethics and Conditioning Little Albert	

Beginnings

2

Chapter Outline and Learning Objectives

Prepare ∧ to Learn

1 **GO** to your **Psychology CourseMate** at **login.cengagebrain.com** and take the **Chapter Pre-Test** to introduce yourself to this chapter's topics and see what you may already know.

2 **READ** the **Learning Objectives** (LOs, in the left sidebars) and begin the chapter.

3 **COMPLETE** the **Online Activities** (in the right sidebars) *as you read each module.* Activities include **videos, animations, readings,** and **quizzes.**

4 **CHECK Your Learning** by going online to take the quiz at the end of each module and review material as necessary.

5 **MEASURE Your Learning** after reading the chapter by taking the online **Chapter Post-Test.** Use the chapter review guide at the end of the chapter as needed.

WATCH for these **Online Activities** icons as you read:

Video

Animation

Reading

Assessment

Online Activities

These online activities are essential to mastering this chapter. Go to login.cengagebrain.com:

 Videos Watch the following videos:

- An Ultrasound
- Prenatal Doctor's Visit
- Twins Research
- Stress and Pregnancy
- Rx Drugs and Development
- Fetal Alcohol Syndrome
- Fathers and Autism
- Birth
- Prenatal Health Issues

 Animations Interact with and visualize important processes, timelines, and concepts:

- The Double Helix of DNA
- Chromosomes and Genes
- Inheriting Eye Color
- Female Reproductive Organs
- Stages of Conception
- Sexual Differentiation
- Organ Development

 Readings Delve deeper into key content:

- Where Are the Girls?
- Selecting the Sex of Your Child
- Fetal Perception
- Highlights of Prenatal Development
- Preventing HIV in the Unborn
- Should Pregnant Women Avoid Caffeine?
- Birthing Options
- Global Birthrates
- Maternal and Infant Mortality

 Assessment Measure your mastery:

- Chapter Pre-Test
- Check Your Learning Quizzes
- Chapter Post-Test

Did you know that—

• Your father determined whether you are female or male?

• Fertility drugs enhance the chances of having multiple births, such as twins?

• Two brown-eyed parents can have a blue-eyed child?

• Males with an XYY sex-chromosomal structure were once referred to as "supermales"?

▼

Let's talk about the facts of life. Here are a few of them:

People cannot breathe underwater (without special equipment).
People cannot fly (without special equipment).
Fish cannot learn to speak French or dance an Irish jig, even if you raise them in enriched environments and send them to finishing school.

We cannot breathe underwater or fly because we have not inherited gills or wings. Fish are similarly limited by their heredity. Heredity defines one's nature—which is based on the biological transmission of traits and characteristics from one generation to another. Because of their heredity, fish cannot speak French or do a jig.

In this module, we explore heredity—the genetic influences in development. We could say that development begins long before conception. Development involves the origins of the genetic structures that determine that human embryos will grow arms rather than wings, lungs rather than gills, and hair rather than scales. Our discussion thus begins with an examination of the building blocks of heredity: genes and chromosomes.

The Influence of Heredity on Development

Heredity makes possible all things human. The structures we inherit make our behavior possible and place limits on it. The field of biology that studies heredity is called **genetics**. Genetics involves both our shared human development and the development of individual differences.

Genetic influences are fundamental in the transmission of physical traits, such as height, hair texture, and eye color. Genetics appears to play a role in psychological

genetics The branch of biology that studies heredity.

chromosome A rod-shaped structure, composed of genes, found within the nuclei of cells.

gene The basic unit of heredity. Genes are composed of deoxyribonucleic acid (DNA).

polygenic Resulting from many genes.

deoxyribonucleic acid (DNA) Genetic material that takes the form of a double helix composed of phosphates, sugars, and bases.

traits such as intelligence, activity level, sociability, shyness, anxiety, empathy, effectiveness as a parent, happiness, and even interest in arts and crafts (Johnson & Krueger, 2006; Knafo & Plomin, 2006; Leonardo & Hen, 2006). Moreover, genetic factors are involved in psychological problems such as schizophrenia, depression, and dependence on nicotine, alcohol, and other substances (Farmer et al., 2005; Metzger et al., 2007).

Chromosomes and Genes

Traits are transmitted by chromosomes and genes. **Chromosomes** are rod-shaped structures found in cells. Typical human cells contain 46 chromosomes organized into 23 pairs. Each chromosome contains thousands of segments called genes. **Genes** are the biochemical materials that regulate the development of traits. Some traits, such as blood type, appear to be transmitted by a single pair of genes, one from each parent. Other traits are **polygenic**, that is, determined by several pairs of genes.

Our heredity is governed by 20,000 to 25,000 genes (Human Genome Sequencing Consortium, 2004). Genes are segments of strands of **deoxyribonucleic acid (DNA)**. DNA takes the form of a double spiral, or helix, similar to a twisting ladder (see Figure 2.1). The rungs of the ladder consist of one of two pairs of bases, either adenine with thymine (A with T) or cytosine with guanine (C with G). The sequence of the rungs is the genetic code that will cause the developing organism to grow arms or wings, skin or scales.

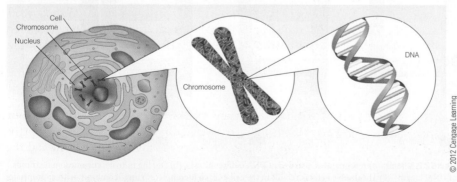

© 2012 Cengage Learning

Figure 2.1 The Double Helix of DNA DNA takes the form of a double spiral, or helix.

DNA's Double Helix

View an interactive version of Figure 2.1.

Mitosis and Meiosis

We begin life as a single cell, or zygote, that divides repeatedly. There are two types of cell division: *mitosis* and *meiosis*. In **mitosis**, strands of DNA break apart, or "unzip" (see Figure 2.2). The double helix then duplicates. The DNA forms two camps, one on either side of the cell, and then the cell divides. Each incomplete rung combines with the appropriate "partner" (i.e., G and C, A and T) to form a new complete ladder. The two resulting identical copies of the DNA strand separate when the cell divides; each becomes a member of a newly formed cell. As a result, the genetic code is identical in new cells unless **mutations** occur through radiation or other environmental influences. Mutations also occur by chance, but not often.

mitosis The form of cell division in which each chromosome splits lengthwise to double in number. Half of each chromosome combines with chemicals to retake its original form and then moves to the new cell.

mutation A sudden variation in a heritable characteristic, as by an accident that affects the composition of genes.

meiosis The form of cell division in which each pair of chromosomes splits so that one member of each pair moves to the new cell. As a result, each new cell has 23 chromosomes.

autosome A member of a pair of chromosomes (with the exception of sex chromosomes).

sex chromosome A chromosome in the shape of a Y (male) or X (female) that determines the gender of a child.

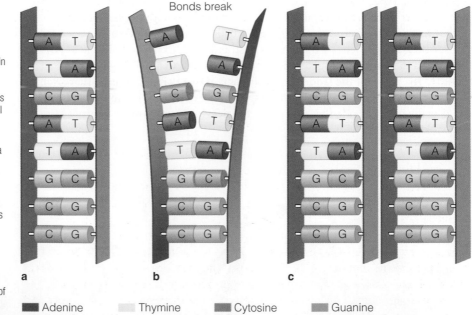

Bonds break

a   b   c

■ Adenine   ■ Thymine   ■ Cytosine   ■ Guanine

© 2012 Cengage Learning

Figure 2.2 Mitosis (a) A segment of a strand of DNA before mitosis. (b) During mitosis, chromosomal strands of DNA "unzip." (c) The double helix is rebuilt in the cell as each incomplete "rung" combines with appropriate molecules.

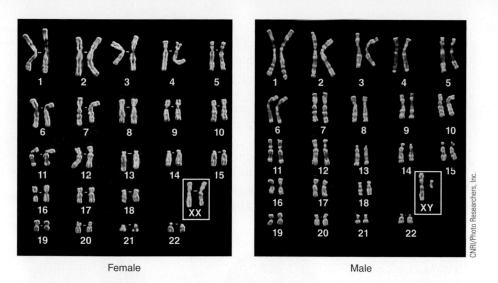

CNRI/Photo Researchers, Inc.

Female   Male

Figure 2.3 The 23 Pairs of Human Chromosomes People normally have 23 pairs of chromosomes. Females have two X sex chromosomes, whereas males have an X and a Y sex chromosome.

Sperm and ova (egg cells) are produced through **meiosis**, or *reduction division*. In meiosis, the 46 chromosomes within the cell nucleus first line up into 23 pairs. The DNA ladders then unzip, leaving unpaired halves of chromosome. When the cell divides, one member of each separated pair goes to each newly formed cell. Each new cell nucleus contains only 23 chromosomes, not 46.

When a sperm cell fertilizes an ovum, we receive 23 chromosomes from our father's sperm cell and 23 from our mother's ovum, and the combined chromosomes form 23 pairs (see Figure 2.3). Twenty-two of the pairs are **autosomes**—pairs that look alike and possess genetic information concerning the same set of traits. The 23rd pair are **sex chromosomes**, which look different from other chromosomes and determine our gender. We all receive an X sex chromosome (so called because of its X shape) from our mothers. The father supplies either a Y or an X sex chromosome. If we receive another X sex chromosome from our fathers, we develop into females, and if a Y (named after its Y shape), males.

Chromosomes and Genes

Learn more about chromosomes and genes, beginning with fertilization.

Identical and Fraternal Twins

Now and then, a zygote divides into two cells that separate so that each develops into an individual with the same genetic makeup. These individuals are identical twins, or **monozygotic (MZ) twins**. If the woman produces two ova in the same month and they are each fertilized by different sperm cells, they develop into fraternal twins, or **dizygotic (DZ) twins**. DZ twins run in families. If a woman is a twin, if her mother was a twin, or if she has previously borne twins, the chances rise that she will bear twins (Martin et al., 2006).

As women reach the end of their childbearing years, **ovulation** becomes less regular, resulting in a number of months when more than one ovum is released. Thus, the chances of twins increase with maternal age (National Guideline Clearinghouse, 2007). Fertility drugs also enhance the chances of multiple births by causing more than one ovum to ripen and be released during a woman's cycle (National Guideline Clearinghouse, 2007).

monozygotic (MZ) twins Twins that derive from a single zygote that has split into two; identical twins. Each MZ twin carries the same genetic code.

dizygotic (DZ) twins Twins that derive from two zygotes; fraternal twins.

ovulation The releasing of an ovum from an ovary.

allele A member of a pair of genes.

homozygous Having two identical alleles.

heterozygous Having two different alleles.

dominant trait A trait that is expressed.

recessive trait A trait that is not expressed when the gene or genes involved have been paired with dominant genes.

Veer/Corbis

Identical, or monozygotic (MZ) twins share 100% of their genes. Fraternal, or dizygotic (DZ) twins, like most siblings, share 50% of their genes.

Dominant and Recessive Traits

Traits are determined by pairs of genes. Each member of a pair of genes is termed an **allele**. When both of the alleles for a trait, such as hair color, are the same, a person is said to be **homozygous** for that trait. When the alleles for a trait differ, a person is **heterozygous** for that trait. Some traits result from an "averaging" of the genetic instructions carried by the parents. When the effects of both alleles are shown, there is said to be incomplete dominance or codominance. When a *dominant* allele is paired with a *recessive* allele, the trait determined by the dominant allele appears in the offspring. For example, the offspring from the crossing of brown eyes with blue eyes have brown eyes, suggesting that brown eyes are a **dominant trait** and blue eyes are a **recessive trait**.

If one parent carried genes for only brown eyes and if the other parent carried genes for only blue eyes, the children would invariably have brown eyes. But brown-eyed parents can also carry recessive genes for blue eyes, as shown in Figure 2.4. If the recessive gene from one parent combines with the recessive gene from the other parent, the recessive trait will be shown. As suggested by Figure 2.4, approximately 25% of the children of brown-eyed parents who carry recessive blue eye color will have blue eyes. Table 2.1 shows a number of dominant and recessive traits in humans.

Table 2.1

Examples of Dominant and Recessive Traits

Dominant Trait	Recessive Trait
Dark hair	Blond hair
Dark hair	Red hair
Curly hair	Straight hair
Normal color vision	Red-green color blindness
Normal vision	Myopia (nearsightedness)
Farsightedness (hyperopia)	Normal vision
Normal pigmentation	Deficiency of pigmentation in skin, hair, and retinas (albinism)
Normal sensitivity to touch	Extremely fragile skin
Normal hearing	Some forms of deafness
Dimples	Lack of dimples
Type A blood	Type O blood
Type B blood	Type O blood
Lactose tolerance	Lactose intolerance

© 2012 Cengage Learning

Inheriting Eye Color

Explore for a closer look at dominant and recessive traits for eye color.

▶ **LO5** Discuss chromosomal disorders.

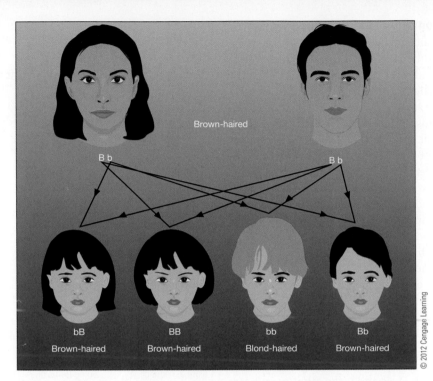

bB — Brown-haired   BB — Brown-haired   bb — Blond-haired   Bb — Brown-haired

© 2012 Cengage Learning

Figure 2.4 Transmission of Dominant and Recessive Traits These two brown-haired parents each carry genes for blond hair as well as brown hair. Their children have an equal opportunity of receiving genes for brown hair and blond hair. However, only a child who receives two genes for blond hair will actually have blond hair.

carrier A person who carries and transmits characteristics but does not exhibit them.

Down syndrome A chromosomal abnormality characterized by mental retardation and caused by an extra chromosome in the 21st pair.

sex-linked chromosomal abnormality An abnormality that is transmitted from generation to generation and carried by a sex chromosome.

People who bear one dominant gene and one recessive gene for a trait are said to be **carriers** of the recessive gene. In the cases of recessive genes that cause illness, carriers of those genes are fortunate to have dominant genes that cancel their effects.

Chromosomal Abnormalities

Chromosomal abnormalities can cause health problems. Some chromosomal disorders reflect abnormalities in the 22 pairs of autosomes (such as Down syndrome); others reflect abnormalities in the sex chromosomes (e.g., XYY syndrome).

People normally have 46 chromosomes. Children with more or fewer chromosomes usually experience health problems or behavioral abnormalities. The risk of chromosomal abnormalities rises with the age of the parents (American Fertility Association, 2009).

Down Syndrome

Down syndrome is usually caused by an extra chromosome on the 21st pair, resulting in 47 chromosomes. The probability of having a child with Down syndrome increases with the age of the parents. People with Down syndrome have characteristic features that include a rounded face, a protruding tongue, a broad, flat nose, and a sloping fold of skin over the inner corners of the eyes, such as the child on the right in Figure 2.5. They show deficits in cognitive development (Rondal & Ling, 2006) and motor development (Virji-Babul et al., 2006) and usually die from cardiovascular problems by middle age, although modern medicine has extended their life expectancy appreciably.

Sex-Linked Chromosomal Abnormalities

A number of disorders stem from an abnormal number of sex chromosomes and are therefore called **sex-linked chromosomal abnormalities**. Most individuals with an abnormal number of sex chromosomes are infertile. Beyond that common finding, there are many differences, some of them associated with "maleness" or "femaleness" (Wodrich, 2006).

Approximately 1 male in 700 to 1,000 has an extra Y chromosome. The Y chromosome is associated with maleness, and the extra Y sex chromosome apparently heightens male secondary sex characteristics. For example, XYY males are somewhat taller than average and

Gary Parker/Photo Researchers, Inc.

Figure 2.5 Down Syndrome

2.1 Genetic Influences on Development

▶ L06 Discuss genetic disorders.

Klinefelter syndrome A chromosomal disorder found among males that is caused by an extra X sex chromosome and characterized by infertility and mild mental retardation.

testosterone A male sex hormone produced mainly by the testes.

Turner syndrome A chromosomal disorder found among females that is caused by having a single X sex chromosome and characterized by infertility.

estrogen A female sex hormone produced mainly by the ovaries.

multifactorial problems Problems that stem from the interaction of heredity and environmental factors.

phenylketonuria (PKU) A genetic abnormality in which phenylalanine builds up and causes mental retardation.

Huntington's disease A fatal genetic neurologic disorder with onset in middle age.

sickle-cell anemia A genetic disorder that decreases the blood's capacity to carry oxygen.

Tay-Sachs disease A fatal genetic neurological disorder.

develop heavier beards. For these kinds of reasons, males with XYY sex chromosomal structure were once called "supermales." However, XYY "supermales" tend to have more problems than XY males. For example, they are often mildly delayed in language development.

Approximately 1 male in 500 has **Klinefelter syndrome**, which is caused by an extra X sex chromosome (an XXY sex-chromosomal pattern). XXY males produce less of the male sex hormone **testosterone** than normal males. As a result, male primary and secondary sex characteristics—such as the testes, deepening of the voice, musculature, and male pattern of body hair—do not develop properly. XXY males usually have enlarged breasts (gynecomastia) and mild intellectual deficiency, particularly in language skills (van Rijn et al., 2006). XXY males are typically treated with testosterone-replacement therapy, which can foster growth of sex characteristics and elevate the mood, but they remain infertile.

Approximately 1 girl in 2,500 has a single X sex chromosome and as a result develops **Turner syndrome**. The external genitals of such girls are normal, but their ovaries are poorly developed and they produce little **estrogen**. Girls with this problem are shorter than average and infertile. Researchers have connected a specific pattern of cognitive deficits with low estrogen levels: problems in visual-spatial skills, mathematics, and nonverbal memory (S. J. Hart et al., 2006).

Approximately 1 girl in 1,000 has an XXX sex-chromosomal structure, *triple X syndrome*. Such girls are normal in appearance but tend to show lower-than-average language skills and poorer memory for recent events. Development of external sexual organs appears normal enough, although there is increased incidence of infertility (Wodrich, 2006).

Genetic Abnormalities

Genetic abnormalities can also give rise to health problems. Some genetic abnormalities, such as cystic fibrosis, are caused by a single pair of genes; others are caused by combinations of genes. Diabetes mellitus, epilepsy, and peptic ulcers are **multifactorial problems**; they reflect both a genetic predisposition and environmental contributors. Genetic abnormalities include phenylketonuria, Huntington's disease, Sickle cell anemia, Tay Sachs disease, cystic fibrosis, hemophilia, and muscular dystrophy.

Phenylketonuria

The enzyme disorder **phenylketonuria (PKU)** is transmitted by a recessive gene and affects about 1 child in 8,000. Children with PKU cannot metabolize an amino acid called phenylalanine, so it builds up in their bodies and impairs the functioning of the central nervous system, resulting in mental retardation, psychological disorders, and physical problems. There is no cure for PKU, but children with PKU can be placed on diets low in phenylalanine within 3 to 6 weeks of birth and develop normally (Brazier & Rowlands, 2006).

Huntington's Disease

Huntington's disease is a fatal, progressive degenerative disorder and a dominant trait, affecting approximately 1 in 18,000 Americans. Physical symptoms include uncontrollable muscle movements (D. M. Jacobs et al., 2006). Psychological symptoms include loss of intellectual functioning and personality change (Robins Wahlin et al., 2007). Because the onset of Huntington's disease is delayed until middle adulthood, many individuals with the defect have borne children only to discover years later that they and possibly half their offspring will inevitably develop it. Medicines can help deal with some symptoms.

Sickle-Cell Anemia

Sickle-cell anemia is caused by a recessive gene. Sickle-cell anemia is most common among African Americans. Nearly 1 in 10 African Americans and 1 in 20 Latin Americans is a carrier. In sickle-cell anemia, red blood cells take on the shape of a sickle and clump together, obstructing small blood vessels and decreasing the oxygen supply. The lessened oxygen supply can impair cognitive skills and academic performance (Hogan et al., 2005; Ogunfowora et al., 2005). Physical problems include painful and swollen joints, jaundice, and potentially fatal conditions such as pneumonia, stroke, and heart and kidney failure.

Tay-Sachs Disease

Tay-Sachs disease is also caused by a recessive gene. It causes the central nervous system to degenerate, resulting in death. The disorder is most commonly found among children in Jewish families of Eastern European background. Approximately 1 in 30 Jewish Americans from this background carries the recessive gene for Tay-Sachs.

▶ **LO7** Describe prenatal testing methods for chromosomal and genetic abnormalities.

cystic fibrosis A fatal genetic disorder in which mucus obstructs the lungs and pancreas.

hemophilia A genetic disorder in which blood does not clot properly.

sex-linked genetic abnormality An abnormality resulting from genes that are found on the X sex chromosome; more likely to be shown by male offspring (who do not have an opposing gene from a second X chromosome) than by female offspring.

muscular dystrophy A chronic disease characterized by a progressive wasting away of the muscles.

genetic counselor A health worker who compiles information about a couple's genetic heritage to advise them as to whether their children might develop genetic abnormalities.

prenatal Before birth.

amniocentesis A procedure for drawing and examining fetal cells sloughed off into amniotic fluid to determine the presence of various disorders.

miscarriage The expulsion of an embryo or fetus before it can sustain life on its own, most often due to defective development.

chorionic villus sampling (CVS) A method for the prenatal detection of genetic abnormalities that samples the membrane enveloping the amniotic sac and fetus.

uterus The hollow organ within females in which the embryo and fetus develop.

Children with the disorder progressively lose control over their muscles, experience sensory losses, develop mental retardation, become paralyzed, and usually die by about the age of 5.

Cystic Fibrosis

Cystic fibrosis, also caused by a recessive gene, is the most common fatal hereditary disease among European Americans. Approximately 30,000 Americans have the disorder, but another 10 million (1 in every 31 people) are carriers (Cystic Fibrosis Foundation, 2007). Children with the disease suffer from excessive production of thick mucus that clogs the pancreas and lungs. Most victims die of respiratory infections in their 20s.

Sex-Linked Genetic Abnormalities

Some genetic defects, such as **hemophilia**, are carried on only the X sex chromosome. For this reason, they are referred to as **sex-linked genetic abnormalities**. These defects also involve recessive genes. Females, who have two X sex chromosomes, are less likely than males to show sex-linked disorders because the genes that cause the disorder would have to be present on both of a female's sex chromosomes for the disorder to be expressed. Sex-linked diseases are more likely to afflict sons of female carriers because males have only one X sex chromosome, which they inherit from their mothers.

One form of **muscular dystrophy**, Duchenne muscular dystrophy, is sex-linked. Muscular dystrophy is characterized by a weakening of the muscles, which can lead to wasting away, inability to walk, and sometimes death. Other sex-linked abnormalities include diabetes, color blindness, and some types of night blindness.

©Photo12/The Image Works

Queen Victoria of England was a carrier of hemophilia and transmitted the blood disorder to many of her children, who in turn carried it into a number of the ruling houses of Europe. For this reason, hemophilia has been dubbed "the royal disease."

Genetic Counseling and Prenatal Testing

It is possible to detect genetic abnormalities that are responsible for many diseases. **Genetic counselors** compile information about a couple's genetic heritage to explore whether their children might develop genetic abnormalities. Couples who face a high risk of passing along genetic defects to their children sometimes elect to adopt or not have children, rather than conceive their own. In addition, **prenatal** testing can indicate whether an embryo or fetus is carrying genetic abnormalities.

Amniocentesis

Amniocentesis is usually performed on the mother at 14–16 weeks after conception, although many physicians now perform the procedure earlier ("early amniocentesis"). In this method, the health professional uses a syringe (needle) to withdraw fluid from the amniotic sac (see Figure 2.6). The fluid contains cells that are sloughed off by the fetus. The cells are separated from the amniotic fluid, grown in a culture, and then examined microscopically for genetic and chromosomal abnormalities.

Amniocentesis has become routine among American women who become pregnant past the age of 35 because the chances of Down syndrome and other chromosomal abnormalities increase dramatically as women approach or pass the age of 40. Amniocentesis also permits parents to learn the gender of their unborn child through examination of the sex chromosomes, but most parents learn the gender of their baby earlier by means of ultrasound. Amniocentesis carries some risk of **miscarriage** (approximately 1 woman in 100 who undergo the procedure will miscarry), so health professionals would not conduct it just to learn the gender of the child.

Chorionic Villus Sampling

Chorionic villus sampling (CVS) is similar to amniocentesis but is carried out between the 9th and 12th week of pregnancy. A small syringe is inserted through the vagina into the **uterus** and sucks out some threadlike projections (villi) from the outer membrane that envelops the amniotic sac and fetus. Results are available within days. CVS has not been used as frequently as amniocentesis because CVS carries a slightly greater risk of miscarriage. More recent studies suggest that both amniocentesis and CVS increase the risk of miscarriage and that the risks might not be equal (Alfirevic et al., 2003; Philip et al., 2004).

Ultrasound

Health professionals also use sound waves that are too high in frequency to be heard by the human ear—**ultrasound**—to obtain information about the fetus. Ultrasound waves are reflected by the fetus, and a computer uses the information to generate a picture of the fetus. The picture is termed a **sonogram** (see Figure 2.7).

Ultrasound

Watch an ultrasound recording.

▶ **LO8** Differentiate between genotypes and phenotypes.

▶ **LO9** Explain how twin studies and adoption studies are used to sort out the effects of nature and nurture.

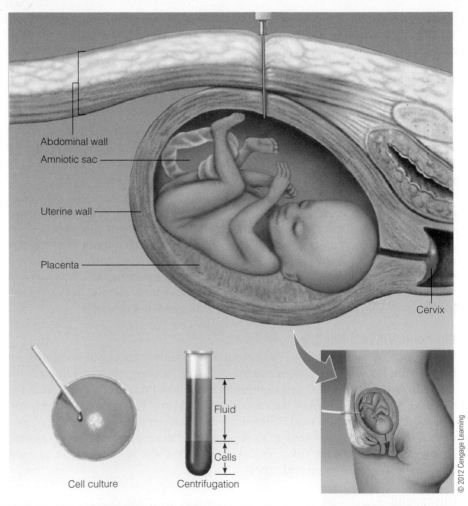

Abdominal wall

Amniotic sac

Uterine wall

Placenta

Cervix

Fluid

Cells

Cell culture

Centrifugation

© 2012 Cengage Learning

Figure 2.6 Amniocentesis Amniocentesis allows prenatal identification of certain genetic and chromosomal disorders by examining genetic material sloughed off by the fetus into amniotic fluid.

alpha-fetoprotein assay A blood test that assesses the mother's blood level of alpha-fetoprotein, a substance linked with fetal neural-tube defects.

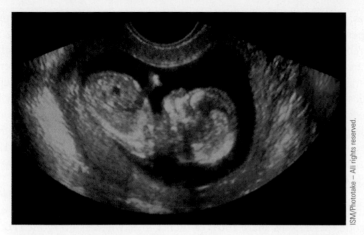

Figure 2.7 Sonogram of a 5-Month-Old Fetus In the ultrasound technique, sound waves are bounced off the fetus and provide a picture that enables professionals to detect various abnormalities.

Ultrasound is used to guide the syringe in amniocentesis and CVS by determining the position of the fetus. It is also used to track the growth of the fetus, determine fetal age and gender, and detect multiple pregnancies and structural abnormalities.

Blood Tests

Parental blood tests can reveal the presence of genetic disorders such as sickle-cell anemia, Tay-Sachs disease, and cystic fibrosis. The **alpha-fetoprotein assay** is used to detect neural-tube defects such as spina bifida and certain chromosomal abnormalities. Neural-tube defects cause an elevation in the level of alpha-fetoprotein in the mother's blood. Elevated levels also are associated with increased risk of fetal death.

Kinship Studies

In addition to inheritance, the development of our traits is also influenced by nutrition, learning, exercise, and— unfortunately—accident and illness. A potential Shakespeare who is reared in poverty and never taught to read or write will not create a *Hamlet*. Our traits and behaviors therefore represent the interaction of heredity and environment. The sets of traits that we inherit from our parents are referred to as our

Prenatal Doctor's Visit

Watch the highlights of a mother-to-be's prenatal visit, including an ultrasound.

Twins Research

Learn how scientists gather research about twins for studies.

genotypes. The actual sets of traits that we exhibit are called our phenotypes. Our **phenotypes** reflect both genetic and environmental influences.

Researchers have developed a number of strategies to help sort out the effects of heredity and the environment on development. In kinship studies, researchers study the appearance of a trait or behavior pattern among relatives with various degrees of genetic closeness. The more closely people are related, the more genes they have in common. Parents and children have a 50% overlap in their genetic endowments, and so do siblings (brothers and sisters). Aunts and uncles have a 25% overlap with nieces and nephews, as do grandparents with grandchildren. First cousins share 12.5% of their genetic endowment. If genes are implicated in a trait, people who are more closely related should be more likely to share it.

Twin Studies: Looking In the Genetic Mirror

Monozygotic (MZ) twins share 100% of their genes, whereas dizygotic (DZ) twins have a 50% overlap, just as other siblings do. If MZ twins show greater similarity on some trait or behavior than DZ twins do, a genetic basis for the trait or behavior is indicated.

MZ twins resemble each other more closely than DZ twins on a number of physical and psychological traits, even when the MZ twins are reared apart and the DZ twins are reared together (Bouchard & Loehlin, 2001). MZ twins are more likely to

genotype The genetic form or constitution of a person as determined by heredity.

phenotype The actual form or constitution of a person as determined by heredity and environmental factors.

autism A developmental disorder characterized by failure to relate to others, communication problems, intolerance of change, and ritualistic behavior.

iStockphoto.com/Carmen Martinez Banús

look alike and be similar in height (Plomin, 2002). Heredity even affects their preference for coffee or tea (Luciano et al., 2005). MZ twins resemble one another more strongly than DZ twins in intelligence and personality traits (Hur, 2005; Johnson et al., 2004; McCrae et al., 2000). MZ twins are also more likely to share psychological disorders such as **autism**, depression, schizophrenia, and vulnerability to alcoholism (Belmonte & Carper, 2006; Plomin, 2002; Ronald et al., 2006).

But one might ask whether MZ twins resemble each other so closely partly because they are often treated so similarly? One way to answer this question is to find and compare MZ twins who were reared apart. Except for the uterine environment, similarities between MZ twins reared apart would appear to be a result of heredity. In the Minnesota Study of Twins Reared Apart (Bouchard et al., 1990; DiLalla et al., 1999; Lykken, 2006), researchers have been measuring the physiological and psychological characteristics of 56 sets of MZ adult twins who were separated in infancy and reared in different homes. The MZ twins reared apart are about as similar as MZ twins reared together on measures of intelligence, personality, temperament, occupational and leisure-time interests, and social attitudes. These traits would thus appear to have a genetic underpinning.

Adoption Studies

Adoption studies in which children are separated from their natural parents at an early age and reared by adoptive parents provide special opportunities for sorting out nature and nurture. When children who are reared by adoptive parents are nonetheless more similar to their natural parents in a trait, a powerful argument is made for a genetic role in the appearance of that trait.

Traits are determined by pairs of genes. One member of each pair comes from each parent in the process called conception, which we discuss in the following module.

Check Your Learning Quiz 2.1

Go to **login.cengagebrain.com** and take the online quiz.

▸ **LO10** Describe the development and release of ova.

▸ **LO11** Describe the development and travels of sperm.

▸ **LO12** Define *conception*.

Did you know that—

- Approximately 120 to 150 boys are conceived for every 100 girls?
- Sperm use the sense of smell to help find ova?
- "Test-tube" babies aren't conceived in test tubes; nor do they develop in test tubes?
- Newly fertilized egg cells survive without any nourishment from the mother for more than a week?
- Fetuses suck their thumbs, sometimes for hours on end?
- A father's age as well as a mother's at the time of conception can influence the development of the fetus?

▼

Conception: Against All Odds

On a balmy day in October, Marta and her partner Jorge rush to catch the train to their jobs in the city. Marta's workday is outwardly the same as any other. Within her body, however, a drama is unfolding. Yesterday, hormones caused an ovarian follicle to rupture, releasing its egg cell, or ovum. How this particular follicle was selected to ripen and release its ovum this month remains a mystery. But starting then, Marta was capable of conceiving for a day or so.

Yesterday morning, Marta used her ovulation-timing kit, which showed that she was about to ovulate. So later that night, Marta and Jorge made love, hoping that Marta would conceive. Jorge ejaculated hundreds of millions of sperm—a normal amount. Sperm do not travel about at random inside the woman's reproductive tract. The direction in which they travel is guided by a change in calcium ions that occurs when an ovum is released, and sperm use a sense of smell to track it.

Only a few thousand of Jorge's sperm survived the journey through the cervix and uterus to the fallopian tube that contained the ovum, released just hours earlier. Of these, a few hundred remained to bombard the ovum. One succeeded in penetrating the ovum's covering, resulting in conception. From a single cell formed by the union of sperm and ovum, a new life begins to form. The zygote is only 1/175 of an inch across—a tiny beginning for the drama about to take place.

conception The union of a sperm cell and an ovum that occurs when the chromosomes of each of these cells combine to form 23 new pairs.

endometrium The inner lining of the uterus.

Marta is 37 years old. Four months into her pregnancy, Marta undergoes amniocentesis in order to check for the presence of chromosomal abnormalities, such as Down syndrome. (Down syndrome is more common among children born to women in their late 30s and older.) Amniocentesis also indicates the gender of the fetus. Although many parents prefer to know the gender of their baby before it is born, Marta and Jorge ask their doctor not to inform them. "Why ruin the surprise?" Jorge tells his friends. So Marta and Jorge are left to debate boys' names and girls' names for the next few months.

Conception is the term used to describe the union of an ovum and a sperm cell. It is the beginning of a new human life, but the cells which combine to form that new life were also living. If another sperm cell had combined with another ovum, your parents would have had someone else—genetically speaking, your brother or your sister. That someone else could have been like you—or not.

Ova

At birth, women already have hundreds of thousands of egg cells, or ova. They are immature in form, however. The ovaries produce the female hormones estrogen and progesterone. At puberty, in response to hormonal command, some ova begin to mature. Each month, an egg (occasionally more than one) is released from its ovarian follicle about midway through the menstrual cycle and enters a nearby fallopian tube (see Figure 2.8). It might take 3 to 4 days for an egg to be propelled by small, hairlike structures called cilia and, perhaps, by contractions in the wall of the tube, along the few inches of the fallopian tube to the uterus. Unlike sperm, eggs do not propel themselves.

If the egg is not fertilized, it is discharged—along with the **endometrium** that had formed to support an embryo—through the uterus and the vagina in the menstrual flow. During a woman's reproductive years, about 400 ova (that is, 1 in 1,000 or so) will ripen and be released.

Ova are much larger than sperm. The chicken egg and the 6-inch ostrich egg are each just one cell, although the sperm of these birds are microscopic. Human ova are barely visible to the eye, but their bulk is still thousands of times larger than that of sperm cells.

Sperm Cells

Sperm cells develop through several stages. They each begin with 23 pairs of chromosomes, or a total of 46 chromosomes. Each pair of sex chromosomes carries an X sex chromosome and a Y sex chromosome. After meiosis, each sperm has

Blend Images/Jupiterimages and Joan Coll/iStockphoto.com

Female Reproductive Organs

Explore an interactive version of Figure 2.8.

▶ **L013** Discuss infertility.

▶ **L014** Discuss preimplantation genetic diagnosis.

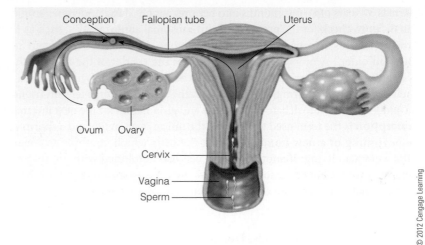

Figure 2.8 Female Reproductive Organs

© 2012 Cengage Learning

23 chromosomes. Half of the sperm cells now carry an X sex chromosome, and half carry a Y sex chromosome. Each sperm cell is about 1/500 of an inch long, one of the smallest types of cells in the body. Sperm with Y sex chromosomes appear to swim faster than sperm with X sex chromosomes. This difference contributes to the conception of 120 to 150 boys for every 100 girls. Male fetuses suffer a higher rate of miscarriage than females, however, often during the first month of pregnancy. At birth, boys outnumber girls by only 106 to 100. Boys also have a higher incidence of infant mortality, which further equalizes the numbers of girls and boys.

The 150 million or so sperm in the ejaculate—which carries bodily fluids as well as sperm cells—may seem to be a wasteful investment because only one sperm can fertilize an ovum, but only 1 in 1,000 sperm will ever approach an ovum. Millions deposited in the vagina flow out of the woman's body because of gravity. Normal vaginal acidity kills many more sperm. Many surviving sperm then have to swim against the current of fluid coming from the cervix (see Figure 2.8).

Sperm that survive these initial obstacles may reach the fallopian tubes 60 to 90 minutes after ejaculation. About half the sperm enter the fallopian tube that does not contain the egg. Perhaps 2,000 enter the correct tube. Fewer still manage to swim the final 2 inches against the currents generated by the cilia that line the tube. Sperm

motility Self-propulsion.

cells do not travel about at random inside the woman's reproductive tract. They are apparently "egged on" (pardon the pun) by a change in calcium ions that occurs when an ovum is released (Angier, 2007).

Of all the sperm swarming around the egg, only one enters (see Figure 2.9). Ova are surrounded by a gelatinous layer that must be penetrated if fertilization is to occur. Many of the sperm that complete their journey to the ovum secrete an enzyme that briefly thins the layer, but it enables only one sperm to penetrate. Once a sperm cell enters, the layer thickens, locking other sperm out.

The chromosomes from the sperm cell line up across from the corresponding chromosomes in the egg cell. They form 23 new pairs with a unique set of genetic instructions.

Medical RF/Phototake

Figure 2.9 Human Sperm Swarming Around an Ovum in a Fallopian Tube Fertilization normally occurs in a fallopian tube. Thousands of sperm may wind up in the vicinity of an ovum, but only one fertilizes it.

Infertility and Alternative Ways of Becoming Parents

Approximately 1 in 6 or 7 American couples has fertility problems (Rebar & DeCherney, 2004). The term *infertility* usually is not applied until the couple has failed to conceive on their own for 1 year. Infertility was once viewed as a problem of the woman, but it turns out that the problem lies with the man in about 40% of cases.

Causes of Infertility

A low sperm count—or lack of sperm—is the most common infertility problem in men. Men's fertility problems have a variety of causes: genetic factors, environmental poisons, diabetes, sexually transmitted infections (STIs), overheating of the testes (which happens now and then among athletes, such as long-distance runners), pressure (as from using narrow bicycle seats), aging, and certain prescription and illicit drugs (Hatcher et al., 2007). Sometimes the sperm count is adequate, but other factors, such as prostate or hormonal problems, deform sperm or deprive them of their **motility**. Motility can also be impaired by scar tissue from infections, such as STIs.

The most common problem in women is irregular ovulation or lack of ovulation. This problem can have many causes, including irregularities among the hormones that govern ovulation, stress, and malnutrition. So-called fertility drugs (e.g., *clomi-*

Stress and Pregnancy

Watch and learn how stress may affect fertility.

phene and *Pergonal*) are made up of hormones that cause women to ovulate. These drugs may cause multiple births by stimulating more than one ovum to ripen during a month (Legro et al., 2007).

Infections may scar the fallopian tubes and other organs, impeding the passage of sperm or ova. **Pelvic inflammatory disease** can result from such infections, whether bacterial or viral, including the STIs gonorrhea and chlamydia. Antibiotics are usually helpful in treating bacterial infections, but infertility may be irreversible.

Endometriosis can obstruct the fallopian tubes, where conception normally takes place. Endometriosis has become fairly common among women who delay childbearing. Each month, tissue develops to line the uterus in case the woman conceives. This tissue—the endometrium—is then sloughed off during menstruation. But some of it backs up into the abdomen through the fallopian tubes. It then collects in the abdomen, where it can cause abdominal pain and lessen the chances of conception. Physicians may treat endometriosis with hormones that temporarily prevent menstruation or through surgery.

Artificial Insemination

pelvic inflammatory disease (PID) An infection of the abdominal region that may have various causes and that may impair fertility.

endometriosis Inflammation of endometrial tissue sloughed off into the abdominal cavity rather than out of the body during menstruation; the condition is characterized by abdominal pain and sometimes infertility.

artificial insemination Injection of sperm into the uterus to fertilize an ovum.

in vitro fertilization (IVF) Fertilization of an ovum in a laboratory dish.

donor IVF The transfer of a donor's ovum, fertilized in a laboratory dish, to the uterus of another woman.

Ejaculations of men with low sperm counts can be collected, combined, and quick-frozen. The larger amount of sperm can then be injected into the woman's uterus at the time of ovulation. This method is one **artificial insemination** procedure. Sperm from men with low sperm motility can also be injected into their partners' uteruses so that the sperm can begin their journey closer to the fallopian tubes. When a man has no sperm or an extremely low sperm count, his partner can be artificially inseminated with the sperm of a donor who resembles the man in physical traits. Some women who want a baby but do not have a partner also use artificial insemination.

In Vitro Fertilization

So called "test-tube babies" are not actually grown in a test tube but are conceived through **in vitro fertilization (IVF)**, a method of conception in which ripened ova are removed surgically from the mother and placed in a laboratory dish. The father's sperm are also placed in the dish. One or more ova are fertilized and then injected into the mother's uterus to become implanted.

IVF may be used when the blocked fallopian tubes prevent ova from travelling through them. If the father's sperm are low in motility, they are sometimes injected directly into the ovum. A variation known as **donor IVF** can be used when the intended mother does not produce ova. An ovum from another woman is fertilized and injected into the uterus of the mother-to-be.

Because only a minority of IVF attempts lead to births, it can take several attempts to achieve a pregnancy. Several embryos may be injected into the uterus at once, heightening the odds that one of the embryos will become implanted. IVF remains costly but is otherwise routine, if not guaranteed.

Surrogate Mothers

Surrogate mothers bring babies to term for other women who are infertile. Surrogate mothers may be artificially inseminated by the partners of infertile women, in which case the baby carries the genes of the father. But sometimes—as with 60-year-old singer-songwriter James Taylor and his 54-year-old wife, Caroline Smedvig—ova are surgically extracted from the biological mother, fertilized in vitro by the biological father, and then implanted in another woman's uterus, where the baby is brought to term. Surrogate mothers are usually paid and sign agreements to surrender the baby.

Adoption

Adoption is another way for people to obtain children. Despite occasional conflicts that pit adoptive parents against biological parents who change their minds about giving up their children, most adoptions result in the formation of loving new families. Many Americans find it easier to adopt infants from other countries or with special needs. Children adopted at younger ages acquire the language and customs of their adoptive parents more readily.

An aspect of adoption that is often not considered is its effects on the relinquishing mother (Aloi, 2009). These mothers often experience feelings of loss and guilt, along with wondering how their child is developing and adjusting.

Junko Kimura/Getty Images

Film actors Angelina Jolie and Brad Pitt derive satisfaction from adopting children even though they are fertile.

Selecting the Gender of Your Child

Today, there is a reliable method for selecting the gender of a child prior to implantation: preimplantation genetic diagnosis. It was developed to detect genetic

▶ **LO15** Describe the stages of prenatal development.

disorders, but it also reveals the sex of the embryo. In the procedure, ova are fertilized in vitro. After a few days of cell division, a cell is extracted from each, and its sex-chromosomal structure is examined microscopically to learn its sex. Embryos of the desired sex are implanted in the woman's uterus, where one or more can grow to term. However, successful implantation cannot be guaranteed.

Prenatal Development

The most rapid and dramatic human developments are literally out of sight, taking place in the uterus. Within 9 months, a fetus develops from a nearly microscopic cell to a neonate about 20 inches long. Its weight increases a billionfold.

We can date pregnancy from the onset of the last menstrual period before conception, which makes the normal gestation period 280 days. We can also date pregnancy from the assumed date of fertilization, which normally occurs 2 weeks after the beginning of the woman's last menstrual cycle. With this accounting method, the gestation period is 266 days.

Prenatal development is divided into three periods: the germinal stage (approximately the first 2 weeks), the embryonic stage (the third through the eighth weeks), and the fetal stage (the third month through birth). Health professionals also commonly speak of prenatal development in terms of three trimesters of 3 months each.

germinal stage The period of development between conception and the implantation of the embryo.

blastocyst A stage within the germinal period of prenatal development in which the zygote has the form of a sphere of cells surrounding a cavity of fluid.

embryonic disk The platelike inner part of the blastocyst that differentiates into the ectoderm, mesoderm, and endoderm of the embryo.

trophoblast The outer part of the blastocyst from which the amniotic sac, placenta, and umbilical cord develop.

umbilical cord A tube that connects the fetus to the placenta.

placenta An organ connected to the uterine wall and to the fetus by the umbilical cord. The placenta serves as a relay station between mother and fetus for the exchange of nutrients and wastes.

The Germinal Stage: Wanderings

Within 36 hours after conception, the zygote divides into two cells. It then divides repeatedly as it undergoes its 3–4 day journey to the uterus. Within another 36 hours, it has become 32 cells. The mass of dividing cells wanders about the uterus for another 3 to 4 days before it begins to implant in the uterine wall. Implantation takes another week or so. The period from conception to implantation is called the **germinal stage** (see Figure 2.10).

A few days into the germinal stage, the dividing cell mass takes the form of a fluid-filled ball of cells called a **blastocyst**. In the blastocyst, cells begin to separate into groups that will eventually become different structures. The inner part of the blastocyst has two distinct layers that form a thickened mass of cells called the **embryonic disk**. These cells will become the embryo and eventually the fetus.

The outer part of the blastocyst, or **trophoblast**, at first consists of a single layer of cells, but it rapidly differentiates into four membranes that will protect and nourish the embryo. One membrane produces blood cells until the embryo's liver develops and takes over this function. Then it disappears. Another membrane develops into the **umbilical cord** and the blood vessels of the **placenta**. A third develops into the amniotic sac, and the fourth becomes the chorion, which will line the placenta.

The cluster of cells that will become the embryo and then the fetus is at first nourished only by the yolk of the egg cell. A blastocyst gains mass only when it receives nourishment from outside. For that to happen, it must be implanted in the uterine wall. Implantation may be accompanied by bleeding, which is usually normal but can also be a sign of miscarriage. Most women who experience implantation bleeding, however, do

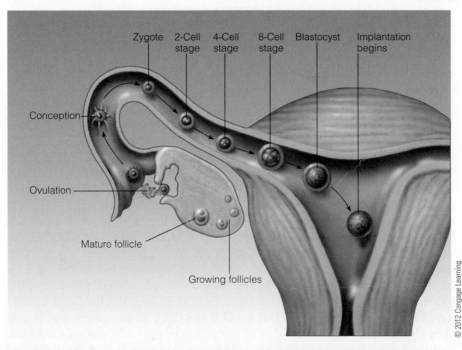

© 2012 Cengage Learning

Figure 2.10 The Ovarian Cycle, Conception, and the Early Days of the Germinal Stage Division of the zygote creates the hollow sphere of cells termed the blastocyst, which becomes implanted in the uterine wall.

Where Are the Girls?

Read about the shortage of female babies born in China.

Sex Selection

Selecting the Gender of Your Child: Fantasy or Reality?

not miscarry, but have normal pregnancies. Miscarriage usually stems from abnormalities in the developmental process. Nearly one third of pregnancies end in miscarriage, with most miscarriages occurring in the first 3 months (Miscarriage, 2007).

The Embryonic Stage

The **embryonic stage** begins with implantation and covers the first 2 months, during which the major organ systems differentiate. Development follows **cephalocaudal** (Latin for "head to tail") and **proximodistal** (Latin for "near to far") trends. Growth of the head takes precedence over growth of the lower parts of the body (see Figure 2.11). You can also think of the body as containing a central axis that coincides with the spinal cord. Growth of the organ systems near the spine occurs earlier than growth of the extremities. Relatively early maturation of the brain and organs that lie near the spine allows them to play key roles in further development.

During the embryonic stage, the outer layer of cells of the embryonic disk, or **ectoderm**, develops into the nervous system, sensory organs, nails, hair, teeth, and outer layer of skin. At approximately 21 days, two ridges appear in the embryo and fold to compose the **neural tube**, from which the nervous system will develop. The inner layer, or **endoderm**, forms the digestive and respiratory systems, the liver, and the pancreas. A bit later, the mesoderm, a middle layer of cells, becomes differentiated. The **mesoderm** develops into the excretory, reproductive, and circulatory systems, the muscles, the skeleton, and the inner layer of the skin.

During the third week after conception, the head and blood vessels begin to form. Your heart started beating when you were only one quarter of an inch long and weighed only a fraction of an ounce. The major organ systems develop during the first 2 months. Arm buds and leg buds begin to appear toward the end of the first month. Eyes, ears, nose, and mouth begin to take shape. By this time, the nervous system, including the brain, has also begun to develop. During the second month, the cells in the nervous system begin to "fire"; that is, they send messages among themselves. Most likely it is random cell firing, and the "content" of such "messages" is anybody's guess. By the end of the second month, the embryo is looking quite human. The head has the lovely, round shape of your own, and the facial features have become quite distinct. All this detail is inscribed on an embryo that is only about 1 inch long and weighs 1/30 of an ounce. By the end of the embryonic period, tooth buds have formed. The embryo's kidneys are filtering acid from the blood, and its liver is producing red blood cells.

embryonic stage The stage of prenatal development that lasts from implantation through the eighth week of pregnancy; it is characterized by the development of the major organ systems.

cephalocaudal From head to tail.

proximodistal From the inner part (or axis) of the body outward.

ectoderm The outermost cell layer of the newly formed embryo from which the skin and nervous system develop.

neural tube A hollowed-out area in the blastocyst from which the nervous system develops.

endoderm The inner layer of the embryo from which the lungs and digestive system develop.

mesoderm The central layer of the embryo from which the bones and muscles develop.

androgens Male sex hormones.

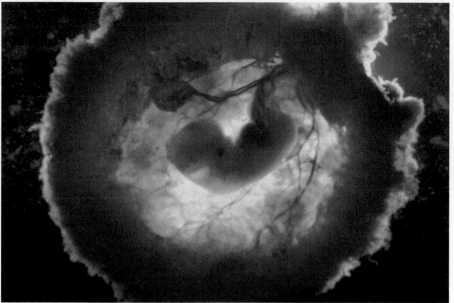

Figure 2.11 A Human Embryo at 7 Weeks The head of the human embryo is oversized in relation to the rest of the body.

Sexual Differentiation

At 5 to 6 weeks, the embryo is only one-quarter to one-half of an inch long. At this stage of development, both the internal and the external genitals resemble primitive female structures. By about the seventh week, the genetic code (XY or XX) begins to assert itself, causing sex organs to differentiate. Genetic activity on the Y sex chromosome causes the testes to begin to differentiate. The ovaries begin to differentiate if the Y chromosome is *absent*. By about 3 months after conception, males and females show distinct external genital structures. Once the testes have developed in the embryo, they begin to produce male sex hormones, or **androgens**, the most important of which is testosterone. Female embryos and fetuses produce small amounts of androgens, but they are usually not enough to cause sexual differentiation along male lines.

Stages of Conception

Explore an animation of Figure 2.10.

Sexual Differentiation

Explore to learn more about sexual differentiation.

The Amniotic Sac

The embryo and fetus develop within a protective **amniotic sac** in the uterus. This sac is surrounded by a clear membrane and contains **amniotic fluid**. The fluid serves as a kind of natural cushion, allowing the embryo and fetus to move around without injury. It also helps maintain an even temperature.

The Placenta: A Filtration System

The pancake-shaped placenta is a mass of tissue that permits the embryo (and, later on, the fetus) to exchange nutrients and wastes with the mother. The placenta is unique in origin. It grows from material supplied by both the mother and the embryo. The fetus is connected to the placenta by the umbilical cord; the mother is connected to the placenta by blood vessels in the uterine wall.

Mother and embryo have separate circulatory systems. The placenta contains a membrane that acts as a filter to permit oxygen and nutrients to reach the embryo from the mother and carbon dioxide and waste products to pass to the mother from the embryo. The mother then eliminates them through her lungs and kidneys. Some harmful substances can also sneak through the placenta, including various "germs," such as the ones that cause syphilis and German measles, but HIV (the virus that causes AIDS) is more likely to be transmitted through childbirth. Some drugs—aspirin, narcotics, alcohol, tranquilizers, and others—cross the placenta and affect the fetus.

The placenta also secretes hormones that preserve the pregnancy, prepare the breasts for nursing, and stimulate the uterine contractions that prompt childbirth. Ultimately, the placenta passes from the birth canal after the baby; for this reason, it is also called the afterbirth.

The Fetal Stage

amniotic sac Sac containing fetus

amniotic fluid Fluid within the amniotic sac that suspends and protects the fetus.

fetal stage The stage of development that lasts from the beginning of the ninth week of pregnancy through birth; it is characterized by gains in size and weight and by maturation of the organ systems.

The **fetal stage** lasts from the beginning of the third month until birth. The fetus begins to turn and respond to external stimulation at about the 9th or 10th week. By the end of the first trimester, the major organ systems have been formed. The fingers and toes are fully formed. The eyes and the gender of the fetus can be clearly seen.

The second trimester is characterized by further maturation of fetal organ systems and dramatic gains in size. The brain continues to mature, contributing to the fetus's ability to regulate its own basic body functions. The fetus advances from 1 ounce to 2 pounds in weight and grows 4 to 5 times in length, from about 3 inches to 14 inches. By the end of the second trimester, the fetus opens and shuts its eyes, sucks its thumb—sometimes for hours on end—alternates between wakefulness and sleep, and perceives light and sounds.

During the third trimester, the organ systems mature further. The fetus gains about 5½ pounds and doubles in length. During the seventh month, the fetus normally turns upside down in the uterus so that delivery will be head first. By the end of the seventh month, the fetus will have almost doubled in weight, gaining another 1 pound 12 ounces, and will have increased another 2 inches in length. If the fetus is born now, chances of survival are nearly 90%; at the end of the eighth month, the odds are overwhelmingly in favor of survival. Newborn boys average about 7½ pounds, and newborn girls about 7 pounds.

Fetal Perception

By the 13th week of pregnancy, the fetus responds to sound waves. L. W. Sontag and Richards (1938) rang a bell near the mother's abdomen, and the fetus responded with movements similar to those of the startle reflex shown after birth. During the third trimester, fetuses respond to sounds of different frequencies through a variety of movements and changes in heart rate, suggesting that they can discriminate pitch (Lecanuet et al., 2000).

An experiment by Anthony DeCasper and William Fifer (1980) was even more intriguing. In this study, women read the Dr. Seuss book *The Cat in the Hat* out loud twice daily during the final month and a half of pregnancy. After birth, their babies were given special pacifiers. Sucking on these pacifiers in one way would activate recordings of their mothers reading *The Cat in the Hat*, and sucking on them in another way would activate their mothers' readings of a book that was written in very different rhythms. The newborns "chose" to hear *The Cat in the Hat*. Fetal learning may be one basis for the development of attachment to the mother (Krueger et al., 2004; Lecanuet et al., 2005).

RubberBall Photography/Veer

No, we're not seriously suggesting that pregnant women "pipe" classical music into their fetuses through headphones or the like. But research has shown that fetuses can hear during the latter part of pregnancy, so some parents attempt to shape their tastes by having the "proper" music in their environments.

Organ Development

Explore the development of a fetus's internal genital organs following conception.

Fetal Perception

Read research on perception in unborn babies.

Fetal Movement

The mother usually feels the first fetal movements in the middle of the fourth month (Adolph & Berger, 2005). By 29–30 weeks, the fetus moves its limbs so vigorously that the mother may complain of being kicked. The fetus also turns somersaults, which are clearly felt by the mother. The umbilical cord will not break or become dangerously wrapped around the fetus, no matter how many acrobatic feats the fetus performs. As the fetus grows, it becomes cramped in the uterus and movement is constricted, so that the fetus becomes markedly less active during the ninth month of pregnancy.

Environmental Influences on Prenatal Development

The developing fetus is subject to many environmental hazards. Scientific advances have made us keenly aware of the types of things that can go wrong and what we can do to prevent these problems.

stillbirth The birth of a dead fetus.

teratogens Environmental influences or agents that can damage the embryo or fetus.

critical period In this usage, a period during which an embryo is particularly vulnerable to a certain teratogen.

A Human Fetus at 12 Weeks

Petit Format/Nestle/ Science Source/ Photo Researchers, Inc.

Nutrition

It is a common misconception that fetuses "take what they need" from their mothers. However, maternal malnutrition has been linked to low birth weight, prematurity, retardation of brain development, cognitive deficiencies, behavioral problems, and even cardiovascular disease (Giussani, 2006; Guerrini et al., 2007; Morton, 2006). The effects of fetal malnutrition are sometimes overcome by a supportive, caregiving environment. Experiments with children who suffered from fetal malnutrition showed that enriched day-care programs enhanced intellectual and social skills by 5 years of age (Ramey et al., 1999). Supplementing the diets of pregnant women who might otherwise have caloric and protein deficiencies also showed modest positive effects on the motor development of infants (Morton, 2006). On the other hand, maternal obesity is linked with a higher risk of **stillbirth** (Fernandez-Twinn & Ozanne, 2006) and neural-tube defects. Over the course of pregnancy, women who do not restrict their diet will normally gain 25–35 pounds. Overweight women may gain less, and slender women may gain more. Regular weight gains of about one half pound per week during the first half of the pregnancy and 1 pound per week thereafter are desirable (Christian et al., 2003; Hynes et al., 2002).

Teratogens and Health Problems of the Mother

Teratogens are environmental agents that can harm the embryo or fetus. They include drugs taken by the mother, such as marijuana and alcohol, and substances that the mother's body produces, such as Rh-positive antibodies. Another class of teratogens is the heavy metals, such as lead and mercury, which are toxic to the embryo. Hormones are healthful in countless ways—for example, they help maintain pregnancy—but excessive quantities are harmful to the embryo. Exposure to radiation can also harm the embryo. Finally, disease-causing organisms—called pathogens—such as bacteria and viruses are also teratogens.

Critical Periods of Vulnerability

Exposure to particular teratogens is most harmful during **critical periods** that correspond to the times when organs are developing. For example, the heart develops rapidly in the third to fifth weeks after conception. As you can see in Figure 2.12, the heart is most vulnerable to certain teratogens at this time. The arms and legs, which develop later, are most vulnerable in the fourth through eighth weeks. Because the major organ systems differentiate during the embryonic stage, the embryo is gener-

Highlights of Prenatal Development

Explore the highlights of prenatal development.

Rx Drugs and Development

Watch and learn about prescription drugs and fetal brain development.

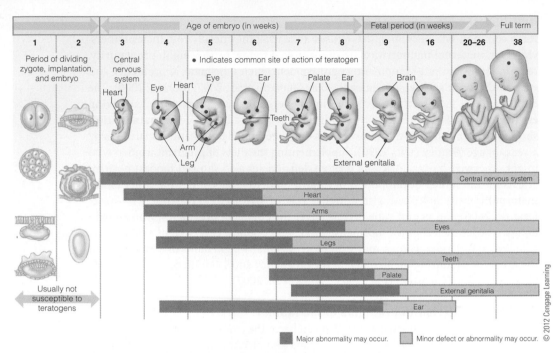

				Age of embryo (in weeks)					Fetal period (in weeks)			Full term
1	2	3	4	5	6	7	8	9	16	20–26	38

Period of dividing zygote, implantation, and embryo

Central nervous system

• Indicates common site of action of teratogen

Heart — Eye — Heart — Eye — Ear — Palate — Ear — Brain — Teeth — Arm — Leg — External genitalia

Usually not susceptible to teratogens

Central nervous system
Heart
Arms
Eyes
Legs
Teeth
Palate
External genitalia
Ear

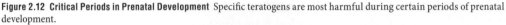

■ Major abnormality may occur. □ Minor defect or abnormality may occur.

© 2012 Cengage Learning

Figure 2.12 Critical Periods in Prenatal Development Specific teratogens are most harmful during certain periods of prenatal development.

syphilis A sexually transmitted infection that attacks major organ systems.

congenital Present at birth and resulting from genetic or chromosomal abnormalities or exposure to the prenatal environment.

HIV/AIDS Human immunodeficiency virus cripples the body's immune system; Acquired Immuno-Deficiency Syndrome weakens the immune system and leaves it vulnerable to diseases it would otherwise fight off.

ally more vulnerable to teratogens than the fetus. Even so, many teratogens are harmful throughout the entire course of prenatal development.

Let's consider the effects of various health problems of the mother. We begin with STIs.

Sexually Transmitted Infections

The **syphilis** bacterium can cause miscarriage, stillbirth, or **congenital** syphilis. Routine blood tests early in pregnancy can diagnose syphilis. The syphilis bacterium is vulnerable to antibiotics. The fetus will probably not contract syphilis if an infected mother is treated with antibiotics before the fourth month of pregnancy (Centers for Disease Control and Prevention, 2006). If the mother is not treated, the baby may be infected in utero and develop congenital syphilis.

HIV/AIDS (human immunodeficiency virus/acquired immunodeficiency syndrome) disables the body's immune system and leaves victims prey to a variety of fatal illnesses, including respiratory disorders and cancer. HIV/AIDS is lethal unless treated with a "cocktail" of antiviral drugs. Even then, the drugs do not work for everyone, and the eventual outcome remains in doubt (Rathus et al., 2011).

HIV can be transmitted by sexual relations, blood transfusions, sharing of hypodermic needles while shooting up drugs, childbirth, and breast feeding. About one fourth of babies born to HIV-infected mothers become infected themselves (Coovadia, 2004). During childbirth, blood vessels in the mother and baby rupture, enabling an exchange of blood and transmission of HIV. HIV is also found in breast milk. An African study found that the probability of transmission of HIV through breast milk was about 1 in 6 (16.2%) (Nduati et al., 2000).

rubella A viral infection that can cause retardation and heart disease in the embryo. Also called German measles.

toxemia (or preeclampsia) A life-threatening disease that can afflict pregnant women, characterized by high blood pressure.

premature Born before the full term gestation. Also referred to as *preterm*.

Rubella

Rubella (German measles) is a viral infection. Women who are infected during the first 20 weeks of pregnancy stand at least a 20% chance of bearing children with birth defects such as deafness, mental retardation, heart disease, or eye problems, including blindness (Food and Drug Administration, 2004; Reef et al., 2004).

Many adult women had rubella as children and became immune in this way. Vaccinating women who are not immune before they become pregnant is best, although they can be inoculated during pregnancy if necessary. Inoculation has led to a dramatic decline in the number of American children born with defects caused by rubella, from approximately 2,000 cases in 1964–1965 to 21 cases in 2001 (Food and Drug Administration, 2004; Reef et al., 2004).

Toxemia

Toxemia (also called **preeclampsia**) is a life-threatening disease, characterized by high blood pressure, that may afflict women late in the second or early in the third trimester. Women with toxemia often have **premature** or undersized babies. Toxemia is also a cause of pregnancy-related maternal deaths (Rumbold et al., 2006). Toxemia appears to be linked to malnutrition, but the causes are unclear. Women who do not receive prenatal care are much more likely to die from toxemia than those who receive prenatal care (J. R. Scott, 2006).

Preventing HIV in the Unborn

Learn how to prevent infecting an unborn baby with HIV.

Rh Incompatibility

In **Rh incompatibility**, antibodies produced by the mother are transmitted to a fetus or newborn infant and cause brain damage or death. Rh is a blood protein found in the red blood cells of some individuals. Rh incompatibility occurs when a woman who does not have this factor—and is thus Rh negative—is carrying an Rh-positive fetus, which can happen if the father is Rh positive. The negative–positive combination occurs in approximately 10% of American couples and becomes a problem in some resulting pregnancies. Rh incompatibility does not affect a first child because women will not have formed Rh antibodies. The chances of an exchange of blood are greatest during childbirth. If an exchange occurs, the mother produces Rh-positive antibodies to the baby's Rh-positive blood. These antibodies can enter the fetal bloodstream during subsequent deliveries, causing anemia, mental deficiency, or death.

If an Rh-negative mother is injected with Rh immunoglobulin within 72 hours after delivery of an Rh-positive baby, she will not develop the antibodies. A fetus or newborn child at risk of Rh disease may receive a blood transfusion to remove the mother's antibodies.

Drugs Taken By the Parents

Rh antibodies can be lethal to children, but many other substances can have harmful effects. Even commonly used medications, such as aspirin, can be harmful to the fetus. If a woman is pregnant or thinks she may be, it is advisable for her to consult her obstetrician before taking any drugs, not just prescription medications. A physician usually can recommend a safe and effective substitute for a drug that could potentially harm a developing fetus.

Thalidomide

Thalidomide was marketed in the 1960s as a treatment for insomnia and nausea, and provides a dramatic example of critical periods of vulnerability to teratogens. A fetus's extremities undergo rapid development during the second month of pregnancy (see Figure 2.12). Thalidomide taken during this period almost invariably causes birth defects, such as missing or stunted limbs. The drug is no longer prescribed for pregnant women.

Rh incompatibility A condition in which antibodies produced by the mother are transmitted to the child, possibly causing brain damage or death.

thalidomide A sedative used in the 1960s that has been linked to birth defects, especially deformed or absent limbs.

progestin A synthetic hormone used to maintain pregnancy that can cause masculinization of the fetus.

DES Diethylstilbestrol, a synthetic estrogen that has been linked to cancer in the reproductive organs of children of women who used it when pregnant.

Hormones

Women at risk for miscarriages have been prescribed hormones to help maintain their pregnancies. **Progestin**—a synthetic version of naturally occurring progesterone—is chemically similar to male sex hormones and can masculinize the external sex organs of female embryos. **DES** (short for diethylstilbestrol), a powerful estrogen often prescribed during the 1940s and 1950s to help prevent miscarriage, has been shown to have caused cervical and testicular cancer in some offspring. Among daughters of DES users, about 1 in 1,000 will develop cancer in the reproductive tract (Federal Interagency Forum on Child and Family Statistic, 2005).

Vitamins

Although pregnant women are often prescribed multivitamins to maintain their own health and to promote the development of their fetuses, high doses of vitamins A and D have been associated with damage to the central nervous system, small head size, and heart defects (National Institutes of Health, 2002).

Corbis Photography / Veer

What drugs are safe for pregnant women? When in doubt, she should ask her obstetrician.

Heroin and Methadone

Maternal addiction to heroin or methadone is linked to low birth weight, prematurity, and toxemia. Narcotics such as heroin and methadone readily cross the placental membrane, and the fetuses of women who regularly use them can become addicted (Lejeune et al., 2006). Addicted newborns may be given the narcotic or a substitute shortly after birth so that they will not suffer serious withdrawal symptoms. The drug is then withdrawn gradually. Addicted newborns may also have behavioral effects, such as delays in motor and language development at the age of 12 months (Bunikowski et al., 1998).

Marijuana (Cannabis)

Smoking marijuana during pregnancy apparently poses a number of risks for the fetus, including slower growth (Hurd et al., 2005) and low birth weight (Visscher et al., 2003). The babies of women who regularly used marijuana showed increased tremors and startling, suggesting immature development of the nervous system (Huestis et al., 2002).

Research into the cognitive effects of maternal prenatal use of marijuana shows mixed results. Some studies have suggested that there may be no impairment (Fried & Smith, 2001). Others have suggested that cognitive skills, including learning and memory, may be impaired (Huizink & Mulder, 2006). One study assessed the behavior of 10-year-olds who had been exposed prenatally to maternal use of marijuana (Goldschmidt et al., 2000), and suggested that prenatal use of marijuana was significantly related to increased hyperactivity, impulsivity, problems in paying attention, and increased delinquency and aggressive behavior.

Cocaine

Pregnant women who abuse cocaine increase the risk of stillbirth, low birth weight, and birth defects. Infants exposed to cocaine prenatally are often excitable and irritable, or lethargic; sleep is disturbed (Schuetze et al., 2006). There are suggestions of delays in cognitive development even at 12 months of age (Singer et al., 2005).

Children who are exposed to cocaine prenatally also show problems at later ages. One study compared 189 children at 4 years of age who had been exposed to cocaine in utero with 185 4-year-olds who had not (B. A. Lewis et al., 2004). The children exposed to cocaine had lower abilities to understand language and to express themselves through language.

Alcohol

Because alcohol passes through the placenta, drinking by a pregnant woman poses risks for the embryo and fetus. Heavy drinking can be lethal and is also connected with deficiencies and deformities in growth. Some children of heavy drinkers develop **fetal alcohol syndrome (FAS)** (Connor et al., 2006; see Figure 2.13). Babies with FAS are often smaller than normal, and so are their brains. The babies have distinct facial features: widely spaced eyes, an underdeveloped upper jaw, and a flattened nose. Psychological characteristics appear to reflect dysfunction of the brain (Guerrini et al., 2007).

fetal alcohol syndrome (FAS) A cluster of symptoms shown by children of women who drank heavily during pregnancy, including characteristic facial features and mental retardation.

The facial deformities of FAS diminish as the child moves into adolescence, and most children catch up in height and weight, but the intellectual, academic, and behavioral deficits of FAS persist (Guerrini et al., 2007). Maladaptive behaviors such as poor judgment, distractibility, and difficulty perceiving social cues are common (Schonfeld et al., 2005). Although some health professionals allow pregnant women a glass of wine with dinner, research suggests that even moderate drinkers place their offspring at increased risk (Newburn-Cook et al., 2002).

Figure 2.13 Fetal Alcohol Syndrome (FAS) The children of many mothers who drink alcohol during pregnancy exhibit FAS. This syndrome is characterized by developmental lags and such facial features as an underdeveloped upper jaw, a flattened nose, and widely spaced eyes.

Caffeine

Many pregnant women consume caffeine in the form of coffee, tea, soft drinks, chocolate, and nonprescription drugs. Research findings on caffeine's effects on the developing fetus have been inconsistent (Signorello & McLaughlin, 2004). Some studies have reported no adverse findings, but other studies have found that pregnant women who take in a good deal of caffeine are more likely than nonusers to have a miscarriage or a low-birth-weight baby (Weng et al., 2008).

Cigarettes

Cigarette smoke contains many ingredients, including the stimulant nicotine, the gas carbon monoxide, and hydrocarbons ("tars"), which are carcinogens. Nicotine and carbon monoxide pass through the placenta and reach the fetus. Nicotine stimulates the fetus, but its long-term effects are uncertain. Carbon monoxide decreases the amount of oxygen available to the fetus. Oxygen deprivation is connected with impaired motor development, academic delays, learning disabilities, mental retardation, and hyperactivity (Secker-Walker & Vacek, 2003).

Pregnant women who smoke are likely to deliver smaller babies than nonsmokers (I.M. Bernstein et al., 2005). Their babies are more likely to be stillborn or to die soon after birth (Cnattingius, 2004). Babies of fathers who smoke have higher rates of birth

Fetal Alcohol Syndrome

Watch and learn more about FAS.

Should Pregnant Women Avoid Caffeine?

Can we trust the research on the effects of caffeine taken during pregnancy?

▶ **LO19** Discuss the risks associated with the age of the parents to the embryo and fetus.

defects, infant mortality, lower birth weights, and cardiovascular problems (Goel et al., 2004).

Environmental Hazards

Mothers know when they are ingesting drugs, but there are many other substances in the environment they may take in unknowingly. These substances are environmental hazards to which we are all exposed, and we refer to them collectively as pollution.

James Leynse/Corbis

Prenatal exposure to heavy metals such as lead, mercury, and zinc threatens to delay mental development at 1 and 2 years of age (Heindel & Lawler, 2006). Polychlorinated biphenyls (PCBs), used in many industrial products, accumulate in fish that feed in polluted waters. Newborns whose mothers consumed PCB-contaminated fish from Lake Michigan were smaller and showed poorer motor functioning and memory defects (Jacobson et al., 1992).

Experiments with mice have shown that fetal exposure to radiation in high doses can damage the eyes, central nervous system, and skeleton (e.g., Hossain et al., 2005). Pregnant women exposed to atomic radiation during the bombings of Hiroshima and Nagasaki in World War II gave birth to babies who were likely to have mental retardation as well as physical deformities (Sadler, 2005). Pregnant women are advised to avoid unnecessary exposure to X-rays. (Ultrasound, which is not an X-ray, has not been shown to harm the fetus.)

Parents' Age

What about the parents' age? Older fathers are more likely to produce abnormal sperm. The mother's age also matters. From a biological vantage point, the 20s may be the ideal age for women to bear children. Teenage mothers have a higher incidence of infant mortality and children with low birth weight (Phipps et al., 2002; Save the Children, 2008). Girls who become pregnant in their early teens may place a burden on bodies that may not have adequately matured to facilitate pregnancy and childbirth (Berg et al., 2003).

For Women, Issues Arise in the 30s

Women's fertility declines gradually until the mid-30s, after which it declines more rapidly. Women possess all their ova in immature form at birth. Over 30 years, these cells are exposed to the slings and arrows of an outrageous environment of toxic wastes, chemical pollutants, and radiation, thus increasing the risk of chromosomal abnormalities such as Down syndrome. Women who wait until their 30s or 40s to have children also increase the likelihood of having stillborn or preterm babies (Berg et al., 2003). With adequate prenatal care, however, the risk of bearing a premature or unhealthy baby is still relatively small, even for older first-time mothers (Berg et al., 2003). (Teenage mothers are discussed in Chapter 6.)

Do Men Really Have All the Time in the World?

The artist Pablo Picasso fathered children in his 70s. Former Senator Strom Thurmond fathered a child in his 90s. It has been widely known that women's chances of conceiving children decline as they age. The traditional message has been "Women, you'd better hurry up. Men, you have all the time in the world."

Not so, apparently. Older fathers are more likely to produce abnormal sperm, leading to fertility problems. But that's only the tip of the iceberg. University of Queensland researchers analyzed data from some 33,000 U.S. children and found that the older the father was at conception, the lower the child's score might be on tests of reading skills, reasoning, memory, and concentration. The ages of 29 and 30 are something of a turning point for men, because children conceived past these ages are at greater risk for the psychological disorders of schizophrenia and bipolar disorder. Children born to men past 40 also have a greater risk of autism, as shown in Figure 2.14 (Archives of General Psychiatry, 2006).

These findings do not mean that the majority of children born to men past their reproductive "prime" will develop these problems, but it does mean that men's age, as women's, is related to risks for their children.

Whatever the age of the mother and father, the events of childbirth provide some of the most memorable moments in the lives of parents. In the next module, we continue our voyage with the process of birth and the characteristics of the newborn child.

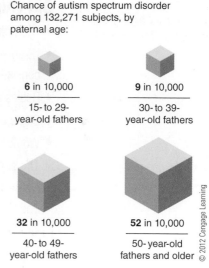

Chance of autism spectrum disorder among 132,271 subjects, by paternal age:

6 in 10,000
15- to 29-year-old fathers

9 in 10,000
30- to 39-year-old fathers

32 in 10,000
40- to 49-year-old fathers

52 in 10,000
50- year-old fathers and older

© 2012 Cengage Learning

Figure 2.14 Risky Business

Fathers and Autism

Learn more about how a father's age affects a child's chances of being born with autism.

Check Your Learning Quiz 2.2

Go to **login.cengagebrain.com** and take the online quiz.

▶**LO20** Describe events that indicate that a baby is ready to be born.

Did you know that—

- The first uterine contractions are usually false contractions?
- "Prepping" the woman prior to delivery, along with the episiotomy, is now considered unnecessary by most women and obstetricians?
- Babies are *not* slapped on the buttocks to stimulate breathing?
- Some anesthesia is used in most deliveries in the United States?
- Women using the Lamaze method still experience some pain during delivery?
- The percentage of American women who deliver their babies by cesarean section has been growing dramatically?
- The United States ranks behind Ireland, Italy, Sweden, the United Kingdom, and Israel in the risk that a woman will die during childbirth?
- A child born in China is 6 times as likely to die during the first year as a child born in Italy?

▼

term The typical 9-month period from conception to childbirth.

Braxton-Hicks contractions The first, usually painless, contractions of childbirth.

cervix The narrow lower end of the uterus, through which a baby passes to reach the vagina.

prostaglandins Hormones that stimulate uterine contractions.

oxytocin A hormone that stimulates labor contractions.

During the last few weeks before she gave birth, Michele explained: "I couldn't get my mind off the pregnancy—what it was going to be like when I finally delivered Lisa. I'd had the amniocentesis, so I knew it was a girl. I'd had the ultrasounds, so all her fingers and toes had been counted, but I was still hoping and praying that everything would turn out all right. To be honest, I was also worried about the delivery. I had always been an A student, and I guess I wanted to earn an A in childbirth as well. Matt was understanding, and he was even helpful, but, you know, it wasn't him."

Nearly all first-time mothers struggle through the last weeks of pregnancy and worry about the mechanics of delivery. Childbirth is a natural function, of course, but so many of them have gone to classes to learn how to do what comes naturally! They worry about whether they'll get to the hospital or birthing center on time ("Is there gas in the car?" "Is it snowing?"). They worry about whether the baby will start breathing on its own properly. They may wonder if they'll do it on their own or need a C-section. They may also worry about whether it will hurt, and how much, and when they should ask for anesthetics, and, well, how to earn that A.

Close to full **term**, Michele and other women are sort of front-loaded and feel bent out of shape, and guess what? They are. The weight of the fetus may also be causing backaches. Will they deliver the baby, or will the baby—by being born—deliver them from discomfort? "Hanging in and having Lisa was a wonderful experience," Michele said in the end. "I think Matt should have had it."

Countdown...

Early in the last month of pregnancy, the head of the fetus settles in the pelvis. This process is called *dropping* or *lightening*. Because lightening decreases pressure on the diaphragm, the mother may, in fact, feel lighter.

The first uterine contractions are called **Braxton-Hicks contractions**, or false labor contractions. They are relatively painless and may be experienced as early as the sixth month of pregnancy. They increase in frequency as the pregnancy progresses and may serve to tone the muscles that will be used in delivery. True labor contractions are more painful and regular, and are usually intensified by walking.

A day or so before labor begins, increased pelvic pressure from the fetus may rupture blood vessels in the birth canal so that blood appears in vaginal secretions. Mucus that had plugged the **cervix** and protected the uterus from infection becomes dislodged. About 1 woman in 10 has a rush of warm liquid from the vagina at this time. This liquid is amniotic fluid, and its discharge means that the amniotic sac has burst. The sac usually does not burst until the end of the first stage of childbirth, as described later. Other signs that labor is beginning include indigestion, diarrhea, an ache in the small of the back, and cramps.

The fetus may actually signal the mother when it is "ready" to be born by secreting hormones that stimulate the placenta and uterus to secrete **prostaglandins** (Snegovskikh et al., 2006). Prostaglandins not only cause the cramping that women may feel before or during menstruation, they also excite the muscles of the uterus to engage in labor contractions. As labor progresses, the pituitary gland releases the hormone **oxytocin**, which stimulates contractions powerful enough to expel the baby.

▶ **LO21** Describe the three stages of childbirth.

The Stages of Childbirth

Regular uterine contractions signal the beginning of childbirth. Childbirth occurs in three stages. In the first stage, uterine contractions **efface** and **dilate** the cervix, which needs to widen to about 4 inches (10 cm) to allow the baby to pass. Dilation of the cervix causes most of the pain of childbirth.

The first stage is the longest stage. Among women undergoing their first deliveries, this stage may last from a few hours to more than a day. Subsequent pregnancies take less time. The first contractions are not usually all that painful and are spaced 10 to 20 minutes apart. They may last from 20 to 40 seconds each. As the process continues, the contractions become more powerful, frequent, and regular. Women are usually advised to go to the hospital or birthing center when the contractions are 4 to 5 minutes apart. The mother is usually in a labor room until the end of the first stage of labor.

If the woman is to be "prepped"—that is, if her pubic hair is to be shaved—it takes place now. The prep is intended to lower the chances of infection during delivery and to facilitate the performance of an **episiotomy**. A woman may be given an enema to prevent an involuntary bowel movement during labor. But many women find prepping and enemas degrading and seek obstetricians (physicians who treat women during pregnancy, labor, and recovery from childbirth) who do not perform them routinely.

During the first stage of childbirth, fetal monitoring may be used. One kind of monitor is an electronic device strapped around the woman's abdomen that measures the fetal heart rate as well as the mother's contractions. An abnormal heart rate alerts the medical staff to possible fetal distress so that appropriate steps can be taken, such as speeding up the delivery. When the cervix is nearly fully dilated, the head of the fetus begins to move into the vagina. This process is called **transition**. During transition, which lasts about 30 minutes or less, contractions are usually frequent and strong.

The second stage of childbirth begins when the baby appears at the opening of the vagina (now called the "birth canal"; see Figure 2.15). The second stage is briefer than the first, possibly lasting minutes or a few hours and ending with the birth of the baby. The woman may be taken to a delivery room for the second stage.

The contractions of the second stage stretch the skin surrounding the birth canal farther and propel the baby along. The baby's head is said to have crowned when it

efface To become thin.

dilate To widen.

episiotomy A surgical incision between the birth canal and anus that widens the vaginal opening.

transition Movement of the head of the fetus into the vagina.

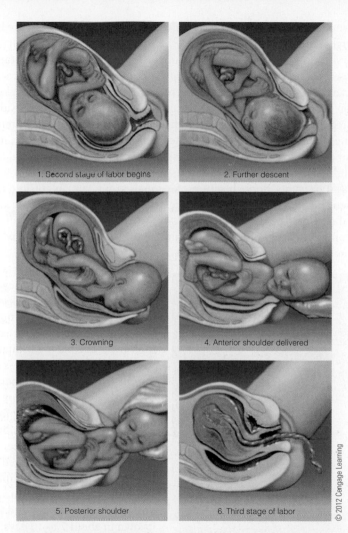

1. Second stage of labor begins

2. Further descent

3. Crowning

4. Anterior shoulder delivered

5. Posterior shoulder

6. Third stage of labor

© 2012 Cengage Learning

Figure 2.15 Stages of Childbirth In the first stage, uterine contractions efface and dilate the cervix. The second stage begins with movement of the baby into the birth canal and ends with birth of the baby. During the third stage, the placenta separates from the uterine wall and is expelled through the birth canal.

begins to emerge from the birth canal. Once crowning has occurred, the baby normally emerges completely within minutes.

The physician or nurse may perform an episiotomy once crowning takes place. The purpose of an episiotomy is to prevent random tearing when the area between the birth canal and the anus becomes severely stretched. Women are unlikely to feel the incision of the episiotomy because the pressure of the crowning head tends to numb the region between the vagina and the anus. The episiotomy, like prepping and the enema, is controversial and is not practiced in Europe. The incision may cause itching and discomfort as it heals. The use of episiotomy in the United States has been declining, with some studies suggesting that the procedure causes as many problems as it prevents. Some health professionals argue that an episiotomy is warranted when the baby's shoulders are wide or if the baby's heart rate declines for a long period of time. The strongest predictor of whether a practitioner will choose to use episiotomy is not the condition of the mother or the baby, but rather whether the physician normally performs an episiotomy.

In old movies, we may see babies held upside down after they are born and slapped on the buttocks to stimulate independent breathing. In fact, babies generally begin breathing on their own. In today's hospitals, mucus is suctioned from the baby's nose and mouth when the head emerges from the birth canal, to clear any obstructions from the passageway for breathing. When the baby is breathing adequately on its own, the umbilical cord is clamped and severed (see Figure 2.16). Mother and infant are now separate beings. The stump of the umbilical cord will dry and fall off on its own in about 7 to 10 days.

Now the baby is frequently whisked away by a nurse, who will perform various procedures, including foot-

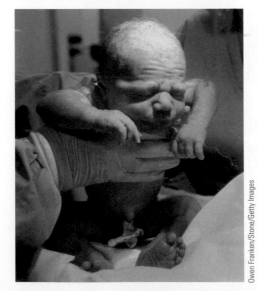

midwife An individual who helps women in childbirth.

anesthetics Agents that lessen pain.

general anesthesia Elimination of pain by putting a person to sleep.

local anesthetic Reduction of pain in an area of the body.

Owen Franken/Stone/Getty Images

Figure 2.16 Cutting the Umbilical Cord The stump of the cord dries and falls off in about 10 days.

printing the baby, supplying an ID bracelet, putting antibiotic ointment or drops of silver nitrate into the baby's eyes to prevent bacterial infections, and giving the baby a vitamin K injection to help its blood clot properly if it bleeds (newborn babies do not manufacture vitamin K). While these procedures go on, the mother is in the third stage of labor.

The third stage of labor, also called the placental stage, lasts from minutes to an hour or more. During this stage, the placenta separates from the uterine wall and is expelled through the birth canal. Some bleeding is normal. The obstetrician sews the episiotomy, if one has been performed.

Methods of Childbirth

Childbirth was once a more intimate procedure that usually took place in the woman's home and involved her, perhaps a **midwife**, and family. This pattern is followed in many less developed nations today, but only rarely in the United States and other developed nations. Contemporary American childbirths usually take place in hospitals, where physicians use sophisticated instruments and anesthetics to protect mother and child from complications and discomfort. Modern medicine has saved lives, but childbearing has also become more impersonal. Some argue that modern methods wrest control over their own bodies from women. They even argue that anesthetics have denied many women the experience of giving birth, although many women admit that they appreciate having the experience "muted."

Anesthesia

Although painful childbirth has historically been seen as the standard for women, today, at least some anesthesia is used in most American deliveries. Two types of **anesthetics** are used to lessen the pain associated with childbirth. **General anesthesia** achieves its anesthetic effect by putting the woman to sleep by means of an injected barbiturate. General anesthesia reduces the responsiveness of the baby shortly after birth, but there is little evidence that it has long-term negative effects (Caton et al., 2002).

Regional or **local anesthetics** deaden pain without putting the mother to sleep. With a *pudendal block*, the mother's external genitals are numbed by local injection. With an *epidural block* and a *spinal block*, anesthesia is injected into the spinal canal or spinal cord and it temporarily numbs the body below the waist. Local anesthesia

A Birth
Watch a video of a baby's birth.

▶ **LO23** Discuss oxygen deprivation during childbirth.

▶ **LO24** Discuss the problems of preterm and low-birth-weight infants.

has minor depressive effects on **neonates** shortly after birth, but the effects have not been shown to linger (Caton et al., 2002; Eltzschig et al., 2003).

In so-called **natural childbirth**, a woman uses no anesthesia. Instead, she is educated about the biological aspects of reproduction and delivery, encouraged to maintain physical fitness, and taught relaxation and breathing exercises.

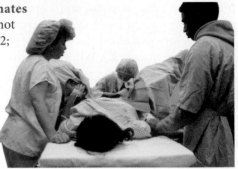

Partner in the Delivery Room. Today, the woman's partner is usually integrated into the process of childbirth. In this case, the father and mother take pride in "their" accomplishments of childbirth.

© Harriet Gans/The Image Works

Prepared Childbirth

In the **Lamaze method**, or prepared childbirth, women engage in breathing and relaxation exercises that lessen fear and pain and distract them from discomfort. The mother-to-be attends Lamaze classes with a "coach"—most often, her partner—who will aid her in the delivery room by doing things such as massaging her, timing the contractions, offering social support, and coaching her in patterns of breathing and relaxation. Women using the Lamaze method often report less pain and ask for less medication (Meldrum, 2003). But this is not to say that labor is pain-free.

Doulas

Social support during labor can be provided by individuals other than a woman's partner, such as a mother, sibling, friend, or another experienced but nonprofessional female companion, such as a *doula* (Guzikowski, 2006). Women with doulas present during birth appear to have shorter labors than women without doulas (D. A. Campbell et al., 2006).

Cesarean Section

In a **cesarean section** (C-section), the physician delivers the baby by surgery. The physician cuts through the mother's abdomen and uterus and physically removes the baby.

Physicians prefer C-sections to vaginal delivery when they believe that normal delivery may threaten the mother or child or be more difficult than desired. About

neonate A newborn infant, especially during the first 4 weeks.

natural childbirth Childbirth without anesthesia.

Lamaze method A childbirth method in which women are educated about childbirth, breathe in patterns that lessen pain during birth, and have a coach present.

cesarean section Delivery of a baby by abdominal surgery.

anoxia Absence of oxygen.

hypoxia Less oxygen than required.

breech (bottom-first) presentation Buttocks-first childbirth.

3 of every 10 births in the United States are currently by C-section (Bakalar, 2005). To gain some perspective, note that C-sections accounted for only 1 in 20 births (5%) in 1965 (Bakalar, 2005). Some of the increase is due to medical advances, but some women request C-sections so they can control the time of the delivery, and some physicians perform them to prevent malpractice suits in case something goes wrong during a vaginal delivery (Maternity Center Association, 2004).

C-sections are also performed when the physician wants to prevent the circulatory systems of the mother and baby from mixing, as might occur when there is (normal) bleeding during vaginal delivery. C-sections in such cases help prevent transmission of the viruses that cause genital herpes and AIDS.

Birth Problems

Although every delivery is usually most remarkable from the parents' point of view, most are unremarkable from a medical standpoint. Still, a number of problems can and do occur.

Oxygen Deprivation

Researchers use two terms to discuss oxygen deprivation: anoxia and hypoxia. **Anoxia** derives from roots meaning "without oxygen." **Hypoxia** derives from roots meaning "under" and "oxygen," the point again being that the baby does not receive enough oxygen in utero to develop properly. Prenatal oxygen deprivation can impair the development of the fetus's central nervous system, leading to cognitive problems, especially in memory and spatial relations, motor problems, and psychological disorders (Golan & Huleihel, 2006; Hogan et al., 2005). Prolonged cutoff of the baby's oxygen supply during delivery can also cause psychological and physical health problems, such as early-onset schizophrenia and cerebral palsy (Rees et al., 2006).

Oxygen deprivation can be caused by maternal disorders such as diabetes, by immaturity of the baby's respiratory system, and by accidents, some of which involve pressure against the umbilical cord during birth. Passage through the birth canal is tight, and the umbilical cord is usually squeezed during the process. If the squeezing is temporary, the effect is like holding one's breath for a moment and no problems are likely to ensue. But if constriction of the umbilical cord is prolonged, problems can result. Prolonged constriction is more likely during a **breech (bottom-first) presentation**, when the baby's body may press the umbilical cord against the birth canal.

Prenatal Health Issues

Watch this video to learn about the importance of prenatal care as it relates to potential teratogens.

Birthing Options

Explore the birthing options available to pregnant women.

Preterm and Low-Birth-Weight Infants

A baby is considered premature or **preterm** when birth occurs at or before 37 weeks of gestation, compared with the normal 40 weeks. A normal birth weight is 5.5 pounds or above. A baby is considered to have a low birth weight when it weighs less than 5.5 pounds (about 2,500 grams). When a baby is low in birth weight, even though it is born at full term, it is referred to as **small for gestational age**. Mothers who smoke, abuse drugs, or are malnourished place their babies at risk of being undersized. Small-for-gestational-age babies tend to remain shorter and lighter than their age-mates and show slight delays in learning and problems in attention when compared with their age-mates (O'Keeffe et al., 2003). Preterm babies are more likely than small-for-gestational-age babies to achieve normal heights and weights. Prematurity is more common in the case of multiple births—even twins (Kogan et al., 2000).

Risks Associated With Prematurity and Low Birth Weight

Neonates weighing between 3.25 and 5.5 pounds are 7 times more likely to die than infants of normal birth weight, whereas those weighing less than 3.3 pounds are nearly 100 times as likely to die (Nadeau et al., 2003). By and large, the lower a child's birth weight, the more poorly he or she fares on measures of neurological development and cognitive functioning throughout the school years (Dorling et al., 2006; Nadeau et al., 2003; Wocadlo & Rieger, 2006).

There are also risks for motor development. One study compared 96 children with very low birth weight (VLBW) with normal-term children at 6, 9, 12, and 18 months, correcting for age according to the expected date of delivery (Jeng et al., 2000). The median age at which the full-term infants began to walk was 12 months, compared with 14 months for the VLBW infants. By 18 months of age, all full-term infants were walking, compared to 89% of the VLBW infants. The outcomes for low-birth-weight children are variable. Studies seem to indicate that the severity of disabilities corresponds to the deficiency of birth weight (Walther et al., 2000).

preterm Born prior to 37 weeks of gestation.

small for gestational age Descriptive of neonates who are small for their age.

lanugo Fine, downy hair on premature babies.

vernix Oily white substance on the skin of premature babies.

respiratory distress syndrome Weak and irregular breathing, typical of preterm babies.

incubator A heated, protective container for premature infants.

Figure 2.17 A Premature Newborn This newborn baby shows lanugo and vernix, both characteristics of prematurity.

Signs of Prematurity

Preterm babies are relatively thin because they have not yet formed the layer of fat that gives full-term children their round, robust appearance. They often have fine, downy hair, referred to as **lanugo**, and an oily white substance on the skin known as **vernix**. If the babies are born 6 weeks or more before term, their nipples will not have emerged. The testicles of boys born this early will not yet have descended into the scrotum. Boys with undescended testes at birth are at higher risk for testicular cancer later in life.

Preterm babies have immature muscles, so their sucking and breathing reflexes are weak. In addition, the walls of the tiny air sacs in their lungs may tend to stick together because the babies do not yet secrete substances that lubricate the walls of the sacs. As a result, babies born more than a month before full term may breathe irregularly or may suddenly stop breathing, evidence of **respiratory distress syndrome**. Preterm infants with respiratory distress syndrome show poorer development in cognitive, language, and motor skills over the first 2 years of development than full-term infants. Injecting pregnant women at risk for delivering preterm babies with corticosteroids increases the babies' chances of survival (Crowther et al., 2006).

Strides have been made in helping low-birth-weight children survive, but children who survive often have below-average verbal ability and academic achievement and various motor and perceptual impairments (Saigal et al., 2006).

Treating Preterm Babies

Because of their physical frailty, preterm infants usually remain in the hospital and are placed in **incubators**, which maintain a temperature-controlled environment and afford some protection from disease. The babies may be given oxygen, although excessive oxygen can cause permanent eye injury.

Parents and Preterm Newborn Babies

Parents often do not treat preterm newborns as well as they treat full-term newborns. For one thing, preterm infants usually do not have the robust, appealing appearance of many full-term babies. Their cries are higher pitched and more grating, and they are more irritable (Bugental & Happaney, 2004; Eckerman et al., 1999). The demands of caring for preterm babies can be depressing to mothers (L. Davis et al., 2003; Drewett et al., 2004). Mothers of preterm babies frequently report that they feel alienated from their babies and harbor feelings of failure, guilt, and low self-esteem (Bugental & Happaney, 2004). Fear of hurting preterm babies can further discourage parents from handling them, but encouraging mothers to massage their preterm infants can help them cope with this fear (Feijó et al., 2006). Once they come home from the hospital, preterm infants remain more passive and less sociable than full-term infants (Larroque et al., 2005; M. McGrath et al., 2005). Preterm infants fare better when they have responsive and caring parents.

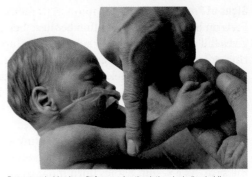

Premature babies benefit from early stimulation, including holding, touching, and rocking. To stimulate this premature infant, light massage is applied to his limbs and body.

Sarah Leen/National Geographic/Getty Images

Intervention Programs

Preterm infants profit from early stimulation just as full-term babies do—being cuddled, rocked, talked to, and sung to; being exposed to recordings of their mothers' voices; having mobiles in view; and having live and recorded music in their environment (Arnon et al., 2006; H.-L. Lai et al., 2006). Other forms of stimulation include massage (Field, 1999) and "kangaroo care" (H.-L. Lai et al., 2006), in which the baby spends time each day lying skin to skin and chest to chest with a parent. By and large, stimulated preterm infants tend to gain weight more rapidly, show fewer respiratory problems, and make greater advances in motor, intellectual, and neurological development than infants who are not stimulated (Caulfield, 2000; Dombrowski et al., 2000).

Maternal and Child Mortality Around the World

Modern medicine has made vast strides in decreasing the rates of maternal and child mortality, but the advances are not equally spread throughout the world. Save the Children, a nonprofit relief and development organization, tracks the likelihood that a woman will die in childbirth and that a child will die during its first 5 years. The likelihood of maternal and child mortality is connected with factors such as the percentage of births that are attended by trained people, the level of education of women, and the participation of women in national government (which is one measure of the extent to which a society empowers women). The safest place for a woman to deliver is Ireland, where her chances of dying during childbirth are about 1 in 47,000. Moreover, in Ireland only 5 infants in 1,000 die during their first 5 years. Ireland also has the greatest estimated number of years of schooling for girls (18 years). In Sweden, where the chances of a woman dying during childbirth are about 1 in 17,000, and where only 3 infants in 1,000 die during the first few years, there is a nearly 100% adult female literacy rate, all recorded births are assisted by trained personnel, and women have the highest participation rate in national government (47%). In Afghanistan, 1 woman in 8 will die as a result of pregnancy, and 257 children of 1,000 will die during their first 5 years. There is little professional assistance during childbirth (12%).

Globally speaking, 6 out of 7 newborn deaths are directly attributable to one of three causes: serious infections, including sepsis (blood poisoning), pneumonia, tetanus, and diarrhea; asphyxia (lack of oxygen); and pre-term birth (UNICEF, 2008).

The United States ranks number six, behind Israel, for material mortality during childbirth and infant mortality. Why isn't the United States ranked higher? One answer is that the United States is a nation made up of nations. States with above-average poverty rates, large rural populations, and below-average levels of education have the highest maternal and child mortality rates. According to a report by the CDC National Center for Health Statistics (2007), African American women had the highest child mortality rate—13.60 per 1,000 live births, as compared to 5.66 per 1,000 among European American women. Cuban Americans had the lowest child mortality rate—4.55 per 1,000 live births. Other child mortality rates were 8.45 for Native Americans, 7.82 for Puerto Ricans, 5.47 for Mexican Americans, 4.67 for Asian Americans, and 4.65 for Central and South Americans. How would you explain these ethnic differences?

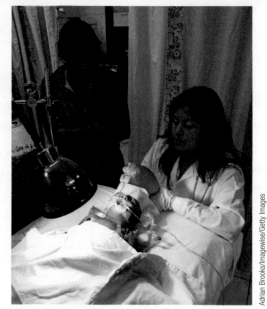

Adrian Brooks/Imagewise/Getty Images

Global Birthrates

Read more about birthrates around the world.

Maternal and Infant Mortality

Read more on how global differences in infant and maternal mortality relates to the empowerment of women.

Check Your Learning Quiz 2.3

Go to **login.cengagebrain.com** and take the online quiz.

GO to your Psychology CourseMate at login.cengagebrain.com and take the Chapter Post-Test to see which Learning Objectives you've mastered and which need more review. Use the chapter review guide below and the online activities—including flashcards to review key terms—to measure your learning.

Module	Learning Objectives
2.1 Genetic Influences on Development 42	
The Influence of Heredity on Development	**LO1** Define *chromosomes* and *genes*. **LO2** Describe mitosis and meiosis. **LO3** Differentiate between identical and fraternal twins. **LO4** Define dominant and recessive traits, and provide examples of each.
Chromosomal Abnormalities	**LO5** Discuss chromosomal disorders.
Genetic Abnormalities	**LO6:** Discuss genetic disorders.
Genetic Counseling and Prenatal Testing	**LO7:** Describe prenatal testing methods for chromosomal and genetic abnormalities.

Online Activities

Key Terms	Video	Animation	Reading	Assessment

Key Terms	Video	Animation	Reading	Assessment
Genetics, chromosome, gene, polygenic, deoxyribonucleic acid (DNA), mitosis, mutation, meiosis, autosome, sex chromosome, monozygotic (MZ) twins, dizygotic (DZ) twins, ovulation, allele, homozygous, heterozygous, dominant trait, recessive trait, carrier		DNA's Double Helix Chromosomes and Genes Inheriting Eye Color		Check Your Learning Quiz 2.1
Down syndrome, sex-linked chromosomal abnormality, Klinefelter syndrome, testosterone, Turner syndrome, estrogen				
Multifactorial problems, phenylketonuria (PKU), Huntington's disease, sickle-cell anemia, Tay-Sachs disease, cystic fibrosis, hemophilia, sex-linked genetic abnormality, muscular dystrophy				
Genetic counselor, prenatal, amniocentesis, miscarriage, chorionic villus sampling (CVS), uterus, ultrasound, sonogram, alpha-fetoprotein assay	Ultrasound Prenatal Doctor's Visit			

13 14 15 16 17 18 19 20 21 22 23
2 3.3 3.4 3.5 3.6 3.7 3.8 3.9 40 4.1 4.2 4.3 4.4 4.5 4.6 4.7 4.8 4.9 50 5.1 5.2 5.3 5.4 5.5 5.6 5.7 58

Measure ^ Your Learning

Key Terms	Video	Animation	Reading	Assessment
Genotype, phenotype, autism	Twins Research			
Conception, endometrium		Female Reproductive Organs		Check Your Learning Quiz 2.2
Motility, pelvic inflammatory disease, endometriosis, artificial insemination, in vitro fertilization (IVF), donor IVF	Stress and Pregnancy			
Germinal stage, blastocyscht, embryonic disk, trophoblast, umbilical cord, placenta, embryonic stage, cephalocaudal, proximodistal, ectoderm, neural tube, endoderm, mesoderm, androgens, amniotic sac, amniotic fluid, fetal stage		Stages of Conception Sexual Differentiation Organ Development	Where Are the Girls? Sex Selection Fetal Perception Highlights of Prenatal Development	
Stillbirth, teratogens, critical period, syphilis, congenital, HIV/AIDS, rubella, toxemia, preeclampsia, premature, Rh incompatibility, thalidomide, progestin, DES, fetal alcohol syndrome (FAS)	Rx Drugs and Development Fetal Alcohol Syndrome		Preventing HIV in the Unborn Should Pregnant Women Avoid Caffeine?	

Measure ^Your Learning

Online Activities

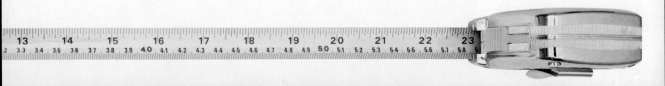

Key Terms	Video	Animation	Reading	Assessment
		Fathers and Autism		
Term				
Braxton-Hicks contractions, cervix, prostaglandins, oxytocin				Check Your Learning Quiz 2.3
Efface, dilate, episiotomy, transition	A Birth			
Midwife, anesthetics, general anesthesia, local anesthetic, neonate, natural childbirth, Lamaze method, cesarean section			Birthing Options	
Anoxia, hypoxia, breech (bottom-first) presentation, preterm, small for gestational age, lanugo, vernix, respiratory distress syndrome, incubator	Prenatal Health Issues			
			Global Birthrates Maternal and Infant Mortality	

Infancy

3

Chapter Outline and Learning Objectives

✓ **Prepare to Learn 100**

Chapter Pre-Test

Online Activities 101

3.1 The Postpartum Period and the Newborn Baby: In the New World 102

LO1 Discuss the kinds of mood problems many women experience during the postpartum period.

LO2 Discuss research on the necessity of early parent–infant contact for bonding.

LO3 Discuss the health, reflexes, and sensory capabilities of neonates.

LO4 Discuss the conditioning of neonates.

LO5 Describe patterns of waking and sleeping among neonates.

LO6 Explain why babies cry and how to soothe them.

LO7 Identify the risk factors for SIDS.

3.2 Physical Development: Infancy 118

LO8 Describe the sequences of physical development.

LO9 Describe patterns of growth in infancy.

LO10 Discuss failure to thrive.

LO11 Discuss the advantages and disadvantages of breast milk.

LO12 Discuss neural development.

LO13 Discuss motor development.

LO14 Describe sensory development.

3.3 Cognitive Development: Infancy 140

LO15 Describe the sensorimotor stage of cognitive development.

LO16 Discuss the strengths and limitations of Piaget's theory of sensorimotor development.

LO17 Discuss infants' memory.

LO18 Discuss imitation during infancy.

LO19 Explain how we measure individual differences in the development of cognitive functioning.

LO20 Describe language development in infancy.

LO21 Discuss theories of language development.

3.4 Social and Emotional Development: Infancy 160

LO22 Describe the development of attachment.

LO23 Explain the benefits of being securely attached.

LO24 Explain the research findings on social deprivation and its effects on humans.

LO25 Define and explain aspects of autism spectrum disorders.

LO26 Describe the effects of day care.

LO27 Discuss the development of emotions.

 Measure Your Learning 182

Chapter Post-Test

99

Prepare ^ to Learn

1 **GO** to your **Psychology CourseMate** at **login.cengagebrain.com** and take the **Chapter Pre-Test** to introduce yourself to this chapter's topics and see what you may already know.

2 **READ** the **Learning Objectives** (LOs, in the left sidebars) and begin the chapter.

3 **COMPLETE** the **Online Activities** (in the right sidebars) *as you read each module*. Activities include **videos, animations, readings,** and **quizzes.**

4 **CHECK Your Learning** by going online to take the quiz at the end of each module and review material as necessary.

5 **MEASURE Your Learning** after reading the chapter by taking the online **Chapter Post-Test.** Use the chapter review guide at the end of the chapter as needed.

Video

Animation

Reading

Assessment

Online Activities

These online activities are essential to mastering this chapter. Go to login.cengagebrain.com:

 Videos Watch the following videos:

- Postpartum Depression
- The Apgar Test
- Reflexes in Infants
- Early Infant Experiences With Smells
- Early Infant Experiences With Tastes
- A Test That Predicts SIDS?
- The Development of Visual Fields in Infants
- Visual Cliff
- Depth Perception in Infancy
- Piaget's Sensorimotor Stage
- Attachment Between Infants and Their Caregivers
- The Social Smile
- Autistic Savant
- Autism in Girls
- Autism Diagnosis
- Pros and Cons of Day Care

 Animations Interact with and visualize important processes, timelines, and concepts:

- The Neonate
- Neuron Anatomy
- Brain Development
- Brain Structures
- The Sensorimotor Stage
- Object Permanence

 Readings Delve deeper into key content:

- Visual Acuity in Infants
- Shape Constancy
- Infants Discriminate the Sounds of Foreign Languages
- The Effects of Early Exposure to Certain Tastes
- Jean Piaget
- Counting in the Crib?
- Sample Items From the Bayley Scales Test
- Milestones of Language Development in Infancy
- Babbling Here, There, and Everywhere

- Teaching an Infant to Use Sign Language
- Universality of Kinds of Two-Word Sentences
- Motherese
- Noam Chomsky
- The Strange Situation

 Assessment Measure your mastery:

- Chapter Pre-Test
- Check Your Learning Quizzes
- Chapter Post-Test

▶ **LO1** Discuss the kinds of mood problems many women experience during the postpartum period.

Did you know that—

- It is normal to feel depressed following childbirth?
- Parents need not have extended early contact with their newborn children for adequate bonding to take place?
- A heart rate of 100–140 beats per minute is normal for a newborn baby?
- Newborn babies will suck almost any object that touches their lips?
- The odors preferred by newborn babies are similar to those preferred by older children and adults?
- Newborn babies spend about two thirds of the time sleeping?
- Babies cry for a reason?
- More children die from sudden infant death syndrome (SIDS) than from cancer, heart disease, pneumonia, child abuse, AIDS, cystic fibrosis, and muscular dystrophy combined?

▼

The **postpartum period** refers to the weeks following delivery, but there is no specific limit. "Parting is such sweet sorrow," Shakespeare has Juliet tell Romeo. The parting from the baby is frequently sweet enough—a happy experience. The family's long wait is over, concerns about pregnancy and labor are over, fingers and toes have been counted, and despite some local discomfort, the mother finds her "load" lightened, most literally. However, according to the American Psychiatric Association (2000, p. 423), about 70% of new mothers have periods of tearfulness, sadness, and irritability, which the association refers to as the "baby blues."

In this module, we discuss two issues of the postpartum period: maternal depression and bonding. Then we focus more directly on the newborn baby, or *neonate*. We see what neonates can do and what they can't do. Much of what they do is built in, but they are also capable of learning. We see how much they sleep, and how much they keep parents awake! Finally, we turn to an issue that troubles many parents for the first few months: sudden infant death syndrome (SIDS).

postpartum period The period immediately following childbirth.

Maternal Depression

Once upon a time, there was a little girl who dreamed of being a mommy. She wanted, more than anything, to have a child and knew her dream would come true one day. She would sit for hours thinking up names to call her baby. Eventually this little girl grew up. Though she'd met and married her Prince Charming, she was having trouble conceiving. She began to realize that her dream wasn't going to come true without a great deal of medical help. So she went on a long journey through the world of fertility treatments. When none of them worked, she got frustrated and depressed. She felt like a failure. And then one day, finally, she became pregnant. She was thrilled beyond belief. She had a wonderful pregnancy and a perfect baby girl. At long last, her dream of being a mommy had come true. But instead of being relieved and happy, all she could do was cry.
—Brooke Shields, Down Came the Rain (2005)

So wrote Brooke Shields in her recounting of her experiences following her pregnancy and the delivery of her daughter, Rowan. We will see that Shields's feelings are far from unique, even though they were more intense than most women's. She was experiencing a form of *postpartum depression* which, for many women, is one of the unfortunate features of the postpartum period.

Problems related to maternal depression include the baby blues and more serious mood disorders ("postpartum-onset mood episodes"), which occasionally include "psychotic features" (American Psychiatric Association, 2000) (see Table 3.1). Postpartum mood problems are so common that they are statistically normal (N. I. Gavin et al., 2005). Researchers believe that they are often due to hormonal changes that follow delivery (Kohl, 2004). They last about 10 days and are generally not severe enough to impair the mother's functioning.

Perhaps as many as 1 in 5 women encounter the more serious mood disorder frequently referred to as

UPI Photo/Roger L. Wollenberg /Landov

Actress Brooke Shields takes part in a press conference on Capitol Hill in Washington, D.C. to encourage the passage of postpartum-depression legislation that would give new mothers access to help, education, and treatment. With Shields is one of the bill's cosponsors, Senator Robert Menendez (D-New Jersey). Shields speaks of her own struggles with postpartum depression after the birth of her daughter, Rowan.

Postpa

Watch
and
de

postpartum depression (PPD), which begins about a month after delivery and may linger for weeks or months. PPD is characterized by serious sadness; feelings of hopelessness, helplessness, and worthlessness; difficulty concentrating; mood swings; and major changes in appetite (usually loss of appetite) and sleep patterns (frequently insomnia). Some women show obsessive concern with the well-being of their babies.

Many researchers suggest that PPD is caused by a sudden drop in estrogen (Kohl, 2004). The focus of PPD is on physiological factors because of the major changes in body chemistry during and after pregnancy and because women around the world seem to experience similar disturbances in mood, even when their life experiences and support systems are radically different from those found in the United States (L. S. Cohen et al., 2006).

According to the American Psychiatric Association (2000), postpartum psychosis may mean a break with reality. Mothers with postpartum psychosis may have delu-

Table 3.1
Kinds of Maternal Depression After Delivery

Types	Incidence	Symptoms	Comments
Baby blues	About 4 new mothers in 5	• Feeling let down • Crying for no apparent reason • Impatience, irritability, restlessness, anxiety	Occurs in first weeks and disappears on its own
Postpartum depression	About 1 new mother in 5	• Frequent sadness, crying, helplessness, despair, possible thoughts of suicide, anxiety, panic, feelings of inadequacy, guilt, shame • Changes in appetite • Insomnia or hypersomnia; fatigue • Lack of feeling for the baby or excessive concern for the baby • Irritability • Difficulty concentrating • Frightening feelings, thoughts, and images • Loss of interest in sex	Occurs within days of delivery or gradually during the first year
Postpartum psychosis	About 1 new mother in 1,000	• Hallucinations • Severe insomnia • Agitation • Bizarre feelings or behavior	Occurs within a few weeks after delivery; an emergency that requires help

© 2012 Cengage Learning

depression (PPD) epression follow- by sad-

sional thoughts about the infant that place the infant at risk of injury or death. Some women experience delusions that the infant is possessed by the devil. Some women have "command hallucinations" and experience a command to kill the infant as though it is coming from the outside.

Women who experience PPD usually profit from a history of high self-esteem, from social support, and from counseling, even if counseling does little more than explain that many women encounter PPD and it usually eases and ends as time goes on. Drugs that increase estrogen levels or act as antidepressants may also help.

Bonding

Bonding—that is, the formation of bonds of attachment between parents and their children—is essential to the survival and well-being of children. Since the publication of controversial research by Marshall Klaus and John Kennell in the 1970s, many have wondered whether extended parent–infant contact is required during the first hours postpartum in order to foster parent–infant bonding (Klaus & Kennell, 1978). In their study, one group of mothers was randomly assigned to standard hospital procedure, in which their babies were whisked away to the nursery shortly after birth. Throughout the remainder of the hospital stay, the babies visited their mothers during feeding. The other group of mothers spent 5 hours a day with their infants during the hospital stay. The hospital staff encouraged and reassured the group of mothers who had extended contact. Follow-ups over 2 years found that mothers with extended contact were more likely than control mothers to cuddle their babies, soothe them when they cried, and interact with them. Critics have noted that the Klaus and Kennell studies did not separate the benefits of extended contact from benefits attributable to parents' knowledge that they were in a special group and from the extra attention of the hospital staff.

Parent–child bonding has been shown to be a complex process involving desire to have the child; parent and child familiarity with each other's sounds,

Are the first hours postpartum a special period for mother–baby bonding?

RubberBall Photography/Veer/Corbis

▶ **LO3** Discuss the health, reflexes, and sensory capabilities of neonates.

odors, and tastes; and caring. On the other hand, serious maternal depression can delay bonding with neonates (Klier, 2006), and a history of rejection by her parents can interfere with a woman's bonding with her own children (Leerkes & Crockenberg, 2006).

Despite the Klaus and Kennell studies, which made a brief splash in the 1970s, it is not necessary that parents have extended early contact with their newborn children for adequate bonding to occur. Many parents, for instance, adopt children later during the first year, or at advanced ages, and bond closely with them. However, adopted children appear to be most secure when they are adopted before 12 months of age (van den Dries et al., 2009).

Characteristics of Neonates

Many newborn babies—neonates—come into the world with a somewhat fuzzy appearance. They are utterly dependent on others, but they are probably more aware of their surroundings than you imagine. Neonates also make rapid adaptations to the world around them.

Assessing the Health of Neonates

The neonate's overall level of health is usually evaluated at birth according to the **Apgar scale** (see Table 3.2). Apgar scores are based on five signs of health: appearance, pulse, grimace, activity level, and respiratory effort. The neonate can receive a score of 0, 1, or

Apgar scale A measure of a newborn's health that assesses appearance, pulse, grimace, activity level, and respiratory effort.

Brazelton Neonatal Behavioral Assessment Scale A measure of a newborn's motor behavior, response to stress, adaptive behavior, and control over physiological state.

reflex An unlearned, stereotypical response to a stimulus.

rooting reflex Turning the mouth and head toward stroking of the cheek or the corner of the mouth.

Table 3.2
The Apgar Scale

Points	0	1	2
Appearance: Color	Blue, pale	Body pink, extremities blue	Entirely pink
Pulse: Heart Rate	Absent (not detectable)	Slow—below 100 beats/minute	Rapid—100–140 beats/minute
Grimace: Reflex irritability	No response	Grimace	Crying, coughing, sneezing
Activity level: Muscle tone	Completely flaccid, limp	Weak, inactive	Flexed arms and legs; resistance to extension
Respiratory effort: Breathing	Absent (infant is apneic)	Shallow, irregular, slow	Regular breathing; lusty crying

© 2012 Cengage Learning

2 on each sign. The total Apgar score can therefore vary from 0–10. A score of 7 or above usually indicates that the baby is not in danger. A score below 4 suggests that the baby is in critical condition and requires medical attention. By 1 minute after birth, most normal babies attain scores of 8–10 (R. Clayton & Crosby, 2006).

The **Brazelton Neonatal Behavioral Assessment Scale** measures neonates' reflexes and other behavior patterns. This test screens neonates for behavioral and neurological problems by assessing four areas of behavior: motor behavior, response to stress, adaptive behavior, and control over physiological state.

Reflexes

Reflexes are simple, automatic, stereotypical responses that are elicited by certain types of stimulation. They occur without thinking. Reflexes are the most complicated motor activities displayed by neonates. Of these reflexes, most are exhibited by neonates very shortly after birth, disappear within a few months, and—if the behaviors still serve a purpose—are replaced by corresponding voluntary actions.

Pediatricians learn about a neonate's neural functioning by testing its reflexes. The absence or weakness of a reflex may indicate immaturity (as in prematurity), slowed responsiveness (which can result from anesthetics used during childbirth), brain injury, or intellectual deficiency.

The rooting and sucking reflexes are basic to survival. In the **rooting reflex**, the baby turns the head and mouth toward a stimulus that strokes the cheek, chin, or corner of the mouth. The rooting reflex facilitates finding the mother's nipple in preparation for sucking. Babies will suck almost any object that touches their lips. The sucking reflex grows stronger during the first days after birth and can be lost if not stimulated. As the months go on, reflexive sucking becomes replaced by voluntary sucking.

(a)   (b)   (c)

The Rooting Reflex

The Apgar Test

Watch an Apgar test administered immediately after birth.

In the startle or **Moro reflex**, the back arches and the legs and arms are flung out and then brought back toward the chest, with the arms in a hugging motion. The Moro reflex occurs when a baby's position is suddenly changed or when support for the head and neck is suddenly lost. It can also be elicited by loud noises, bumping the baby's crib, or jerking the baby's blanket. The Moro reflex is usually lost within 6–7 months after birth. Absence of the Moro reflex can indicate immaturity or brain damage.

The Moro Reflex

During the first few weeks following birth, babies show an increasing tendency to reflexively grasp fingers or other objects pressed against the palms of their hands. In this **grasping reflex**, or palmar reflex, they use four fingers only (the thumbs are not included). Absence of the grasping reflex may indicate depressed activity of the nervous system, which can stem from use of anesthetics during childbirth. The grasping reflex is usually lost within 3–4 months, and babies generally show voluntary grasping within 5–6 months.

The Grasping Reflex

Within 1 or 2 days after birth, babies show a reflex that mimics walking. When held under the arms and tilted forward so that the feet press against a solid surface, a baby will show a **stepping reflex** in which the feet advance one after the other. A full-term baby "walks" heel to toe, whereas a preterm infant is more likely to remain on tiptoe. The stepping reflex usually disappears by about 3 or 4 months of age.

In the **Babinski reflex**, the neonate fans or spreads the toes in response to stroking of the underside of the foot from heel to toes. The Babinski reflex normally disappears

The Stepping Reflex

toward the end of the first year, to be replaced by curling downward of the toes.

The **tonic-neck reflex** is observed when the baby is lying on its back and turns its head to one side. The arm and leg on that side extend, while the limbs on the opposite side flex.

Some reflexes, such as breathing regularly and blinking the eye in response to a puff of air, remain with us for life. Others, such as the sucking and grasping reflexes,

Moro reflex Arching the back, flinging out the arms and legs, and drawing them back to the chest in response to a sudden change in position.

grasping reflex Grasping objects that touch the palms.

stepping reflex Taking steps when held under the arms and leaned forward so the feet press the ground.

Babinski reflex Fanning the toes when the soles of the feet are stroked.

tonic-neck reflex Turning the head to one side, extending the arm and leg on that side, and flexing the limbs on the opposite side.

visual accommodation Automatic adjustments of the lenses to focus on objects.

convergence Inward movement of the eyes to focus on an object that is drawing nearer.

are gradually replaced after a number of months by voluntary sucking and grasping. Still others, such as the Moro and Babinski reflexes, disappear, indicating that the nervous system is maturing on schedule.

Sensory Capabilities

In 1890, William James, a founder of modern psychology, wrote that the neonate must sense the world "as one great blooming, buzzing confusion" (p. 462). The neonate emerges from being literally suspended in a temperature-controlled environment to being—again in James's words—

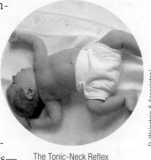

The Tonic-Neck Reflex

"assailed by eyes, ears, nose, skin, and entrails at once" (p. 462). We now describe the sensory capabilities of neonates, and we see that James, for all his eloquence, exaggerated their disorganization.

Vision

Neonates can see, but they are nearsighted. They can best see objects that are about 7–9 inches from their eyes (Kellman & Arterberry, 2006). They also do not have the peripheral vision of older children (Candy et al., 1998). Neonates can visually detect movement, and many neonates can visually follow, or track, movement the first day after birth. In fact, they appear to prefer (i.e., they spend more time looking at) moving objects to stationary objects (Kellman & Arterberry, 2006).

Visual accommodation refers to the self-adjustments made by the eye's lens to bring objects into focus. Neonates show little or no visual accommodation; rather, they see as through a fixed-focus camera. As noted, objects placed about 7–9 inches away are in clearest focus for most neonates, but visual accommodation improves dramatically during a baby's first 2 months (Kellman & Arterberry, 2006).

Neonates do not have the muscle control to converge their eyes on an object that is close to them. For this reason, one eye may be staring off to the side while the other fixates on an object straight ahead. **Convergence** does not occur until 7 or 8 weeks of age for nearby objects (Kellman & Arterberry, 2006).

The degree to which neonates perceive color remains an open question. By 4 months, however, infants can see most, if not all, of the colors of the visible spectrum (Franklin et al., 2005).

Even at birth, babies do not just passively respond to visual stimuli. Babies placed in absolute darkness open their eyes wide and search around (Kellman & Arterberry, 2006).

Visual Acuity in Infants

Read and explore visual acuity in infants.

Reflexes in Infants

Watch reflex tests administered to babies.

Hearing

Fetuses respond to sound for months before they are born. Although the auditory pathways in the brain are not fully developed prior to birth, fetuses' middle and inner ears normally reach their mature shapes and sizes before birth. Normal neonates hear well unless their middle ears are clogged with amniotic fluid (Priner et al., 2003). Most neonates turn their heads toward unusual sounds, such as the shaking of a rattle.

Neonates have the capacity to respond to sounds of different **pitch** and **amplitude**. They are more likely to respond to high-pitched sounds than to low-pitched sounds (Trehub & Hannon, 2006). Speaking or singing to infants softly, in a relatively low-pitched voice, can have a soothing effect (Volkova et al., 2006).

The sense of hearing may play a role in the formation of bonds of affection between neonates and mothers that goes well beyond the soothing potential of the mothers' voices. Neonates prefer their mothers' voices to those of other women, but they do not show similar preferences for the voices of their fathers (DeCasper & Prescott, 1984; Freeman et al., 1993). This preference may reflect prenatal exposure to sounds produced by their mothers.

Neonates are particularly responsive to the sounds and rhythms of speech, although they do not show preferences for specific languages. Neonates can discriminate different speech sounds (Dehaene-Lambertz et al., 2004), and they can discriminate new sounds of speech from those they have heard before (L R. Brody et al., 1984).

Smell: The Nose Knows—Early

Neonates can discriminate distinct odors, such as those of onions and licorice. They show more rapid breathing patterns and increased bodily movement in response to powerful odors. They also turn away from unpleasant odors, such as ammonia and vinegar, as early as the first day after birth (Werner & Bernstein, 2001). The nasal preferences of neonates are similar to those of older children and adults (L. A. Werner & Bernstein, 2001).

The sense of smell, like hearing, may provide a vehicle for mother–infant recognition and attachment (Macfarlane, 1975, 1977). Neonates may be sensitive to the smell of milk: When held by the mother, they tend to turn toward her nipple before they have had a chance to see or touch it. In one experiment, Macfarlane placed nursing pads above and to the sides of neonates' heads. One pad had absorbed milk from the mother, the other was clean. Neonates less than 1 week old spent more time turning to look at their mothers' pads than at the new pads.

Breast-fed 15-day-old infants also prefer their mother's underarm odor to odors produced by other milk-producing women and by other women. Bottle-fed infants

pitch Highness or lowness (of a sound), as determined by the frequency of sound waves.

amplitude Loudness (of sound).

Figure 3.1 Facial Expressions Elicited by Sweet, Sour, and Bitter Solutions Neonates are sensitive to different tastes, as shown by their facial expressions when tasting (a) sweet, (b) sour, and (c) bitter solutions.

a   b   c

Rosenstein, D.S. & Oster, H. (1988). Differential facial responses to four basic tastes in newborns. *Child Development*, 59, 1555-1568.

do not show this preference (Cernoch & Porter, 1985; R. H. Porter et al., 1992). Underarm odor, along with odors from breast secretions, might contribute to the early development of recognition and attachment.

Taste

Neonates are sensitive to different tastes, and their preferences, as suggested by their facial expressions in response to various fluids, are like those of adults (Werner & Bernstein, 2001). Neonates swallow without showing any facial expression suggestive of a positive or negative response when distilled water is placed on their tongues. Sweet solutions are met with smiles, licking, and eager sucking, as in Figure 3.1a (Rosenstein & Oster, 1988). Neonates discriminate among solutions with salty, sour, and bitter tastes, as suggested by reactions in the lower part of the face (Rosenstein & Oster, 1988). Sour fluids elicit pursing of the lips, nose wrinkling, and eye blinking (see Figure 3.1b). Bitter solutions stimulate spitting, gagging, and sticking out the tongue (see Figure 3.1c).

Sweet solutions have a calming effect on neonates (E. M. Blass & Camp, 2003). One study found that sweeter solutions increase the heart rate, suggesting heightened arousal, but also slow down the rate of sucking (Crook & Lipsitt, 1976). Researchers interpreted this finding to suggest an effort to savor the sweeter solution, to make the flavor last.

Touch

The sense of touch is an extremely important avenue of learning and communication for babies. Not only do the skin senses provide information about the external world, but the sensations of skin against skin also appear to provide feelings of comfort and security that may be major factors in the formation of bonds of attachment between infants and their caregivers. Many reflexes—including the rooting, sucking, Babinski, and grasping reflexes, to name a few—are activated by pressure against the skin.

Infants and Smell

Watch an infant and her early experiences with odors.

Infants and Taste

Observe an infant's early experiences with and reaction to different tastes.

The Neonate

Explore an animated learning module to expand your knowledge of neonate sense development.

▸ **LO4** Discuss the conditioning of neonates.

▸ **LO5** Describe patterns of waking and sleeping among neonates.

▸ **LO6** Explain why babies cry and how to soothe them.

Learning: Really Early Childhood "Education"

The somewhat limited sensory capabilities of neonates suggest that they may not learn as rapidly as older children do. After all, we must sense clearly those things we are to learn about. Neonates do, however, seem capable of conditioning.

Classical Conditioning of Neonates

In classical conditioning of neonates, involuntary responses are conditioned to new stimuli. In a typical study (Lipsitt, 2002), neonates were taught to blink in response to a tone. Blinking (the unconditioned response) was elicited by a puff of air directed toward the infant's eye (the unconditioned stimulus). A tone was sounded (the conditioned stimulus) as the puff of air was delivered. After repeated pairings, sounding the tone caused the neonate to blink (the conditioned response). As any new parent will relate, neonates quickly learn to associate crying with being picked up, and being picked up with nursing.

Operant Conditioning of Neonates

Operant conditioning, like classical conditioning, can take place in neonates. In Module 2.2 we described an experiment in which neonates learned to suck on a pacifier in such a way as to activate a recording of their mothers reading *The Cat in the Hat* (DeCasper & Fifer, 1980; DeCasper & Spence, 1991). The mothers had read this story aloud during the final weeks of pregnancy. In this example, the infants' sucking reflexes were modified through the reinforcement of hearing their mothers read a familiar story.

The younger the child, the more important it is that reinforcers be administered rapidly. Among neonates, it seems that reinforcers must be administered within a second after the desired behavior is performed if learning is to occur. Infants aged 6–8 months can learn if the reinforcer is delayed by 2 seconds, but if the delay is 3 seconds or more, learning does not take place (Millar, 1990). In the example of neonatal crying in the previous section, once neonates learn that crying leads to being picked up and fed, they will cry simply in order to be picked up, hungry or not.

rapid-eye-movement (REM) sleep A sleep period when dreams are likely, as suggested by rapid eye movements.

non-rapid-eye-movement (non-REM) sleep A sleep period when dreams are unlikely.

Sleeping and Waking in Infancy

As adults, we spend about one third of our time sleeping. Neonates greatly outdo us, spending two thirds of their time, or about 16 hours per day, in sleep. And, in one of life's basic challenges to parents, neonates do not sleep their 16 hours consecutively.

A number of different states of sleep and wakefulness have been identified in neonates and infants (Cornwell & Feigenbaum, 2006; Salzarulo & Ficca, 2002; Wulff & Siegmund, 2001):

- **Quiet sleep (non-REM):** Regular breathing, eyes closed, no movement
- **Active sleep (REM):** Irregular breathing, eyes closed, rapid eye movement, muscle twitches
- **Drowsiness:** Regular or irregular breathing, eyes open or closed, little movement
- **Alert inactivity:** Regular breathing, eyes open, looking around, little body movement
- **Alert activity:** Irregular breathing, eyes open, active body movement
- **Crying Irregular:** breathing, eyes open or closed, thrashing of arms and legs, crying

Although individual babies differ in the amount of time they spend in each of these states, sleep clearly predominates over wakefulness in the early days and weeks of life.

Different infants require different amounts of sleep and follow different patterns of sleep, but virtually all infants distribute their sleeping throughout the day and night through a series of naps. The typical infant has about six cycles of waking and sleeping in a 24-hour period. The longest nap typically approaches 4½ hours, and the neonate is usually awake for a little more than 1 hour during each cycle.

After a month or so, the infant has fewer but longer sleep periods and will usually take longer naps during the night. By the age of about 6 months to 1 year, many infants begin to sleep through the night. Some infants start sleeping through the night even earlier (Salzarulo & Ficca, 2002). A number of infants begin to sleep through the night for a week or so and then revert to their wakeful ways again for a while.

REM and Non-REM Sleep

Sleep can be divided into **rapid-eye-movement (REM) sleep** and **non-rapid-eye-movement (non-REM) sleep** (see Figure 3.2). REM sleep is characterized by rapid eye movements that can be observed beneath closed lids. Adults who are roused during REM sleep report that they have been dreaming about 80% of the time. Is the same true of neonates?

Note from Figure 3.2 that neonates spend about half their sleeping time in REM sleep. As they develop, the percentage of sleeping time spent in REM sleep declines. By 6 months or so, REM sleep accounts for only about 30% of the baby's sleep. By 2–3 years,

REM sleep drops off to about 20%–25% (Salzarulo & Ficca, 2002). There is a dramatic falling off in the total number of hours spent in sleep as we develop (Salzarulo & Ficca, 2002).

What is the function of REM sleep in neonates? Research with humans and other animals, including kittens and rat pups, suggests that the brain requires a certain amount of stimulation for the creation of proteins that are involved in the development

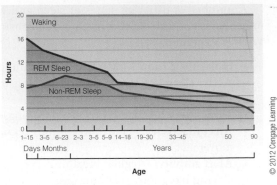

Figure 3.2 REM Sleep and Non-REM Sleep The percentage of time spent in REM sleep declines as people age. Source: Roffwarg et al. (1966).

of neurons and synapses (Dang-Vu et al., 2006). Perhaps neonates create this stimulation by means of REM sleep, which most closely parallels the waking state in terms of brain waves. Preterm babies spend an even greater proportion of their time in REM sleep, perhaps because they need relatively more stimulation of the brain.

Crying

No discussion of the sleeping and waking states of neonates would be complete without mentioning crying—a comment that parents will view as an understatement. The main reason babies cry seems to be simple enough. Studies suggest a one-word answer: pain (Gormally et al., 2001; Zeifman, 2004). Whether crying is healthful remains an open question, but some crying among babies seems to be universal.

Before parenthood, many people wonder whether they will be able to recognize the meaning of their baby's cries, but it usually does not take them long to do so. Parents typically learn to distinguish cries that signify hunger, anger, and pain. The pitch of an infant's cries appears to provide information (Zeifman, 2004). Adults perceive high-pitched crying to be more urgent, distressing, and sick sounding than low-pitched crying (Zeifman, 2004). A sudden, loud, insistent cry associated with flexing and kicking of the legs may indicate colic, that is, pain resulting from gas or other sources of distress in the digestive tract. Crying from colic can be severe and persistent; it may last for hours (Barr, et al., 2005). Much to the relief of parents, colic tends to disappear by the third to sixth month, as the baby's digestive system matures.

pacifier A device such as an artificial nipple or teething ring that soothes babies when it is sucked.

Certain high-pitched cries, when prolonged, may signify health problems. The cries of chronically distressed infants differ from those of nondistressed infants in both rhythm and pitch. Patterns of crying may be indicative of chromosomal abnormalities, infections, fetal malnutrition, and exposure to narcotics (Zeifman, 2004).

Peaks of crying appear to be concentrated in the late afternoon and early evening (McGlaughlin & Grayson, 2001). Although some cries may seem extreme and random at first, they tend to settle into a recognizable pattern. Infants seem to produce a consistent number of crying bouts throughout the first 9 months or so, the duration of the bouts lessens during this period (van IJzendoorn & Hubbard, 2000). The response of the caregiver influences crying. It turns out that the more frequently mothers ignore their infants' crying bouts in the first 9 weeks, the less frequently their infants cry in the following 9-week period (van IJzendoorn & Hubbard, 2000). This finding should certainly not be interpreted to mean that infant crying is best ignored. At least at first, crying communicates pain and hunger, and these are conditions that it is advisable to correct. Persistent crying can strain the mother–infant relationship (Reijneveld et al., 2004).

Soothing

Sucking seems to be a built-in tranquilizer. Sucking on a **pacifier** decreases crying and agitated movement in hungry neonates (T. Field, 1999). Therefore, the soothing function of sucking need not be learned through experience. Sucking (drinking) a sweet solution also appears to have a soothing effect (B. Stevens et al., 2005).

Parents soothe infants by picking them up, patting them, caressing and rocking them, swaddling them (wrapping them in a blanket, reminiscent of the womb), and speaking to them in a low voice. Parents then usually try to find the specific cause of the distress by offering a bottle or pacifier or checking the diaper. Parents learn by trial and error what types of embraces and movements are likely to soothe their child, and infants learn quickly that crying is followed by being picked up or other interventions. Parents sometimes worry that if they pick up a crying baby quickly, they are reinforcing the baby for crying. In this way, they believe, the child may become spoiled and find it progressively more difficult to engage in self-soothing to get to sleep.

Fortunately, as infants mature and learn, crying tends to become replaced by less upsetting verbal requests for intervention. Among adults, of course, soothing techniques take very different forms—such as admission that one started the argument.

This father is soothing his baby by picking him up and caressing him.

Rubberball 2009/Veer

▶ **LO7** Identify the risk factors for SIDS.

Sudden Infant Death Syndrome (SIDS)

More children die from **sudden infant death syndrome** (SIDS) than from cancer, heart disease, pneumonia, child abuse, AIDS, cystic fibrosis, and muscular dystrophy combined (Lipsitt, 2003). SIDS—also known as *crib death*—is a disorder of **infancy** that apparently strikes while a baby is sleeping. In the typical case, a baby goes to sleep, apparently in perfect health, and is found dead the next morning. There is no sign that the baby struggled or was in pain.

The incidence of SIDS has been declining, but some 2,000–3,000 infants in the United States still die each year of SIDS. It is the most common cause of death during the first year, with most of these deaths occuring between 2 and 5 months of age (Paterson et al., 2006). New parents frequently live in dread of SIDS and check regularly through the night to see if their babies are breathing. It is not abnormal, by the way, for babies occasionally to suspend breathing for a moment.

SIDS is more common among the following groups (Hunt & Hauck, 2006; Paterson et al., 2006):

- Babies aged 2–4 months
- Babies who are put to sleep on their stomachs or their sides
- Premature and low-birth-weight infants
- Male babies
- Babies in families of lower socioeconomic status
- African American babies
- Babies of teenage mothers
- Babies whose mothers smoked during or after pregnancy or whose mothers used narcotics during pregnancy

The prevention of SIDS begins during pregnancy. Smoking and using other drugs during pregnancy increases the risk of SIDS. Mothers should obtain adequate nutrition and health care during pregnancy.

The Children's Hospital Boston Study

Perhaps the most compelling study to date about the causes of SIDS was led by health professionals at Children's Hospital Boston (Paterson et al., 2006). The study focused on an area in the brainstem called the **medulla** (see Figure 3.3), which

sudden infant death syndrome (SIDS) The death, while sleeping, of apparently healthy babies who stop breathing.

infancy The period of very early childhood, characterized by lack of complex speech; the first 2 years after birth.

medulla A part of the brain stem that regulates vital and automatic functions such as breathing and the sleep–wake cycle.

is involved in basic functions such as breathing and sleep–wake cycles. The medulla causes us to breathe if we are in need of oxygen. Researchers compared the medullas of babies who had died from SIDS with those of babies who had died at the same ages from other causes. They found that the medullas of the babies who died from SIDS were less sensitive to the brain chemical *serotonin*, which helps keep the medulla responsive. The problem was particularly striking in the brains of the boys, which could account for the gender difference in the incidence of SIDS.

Medulla

© 2012 Cengage Learning

Figure 3.3 The Medulla Sudden infant death syndrome (SIDS) may be caused by low sensitivity of the medulla to serotonin.

Perhaps within a few years we will have a screening test for SIDS and a method for preventing or controlling it. Meanwhile, what should you do about SIDS? Check out the recommendations of the American Academy of Pediatrics (Task Force on SIDS, 2005):

- Place infants in a supine position (wholly on the back) for every sleep period.
- Use a firm mattress or other sleep surface, preferably covered by a sheet.
- Keep soft objects such as pillows, comforters, quilts, and stuffed toys away from the infant's sleeping environment. Bumper pads, if used, should be firm, thin, and well secured so they are less likely to cover the infant's face.
- Avoid smoking during pregnancy.
- Use a separate but nearby sleeping environment, such as a crib, bassinet, or cradle, preferably in the same room as the parent.
- Consider using a pacifier at sleep time for the first year.
- Do not overheat the sleep environment.
- Do not use commercial devices marketed as reducing the risk of SIDS.
- Do not use home monitors for detecting sleep patterns prior to SIDS. (Monitors may be appropriate for other purposes; ask your obstetrician.)
- Encourage "tummy time" (or "kangaroo care") when the infant is awake..

Preventing SIDS

Watch and learn whether a simple hearing test can identify SIDS susceptibility.

Check Your Learning Quiz 3.1

Go to **login.cengagebrain.com** and take the online quiz.

▶ **LO8** Describe the sequences of physical development.

▶ **LO9** Describe patterns of growth in infancy.

▶ **LO10** Discuss failure to thrive.

Did you know that—

- The head of a newborn child doubles in length by adulthood, but the legs grow about 5 times as long?
- Infants triple their birth weight within a year?
- A child's brain reaches half its adult weight by the age of 1 year?
- The cerebral cortex—the outer layer of the brain, which is vital to human thought and reasoning—is only one eighth of an inch thick?
- Native American Hopi infants spend the first year of life strapped to a board, yet they begin to walk at about the same time as children who are reared in other cultures?

▼

Physical Growth and Development

What a fascinating creature the newborn is: tiny, delicate, apparently oblivious to its surroundings, yet perfectly formed and fully capable of letting its caregivers know when it is hungry, thirsty, or uncomfortable. And what a fascinating creature is this same child 2 years later: running, playing, talking, hugging, and kissing.

It is hard to believe that only 2 short years—the years of infancy—bring about so many changes. It seems that nearly every day brings a new accomplishment. But as we will see, not all infants share equally in the explosion of positive developments. Therefore, we will also enumerate some developmental problems and what can be done about them.

Sequences of Physical Development: Head First?

Three key sequences of physical development are **cephalocaudal** development, **proximodistal** development, and differentiation.

cephalocaudal from head to tail

proximodistal from the inner part (or axis) of the body outward.

differentiation The processes by which behaviors and physical structures become specialized.

1. Cephalocaudal Development

Development proceeds from the upper part of the head to the lower parts of the body. When we consider the central role of the brain, which is contained within the skull, the cephalocaudal sequence appears quite logical. The brain regulates essential functions, such as the heartbeat. Through the secretion of hormones, the brain also regulates the growth and development of the body and influences basic drives, such as hunger and thirst.

The head develops more rapidly than the rest of the body during the embryonic stage. By 8 weeks after conception, the head constitutes half the entire length of the embryo. The brain develops more rapidly than the spinal cord. Arm buds form before leg buds. Most newborn babies have a strong, well-defined sucking reflex, although their legs are spindly and their limbs move back and forth only in diffuse excitement or agitation. Infants can hold up their heads before they gain control over their arms, their torsos, and, finally, their legs. They can sit up before they can crawl and walk.

The lower parts of the body, because they get off to a later start, must do more growing to reach adult size. The head doubles in length between birth and maturity, but the torso, arms, and legs must do more than double to reach their mature lengths; they increase in length by 3, 4, and 5 times, respectively.

2. Proximodistal Development

Growth and development also proceed from the trunk outward, from the body's central axis toward the periphery. The proximodistal principle, too, makes sense. The brain and spinal cord follow a central axis down through the body, and it is essential that the nerves be in place before infants can gain control over their arms and legs. Consider also that the life functions of the newborn baby—heartbeat, respiration, digestion, and elimination of wastes—are all carried out by organ systems close to the central axis. These functions must be in operation or ready to operate when the child is born.

In terms of motor development, infants gain control over their trunks and their shoulders before they can control their arms, hands, and fingers. Similarly, infants gain control over their hips and upper legs before they can direct their lower legs, feet, and toes.

3. Differentiation

As children mature, their physical reactions become less global and more specific. The tendency of behavior and physical structures to become more specific and distinct is called differentiation. If a neonate's finger is pricked or burned, he or she may withdraw the finger but also thrash about, cry, and show general signs of distress. Toddlers may also cry, show distress, and withdraw the finger, but they are less likely to thrash about wildly. Thus, the response to pain has become more specific. An older child or adult is also likely to withdraw the finger, but less likely to wail (sometimes) and show general distress.

Growth Patterns in Height and Weight

The most dramatic gains in height and weight occur during prenatal development. Within a span of 9 months, children develop from a zygote about 1/175 of an inch long to a neonate about 20 inches in length. Weight increases by billions.

During the first year after birth, gains in height and weight are also dramatic, although not by the standards of prenatal gains. Infants usually double their birth weight in about 5 months and triple it by the first birthday (Kuczmarski et al., 2000). Their height increases by about 50% in the first year, so that a child whose length at birth was 20 inches is likely to be about 30 inches tall at 12 months.

Growth in infancy has long been viewed as a slow and steady process. Growth charts in pediatricians' offices are smooth, continuous curves, but research suggests that infants actually grow in spurts. About 90%–95% of the time, they are not growing at all. One study measured the height of infants throughout their first 21 months (Lampl et al., 1992). The researchers found that the infants would remain the same size for 2–63 days and then would shoot up in length by one fifth of an inch (0.5 centimeter) to a full inch (2.5 centimeters) in less than 24 hours.

Infants grow another 4–6 inches during the second year and gain another 4–7 pounds. Boys generally reach half their adult height by their second birthday. Girls, however, mature more quickly than boys and are likely to reach half their adult height at the age of 18 months (Tanner, 1989). The growth rates of taller-than-average infants, as a group, tend to slow down. Those of shorter-than-average infants, as a group, tend to speed up. I am not suggesting that there is no relationship between infant and adult heights or that we all wind up in an average range. Tall infants, as a group, wind up taller than short infants, but in most cases not by as much as seemed likely during infancy.

Changes in Body Proportions

As mentioned earlier, development proceeds in a cephalocaudal manner. A few weeks after conception, an embryo is almost all head. At the beginning of the fetal stage, the head is about half the length of the unborn child. In the neonate, it is about one fourth the length of the body. The head gradually diminishes in proportion to the rest of the body, even though it doubles in size by adulthood.

Typically, an adult's arms are nearly 3 times the length of the head. The legs are about 4 times as long. Among neonates, the arms and legs are about equal in length. Each is only about 1½ times the length of the head. By the first birthday, the neck has begun to lengthen, as have the arms and legs. The arms grow more rapidly than the

failure to thrive (FTT) A disorder of infancy and early childhood characterized by variable eating and inadequate gains in weight.

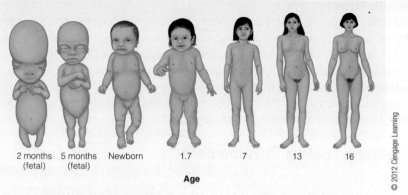

2 months (fetal) 5 months (fetal) Newborn 1.7 7 13 16

Age

© 2012 Cengage Learning

Figure 3.4 Changes in the Proportions of the Body Development proceeds in a cephalocaudal direction. The head is proportionally larger during fetal development and among younger children.

legs at first; by the second birthday, the arms are actually longer than the legs, but soon the legs catch up with and surpass the arms in length (see Figure 3.4).

Failure to Thrive

Haley is 4 months old. Her mother, as she puts it, is breast-feeding Haley "all the time" because she is not gaining weight. Not gaining weight for a while is normal, but Haley also is irritable and feeds fitfully, sometimes refusing the breast entirely. Her pediatrician is evaluating her for a syndrome called **failure to thrive** (FTT).

FTT is a serious disorder that impairs growth in infancy and early childhood (Simonelli et al., 2005). Yet FTT is sometimes a fuzzy diagnosis. Historically, researchers have spoken of biologically based (or "organic") FTT versus nonbiologically based ("nonorganic") FTT. The idea is that in organic FTT, an underlying health problem accounts for FTT. Nonorganic FTT apparently has psychological roots, social roots, or both. In either case, the infant does not make normal gains in weight and size (Simonelli et al., 2005).

Regardless of the cause or causes, feeding problems are central. As in Haley's case, infants are more likely to be described as variable eaters and less often as hungry (C. Wright & Birks, 2000). FTT is linked not only to slow physical growth but also to cognitive, behavioral, and emotional problems (Simonelli et al., 2005). At the age of 8½, children who had been diagnosed with FTT in infancy were smaller, less cognitively advanced, and more emotionally disturbed than normal children (Dykman et al., 2001).

▶ **LO11** Discuss the advantages and disadvantages of breast milk.

Catch-Up Growth

A child's growth can be slowed from its genetically predetermined course by many organic factors, including illness and malnutrition. If the problem is alleviated, the child's rate of growth frequently accelerates to approximate its normal course (van IJzendoorn & Juffer, 2006). The tendency to return to one's genetically determined pattern of growth is referred to as **canalization**. Once Haley's parents receive counseling and once Haley's FTT is overcome, Haley will put on weight rapidly and almost catch up to the norms for her age.

Nutrition: Fueling Development

The nutritional status of most children in the United States is good compared with that of children in developing countries (Arija et al., 2006). However, infants and young children from low-income families are more likely than other children to display signs of poor nutrition, such as anemia (a reduced number of red blood cells, causing paleness and weakness) and FTT (National Center for Children in Poverty, 2009).

From birth, infants should be fed either breast milk or an iron-fortified infant formula. The introduction of solid foods is not recommended until about 4–6 months of age, although the American Academy of Pediatrics recommends that infants be fed breast milk throughout the first year and longer if possible (American Academy of Pediatrics, 2007). The first solid food is usually iron-enriched cereal, followed by strained fruits, vegetables, meats, poultry, and fish. Whole cow's milk is normally delayed until the infant is 9–12 months old. Finger foods such as teething biscuits are introduced in the latter part of the first year.

Here are some useful guidelines for infant nutrition (Infant and Newborn Nutrition, 2007):

- Build up to a variety of foods. Introduce new foods one at a time. The infant may be allergic to a new food, and introducing foods one at a time helps isolate their possible effects.
- Pay attention to the infant's appetite to help avoid overfeeding or underfeeding.
- Do not restrict fat and cholesterol too much. Infants need calories and some fat.
- Do not overdo high-fiber foods.
- Generally avoid items with added sugar and salt.
- Encourage eating of high-iron foods; infants need more iron, pound for pound, than adults do.

canalization The tendency of growth rates to return to normal after undergoing environmentally induced change.

Breast-Feeding Versus Bottle-Feeding

In many developing nations, mothers have to breast-feed. Even in developed nations, where formula is readily available, breast milk is considered by most health professionals to be the "medical gold standard" (Knaak, 2005). Perhaps for this reason, popular magazines in the United States tend to carry more articles on breast-feeding than on bottle-feeding (Frerichs et al., 2006).

Over the past few decades, breast-feeding has become more popular, largely because of increased knowledge of its health benefits (Sloan et al., 2006). Today, most American mothers—more than 70%—breast-feed their children for at least a while, but only about 2 women in 5 continue to breast-feed after 6 months, and only 1 in 5 is still breast feeding after 1 year (Breastfeeding, 2006).

Many women bottle-feed because they return to work after childbirth and are unavailable to breast-feed. Their partners, extended families, nannies, or child-care workers give their children bottles during the day. Some mothers pump their milk and bottle it for use when they are away. Some parents bottle-feed because it permits both parents to share in feeding.

Advantages and Disadvantages of Breast-Feeding

The American Academy of Pediatrics recommends breast-feeding for the following reasons:

- Breast milk conforms to human digestion processes (i.e., it is unlikely to upset the infant's stomach).
- Breast milk alone is generally perceived to be adequate for the first 6 months after birth.
- As the infant matures, the composition of breast milk changes to help meet the infant's changing needs.
- Breast milk contains the mother's antibodies and helps the infant ward off health problems ranging from ear infections, pneumonia, wheezing, bronchiolitis, and tetanus to chicken pox, bacterial meningitis, and typhoid fever.
- Breast milk helps protect against the form of cancer known as childhood lymphoma (a cancer of the lymph glands).
- Breast milk decreases the likelihood of developing serious cases of diarrhea.
- Infants who are nourished by breast milk are less likely to develop allergic responses and constipation.
- Breast-fed infants are less likely to develop obesity later in life.

▶ **LO12** Discuss neural development.

- Breast-feeding is associated with better neural and behavioral organization in the infant.

Breast-feeding also has health benefits for the mother: It reduces the risk of early breast cancer and ovarian cancer, and it builds the strength of bones, which can reduce the likelihood of hip fractures that result from osteoporosis following menopause. Breast-feeding also helps shrink the uterus after delivery.

But there are also downsides to breast-feeding. For example, breast milk is one of the bodily fluids that transmit HIV. As many as one third of the world's infants who have HIV/AIDS were infected in this manner (UNAIDS, 2006). Alcohol, many drugs, and environmental hazards such as polychlorinated biphenyls can also be transmitted through breast milk. Moreover, for breast milk to contain the necessary nutrients, mothers must be adequately nourished themselves. The mother also encounters the physical demands of producing and expelling milk, a tendency for soreness in the breasts, and the inconvenience of being continually available to meet the infant's feeding needs.

nerve A bundle of axons from many neurons.

neuron A cell in the nervous system that transmits messages.

dendrite A rootlike part of a neuron that receives impulses from other neurons.

axon A long, thin part of a neuron that transmits impulses to other neurons through branching structures called *axon terminals*.

neurotransmitter A chemical that transmits a neural impulse across a synapse from one neuron to another.

myelin sheath A fatty, whitish substance that encases and insulates axons.

myelination The coating of axons with myelin.

multiple sclerosis A disorder in which hard fibrous tissue replaces myelin, impeding neural transmission.

Development of the Brain and Nervous System

The nervous system is a system of **nerves** involved in heartbeat, visual–motor coordination, thought and language, and so on.

Development of Neurons

The basic units of the nervous system are cells called **neurons**. Neurons receive and transmit messages from one part of the body to another. The messages account for phenomena such as reflexes, the perception of an itch from a mosquito bite, the visual–motor coordination of a skier, the composition of a concerto, and the solution of a math problem.

People are born with about 100 billion neurons, most of which are in the brain. Neurons vary according to their functions and locations in the body. Some neurons in the brain are only a fraction of an inch in length, whereas neurons in the leg can grow several feet long. Each neuron possesses a cell body, dendrites, and an axon (see Figure 3.5). **Dendrites** are short fibers that extend from the cell body and receive incoming messages from up to 1,000 adjoining transmitting neurons. The **axon** extends trunklike from the cell body and accounts for much of the difference in length in neurons. An axon can be up to several feet in length if it is carrying messages from the toes upward. Messages are released from axon terminals in the form of chemicals called **neurotransmitters**. These messages are received by the dendrites of adjoining neurons, muscles, or glands. As the child matures, axons lengthen and dendrites and axon terminals proliferate.

Myelin

Many neurons are tightly wrapped with white, fatty **myelin sheaths** that give them the appearance of a string of white sausages. The high fat content of the myelin sheath insulates the neuron from electrically charged atoms in the fluids that encase the nervous system. In this way, leakage of the electric current being carried along the axon is minimized and messages are conducted more efficiently.

The term **myelination** refers to the process by which axons are coated with myelin. Myelination is not complete at birth, but rather is part of the maturation process that leads to crawling and walking during the first year after birth. Myelination of the brain's prefrontal matter continues into the second decade of life and is connected with advances in working memory and language ability (Aslin & Schlaggar, 2006; Pujol et al., 2006). Breakdown of myelin is believed to be associated with Alzheimer's disease, a source of cognitive decline that begins later in life.

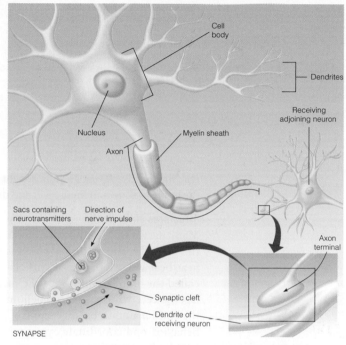

Figure 3.5 Anatomy of a Neuron "Messages" enter neurons through dendrites, are transmitted along the axon, and then are sent through axon terminals to muscles, glands, and other neurons. Neurons develop by means of proliferation of dendrites and axon terminals, and through myelination.

In the disease **multiple sclerosis**, myelin is replaced by hard, fibrous tissue that disrupts the timing of neural transmission, interfering with muscle control (Stankoff et al., 2006). Phenylketonuria causes mental retardation by inhibiting the formation of myelin in the brain (Sirrs et al., 2007).

Development of the Brain

The brain of the neonate weighs a little less than a pound, or nearly one fourth its adult weight. In keeping with the principles of cephalocaudal growth, an infant's brain reaches a good deal more than half its adult weight by the first birthday. In fact, it triples in weight,

Neuron Anatomy

Explore an animation of the neuron's anatomy.

Brain Development

Explore an animated learning module to expand your knowledge of infant brain development.

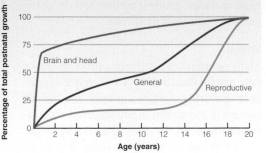

Figure 3.6 Growth of Body Systems as a Percentage of Total Postnatal Growth The brain of the neonate weighs about one fourth of its adult weight. In keeping with the principle of cephalocaudal growth, the brain will triple in weight by the infant's first birthday, reaching nearly 70% of its adult weight.

reaching nearly 70% of its adult weight by the age of 1 year (see Figure 3.6). Let's look at the brain, as shown in Figure 3.7, and discuss the development of the structures within.

Structures of the Brain

Many nerves that connect the spinal cord to higher levels of the brain pass through the medulla. The medulla, which is vital in the control of basic functions such as heartbeat and respiration, is part of an area called the brain stem. Above the medulla lies the **cerebellum**. The cerebellum helps the child maintain balance, control motor behavior, and coordinate eye movements with bodily sensations.

The **cerebrum** is the crowning glory of the brain. It makes possible the breadth and depth of human learning, thought, memory, and language. The surface of the cerebrum consists of two hemispheres that become increasingly wrinkled as the child develops, coming to show ridges and valleys called *fissures*. This surface is the cerebral cortex. The cerebral cortex is only one eighth of an inch thick, yet it is the seat of thought and reason. It is here that we receive sensory information from the world outside and command muscles to move.

cerebellum The part of the brain stem involved in coordination and balance.

cerebrum The part of the brain responsible for learning, thought, memory, and language.

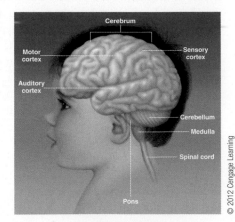

Figure 3.7 Structures of the Brain The convolutions of the cortex increase its surface area and, apparently, its intellectual capacity. (In this case, wrinkles are good.) The medulla is involved in vital functions such as respiration and heartbeat; the cerebellum is involved in balance and coordination.

Figure 3.8 Increase in Neural Connections in the Brain A major growth spurt in the brain occurs between the 25th week of prenatal development and the end of the second year after birth. This growth spurt is due primarily to the proliferation of dendrites and axon terminals. Source: Conel (1959).

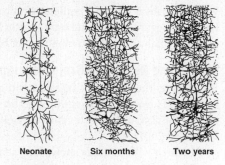

Neonate   Six months   Two years

Growth Spurts of the Brain

The first major growth spurt of the brain occurs during the fourth and fifth months of prenatal development, when neurons proliferate. A second growth spurt in the brain occurs between the 25th week of prenatal development and the end of the second year after birth. Whereas the first growth spurt of the brain is due to the formation of neurons, the second growth spurt is due primarily to the proliferation of dendrites and axon terminals (see Figure 3.8).

Brain Development in Infancy

There is a link between what infants can do and myelination. At birth, the parts of the brain involved in heartbeat and respiration, sleeping and arousal, and reflex activity are fairly well myelinated and functional. Neonates can show stereotyped reflexes thanks to myelination of motor pathways, but otherwise their physical activity tends to be random and ill organized. Myelin develops rapidly along the major motor pathways from the cerebral cortex during the last month of gestation and continues after birth. The development of intentional physical activity coincides with myelination as the unorganized movements of the neonate come under increasing control. Myelination of the nerves to muscles is largely developed by the age of 2 years, although myelination continues to some degree into adolescence (Wozniak & Lim, 2006).

Although neonates respond to touch and can see and hear quite well, the areas of the cortex that are involved in vision, hearing, and the skin senses are less well myelinated at birth. As myelination progresses and the interconnections between the various areas of the cortex thicken, children become increasingly capable of complex and integrated sensorimotor activities (Wozniak & Lim, 2006).

Myelination of the neurons involved in the sense of hearing begins at about the sixth month of gestation. Myelination of these pathways is developing rapidly at the time

Brain Structures

Explore an animation of the structures of the brain.

▶ **L013** Discuss motor development.

when the baby is born and continues until about the age of 4 years. The neurons involved in vision begin to myelinate only shortly before full term, but then they complete the process rapidly. Within 5–6 months after birth, vision has become the dominant sense.

Nature and Nurture in Brain Development

Brain areas that control sensation and movement develop because of maturation (nature). However, sensory stimulation and physical activity in early infancy help these brain structures develop as well (nurture) (Güntürkün, 2006; Posner & Rothbart, 2007).

Research with animals shows how sensory stimulation sparks growth of the cortex. Researchers have given rats "amusement parks" with toys such as ladders, platforms, and boxes to demonstrate the effects of enriched environments. In these studies, rats exposed to the more complex environments develop heavier brains than control animals. The weight differences in part reflect more synapses per neuron (Briones et al., 2004). On the other hand, animals reared in darkness show shrinkage of the visual cortex, impaired vision, and impaired visual–motor coordination (Klintsova & Greenough, 1999). If they don't use it, they lose it.

The brain is also affected by experience. Infants actually have more connections among neurons than adults do. Connections that are activated by experience survive; others do not (Tsuneishi & Casaer, 2000; Weinberg, 2004).

The great adaptability of the brain appears to be a double-edged sword. Adaptability allows us to develop different patterns of neural connections to meet the demands of different environments, but lack of stimulation—especially during critical early periods of development—can impair adaptability.

Motor Development: How Moving

Motor development involves the activity of muscles, leading to changes in posture, movement, and coordination of movement with the infant's developing sensory apparatus. Motor development provides some of the most fascinating changes in infants, because so much happens so fast.

Like physical development, motor development follows cephalocaudal and proximodistal patterns and differentiation. Infants gain control of their heads and upper torsos before they can effectively use their arms. This trend illustrates cephalocaudal development. Infants also can control their trunks and shoulders before they can use their hands and fingers, demonstrating the proximodistal trend.

ulnar grasp Grasping objects between the fingers and the palm.

pincer grasp Grasping objects between the fingers and the thumb.

Lifting and Holding the Torso and Head

Neonates can move their heads slightly to the side. They can thus avoid suffocation if they are lying face down and their noses or mouths are obstructed by bedding. At about 1 month, infants can raise their heads. By about 2 months, they can also lift their chests while lying on their stomachs.

When neonates are held, their heads must be supported. But by 3–6 months of age, infants generally manage to hold their heads quite well, so supporting the head is no longer necessary. Unfortunately, infants who can normally support their heads cannot do so when they are lifted or moved about in a jerky manner; infants who are handled carelessly can thus develop neck injuries.

Control of the Hands: Getting a Grip

The development of hand skills is an example of proximodistal development. Infants will track slowly moving objects with their eyes shortly after birth, but they will not reach for them. Voluntary reaching and grasping require visual–motor coordination. By about 3 months, infants will make clumsy swipes at objects. Between 4 and 6 months, infants become more successful at grasping objects (Piek, 2006; Santos et al., 2000). However, they may not know how to let go and may hold an object indefinitely, until their attention is diverted and the hand opens accidentally. Between 4 and 6 months is a good age for giving children rattles, large plastic spoons, mobiles, and other brightly colored hanging toys that can be grasped but are harmless when they wind up in the mouth.

Infants first hold objects between their fingers and palm. Once the opposable thumb comes into play at about 9–12 months of age, infants are able to pick up tiny objects using what is termed a pincer grasp.

Grasping is reflexive at first. Voluntary holding replaces reflexive grasping by 3–4 months. Infants first use an **ulnar grasp**, holding objects clumsily between their fingers and their palm. By 4–6 months, they can transfer objects back and forth between hands. The opposable thumb comes into play at about 9–12 months, enabling infants to pick up tiny objects in a **pincer grasp**. By about 11 months, infants can hold objects in each hand and inspect them in turn.

Another aspect of visual–motor coordination is stacking blocks. On average, children can stack two blocks at 15 months, three blocks at 18 months, and five blocks at 24 months (Wentworth et al., 2000).

Locomotion: Getting a Move On

Locomotion is movement from one place to another. Children gain the capacity to move their bodies through a sequence of activities that includes rolling over, sitting up, crawling, creeping, walking, and running (see Figure 3.9). There is much variation in the ages at which infants first engage in these activities. Although the sequence mostly remains the same, some children will skip a step. For example, an infant may creep without ever having crawled.

Most infants can roll over from back to stomach and from stomach to back by about the age of 6 months. By about 7 months, infants usually begin to sit up by themselves. At about 8–9 months, most infants begin to crawl, a motor activity in which they lie on their bellies and use their arms to pull themselves along. Creeping, in which infants move themselves along on their hands and knees, usually appears a month or so after crawling.

Standing overlaps with crawling and creeping. Most infants can remain in a standing position by holding on to something at about the age of 10 months. At this age, they may also be able to walk a bit with support and can pull themselves to a standing position by holding on to the sides of their cribs or other objects and can stand briefly without holding on. By 12–15 months or so, they walk by themselves, earning them the name **toddler**.

Toddlers soon run about, supporting their relatively heavy heads and torsos by spreading their legs in a bowlegged fashion. Because they are top-heavy and inexperienced, they fall frequently. Many toddlers are skillful at navigating slopes (Adolph & Berger, 2005). They walk down shallow slopes but prudently choose to slide or crawl down steep ones. Walking lends children new freedom. It allows them to get about rapidly and to grasp objects that were formerly out of reach. Give toddlers a large ball to toss and run after; it is an inexpensive and most enjoyable toy.

As children mature, their muscle strength, bone density, and balance and coordination improve (Metcalfe et al., 2005). By the age of 2 years, they can climb steps one at a time, placing both feet on each step. They can run well, walk backward, kick a large ball, and jump several inches.

Both maturation (nature) and experience (nurture) are involved in motor development. Certain voluntary motor activities are not possible until the brain has matured in terms of myelination and the differentiation of the motor areas of the cortex. Although the neonate shows stepping and swimming reflexes, these behaviors are controlled by more primitive parts of the brain. They disappear when cortical development inhibits

locomotion Movement from one place to another.

toddler A child who walks with short, uncertain steps.

some functions of the lower parts of the brain; and when they reappear, they differ in quality.

Infants also need some opportunity to experiment before they can engage in milestones such as sitting up and walking. Even so, many of these advances can apparently be attributed to maturation. In classic research, Wayne and Marsena Dennis (1940) reported on the motor development of Native American Hopi children who spent their first year strapped to a cradleboard. Although denied a full year of experience in locomotion, the Hopi infants gained the capacity to walk early in their second year, about when other children do (Figure 3.10).

Can training accelerate the appearance of motor skills? In a classic study with identical twins, Arnold Gesell (1929) gave one twin extensive training in hand coordination, block building, and stair climbing from early infancy. The other twin was allowed to develop on his own. At first, the trained twin had better skills, but as time passed, the untrained twin became just as skilled. The development of motor skills can be accelerated by training (Adolph & Berger, 2005; Zelazo, 1998), but the effect seems slight.

Although being strapped to a cradleboard did not permanently prevent the motor development of Hopi infants, Wayne Dennis (1960) reported that infants in an Iranian orphanage who were exposed to extreme social and physical deprivation were significantly retarded in their motor development. They grew apathetic, and all

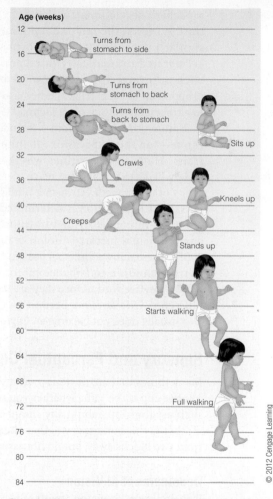

Age (weeks)

Turns from stomach to side
Turns from stomach to back
Turns from back to stomach
Sits up
Crawls
Kneels up
Creeps
Stands up
Starts walking
Full walking

© 2012 Cengage Learning

Figure 3.9 Motor Development in Infancy Motor development proceeds in an orderly sequence, but there is considerable variation in the timing of the marker events shown in this figure. An infant who is a bit behind will most likely develop without problems, and a precocious infant will not necessarily become a rocket scientist (or gymnast).

aspects of development suffered. By contrast, however, the motor development of similar infants in a Lebanese orphanage accelerated dramatically in response to such minimal intervention as being propped up in their cribs and being given a few colorful toys (Sayegh & Dennis, 1965).

Nature provides the limits—the reaction range—for the expression of inherited traits. Nurture determines whether the child will develop skills that reach the upper limits of the range. Even such a fundamental skill as locomotion is determined by a complex interplay of maturational and environmental factors (Adolph & Berger, 2005). There may be little purpose in trying to train children to enhance motor skills

Figure 3.10 **A Native American Hopi Infant Strapped to a Cradleboard** Researchers have studied Hopi children, who are strapped to cradleboards during their first year, to see whether their motor development is significantly delayed. Once released from their boards, Hopi children advance rapidly in their motor development, suggesting the important role of maturation in motor development.

before they are ready. Once they are ready, however, teaching and practice do make a difference. One does not become an Olympic athlete without "good genes," but one also usually does not become an Olympic athlete without solid training.

Sensory and Perceptual Development: Taking In the World

Many things that are obvious to us are not so obvious to infants. You may know that a coffee cup is the same whether you see it from above or from the side, but make no such assumptions about the infant's knowledge. You may know that an infant's mother is the same size whether she is standing next to the infant or approaching from two blocks away, but do not assume that the infant agrees with you.

Development of Vision

Development of vision involves the development of visual acuity or sharpness, peripheral vision (seeing things at the sides while looking ahead), visual preferences, depth perception, and perceptual constancies, such as knowing that an object remains the same object even though it may look different when seen from a different angle.

Development of Visual Acuity and Peripheral Vision

Newborns are extremely nearsighted, with vision beginning at about 20/600 (that is, objects that are only 20 ft away may look as "fuzzy" as objects that are 600 ft away). The most dramatic gains in visual acuity are made between birth and 6 months of age, with acuity reaching about 20/50 (Haith, 1990; Skoczenski, 2002). By 3–5 years, visual acuity generally approximates adult levels (20/20 in the best cases).

Neonates also have poor peripheral vision (Cavallini et al., 2002; Skoczenski, 2002). Adults can perceive objects that are nearly 90° off to the side (i.e., directly to the left or right), although objects at these extremes are unclear. Neonates cannot perceive visual stimuli that are off to the side by an angle of more than 30°, but their peripheral vision expands to an angle of about 45° by the age of 7 weeks. By 6 months, their peripheral vision is about equal to that of an adult.

Let us now consider the development of visual perception. We will see that infants frequently prefer the strange to the familiar and will avoid going off the deep end—sometimes.

Visual Preferences: How Do You Capture an Infant's Attention?

Neonates look at stripes longer than at blobs. This finding has been used in much of the research on visual acuity. Classic research found that by the age of 8–12 weeks, most infants also show distinct preferences for curved lines over straight ones (Fantz et al., 1975).

Robert Fantz (1961) also wondered whether there was something intrinsically interesting about the human face that drew the attention of infants. To investigate this question, he showed 2-month-old infants six disks. One disk contained human features, another newsprint, and still another a bull's-eye. The remaining three disks were featureless but colored red, white, and yellow. In this study, the infants fixated significantly longer on the human face.

Some studies suggest that the infants in Fantz's (1961) study may have preferred the human face because it had a complex, intriguing pattern of dots (eyes) within an outline, not because it was a face. But de Haan and Groen (2006) have asserted that "reading" faces (interpreting facial expressions) is important to infants because they do not understand verbal information as communicated through language.

Researchers therefore continue to ask whether humans come into the world "prewired" to prefer human stimuli to other stimuli that are just as complex, and—if so—what it is about human stimuli that draws attention. Some researchers—unlike de Haan and Groen—argue that neonates do not prefer faces because they are faces per se but because of the structure of their immature visual systems (Simion et al., 2001). A supportive study of 34 neonates found that the longer fixations on facelike stimuli resulted from a larger number of brief fixations (looks) rather than from a few prolonged fixations (Cassia et al., 2001). The infants' gaze, then, was sort of bouncing around from feature to feature rather than staring at the face in general. The researchers interpreted the finding to show that

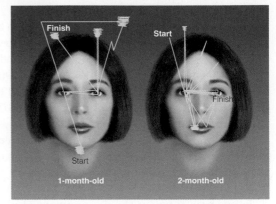

Figure 3.11 Eye Movements of 1- and 2-Month-Olds One-month-olds direct their attention to the edges of objects. Two-month-olds move in from the edge. Source: Salapatek (1975).

the stimulus properties of the visual object are more important than the fact that it represents a human face. Even so, of course, the immature visual system would be providing some prewired basis for attending to the face. Learning also plays a role. For example, neonates can discriminate their mother's face from a stranger's after 8 hours of mother–infant contact spread over 4 days (I. W. R. Bushnell, 2001).

Neonates appear to direct their attention to the edges of objects. This pattern persists for the first several weeks (Bronson, 1991). When they are given the opportunity to look at human faces, 1-month-old infants tend to pay most attention to the "edges," that is, the chin, an ear, or the hairline. The eye movements of 2-month-old infants move in from the edge (see Figure 3.11). The infants focus particularly on the eyes, although they also inspect other features, such as the mouth and nose (C. A. Nelson & Ludemann, 1989).

Some researchers (e.g., Haith, 1979) have explained infants' tendencies to scan from the edges of objects inward by noting that for the first several weeks, infants seem to be concerned with *where* things are. Their attention is captured by movement and sharp contrasts in brightness and shape, such as those found where the edges of objects stand out against their backgrounds. But by about 2 months, infants tend to focus on *what* things are, scanning systematically within the boundaries of objects (Bronson, 1990, 1997).

perceptual constancy Perceiving objects as maintaining their identity although sensations from them change as their positions change.

Development of Depth Perception

Infants generally respond to cues for depth by the time they are able to crawl (6–8 months of age or so), and most have the good sense to avoid going off the deep end, that is, crawling off ledges and tabletops into open space (Campos, et al., 1978).

In a classic study on depth perception, Gibson and Walk (1960) placed infants of various ages on a fabric-covered run-way that ran across the center of a clever device called a visual cliff. The visual cliff is a sheet of Plexiglas that covers a cloth with a checkerboard pattern. On one side, the cloth is placed immediately beneath the Plexiglas; on the other, it is dropped about 4 feet. In the Gibson and Walk study, 8 out of 10 infants who had begun to crawl refused to venture onto the seemingly unsupported surface, even when their mothers beckoned encouragingly from the other side.

On a visual cliff, this young explorer has the good sense not to crawl out onto a (visually) unsupported surface. Do infants have to experience some of life's "bumps" before they avoid "going off the deep end," or does fear of heights "mature" at about the same time infants gain the ability to move around?

© 2012 Cengage Learning

Psychologists can assess infants' emotional responses to the visual cliff long before infants can crawl. For example, Campos and his colleagues (1970) found that 1-month-old infants showed no change in heart rate when placed face down on the "cliff." They apparently did not perceive the depth of the cliff. At 2 months, infants showed decreases in heart rate when so placed, which psychologists interpreted as a sign of interest. But the heart rates of 9-month-olds accelerated on the cliff, which was interpreted as a fear response. The study appears to suggest that infants profit from some experience crawling about (and, perhaps, accumulating some bumps) before they develop fear of heights. The 9-month-olds but not the 2-month-olds had had such experience. Other studies support the view that infants usually do not develop fear of heights until they can move around (Sorce et al., 2000; Witherington et al., 2005).

Development of Perceptual Constancies

It may not surprise you that a 12-inch ruler is the same length whether it is 2 feet or 6 feet away, or that a door across the room is a rectangle whether closed or ajar. Awareness of these facts depends not on sensation alone but on the development of perceptual constancies. **Perceptual constancy** is the tendency to perceive an object to be the same, even though the sensations produced by the object may differ under various conditions.

Consider again the example of the ruler. When it is 2 feet away, its image, as focused on the retina, has a certain retinal size. From 6 feet away, the 12-inch ruler is

Visual Field Development

Watch how infants' vision improves as they grow.

Visual Cliff

Watch an infant refuse to crawl across a visual cliff.

only one third as long in terms of retinal size, but we perceive it as being the same size because of size constancy. *Size constancy* is the tendency to perceive an object as having the same size even though its retinal size varies as a function of distance. From 6 feet away, a 36-inch yardstick casts an image equal in retinal size to the 12-inch ruler at 2 feet, but—if recognized as a yardstick—it is perceived as longer, again because of size constancy.

T. G. R. Bower (1974) conditioned infants aged 2½ to 3 months to turn their heads to the left when shown a 12-inch cube from a distance of 3 feet. He then presented them with three experimental stimuli: (1) a 12-inch cube 9 feet away, whose retinal size was smaller than that of the original cube; (2) a 36-inch cube 3 feet away, whose retinal size was larger than that of the original cube; and (3) a 36-inch cube 9 feet away, whose retinal size was the same as that of the original cube. The infants turned their heads most frequently in response to the first experimental cube, although its retinal image was only one third the length of that to which they had been conditioned, suggesting that they had achieved size constancy. Later studies have confirmed Bower's finding that size constancy is present in early infancy. Some research suggests that even neonates possess rudimentary size constancy (Slater, 2000; Slater et al., 1990).

Shape constancy is the tendency to perceive an object as having the same shape even though, when perceived from another angle, the shape projected onto the retina may change dramatically. When the top of a cup or a glass is seen from above, the visual sensations are in the shape of a circle. When seen from a slight angle, the sensations are elliptical. However, because of our familiarity with the object, we still perceive the rim of the cup or glass as being a circle. In the first few months after birth, infants see the features of their caregivers, bottles, cribs, and toys from all different angles, so that by the time they are 4 or 5 months old, a broad grasp of shape constancy seems to be established, at least under certain conditions (Slater, 2000).

Development of Hearing: The Better to Hear You With

Neonates can crudely orient their heads in the direction of a sound (Saffran et al., 2006). By 18 months of age, the accuracy of sound-localizing ability approaches that of adults. Sensitivity to sounds increases in the first few months of life (Saffran et al., 2006). As infants mature, the range of the pitch of the sounds they can sense gradually expands to include the adult's range of 20–20,000 cycles per second. The ability to detect differences in the pitch and loudness of sounds improves considerably throughout the preschool years. Auditory acuity also improves gradually over the

habituation The process of becoming used to a stimulus such that one discontinues responding to it.

first several years (Saffran et al., 2006), although infants' hearing can be so acute that many parents complain their napping infants will awaken at the slightest sound. This is especially true if parents have been overprotective in attempting to keep their rooms as silent as possible. Infants who are normally exposed to a backdrop of moderate noise levels become habituated to them and are not likely to awaken unless there is a sudden, sharp noise.

By the age of 1 month, infants perceive differences between speech sounds that are highly similar. In a classic study relying on the **habituation** method, infants of this age could activate a recording of "bah" by sucking on a nipple (Eimas et al., 1971). As time went on, habituation occurred, as shown by decreased sucking to hear the "bah" sound. Then the researchers switched from "bah" to "pah." If the sounds had seemed the same to the infants, their lethargic sucking patterns would have continued, but they immediately sucked harder, suggesting that they perceived the difference. Other researchers have found that within another month or two, infants reliably discriminate three-syllable words such as *marana* and *malana* (Kuhl et al., 2006).

Infants can discriminate the sounds of their parent's voices by 3½ months of age. In classic research (Spelke & Owsley, 1979), infants of this age were oriented toward their parents as they reclined in infant seats. The experimenters played recordings of the mother's or father's voice while the parents themselves remained inactive. The infants reliably looked at the parent whose voice was being played.

Young infants are capable of perceiving most of the speech sounds present in the world's languages. But after exposure to one's native language, infants gradually lose the capacity to discriminate those sounds that are not found in the native language (Werker et al., 2007), as shown in Figure 3.14 (Werker, 1989).

Infants also learn, as early as 6 months of age, to ignore small, meaningless variations in the sounds of their native language, for instance those caused by accents or head colds (Kuhl et al., 2006). Kuhl and her colleagues (1997) presented American and Swedish infants with pairs of sounds in either their own language or the other one. The infants were trained to look over their shoulder when they heard a difference in the sounds and to ignore sound pairs that seemed to be the same. The infants routinely ignored variations in sounds that were part of their language, because they apparently perceived them as the same sound. But the infants noticed slight variations in the sounds of the other language. Another study demonstrated the same ability in infants as young as 2 months (Marean et al., 1992).

Shape Constancy

Learn more about shape constancy.

Infants and Foreign Languages

Explore more about infants and their ability to discriminate the sounds of foreign languages.

Development of Coordination of the Senses: If I Can See It, Can I Touch It?

Young infants can recognize that objects experienced through one sense (e.g., vision) are the same as those experienced through another sense (e.g., touch). This ability has been demonstrated in infants as young as 1 month (E. W. Bushnell, 1993). One experiment demonstrating such understanding in 5-month-olds showed that infants of this age tend to look longer at novel rather than familiar sources of stimulation. Féron and her colleagues (2006) first allowed 5-month-old infants to handle groups of either two or three objects, presented one by one to their right hand. The infants were then shown visual displays of either two or three objects. The infants looked longer at the group of objects that differed from the ones they had handled, showing a transfer of information from the sense of touch to the sense of vision.

The Active–Passive Controversy in Perceptual Development

Newborn children may have more sophisticated sensory capabilities than you expected. Still, their ways of perceiving the world are largely mechanical, or passive. Neonates seem to be generally at the mercy of external stimuli. When a bright light strikes, they attend to it. If the light moves slowly across the plane of their vision, they track it.

As time passes, broad changes occur in the perceptual processes of children, and the child's role in perception appears to become decidedly more active. Developmental psychologist Eleanor Gibson (1969, 1991) noted a number of these changes:

1. **Intentional action replaces "capture" (automatic responses to stimulation).** As infants mature and gain experience, purposeful scanning and exploration of the environment take the place of mechanical movements and passive responses to stimulation.
2. **Systematic search replaces unsystematic search.** Over the first few years of life, children become more active as they develop systematic ways of exploring the environment. They come to pay progressively more attention to details of objects and people and to make finer and finer discriminations.
3. **Attention becomes selective.** Older children become capable of selecting the information they need from the welter of confusion in the environment.
4. **Irrelevant information becomes ignored.** Older children gain the capacity to screen out or deploy their attention away from stimuli that are irrelevant to the task at hand. That might mean shutting out the noise of cars in the street or radios in the neighborhood so as to focus on a book.

In short, children develop from passive, mechanical reactors to the world about them into active, purposeful seekers and organizers of sensory information.

Nature and Nurture in Perceptual Development

The nature–nurture issue is found in perceptual development, as in other areas of development.

Evidence for the Role of Nature

Compelling evidence supports the idea that inborn sensory capacities play a crucial role in perceptual development. Neonates arrive in the world with a good number of perceptual skills. They can see nearby objects quite well, and their hearing is usually fine. They are born with tendencies to track moving objects, to systematically scan the horizon, and to prefer certain kinds of stimuli. Preferences for different kinds of visual stimuli appear to unfold on schedule as the first months wear on. Sensory changes, as with motor changes, appear to be linked to maturation of the nervous system.

Evidence for the Role of Nurture

Evidence that experience plays a crucial role in perceptual development is also compelling. Children and lower animals have critical periods in their perceptual development. Failure to receive adequate sensory stimulation during these periods can result in permanent sensory deficits (Greenough et al., 2002). For example, newborn kittens raised with a patch over one eye wind up with few or no cells in the visual area of the cerebral cortex that would normally be stimulated by light that enters that eye. In effect, that eye becomes blind, even though sensory receptors in the eye itself may fire in response to light. On the other hand, if the eye of an adult cat is patched for the same amount of time, the animal will not lose vision. The critical period will have passed. Similarly, if health problems require that a child's eye must be patched for an extensive period of time during the first year, the child's visual acuity in that eye may be impaired.

Today most developmentalists would agree that nature and nurture interact to shape perceptual development. In the next module, we see how nature and nurture influence the development of thought and language in infants.

Early Exposure to Tastes

Learn more about the effects of early exposure to certain tastes.

Depth Perception in Infants

Watch a video on sensation and perception in infancy.

Check Your Learning Quiz 3.2

Go to **login.cengagebrain.com** and take the online quiz.

▶ **LO15** Describe the sensorimotor stage of cognitive
development.

▶ **LO16** Discuss the strengths
and limitations of Piaget's theory of sensorimotor development.

Did you know that—

- For 2-month-old infants, out of sight is truly out of mind?

- A 1-hour-old infant may imitate an adult who sticks out his or her tongue?

- Psychologists can begin to measure intelligence in infancy?

- Infant crying is not a primitive form of language?

- Infants all around the world initially babble the same sounds?

- You may slow down a child's development of pronunciation by correcting his
  or her errors?

- Children are prewired to listen to language in such a way that they come to
  understand rules of grammar?

▼

*Laurent … resumes his experiments of the day before. He grabs in succession a celluloid
swan, a box, etc., stretches out his arm and lets them fall. He distinctly varies the position of the fall. Sometimes he stretches out his arm vertically, sometimes he holds it
obliquely, in front of or behind his eyes, etc. When the object falls in a new position, he
lets it fall two or three times more on the same place, as though to study the spatial relation; then he modifies the situation (Source: Piaget, 1963).*

Is this a description of a scientist at work? In a way, it is. Although Swiss psychologist Jean Piaget (1936/1963) was describing his 11-month-old son Laurent, children
of this age frequently act like scientists, performing what Piaget called "experiments
in order to see."

Cognitive Development: Jean Piaget

sensorimotor stage Piaget's
first stage of cognitive development,
which lasts through infancy and is
generally characterized by increasingly complex coordination of sensory experiences with motor
activity.

primary circular reactions
The repetition of actions that first
occurred by chance and that focus
on the infant's own body.

secondary circular reactions
The repetition of actions that produce an effect on the environment.

Cognitive development focuses on the development of children's ways of perceiving
and mentally representing the world. Piaget labeled children's concepts of the world
schemes. He hypothesized that children try to use *assimilation* to absorb new events
into existing schemes. When assimilation does not allow children to make sense of
novel events, they try to modify existing schemes through *accommodation*.

Piaget (1936/1963) hypothesized that cognitive processes develop in an orderly
sequence of stages. Some children may advance more quickly than others, but the

sequence remains constant (Flavell et al., 2002; Siegler & Alibali, 2005). Piaget identified four stages of cognitive development: sensorimotor, preoperational, concrete operational, and formal operational. In this module, we discuss the sensorimotor stage.

The Sensorimotor Stage

Piaget's **sensorimotor stage** refers to the first 2 years of cognitive development, a time during which infants progress from responding to events with reflexes, or ready-made schemes, to goal-oriented behavior. Piaget divided the sensorimotor stage into six substages:

1. **Simple Reflexes.** The first substage covers the first month after birth. It is dominated by the assimilation of sources of stimulation into inborn reflexes such as grasping or visual tracking. At birth, reflexes seem stereotypical and inflexible. But even within the first few hours, neonates begin to modify reflexes as a result of experience. For example, infants will adapt patterns of sucking to the shape of the nipple and the rate of flow of fluid. During the first month or so, however, infants apparently make no connection between stimulation perceived through different sensory modalities. They make no effort to grasp objects that they visually track.

2. **Primary Circular Reactions.** The second substage, primary circular reactions, lasts from about 1 to 4 months of age and is characterized by the beginnings of the ability to coordinate various sensorimotor schemes. Infants tend to repeat stimulating actions that first occurred by chance. They may lift an arm repeatedly to bring it into view. **Primary circular reactions** focus on the infant's own body rather than on the external environment. Because infants will repeat actions that allow them to see, cognitive-developmental psychologists consider sensorimotor coordination self-reinforcing.

3. **Secondary Circular Reactions**. The third substage lasts from about 4 to 8 months and is characterized by **secondary circular reactions**, in which patterns of activity are repeated because of their effect on the environment. In the second substage (primary circular reactions), infants are focused on their own bodies, as in the example given with Laurent. In the third substage (secondary circular reactions), the focus shifts to objects and environmental events. Infants may now learn to pull strings in order to make a plastic face appear, or to shake an object in order to hear it rattle.

Jean Piaget

Read more about Jean Piaget.

The Sensorimotor Stage

Access this special animated learning module to delve deeper into this stage's six sub-stages and the theory's central concepts.

4. **Coordination of Secondary Schemes.** In the fourth substage, which lasts from about 8 to 12 months of age, infants can coordinate schemes to attain specific goals. Infants begin to show intentional, goal-directed behavior in which they differentiate between the means of achieving a goal and the goal or end itself. For example, they may lift a piece of cloth to reach a toy that they saw a parent place under the cloth earlier. In this example, the scheme of picking up the cloth (the means) is coordinated with the scheme of reaching for the toy (the goal or end). Infants also gain the capacity to imitate gestures and sounds that they previously ignored. The imitation of a facial gesture implies that infants have mentally represented their own faces and can tell what parts of their faces they are moving through feedback from facial muscles.

David Mendelsohn/Masterfile

Tertiary circular reactions. In this substage, infants vary their actions in a trial-and-error fashion to learn how things work. This child is fascinated by the results of pulling on the end of a roll of toilet paper.

5. **Tertiary Circular Reactions.** In the fifth substage, which lasts from about 12 to 18 months of age, Piaget looked on the behavior of infants as characteristic of budding scientists. Infants now engage in **tertiary circular reactions,** or purposeful adaptations of established schemes to specific situations. Behavior takes on a new experimental quality, and infants may vary their actions dozens of times in a deliberate trial-and-error fashion to learn how things work.

6. **Invention of New Means through Mental Combinations.** The sixth substage lasts from about 18 to 24 months of age. It serves as a transition between sensorimotor development and the development of symbolic thought. External exploration is replaced by mental exploration. At about 18 months, children may also use imitation to symbolize or stand for a plan of action.

tertiary circular reactions The purposeful adaptation of established schemes to new situations.

object permanence Recognition that objects continue to exist when they are not in view.

A-not-B error The error made when an infant selects a familiar hiding place (A) for an object rather than a new hiding place (B), even after the infant has seen the object hidden in the new place.

Development of Object Permanence

The appearance of **object permanence** is an important aspect of sensorimotor development. Object permanence is the recognition that an object or person continues to exist when out of sight. For example, your textbook continues to exist when you leave it in the library after studying for the big test, and an infant's mother continues to exist even when she is in another room. The development of object permanence is tied into the development of infants' working memory and reasoning ability (Aguiar & Baillargeon, 2002; Saiki & Miyatsuji, 2007).

Neonates do not respond to objects that are not within their immediate sensory grasp. By the age of 2 months, infants may show some surprise if an object (such as a toy duck) is placed behind a screen and then removed, so that when the screen is lifted, it is absent. However, they make no effort to search for the missing object. (See Figure 3.12.) Through the first 6 months or so, when the screen is placed between the object and the infant, the infant behaves as though the object is no longer there. Out of sight is out of mind for 2-month-olds: They do not yet appear to reliably mentally represent objects they see.

Figure 3.12 Development of Object Permanence To the infant who is in the early part of the sensorimotor stage, out of sight is truly out of mind. Once a sheet of paper is placed between the infant and the toy monkey (top two photos), the infant loses all interest in the toy. From evidence of this sort, Piaget concluded that the toy is not mentally represented. The bottom series of photos shows a child in a later part of the sensorimotor stage. This child does mentally represent objects, and pushes through a towel to reach an object that has been screened from sight.

By about the sixth month (Piaget's substage 3), an infant will tend to look for an object that has been dropped, behavior that suggests some form of object permanence. By 8–12 months of age (Piaget's substage 4), infants will seek to retrieve objects that have been completely hidden. But in observing his own children, Piaget (1936/1963) noted an interesting error known as the **A-not-B error**. Piaget repeatedly hid a toy behind a screen (A), and each time, his infant removed the screen and retrieved the toy. Then, as the infant watched, Piaget hid the toy behind another screen (B) in a different place. Still, the infant tried to recover the toy by pushing aside the first screen (A). It is as though the child had learned that a certain motor activity would reinstate the missing toy. The child did not, at this age, recognize that

Piaget's Sensorimotor Stage

Watch as children progress through Piaget's sensorimotor period.

Object Permanence

Explore and interact with an animation of an important aspect of sensorimotor development, object permanence.

▶ **LO17** Discuss infants' memory.

▶ **LO18** Discuss imitation during infancy.

objects usually remain in the place where they have been most recently mentally represented.

Evaluation of Piaget's Theory

The sequence of events Piaget described has been observed among American, European, African, and Asian infants (E. E. Werner, 1988). Still, research has raised questions about the validity of other of Piaget's views (Siegler & Alibali, 2005). For example, most researchers now agree that cognitive development is not as tied to discrete stages as Piaget suggested (Krojgaard, 2005; Siegler & Alibali, 2005). The process may be more gradual. Moreover, Piaget emphasized the role of maturation almost to the point of excluding adult and peer influences on cognitive development. However, research has shown that interpersonal influences play roles in cognitive development (Kuhn, 2007; Maratsos, 2007).

Piaget also appears to have underestimated infants' competence (Siegler & Alibali, 2005). For example, infants display object permanence earlier than he believed (S. H. Wang et al., 2005). Also, consider studies on **deferred imitation** (imitation of an action that may have occurred hours, days, or even weeks earlier). The presence of deferred imitation suggests that children have mentally represented behavior patterns. Piaget believed that deferred imitation appears at about 18 months, but others have found that infants show deferred imitation as early as 6–9 months. In Meltzoff's (1988) study, 9-month-old infants watched an adult perform behaviors such as pushing a button to produce a beep. When given a chance to play with the same objects a day later, many infants imitated the actions they had witnessed.

Information Processing

The **information-processing approach** to cognitive development focuses on how children manipulate or process information coming in from the environment or already stored in the mind. Infants' tools for processing information include memory and imitation.

Memory

Many of the cognitive capabilities of infants—recognizing the faces of familiar people, developing object permanence, and, in fact, learning in any form—depend on one critical aspect of cognitive development: their memory (Daman-Wasserman

deferred imitation The imitation of people and events that occurred in the past.

information-processing approach The view of cognitive development that focuses on how children manipulate sensory information or information stored in memory.

et al., 2006; Hayne & Fagen, 2003). Even neonates demonstrate memory for stimuli to which they have been exposed previously. For example, neonates adjust their rate of sucking to hear a recording of their mother reading a story she had read aloud during the last weeks of pregnancy, as discussed in Chapter 2 (DeCasper & Fifer, 1980; DeCasper & Spence, 1991).

Memory improves dramatically between 2 and 6 months of age and then again by 12 months (Pelphrey et al., 2004; S. A. Rose, Feldman, & Jankowski, 2001). The improvement may indicate that older infants are more capable than younger ones of encoding (i.e., storing) information, retrieving information already stored, or both (Hayne & Fagen, 2003).

A fascinating series of studies by Carolyn Rovee-Collier and her colleagues (Rovee-Collier, 1993) illustrated some of these developmental changes in infant memory. One end of a ribbon was tied to a brightly colored mobile suspended above the infant's crib. The other end was tied to the infant's ankle, so that when the infant kicked, the mobile moved. Infants quickly learned to increase their rate of kicking. To measure memory, the infant's ankle was again fastened to the mobile after a period of 1 or more days had elapsed. In one study, 2-month-olds remembered how to make the mobile move after delays of up to 3 days, and 3-month-olds remembered for more than a week (Greco et al., 1986).

Imitation: Infant See, Infant Do?

Imitation is the basis for much of human learning. Deferred imitation—that is, the imitation of actions after a time delay—occurs as early as 6 months of age (Barr et al., 2005; Campanella & Rovee-Collier, 2005). To help them remember the imitated act, infants are usually permitted to practice it when they learn it. But in one study, 12-month-old infants were prevented from practicing the behavior they imitated. Yet they were able to demonstrate it 4 weeks later, suggesting that they had mentally represented the act (Klein & Meltzoff, 1999).

But infants can imitate certain actions at a much earlier age. Neonates only 42 minutes to 71 hours old have been found to imitate adults who open their mouths or stick out their tongues (Meltzoff & Prinz, 2002; Rizzolatti et al., 2002;

Counting in the Crib?

Can infants add and subtract?

© Gross L (2006) Evolution of Neonatal Imitation. PLoS Biol 4(9): e311. doi:10.1371/journal. pbio.0040311

▶ **LO19** Explain how we measure individual differences in the development of cognitive functioning.

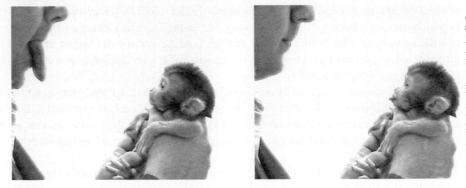

Figure 3.13 Mirror Neurons A newborn rhesus monkey imitates protrusion of the tongue, a feat made possible by mirror neurons, not by learning. Newborn humans show similar patterns of imitation.

see Figure 3.13). Such early imitation is apparently built-in—enabled by the presence of so-called *mirror neurons* in the brain. Mirror neurons are found in newborn monkeys as well as newborn humans.

Studies that have found imitation generally have been done with very young infants—up to 2 weeks old—whereas the studies that have not found imitation have tended to use older infants. This is further evidence that imitation in neonates is inborn. Thus, built-in imitation might disappear when reflexes are "dropping out" and reemerge when it has a firmer cognitive footing. Why might newborns possess some sort of imitation reflex? One possibility is that mirror neurons enabling imitation would be maintained by evolutionary forces because they enhance the probability of survival as a result of caregiving (Oztop et al., 2006; Rizzolatti et al., 2002).

Individual Differences in Cognitive Functioning Among Infants

Cognitive development does not proceed in the same way or at the same pace for all infants (R. Newman et al., 2006; S. A. Rose, Feldman, & Jankowski, 2005). Efforts to understand infant differences in cognitive development have relied on so-called scales of infant development or infant intelligence.

Measuring cognition or intelligence in infants is quite different from measuring it in adults. Infants cannot, of course, be assessed by asking them to explain the meanings of words, the similarity between concepts, or the rationales for social rules. One of the most important tests of intellectual development among infants—the Bayley Scales of Infant Development, constructed in 1933 by psychologist Nancy Bayley and revised since—contains very different kinds of items.

The Bayley test currently consists of 178 mental-scale items and 111 motor-scale items. The mental scale assesses verbal communication, perceptual skills, learning and memory, and problem-solving skills. The motor scale assesses gross motor skills, such as standing, walking, and climbing, and fine motor skills, as shown by the ability to manipulate the hands and fingers. A behavior rating scale, based on examiner observation of the child during the test, is also used. The behavior rating scale assesses attention span, goal-directedness, persistence, and aspects of social and emotional development.

Even though psychologists can begin to measure intelligence in infancy, they use items that differ from the kinds of items used with older children and adults. It remains unclear how well results obtained in infancy predict intellectual functioning at later ages.

Testing Infants: Why and With What?

As you can imagine, it is no easy matter to test an infant. The items must be administered on a one-to-one basis by a patient tester, and it can be difficult to judge whether the infant is showing the targeted response. Why, then, do we test infants?

One reason is to screen infants for disabilities. A tester may be able to detect early signs of sensory or neurological problems, as suggested by development of visual–motor coordination. In addition to the Bayley scales, a number of tests have been developed to screen infants for such difficulties, including the Brazelton Neonatal Behavioral Assessment Scale and the Denver Developmental Screening Test.

Instability of Intelligence Scores Attained in Infancy

Researchers have also tried to use infant scales to predict development, but this effort has been less than successful. One study found that scores obtained during the first year of life correlated moderately at best with scores obtained a year later

The Bayley Scales Test

View sample items from the Bayley Scales of Infant Development.

(S. R. Harris et al., 2005). Certain items on the Bayley scales appear to predict related intellectual skills later in childhood. For example, Bayley items measuring infant motor skills predict subsequent fine motor and visual–spatial skills at 6–8 years of age (L. S. Siegel, 1992). Bayley language items also predict language skills at the same age (Siegel, 1992).

One study found that the Bayley scales and socioeconomic status were able to predict cognitive development among low-birth-weight children from 18 months to 4 years of age (Dezoete et al., 2003). But overall scores on the Bayley and other infant scales apparently do not predict school grades or IQ scores among schoolchildren very well (Colombo, 1993). Perhaps the sensorimotor test items used during infancy are not that strongly related to the verbal and symbolic items used to assess intelligence at later ages.

The overall conclusion seems to be that the Bayley scales can identify gross lags in development and relative strengths and weaknesses. However, they are only moderate predictors of intelligence scores even 1 year later, and are still poorer predictors of scores when the time between testing expands.

Use of Visual Recognition Memory

In a continuing effort to find aspects of intelligence and cognition that might remain consistent from infancy through later childhood, a number of researchers have focused on *visual recognition memory* (Courage et al., 2004). **Visual recognition memory** is the ability to discriminate previously seen objects from novel objects. This procedure is based on *habituation*.

Let us consider longitudinal studies of this type. Susan Rose and her colleagues (S. A. Rose, Feldman, & Wallace, 1992) showed 7-month-old infants pictures of two identical faces. After 20 seconds, the pictures were replaced with one picture of a new face and a second picture of the familiar face. The amount of time the infants spent looking at each face in the second set of pictures was recorded. Some infants spent more time looking at the new face than at the older face, suggesting that they had better memory for visual stimulation. The children were given standard IQ tests yearly from ages 1 through 6. It was found that the children with greater visual recognition memory later attained higher IQ scores.

Rose and her colleagues (S. A. Rose, Feldman, & Jankowski, 2001) also showed that, from age to age, individual differences in capacity for visual recognition mem-

visual recognition memory The kind of memory shown in an infant's ability to discriminate previously seen objects from novel objects.

prelinguistic vocalization A vocalization made by an infant before the use of language.

cooing Prelinguistic vowel-like sounds that reflect feelings of positive excitement.

ory remain stable. This finding is important because intelligence—the quality that many researchers seek to predict from visual recognition memory—is also theorized to be a reasonably stable trait.

A number of other studies have examined the relationship between either infant visual recognition memory or preference for novel stimulation (which is a related measure) and later IQ scores. In general, they show good predictive validity for broad cognitive abilities throughout childhood, including measures of intelligence and language ability (Heimann et al., 2006; S. A. Rose, Feldman, & Jankowski, 2004).

Now let us turn our attention to a fascinating aspect of cognitive development, the development of language.

Language Development: The 2-Year Explosion

As children develop language skills, they often begin speaking about things closely connected with their environments and their needs. They indicate that they're hungry or want a treat and that Mommy is leaving or coming home. Children enjoy playing with language. In physical development, the most dramatic developments come early—fast and furious—long before the child is born. Language does not come quite as early, and its development may not seem quite so fast and furious. Nevertheless, during the years of infancy, most infants develop from creatures without language to little people who understand nearly all the things that are said to them and who relentlessly sputter words and simple sentences for all the world to hear.

Early Vocalizations

Children develop language according to an invariant sequence of steps, or stages. We begin with the **prelinguistic vocalizations**. True words are symbols of objects and events. Prelinguistic vocalizations, such as *cooing* and *babbling*, do not represent objects or actions, so infant crying is not a primitive form of language.

Newborn children, as parents are well aware, have an unlearned but highly effective form of verbal expression: crying and more crying. During the second month, infants begin **cooing**. Infants use their tongues when they coo. For this reason, coos are more articulated than cries. Coos are often vowel-like and may resemble extended "oohs" and "ahs." Cooing appears linked to feelings of pleasure or positive excitement. Infants tend not to coo when they are hungry, tired, or in pain.

Cries and coos are innate but can be modified by experience (Volterra et al., 2004). When parents respond positively to cooing by talking to their infants, smiling at them, and imitating them, cooing increases. Early parent–child "conversations," in which parents respond to coos and then pause as the infant coos, may foster infant awareness of taking turns as a way of verbally relating to other people.

By about 8 months of age, cooing decreases markedly. Somewhere between 6 and 9 months, children begin to babble. **Babbling** is the first vocalizing that sounds like human speech. In babbling, infants frequently combine consonants and vowels, as in *ba*, *ga*, and, sometimes, the much valued *dada* (Stoel-Gammon, 2002). At first, *dada* is purely coincidental (sorry, you dads), despite the family's jubilation over its appearance.

In verbal interactions between infants and adults, the adults frequently repeat the syllables produced by their infants. They are likely to say "dadada" or "bababa" instead of simply "da" or "ba." Such redundancy apparently helps infants discriminate these sounds from others and further encourages them to imitate their parents (Elkind, 2007; Tamis-LeMonda et al., 2006).

After infants have been babbling for a few months, parents often believe that their children are having conversations with themselves. At 10–12 months, infants tend to repeat syllables, showing what linguists refer to as **echolalia**. Parents overhear them going on and on, repeating consonant–vowel combinations ("ah-bah-bah-bah-bah"), pausing, and then switching to other combinations.

Toward the end of the first year, infants are also using patterns of rising and falling **intonation** that resemble the sounds of adult speech. It may sound as though the infant is trying to speak the parents' language. Parents may think that their children are babbling in English or in whatever tongue is spoken in the home.

Development of Vocabulary

Vocabulary development refers to the child's learning the meanings of words. In general, children's **receptive vocabulary** outpaces their **expressive vocabulary** in development (Lickliter, 2001; Ouellette, 2006). In other words, at any given time, children can understand more words than they can use. One study, for example, found that 12-month-olds could speak an average of 13 words but could comprehend the meaning of 84 (Tamis-LeMonda et al., 2006). Infants usually understand much of what others are saying well before they themselves utter any words at all. Their ability to

babbling The child's first vocalizations that have the sounds of speech.

echolalia The automatic repetition of sounds or words.

intonation The use of pitches of varying levels to help communicate meaning.

receptive vocabulary The number of words one understands.

expressive vocabulary The number of words one can use in the production of language.

referential language style The use of language primarily as a means for labeling objects.

segment speech sounds into meaningful units—or words—before 12 months is a good predictor of their vocabulary at 24 months (R. Newman et al., 2006).

The Child's First Words

Ah, that long-awaited first word! What a milestone! Sad to say, many parents miss it. They are not quite sure when their infants utter their first word, often because the first word is not pronounced clearly or because pronunciation varies from usage to usage.

A child's first word typically is spoken between the ages of 11 and 13 months, but a range of 8–18 months is considered normal (Hoff, 2006; Tamis-LeMonda et al., 2006). First words tend to be brief, consisting of one or two syllables. Each syllable is likely to consist of a consonant followed by a vowel. Vocabulary acquisition is slow at first. It may take children 3 or 4 months to achieve a vocabulary of 10–30 words after the first word is spoken (de Villiers & de Villiers, 1999).

By about 18 months of age, children may be producing up to 50 words. Many of them are quite familiar, such as *no, cookie, mama, hi,* and *eat.* Others, such as *all gone* and *bye-bye,* may not be found in the dictionary, but they function as words. That is, they are used consistently to symbolize the same meaning.

More than half (65%) of children's first words comprise general nominals and specific nominals (Hoff, 2006; K. Nelson, 1973). General nominals are similar to nouns in that they include the names of classes of objects (*car, ball*), animals (*doggy, cat*), and people (*boy, girl*), but they also include both personal and relative pronouns (*she, that*). Specific nominals are proper nouns, such as *Daddy* and *Rover.* Words expressing movement are also frequently found in early speech.

At about 18–22 months of age, there is a rapid burst in vocabulary (Tamis-LeMonda et al., 2006). The child's vocabulary may increase from 50 to more than 300 words in only a few months. This vocabulary spurt could also be called a naming explosion, because almost 75% of the words added during this time are nouns. The rapid pace of vocabulary growth continues through the preschool years, with children acquiring an average of nine new words per day (Hoff, 2006).

Referential and Expressive Styles in Language Development

Some children prefer a referential approach in their language development, whereas others take a more expressive approach (Hoff, 2006; K. Nelson, 1981). Children who show a **referential language style** use language primarily to label objects in their

Language Development Milestones

Explore the milestones of language development in infancy.

Babbling Here, There, and Everywhere

Read more about infant babbling.

Infants and Sign Language

Can infants be taught sign language?

environments. Children who use an **expressive language style** use language primarily as a means for engaging in social interactions. Children with an expressive style use more pronouns and many words involved in social routines, such as *stop, more,* and *all gone.* More children use an expressive style than a referential style (Tamis-LeMonda et al., 2006), but most use a combination of the styles.

Overextension
Young children try to talk about more objects than they have words for. To accomplish their linguistic feats, children often extend the meaning of one word to refer to things and actions for which they do not have words (McDonough, 2002). This process is called **overextension**. Eve Clark (1973, 1975) studied diaries of infants' language development and found that overextensions are generally based on perceived similarities in function or form between the original object or action and the new one. She provided the example of the word *mooi*, which one child originally used to designate the moon. The child then overextended *mooi* to designate all round objects, including the letter O and cookies and cakes. Overextensions gradually pull back to their proper references as the child's vocabulary and ability to classify objects develop (McDonough, 2002).

Development of Sentences: Telegraphing Ideas
The infant's first sentences are typically one-word utterances, but they express complete ideas and therefore can be thought of as sentences. Roger Brown (1973) called brief expressions that have the meanings of sentences **telegraphic speech**. Adults who write telegrams use principles of syntax to cut out all the unnecessary words. "Home Tuesday" might stand for "I expect to be home on Tuesday." Similarly, only the essential words are used in children's telegraphic speech—in particular, nouns, verbs, and some modifiers.

Mean Length of Utterance
The **mean length of utterance** (MLU) is the average number of **morphemes** that communicators use in their sentences (Pancsofar & Vernon-Feagans, 2006; Saaristo-Helin et al., 2006). Morphemes are the smallest units of meaning in a language. A morpheme may be a whole word or part of a word, such as a prefix or suffix. For example, the word *walked* consists of two morphemes: the verb *walk* and the suffix *-ed*, which changes the verb to the past tense. In Figure 3.14, we see the relationship between chronological age and MLU for three children tracked by Roger Brown

expressive language style The use of language primarily as a means for engaging in social interaction.

overextension The use of words in situations in which their meanings become extended.

telegraphic speech A type of speech in which only the essential words are used.

mean length of utterance (MLU) The average number of morphemes used in an utterance.

morpheme The smallest unit of meaning in a language.

holophrase A single word that is used to express complex meanings.

(1973, 1977): Lin, Victor, and Sarah.

The patterns of growth in MLU are similar for each child, showing swift upward movement broken by intermittent and brief regressions. Figure 3.14 also shows us something about individual differences. Lin was precocious compared with Victor and Sarah, extending her MLU at much earlier ages. But as suggested earlier, the receptive language of all three children would have exceeded their expressive language at any given time. Also, Lin's earlier extension of MLU does not guarantee that she will show more complex expressive language than Victor and Sarah at maturity.

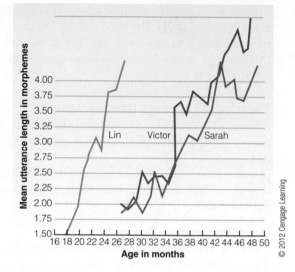

Figure 3.14 **Mean Length of Utterance for Three Children** Some children begin speaking earlier than others. However, the mean length of utterance (MLU) increases rapidly once speech begins.

Let us now consider the features of two types of telegraphic speech: the holophrase and two-word sentences.

Holophrases

Holophrases are single words that are used to express complex meanings. For example, "Mama" may be used by the child to signify meanings as varied as "There goes Mama," "Come here, Mama," and "You are Mama." Most children readily teach their parents what they intend by augmenting their holophrases with gestures, intonations, and reinforcers. That is, they act delighted when parents do as requested and howl when they do not (Tamis-LeMonda et al., 2006).

Two-Word Sentences

When the child's vocabulary consists of 50–100 words (typically somewhere between 18 and 24 months of age), telegraphic two-word sentences begin to appear (Tamis-LeMonda et al., 2006). In the sentence "That ball," the words *is* and *a* are implied.

Two-Word Sentences

Read more about the universality of kinds of two-word sentences.

Two-word sentences, although brief and telegraphic, show understanding of **syntax** (Slobin, 2001). The child will say "Sit chair," not "Chair sit," to tell a parent to sit in a chair. The child will say "My shoe," not "Shoe my," to show possession. "Mommy go" means Mommy is leaving, whereas "Go, Mommy" expresses the wish for Mommy to go away.

Theories of Language Development

Billions of children have learned the languages spoken by their parents and have passed them down, with minor changes, from generation to generation. But how do they do so? In discussing this question—and so many others—we refer to the possible roles of nature and nurture. Learning theorists have come down on the side of nurture, and those who point to a basic role for nature are said to hold a nativist view.

Views That Emphasize Nurture

Learning plays an obvious role in language development. Children who are reared in English-speaking homes learn English, not Japanese or Russian. Learning theorists usually explain language development in terms of imitation and reinforcement.

The Role of Imitation

From a social cognitive perspective, parents serve as **models**. Children learn language, at least in part, by observation and imitation. Many vocabulary words, especially nouns and verbs, are learned by imitation. But imitative learning does not explain why children spontaneously utter phrases and sentences that they have not observed (Tamis-LeMonda et al., 2006). Parents, for example, are unlikely to model utterances such as "Bye-bye sock" and "All gone, Daddy" but children say them. And children sometimes steadfastly avoid imitating certain language forms suggested by adults, even when the adults are insistent. Note the following exchange between 2-year-old Ben and a (very frustrated) adult (Kuczaj, 1982, p. 48):

> **Ben:** *I like these candy. I like they.*
> **Adult:** *You like them?*
> **Ben:** *Yes, I like they.*
> **Adult:** *Say "them."*
> **Ben:** *Them.*
> **Adult:** *Say "I like them."*

syntax The rules in a language for placing words in order to form sentences.

model In learning theory, a person whose behaviors are imitated by others.

extinction Decrease in frequency of a response due to absence of reinforcement.

shaping Gradual building of complex behavior through reinforcement of successive approximations to the target behavior.

Ben: I like them.
Adult: Good.
Ben: I'm good. These candy good too.
Adult: Are they good?
Ben: Yes. I like they. You like they?

Ben is not resisting the adult because of obstinacy. He does repeat "I like them" when asked to do so. But when given the opportunity afterward to construct the objective *them*, he reverts to using the subjective form *they*. Ben is likely at this period in his development to use his (erroneous) understanding of syntax spontaneously to actively produce his own language, rather than just imitate a model.

B. F. Skinner (1957) allowed that prelinguistic vocalizations such as cooing and babbling may be inborn. But parents reinforce children for babbling that approximates the form of real words, such as *da*, which in English resembles *dog* or *daddy*. Children, in fact, do increase their babbling when it results in adults smiling at them, stroking them, and talking back to them. As the first year progresses, children babble the sounds of their native tongues with increasing frequency; foreign sounds tend to drop out. The behaviorist explains this pattern of changing frequencies in terms of reinforcement of the sounds of the adults' language and **extinction** of foreign sounds. Another (nonbehavioral) explanation is that children actively attend to the sounds in their linguistic environments and are intrinsically motivated to utter them.

From Skinner's perspective, children acquire their early vocabularies through **shaping**. That is, parents require that children's utterances be progressively closer to actual words before they are reinforced. In support of Skinner's position, research has shown that reinforcement accelerates the growth of vocabulary in children (August et al., 2005; Kroeger & Nelson, 2006).

But recall Ben's refusal to be shaped into correct syntax. If the reinforcement explanation of lan-

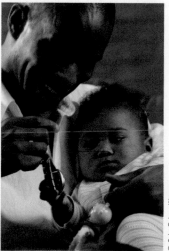

© Gabe Palmer/Alamy

Language growth in young children is enhanced when parents and caregivers engage the infant in "conversation" about activities and objects in the environment.

guage development were sufficient, parents' reinforcement would facilitate children's learning of syntax and pronunciation. However, parents are more likely to reinforce their children for the accuracy, or truth value, of their utterances than for their grammatical correctness (R. Brown, 1973). The child who points down and says "The grass is purple" is not likely to be reinforced, despite correct syntax. But the enthusiastic child who shows her empty plate and blurts out "I eated it all up" is likely to be reinforced, despite the grammatical incorrectness of "eated."

Selective reinforcement of children's pronunciation can also backfire. Children whose parents reward proper pronunciation but correct poor pronunciation develop vocabulary more slowly than children whose parents are more tolerant about pronunciation (K. Nelson, 1973).

Learning theory also cannot account for the invariant sequences of language development and for children's spurts in acquisition. The types of questions used, passive versus active sentences and so on, all emerge in the same order.

On the other hand, aspects of the child's language environment do influence the development of language. Studies show that language growth in young children is enhanced when adults (Tamis-LeMonda et al., 2006):

- Use a simplified form of speech known as infant-directed speech or, less formally, as "motherese."
- Use questions that engage the child in conversation.
- Respond to the child's expressive language efforts in a way that is "attuned"; for example, adults relate their speech to the child's utterance by saying "Yes, your doll is pretty" in response to the child's statement "My doll."
- Join the child in paying attention to a particular activity or toy.
- Gesture to help the child understand what they are saying.
- Describe aspects of the environment occupying the infant's current focus of attention.
- Read to the child.
- Talk to the child a great deal.

Views That Emphasize Nature

The nativist view of language development holds that inborn factors cause children to attend to and acquire language in certain ways. From this perspective, children bring an inborn tendency in the form of neurological prewiring to

psycholinguistic theory The view that language learning involves an interaction between environmental influences and an inborn tendency to acquire language.

language acquisition device Neural prewiring that eases the child's learning of grammar.

surface structure The superficial grammatical constructions in a language.

deep structure The underlying meanings in a language.

language learning. According to Steven Pinker and Ray Jackendoff (2005), the structures that enable humans to perceive and produce language evolved in bits and pieces. Those individuals who possessed these bits and pieces were more likely to reach maturity and transmit their genes from generation to generation because communication ability increased their chances of survival.

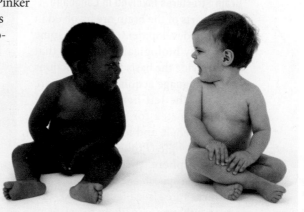

Masterfile (Royalty-Free Div.)

Do infants have an inborn language acquisition device? According to psycholinguistic theory, humans have an inborn "language acquisition device" that leads to commonalities in language development in all cultures. Babbling, for example, emerges at about the same time everywhere and, at about the same time, infants begin to sound as if they are babbling the sounds in the language spoken in the home.

Psycholinguistic Theory

According to **psycholinguistic theory**, language acquisition involves an interaction between environmental influences—such as exposure to parental speech and reinforcement—and an inborn tendency to acquire language. Noam Chomsky (1988, 1990) labeled this innate tendency a **language acquisition device**. Evidence for an inborn tendency is found in the universality of human language abilities; in the regularity of the early production of sounds, even among deaf children; and in the invariant sequences of language development among all languages (L. Bloom, 1998; Volterra et al., 2004).

The inborn tendency primes the nervous system to learn grammar. On the surface, languages differ much in vocabulary and grammar. Chomsky labels these elements the **surface structure** of language. However, Chomsky believes that the language acquisition device serves children all over the world because languages share a "universal grammar"—an underlying **deep structure** or set of rules for transforming ideas into sentences. From Chomsky's perspective, children are genetically prewired to attend to language and deduce the rules for constructing sentences from ideas. That is, it appears that children are prewired to listen to language in such a way that they come to understand rules of grammar.

Brain development suggests that there is a biological component to language acquisition.

Motherese

Read more about infant-directed speech used by parents.

Noam Chomsky

Read more about Noam Chomsky.

Brain Structures Involved in Language

Many parts of the brain are involved in language development; however, some of the key biological structures that may provide the basis for the functions of the language acquisition device are based in the left hemisphere of the cerebral cortex for nearly all right-handed people and for 2 out of 3 left-handed people (Pinker, 1994). In the left hemisphere, the two areas most involved in speech are Broca's area and Wernicke's area (see Figure 3.15). Damage to either area is likely to cause an **aphasia**—a disruption in the ability to understand or produce language.

Broca's area is located near the section of the motor cortex that controls the muscles of the tongue, throat, and other areas of the face that are used in speech. When Broca's area is damaged, people speak laboriously in a pattern termed **Broca's aphasia**. But they can readily understand speech. Wernicke's area lies near the auditory cortex and is connected to Broca's area by nerves. People with damage to Wernicke's area may show **Wernicke's aphasia**, in which they speak freely and with proper syntax but have trouble understanding speech and finding the words to express themselves.

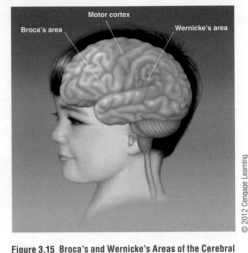

Figure 3.15 Broca's and Wernicke's Areas of the Cerebral Cortex Broca's area and Wernicke's area of the (usually left) hemisphere are most involved in speech. Damage to either area can produce an aphasia—an impairment in the ability to understand or produce language.

© 2012 Cengage Learning

The Sensitive Period

Language learning is most efficient during the **sensitive period**, which begins at about 18–24 months and last until puberty (Clancy & Finlay, 2001; Uylings, 2006). During these periods, neural development provides plasticity of the brain.

Evidence for a sensitive period is found in recovery from brain injuries in some people. Injuries to the hemisphere that controls language (usually the left hemisphere) can impair or destroy the ability to speak (Werker & Tees, 2005). But before puberty, children suffering left-hemisphere injuries frequently recover a good deal of

aphasia A disruption in the ability to understand or produce language.

Broca's aphasia An aphasia caused by damage to Broca's area and characterized by difficulty speaking.

Wernicke's aphasia An aphasia caused by damage to Wernicke's area and characterized by impaired comprehension of speech and difficulty producing the right word.

sensitive period The period from about 18 months of age to puberty when the brain is especially capable of learning language.

speaking ability. In young children, left-hemisphere damage may encourage the development of language functions in the right hemisphere. But adaptation ability wanes in adolescence, when brain tissue has reached adult levels of differentiation (Snow, 2006).

The most effective way to determine whether people are capable of acquiring language once they have passed puberty would be to run an experiment in which one or more children were reared in such severe isolation that they were not exposed to language until puberty. Of course, such an experiment could not be run for ethical reasons. However, the disturbing case history of Genie offers insights into whether there is a sensitive period for language development (Fromkin et al., 2004; LaPointe, 2005).

Genie's father locked her in a small room at the age of 20 months and kept her there until she was 13 years old. Her social contacts during this period were limited to feedings by her mother and beatings by her father. When Genie was rescued, she weighed only about 60 pounds, did not speak, was not toilet trained, and could barely stand. She was placed in a foster home, and thereafter her language development followed the normal sequence of much younger children in a number of ways. Five years after her liberation, however, Genie's language remained largely telegraphic. She still showed significant problems with syntax, such as failing to reverse subjects and verbs to phrase questions.

Genie's language development provides support for the sensitive-period hypothesis, although her language problems might also be partly attributed to her years of malnutrition and abuse. Her efforts to acquire English after puberty were laborious, and the results were substandard compared even with the language of many 2- and 3-year-olds.

In sum, the development of language in infancy represents the interaction of environmental and biological factors. The child brings a built-in readiness to the task of language acquisition, whereas houseplants and other organisms do not. The child must also have the opportunity to hear spoken language and to interact verbally with others. In the next chapter, we see how interaction with others affects social development.

Check Your Learning Quiz 3.3

Go to **login.cengagebrain.com** and take the online quiz.

▶ **LO22** Describe the development of attachment.

▶ **LO23** Explain the benefits of being securely attached.

Did you know that—

- You can cause baby ducks and geese to become attached to you by being present when they hatch and allowing them to follow you?
- Autism is 4 or 5 times more common among boys than among girls?
- Autistic children may respond to people as though they were pieces of furniture?
- Children placed in day care are more aggressive than children who are cared for in the home?
- Fear of strangers is normal among infants?
- Children become aware of themselves—their own existence—at about the age of 18 months?

▼

attachment An affectional bond characterized by seeking closeness with another and distress upon separation.

separation anxiety Fear of separation from a target of attachment.

secure attachment A type of attachment characterized by being mildly distressed at leave-takings and readily soothed by reunion.

insecure attachment A type of attachment characterized by avoiding the caregiver, excessive clinging, or inconsistency.

avoidant attachment A type of insecure attachment characterized by apparent indifference to leave-takings from and reunions with an attachment figure.

ambivalent/resistant attachment A type of insecure attachment characterized by severe distress at leave-takings from and ambivalent behavior at reunions.

Attachment: Bonds That Endure

Attachment is what most people refer to as affection or love. Mary Ainsworth (1989), a preeminent researcher on attachment, defined it as an enduring emotional bond between one animal or person and another. John Bowlby (1988) added that attachment is essential to the survival of the infant. He noted that babies are born with behaviors—crying, smiling, clinging—that stimulate caregiving from adults.

Infants try to maintain contact with caregivers to whom they are attached. They engage in eye contact, pull and tug at them, and ask to be picked up. When they cannot maintain contact, they show **separation anxiety**—they thrash about, fuss, cry, screech, or whine.

Patterns of Attachment

Ainsworth and her colleagues (Ainsworth et al., 1978) identified various patterns of attachment. Broadly, infants show **secure attachment** or **insecure attachment**. Most infants in the United States are securely attached (Belsky, 2006a; McCartney et al., 2004).

Ainsworth developed the *strange-situation method* as a way of measuring the development of attachment. In this method, an infant is exposed to a series of separations from and reunions with a caregiver (usually the mother) and a stranger who is a confederate of the researchers. In the test, secure infants mildly protest their mother's departure, seek interaction upon reunion, and are readily comforted by her.

There are two major types of insecurity, or insecure attachment: **avoidant attachment** and **ambivalent/resistant attachment**. Infants who show avoidant attachment are least distressed by their mothers' departure. They play without fuss when alone and ignore their mothers upon reunion. Ambivalent/resistant babies are the most emotional. They show severe signs of distress when their mothers leave and show ambivalence upon reunion by alternately clinging to their mothers and pushing them away.

Secure infants and toddlers are happier, more sociable, and more cooperative with caregivers. At ages 5 and 6, they get along better with peers and are better adjusted in school than insecure children (Belsky, 2006a; McCartney et al., 2004; Spieker et al., 2003). Insecure attachment at the age of 1 year predicts psychological disorders at the age of 17 (Sroufe, 1998; H. Steele, 2005).

Establishing Attachment

Attachment is related to the quality of infant care (Belsky, 2006a; Coleman, 2003). Parents of secure infants are more affectionate, cooperative, and predictable than parents of insecure infants. They respond more sensitively to their infants' smiles and cries (J. Harel & Scher, 2003).

Security is also connected with the infant's temperament (Belsky, 2006a; Kerns et al., 2007). The mothers of "difficult" children are less responsive to them and report feeling more distant from them (Morrell & Steele, 2003; Stams et al., 2002).

Involvement of Fathers

How involved is the average father with his children? The brief answer, in developed nations, is "more so than in the past" (Grossmann et al., 2002). But mothers engage in more interactions with their infants. Most fathers are more likely to play with their children than to feed or clean them (Laflamme et al., 2002). Fathers more often than mothers engage in rough-and-tumble play, whereas mothers are more likely to play games involving toys, and patty-cake and peekaboo (Làflamme et al., 2002).

How strongly, then, do infants become attached to their fathers? The more affectionate the interaction between father and infant is, the stronger the attachment (R. A. Thompson et al., 2003).

The Strange Situation

Explore photos from the Strange Situation study.

Infant Attachment

Watch and learn more about attachment between infants and their caregivers.

Stability of Attachment

Patterns of attachment tend to persist when caregiving conditions remain constant (Ammaniti et al., 2005; Karavasilis et al., 2003). Children can also become less securely attached to caregivers when home life deteriorates (Belsky, 2006a). Children adopted at various ages can become securely attached to adoptive parents (Veríssimo & Salvaterra, 2006). Early attachment patterns tend to endure into middle childhood, adolescence, and even adulthood (Ammaniti et al., 2005; Karavasilis et al., 2003).

Stages of Attachment

Cross-cultural studies have led to a theory of stages of attachment. In one study, Ainsworth (1967) tracked the behavior of Ugandan infants. Over a 9-month period, she noted their efforts to maintain contact with the mother, their protests when separated, and their use of the mother as a base for exploring the environment. At first, the Ugandan infants showed **indiscriminate attachment**—no particular preferences for a familiar caregiver. Specific attachment to the mother, as evidenced by separation anxiety and other behavior, began to develop at about 4 months of age and grew intense by about 7 months. Fear of strangers developed 1 or 2 months later.

In another study, Scottish infants showed indiscriminate attachment during the first 6 months or so after birth (Schaffer & Emerson, 1964). Then indiscriminate attachment waned. Specific attachments to the mother and other familiar caregivers intensified, as demonstrated by the appearance of separation anxiety, and remained at high levels through the age of 18 months. Fear of strangers occurred a month or so after the intensity of specific attachments began to mushroom. In both this and the Ugandan study, fear of strangers followed separation anxiety and the development of specific attachments by weeks.

From such studies, Ainsworth and her colleagues (1978) identified the following three phases of attachment:

1. The **initial-preattachment phase** lasts from birth to about 3 months and is characterized by indiscriminate attachment.
2. The **attachment-in-the-making phase** occurs at about 3 or 4 months and is characterized by a preference for familiar figures.
3. The **clear-cut-attachment phase** occurs at about 6 or 7 months and is characterized by intensified dependence on the primary caregiver, usually the mother.

indiscriminate attachment The display of attachment behaviors toward any person.

initial-preattachment phase The first phase in the development of attachment, characterized by indiscriminate attachment.

attachment-in-the-making phase The second phase in the development of attachment, characterized by preference for familiar figures.

clear-cut-attachment phase The third phase in the development of attachment, characterized by intensified dependence on the primary caregiver.

But most infants have more than one adult caregiver and are likely to form multiple attachments: to the father, day-care providers, grandparents, and other caregivers, as well as the mother.

Theories of Attachment

There are several theories of the development of attachment.

Cognitive View of Attachment

The cognitive view suggests that an infant must develop the concept of object permanence before specific attachment becomes possible. If caregivers are to be missed when absent, the infant must perceive that they continue to exist. We have seen that infants tend to develop specific attachments at about the age of 6 to 7 months. Basic object permanence develops somewhat earlier (see Module 3.3).

Behavioral View of Attachment

Early in the twentieth century, behaviorists argued that attachment behaviors are conditioned. Caregivers feed their infants and tend to their other physiological needs. Thus, infants associate their caregivers with gratification and learn to approach them to meet their needs. From this perspective, a caregiver becomes a conditioned reinforcer.

Psychoanalytic Views of Attachment

According to psychoanalytic theorists, the caregiver, usually the mother, becomes not just a reinforcer but also a love object who forms the basis for all later attachments. Sigmund Freud emphasized the importance of oral activities, such as eating, in the first year. Freud believed that the infant becomes emotionally attached to the mother during this time because she is the primary satisfier of the infant's needs for food and sucking.

Erik Erikson characterized the first year of life as the stage of *trust versus mistrust*. Erikson believed that the first year is critical for developing a sense of trust in the mother, which fosters attachment. The mother's general sensitivity to the child's needs, not just the need for food, fosters the development of trust and attachment.

Contact Comfort

Harry and Margaret Harlow conducted classic experiments to demonstrate that feeding is not as critical to the attachment process as Freud suggested (H. F. Harlow & Harlow, 1966). In one study, the Harlows placed infant rhesus monkeys in cages with

▶ **LO24** Explain the research findings on social deprivation and its effects on humans.

▶ **LO25** Define and explain aspects of autism spectrum disorders.

two surrogate mothers (see Figure 3.16). One "mother" was made from wire mesh from which a baby bottle was extended. The other surrogate mother was made of soft, cuddly terry cloth. Infant monkeys spent most of their time clinging to the cloth mother, even though it did not offer food. The Harlows concluded that monkeys—and perhaps humans—have a need for **contact comfort** that is as basic as the need for food.

Ethological View of Attachment

Ethologists note that for many animals, attachment is an inborn or instinctive response to a specific stimulus. Some researchers theorize that a baby's cry stimulates caregiving in women. By 2–3 months of age, to help ensure survival by gaining the affection of caregivers, infants begin to respond to the human face with a **social smile** (Ainsworth & Bowlby, 1991; Bowlby, 1988). And in turn, the caregiver's

Figure 3.16 Contact Comfort as a Key to Attachment Although this infant rhesus monkey is fed by the wire-mesh "mother," it spends most of its time clinging to the soft, cuddly, terry-cloth "mother."

Nina Leen//Time Life Pictures/Getty Images

contact comfort The pleasure derived from physical contact with another.

ethologist A scientist who studies the behavior patterns characteristic of various species.

social smile A smile that occurs in response to a human voice or face.

critical period A period during which imprinting can occur.

imprinting The process by which waterfowl become attached to the first moving object they follow.

social response to the infant's face causes the infant to smile by 8 months of age (Jones & Hong, 2005). The pattern contributes to a mutual attachment.

In many nonhumans, attachment occurs during a **critical period** of life. Waterfowl become attached during this period to the first moving object they encounter. Because the image of the moving object seems to become "imprinted" on the young animal, the process is termed **imprinting**.

Ethologist Konrad Lorenz (1962, 1981) acquired his "family" of goslings by being present when they hatched and allowing them to follow him (see Figure 3.17). The critical period for geese and ducks begins when they first engage in locomotion and ends when they develop fear of strangers. The goslings followed Lorenz persistently, ran to him when frightened, honked with distress at his departure, and tried to overcome barriers placed between them. If you substitute crying for honking, it sounds quite human.

Ethology, Ainsworth, and Bowlby

Ainsworth and Bowlby wrote that "the distinguishing characteristic of the theory of attachment that we have jointly developed is that it is an ethological approach" (1991). But their ethological approach differs from Lorenz's in a number of ways. For example, Ainsworth and Bowlby wrote that caregiving in humans is largely learned and not inborn. They also noted that the critical period for attachment in humans—if one exists—extends to months or years (Ainsworth & Bowlby, 1991; Veríssimo & Salvaterra, 2006). Caregiving itself and infant responsiveness, such as smiling, also promote attachment.

Figure 3.17 Imprinting: A Source of Attachment in Ethological Theory Konrad Lorenz may not look like Mommy to you, but these goslings became attached to him because he was the first moving object they perceived and followed. This type of attachment process is referred to as imprinting.

Nina Leen/Time Life Pictures/Getty Images

When Attachment Fails

What happens when children are reared with little or no contact with caregivers? When parents neglect or abuse their children? In the case of autism spectrum disorders?

Social Deprivation

Studies of children reared in institutions where they receive little social stimulation from caregivers are limited in that they are correlational. In other words, family factors that led to the children's placement in institutions may also have contributed to their developmental problems. Ethical considerations prevent us from conducting experiments in which we randomly assign children to social deprivation. However, experiments of this kind have been undertaken with rhesus monkeys, and the results are consistent with those of the correlational studies of children.

The Social Smile

Watch and learn more about the development of social smiling — another "endearing" quality of infants that solidifies the caregiver-infant bonds of attachment.

Experiments With Monkeys

Rhesus monkeys were "reared by" wire-mesh and terry-cloth surrogate mothers in studies conducted by Harlow and his colleagues. In later studies, rhesus monkeys were reared without even terry-cloth surrogate mothers—without seeing any other animal, monkey or human (H. F. Harlow et al., 1971).

The researchers found that infant rhesus monkeys reared in this most solitary confinement later avoided other monkeys. Instead, they cowered in the presence of others. Nor did they try to fend off attacks by other monkeys. Rather, they sat in the corner, clutching themselves, and rocking back and forth. The females who later bore children ignored or abused them.

Can the damage from social deprivation be overcome? When monkeys deprived for 6 months or more are placed with younger, 3- to 4-month-old females for a couple of hours a day, the younger monkeys attempt to interact with their deprived elders. Many of the deprived monkeys begin to play with the youngsters after a few weeks, and many eventually expand their social contacts to older monkeys (Suomi et al., 1972).

Studies With Children

Institutionalized children whose material needs are met but who receive little social stimulation from caregivers encounter problems in all areas of development (Ganesh & Magdalin, 2007; Rutter, 2006b). René A. Spitz (1965) found that many institutionalized children show withdrawal and depression. In one institution, infants were maintained in separate cubicles for most of their first year to ward off infectious diseases (Provence & Lipton, 1962). Adults tended to them only to feed them and change their diapers. As a rule, baby bottles were propped up in the cribs. Attendants rarely responded to the infants' cries; they were rarely played with or spoken to. By the age of 4 months, the infants showed little interest in adults. A few months later, some of them sat withdrawn in their cribs and rocked back and forth, almost like the Harlows' monkeys. None were speaking at 12 months.

Why do children whose material needs are met show such dramatic deficiencies? The answer may depend, in part, on the age of the child. Research by Leon Yarrow and his colleagues (Yarrow et al., 1971; Yarrow & Goodwin, 1973) suggests that deficiencies in sensory stimulation and social interaction may cause more problems than lack of love in infants who are too young to have developed specific attachments. But once infants have developed specific attachments, separation from their primary caregivers can lead to problems.

The Capacity to Recover From Social Deprivation

Infants also have powerful capacities to recover from deprivation. One study showed how many children may be able to recover fully from 13 or 14 months of deprivation (J. Kagan & Klein, 1973). The natives in an isolated Guatemalan village believe that fresh air and sunshine will sicken children. Children are thus kept in windowless huts until they can walk, and are played with infrequently. During their isolation, the infants behave apathetically. They are physically and socially retarded when they start to walk. But by 11 years of age they are as alert and active as U.S. children of the same age.

A classic longitudinal study of orphanage children also offered evidence of the ability of children to recover from social deprivation (Skeels, 1966). In this study, a group of 19 month-old mildly intellectually deficient children were placed in the care of older institutionalized girls. The girls spent a great deal of time playing with and nurturing them. Four years after being placed with the girls, the "retarded" children made dramatic gains in IQ scores, whereas children remaining in the orphanage showed declines in IQ.

Child Abuse and Neglect

Consider the following statistics from national surveys (Straus & Field, 2003; U.S. Department of Health and Human Services [USDHHS], 2004): By the time a child is 2 years of age, 90% of parents have engaged in some sort of psychological or emotional abuse; 55% of parents have slapped or spanked their children; and 31% of parents have pushed, grabbed, or shoved their children.

According to the U.S. Department of Health and Human Services (2004), some three million American children are neglected or abused each year by their parents or caregivers. More than 150,000 of the three million are sexually abused (Letourneau et al., 2004; USDHHS, 2004). But researchers believe that 50%–60% of cases of abuse and neglect go unreported, so the true incidences are higher (USDHHS, 2004). Neglect causes more injuries and deaths than abuse (USDHHS, 2004).

The true incidence of child sexual abuse is unknown (Hines & Finkelhor, 2007). Although most sexually abused children are girls, one quarter to one third are boys (Edwards et al., 2003). One survey suggested that the prevalence of sexual abuse among boys is about 18%, and among girls, about 25% (Edwards et al., 2003).

Effects of Child Abuse

Abused children show a high incidence of personal and social problems and psychological disorders (Letourneau et al., 2004). In general, abused children are less securely attached to their parents. They are less intimate with peers and more aggressive, angry, and noncompliant than other children (P. T. Joshi et al., 2006). They have lower self-esteem and perform more poorly in school (Shonk & Cicchetti, 2001). Later on, abused children are at greater risk for delinquency, risky sexual behavior, and substance abuse (Haapasalo & Moilanen, 2004). When they reach adulthood, they are more likely to act aggressively toward their partners (Malinosky-Rummell & Hansen, 1993).

Causes of Child Abuse

Various factors contribute to child abuse, including stress, a history of abuse in at least one parent's family of origin, lack of adequate coping and child-rearing skills, unrealistic expectations of children, and substance abuse (Maluccio & Ainsworth, 2003; Merrill et al., 2004). Stress has many sources, including divorce, job loss, moving, and the birth of a new family member (P. T. Joshi et al., 2006).

Ironically, infants who are already in pain of some kind and difficult to soothe are more likely to be abused (Frodi, 1985). Abusive parents may find the cries of their infants particularly aversive, so infants' crying may precipitate abuse (Schuetze, Zeskind, et al., 2003). Children who are disobedient, inappropriate, or unresponsive are also at greater risk (Bugental & Happaney, 2004).

What to Do

Many states require helping professionals such as psychologists and physicians to report any suspicion of child abuse. Some legally require *anyone* who suspects child abuse to report it to authorities.

A number of techniques have been developed to help prevent child abuse. One approach focuses on strengthening parenting skills among the general population (P. T. Joshi et al., 2006). Another approach targets groups at high risk for abuse, such as poor, single, teen mothers (P. T. Joshi et al., 2006). In some programs, home visitors help new parents develop skills in caregiving and home management (Duggan et al., 2004).

A third technique focuses on presenting information about abuse and providing support to families. For instance, many locales have child-abuse hotlines. Readers who suspect child abuse may call for advice. Parents having difficulty controlling aggressive impulses toward their children are also encouraged to call.

Autism Spectrum Disorders

Autism spectrum disorders (ASDs) are characterized by impairment in communication skills and social interaction and by repetitive, stereotyped behavior: (Strock, 2004).

autism spectrum disorders (ASDs) Developmental disorders characterized by impairment in communication and social skills and by repetitive, stereotyped behavior.

autism A disorder characterized by extreme aloneness, communication problems, preservation of sameness, and ritualistic behavior.

mutism Refusal to speak.

Key Indicators

- Does not babble, point, or make meaningful gestures by 1 year of age
- Does not speak one word by 16 months
- Does not combine two words by 2 years
- Does not respond to name
- Loses language or social skills

Other Indicators

- Exhibits poor eye contact
- Doesn't seem to know how to play with toys
- Excessively lines up toys or other objects
- Is attached to one particular toy or object
- Doesn't smile
- Seems at times to be hearing impaired

Source: Adapted from Strock (2004).

ASDs tend to become evident by the age of 3 and sometimes before the end of the first year. A CDC study of 407,578 children from 14 parts of the United States identified 1 in every 152 children as having an ASD (Rice, 2007). There are several variations of ASDs, but autism is the major type. Other forms of ASDs include:

- *Asperger's disorder:* Characterized by social deficits and stereotyped behavior but without the significant cognitive or language delays associated with autism.
- *Rett's disorder:* Characterized by a range of physical, behavioral, motor, and cognitive abnormalities that begin after a few months of normal development.
- *Childhood disintegrative disorder:* Characterized by abnormal functioning and loss of previously acquired skills that begins after about 2 years of apparently normal development.

Autism

Autism is 4 to 5 times more common among boys than girls. Children with autism do not show interest in social interaction and may avoid eye contact. Attachment to others is weak or absent.

Other features of autism include communication problems, intolerance of change, and ritualistic or stereotyped behavior (Georgiades et al., 2007). Parents of autistic children often say they were "good babies," which usually means they made few demands. But as autistic children develop, they tend to shun affectionate contacts such as hugging, cuddling, and kissing.

Development of speech lags. There is little babbling and communicative gesturing during the first year. Autistic children may show **mutism**, echolalia, and pronoun reversal, referring to themselves as "you" or "he." About half use language by middle childhood, but their speech is unusual and troubled.

Autistic Savant

Watch and learn about the various aspects of autism from a man who is an autistic savant.

Autism in Girls

Is autism underdiagnosed in females? Watch and learn.

Autism Diagnosis

Watch and learn about the methods used to diagnose autism.

▸**LO26** Describe the effects of day care.

Autistic children become bound by ritual. Even slight changes in routines or the environment may cause distress. The teacher of a 5-year-old autistic girl would greet her each morning with, "Good morning, Lily, I am very, very glad to see you." Lily would ignore the greeting, but she would shriek if the teacher omitted even one of the *very*s. This feature of autism is termed *preservation of sameness*. When familiar objects are moved from their usual places, children with autism may throw tantrums or cry until they are restored. They may insist on eating the same food every day. Autistic children show deficits in peer play, imaginative play, imitation, and emotional expression. Many sleep less than their age-mates (Georgiades et al., 2007).

Some autistic children mutilate themselves, even as they cry out in pain. They may bang their heads, slap their faces, bite their hands and shoulders, or pull out their hair.

The most poignant feature of autism is the child's utter aloneness. Autism is rather rare, but is more common in boys than in girls. Symptoms include communication problems, intolerance of any change, and ritualistic or stereotyped behavior.

Causes of Autism

Contrary to what some theorists say, research evidence finds no correlation between the development of autism and deficiencies in child rearing (Mackic-Magyar & McCracken, 2004). Various lines of evidence suggest a key role for biological factors. For example, very low birth weight and advanced maternal age may heighten the risk of autism (Maimburg & Væth, 2006). A role for genetic mechanisms has been suggested by kinship studies (Constantino et al., 2006; Gutknecht, 2001). The concordance (agreement) rates for autism are about 60% among pairs of identical (MZ) twins, who fully share their genetic heritage, compared with about 10% for pairs of fraternal (DZ) twins, whose genetic codes overlap by half (Plomin, Owen, et al., 1994).

Biological factors focus on neurological involvement. Many children with autism have abnormal brain-wave patterns or seizures (Canitano, 2007; Roulet-Perez &

Deonna; 2006). Other researchers have found that the brains of children with autism have abnormal sensitivities to neurotransmitters such as serotonin, dopamine, acetylcholine, and norepinephrine (Bauman et al., 2006). Still other researchers have noted unusual activity in the motor region of the cerebral cortex (R. Mueller et al., 2001) and less activity in some other areas of the brain (K. S. L. Lam et al., 2006; Penn, 2006).

Treatment of Autism

Treatment of autism is mainly based on principles of learning, although investigation of biological approaches is also under way (Strock, 2004). Behavior modification has been used to increase the child's ability to attend to others, play with other children, and discourage self-mutilation.

Because children with autism show behavioral deficits, behavior modification is used to help them develop new behavior. Though autistic children often relate to people as if they were furniture, many can be taught to accept people rather than objects as reinforcers by pairing praise with food treats (Drasgow et al., 2001). The most effective treatment programs have individualized instruction (Rapin, 1997). In a classic study conducted by Lovaas (Lovaas et al., 1989), autistic children received more than 40 hours of one-to-one behavior modification a week for at least 2 years. Significant intellectual and educational gains were reported for 9 of 19 children (47%) in the program (Stahmer et al., 2004).

Biological approaches for the treatment of autism are under study. Drugs that enhance serotonin activity (selective serotonin reuptake inhibitors) can apparently help prevent self-injury, aggressive outbursts, depression, anxiety, and repetitive behavior (Kwok, 2003). Drugs that are usually used to treat schizophrenia—so-called major tranquilizers—are helpful with stereotyped behavior, hyperactivity, and self-injury, but not with cognitive and language deficits (Kwok, 2003; McClellan & Werry, 2003).

Autistic behavior generally continues into adulthood to one degree or another. Nevertheless, some autistic people go on to achieve college degrees and function independently (Rapin, 1997).

Day Care

Most American parents, including mothers with infants, are in the workforce (Carey, 2007). As a result, of the more than 10 million American children under the age of 5, more than 20% are cared for in day-care centers.

▶ **L027** Discuss the development of emotions.

Many parents wonder whether day care will affect their children's attachment to them. Some studies have found that infants who are in full-time day care are more likely than other children to show insecure attachment (Brandtjen & Verny, 2001). Even so, the likelihood of insecure attachment is not much greater in infants placed in day care than in those cared for in the home. Most infants in both groups are securely attached (Timmerman, 2006).

Not all child-care arrangements are equal. Some studies report that infants with positive day-care experiences are more peer oriented and play at higher developmental levels than home-reared infants. Children in high-quality day care are more likely to share their toys. They are more independent, self-confident, outgoing, and affectionate, as well as more helpful and cooperative with peers and adults (Lamb & Ahnert, 2006; Pierce & Vandell, 2006). Participation in good-quality day care is also linked with better academic performance in elementary school (Belsky, 2006b).

A study funded by the National Institute of Child Health and Human Development agreed that high-quality day care can result in scores on cognitive-skill tests that rival or exceed those of children reared in the home by their mothers (Belsky et al., 2007). The quality of the day care was defined in terms of the richness of the learning environment (availability of toys, books, and other materials), the ratio of caregivers to children (high quality meant more caregivers), the amount of individual attention received by the child, and the extent to which caregivers talked to the children and asked them questions.

However, the researchers also found that children placed in day care may be less cooperative and more aggressive toward peers and adults than children who are reared in the home. The more time spent away from their mothers, the more likely these children were to be rated as defiant, aggressive, and disobedient once they got to kindergarten.

Teacher ratings found that once children who were in day care are in school, they are significantly more likely than children cared for in the home to interrupt in class and tease or bully other children (Belsky et al., 2007). The degree of disturbance generally remained "within normal limits." That is, the children who had been in day care could not be labeled criminals and were not being expelled. *The quality of the day-care center made no difference.* Children from high-quality day-care centers were also more likely to be disruptive than children cared for in the home. Moreover, the behavioral difference persisted through the sixth grade.

Now let us note some limitations of the study. Although the differences in disruptive behavior between children in full-time day care and children cared for in the home are statistically significant—meaning that they are unlikely to be due to chance—they are small. The study implies that day care *causes* the disruptive behavior of concern later on, but there was no control group (J. R. Harris, 2007). Children are *not* assigned at random to day care or care in the home. Therefore, it may be that children placed in day care are those whose caregivers are most stressed by work through their children's primary school years (C. Taylor, 2007).

In any case, reality intrudes. Millions of parents do not have the option of deciding whether to place their children in day care; their only choice is where. And some parents, given their financial and geographic circumstances, might not even have that choice.

Emotional Development

To determine the emotional states of babies, we have to observe how they behave, including their facial expressions (Oster, 2005). Facial expressions appear to be universal in that they are recognized in different cultures around the world, so they are considered a reliable index of emotion.

Do the emotional expressions of newborns begin as a combination of many emotions or simply excitement? Researchers try to answer this question by asking if newborn baby's cries express discomfort or if infants' facial expressions reflect internal states of feeling (Soussignan & Schaal, 2005). They have asked whether the newborn baby's crying is nothing more than a reflex in response to discomfort. They have even asked whether the facial expressions of infants, which many researchers claim to express emotions such as anger, joy, fear, and excitement within a few months after birth, actually reflect internal states of feeling. It seems clear enough that as infants develop through the first year, their cognitive appraisal of events, including their interaction with their caregivers, becomes a key part of their emotional life and their emotional expression (Camras et al., 2007; Soussignan & Schaal, 2005).

Infants' initial emotional expressions appear to comprise two basic states of emotional arousal: a positive attraction to pleasant stimulation, such as the caregiver's voice or being held, and a withdrawal from aversive stimulation, such as a sudden loud noise. By the age of 2–3 months, social smiling has replaced reflexive smiling. Social smiling is usually highly endearing to caregivers. At 3–5 months, infants laugh at active stimuli, such as repetitively touching their bellies or playing "Ah, boop!"

Daycare Pros and Cons

Watch and learn about research on the benefits and consequences for children in day care.

In sum, researchers agree that infants show only a few emotions during the first few months. They agree that emotional development is linked to cognitive development and social experience. They do not necessarily agree on exactly when specific emotions are first shown or whether discrete emotions are present at birth (Camras et al., 2007).

Emotional Development and Patterns of Attachment

Emotional development has been linked with various histories of attachment. In a longitudinal study of 112 children at ages 9, 14, 22, and 33 months, Kochanska (2001) studied the development of fear, anger, and joy by using laboratory situations designed to evoke these emotions. Patterns of attachment were assessed using the strange-situation method. Differences in emotional development could first be related to attachment at the age of 14 months. Resistant children were most fearful and they frequently responded with distress even in episodes designed to evoke joy. When they were assessed repeatedly over time, it became apparent that securely attached children were becoming significantly less angry. By contrast, the negative emotions of insecurely attached children rose: Avoidant children grew more fearful, and resistant children became less joyful. At 33 months of age, securely attached children were less likely to show fear and anger, even when they were exposed to situations designed to elicit these emotions.

Fear of Strangers

When my daughter Jordan was 1 year old, her mother and I needed a nanny for a few hours a day so that we could teach, write, breathe, and engage in other life activities. We hired a social-work graduate student who had a mild, engaging way about her. She nurtured Jordan and played with her for about 4 months, during which time Jordan came to somewhat grudgingly accept her, most of the time. Even so,

social referencing Using another person's reaction to a situation to form one's own response.

emotional regulation Techniques for controlling one's emotional states.

© David Young-Wolff / Alamy

Jordan was never completely comfortable with her and often let out a yowl as if buildings were collapsing around her, although the nanny did nothing except calmly try to soothe her.

Unfortunately, Jordan met the nanny during the period when she had developed fear of strangers. The fear would eventually subside, as these fears do, but during her entire encounter with the nanny, the nanny wondered what she was doing wrong. The answer was simple: She was existing, within sight of Jordan.

Fear of strangers—also called *stranger anxiety*—is normal. Most infants develop it. Stranger anxiety appears at about 6–9 months of age. By 4 or 5 months of age, infants may compare the faces of strangers and their mothers, looking back and forth. Somewhat older infants show distress by crying, whimpering, gazing fearfully, and crawling away. Fear of strangers often peaks at 9–12 months and declines in the second year.

Children with fear of strangers show less anxiety when their mothers are present (R. A. Thompson & Limber, 1990). Children also are less fearful when they are in familiar surroundings, such as their homes, rather than in the laboratory (Sroufe, Waters, et al., 1974).

Social Referencing: What Should I Do Now?

Social referencing is the seeking out of another person's perception of a situation to help us form our own view of it (Hertenstein & Campos, 2004). Leslie Carver and Brenda Vaccaro (2007) suggested that social referencing requires three components: (1) looking at another, usually older individual in a novel, ambiguous situation; (2) associating that individual's emotional response with the unfamiliar situation; and (3) regulating one's own emotional response in accord with the response of the older individual.

Infants also display social referencing, as early as 6 months of age. They use caregivers' facial expressions or tone of voice as clues on how to respond (Hertenstein & Campos, 2004). In one study, 8-month-old infants were friendlier to a stranger when their mothers exhibited a friendly facial expression in the stranger's presence than when she looked worried (Boccia & Campos, 1989).

Emotional Regulation: Keeping on an Even Keel

Emotional regulation refers to the ways in which young children control their own emotions. Even infants display certain behaviors to control unpleasant emotional states. They may look away from a disturbing event or suck their thumbs (Rothbart &

Sheese, 2007). Caregivers help infants learn to regulate their emotions. A two-way communication system develops, in which the infant signals the caregiver that help is needed and the caregiver responds. Claire Kopp provided an example of such a system:

> A 13-month-old, playing with a large plastic bottle, attempted to unscrew the cover, but could not. Fretting for a short time, she initiated eye contact with her mother and held out the jar. As her mother took it to unscrew the cover, the infant ceased fretting. (1989, p. 347)

Research evidence suggests that the children of secure mothers are not only likely to be securely attached but also are likely to regulate their own emotions in a positive manner (Grolnick, McMenamy, et al., 2006; R. A. Thompson & Meyer, 2007).

Personality Development

In this section, we look at the emergence of the self-concept. We then turn to a discussion of temperament. Finally, we consider gender differences in behavior.

Self-Concept

At birth, we may find the world to be a confusing blur of sights, sounds, and inner sensations—yet the "we" may be missing, at least for a while. When our hands first come into view, there is little evidence that we realize the hands "belong" to us and we are separate and distinct from the world outside.

The self-concept appears to emerge gradually during infancy. At some point, infants understand that the hands they are moving in and out of sight are their hands. At some point, they understand that their own bodies extend only so far and then external objects and the bodies of others begin.

Development of the Self-Concept

Psychologists have devised ingenious methods to assess the development of the self-concept in infants. One is the *mirror technique*, which involves the use of a mirror and a dot of rouge. Before the experiment begins, the researcher observes the infant for baseline data on how frequently the infant touches his or her nose. Then the mother places rouge on the infant's nose, and the infant is placed before a mirror. Not

separation–individuation The process of becoming separate from and independent of the mother.

until about the age of 18 months do infants begin to touch the rouge on their own noses upon looking in the mirror (A. Campbell et al., 2000; H. Keller et al., 2005). Nose touching suggests that children recognize themselves and that they perceive that the dot of rouge is an abnormality. Most 2-year-olds can point to pictures of themselves, and they begin to use *I* or their own name spontaneously (P. A. Smiley & Johnson, 2006).

In the middle of the second year, infants begin to develop self-awareness, which has a powerful effect on social and emotional development.

Self-awareness permits the infant and child to develop notions of sharing and cooperation (Foley, 2006). In one study, 2-year-olds with a better developed sense of self were more likely to cooperate with other children (Brownell & Carriger, 1990).

Self-awareness also facilitates the development of "self-conscious" emotions such as embarrassment, envy, empathy, pride, guilt, and shame (Foley, 2006). In one study, Deborah Stipek and her colleagues (1992) found that children older than 21 months often seek their mother's attention and approval when they have successfully completed a task, whereas younger toddlers do not.

Psychoanalytic Views of the Self-Concept

Margaret Mahler, a psychoanalyst, proposed that development of the self-concept comes about through a process of **separation–individuation**, which lasts from about 5 months until 3 years of age (Mahler et al., 1975). Separation involves the child's growing perception that her mother is separate from herself. Individuation refers to the child's increasing sense of independence and autonomy.

One of the ways toddlers demonstrate growing autonomy, much to the dismay of caregivers, is by refusing to comply with caregivers' requests. Studies of toddlers and preschoolers between the ages of 1½ and 5 years have found that as children grow older, they adopt more skillful ways of expressing resistance to caregivers' requests (C. L. Smith et al., 2004; Stifter & Wiggins, 2004). For example, young toddlers are more likely to ignore a caregiver's request or defy it. Older toddlers and preschoolers are more likely to make excuses or negotiate.

Temperament: Easy, Difficult, or Slow to Warm Up?

Each child has a characteristic **temperament**, a stable way of reacting and adapting to the world that is present early in life (Wachs, 2006). Many researchers believe that temperament involves a strong genetic component (Goldsmith et al., 2003; Wachs, 2006). The child's temperament includes many aspects of behavior, such as activity level, smiling and laughter, regularity in eating and sleep habits, approach or withdrawal, adaptability to new situations, intensity of responsiveness, general cheerfulness or unpleasantness, distractibility or persistence, and soothability (Gartstein et al., 2003; A. Thomas & Chess, 1989).

Types of Temperament

Alexander Thomas and Stella Chess (1989) found that from the first days of life, many of the children in their study (65%) could be classified into one of three types of temperament: "easy" (40% of their sample), "difficult" (10%), and "slow to warm up" (15%). Some of the differences among these three types of children are shown in Table 3.3. The easy child has regular sleep and feeding schedules, approaches new

Table 3.3
Types of Temperament

Temperament Category	Easy	Difficult	Slow to Warm Up
Regularity of biological functioning	Regular	Irregular	Somewhat irregular
Response to new stimuli	Positive approach	Negative withdrawal	Negative withdrawal
Adaptability to new situations	Adapts readily	Adapts slowly or not at all	Adapts slowly
Intensity of reaction	Mild or moderate	Intense	Mild
Quality of mood	Positive	Negative	Initially negative; gradually more positive

Sources: Chess & Thomas (1991); A. Thomas & Chess (1989).

temperament An individual difference in style of reaction that is present early in life.

goodness of fit An agreement between the parents' expectations of a child and the child's temperament.

situations (such as a new food or a new school) with enthusiasm and adapts to them easily, and is generally cheerful. Some children are more inconsistent and show a mixture of temperament traits. For example, a toddler may have a pleasant disposition but be frightened of new situations.

The difficult child, on the other hand, has irregular sleep and feeding schedules, is slow to accept new people and situations, takes a long time to adjust to new routines, and responds to frustrations with tantrums and crying. The child who is slow to warm up falls between the other two.

Stability of Temperament

There is at least moderate consistency in the development of temperament from infancy onward (Wachs, 2006). The infant who is highly active and cries in novel situations often becomes a fearful toddler. Difficult children in general are at greater risk for developing psychological disorders and adjustment problems later in life (Pauli-Pott et al., 2003; Rothbart et al., 2004). A longitudinal study tracked the progress of infants with a difficult temperament from 1½ through 12 years of age (D. W. Guerin et al., 1997). A difficult temperament correlated with parental reports of behavioral problems from ages 3 to 12, and with teachers' reports of short attention span and aggression.

Goodness of Fit: The Role of the Environment

Our daughter was a difficult infant, but we weathered the storm. At the age of 15, she was climbing out the second-story bedroom window at 2 a.m. to be with friends. When we discovered it, she sarcastically asked if we disapproved. "Yes," we said. "Use the front door; you're less likely to get hurt." She graduated college with honors. She has occasional outbursts, but that's her boyfriend's problem. And they love her on the job. She's a hard worker and the most creative thing they've ever seen.

The environment also affects the development of temperament. An initial biological predisposition to a certain temperament may be strengthened or weakened by the parents' reactions. Parents may react rigidly to a difficult child, which in turn can cause the child to become even more difficult (Schoppe-Sullivan et al., 2007). This example illustrates a poor fit between the child's behavior style and the parents' response.

On the other hand, parents may modify a child's initial temperament in a more positive direction to achieve a **goodness of fit** between child and parent. Realization that their youngster's behavior does not mean that the child is weak or deliberately disobedient, or that they are bad parents, helps parents modify their attitudes and behavior toward the child, whose behavior may then improve (Bird et al., 2006; Schoppe-Sullivan et al., 2007).

Gender Differences

All cultures distinguish between females and males and have expectations about how they ought to behave. Children's gender is a key factor in their society's efforts to shape their personality and behavior.

Behavior of Infant Girls and Boys

Girls tend to advance more rapidly in their motor development in infancy: They sit, crawl, and walk earlier than boys (Matlin, 2008). Evidence is mixed as to whether infant boys are more active and irritable than girls (Matlin, 2008). Girls and boys are similar in social behavior. They are equally likely to smile at people's faces, for example, and they do not differ in their dependency on adults (Maccoby & Jacklin, 1974). Girls and boys do begin to differ early in their preference for certain toys and play activities. One study found that children show gender-typed play by the age of 13 months (Knickmeyer et al., 2005). Another study investigated the gender-typed visual preferences of 30 human infants at the early ages of 3–8 months (G. M. Alexander et al., 2009). The researchers assessed interest in a toy truck and a doll by using eye-tracking technology to indicate the direction of visual attention. They found that girls showed a visual preference for the doll over the truck (that is, they made a greater number of visual fixations on the doll), and boys showed a visual preference for the truck. Gender differences that show up later, such as differences in spatial relations skills, are not all that evident in infancy (Örnkloo & von Hofsten, 2007). By 24 months, both girls and boys appear to be aware of which behaviors are considered appropriate or inappropriate for their gender, according to cultural stereotypes (S. E. Hill & Flom, 2007). Thus it appears girls and boys may show a preference for gender-typed toys before they have been socialized and possibly before they are aware of their own gender.

Adults' Behavior Toward Infants

Most adults interact differently with girls and boys. Researchers have presented American adults with an unfamiliar infant who is dressed in boy's clothes and has a boy's name or an infant who is dressed in girl's clothing and has a girl's name. (In reality, it is the same baby who simply is given different names and clothing.) When adults believe they are playing with a girl, they are more likely to offer "her" a doll; when they think the child is a boy, they are more likely to offer a football or a hammer. "Boys" also are encouraged to engage in more physical activity than "girls" (Worell & Goodheart, 2006).

Parents, especially fathers, are more likely to encourage rough-and-tumble play in sons than daughters (Eccles et al., 2000; Fagot et al., 2000). On the other hand, parents talk more to infant daughters, smile more at them, and are more emotionally expressive toward them (Powlishta et al., 2001).

Infant girls are likely to be decked out in a pink or yellow dress and embellished with ruffles and lace, whereas infant boys wear blue or red (Eccles et al., 2000; Powlishta et al., 2001). Examination of the contents of rooms of children from 5 months to 6 years of age found that boys' rooms were often decorated with animal themes and with blue bedding and curtains. Girls' rooms featured flowers, lace, ruffles, and pastels. Girls owned more dolls; boys had more vehicles, military toys, and sports equipment.

Parents react favorably when their infant daughters play with "girls' toys" and their sons play with "boys' toys." Adults, especially fathers, show more negative reactions when infants play with "gender-inappropriate" toys (C. L. Martin et al., 2002; Worell & Goodheart, 2006).. Parents thus try to shape their children's behavior during infancy and lay the foundation for development in early childhood.

Check Your Learning Quiz 3.4

Go to **login.cengagebrain.com**
and take the online quiz.

GO to your Psychology CourseMate at login.cengagebrain.com and take the Chapter Post-Test to see which Learning Objectives you've mastered and which need more review. Use the chapter review guide below and the online activities—including flashcards to review key terms—to measure your learning.

Online Activities

Key Terms	Video	Animation	Reading	Assessment
Postpartum period, postpartum depression (PPD)	Postpartum Depression			Check Your Learning Quiz 3.1
Bonding				
Apgar scale, Brazelton Neonatal Behavioral Assessment Scale, reflex, rooting reflex, Moro reflex, grasping reflex, stepping reflex, Babinski reflex, tonic-neck reflex, visual accommodation, convergence, pitch, amplitude	The Apgar Test Reflexes in Infants Infants and Smell Infants and Taste	The Neonate	Visual Acuity in Infants	
Rapid-eye-movement (REM) sleep, non-rapid-eye-movement (non-REM) sleep, pacifier				
Sudden infant death syndrome (SIDS), infancy, medulla	Preventing SIDS			

Online Activities

Key Terms	Video	Animation	Reading	Assessment
Cephalocaudal, proximodistal, differentiation, failure to thrive (FTT), canalization				Check Your Learning Quiz 3.2
Nerve, neuron, dendrite, axon, neurotransmitter, myelin sheath, myelination, multiple sclerosis, cerebellum, cerebrum		Neuron Anatomy Brain Development Brain Structures		
Ulnar grasp, pincer grasp, locomotion, toddler				
Perceptual constancy, habituation	Visual Field Development Visual Cliff Depth Perception in Infants		Shape Constancy Infants and Foreign Languages Early Exposures to Tastes	
Sensorimotor stage, primary circular reactions, secondary circular reactions, tertiary circular reactions, object permanence, A-not-B error, deferred imitation	Piaget's Sensorimotor Stage	The Sensorimotor Stage Object Permananence	Jean Piaget	Check Your Learning Quiz 3.3
Information-processing approach			Counting in the Crib?	
Visual recognition memory			The Bayley Scales Test	

Measure
^Your Learning

Online Activities

Key Terms	Video	Animation	Reading	Assessment
Prelinguistic vocalization, cooing, babbling, echolalia, intonation, receptive vocabulary, expressive vocabulary, referential language style, expressive language style, overextension, telegraphic speech, mean length of utterance (MLU), morpheme, holophrase, syntax, model, extinction, shaping, psycholinguistic theory, language acquisition device, surface structure, deep structure, aphasia, Broca's aphasia, Wernicke's aphasia, sensitive period			Language Development Milestones Babbling Here, There and Everywhere Infants and Sign Language Two-Word Sentences Motherese Noam Chomsky	
Attachment, separation anxiety, secure attachment, insecure attachment, avoidant attachment, ambivalent/resistant attachment, indiscriminate attachment, initial-preattachment phase, attachment-in-the-making phase, clear-cut-attachment phase, contact comfort, ethologist, social smile, critical period, imprinting	Infant Attachment The Social Smile		The Strange Situation	Check Your Learning Quiz 3.4
Autism spectrum disorders (ASDs), autism, mutism	Autistic Savant Autism in Girls Autism Diagnosis			
	Daycare Pros and Cons			
Social referencing, emotional regulation				
Separation-individuation, temperament, goodness of fit				

Early Childhood

4

Prepare ^ to Learn

1 **GO** to your **Psychology CourseMate** at **login.cengagebrain.com** and take the **Chapter Pre-Test** to introduce yourself to this chapter's topics and see what you may already know.

2 **READ** the **Learning Objectives** (LOs, in the left sidebars) and begin the chapter.

3 **COMPLETE** the **Online Activities** (in the right sidebars) *as you read each module.* Activities include **videos, animations, readings,** and **quizzes.**

4 **CHECK Your Learning** by going online to take the quiz at the end of each module and review material as necessary.

5 **MEASURE Your Learning** after reading the chapter by taking the online **Chapter Post-Test.** Use the chapter review guide at the end of the chapter as needed.

WATCH for these **Online Activities** icons as you read:

Video

Animation

Reading

Assessment

These online activities are essential to mastering this chapter. Go to login.cengagebrain.com:

Videos Watch the following videos:

- The Brain's Hemispheres: The Long Fissure
- Visual Spatial Processing in Children
- Gross Motor Control in Early Childhood
- Fine Motor Skills in Early Childhood
- The Preoperational Stage
- Zone of Proximal Development
- False Beliefs
- Rehearsal Strategies
- Children and Vocabulary
- Parenting Styles
- Types of Play
- Gender Roles and Children
- Relational Aggression

Animations Interact with and visualize important processes, timelines, and concepts:

- Motor Development
- Piaget's Preoperational Stage
- Piaget: Conservation of Volume
- Parenting

Readings Delve deeper into key content:

- Gender Differences in Motor Activity
- Sample Meal Plan
- 10 Things You Need to Know About Immunizations
- Immunization Coverage Estimates In the United States
- The U.S. Recommended Immunization Schedule
- Leading Causes of Death for American Children
- Cross-Cultural Differences in Sleeping Arrangements
- Children's Concepts of Race and Ethnicity
- Highlights of the Preoperational Stage
- Research on Scaffolding
- Mixed-Aged Classrooms
- Helping Children Wisely Choose TV Programming
- Where Are the Missing American Fathers?
- Individualism, Collectivism, and Patterns of Child Rearing
- Do Children Have to Be Taught to Hate?
- Gender Stereotypes

Assessment Measure your mastery:

- Chapter Pre-Test
- Check Your Learning Quizzes
- Chapter Post-Test

Did you know that—

- Even though some people may be called left-brained or right-brained, both sides of the brain normally work together?
- A disproportionately high percentage of math whizzes are left-handed?
- It is normal to have certain diseases during childhood?
- Nearly one third of children in the United States suffer from a major chronic illness?
- It is only a myth that competent parents toilet train their children by their second birthday?
- Accidents are the most common single cause of death in early childhood in the United States?
- It is not dangerous to awaken a sleepwalker?

▼

The years from 2 to 6 are referred to as **early childhood** or the preschool years. During early childhood, physical growth is slower than in infancy. Children become taller and leaner, and by the end of early childhood they look more like adults than like infants. Motor skills develop. Children become stronger, faster, and better coordinated.

Language improves enormously, and children come to carry on conversations with others. As cognitive skills develop, a new world of make-believe or pretend play emerges. Most preschoolers are curious and eager to learn. Increased physical and cognitive capabilities enable children to emerge from total dependence on caregivers to become part of the broader world outside the family.

early childhood The period of childhood from the ages of 2 to 6, roughly following infancy and ending with entry into first grade.

Growth Patterns

During the preschool years, physical and motor development proceeds, literally, by leaps and bounds.

height in a
e slows dur-
ırski et al.,
ain about
d weight
5 pounds
rly slen-
d some
ightly
varia-
l.

ın
ıt

© Ocean/Corbis

though the body weight of the 5-year-
dult (Tanner, 1989).

he continuing myelination of nerve
pathways that link the cerebellum to
motor skills, balance, and coordi-
999).

information (Yamada et al.,
that enable the child to sus-
ingly myelinated between
enabling most children to
ormation improves through-
dolescence (Chou et al., 2006;

The Brain's Hemispheres: The Long Fissure

See a brain slice showing the long fissure of the brain, and the division between the left and right hemispheres.

Visual Spatial Processing in Children

Watch and learn how scientists use fMRI to study developing children's visual-spatial processing skills.

▶ **LO4** Describe the development of motor skills in early childhood.

Right Brain, Left Brain?

We often hear people described as being righ[...] notion is that the hemispheres of the brain are in[...] lectual and emotional activities. Research does s[...] viduals, the left hemisphere is relatively more inv[...] that require logical analysis and problem sol[...] (Grindrod & Baum, 2005; O'Shea & Corballis[...] right hemisphere) is usually superior in visu[...] puzzles together), aesthetic and emotion[...] metaphors.

But it is not true that some children a[...] brained. The functions of the left and righ[...] spheres respond simultaneously when we [...] aided in cooperation by the myelination o[...] nerve fibers that connects the hemisph[...] largely complete by the age of 8, enablin[...] functioning.

Plasticity of the Brain

Many parts of the brain have specialize[...] complex. But it also means that injuri[...] of these functions. However, the bra[...] pensate for injuries to particular are[...] and then gradually declines (Kolb[...] adults suffer damage to the areas [...] ability to speak or understand[...] assume these functions in pr[...] may regain the ability to spe[...] Neurological factors that [...] ("sprouting") and the red[...] Szaflarski et al., 2006).

Motor Development

The preschool years witness an [...] tems mature and their movement[...]

corpus callosum The thick bundle of nerve fibers that connects the left and right hemispheres of the brain.

plasticity The tendency of other parts of the brain to take up the functions of injured parts.

gross motor skills Skills employing the large muscles used in locomotion.

Height and Weight

Following the dramatic gains in
child's first 2 years, the growth rate
ing the preschool years (Kuczma
2000). Girls and boys tend to g
2–3 inches in height per year, an
gains remain fairly even at about 4–
per year. Children become increasing
der as they gain in height and she
"baby fat." Boys as a group become s
taller and heavier than girls. Noticeable
tions in growth occur from child to chil

Development of the Brain

The brain develops more quickly tha
any other organ in early childhood. A
2 years of age, the brain already has attaine
75% of its adult weight. By the age of 5, the
brain has reached 90% of its adult weight, ever
old is barely one third of what it will be in the a

The increase in brain size is due in part to
fibers. Completion of myelination of the neu
the cerebral cortex facilitates development
nation (C. A. Nelson & Luciana, 2001; Pau

Brain Development and Visual Skills

Brain development also improves pro
2000), facilitating learning to read. Th
tain attention and screen out distrac
the ages of about 4 and 7 (C. A. Nel
focus on schoolwork. The speed of
out childhood, reaching adult le
Paus et al., 1999).

t-brained or left-brained. The
volved in different kinds of intel-
uggest that in right-handed indi-
volved in intellectual undertakings
ving, language, and computation
, 2005). The other hemisphere (the
ospatial functions (such as piecing
al responses, and understanding

re left-brained and others are right-
t hemispheres overlap, and the hemi-
focus on one thing or another. They are
f the **corpus callosum**, a thick bundle of
eres (Kinsbourne, 2003). This process is
g the integration of logical and emotional

d functions, allowing our behavior to be more
s to certain parts of the brain can result in loss
also shows **plasticity**, or the ability to com-
Plasticity is greatest at about 1–2 years of age
b, 2007; Nelson et al., 2006). When we as
ain that control language, we may lose the
However, other areas of the brain may
suffer such damage. As a result, they
d language (C. A. Nelson et al., 2006).
clude the growth of new dendrites
nections (C. A. Nelson et al., 2006;

ills, as children's nervous sys-
e and coordinated.

Gross Motor Skills

Gross motor skills involve the large muscles used in locomotion. At about the age of 3, children can balance on one foot. By age 3 or 4, they can walk up stairs as adults do, by placing a foot on each step. By age 4 or 5, they can skip and pedal a tricycle (McDevitt & Ormrod, 2002). Older preschoolers are better able to coordinate two tasks, such as singing and running at the same time. In general, preschoolers appear to acquire motor skills by teaching themselves and observing other children. Imitating other children seems more important than adult instruction at this age.

Throughout early childhood, girls and boys are similar in motor skills. Girls are somewhat better at balance and precision. Boys show some advantage in throwing and kicking (McDevitt & Ormrod, 2002).

Individual differences are larger than gender differences throughout early and middle childhood. Some children are genetically predisposed to developing better coordination or more strength. Motivation and practice also are important. Motor experiences in infancy may affect the development of motor skills in early childhood. For example, children with early crawling experience perform better on tests of motor skills than those who do not crawl early (McEwan et al., 1991).

Gross Motor Skills. During the preschool years, children make great strides in the development of gross motor skills. By age 4 or 5, they can pedal a tricycle quite skillfully.

GeoM/Shutterstock.com

Gross Motor Control and Children

Learn about the gross motor control of young children in preschool and early elementary.

Motor Development

Explore the hallmarks of gross motor development, including gender differences.

Physical Activity

Preschoolers spend an average of more than 25 hours a week in large-muscle activity (D. W. Campbell et al., 2002). Younger preschoolers are more likely than older preschoolers to engage in physically oriented play, such as grasping, banging, and mouthing objects (D. W. Campbell et al., 2002).

Motor-activity level begins to decline after 2 or 3 years of age. Children become less restless and are able to sit still longer. Between the ages of 2 and 4, children show an increase in sustained, focused attention.

Rough-and-Tumble Play

Rough-and-tumble play consists of running, chasing, fleeing, wrestling, hitting with an open hand, laughing, and making faces. Rough-and-tumble play, which is more common among boys than among girls, is not the same as aggressive behavior, which involves hitting, pushing, taking, grabbing, and angry looks. Rough-and-tumble play helps develop physical and social skills (Fry, 2005; Smith, 2005).

Fine Motor Skills. Control over the wrists and fingers enables children to hold a pencil, play a musical instrument, and, as shown in this photograph, play with clay.

Robert Brenner / PhotoEdit, Inc.

Individual Differences in Activity Level

Physically active parents are likely to have physically active children (Eveland et al., 2006; Welk et al., 2003). Several reasons may explain this relationship. First, active parents may serve as role models for activity. Second, sharing of activities by family members may be responsible. Active parents may also encourage their child's participation in physical activity. Twin studies also suggest there is a genetic tendency for activity level (Saudino & Eaton, 1993; Stevenson, 1992).

Fine Motor Skills

fine motor skills Skills employing the small muscles used in manipulation, such as those in the fingers.

Fine motor skills involve the small muscles used in manipulation and coordination. These skills develop gradually, a bit more slowly than gross motor skills. Control over the wrists and fingers enables children to hold a pencil properly, dress themselves, and stack blocks. Preschoolers can labor endlessly in attempting to tie their shoelaces and get their jackets zipped.

Children's Drawings

The development of drawing is linked to the development of motor and cognitive skills. Children first begin to scribble during the second year of life. Initially, they seem to make marks for the sheer joy of it (Eisner, 1990). Rhoda Kellogg (1959, 1970) found a meaningful pattern in the scribbles. She identified 20 basic scribbles that she considered the building blocks of art (see Figure 4.1).

Source: Kellogg (1970).

Figure 4.1 The 20 Basic Scribbles By the age of 2, children can scribble. Rhoda Kellogg has identified these 20 basic scribbles as the building blocks of the young child's drawings.

Children progress through four stages from making scribbles to drawing pictures: the *placement*, *shape*, *design*, and *pictorial* stages (see Figure 4.2). Two-year-olds scribble in various locations on the page (e.g., in the middle of the page or near one of the borders). By age 3, children are starting to draw basic shapes: circles, squares, triangles, crosses, Xs, and odd shapes. As soon as they can draw shapes, children begin to combine them in the design stage. Between ages 4 and 5, children reach the pictorial stage, in which designs begin to resemble recognizable objects.

Children's early drawings tend to be symbolic of broad categories rather than specific. A child might draw the same simple building whether asked to draw a school or a house (Tallandini & Valentini, 1991). Children between 3 and 5 usually do not set out to draw a particular thing. They are more likely to see what they have drawn, then name it. As motor and cognitive skills develop beyond the age of 5, children become able to draw an object they have in mind (Matthews, 1990). They also improve at copying figures (Karapetsas & Kantas, 1991; Pemberton, 1990).

Gender and Motor Activity

Does gender affect activity levels during childhood? Read and find out.

Fine Motor Skills in Early Childhood

Observe children with different levels of fine motor control.

▶ **L05** Discuss handedness.

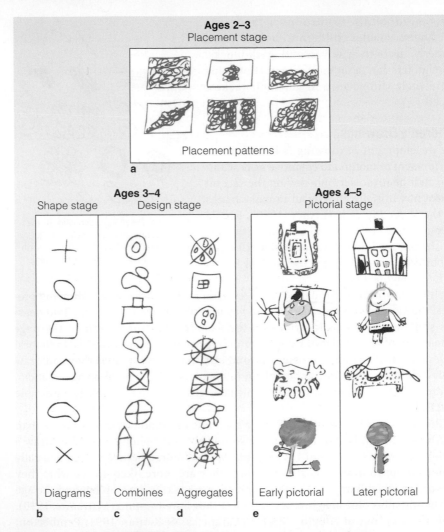

Figure 4.2 Four Stages in Children's Drawings Children go through four stages in drawing pictures. (a) They first place their scribbles in various locations on the page. (b) They then draw basic shapes and (c, d) combine shapes into designs. (e) Finally they draw recognizable objects.

Source: Kellogg (1970).

Handedness

Handedness emerges during infancy. By the age of 2–3 months, a rattle placed in an infant's hand is held longer with the right hand than the left (H. E. Fitzgerald et al., 1991). By 4 months of age, most infants show a clear-cut right-hand preference in exploring objects (Streri, 2002). Preference for grasping with one hand or the other increases markedly between 7 and 11 months (Hinojosa et al., 2003). Handedness becomes more strongly established during early childhood (I. C. McManus et al., 1988). Most people are right-handed; studies vary as to how many are left-handed.

The origins of handedness apparently have a genetic component (D. H. Geschwind, 2000; C. McManus, 2003). If both of your parents are right-handed, your chances of being right-handed are about 92%. If both of your parents are left-handed, your chances of being left-handed are about 50% (Annett, 1999; Clode, 2006).

Left-Handedness

Being a "lefty" was once seen as a deficiency. The English language still swarms with slurs on lefties. We speak of left-handed compliments or of having two left feet. Being left-handed may matter because it appears to be connected with language problems, such as dyslexia and stuttering, and with health problems, such as high blood pressure and epilepsy (Andreou et al., 2002; Bryden et al., 2005). Left-handedness is also apparently connected with psychological disorders, including schizophrenia and depression (Annett & Moran, 2006; Dollfus et al., 2005).

Even so, there may be advantages to being left-handed. A disproportionately high percentage of math whizzes are left-handed, as found on the math part of the SAT among 12- and 13-year-olds (O'Boyle & Benbow, 1990). Twenty percent of the highest-scoring group was left-handed, while only 10% of the general population is left-handed.

Left-handedness (or use of both hands) also has been associated with success in athletic activities such as handball, fencing, boxing, basketball, and baseball (Coren, 1992; Dane & Erzurumluoglu, 2003). Higher frequencies of left-handedness are found among musicians, architects, and artists (Natsopoulos et al., 1992).

Nutrition

The average 4- to 6-year-old needs about 1,400 calories, compared with about 1,000–1,300 calories for the average 1- to 3-year-old (American Academy of Family Physicians, 2006).

Patterns of Eating

During the second and third years, a child's decreasing, erratic appetite often worries parents. But because the child is growing more slowly now, he or she needs fewer calories. Also, young children who eat less at one meal typically compensate by eating more at another. Children may develop strong (and strange) preferences for certain foods (Cooke et al., 2003). At one time during her third year, my daughter Allyn wanted to eat nothing but SpaghettiOs.

Many children (and adults) consume excessive amounts of sugar and salt, which can be harmful to their health. Infants seem to be born liking the taste of sugar, although they are fairly indifferent to salty tastes. But preference for both sweet and salty foods increases if children are repeatedly exposed to them during childhood. Parents also serve as role models in the development of food preferences. If a parent—especially the parent who usually prepares meals—displays an obvious dislike for vegetables, children may develop a similar dislike (Hannon, et al., 2003).

What is the best way to get children to eat their green peas or spinach or other healthful foods they may dislike? (Notice that it is rarely dessert that the child refuses to eat.) One method is to encourage the child to taste tiny amounts of the food 8 or 10 times within a period of a few weeks so that it becomes more familiar. Familiarity with food may breed content, not contempt.

Health and Illness

Almost all children get ill now and then. Some seem to be ill every other week or so. Most illnesses are minor, and children seem to eventually recover from or outgrow many of them. Fortunately, we can prevent or cure many others.

Minor Illnesses

Minor illnesses are respiratory infections, such as colds, and gastrointestinal upsets, such as nausea, vomiting, and diarrhea. These diseases are normal in that most children come down with them. They typically last a few days or less and are not life threatening. Although diarrheal illness in the United States is usually mild, it is a leading killer of children in developing countries (UNICEF, 2006).

American children between the ages of 1 and 3 average eight to nine minor illnesses a year. Between the ages of 4 and 10, the average drops to four to six. Childhood illnesses can lead to the creation of antibodies that may prevent children from coming down with the same illnesses in adulthood, when they can do more harm.

Major Illnesses

Let's travel around the world and consider some facts about illnesses that afflict children (Save the Children, 2008):

- Pneumonia kills more children under the age of 5 than AIDS, malaria, and measles combined—as many as three million children a year. Antibiotics that would vanquish bacterial pneumonia cost less than 30 cents a dose, but only 20% of children with pneumonia receive them.
- Diarrhea kills almost two million under-5 children each year (Patel et al., 2009). The treatment to prevent children from dying from diarrhea is *oral rehydration therapy* with salts, which costs under 50 cents. But only 38% of children with diarrhea receive this therapy.
- Malaria, which is transmitted to people by mosquitoes, kills some 800,000 under-5 children in sub-Saharan Africa annually.
- Measles kills some 240,000 children each year. It is one of the world's leading causes of death that is preventable by vaccination.
- Malnutrition is connected with half of the deaths of children under the age of 5. Poorly nourished children have lower resistance to infection.

Advances in immunization, along with the development of antibiotics and other medications, have dramatically reduced the incidence of serious and potentially fatal childhood diseases in the United States. Because most preschoolers and school-children have been inoculated against major childhood illnesses such as rubella (German measles), measles, tetanus, mumps, whooping cough, diphtheria, and polio, these diseases no longer pose the threat they once did.

Nearly one third of the children in the United States younger than 18 years—about 20 million children—suffer from a chronic illness (Agency for Healthcare Research and Quality, 2004). The illnesses include such major disorders as arthritis, diabetes, cerebral palsy, and cystic fibrosis. Other chronic medical problems such

Sample Meal Plan

Explore an ideal diet for a young child.

Immunizations

Read 10 things you need to know about immunizations.

Immunization Coverage in the U.S.

Read about immunization coverage estimates in the United States.

Recommended Immunization Schedule

Read about the U.S. recommended immunization schedule.

Causes of Death in Young Children

What are the top ten causes of death in young children?

▶ **LO8** Discuss sleep during early childhood.

as asthma and migraine headaches are less serious but still require extensive health care.

Although many major childhood diseases have been largely eradicated in the United States and other industrialized nations, they remain fearsome killers of children in developing countries. Around the world, more than 13 million children die each year. Two thirds of them die of just six diseases: pneumonia, diarrhea, measles, tetanus, whooping cough, and tuberculosis (UNICEF, 2006). Diarrheal diseases are almost completely related to unsafe drinking water and a general lack of sanitation and hygiene. Children's immune systems and detoxification mechanisms are not as strong as those of adults, and children are thus more vulnerable to chemical, physical, and biological hazards in the water, soil, and air.

Unintentional Injuries

Accidents cause more deaths in early childhood than the next six most frequent causes combined (National Center for Injury Prevention and Control, 2007a). The single most common cause of death in early childhood is motor-vehicle accidents.

Boys are more likely than girls to incur accidental injuries at all ages and in all socio-economic groups. Poor children are 5 times as likely to die from fires and more than twice as likely to die in motor-vehicle accidents than other children (National Center for Injury Prevention and Control, 2007a). The high accident rate for low-income children may result partly from living in dangerous housing and neighborhoods.

Sleep

Preschoolers do not need as much sleep as infants. Most preschoolers sleep 10–11 hours in a 24-hour period (National Sleep Foundation, 2009b). A common pattern is 9–10 hours at night and a nap of 1–2 hours. Many children resist going to bed or going to sleep (Christophersen & Mortweet, 2003). Getting to sleep late can be a problem,

sleep terrors Frightening dream-like experiences that occur during the deepest stage of non-REM sleep, shortly after the child has gone to sleep.

somnambulism Sleepwalking.

iStockphoto.com/Ana Abejon

Automobile Safety. Automobile accidents are the most common cause of death in young children in the United States. All 50 states now require child restraint seats in automobiles. These laws have contributed to a reduction in child deaths and injuries.

because preschoolers tend not to make up fully for lost sleep (Kohyama et al., 2002). Many young children take a so-called transitional object—such as a favored blanket or a stuffed animal—to bed with them (Morelli et al., 1992).

Sleep Disorders

In this section, we focus on the sleep disorders of sleep terrors, nightmares, and sleepwalking.

Sleep Terrors and Nightmares

Sleep terrors are more severe than the anxiety dreams we refer to as nightmares. Sleep terrors usually occur during deep sleep. Nightmares take place during lighter rapid-eye-movement (REM) sleep, when about 80% of normal dreams occur.

Sleep terrors usually begin in childhood or early adolescence and are outgrown by late adolescence. They are sometimes associated with stress, as in moving to a new neighborhood, beginning school, adjusting to parental divorce, or being in a war zone. Children with sleep terrors may wake suddenly with a surge in heart and respiration rates, talk incoherently, and thrash about. Children may then fall back into more restful sleep. The incidence of sleep terrors wanes as children develop.

Children who have frequent nightmares or sleep terrors may come to fear going to sleep. They may show distress at bedtime, refuse to get into their pajamas, and insist that the lights be kept on. As a result, they can develop insomnia. Children with frequent nightmares or sleep terrors need caregivers' understanding and affection. They also profit from a regular routine in which they are expected to get to sleep at the same time each night (Christophersen & Mortweet, 2003).

Sleepwalking

Sleepwalking, or **somnambulism**, is more common among children than adults. As with sleep terrors, sleepwalking tends to occur during deep sleep (Stores & Wiggs, 2001). Onset is usually between the ages of 3 and 8.

When children sleepwalk, they may rearrange toys, go to the bathroom, or go to the refrigerator and have a glass of milk. They then return to their rooms and go back to bed. There are myths about sleepwalking, for instance that sleepwalkers' eyes are closed, that they will avoid harm, and that they will become violently agitated if they are awakened during an episode. All these notions are false.

Culture and Sleeping Arrangements

Read about cross-cultural differences in sleeping arrangements.

▶ **LO9** Discuss elimination problems.

Sleepwalking in children is assumed to reflect immaturity of the nervous system. As with sleep terrors, the incidence of sleepwalking drops as children develop. It may help to discuss a child's persistent sleep terrors or sleepwalking with a health professional.

Elimination Disorders

The elimination of waste products occurs reflexively in neonates. As children develop, they learn to inhibit the reflexes that govern urination and bowel movements. How parents teach their children to inhibit these reflexes is referred to as *toilet training*.

In toilet training, maturation plays a crucial role. During the first year, only an exceptional child can be toilet trained. Most American children are toilet trained between the ages of 3 and 4 (Scheres & Castellanos, 2003). They may have nighttime "accidents" for another year or so. Children who do not become toilet trained within reasonable time frames may be diagnosed with enuresis, encopresis, or both.

Enuresis

Enuresis is failure to control the bladder (urination) once the "normal" age for achieving bladder control has been reached. The American Psychiatric Association (2000) places the cutoff age at 5 years and does not consider "accidents" to represent enuresis unless they occur at least twice a month for 5- and 6-year-olds.

A nighttime "accident" is termed **bed-wetting**. Nighttime control is more difficult to achieve than daytime control. At night, children must first wake up when their bladders are full. Only then can they go to the bathroom. Overall, 8%–10% of American children wet their beds (Mellon & Houts, 2006), with the problem about twice as common among boys. Bed-wetting tends to occur during the deepest stage of sleep. That is also the stage when sleep terrors and sleepwalking take place.

enuresis Failure to control the bladder (urination) once the normal age for control has been reached.

bed-wetting Failure to control the bladder during the night.

encopresis Failure to control the bowels once the normal age for bowel control has been reached. Also called *soiling*.

Piotr Powietrzynski/Getty Images

Toilet Training. If parents wait until the third year to begin toilet training, the process usually goes relatively rapidly and smoothly.

It is believed that enuresis might have organic causes, most often immaturity of the motor cortex of the brain (von Gontard, 2006). Just as children outgrow sleep terrors and sleepwalking, they tend to outgrow bed-wetting (Mellon & Houts, 2006).

Encopresis

Soiling, or **encopresis**, is lack of control over the bowels. Soiling, like enuresis, is more common among boys. About 1%–2% of children at the ages of 7 and 8 have continuing problems controlling their bowels (Mellon, 2006; von Gontard, 2006). Soiling, in contrast to enuresis, is more likely to occur during the day. Thus, it can be embarrassing to the child, especially in school.

Encopresis stems from both physical causes, such as chronic constipation, and psychological factors (Mellon, 2006; von Gontard, 2006). Soiling may follow harsh punishment of toileting accidents, especially in children who are already anxious or under stress. Punishment may cause the child to tense up on the toilet, when moving one's bowels requires that one relax the anal sphincter muscles. Soiling, punishment, and anxiety can become a vicious cycle.

Check Your Learning Quiz 4.1

Go to **login.cengagebrain.com** and take the online quiz.

▶ **L010** Describe how preoperational children think and behave.

Did you know that—

- A preschooler's having imaginary playmates is *not* a sign of loneliness or psychological problems?

- Two-year-olds tend to assume that their parents are aware of everything that is happening to them, even when their parents are not present?

- "Because Mommy wants me to" may be a perfectly good explanation—for a 3-year-old?

- Children's levels of intelligence—not just their knowledge—are influenced by early learning experiences?

- Three-year-olds usually say "Daddy goed away" instead of "Daddy went away" because they *do* understand rules of grammar?

▼

I was confused when one of my daughters, at the age of 2½, insisted that I continue to play "Billy Joel" on the stereo. Put aside the question of her taste in music. My problem stemmed from the fact that when she asked for Billy Joel—the name of the singer—she could be satisfied only by my playing the song "Movin' Out." When "Movin' Out" ended and the next song, "The Stranger," began to play, she would insist that I play "Billy Joel" again. "That *is* Billy Joel," I would protest. "No, no," she would insist, "I want Billy Joel!"

Finally, it dawned on me that, for her, *Billy Joel* symbolized the song "Movin' Out," not the name of the singer. She was conceptualizing *Billy Joel* as a property of a particular song, not as the name of someone who could sing many songs.

Children between the ages of 2 and 4 tend to show confusion between symbols and the objects they represent. They do not yet recognize that words are arbitrary symbols for objects and events and that people can use different words. They tend to think of words as inherent properties of objects and events.

In this module we discuss cognitive development during early childhood. First, we examine Piaget's preoperational stage of cognitive development.

preoperational stage The second stage in Piaget's scheme, characterized by inflexible and irreversible mental manipulation of symbols.

symbolic play Play in which children make believe that objects and toys are other than what they are. Also called *pretend play*.

Jean Piaget's Preoperational Stage

According to Piaget, the **preoperational stage** of cognitive development lasts from about age 2 to age 7. *Operations* are mental manipulations of information, and at this stage, Piaget believed that young children's logic is at best "under construction."

Symbolic Thought

Preoperational thought is characterized by the use of symbols to represent objects and relationships among them. Perhaps the most important kind of symbolic activity of young children is language, but children's early use of language leaves something to be desired in the realm of logic. According to Piaget, preschoolers' drawings are symbols of objects, people, and events in children's lives. Symbolism is also expressed as symbolic or pretend play.

Symbolic or Pretend Play: "Let's Make Believe"

Children's **symbolic play**—the "let's pretend" type of play—may seem immature to busy adults meeting the realistic demands of the business world, but it requires cognitive sophistication (Feldman & Masalha, 2007; Keen et al., 2007).

Piaget (1946/1962) wrote that pretend play usually begins in the second year, when the child begins to symbolize objects. The ability to engage in pretend play is based on the use and recollection of symbols, that is, on mental representations of things children have experienced or heard about.

Children first engage in pretend play at about 12 or 13 months. They make believe that they are performing familiar activities, such as sleeping or feeding themselves. By 15–20 months, they can shift their focus from themselves to others. A child may pretend to feed a doll. By 30 months, she or he can make believe that the other object takes an active role. The child may pretend that the doll is feeding itself (Paavola et al., 2006).

The quality of preschoolers' pretend play has implications for subsequent development. For example, preschoolers who engage in violent pretend play are less empathic, less likely to

Symbolic play—also called *pretend play*—usually begins in the second year, when the child begins to form mental representations of objects. This 2½-year-old may engage in a sequence of play acts such as making a doll sit down at the table and offering it a make-believe cup of tea.

help other children, and more likely to engage in antisocial behavior later on (J. Dunn & Hughes, 2001). The quality of pretend play is connected with preschoolers' academic performance later on, their creativity, and their social skills (Russ, 2006; Stagnitti et al., 2000).

Imaginary friends are an example of pretend play. As many as 65% of preschoolers have imaginary friends; they are most common among firstborn and only children (T. R. Gleason, Sebanc, et al., 2003). Having an imaginary playmate does not mean that the child has problems with real relationships (T. R. Gleason, 2004; E. Hoff, 2005). In fact, children with imaginary friends are less aggressive, more cooperative, and more creative than children without them (T. R. Gleason, 2002). They have more real friends, show greater ability to concentrate, and are more advanced in language development (M. Taylor, 1999).

Egocentrism: It's All About Me

Sometimes the attitude "It's all about me" is a sign of early childhood, not of selfishness. One consequence of one-dimensional thinking is **egocentrism**. Egocentrism, in Piaget's use of the term, means that preoperational children do not understand that

egocentrism Putting oneself at the center of things such that one is unable to perceive the world from another person's point of view.

precausal A type of thought in which natural cause-and-effect relationships are attributed to will and other preoperational concepts.

transductive reasoning Reasoning from the specific to the specific.

animism The attribution of life and intentionality to inanimate objects.

artificialism The belief that environmental features were made by people.

other people may have different perspectives on the world. Two-year-olds may, in fact, assume that their parents are aware of everything that is happening to them, even when their parents are not present. When I asked a daughter aged 2½ to tell me about a trip to the store with her mother, she answered, "You tell me." It did not occur to her that I could not see the world through her eyes.

Piaget used the "three-mountains test" (see Figure 4.3) to show that egocentrism prevents young children from taking the viewpoints of others. In this demonstration, the child sits at a table before a model of three mountains. One has a house on it, and another has a cross at the summit.

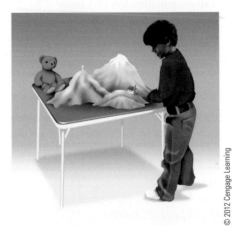

© 2012 Cengage Learning

Figure 4.3 The Three-Mountains Test Piaget used the three-mountains test to learn whether children at certain ages are egocentric or can take the viewpoints of others.

Piaget then placed a doll elsewhere on the table and asked the child what the doll sees. The language abilities of very young children do not permit them to provide verbal descriptions of what can be seen from where the doll is situated, so they can answer in one of two ways: They can either select a photograph taken from the proper vantage point or construct another model of the mountains as they would be seen by the doll. The results of an experiment with the three-mountains test suggested that 5- and 6-year-olds usually select photos or build models that correspond to their own viewpoints (Laurendeau & Pinard, 1970).

Causality: Why? Because.

Preoperational children's responses to questions such as "Why does the sun shine?" show other facets of egocentrism. At the age of 2 or so, they may answer that they do not know or change the subject. Three-year-olds may report themselves as doing things because they want to do them or "because Mommy wants me to." This explanation of behavior is egocentrically extended to inanimate objects. The sun shines because it wants to shine or someone wants it to shine.

Piaget labels this structuring of cause and effect **precausal**. Consider the question "Why does it get dark outside?" The preoperational child usually does not have knowledge of Earth's rotation and is likely to answer something like, "So I can go to sleep."

In **transductive reasoning**, children reason by going from one specific isolated event to another. For example, a 3-year-old may argue that she should go on her swings in the backyard *because* it is light outside or that she should go to sleep *because* it is dark outside. That is, separate events, daylight and going on the swings (or being awake), are thought of as having cause-and-effect relationships.

Preoperational children also show **animism** and **artificialism** in their attributions of causality. In animistic thinking, they attribute life and intentions to inanimate objects, such as the sun and the moon. ("Why is the moon gone during the day?" "It is afraid of the sun.") Artificialism assumes that environmental features such as rain and thunder have been designed and made by people.

Confusion of Mental and Physical Events

What would you do if someone asked you to pretend you were a galaprock? Chances are, you might inquire what a galaprock is and how it behaves. So might a 5-year-old child. But a 3-year-old might not think that such information is necessary (Gottfried et al., 2003).

According to Piaget, the preoperational child has difficulty distinguishing between mental and physical events. Children between the ages of 2 and 4 show confusion between symbols and the things they represent. Egocentrism contributes to the assumption that their thoughts exactly reflect external reality. They do not recognize that words are arbitrary and that people can use different words to refer to things. Piaget (1946/1962) asked a 4-year-old child, "Could you call this table a cup and that cup a table?" "No," the child responded. "Why not?" "Because," explained the child, "you can't drink out of a table!" Another example of the preoperational child's confusion of the mental and the physical is the tendency of many 4-year-olds to believe that dreams are real (S. Meyer & Shore, 2001).

Focus on One Dimension at a Time

To gain further insight into preoperational thinking, consider these two problems. First, imagine that you pour the water from a low, wide glass into a tall, thin glass, as in Figure 4.4b. Now, does the tall, thin glass contain more than, less than, or the same amount of water as in the low, wide glass? We won't keep you in suspense. If you said the same amount, you were correct.

Next, if you flatten a ball of clay into a pancake, do you wind up with more, less, or the same amount of clay? If you said the same amount, you are correct once more.

To arrive at the correct answers to these questions, you must understand the law of **conservation**. The law of conservation holds that properties of substances such as volume, mass, and number remain the same—or are conserved—even if you change their shape or arrangement.

Conservation requires the ability to focus on two aspects of a situation at once, such as height and width. A preoperational child focuses or centers on only one dimension at a time, a characteristic of thought that Piaget called **centration**. First, the child is shown two squat glasses of water and agrees that they have the same amount of water (see Figure 4.4). Then, as he watches, water is poured from one squat glass into a tall, thin glass. Asked which glass has more water, he points to the tall glass. Why? When he looks at the glasses, he is swayed by the fact that the thinner glass is taller.

The preoperational child's failure to show conservation also comes about because of *irreversibility*. In the case of the water, the child does not realize that pouring water from the wide glass to the tall glass can be reversed, restoring things to their original condition.

conservation In cognitive psychology, the principle that properties of substances such as weight and mass remain the same (are conserved) when superficial characteristics such as their shapes or arrangement are changed.

centration Focusing on an aspect or characteristic of a situation or problem.

class inclusion Categorizing a new object or concept as belonging to a broader group of objects or concepts.

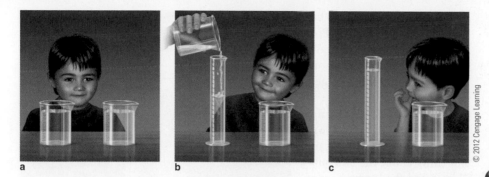

a b c

Figure 4.4 Conservation (a) The boy in this illustration agreed that the amount of water in two identical containers is equal. (b) He then watched as water from one container was poured into a tall, thin container. (c) When asked whether the amounts of water in the two containers are now the same, he said no.

After you have tried the experiment with the water, try this experiment on conservation of number. Make two rows with four pennies in each. As the 3-year-old child watches, move the pennies in the second row to about 1 inch apart, as in Figure 4.5. Then ask the child which row has more pennies. What do you think the child will say? Why?

Class Inclusion

Class inclusion, as we are using it here, means including new objects or categories in broader mental classes or categories. Class inclusion also requires children to focus on two aspects of a situation at once. In one of Piaget's class-inclusion tasks, the child is shown several pictures from two subclasses of a larger class, for example, four cats and six dogs (see Figure 4.6). He is asked whether there are more

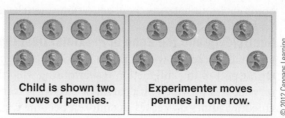

| Child is shown two rows of pennies. | Experimenter moves pennies in one row. |

Figure 4.5 Conservation of Number In this demonstration, we begin with two rows of pennies that are spread out equally, as shown on the left. Then one row of pennies is spread out more, as shown on the right. We then ask the child, "Do the two rows still have the same number of pennies?" Do you think that a preoperational child will conserve the number of pennies or focus on the length of the longer row in arriving at an answer?

The Preoperational Stage

Examine the features of Piaget's second stage of cognitive development, including conservation.

Concepts of Race and Ethnicity

How do children develop concepts of ethnicity and race?

Highlights of the Preoperational Stage

Review the highlights of the preoperational stage.

Piaget's Preoperational Stage

Explore to learn features of Piaget's second stage of cognitive development, conservation, and limitations of Piaget's theory.

Conservation of Volume

Explore Piaget's conservation of volume task and how preoperational and concrete operational children perform on it.

▶ **LO11** Describe factors that influence cognitive development in early childhood.

dogs or more animals. What do you think he will say? Preoperational children typically answer that there are more dogs than animals (Piaget, 1936/1963).

Why do preoperational children make this error? According to Piaget, they cannot think about the two subclasses and the larger class at the same time. Therefore, they cannot easily compare them. Children view dogs as dogs, or as animals, but find it difficult to see them as both dogs and animals at once (Branco & Lourenço, 2004).

© 2012 Cengage Learning

Figure 4.6 Class Inclusion A typical 4-year-old child will say there are more dogs than animals in the example.

Factors in Cognitive Development: The HOME Environment, Preschool, and Television

Vygotsky hypothesized two processes that foster cognitive development in early childhood: scaffolding and the zone of proximal development. Others include the home environment, preschool education, and television.

Scaffolding and the Zone of Proximal Development

scaffolding Vygotsky's term for temporary cognitive structures or methods of solving problems that help the child as he or she learns to function independently.

zone of proximal development Vygotsky's term for the situation in which a child carries out tasks with the help of someone who is more skilled, frequently an adult who represents the culture in which the child develops.

Parental interaction with children is a key ingredient in their cognitive development. One aspect of this interaction is **scaffolding**. Cognitive scaffolding refers to temporary support provided by a parent or teacher to learning children. The guidance provided by adults decreases as children become capable of carrying out the task on their own (Lengua et al., 2007; Sylva et al., 2007).

A related concept is Vygotsky's **zone of proximal development**. The zone refers to the area in which children develop new cognitive skills as a function of working with more skilled people. Adults or older children can best guide children through this zone by gearing their assistance to children's capabilities (Lantolf & Thorne, 2007; Wennergren & Rönnerman, 2006). Researchers have argued that children's cognitive skills develop through interaction with older, more experienced individuals. In a related study, K. Alison Clarke-Stewart and Robert Beck (1999) had 31 5-year-olds observe a videotaped film segment with their mothers, talk about it with their mothers, and then retell the story to an experimenter. Children whose mothers focused the children's attention on the tape, asked their children to talk about it, and discussed the feelings of the characters told better stories than children whose mothers did not use such scaffolding strategies and than children in a control group who did not discuss the story at all.

The "HOME" Environment

Bettye Caldwell and her colleagues (Bradley, Caldwell, & Corwyn, 2003) developed a measure for evaluating children's home environments labeled, appropriately enough, HOME (an acronym for Home Observation for the Measurement of the Environment). With this method, researchers directly observe parent–child interaction in the home. The HOME inventory contains six subscales:

1. Parental emotional and verbal responsiveness
2. Avoidance of restriction and punishment
3. Organization of the physical environment
4. Provision of appropriate play materials
5. Parental involvement with child
6. Opportunities for variety in daily stimulation

The HOME inventory items are better predictors of young children's later IQ scores than social class, mother's IQ, or infant IQ scores (Bradley, 2006). Longitudinal research has also shown that the home environment is connected with occupational success as an adult (Huesmann, Dubow, et al., 2006).

Effects of Early Childhood Education

How important are academic experiences in early childhood? Do they facilitate cognitive development? Research suggests that preschool education enables children to get an early start on achievement in school.

Children reared in poverty generally perform less well on standardized intelligence tests than children of higher socioeconomic status, and they are at greater risk for school failure (Stipek & Hakuta, 2007; Whitehouse, 2006). As a result, preschool

Research on Scaffolding

Does scaffolding help children better remember and retell stories? Read and find out.

Zone of Proximal Development

Watch and learn more about Vygotsky's zone of proximal development.

▶ **LO12** Explain how young children believe the mind works.

The Home Environment and Head Start. The home environment of the young child is linked to intellectual development and later academic achievement. Key aspects of the home environment include the parents' involvement and encouragement of the child, the availability of toys and learning materials, and the variety of experiences to which the child is exposed. Preschoolers enrolled in Head Start programs have made dramatic increases in readiness for elementary school and in intelligence test scores. Head Start and similar programs also can have long-term effects on educational and employment outcomes.

programs were begun in the 1960s to enhance their cognitive development and readiness for elementary school. Children in these programs typically are exposed to letters and words, numbers, books, exercises in drawing, pegs and pegboards, puzzles, and toy animals and dolls—materials and activities that middle-class children usually take for granted.

Studies of Head Start and other intervention programs show that environmental enrichment can enhance the cognitive development of economically disadvantaged children (Stipek & Hakuta, 2007; P. Wilson, 2004). In the Milwaukee Project, poor children of low-IQ mothers were provided with enriched day care from the age of 6 months. By the late preschool years, the children's IQ scores averaged about 121, compared with an average of 95 for peers who did not receive day care (Garber, 1988).

Television

American children spend more time watching television than they do in school. By the time he or she turns 3, the average child already watches 2–3 hours of television a day (E. L. Palmer, 2003). Television has great potential for teaching a variety of cognitive skills, social behaviors, and attitudes. The Children's Television Act requires that networks devote a number of hours per week to educational television. Many but not all of the resultant programs have been shown to have mild to moderate positive effects on preschoolers' cognitive development (Calvert & Kotler, 2003).

theory of mind A commonsense understanding of how the mind works.

Sesame Street is the most successful children's educational television program. The goal of *Sesame Street* is to promote the intellectual growth of preschoolers, particularly those of lower socioeconomic status. Large-scale evaluations of the effects of the program have concluded that regular viewing increases children's learning of numbers, letters, and cognitive skills such as sorting and classification (Fisch, 2004).

Sesame Street is viewed regularly by an estimated 50%–60% of children in the United States between the ages of 2 and 3 years. Research shows that regular viewing of the program improves children's cognitive and language skills.

Theory of Mind: What Is the Mind? How Does It Work?

Adults appear to have a commonsense understanding of how the mind works—that is, a **theory of mind**. We understand that we can gain knowledge through our senses or through hearsay. We know the distinction between actual and mental events and between how things appear and how they really are. We can infer the perceptions, thoughts, and feelings of others. We understand that mental states affect behavior.

Piaget might have predicted that preoperational children are too egocentric and too focused on misleading external appearances to have a theory of mind, but research has shown that even preschoolers can accurately predict and explain human action and emotion in terms of mental states (Wellman et al., 2006).

False Beliefs: Where Are Those Crayons?

One indication of preschoolers' understanding that mental states affect behavior is the ability to understand false beliefs. This concept involves children's ability to separate their beliefs from those of another person who has false knowledge of a situation. It was illustrated in a study of 3-year-olds by Louis Moses and John Flavell (1990). The children were shown a videotape in which a girl named Cathy found some crayons in a bag

Mixed-Aged Classrooms

Read about the benefits of mixed-age classrooms.

TV Choices for Children

Learn how to help children choose TV wisely.

False Beliefs

Watch and learn more about when children attribute beliefs to others.

▶ **LO13** Discuss the development of autobiographical memory.

▶ **LO14** Define factors that affect memory in early childhood.

© 2012 Cengage Learning

Figure 4.7 False Beliefs John Flavell and his colleagues showed preschoolers a videotape in which (a) a girl named Cathy found crayons in a bag. (b) When Cathy left the room, a clown entered, removed the crayons from the bag, hid them in a drawer, and (c) filled the bag with rocks. When asked whether Cathy thought there would be rocks or crayons in the bag, most 3-year-olds said "rocks." Most 4-year-olds correctly answered "crayons," showing the ability to separate their own beliefs from those of someone who has erroneous knowledge of a situation.

(Figure 4.7). When Cathy left the room briefly, a clown entered the room. The clown removed the crayons from the bag, hid them in a drawer, and put rocks in the bag instead. When Cathy returned, the children were asked whether Cathy thought there would be rocks or crayons in the bag. Most of the 3-year-olds incorrectly answered "rocks," demonstrating their difficulty in understanding that the other person's belief would be different from their own. But by the age of 4–5 years, children do not have trouble with this concept and correctly answer "crayons" (Flavell, 1993).

Origins of Knowledge

appearance–reality distinction The difference between real events, on the one hand, and mental events, fantasies, and misleading appearances, on the other hand.

Another aspect of theory of mind is how we acquire knowledge. By age 3, most children begin to realize that people gain knowledge about something by looking at it (Pratt & Bryant, 1990). By age 4, children understand that particular senses provide information about only certain qualities of an object; for example, we come to know an object's color through our eyes, but we learn about its weight by feeling it (O'Neill & Chong, 2001). In a study by Daniela O'Neill and Alison Gopnik (1991), 3-, 4-, and 5-year-olds learned about the contents of a toy tunnel in three different ways: They saw the contents, were told about them, or felt them. The children were then asked to state what was in the tunnel and how they knew. Although the 4- and 5-year-olds did not have any trouble identifying the sources of their knowledge, the 3-year-olds did. For example, after feeling but not seeing a ball in the tunnel, a number of 3-year-olds told the experimenter that they could tell it was a blue ball. The children did not realize they could not learn the ball's color by feeling it.

The Appearance–Reality Distinction

Children must acquire an understanding of the difference between real events, on the one hand, and mental events, fantasies, and misleading appearances, on the other hand (Bialystok & Senman, 2004; Flavell et al., 2002). This understanding is known as the **appearance–reality distinction**.

Piaget's view was that children do not differentiate reality from appearances or mental events until the age of 7 or 8. In a study by Marjorie Taylor and Barbara Hort (1990), children aged 3–5 were shown objects that had misleading appearances, such as an eraser that looked like a cookie. The children initially reported that the eraser looked like a cookie. However, once they learned that it was actually an eraser, they tended to report that it looked like an eraser. Apparently, the children could not mentally represent the eraser as both being an eraser and looking like a cookie.

Three-year-olds also apparently cannot understand changes in their mental states. In one study (Gopnik & Slaughter, 1991), 3-year-olds were shown a crayon box with candles inside. Before it was opened, they consistently said they thought crayons were inside. When asked what they had thought was in the box before it was opened, the children now said "candles."

Development of Memory: Creating Documents, Storing Them, Retrieving Them

Children, like adults, often remember what they want to remember (Ghetti & Alexander, 2004; Sales et al., 2003). Paying attention to a stimulus or a situation is a general requirement for remembering it. Preschoolers tend to pay attention to stimuli that are salient—that is, stimuli that stand out from the background. Toddlers tend to shift their attention from one thing to another, but preschoolers may watch television or a DVD for a half hour or more. At the age of 3, one of my daughters almost drove a babysitter out of the house by insisting on watching *Grease* over and over again. (And over again.)

By the age of 4, children can remember events that occurred at least 1½ years earlier (Fivush & Hammond, 1990). Katherine Nelson (1990, 1993) interviewed children aged 2–5 to study their memory for recurring events in their lives, such as having dinner, playing with friends, and going to birthday parties. She found that 3-year-olds can present coherent, orderly accounts of familiar events. Furthermore, young children seem to form **scripts**, which are abstract, generalized accounts of repeated events. For example, in describing what happens during a birthday party, a child might say, "You play games, open presents, and eat cake" (Fivush, 2002). However, an unusual experience, such as a hurricane, may be remembered in detail for years (Fivush, Sales, et al., 2004).

Even though children as young as 1 and 2 years of age can remember events, these memories seldom last into adulthood. This memory of specific events—known as **autobiographical memory** or *episodic memory*—is facilitated when children talk about the events with others (K. Nelson & Fivush, 2004).

Factors Influencing Memory

Factors that affect memory include what the child is asked to remember, how interested the child is, whether retrieval cues or reminders are available, and what memory measure we are using. First, children find it easier to remember events that follow a fixed and logical order than events that do not. For instance, 3- and 5-year-olds have a better memory for the activities involved in making pretend cookies out of Play-Doh (you put the ingredients in the bowl, then mix the ingredients, then roll out the dough, and so on) than they do for the activities involved in sand play, which can occur in any order (Fivush et al., 1992).

script An abstract, generalized account of a familiar, repeated event.

autobiographical memory The memory of specific episodes or events.

CARLOS BARRIA/Reuters /Landov

Childhood Memory. Despite his youth, this boy will most likely remember this traumatic experience in detail for years to come.

Brad Wrobleski / Masterfile

Memory functioning in ealy childhood—and at other ages—is aided when adults provide cues to help children remember. Adults can help by elaborating on the child's experiences and asking questions that encourage the child to contribute information.

Research consistently shows that (most) preschool boys are more interested in playing with toys such as cars and weapons, whereas (most) preschool girls are more interested in playing with dolls, dishes, and teddy bears. Later, the children typically show better recognition and recall for the toys in which they were interested (C. L. Martin & Ruble, 2004).

Although young children can remember a great deal, they depend more than older children do on cues provided by others to help them retrieve their memories. Elaborating on the child's experiences and asking questions that encourage the child to contribute information to the narrative generally help a child remember an episode (K. Nelson & Fivush, 2004).

Children's memory can often be measured or assessed by asking them to say what they remember. But verbal reports, especially from preschoolers, appear to underestimate children's memory (Mandler, 1990). In one longitudinal study, children's memory for certain events was tested at age 2½ and again at age 4. Most of the information recalled at age 4 had not been mentioned at age 2½, indicating that when they were younger, the children remembered more than they reported (Fivush & Hammond, 1990). One study found that when young children were allowed to use dolls to reenact an event, their recall was better than when they gave a verbal report (G. S. Goodman et al., 1990).

Rehearsal Strategies

Watch and learn how children develop strategies to retain information.

▶ **LO15** Describe language development in early childhood.

Memory Strategies: Remembering to Remember

Adults and older children use strategies to help them remember things. One strategy is mental repetition, or **rehearsal**. If you are trying to remember a new friend's phone number, for example, you might repeat it several times. Another strategy is to organize things to be remembered into categories. Most preschoolers do not engage in spontaneous rehearsal until about 5 years of age (Labrell & Ubersfeld, 2004). They also rarely group objects into related categories to help them remember. By about age 5, many children have learned to verbalize information silently to themselves by counting mentally, for example, rather than aloud.

Having preschoolers sort objects into categories enhances memory (Howe, 2006; Lange & Pierce, 1992). Even 3- and 4-year-olds will use rehearsal and labeling if they are asked to try to remember something.

Language Development: Why "Daddy Goed Away"

Children's language skills mushroom during the preschool years. By the fourth year, children are asking adults and each other questions, taking turns talking, and having lengthy conversations.

Development of Vocabulary

Vocabulary development proceeds rapidly. Word learning can be characterized as a **fast-mapping** process, in which the child quickly attaches a new word to its appropriate concept (Homer & Nelson, 2005; Waxman & Lidz, 2006). Preschoolers learn an average of nine new words per day (Tamis-LeMonda et al., 2006). But how can that be possible when each new word has so many potential meanings?

Consider the following example: A toddler observes a small, black dog running through the park. His older sister points to the animal and says, "Doggy." The word *doggy* could mean this particular dog, or all dogs, or all animals. It could refer to one part of the dog (e.g., its tail) or to its behavior

rehearsal Repetition.

fast mapping A process of quickly determining a word's meaning, which facilitates children's vocabulary development.

whole-object assumption The assumption that words refer to whole objects and not to their component parts or characteristics.

contrast assumption The assumption that objects have only one label.

overregularization The application of regular grammatical rules for forming inflections to irregular verbs and nouns.

Vocabulary Development. When this adult points to the goat and says "goat," the child assumes that "goat" refers to the whole animal, rather than to its horns, fur, size, or color. This bias, known as the whole-object assumption, helps children acquire a large vocabulary in a relatively short period of time.

(running, barking) or to its characteristics (small, black) (Waxman & Lidz, 2006). Does the child consider all these possibilities? Children assume that words refer to whole objects and not to their component parts or their characteristics, such as color, size, or texture (P. Bloom, 2002). This bias is called the **whole-object assumption**. Therefore, the young child assumes that the word *doggy* refers to the dog rather than to its tail, its color, or its barking.

Children also seem to assume that objects have only one label. Therefore, novel terms must refer to unfamiliar objects and not to familiar objects that already have labels. This concept is the **contrast assumption**, which is also known as the *mutual exclusivity assumption* (P. Bloom, 2002; Waxman & Lidz, 2006). Suppose that a child is shown two objects, one of which has a known label ("doggy") and one of which is unknown. Let's further suppose that an adult now says, "Look at the lemur." If the child assumes that "doggy" and "lemur" each can refer to only one object, the child would correctly figure out that "lemur" refers to the other object and is not just another name for "doggy" (Homer & Nelson, 2005; Waxman & Lidz, 2006).

Development of Grammar

There is a "grammar explosion" during the third year (Tamis-LeMonda et al., 2006) (Table 4.1). Children's sentence structure expands to include words missing in telegraphic speech. Children usually add to their vocabulary an impressive array of articles (*a*, *an*, *the*), conjunctions (*and*, *but*, *or*), possessive adjectives (*your*, *her*), pronouns (*she*, *him*, *one*), and prepositions (*in*, *on*, *over*, *around*, *under*, *through*). Usually between the ages of 3 and 4, children show knowledge of rules for combining clauses into complex sentences, as in "You goed and Mommy goed, too."

Overregularization

The apparent basis of one of the more intriguing language developments—**overregularization**—is that children acquire grammatical rules as they learn language. At young ages they tend to apply these rules rather strictly, even in cases that call for exceptions (Jacobson & Schwartz, 2005; Stemberger, 2004). Consider the formation of the past tense and plurals in English. We add *-d* or *-ed* to regular verbs and *-s* to regular nouns. Thus, *walk* becomes *walked* and *doggy* becomes *doggies*. But then there are irregular verbs and irregular nouns. For example, *sit* becomes *sat* and *go* becomes *went*. *Sheep* remains *sheep* (plural) and *child* becomes *children*.

Children and Vocabulary

Watch and learn how children develop language and vocabulary skills.

Table 4.1
Development of Language Skills in Early Childhood

Age	Developments	Typical Sentences
2½ years	There is rapid increase in vocabulary, with new additions each day. There is no babbling. Intelligibility is still not very good. Child uses 2–3 words in sentences. Child uses plurals. Child uses possessives. Child uses past tense. Child uses some prepositions.	Two cups. Sarah's car. It broke. Keisha in bed
3 years	Child has vocabulary of some 1,000 words. Speech nears 100% intelligibility. Articulation of *l* and *r* is frequently faulty. Child uses 3–4 words in sentences. Child uses yes–no questions. Child uses *wh* questions. Child uses negatives. Child embeds one sentence within another.	Will I go? Where is the doggy? I not eat yucky peas. That's the book Mommy buyed me.
4 years	Child has vocabulary of 1,500–1,600 words. Speech is fluent. Articulation is good except for *sh, z, ch,* and *j* sounds. Child uses 5–6 words in sentences. Child coordinates two sentences.	I went to Allie's and I had cookies.

As children become aware of the syntactic rules for forming the past tense and plurals in English, they often misapply them to irregular words. As a result, they tend to make charming errors (Stemberger, 2004). Some 3- to 5-year-olds are more likely to say "Mommy sitted down" than "Mommy sat down" or talk about the "sheeps" they "seed" on the farm and about all the "childs" they ran into at the playground.

Some parents recognize that their children were at first forming the past tense of irregular verbs correctly but then began to make errors. Some of these parents become concerned that their children are "slipping" in their language development and attempt to correct them. However, overregularization reflects accurate knowl-

pragmatics The practical aspects of communication, such as adaptation of language to fit the social situation.

edge of grammar, not faulty language development. In another year or two, *mouses* will be boringly transformed into *mice* and Mommy will no longer have sitted down. Parents might as well enjoy overregularization while they can.

Asking Questions

Children's first questions are telegraphic and characterized by a rising pitch (which signifies a question mark in English) at the end. Depending on the context, "More milky?" can be translated into "May I have more milk?," "Would you like more milk?," or "Is there more milk?" It is usually toward the latter part of the third year that the *wh* questions appear. Consistent with the child's general cognitive development, certain *wh* questions (*what*, *who*, and *where*) appear earlier than others (*why*, *when*, *which*, and *how*) (Tamis-LeMonda et al., 2006). *Why* is usually too philosophical for a 2-year-old, and *how* is too involved. Two-year-olds are also likely to be now-oriented, so *when* is of less than immediate concern. By the fourth year, most children are spontaneously producing *why*, *when*, and *how* questions. These *wh* words are initially tacked on to the beginnings of sentences. "Where Mommy go?" can stand for "Where is Mommy going?," "Where did Mommy go?," or "Where will Mommy go?," and its meaning must be derived from context. Later on, the child will add the auxiliary verbs *is*, *did*, and *will* to indicate whether the question concerns the present, past, or future.

Passive Sentences

Passive sentences, such as "The food is eaten by the dog," are difficult for 2- and 3-year-olds to understand, and so young preschoolers almost never produce them. In a study of children's comprehension (Strohner & Nelson, 1974), 2- to 5-year-olds used puppets and toys to act out sentences that were read to them. Two- and 3-year-olds made errors in acting out passive sentences (e.g., "The car was hit by the truck") 70% of the time. Older children had less difficulty interpreting the meanings of passive sentences correctly. However, most children usually do not produce passive sentences spontaneously even at the ages of 5 and 6.

Pragmatics

Pragmatics refers to the practical aspects of communication. Children show pragmatism when they adjust their speech to fit the social situation (K. Nelson, 2006). For example, children show greater formality in their choice of words and syntax when they are role-playing high-status figures, such as teachers or physicians, in their games. They say *please* more often when making requests of high-status people, or when they use motherese in talking to an infant.

Preschoolers tend to be egocentric; therefore, a 2-year-old telling another child "Gimme my book," without specifying which book, may assume that the other child knows what she herself knows. Once children can perceive the world through the eyes of others, they advance in their abilities to make themselves understood. Now the child recognizes that the other child will require a description of the book or of its location to carry out the request.

Language and Cognition

Language and cognitive development are interwoven (Homer & Nelson, 2005; Waxman & Lidz, 2006). For example, the child gradually gains the capacity to discriminate between animals on the basis of distinct features, such as their size, their patterns of movement, and the sounds they make. At the same time, the child also is acquiring words that represent broader categories, such as *mammal* and *animal*.

But which comes first? Does the child first develop concepts and then acquire the language to describe them, or does the child's increasing language ability lead to the development of new concepts?

Does Cognitive Development Precede Language Development?

Piaget (1976) believed that cognitive development precedes language development. He argued that children must understand concepts before they use words to describe them. From Piaget's perspective, children learn words to describe classes or categories that they have already created (K. Nelson, 2005). Children can learn the word *kitty* because they have perceived the characteristics that distinguish cats from other things.

inner speech Vygotsky's concept of the ultimate binding of language and thought; originates in vocalizations that may regulate the child's behavior and become internalized by age 6 or 7.

Some studies have supported the notion that cognitive concepts may precede language. For example, the vocabulary explosion that occurs at about 18 months of age is related to the child's ability to group a set of objects into two categories, such as "dolls" and "cars" (Gopnik & Meltzoff, 1992). Other research suggests that young children need to experience an action themselves or by observation to learn the meaning of a verb (Pulverman et al., 2006).

Does Language Development Precede Cognitive Development?

Although many theorists argue that cognitive development precedes language development, others have reversed the causal relationship and claimed that children create cognitive classes to understand things that are labeled by words (Clark, 1973). When children hear the word *dog*, they try to understand it by searching for characteristics that separate dogs from other things.

The Interactionist View: Outer Speech and Inner Speech

Today, most developmentalists find something of value in each of these cognitive views (Waxman & Lidz, 2006). In the early stages of language development, concepts often precede words, and many of the infant's words describe classes that have already developed. But later language influences thought.

Vygotsky believed that during most of the first year, vocalizations and thought are separate. But during the second year, thought and speech combine forces. Children discover that objects have labels. Learning labels becomes more self-directed. Children ask what new words mean. Learning new words fosters creation of new categories, and new categories become filled with labels for new things.

Vygotsky's concept of **inner speech** is a key feature of his position. At first children's thoughts are spoken aloud. You can hear the 3-year-old instructing herself as she plays with toys. At this age, her vocalizations serve to regulate her behavior, but they gradually become internalized. What was spoken aloud at 4 and 5 becomes an internal dialogue by 6 or 7. Inner speech is the ultimate binding of language and thought. It is involved in the development of planning and self-regulation, and facilitates learning.

Check Your Learning Quiz 4.2

Go to **login.cengagebrain.com** and take the online quiz.

Did you know that—

• Parents who are restrictive and demand mature behavior wind up with more competent and achieving children?

• Firstborn children are more highly motivated to achieve than later-born children?

• Children who are physically punished are more likely to be aggressive than children who are not?

• Children who watch 2–4 hours of TV a day will see 8,000 murders and another 100,000 acts of violence by the time they have finished elementary school?

• Children do not necessarily imitate the aggressive behavior they view in the media?

• Preschoolers are most likely to fear animals and the dark than social disapproval?

▼

Jeremy and Jessica are both 2½ years old. They are standing at the water table in the preschool classroom. Jessica is filling a plastic container with water and spilling it out. She watches the water splash down the drain. Jeremy watches and then goes to get another container. He, too, fills his container with water and spills it out. The children stand side by side. They empty and refill their plastic pails; they glance at each other and exchange a few words. They continue playing like this for several minutes, until Jessica drops her pail and runs off to ride the tricycle. Soon after, Jeremy also loses interest and finds something else to do.

Meanwhile, 4½-year-olds Melissa and Mike are building in the block corner, making a huge rambling structure that they have decided is a spaceship. They talk animatedly as they work, negotiating who should be captain of the ship and who should be the alien from outer space. Mike and Melissa take turns adding blocks. They continue to build, working together and talking as they play.

In these children we see some of the changes that occur in social development during early childhood. When toddlers play "together," they may spend time watching and imitating each other, but they do not interact very much. Older preschoolers are more likely to take turns, work cooperatively toward a goal, and share. They often engage in fantasy that involves adopting adult roles.

This module is about social and emotional development in early childhood. We consider the roles played by parents, siblings, and peers. We examine child's play, helping and sharing, and aggression. Then we look at personality and emotional development.

Dimensions of Child Rearing

Preschoolers usually spend most of their time with the family. Most parents want preschoolers to develop a sense of responsibility and develop into well-adjusted individuals. They want them to acquire social skills. How do parents try to achieve these goals? What role do siblings play? How do children's peers influence social and emotional development?

Parents have different approaches to rearing their children. Investigators of parental patterns of child rearing have found it useful to classify them according to two broad dimensions: warmth–coldness and restrictiveness–permissiveness (Baumrind, 1989, 2005).

Warm parents are affectionate toward their children. They tend to hug and kiss them and smile at them frequently. Warm parents are caring and supportive. They communicate their enjoyment in being with their children. Warm parents are less likely than cold parents to use physical discipline (Bender et al., 2007).

Cold parents may not enjoy their children and may have few feelings of affection for them. They are likely to complain excessively about their children's behavior, saying they are naughty or have "minds of their own."

It requires no stretch of the imagination to conclude that it is better to be warm than cold toward children. The children of parents who are warm and accepting are more likely to develop internal standards of conduct—a moral sense or conscience (Bender et al., 2007; A. S. Lau et al., 2006). Parental warmth also is related to the child's social and emotional well-being (A. S. Lau et al., 2006; Leung et al., 2004).

Where does parental warmth come from? Some of it reflects parental beliefs about how to best rear children, and some reflects parents' tendencies to imitate the behavior of their own parents. But research by Hetherington and her colleagues (Feinberg, Neiderhiser, et al., 2001) suggests that genetic factors may be involved as well.

Parents decide how restrictive they will be. How will they respond when children make excessive noise, play with dangerous objects, damage property, mess up their rooms, hurt others, or masturbate? Parents who are restrictive tend to impose rules and watch their children closely.

Parents who are strict and demand mature behavior do not invariably wind up with rebellious children. Consistent control and firm enforcement of rules can have positive consequences for the child, particularly when combined with strong support and affection (Grusec, 2006). This parenting style is termed the *authoritative style*. On the other hand, if restrictiveness means physical punishment, interference, or intrusiveness, it can give rise to disobedience, rebelliousness, and lower levels of cognitive development (Paulussen-Hoogeboom et al., 2007; Rudy & Grusec, 2006).

Permissive parents supervise their children less closely than restrictive parents do. Permissive parents allow their children to do what is "natural," such as make noise, treat toys carelessly, and experiment with their bodies. They may also allow their children to show some aggression, intervening only when another child is in danger.

How Parents Enforce Restrictions

Regardless of their general approaches to child rearing, most parents are restrictive now and then, even if only when they are teaching their children not to run into the street or to touch a hot stove. Parents tend to use the methods of induction, power assertion, and withdrawal of love.

Inductive methods aim to teach knowledge that will enable children to generate desirable behavior on their own. The main inductive technique is reasoning, or explaining why one kind of behavior is good and another is not. Reasoning with a 1- or 2-year-old can be basic. "Don't do that—it hurts!" qualifies as reasoning with toddlers. "It hurts!" is an explanation, though brief. The inductive approach helps the child understand moral behavior and fosters prosocial behavior such as helping and sharing (Paulussen-Hoogeboom et al., 2007).

Power-assertive methods include physical punishment and denial of privileges. Parents often justify physical punishment with sayings such as "Spare the rod, spoil the child." Parents may insist that power assertion is necessary because their children are noncompliant. However, use of power assertion is related to parental authoritarianism as well as children's behavior (Roopnarine et al., 2006; Rudy & Grusec, 2006). Parental power assertion is associated with lower acceptance by peers, poorer grades, and more antisocial behavior in children. The more parents use power-assertive techniques, the less children appear to develop internal standards of conduct. Parental punishment and rejection are often linked with aggression and delinquency.

Some parents control children by threatening withdrawal of love. They isolate or ignore misbehaving children. Because most children need parental approval and

inductive Characteristic of disciplinary methods, such as reasoning, that attempt to foster understanding of the principles behind parental demands.

authoritative A child-rearing style in which parents are restrictive and demanding yet communicative and warm.

authoritarian A child-rearing style in which parents demand submission and obedience.

contact, loss of love can be more threatening than physical punishment. Withdrawal of love may foster compliance but also instill guilt and anxiety (Grusec, 2002).

Preschoolers more readily comply when asked to do something than when asked to *stop* doing something (Kochanska et al., 2001). One way to manage children who are doing something wrong or bad is to involve them in something else.

Parenting Styles: How Parents Transmit Values and Standards

Diana Baumrind (1989, 1991b) focused on the relationship between parenting styles and the development of competent behavior in young children. She used the dimensions of warmth–coldness and restrictiveness–permissiveness to develop a grid of four parenting styles based on whether parents are high or low in each dimension (see Table 4.2).

Inductive Reasoning. Inductive methods for enforcing restrictions attempt to teach children the principles they should use in guiding their own behavior. This mother is using the inductive technique of reasoning.

The parents of the most capable children are rated high in both dimensions (see Table 4.2). They are highly restrictive and make strong demands for maturity. However, they also reason with their children and show strong support and feelings of love. Baumrind applied the label **authoritative** to these parents; they know what they want their children to do but also respect their children and are warm toward them. Compared with other children, the children of authoritative parents tend to show self-reliance and independence, high self-esteem, high levels of activity and exploratory behavior, and social competence. They are highly motivated to achieve and do well in school (Baumrind, 1989, 1991b; Grusec, 2006).

"Because I say so" could be the motto of parents that Baumrind labeled **authoritarian**. Authoritarians value obedience for its own sake. They have strict guidelines for right and wrong and demand that their children accept them. Like authoritative parents, they are controlling. But unlike authoritative parents, their enforcement methods rely on force. Moreover, authoritarian parents do not communicate well

Parenting

Explore to learn more about the Baumrind's four parenting styles.

Table 4.2
Baumrind's Patterns of Parenting

	Parental Behavior Patterns	
Parental Style	**Restrictiveness and Control**	**Warmth and Responsiveness**
Authoritative	High	High
Authoritarian	High	Low
Permissive–Indulgent	Low	High
Rejecting–Neglecting	Low	Low

with their children or respect their children's viewpoints. Most researchers find them to be generally cold and rejecting (Grusec, 2002). |

Baumrind found the sons of authoritarian parents to be relatively hostile and defiant and the daughters to be low in independence and dominance (Baumrind, 1989). Other researchers have found that the children of authoritarian parents are less competent socially and academically than those of authoritative parents. They are anxious, irritable, and restrained in their social interactions (Grusec, 2002). As adolescents, they may be conforming and obedient yet have low self-reliance and self-esteem.

Baumrind found two types of parents who are permissive as opposed to restrictive. One is permissive–indulgent and the other rejecting–neglecting.|**Permissive-indulgent** parents are low in their attempts to control their children and in their demands for mature behavior. They are easygoing and unconventional. Their brand of permissiveness is accompanied by high nurturance (warmth and support).

Rejecting–neglecting parents are also low in their demands for mature behavior and attempts to control their children. Unlike indulgent parents, they are low in support and responsiveness.|The children of rejecting–neglecting parents are the least competent, responsible, and mature. The children of permissive–indulgent parents, like those of rejecting–neglecting parents, are less competent in school and show more misconduct and substance abuse than children of more restrictive, controlling parents. But children from permissive–indulgent homes, unlike those from rejecting–neglecting homes, are fairly high in social competence and self-confidence (Baumrind, 1991a).

permissive–indulgent A child-rearing style in which parents are warm and not restrictive.

rejecting–neglecting A child-rearing style in which parents are neither restrictive and controlling nor supportive and responsive.

Advice for parents to control and guide young children's behavior includes:

Do...
- Reward good behavior with praise, smiles, and hugs.
- Give clear, simple, realistic rules appropriate to the child's age.
- Enforce rules with reasonable consequences.
- Ignore annoying behavior such as whining and tantrums.
- Childproof the house, putting dangerous and breakable items out of reach. Then establish limits.
- Be consistent.

Don't...
- Pay attention only to a child's misbehavior.
- Issue too many rules or enforce them haphazardly.
- Try to control behavior solely in the child's domain, such as thumb sucking, which can lead to frustrating power struggles.
- Nag, lecture, shame, or induce guilt.
- Yell or spank.
- Be overly permissive.

Effects of the Situation and the Child on Parenting Styles

Parenting styles are not a one-way street, from parent to child. They also depend partly on the situation and partly on the characteristics of the child (Grusec, 2006). For example, parents are most likely to use power-assertive techniques when dealing with aggressive behavior (Casas et al., 2006; Lipman et al., 2006). Parents prefer power assertion to induction when they believe that children understand the rules they have violated and are capable of acting appropriately. Stress also contributes to use of power.

Baumrind's research suggests that we can make an effort to avoid some of the pitfalls of being authoritarian or overly permissive.

Permissive Parents. Some parents are considered permissive and demand little of their children in terms of mature behavior or control. Permissive–indulgent parents still provide plenty of warmth and support for their children, whereas rejecting–neglecting parents tend to neglect or ignore their children.

Joel Gordon Photography

Missing Fathers

Where are the missing American Fathers?

Child Rearing

Read about culture and child-rearing patterns.

Parenting Styles

Watch and learn how three mothers describe their parenting styles.

Social Behaviors: In the World, Among Others

During early childhood, children advance in social skills and behavior. Their play increasingly involves other children. They learn how to share, cooperate, and comfort others. But young children, like adults, can be aggressive as well as loving and helpful.

Influence of Siblings

Siblings serve many functions, including giving physical care, providing emotional support and nurturance, offering advice, serving as role models, providing social interaction that helps develop social skills, making demands, and imposing restrictions (McHale et al., 2006; Parke & Buriel, 2006).

In early childhood, siblings' interactions have positive aspects (cooperation, teaching, nurturance) and negative aspects (conflict, control, competition) (Parke & Buriel, 2006). Older siblings tend to be more caring but also more dominating than younger siblings. Younger siblings are more likely to imitate older siblings and accept their direction. In many cultures, older girls care for younger siblings (J. Clark, 2005).

Parents often urge their children to stop fighting among themselves, but garden-variety conflict between siblings can enhance their social competence, their development of self-identity (who they are and what they stand for), and their ability to rear their own children (H. Ross et al., 2006).

Tony Freeman/PhotoEdit, Inc.

regression A return to behavior characteristic of earlier stages of development.

Siblings make a unique contribution to one another's social, emotional, and cognitive development. In many cultures, older girls are expected to care for younger siblings.

There is more conflict between siblings when the parents play favorites (Scharf et al., 2005). Conflict between siblings is also greater when the relationships between the parents or between the parents and children are troubled (J.-Y. Kim et al., 2006).

Adjusting to the Birth of a Sibling

The birth of a sister or brother is often a source of stress for preschoolers because of changes in family relationships (Volling, 2003). When a new baby comes into the home, the mother pays relatively more attention to that child and spends less time with the older child. The older child may feel displaced and resentful.

Children show a mixture of negative and positive reactions to the birth of a sibling. These include **regression** to babylike behaviors, such as increased clinging, crying, and toilet accidents. Anger and naughtiness may increase. But the same children may also show increased independence and maturity, insisting on feeding or dressing themselves and helping to care for the baby (Volling, 2003). Parents can help a young child cope with the arrival of a baby by explaining in advance what is to come (Kavcic & Zupancic, 2005).

Birth Order

Differences in personality and achievement have been linked to birth order. Firstborn children, as a group, are more highly motivated to achieve than later-born children (Latham & Budworth, 2007). Firstborn and only children perform better academically and are more cooperative (Healy & Ellis, 2007). They are more adult-oriented and less aggressive than later-born children (E. Beck et al., 2006; Zajonc, 2001a). They obtain higher standardized test scores, including IQ and SAT scores (Kristensen & Bjerkedal, 2007; Sulloway, 2007). On the negative side, firstborn and only children show greater anxiety and are less self-reliant than later-born children.

The birth of a sister or brother is often a source of stress in early childhood because of changes in family relationships.

Alloy Photography/Jupiterimages

Later-born children may learn to act aggressively to compete for the attention of their parents and older siblings (Carey, 2007). Their self-concepts tend to be lower than those of firstborn or only children, but the social skills later-born children acquire from dealing with their family position seem to translate into greater popularity with peers (Carey, 2007). They also tend to be more rebellious and liberal than firstborn children (E. Beck et al., 2006; Zweigenhaft & Von Ammon, 2000).

By and large, parents are more relaxed and flexible with later-born children. Many parents see that the firstborn child is turning out well and perhaps assume that later-born children will also turn out well.

Peer Relationships

Peer interactions foster social skills—sharing, helping, taking turns, and dealing with conflict. Groups teach children how to lead and how to follow. Physical and cognitive skills develop through peer interactions. Peers also provide emotional support (Dishion & Stormshak, 2007; Grusec, 2006).

By about 2 years of age, children imitate one another's play and engage in social games such as follow-the-leader (Fontaine, 2005; Kavanaugh, 2006). By the age of 2,

Friendship takes on different meanings as children develop. Preschoolers focus on sharing toys and activities. Five- to 7-year-olds report that friends are children with whom they have fun. Sharing confidences becomes important in late childhood and adolescence.

dramatic play Play in which children enact social roles.

children show preferences for particular playmates—an early sign of friendship (Sherwin-White, 2006). Friendship is characterized by shared positive experiences and feelings of attachment (Grusec, 2002). Even early friendships can be fairly stable (Rubin et al., 2006).

When preschoolers are asked what they like about their friends, they typically mention the toys and activities they share (T. R. Gleason & Hohmann, 2006). Primary schoolchildren usually report that their friends are the children with whom they do things and have fun (T. R. Gleason & Hohmann, 2006). Not until late childhood and adolescence do friends' traits and notions of trust, communication, and intimacy become important.

Play—Child's Play, That Is

Play is more than fun; it is also meaningful, voluntary, and internally motivated (Elkind, 2007). Play helps children develop motor skills and coordination. It contributes to social development because children learn to share play materials, take turns, and, through **dramatic play**, try on new roles (Elkind, 2007). It supports the development of such cognitive qualities as curiosity, exploration, symbolic thinking, and problem solving. Play may even help children learn to control impulses (Elkind, 2007).

Play and Cognitive Development

Play contributes to and expresses milestones in cognitive development. Jean Piaget (1946/1962) identified kinds of play, each characterized by increasing cognitive complexity:

- *Functional play.* Beginning in the sensorimotor stage, the first kind of play involves repetitive motor activity, such as rolling a ball or running and laughing.
- *Symbolic play.* Also called *pretend play*, *imaginative play*, or *dramatic play*, symbolic play emerges toward the end of the sensorimotor stage and increases during early childhood. In symbolic play, children create settings, characters, and scripts (Kavanaugh, 2006).
- *Constructive play.* Children use objects or materials to draw something or make something, such as a tower of blocks.
- *Formal games.* Games with rules include board games—which are sometimes enhanced or invented by children—and games involving motor skills, such as marbles and hopscotch, ball games involving sides or teams, and video

games. Such games may involve social interaction as well as physical activity and rules. People play such games for a lifetime.

Simple repetition and pretend play develop into play with games that have rules.

Parten's Types of Play

In classic research on children's play, Mildred Parten (1932) observed the development of six types of play among 2- to 5-year-old nursery schoolchildren: unoccupied play, solitary play, onlooker play, parallel play, associative play, and cooperative play (see Table 4.3). Solitary play and onlooker play are considered **nonsocial play**, that is, play in which children do not interact socially. Nonsocial play occurs more often in 2- and 3-year-olds than in older preschoolers. Parallel play, associative play, and cooperative play are considered **social play**. In each case, children are influenced by other children as they play. Parten found that associative play and cooperative play become common by age 5. They are more likely to be found among older and more experienced preschoolers (Dyer & Moneta, 2006). Girls are somewhat more likely than boys to engage in social play (Zheng & Colombo, 1989).

But there are exceptions. Nonsocial play can involve educational activities that foster cognitive development. In fact, many 4- and 5-year-olds spend a good deal of time in parallel constructive play. For instance, they may work on puzzles or build with blocks near other children. Parallel constructive players are frequently perceived by teachers to be socially skillful and are popular with their peers (Coplan et al., 1994). Two-year-olds with older siblings or with group experience may engage in advanced social play.

Prosocial Behavior

Prosocial behavior, also known as *altruism*, is intended to benefit another without expectation of reward. Prosocial behavior includes sharing, cooperating, and helping and comforting others in distress (J. Strayer & Roberts, 2004). It is shown by the preschool and early school years (Knafo & Plomin, 2006a, 2006b) and is linked to the development of empathy and perspective taking.

Empathy

Empathy is sensitivity to the feelings of others and is connected with sharing and cooperation. Infants frequently begin to cry when they hear other children crying, although this early agitated response may be largely reflexive (J. Strayer & Roberts, 2004). Empathy promotes prosocial behavior and decreases aggressive behavior, and

nonsocial play Forms of play in which children do not interact with other children.

social play Play in which children interact with and are influenced by others.

prosocial behavior Behavior that benefits other people, generally without expectation of reward.

Table 4.3
Parten's Types of Play

Category	Nonsocial or Social?	Description
Unoccupied play	Nonsocial	Children do not appear to be playing. They may engage in random movements that seem to be without a goal. Unoccupied play appears to be the least frequent kind of play in nursery schools.
Solitary play	Nonsocial	Children play with toys by themselves, independently of the children around them. Solitary players do not appear to be influenced by children around them. They make no effort to approach them.
Onlooker play	Nonsocial	Children observe other children who are at play. Onlookers frequently talk to the children they are observing and may make suggestions, but they do not overtly join in.
Parallel play	Social	Children play with toys similar to those of surrounding children. However, they treat the toys as they choose and do not directly interact with other children.
Associative play	Social	Children interact and share toys. However, they do not seem to share group goals. Although they interact, individuals still treat toys as they choose. The association with the other children appears to be more important than the nature of the activity. They seem to enjoy each other's company.
Cooperative play	Social	Children interact to achieve common, group goals. The play of each child is subordinated to the purposes of the group. One or two group members direct the activities of others. There is also a division of labor, with different children taking different roles. Children may pretend to be members of a family, animals, space monsters, and all sorts of creatures.

Types of Play

Watch to learn more about play types for different developmental stages.

Taught to Hate

Are children taught prejudices?

these links are evident by the second year (Hastings et al., 2000). During the second year, many children approach other children and adults who are in distress and try to help them. They may hug a crying child or tell the child not to cry. Toddlers who are rated as emotionally unresponsive to the feelings of others are more likely to behave aggressively throughout the school years (Olson, Bates, et al., 2000).

Associative play is a form of social play in which children interact and share toys.

Michael Newman/PhotoEdit Inc.

Perspective Taking

According to Piaget, preoperational children tend to be egocentric. They tend not to be able to see things from the vantage points of others. It turns out that various cognitive abilities, such as being able to take another person's perspective, are related to knowing when someone is in need or distress. Perspective-taking skills improve with age, and so do prosocial skills. Among children of the same age, those with better-developed perspective-taking ability also show more prosocial behavior and less aggressive behavior (Hastings et al., 2000).

Influences on Prosocial Behavior

Although prosocial behavior can occur in the absence of rewards or the expectations of rewards, it is influenced by rewards and punishments. The peers of nursery school-children who are cooperative, friendly, and generous respond more positively to them than they do to children whose behavior is self-centered (Hartup, 1983). Children who are rewarded for acting prosocially are likely to continue these behaviors (Knafo & Plomin, 2006a, 2006b).

Parents foster prosocial behavior when they use inductive techniques such as explaining how behavior affects others ("You made Josh cry. It's not nice to hit."). Parents of prosocial children are more likely to expect mature behavior from their children. They are less likely to use power-assertive techniques of discipline (J. Strayer & Roberts, 2004).

Development of Aggression

Children, like adults, can be not only loving and altruistic, but also aggressive. Some children, of course, are more aggressive than others. Aggression refers to behavior intended to hurt or injure another person.

Aggressive behavior, as other social behavior, seems to follow developmental patterns. The aggression of preschoolers is frequently instrumental or possession oriented (Persson, 2005). Younger preschoolers tend to use aggression to obtain the toys and situations they want, such as a favored seat at the table or in the car. Older preschoolers are more likely to resolve conflicts over toys by sharing rather than fighting (M. Caplan et al., 1991). Anger and aggression in preschoolers usually cause other preschoolers to reject them (D. Henry et al., 2000; Walter & LaFreniere, 2000).

By age 6 or 7, aggression becomes hostile and person-oriented. Children taunt and criticize one another and call one another names; they also attack one another physically.

Aggressive behavior appears to be generally stable and predictive of social and emotional problems later on, especially among boys (Nagin & Tremblay, 2001; Tapper & Boulton, 2004). Toddlers who are perceived as difficult and defiant are more likely to behave aggressively throughout the school years (Olson, Bates, et al., 2000). A longitudinal study of more than 600 children found that aggressive 8-year-olds tended to remain more aggressive than their peers 22 years later, at age 30 (Eron et al., 1991). Aggressive children of both sexes are more likely to have criminal convictions as adults, to abuse their spouses, and to drive while drunk.

Theories of Aggression

What causes some children to be more aggressive than others? Aggression in childhood appears to result from a complex interplay of biological factors and environmental factors such as reinforcement and modeling.

Evidence suggests that genetic factors may be involved in aggressive behavior, including criminal and antisocial behavior (Hicks et al., 2007; Lykken, 2006a; E. O. Wilson, 2004). There is a greater agreement rate for criminal behavior between monozygotic (MZ) twins, who fully share their genetic code, than dizygotic (DZ) twins, who, like other brothers and sisters, share only half of their genetic code (Tehrani & Mednick, 2000). If genetics is involved in aggression, genes may do some of their work through the male sex hormone testosterone. Testosterone is apparently connected with self-confidence, high activity levels, and—the negative side—aggressiveness (J. Archer, 2006; Cunningham & McGinnis, 2007; Popma et al., 2007).

Cognitive research with primary schoolchildren finds that children who believe in the legitimacy of aggression are more likely to behave aggressively when they are presented with social provocations (Tapper & Boulton, 2004). Aggressive children are also often found to be lacking in empathy and the ability to see things from the perspective of other people (Hastings et al., 2000). They fail to conceptualize the experiences of their victims and are thus less likely to inhibit aggressive impulses.

Social cognitive explanations of aggression focus on environmental factors such as reinforcement and observational learning. When children repeatedly push, shove, and hit to grab toys or break into line, other children usually let them have their way (Kempes et al., 2005). Children who are thus rewarded for acting aggressively are likely to continue to use aggressive means, especially if they do not have alternative means to achieve their ends. Aggressive children may also associate with peers who value and encourage aggression (Stauffacher & DeHart; 2006).

Children who are physically punished are more likely to be aggressive themselves than children who are not physically punished (G. R. Patterson, 2005). Physically aggressive parents serve as models for aggression and also stoke their children's anger.

Media Influences

Real people are not the only models of aggressive behavior in children's lives. A classic study by Albert Bandura and his colleagues (Bandura, Ross, et al., 1963) suggested that televised models had a powerful influence on children's aggressive behavior. One group of preschoolers observed a film of an adult model hitting and kicking an inflated Bobo doll, whereas a control group saw an aggression-free film. The experimental and control children were then left alone in a room with the same doll as hidden observers recorded their behavior. The children who had observed the aggressive model showed significantly more aggressive behavior toward the doll themselves (see Figure 4.8). Since this groundbreaking study, Bandura and many other psychologists have run studies that essentially replicate the findings.

Television is a fertile source of aggressive models (Villani, 2001). Children are routinely exposed to TV scenes of murder, beating, and sexual assault. Children who watch 2–4 hours of TV a day will see 8,000 murders and another 100,000 acts of violence by the time they have finished elementary school (Eron, 1993).

Consider a number of ways in which depictions of violence contribute to violence:

disinhibit To encourage a response that has been previously suppressed.

- *Observational learning.* Children learn from observation (J. J. Holland, 2000). TV violence supplies models of aggressive "skills," which children may acquire.

- *Disinhibition.* Punishment inhibits behavior. Conversely, media violence may **disinhibit** aggressive behavior, especially when characters "get away" with it.
- *Increased arousal.* Media violence and aggressive video games increase viewers' level of arousal. We are more likely to be aggressive under high levels of arousal.
- *Priming of aggressive thoughts and memories.* Media violence "primes" or arouses aggressive ideas and memories (Bushman, 1998; Meier et al., 2006).
- *Habituation.* We become used to repeated stimuli. Children exposed to violence are more likely to assume that violence is acceptable or normal and become desensitized to it (Holland, 2000).

Though exposure to violence in the media increases the probability of violence, there is no simple one-to-one connection between media violence and violence in

© Albert Bandura/Dept. of Psychology, Stanford University

Figure 4.8 Photos from Albert Bandura's Classic Experiment in the Imitation of Aggressive Models In the top row, an adult model strikes a clown doll. The second and third rows show a boy and a girl imitating the aggressive behavior.

▶ **LO24** Describe the development of the self in early childhood.

▶ **LO25** Describe the development of childhood fears.

real life. According to social cognitive theory, we also choose whether to imitate the behavior we observe.

Personality and Emotional Development

In early childhood, children's sense of self—who they are and how they feel about themselves—develops and grows more complex. They begin to acquire a sense of their own abilities and their increasing mastery of the environment. As they move out into the world, they also face new experiences that may cause them to feel fearful and anxious.

The Self

The sense of self, or the **self-concept**, emerges gradually during infancy. Infants and toddlers visually begin to recognize themselves and differentiate from other individuals, such as their parents.

In the preschool years, children continue to develop their sense of self. Almost as soon as they begin to speak, they describe themselves in terms of certain categories, such as age groupings (baby, child, adult) and gender (girl, boy). Self-definitions that refer to concrete external traits have been called the **categorical self**.

Children as young as 3 years are able to describe themselves in terms of behaviors and internal states that occur often and are fairly stable over time (Eder, 1989, 1990). For example, in response to the question "How do you feel when you're scared?" young children frequently respond, "Usually like running away" (Eder, 1989). In answer to the question "How do you usually act around grown-ups?" a typical response might be, "I mostly been good with grown-ups."

One aspect of the self-concept is self-esteem. Children with high self-esteem are more likely to be securely attached and have parents who are attentive to their needs (Booth-LaForce et al., 2006; M. M. Patterson & Bigler, 2006). They also are more likely to show prosocial behavior (Salmivalli et al., 2005).

Preschool children begin to make evaluative judgments about two different aspects of themselves by the age of 4 (Harter & Pike, 1984). One is their cognitive and physical competence (e.g., being good at puzzles, counting, swinging, tying shoes), and the second is their social acceptance by peers and parents (e.g., having lots of friends, being read to by Mom). Children also become increasingly capable of self-regulation in early childhood. They become more capable of controlling their eliminatory processes, controlling aggressive behavior, playing with other children, and

self-concept One's self-description and self-evaluation according to various categories, such as child, adolescent, or adult, one's gender, and one's skills.

categorical self Definitions of the self that refer to external traits.

focusing on cognitive tasks such as learning to count and to sound out letters. Self-regulatory abilities are connected with maturation of the brain and the rearing practices of caregivers.

Initiative Versus Guilt

As preschoolers continue to develop a separate sense of themselves, they increasingly move out into the world and take the initiative in learning new skills. Erik Erikson (1963) referred to these early childhood years as the stage of *initiative versus guilt*.

Children in this stage strive to achieve independence from their parents and master adult behaviors. They are curious, try new things, and test themselves. Children learn that not all their plans, dreams, and fantasies can be realized. Adults prohibit children from doing certain things, and children begin to internalize adult rules. Fear of violating the rules may cause the child to feel guilty and may curtail efforts to master new skills. Parents can help children develop and maintain a healthy sense of initiative by encouraging their attempts to learn and explore.

Fears: The Horrors of Early Childhood

Children's fears change as they move from infancy into the preschool years. The number of fears seems to peak between 2½ and 4 years and then tapers off (S. M. Miller et al., 1990). The preschool period is marked by a decline in fears of loud noises, falling, sudden movement, and strangers. In Erikson's view, fear of violating parental prohibitions can be a powerful force in the life of a young child, but preschoolers are most likely to fear animals, imaginary creatures, the dark, and personal danger, not social disapproval (A. P. Field, 2006; Muris et al., 2003). The fantasies of young children frequently involve stories they are told and media imagery. Although fears taper off after the age of 4, many preschoolers are reluctant to have the lights turned off at night for fear that imaginary creatures may assault them. Real objects and situations also cause many preschoolers to fear for their safety—lightning, thunder, other loud noises, high places, sharp objects, blood, unfamiliar people, and stinging and crawling insects.

During middle childhood, children become less fearful of imaginary creatures, but fears of bodily harm and injury remain common. Children grow more fearful of failure and criticism in school and in social relationships (Ollendick & King, 1991).

Check Your Learning Quiz 4.3

Go to **login.cengagebrain.com** and take the online quiz.

▶ **L026** Discuss the development of gender roles.

▶ **L027** Discuss gender differences in play, aggression, and empathy.

Did you know that—

- Preschool boys—but not girls—are rejected by their peers when they show distress?
- Girls and boys both see themselves as being nicer than the other gender?
- Girls choose to play with "boys' toys" such as cars and trucks more often than boys choose to play with dolls and other "girls' toys"?
- Children begin to prefer playmates of their own gender by about the age of 2?
- Girls tend to be more sensitive to the feelings of others than boys are?
- According to evolutionary psychology, evolutionary forces favored the survival of women who desire status in their mates and men who emphasized physical allure, because these preferences provided reproductive advantages?
- One study found that female infants prefer to look at dolls and male infants prefer to look at toy trucks at the early ages of 3–8 months?

▼

I am woman, hear me roar …
I am strong
I am invincible
I am woman

These lyrics are from the song "I Am Woman" by Helen Reddy and Ray Burton. They caught attention because they counter the **stereotype** of the vulnerable woman who needs the protection of a man. The stereotype of the vulnerable woman is a fixed, oversimplified, and conventional idea. So is the stereotype of the chivalrous, protective man. Unfortunately, these stereotypes create demands and limit opportunities for both sexes.

Cultural stereotypes of males and females are broad expectations of behavior that we call **gender roles**. In our culture, the feminine gender-role stereotype includes such traits as dependence, gentleness, helpfulness, warmth, emotionality, submissiveness, and a home orientation. The masculine gender-role stereotype includes aggressiveness, self-confidence, independence, competitiveness, and competence in business, math, and science (C. F. Miller et al., 2006).

stereotype A fixed, conventional idea about a group.

gender role A cluster of traits and behaviors that are considered stereotypical of females or males.

Development of Gender Roles

Gender-role stereotypes develop in stages. First, children learn to label the sexes. At about 2–2½ years of age, they can identify pictures of girls and boys (Fagot & Leinbach, 1993). By age 3, they display knowledge of gender stereotypes for toys, clothing, work, and activities (Campbell et al., 2000). Children of this age generally agree that boys play with cars and trucks, help their fathers, and tend to hit others. They agree that girls play with dolls, help their mothers, and do not hit others (Cherney et al., 2006). One study found that preschool boys but not girls were rejected by their peers when they showed distress, suggesting that boys are expected to be "tougher" (Walter & LaFreniere, 2000).

Children become increasingly traditional in their stereotyping of activities, jobs, and personality traits between the ages of 3 and 9 or 10 (C. F. Miller et al., 2006). For example, traits such as "cruel" and "repairs broken things" are viewed as masculine, and traits such as "often is afraid" and "cooks and bakes" are seen as feminine.

Children and adolescents perceive their own gender in a somewhat better light. For example, girls perceive other girls as nicer, more hardworking, and less selfish than boys. Boys, on the other hand, think that they are nicer, more hardworking, and less selfish than girls (Matlin, 2008; C. F. Miller et al., 2006).

Gender Differences

Clearly, females and males are anatomically different. And according to gender-role stereotypes, people believe that females and males also differ in their behaviors, personality characteristics, and abilities (Amanatullah & Morris, 2010; Lippa, 2010). Gender differences in infancy are small and rather inconsistent. Preschoolers display some

Creatas/Jupiter Images

Gender Stereotypes

Explore a world view of gender stereotypes.

Gender Roles and Children

Watch and learn more about how children view gender.

Are there such things as "boys' toys"? As "girls' toys"? Where do such ideas come from?

differences in their choices of toys and play activities. Boys engage in more rough-and-tumble play and are more aggressive. Girls tend to show more empathy and to report more fears. Girls show somewhat greater verbal ability than boys, whereas boys show somewhat greater visuospatial ability than girls.

Gender Differences in Play

Lisa Serbin and her colleagues (2001) explored infants' visual preferences for gender-stereotyped toys using the assumption that infants spend more time looking at objects that are of greater interest. They found that both girls and boys showed significant preferences for gender-stereotyped toys by 18 months of age. Although preferences for gender-stereotyped toys are well developed by 15–36 months, girls are more likely to stray from the stereotypes (Bussey & Bandura, 1999). Girls ask for and play with "boys' toys" such as cars and trucks more often than boys choose dolls and other "girls' toys."

Girls and boys differ not only in toy preferences but also in their choice of play environments and activities. During the preschool and early elementary school years, boys prefer vigorous physical outdoor activities such as climbing, playing with large vehicles, and rough-and-tumble play (Else-Quest et al., 2006). In middle childhood, boys spend more time than girls in play groups of five or more children and in competitive play (Crombie & Desjardins, 1993; Else-Quest et al., 2006). Girls are more likely than boys to engage in arts and crafts and to play house. Girls' activities are more closely directed by adults (A. Campbell et al., 2002). Girls spend more time than boys playing with one other child or a small group (Crombie & Desjardins, 1993).

Why do children show these early preferences for gender-stereotyped toys and activities? Biological factors may play a role, for example, boys' slightly greater strength and activity levels and girls' slightly greater physical maturity and coordination. But adults treat girls and boys differently. They provide gender-stereotyped toys and room furnishings and encourage gender-typing in play and household chores (Leaper, 2002). Children, moreover, tend to seek out information on which kinds of toys and play are "masculine" or "feminine" and then to conform to the label (C. L. Martin & Ruble, 2004).

Some studies have found that children who "cross the line" by showing interest in toys or activities considered appropriate for the other gender are often teased, ridiculed, rejected, or ignored by their parents, teachers, other adults, and peers. Boys are more likely than girls to be criticized (Fagot & Hagan, 1991; Garvey, 1990).

Another well-documented finding is that children begin to prefer playmates of the same gender by the age of 2. Girls develop this preference somewhat earlier than boys (Fagot, 1990; D. F. Hay et al., 2004). The tendency strengthens during middle childhood. Eleanor Maccoby (1990) believes that two factors are involved in the choice of the gender of playmates in early childhood. One is that boys' play is more oriented toward dominance, aggression, and roughness. The other is that boys are not very responsive to girls' (relatively) polite suggestions. Boys may avoid girls because they see them as inferior (P. J. Caplan & Larkin, 1991).

Gender Differences in Aggression and Empathy

In Module 4.3 it was noted that the male sex hormone testosterone is apparently connected with self-confidence, high activity levels, and, on the negative side, aggres-

American Images Inc/Digital Vision/Getty Images

Why are children—especially boys—aggressive? Why are some children more aggressive than others?

Relational Aggression

Watch and learn about this non-physical form of aggression more common among females.

▶ **LO28** Discuss gender-typing.

siveness (J. Archer, 2006; Cunningham & McGinnis, 2007; Popma et al., 2007). Boys produce more testosterone than girls do, and they are also more aggressive than girls are.

Girls show more empathy than boys do, which is another reason that girls are less likely than boys to behave aggressively (Proverbio et al., 2010; Yamasue et al., 2008). Empathy encourages children to sense what other people are feeling and to see things from the perspectives of others, abilities that discourage them from attacking other children. Empathy tends to encourage helping behavior, not aggression. This gender difference may involve differences in mirror neurons, which are connected with emotions as well as the kinds of imitative behavior we find in newborn babies. Certain regions of the brain—particularly in the frontal lobe—are active when people experience emotions such as disgust, happiness, and pain, and also when they observe another person experiencing an emotion (Iacoboni, 2009a, 2009b). It thus appears that there is a neural basis for empathy—that is, the identification or vicarious experiencing of feelings in other people based on the observation of visual and other cues.

Girls also report more fears and higher levels of anxiety than boys (Kushnir & Sadeh, 2009)—yet another factor which might contribute to lesser aggressiveness.

Biological Theories of Gender-Typing

Why is it that little girls (often) grow up to behave according to the cultural stereotypes of what it means to be female? Why is it that little boys (often) grow up to behave like male stereotypes? The process of developing stereotypical masculine and feminine behavior patterns is termed *gender-typing*. In this section we discuss the roles of evolution and heredity, brain organization, and sex hormones in gender-typing.

The Roles of Evolution and Heredity

According to evolutionary psychologists, gender differences were fashioned by natural selection in response to problems in adaptation that were repeatedly encountered by humans over thousands of generations (Buss & Duntley, 2006; Geary, 2006). The story of the survival of our ancient ancestors is etched in our genes. Genes that bestow attributes that increase an organism's chances of surviving to produce viable offspring are most likely to be transmitted to future generations. We thus possess the genetic codes for traits that helped our ancestors survive and reproduce. These traits include structural gender differences, such as those found in the brain, and differences in body chemistry, such as hormones.

According to the evolutionary perspective, men's traditional roles as hunters and warriors and women's roles as caregivers and gatherers of fruits and vegetables are bequeathed to us in our genes (Confer et al., 2010). Men are better suited to war and the hunt because of physical attributes passed along since ancestral times. Upper-body strength, for example, would have enabled them to throw spears and overpower adversaries. Men also possess perceptual-cognitive advantages, such as superior visual–motor skills, that favor aggression. Visual–motor skills would have enabled men to aim spears or bows and arrows.

Women, it is argued, are genetically predisposed to be empathic and nurturant because these traits enabled ancestral women to respond to children's needs and to enhance the likelihood that their children would flourish and eventually reproduce, thereby transmitting their own genetic legacy to future generations (Confer et al., 2010). Prehistoric women thus tended to stay close to home, care for the children, and gather edible plants, whereas men ventured from home to hunt and raid their neighbors' storehouses.

Why do males tend to place relatively more emphasis than females on physical appearance in mate selection? Why do females tend to place relatively more emphasis on personal factors such as financial status and reliability? Evolutionary psychologists believe that evolutionary forces favor the survival of women who desire status in their mates and men who emphasize physical allure because these preferences provide reproductive advantages. Some physical features such as cleanliness, good complexion, clear eyes, strong teeth and healthy hair, firm muscle tone, and a steady gait are universally appealing to both males and females (Buss, 2009). Perhaps such traits have value as markers of better reproductive potential in prospective mates. According to the "parental investment model," a woman's appeal is more strongly connected with her age and health, both of which are markers of reproductive capacity (Confer et al., 2010). The value of men as reproducers, however, is more intertwined with factors that contribute to a stable environment for child rearing—such as social standing and reliability (Schmitt, 2008). For such reasons, evolutionary psychologists speculate that these qualities may have grown relatively more alluring to women over the millennia (Schmitt, 2008).

The evolutionary perspective is steeped in controversy (Confer et al., 2010). Although scientists do not dispute the importance of evolution in determining physical attributes, many are reluctant to attribute complex social behaviors and gender roles to heredity. The evolutionary perspective implies that stereotypical gender roles—men as breadwinners and women as homemakers, for example—reflect the natural order of things. Critics contend that, among humans, biology is not destiny. The human brain has also evolved to where it is today, and the brain permits us to make choices.

The Role of Prenatal Brain Organization

Researchers have also sought the origins of gender-typed behavior in the organization of the brain. Is it possible that the cornerstone of gender-typed behavior is laid in the brain before the first breath is taken?

The organization of the brain is largely genetically determined (W. A. Collins et al., 2000; Maccoby, 2000). The hemispheres of the brain are specialized to perform certain functions (Brugger et al., 2009; Haier et al., 2009). In most people, the left hemisphere ("left brain") appears more essential to verbal functions, such as speech. The right hemisphere ("right brain") appears specialized to perform visuospatial tasks. Testosterone in the brains of male fetuses spurs greater growth of the right hemisphere and slows the rate of growth of the left hemisphere (Cohen-Bendahan et al., 2005; Siegel-Hinson & McKeever, 2002). This difference may partly explain females' superiority at verbal tasks and males' superiority at spatial-relations tasks, such as interpreting road maps and visualizing objects in space. Hemispheric specialization also leads to superior maze learning by male rats.

Although both males and females have a left hemisphere and a right hemisphere, they may not use them in quite the same way. Consider the hippocampus, a brain structure that is involved in the formation of memories and the relay of incoming sensory information to other parts of the brain (Ohnishi et al., 2006). Matthias Riepe and his colleagues (Grön et al., 2000) have studied the ways in which humans and rats use the hippocampus when they are navigating routes or mazes. Males use the hippocampus in both hemispheres when they are navigating (Grön et al., 2000). Women, however, rely on the hippocampus in the right hemisphere along with the right prefrontal cortex, an area of the brain that evaluates information and makes plans. Riepe and his colleagues wondered whether different patterns of brain activities might contribute to preference for using landmarks or maps.

The Role of Sex Hormones

Researchers are interested in determining the amount of testosterone in the bodily fluids of fetuses so that they can relate the quantity of the hormone to the sex of the individual and also to the behavior of the individual after birth. They do not draw blood directly from the fetus to do so. Instead, because testosterone is diffused into fetal amniotic fluid through the skin of the fetus, and later by fetal urination, researchers can draw a sample of the amniotic fluid. Examining the amniotic fluid enables them to estimate the amount of testosterone in the fetus.

The amount of testosterone in amniotic fluid is variable in both males and females, but higher on average in males. Studies attempting to correlate the variability of fetal testosterone with subsequent gender-typed play in boys and girls have shown mixed results, with many studies finding no relationship (e.g., Knickmeyer et al., 2005; van de Beek et al., 2009). However, one study conducted by Bonnie Auyeung and her colleagues (2009) did find a relationship. In that study, fetal testosterone was measured in the amniotic fluid in 212 pregnant women and related to the subsequent gender-typed behavior of their children at the age of 8½ years. The correlation between testosterone and masculine-typed play was positive and large enough to be not due to chance variation.

However, children in Auyeung's sample were old enough to have been influenced by the gender-role expectations of their caregivers, their educators, and society at large. Other studies have shown that children display gender-typed preferences at very early ages. One study found that children show gender-typed play by the age of 13 months (Knickmeyer et al., 2005). Another study investigated the gender-typed visual preferences of 30 human infants at the early ages of 3–8 months (G. M. Alexander et al., 2009). The researchers assessed interest in a toy truck and a doll by using eye-tracking technology to indicate the direction of visual attention. They found that girls showed a visual preference for the doll over the truck (that is, they made a greater number of visual fixations on the doll), and boys showed a visual preference for the truck. These gender differences appear to strengthen the case for the role of prenatal sex hormones, because there has been relatively little time for social influences to take effect among 3- to 8-month-old infants. At such an early age, infants are not even aware of their own gender.

▶ **LO29** Discuss the four theories of gender-typing.

What is this boy learning about construction equipment?

Psychological Theories of Gender-Typing

Biological theories of gender-typing address what is natural—at least in the sense of biological gender differences. But we should note that there is no perfect relationship between biological differences and behavior patterns. We usually speak of group differences rather than the destiny of the individual.

In this section we review a number of psychological theories of gender-typing: psychodynamic theory, cognitive-developmental theory, social cognitive theory, and gender-schema theory. Generally speaking, they do not find female–male differences to be as hardwired as do the biological theories. They also point out that there are psychological, social, and cultural reasons as well as biological reasons for the development of stereotyped behavior.

Psychodynamic Theory

Sigmund Freud explained the development of gender-typed behavior in terms of identification. Appropriate gender-typing, in Freud's view, requires that boys come to identify with their fathers and girls with their mothers. Identification is completed, in Freud's view, as children resolve the Oedipus complex (called the *Electra complex* in girls).

According to Freud, the Oedipus complex occurs during the phallic period of psychosexual development, from ages 3–5. During this period, the child develops incestu-

gender identity The knowledge that one is female or male.

gender stability The concept that one's gender is unchanging.

gender constancy The concept that one's gender remains the same despite changes in appearance or behavior.

ous wishes for the parent of the other gender and comes to perceive the parent of the same gender as a rival. The complex is resolved by the child's forsaking incestuous wishes for the parent of the other gender and identifying with the parent of the same gender. Through identification with the same gender parent, the child comes to develop preferences and behavior patterns that are typically associated with that gender. But children display stereotypical gender-typed behaviors earlier than Freud would have predicted. As noted earlier, babies show visual preferences for gender-typed toys at 3–8 months (Alexander et al., 2009). During the first year, boys are more independent than girls. Girls are more quiet and restrained. Because of their lack of empirical support, many researchers believe that Freud's views are now of historical interest only.

Cognitive-Developmental Theory

Lawrence Kohlberg (1966) proposed a cognitive-developmental view of gender-typing. According to this perspective, children form concepts about gender and then fit their behavior to the concepts (C. L. Martin & Ruble, 2004). These developments occur in stages and are entwined with general cognitive development.

According to Kohlberg, gender-typing involves the emergence of three concepts: gender identity, gender stability, and gender constancy. The first step in gender-typing is attaining **gender identity**—the knowledge that one is male or female. At 2 years, most children can say whether they are boys or girls. By the age of 3, many children can discriminate anatomic gender differences (Campbell et al., 2002; Ruble et al., 2006).

At around age 4 or 5, most children develop the concept of **gender stability**, according to Kohlberg. They recognize that people retain their gender for a lifetime. Girls no longer believe that they can grow up to be daddies, and boys no longer think that they can become mommies.

By the age of 5–7 years, Kohlberg believes, most children develop the more sophisticated concept of **gender constancy** and recognize that people's gender does not change, even if they change their dress or behavior. A woman who cuts her hair short remains a woman. A man who dons an apron and cooks remains a man. Once children have established concepts of gender stability and constancy, they seek to behave in ways that are consistent with their gender (C. L. Martin & Ruble, 2004).

Cross-cultural studies in the United States, Samoa, Nepal, Belize, and Kenya have found that the concepts of gender identity, gender stability, and gender constancy emerge in the order predicted by Kohlberg (S. P. Leonard & Archer, 1989; Munroe et al., 1984). However, gender constancy and gender-typed play emerge earlier than predicted by Kohlberg. Girls show preferences for dolls and soft toys, and boys for hard transportation toys, by the age of 1½–3 (G. M. Alexander, 2003; Campbell et al., 2004; Powlishta, 2004). At this age, children may have a sense of gender identity, but gender stability and gender constancy remain a year or two away.

Social Cognitive Theory

Social cognitive theorists explain the development of gender-typed behavior in terms of processes such as observational learning, identification, and socialization (Golombok et al., 2008; Zosuls et al., 2009). Children observe the behavior of adult role models and may come to assume that their behavior should conform to that of adults of the same gender. In social cognitive theory, identification is seen as a continuous learning process in which rewards and punishments influence children to imitate adult models of the same gender. In identification, the child not only imitates the behavior of the model but tries to become broadly like the model. These models may be their parents, other adults, other children, or characters in electronic media such as TV and video games.

Socialization is thought to play a role in gender-typing (Golombok et al., 2008; Zosuls et al., 2009). Almost from the moment a baby comes into the world, she or he is treated in ways that are consistent with gender stereotypes. Parents tend to talk more to baby girls, and fathers especially engage in more roughhousing with boys. When children are old enough to speak, caregivers and even other children begin to tell them how they are expected to behave. Parents may reward children for behavior they consider gender appropriate and punish (or fail to reinforce) them for behavior they consider inappropriate for their gender. Girls are encouraged to practice caregiving behaviors, which are intended to prepare them for traditional feminine adult roles. Boys are handed Legos or doctor sets to help prepare them for traditional masculine adult roles. Boys are encouraged to be independent, whereas girls are more likely to be restricted. Boys are allowed to roam farther from home at an earlier age and are more likely to be left unsupervised after school (C. F. Miller et al., 2006).

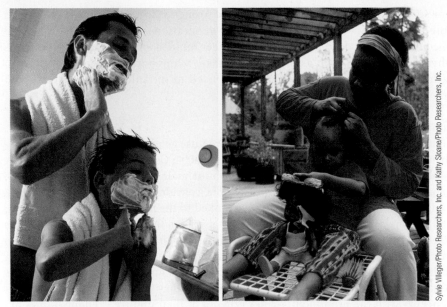

Sylvie Villeger/Photo Researchers, Inc. and Kathy Sloane/Photo Researchers, Inc.

Acquiring Gender Roles. What psychological factors contribute to the acquisition of gender roles? Psychoanalytic theory focuses on the concept of identification. Social cognitive theory focuses on imitation of the behavior patterns of same-sex adults and reinforcement by parents and peers.

Fathers generally encourage their sons to develop assertive, instrumental behavior (that is, behavior that gets things done or accomplishes something) and their daughters to develop nurturant, cooperative behavior. Fathers are likely to cuddle their daughters gently. They are likely to carry their sons like footballs or toss them into the air. Fathers also tend to use heartier and harsher language with their sons, such as "How're yuh doin', Tiger?" and "Hey you, get your keester over here."

Primary schoolchildren show less stereotyping if their mothers frequently engage in traditionally "masculine" tasks such as washing the car, taking children to ball games, or assembling toys (Powlishta, 2004). Maternal employment is associated with less polarized gender-role concepts for girls and boys (Sabattini & Leaper, 2004; Powlishta, 2004). With more mothers working outside the home in our society, daughters are exposed to more women who represent career-minded role models than was the case in earlier generations. More parents today are encouraging their daughters to become career minded and to engage in strenuous physical activities, such as organized sports. Many boys today are exposed to fathers who take a larger role than men used to in child care and household responsibilities.

Gender-Schema Theory

Gender-schema theory proposes that children use gender as one way of organizing their perceptions of the world (Campbell et al., 2004; C. L. Martin & Ruble, 2004). A gender schema is a cluster of concepts about male and female physical traits, behaviors, and personality traits. For example, consider the dimension of strength–weakness. Children learn that strength is linked to the male gender-role stereotype and weakness to the female stereotype. They also learn that some dimensions, such as strength–weakness, are more relevant to one gender than the other—in this case, to males. Once children acquire a gender schema in early childhood, they begin to judge themselves according to traits considered appropriate for their gender (Grace et al., 2008; Most et al., 2007). In doing so, they blend their developing self-concepts with the prominent gender schema of their culture (Tenenbaum et al., 2010). Children with self-concepts that are consistent with the prominent gender schema of their culture are likely to develop higher self-esteem than children whose self-concepts are inconsistent. Jack learns that muscle strength is a characteristic associated with "manliness." He is likely to think more highly of himself if he perceives himself as embodying this attribute than if he does not. Jill is likely to discover that the dimension of kindness–cruelty is more crucial than strength–weakness to the way women are perceived in society.

According to gender-schema theory, once children come to see themselves as female or male, they begin to seek information concerning gender-typed traits and try to live up to them (Tenenbaum et al., 2010). Jack will retaliate when provoked because boys are expected to do so. Jill will be "sugary and sweet" if such is expected of little girls. But gender-schema theory cannot explain why boys and girls tend to show visual preferences for gender-typed toys before they are 1 year old (G. M. Alexander et al., 2009).

gender-schema theory The view that one's knowledge of the gender schema in one's society guides one's assumption of gender-typed preferences and behavior patterns.

From the viewpoint of gender-schema theory, gender identity alone can inspire "gender-appropriate" behavior (Ruble et al., 2006). As soon as children understand the labels "girl" and "boy," they seek information concerning gender-typed traits and try to live up to them. A boy may fight back when provoked because boys are expected to do so. A girl may be gentle and kind because that is expected of girls. Both boys' and girls' self-esteem will depend on how they measure up to the gender schema.

Studies indicate that children organize information according to a gender schema. For example, boys show better memory for "masculine" toys, activities, and occupations, whereas girls show better memory for "feminine" toys, activities, and occupations (C. L. Martin & Ruble, 2004). However, gender-schema theory does not address the issue of whether biological forces also play a role in gender-typing.

In sum, it would appear that both biological and psychological factors contribute to gender-typing. The weight of research evidence suggests that biological gender differences are connected with early childhood preferences for toys and styles of play. In Chapter 5, we will explore further whether or not they are also connected with differences in cognitive skills that tend to develop or be expressed at later ages. But there is also evidence that boys and girls learn what societies expect of them through experience with parents, peers, other people, and the media. Social influences, moreover, appear to affect the degree to which children believe they should conform to gender-role stereotypes. To what degree do you, as an individual, feel bound by or free from gender-role stereotypes?

Check Your Learning Quiz 4.4

Go to **login.cengagebrain.com** and take the online quiz.

GO to your Psychology CourseMate at login.cengagebrain.com and take the Chapter Post-Test to see which Learning Objectives you've mastered and which need more review. Use the chapter review guide below and the online activities—including flashcards to review key terms—to measure your learning.

Measure
^Your Learning

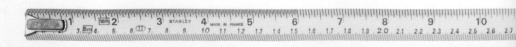

Online Activities

Key Terms	Video	Animation	Reading	Assessment
Early childhood, corpus callosum, plasticity	The Brain's Hemispheres: The Long Fissure Visual Spatial Processing in Children			Check Your Learning Quiz 4.1
Gross motor skills, fine motor skills	Gross Motor Control and Children Fine Motor Skills in Early Childhood	Motor Development	Gender and Motor Activity	
			Sample Meal Plan	
			Immunizations Immunization Coverage in the U.S. Recommended Immunization Schedule Causes of Death in Young Children	
Sleep terrors, somnambulism			Culture and Sleeping Arrangements	
Enuresis, bed-wetting, encopresis				

Measure ^Your Learning

Online Activities

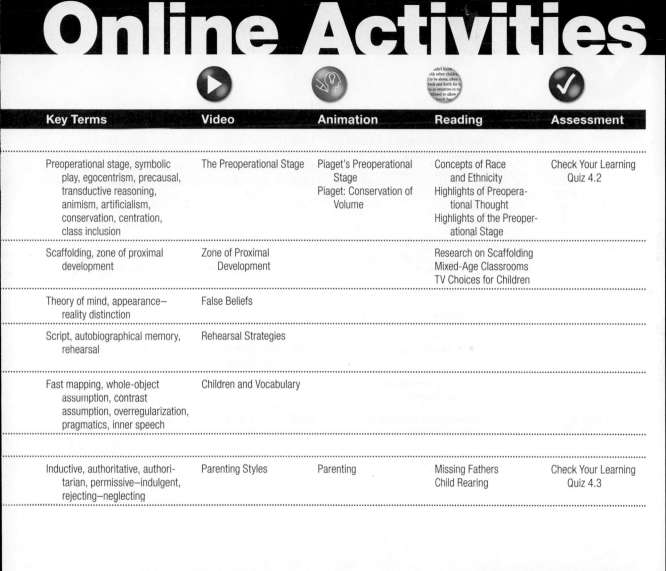

Key Terms	Video	Animation	Reading	Assessment
Preoperational stage, symbolic play, egocentrism, precausal, transductive reasoning, animism, artificialism, conservation, centration, class inclusion	The Preoperational Stage	Piaget's Preoperational Stage Piaget: Conservation of Volume	Concepts of Race and Ethnicity Highlights of Preoperational Thought Highlights of the Preoperational Stage	Check Your Learning Quiz 4.2
Scaffolding, zone of proximal development	Zone of Proximal Development		Research on Scaffolding Mixed-Age Classrooms TV Choices for Children	
Theory of mind, appearance–reality distinction	False Beliefs			
Script, autobiographical memory, rehearsal	Rehearsal Strategies			
Fast mapping, whole-object assumption, contrast assumption, overregularization, pragmatics, inner speech	Children and Vocabulary			
Inductive, authoritative, authoritarian, permissive–indulgent, rejecting–neglecting	Parenting Styles	Parenting	Missing Fathers Child Rearing	Check Your Learning Quiz 4.3

Measure ^Your Learning

Online Activities

Key Terms	Video	Animation	Reading	Assessment
Regression, dramatic play, nonsocial play, social play, prosocial behavior, disinhibit	Types of Play		Taught to Hate	
Self-concept, categorical self				
Stereotype, gender role	Gender Roles and Children		Gender Stereotypes	Check Your Learning Quiz 4.4
	Relational Aggression			
Gender identity, gender stability gender constancy, gender-schema theory				

Middle Childhood

Chapter Outline and Learning Objectives

Prepare ^ to Learn

1 **GO** to your **Psychology CourseMate** at **login.cengagebrain.com** and take the **Chapter Pre-Test** to introduce yourself to this chapter's topics and see what you may already know.

2 **READ** the **Learning Objectives** (LOs, in the left sidebars) and begin the chapter.

3 **COMPLETE** the **Online Activities** (in the right sidebars) *as you read each module.* Activities include **videos, animations, readings,** and **quizzes.**

4 **CHECK Your Learning** by going online to take the quiz at the end of each module and review material as necessary.

5 **MEASURE Your Learning** after reading the chapter by taking the online **Chapter Post-Test.** Use the chapter review guide at the end of the chapter as needed.

WATCH for these **Online Activities** icons as you read:

Video

Animation

Reading

Assessment

These online activities are essential to mastering this chapter. Go to login.cengagebrain.com:

Videos Watch the following videos:

- Motor Skills in School
- Sleep Deprivation and Obesity?
- Why So Many Children Are Overweight
- Medication for ADHD
- Concrete-Operational Children Performing Tasks of Conservation
- Moral Judgments
- Moral Development
- False Memories and Suggestibility
- Measures of IQ
- Closing the Achievement Gap
- Bias in Intelligence Testing
- Social-Emotional Learning
- Self-Concept
- Selective Mutism
- Peer Acceptance
- Emotional Bullying
- Self-Fulfilling Prophecies

Animations Interact with and visualize important processes, timelines, and concepts:

- Kohlberg's Theory of Moral Development
- The Structures of Memory
- IQ Test Items
- Self-Esteem

Readings Delve deeper into key content:

- Helping Overweight Children Manage Their Weight
- Motor Skill Development During Middle Childhood
- African American Youth and ADHD
- Types of Learning Disabilities
- Working Memory and Individual Differences in Achievement in Mathematics
- Emotional and Social Intelligence
- Alfred Binet
- Alison: A Case of Separation Anxiety Disorder

Assessment Measure your mastery:

- Chapter Pre-Test
- Check Your Learning Quizzes
- Chapter Post-Test

▶ **LO1** Describe patterns of growth in middle childhood.

Did you know that—

• The average child's body weight doubles during middle childhood?

• Most foods in school cafeterias and fast-food restaurants are heavy in sugar, animal fats, and salt?

• Despite the belief that children outgrow "baby fat," most overweight children become overweight adults?

• Hyperactivity is not caused by chemical food additives?

• Stimulants are often used to treat children who are already hyperactive?

• Some children who are average in intelligence or above cannot learn to read?

It is 6-year-old Jessica's first day of school. During recess, she runs to the jungle gym in the schoolyard and climbs to the top. As she reaches the top, she announces to the other children, "I'm coming down." She then walks to the parallel bars, goes halfway across, lets go, and tries again.

Steve and Mike are 8-year-olds. They are riding their bikes up and down the street. Steve tries riding with no hands on the handlebars. Mike starts riding fast, standing up on the pedals. Steve shouts, "Boy, you're going to break your neck!"

Middle childhood is a time for learning many new motor skills. Success in both gross and fine motor skills reflects children's increasing physical maturity, their opportunities to learn, and personality factors such as their persistence and self-confidence. Competence in motor skills enhances children's self-esteem and their acceptance by their peers.

In this module, we examine physical and motor development during middle childhood. We also discuss children with certain disorders.

middle childhood The years between 6 and 12, sometimes called "the school years" and defining the period between early childhood and the onset of adolescence.

growth spurt A period during which growth advances at a dramatically rapid rate compared with other periods.

Growth Patterns

Middle childhood is typically defined as the ages from 6 to 12, beginning with the school years and ending with the start of the adolescent **growth spurt**. Following the growth trends of early childhood, boys and girls continue to gain a little over 2 inches in height per year until the spurt begins. The average gain in weight during middle childhood is 5–7 pounds a year, but children grow less stocky and more slender (Kuczmarski et al., 2000).

Nutrition and Growth

In middle childhood, the average child's body weight doubles. Children also spend a good deal of energy in physical activity and play. To fuel this growth and activity, schoolchildren eat more than preschoolers. The typical 4- to 6-year-old needs 1,400–1,800 calories per day, but the typical 7- to 10-year-old requires 2,000 calories.

Nutrition involves more than calories. It is healthful to eat fruits and vegetables, fish, poultry (without skin), and whole grains, and to limit intake of fats, sugar, and starches. However, most foods in school cafeterias and elsewhere are heavy in sugar, animal fats, and salt (K. W. Bauer et al., 2004). Portions have also grown over the decades, especially at fast-food restaurants (Nielsen & Popkin, 2003).

Gender Similarities and Differences in Physical Growth

Like mother, like daughter? Weight problems run in families, but environmental and genetic factors both appear to be involved.

© Ashley Cooper/Corbis

Boys are slightly heavier and taller than girls through the age of 9 or 10. Girls then begin their adolescent growth spurt and surpass boys in height and weight until about 13 or 14. Then boys spurt and grow taller and heavier than girls. The steady gains in height and weight in middle childhood are paralleled by increased muscle strength in both genders. Beginning at about age 11, boys develop relatively more muscle, and girls develop relatively more fat.

Overweight in Children

Between 16% and 25% of children and adolescents in the United States are overweight or obese (see Figure 5.1). Although parents often assume that heavy children will "outgrow" the "baby fat," most overweight children become overweight adults (S. R. Daniels, 2006).

Overweight children are often rejected by peers or are targets of derision (Storch et al., 2007). They are usually poor at sports and less likely to be consid-

Overweight Children

Watch and learn why so many children are overweight.

Sleep Deprivation and Obesity

Is there a link between obesity in children and insufficient sleep?

Weight Management for Children

Explore ways to help overweight children manage their weight.

▸ **LO2** Describe motor development in middle childhood.

▸ **LO3** Discuss gender differences in motor skills.

▸ **LO4** Discuss whether children in the United States are physically fit.

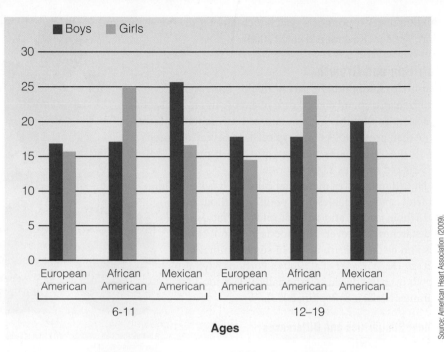

Source: American Heart Association (2009).

Figure 5.1 Overweight Children in America Percentage of children (ages 6–11) and adolescents (ages 12–19), by ethnicity, who are overweight according to the American Heart Association.

ered attractive in adolescence (Storch et al., 2007). Overweight children are also at greater risk of health problems throughout life (American Heart Association, 2007).

Causes of Overweight

Heredity plays a role in being overweight. Some people inherit a tendency to burn up extra calories, whereas others inherit a tendency to turn extra calories into fat (Kolata, 2007).

Family, peers, and other environmental factors play roles in children's eating habits too (Moens et al., 2007). Overweight parents may model poor exercise habits,

reaction time The amount of time required to respond to a stimulus.

encourage overeating, and keep unhealthful foods in the home. Children who watch TV extensively burn fewer calories than children who exercise frequently, and they are more likely to become overweight as adolescents (Schumacher & Queen, 2007).

Motor Development

The school years are marked by increases in the child's speed, strength, agility, and balance. These developments lead to more skillful motor activities.

Gross Motor Skills

Throughout middle childhood, children show steady improvement in their ability to perform gross motor skills. Children are hopping, jumping, and climbing by age 6 or so; by age 6 or 7, they are usually capable of pedaling and balancing on a bicycle. By the ages of 8 to 10, children are showing the balance, coordination, and strength that allow them to engage in gymnastics and team sports.

During these years, muscles grow stronger and neural pathways that connect the cerebellum to the cortex become more myelinated. Experience refines sensorimotor abilities, but there are also inborn differences. Some people have better visual acuity, depth perception, or coordination than others.

Reaction time is basic to the child's timing a swing of the bat or hitting a tennis ball. It gradually improves (decreases) from early childhood to about age 18, but there are individual differences (Karatekin et al., 2007). Reaction time increases again in adulthood.

Fine Motor Skills

By the age of 6 to 7, children can usually tie their shoelaces and hold pencils as adults do. Their abilities to fasten buttons, zip zippers, brush their teeth, wash themselves, coordinate a knife and fork, and use chopsticks all develop during the early school years and improve during childhood (Beilei et al., 2002).

Gender Differences

Throughout middle childhood, boys and girls perform similarly in most motor activities. Boys show slightly greater strength, especially more forearm strength, which aids them in swinging a bat and throwing a ball (Butterfield & Loovis, 1993).

Motor Skills in School

Watch school-aged children perform tasks that require certain motor skills.

Motor Skill Development during Middle Childhood

Review your understanding of motor skill development during middle childhood.

▶ **LO5** Discuss attention deficit/ hyperactivity disorder and learning disorders.

Girls show somewhat greater limb coordination and overall flexibility, which is valuable in dancing, balancing, and gymnastics (Abdelaziz et al., 2001; Cumming et al., 2005).

At puberty, gender differences favoring boys increase (Smoll & Schultz, 1990). But prior to that, boys are more likely than girls to receive encouragement and opportunities in sports (A. M. Thompson et al., 2003). Between middle childhood and adolescence, physical activities become increasingly stereotyped by children as being masculine (e.g., football) or feminine (e.g., dance) (Meaney et al., 2002).

Exercise and Fitness

Exercise reduces the risk of heart disease, stroke, diabetes, and certain forms of cancer (G. Atkinson & Davenne, 2007). Physically active adolescents also have a better self-image and better coping skills than those who are inactive (Kirkcaldy et al., 2002). Yet most children in the United States are not physically fit (Schumacher & Queen, 2007).

Cardiac and muscular fitness is developed by participation in aerobic exercises such as running, walking quickly, swimming laps, bicycling, or jumping rope for several minutes at a time. However, schools and parents tend to focus on sports such as baseball and football, which are less apt to promote fitness.

Children With Disabilities

Certain disabilities of childhood are most apt to be noticed in the middle childhood years, when the child enters school. The school setting requires that a child sit still, pay attention, and master certain academic skills. But some children have difficulty with these demands.

Attention Deficit/Hyperactivity Disorder (ADHD)

attention deficit/hyperactivity disorder (ADHD) A disorder characterized by excessive inattention, impulsiveness, and hyperactivity.

hyperactivity Excessive restlessness and overactivity; a characteristic of ADHD.

Nine-year-old Eddie is a problem in class. His teacher complains that he is so restless and fidgety that the rest of the class cannot concentrate on their work. He … is in constant motion, roaming the classroom, talking to other children while they are working. He has been suspended repeatedly for outrageous behavior, most recently swinging from a fluorescent light fixture. … He has never needed much sleep and always awakened before anyone else in the family, … wrecking things in the living room and kitchen. Once, at the age of 4, he unlocked the front door and wandered into traffic, but was rescued by a passerby. Psychological testing shows Eddie to be average in academic ability but to have a "virtually nonexistent" attention span. He shows no interest in television or in games or toys that require some concentration.

—Adapted from R. L. Spitzer et al., 2002

In **attention deficit/hyperactivity disorder (ADHD)**, the child shows excessive inattention, impulsivity, and **hyperactivity**. The degree of hyperactive behavior is crucial, because many normal children are overactive and fidgety from time to time.

ADHD typically occurs by age 7. The hyperactivity and restlessness impair children's ability to function in school: They cannot sit still. They have difficulty getting along with others. ADHD is diagnosed in about 1%–5% of school-age children and is many times more common in boys than girls.

ADHD is sometimes "overdiagnosed" (Weisler & Sussman, 2007). Some children who misbehave in school are diagnosed with ADHD and medicated to encourage more acceptable behavior (Reddy & De Thomas, 2007).

Causes of ADHD

There may be a genetic component to ADHD involving the brain chemical dopamine (Thapar et al., 2007; Walitza et al., 2006). Studies in brain imaging have found differences in the brain chemistry of children with ADHD.

Though it was widely believed in the 1970s that food coloring and preservatives cause ADHD, research has not borne out this point of view (Cruz & Bahna, 2006). Joel Nigg and his colleagues (Nigg, Hinshaw, et al., 2006) noted that ADHD is due to a lack of executive control of the brain over motor and more primitive functions.

Al Cook Photography

Hyperactive children are continually on the go, as if their motors are constantly running. The psychological disorder we refer to as hyperactivity is not to be confused with the normal high energy levels of children. However, it is sometimes difficult to tell where one ends and the other begins.

African-American Children and ADHD

Read about prevalence of ADHD among African American youth.

Medication for ADHD

Watch and learn about the pros and cons of treating ADHD with Ritalin.

Treatment and Outcome

Stimulants such as Ritalin are the most widespread treatment for ADHD, promoting the activity of the brain chemicals dopamine and noradrenaline, which stimulate the "executive center" of the brain to control the parts of the brain that function more automatically. Stimulants increase children's attention spans and improve their academic performance (Posey et al., 2007). Most children with ADHD continue to have problems in attention, conduct, or learning into adolescence and adulthood (Nigg, Goldsmith, et al., 2004).

Dyslexia

Some children who are intelligent and provided with enriched home environments cannot learn how to read (a condition termed **dyslexia**) or do simple math problems. Many such children have **learning disorders** in math, writing, or reading. Some have difficulties in articulating the sounds of speech or understanding spoken language. Others have problems in motor coordination. Children are usually diagnosed with a learning disorder when they are performing below the level expected for their age and intelligence, and when there is no evidence of other disabilities such as vision or hearing problems, intellectual deficiency, or socioeconomic disadvantage (R. M. Joshi, 2003; Lyon et al., 2003). Learning disorders may persist through life, but with early recognition and remediation, many children can learn to compensate for their disability (Vellutino et al., 2004).

It has been estimated that dyslexia affects anywhere from 5% to 17.5% of American children (S. E. Shaywitz, 1998). Most studies show that dyslexia is much more common in boys than in girls. Figure 5.2 shows a writing sample from a dyslexic child.

stimulant A drug that increases the activity of the nervous system.

dyslexia A reading disorder characterized by letter reversals, mirror reading, slow reading, and reduced comprehension.

learning disorder A disorder characterized by inadequate development of specific academic, language, and speech skills.

mainstreaming Placing disabled children in classrooms with nondisabled children.

© Will and Deni McIntyre/Photo Researchers

Figure 5.2 Writing Sample of a Dyslexic Child Dyslexic children may perceive letters as upside down (confusing *w* with *m*) or reversed (confusing *b* with *d*), leading to rotations or reversals in writing, as shown here.

Origins of Dyslexia

Theories of dyslexia focus on the ways in which sensory and neurological problems may contribute to the reading problems we find in dyslexic individuals. Genetic factors appear to be involved; from 25% to 65% of children who have one dyslexic parent are dyslexic themselves (Plomin & Walker, 2003). About 40% of the siblings of children with dyslexia are dyslexic.

Genetic factors may give rise to neurological problems or circulation problems in the left hemisphere of the brain (Grigorenko, 2007). The circulation problems would result in oxygen deficiency. The part of the brain called the angular gyrus "translates" visual information, such as written words, into auditory information (sounds). Problems in the angular gyrus may give rise to reading problems by making it difficult for the reader to associate letters with sounds (Grigorenko, 2007; Shaywitz et al., 2006b).

Most researchers also focus on *phonological processing*. That is, dyslexic children may not discriminate sounds as accurately as other children do (Halliday & Bishop, 2006). As a result, *b*, *d* and *p* may be hard to tell apart, creating confusion that impairs reading ability (B. A. Shaywitz et al., 2006).

Educating Children With Dyslexia and Other Disabilities

In childhood, treatment of dyslexia focuses on remediation (Bakker, 2006). Children are given highly structured exercises to help them become aware of how to blend sounds to form words, such as identifying word pairs that rhyme and do not rhyme. Later in life, the focus tends to be on accommodation rather than on remediation. For example, college students with dyslexia may be given extra time to do the reading involved in taking tests.

Evidence is mixed on whether placing children with disabilities in separate classes stigmatizes and segregates them from other children. In **mainstreaming**, children with special needs are placed in regular classrooms that have been adapted to their needs. Most students with mild learning disabilities spend most of the school day in regular classrooms (Fergusson, 2007).

Learning Disabilities

Expand your knowledge about types of learning disabilities.

Check Your Learning Quiz 5.1

Go to **login.cengagebrain.com** and take the online quiz.

▶ **LO6** Describe Piaget's stage of concrete operations.

Did you know that—

- If A is larger than B, and B is larger than C, then A is larger than C?
- "Because that's the way to do it" is a perfectly fine explanation for a 5-year-old?
- Jean Piaget "remembered" an attempt to kidnap him when he was a baby, but it never happened?
- We read many words by the way they look rather than trying to figure out the way they sound from the letters?
- Most linguists consider it advantageous for children to be bilingual because knowledge of more than one language contributes to the complexity of the child's cognitive processes?

▼

Did you hear the one about the judge who pounded her gavel and yelled, "Order! Order in the court!"? "A hamburger and French fries, Your Honor," responded the defendant. Such children's jokes are based on ambiguities in the meanings of words and phrases. Most 7-year-olds will find the joke about order in the court funny because they recognize that the word *order* has more than one meaning. At about the age of 11, children can understand ambiguities in grammatical structure. Children make enormous strides in their cognitive development during middle childhood as their thought processes and language become more logical and complex.

Piaget: The Concrete-Operational Stage

concrete operations The third stage in Piaget's scheme, characterized by flexible, reversible thought concerning tangible objects and events.

decentration Simultaneous focusing on more than one aspect or dimension of a problem or situation.

According to Jean Piaget, the typical child is entering the stage of **concrete operations** by the age of 7. In this stage, which lasts until about age 12, children show the beginnings of adult logic but generally focus on tangible objects rather than abstract ideas, which is why they are *concrete*.

Concrete-operational thought is reversible and flexible. Adding the numbers 2 and 3 to get 5 is an operation. Subtracting 2 from 5 to get 3 reverses the operation. Subtracting 3 from 5 to get 2 demonstrates flexibility.

Concrete-operational children are less egocentric than preoperational children. They recognize that people see things in different ways because of different situations and values. Concrete-operational children also engage in **decentration**. They can focus on multiple parts of a problem at once.

Conservation

Concrete-operational children show understanding of the laws of conservation. The 7-year-old child in Figure 5.3 would say that the flattened ball of clay from the example in Module 4.2 (Chapter 4) still has the same amount of clay as the round one "because you can roll it up again." The concrete-operational child knows that objects can have several properties or dimensions. By attending to both the height and the width of the clay, the child recognizes that the loss in height compensates for the gain in width.

© Judy Allen Biggs

Figure 5.3 Conservation of Mass This 7-year-old girl is in the concrete-operational stage of cognitive development. She has rolled two clay balls. In the photo on the left, she agrees that both have the same amount (mass) of clay. In the photo on the right, she (gleefully) flattens one clay ball. When asked whether the two pieces still have the same amount of clay, she answers yes.

Tasks of Conservation

Watch concrete-operational children perform tasks of conservation.

Transitivity

If your parents are older than you are and you are older than your children, are your parents older than your children? The answer, of course, is yes. But how did you arrive at this answer? If you said yes simply on the basis of knowing that your parents are older than your children (e.g., 58 and 56 compared with 5 and 3), your answer did not require concrete-operational thought. One aspect of such thought is the principle of **transitivity**: If A exceeds B in some property (say, age or height) and if B exceeds C, then A must also exceed C.

Researchers can assess whether children understand the principle of transitivity by asking them to place objects in a series, or order, according to some property, such as lining up family members according to age, height, or weight. Placing objects in a series is termed **seriation**.

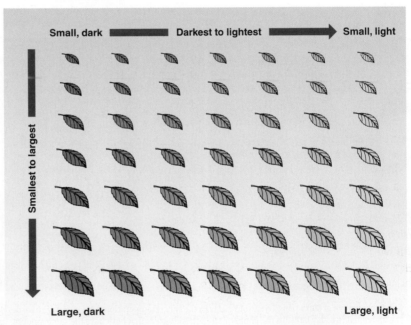

transitivity The principle that if A is greater than B and B is greater than C, then A is greater than C.

seriation Placing objects in an order or series according to a property or trait.

Figure 5.4 A Grid for Demonstrating the Development of Seriation To classify these leaves, children must focus on two dimensions at once: size and lightness. They must also understand the principle of transitivity—that if A is greater than B and B is greater than C, then A is greater than C.

© 2012 Cengage Learning

Piaget assessed children's abilities at seriation by asking them to place 10 sticks in order of size. Children who are 4 or 5 usually place the sticks in a random sequence, or in small groups, as in small, medium, or large. But consider the approach of 7 and 8-year-olds who are capable of concrete operations. They look over the array, then select either the longest or shortest and place it at the point from which they will begin. Then they select the next longest (or shortest) and continue until the task is complete.

Concrete-operational children also have the decentration capacity to allow them to seriate in two dimensions at once, unlike preoperational children. Consider a seriation task used by Piaget and Inhelder (1962): In this test, children were given 49 leaves and asked to classify them according to size and brightness (from small to large and from dark to light) (see Figure 5.4). As the grid is completed from left to right, the leaves become lighter. As it is filled in from top to bottom, the leaves become larger.

Class Inclusion

In Module 4.2, a 4-year-old was shown pictures of four cats and six dogs. When asked whether there were more dogs or more animals, he said more dogs. This preoperational child apparently could not focus on the two subclasses (dogs, cats) and the larger class (animals) at the same time (see Figure 5.5). But concrete-operational children can do so. Therefore, they are more likely to answer the question about the dogs and the animals correctly (Chapman & McBride, 1992).

Applications of Piaget's Theory to Education

Piaget believed that learning involves active discovery. Also, instruction should be geared to the child's level of development. When teaching a concrete-operational child about fractions, for example, the teacher should not only lecture but should also allow the child to divide concrete objects into parts. Third, Piaget believed that learning to take into account the perspectives of others is a key ingredient in the development of both cognition and morality.

© 2012 Cengage Learning

Figure 5.5 Class Inclusion Here are 10 animals, including six dogs. When asked whether there are more dogs or animals, the preoperational child focusing on one aspect of the problem at a time may see that there are more dogs than cats and say "dogs." The concrete-operational child is more likely to recognize that the class "animals" includes both dogs and cats, and will thus answer "animals."

Moral Development: The Child as Judge

On a cognitive level, moral development concerns the basis on which children judge actions as right or wrong. Jean Piaget and Lawrence Kohlberg believed that moral reasoning undergoes the same cognitive-developmental pattern in children around the world. The moral considerations that children weigh at a given age may be influenced by the values of the cultural settings in which they are reared, but they also reflect the orderly unfolding of cognitive processes (Lapsley, 2006). Moral reasoning is related to the child's overall cognitive development.

Piaget's Theory of Moral Development

Piaget observed children playing games such as marbles and judging the seriousness of the wrongdoing of characters in stories they were told. On the basis of these observations, he concluded that children's moral judgments develop in two overlapping stages: *moral realism* and *autonomous morality* (Piaget, 1932).

The first stage is usually referred to as the stage of **moral realism** or **objective morality**. During this stage, which emerges at about the age of 5, children consider behavior correct when it conforms to authority or to the rules of the game. When asked why something should be done in a certain way, the 5-year-old may answer "Because that's the way to do it" or "Because my Mommy says so." Five-year-olds perceive rules as embedded in the structure of things. Rules, to them, reflect ultimate reality, hence the term *moral realism*. Rules and right and wrong are seen as absolute, not as deriving from people to meet social needs.

Another consequence of viewing rules as embedded in the fabric of the world is **immanent justice**, or automatic retribution. This involves thinking that negative experiences are punishment for prior misdeeds, even when realistic causal links are absent (Callan et al., 2006).

Preoperational children tend to focus on only one dimension at a time. Therefore, they judge the wrongness of an act only in terms of the amount of damage done, not in terms of the intentions of the wrongdoer. Consider children's response to Piaget's story about the broken cups. Piaget told children a story in which one child breaks 15 cups accidentally and another child breaks one cup deliberately. Children in the stage of moral realism typically say that the child who did the most damage is the naughtiest and should be punished most (Piaget, 1932).

Piaget found that when children reach the ages of 9 to 11, they begin to show **autonomous morality**. Their moral judgments tend to become more self-governed,

moral realism The first stage in Piaget's cognitive-developmental theory of moral development, in which the child judges acts as moral when they conform to authority or to the rules of the game.

objective morality The perception of morality as objective, that is, as existing outside the cognitive functioning of people.

immanent justice The view that retribution for wrongdoing is a direct consequence of the wrongdoing.

autonomous morality The second stage in Piaget's cognitive-developmental theory of moral development, in which children base moral judgments on the intentions of the wrongdoer and on the amount of damage done.

as children come to view social rules as social agreements that can be changed. Children realize that circumstances can warrant breaking rules. Those who show autonomous morality can focus simultaneously on multiple dimensions, so they consider social rules and the motives of the wrongdoer.

Children in this stage also show a greater capacity to take the point of view of others, to empathize with them. Decentration and increased empathy prompt children to weigh the intentions of the wrongdoer more heavily than the amount of damage done. The child who broke one cup deliberately may be seen as deserving of more punishment than the child who broke 15 cups accidentally. Accidents are less likely to be considered crimes.

Kohlberg's Theory of Moral Development

Kohlberg (1981a, 1985) advanced the cognitive-developmental theory of moral development by elaborating on the kinds of information children use and on the complexities of moral reasoning. Before we discuss Kohlberg's views, read the tale that Kohlberg used in his research and answer the questions that follow.

Mina Chapman/Corbis Super RF/Alamy

Moral realism. It looks bad, but Mom asked her to find the car keys. Mom wasn't thinking of having her go through her purse, however. If the girl breaks things or drops them on the floor in the effort, is she being "bad"? Children in the stage of moral realism might well say yes, because they focus on the damage done, not on the intentions of the wrongdoer.

In Europe, a woman was near death from a special kind of cancer. There was one drug that the doctors thought might save her. It was a form of radium that a druggist in the same town had recently discovered. The drug was expensive to make, but the druggist was charging 10 times what the drug cost him to make. He paid $200 for the radium and charged $2,000 for a small dose of the drug. The sick woman's husband, Heinz, went to everyone he knew to borrow the money, but he could only get together about $1,000, which was half of what it cost. He told the druggist that his wife was dying and asked him to sell it cheaper or let him pay later. But the druggist said: "No, I discovered the drug and I'm going to make money from it." So Heinz got desperate and broke into the man's store to steal the drug for his wife. (Kohlberg, 1969)

Kohlberg emphasized the importance of being able to view the moral world from the perspective of another person (Krebs & Denton, 2005). Look at this situation from Heinz's perspective. What do you think? Should Heinz have tried to steal the

Moral Judgments

Is morality an innate biological function evident in children? Watch and learn.

drug? Was he right or wrong? As you can see from Table 5.1, the issue is more complicated than a simple yes or no. Heinz is caught in a moral dilemma in which legal or social rules (in this case, laws against stealing) are pitted against a strong human need (his desire to save his wife). According to Kohlberg's theory, children and adults arrive at yes or no answers for different reasons. These reasons can be classified according to the level of moral development they reflect.

Why do some children cheat, while others do their own work?

Alloy Photography/Veer

Children (and adults) are faced with many moral dilemmas. Consider cheating in school. When children fear failing a test, they may be tempted to cheat. Different children may decide not to cheat for different reasons. One child may fear getting caught. Another may decide that it is more important to live up to her moral principles than to get the highest possible grade. In each case, the child's decision is not to cheat. However, the decisions reflect different levels of reasoning.

Kohlberg argued that the developmental stages of moral reasoning follow the same sequence in all children. Children progress at different rates, and not everyone reaches the highest stage; but children must experience Stage 1 before Stage 2, and so on. Kohlberg theorized three levels of moral development and two stages within each level.

The Preconventional Level

At the **preconventional level**, children base their moral judgments on the consequences of their behavior. Stage 1 is oriented toward obedience and punishment. Good behavior means being obedient so one can avoid punishment. In Stage 2, good behavior allows people to satisfy their own needs and, perhaps, the needs of others. In a study of American children aged 7–16, Kohlberg (1963) found that Stage 1 and 2 types of moral judgments were offered most frequently by 7- to 10-year-olds. Stage 1 and 2 judgments fell off steeply after age 10.

preconventional level According to Kohlberg, a period during which moral judgments are based largely on expectations of rewards or punishments.

Table 5.1
Kohlberg's Levels and Stages of Moral Development

Stage of Development	Examples of Moral Reasoning That Support Heinz's Stealing the Drug	Examples of Moral Reasoning That Oppose Heinz's Stealing the Drug
Level I: Preconventional—Typically Begins in Early Childhood[a]		
Stage 1: Judgments guided by obedience and the prospect of punishment (the consequences of the behavior)	It is not wrong to take the drug. Heinz did try to pay the druggist for it, and it is only worth $200, not $2,000.	Taking things without paying is wrong because it is against the law. Heinz will get caught and go to jail.
Stage 2: Naively egoistic, instrumental orientation (things are right when they satisfy people's needs)	Heinz ought to take the drug because his wife really needs it. He can always pay the druggist back.	Heinz should not take the drug. If he gets caught and winds up in jail, it won't do his wife any good.
Level II: Conventional—Typically Begins in Middle Childhood		
Stage 3: Good-boy/good-girl orientation (moral behavior helps others and is socially approved)	Stealing is a crime, so it is bad, but Heinz should take the drug to save his wife or else people would blame him for letting her die.	Stealing is a crime. Heinz should not just take the drug, because his family will be dishonored and they will blame him.
Stage 4: Law-and-order orientation (moral behavior is doing one's duty and showing respect for authority)	Heinz must take the drug to do his duty to save his wife. Eventually, he has to pay the druggist for it, however.	If we all took the law into our own hands, civilization would fall apart, so Heinz should not steal the drug.
Level III: Postconventional—Typically Begins in Adolescence[b]		
Stage 5: Contractual, legalistic orientation (one must weigh pressing human needs against society's need to maintain social order)	This thing is complicated because society has a right to maintain law and order, but Heinz has to take the drug to save his wife.	I can see why Heinz feels he has to take the drug, but laws exist for the benefit of society as a whole and cannot simply be cast aside.
Stage 6: Universal ethical-principles orientation (people must follow universal ethical principles and their own consciences, even if it means breaking the law)	In this case, the law comes into conflict with the principle of the sanctity of human life. Heinz must take the drug because his wife's life is more important than the law.	If Heinz truly believes that stealing the drug is worse than letting his wife die, he should not take it. People have to make sacrifices to do what they think is right.

[a]Tends to be used less often in middle childhood.
[b]May not develop at all.

© 2012 Cengage Learning

Moral Development

Watch children at the preconventional and conventional levels of moral development respond to Heinz's dilemma.

Kohlberg's Theory of Moral Development

Explore to learn more about each of the six stages of Kohlberg's theory.

▸ **LO9** Describe the information-processing approach to cognitive development.

▸ **LO10** Discuss memory development in middle childhood.

▸ **LO11** Explain children's understanding of their cognitive processes.

The Conventional Level

At the **conventional level** of moral reasoning, right and wrong are judged by conformity to conventional (family, religious, societal) standards of right and wrong. According to the Stage 3 "good-boy/good-girl orientation," it is good to meet the needs and expectations of others. Moral behavior is what is "normal," what the majority does. In Stage 4, moral judgments are based on rules that maintain the social order. Showing respect for authority and duty is valued highly. Many people do not develop beyond the conventional level. Kohlberg (1963) found that Stage 3 and 4 types of judgments emerge during middle childhood. They are all but absent among 7-year-olds. However, they are reported by about 20% of 10-year-olds and by higher percentages of adolescents.

The Postconventional Level

At the **postconventional level**, moral reasoning is based on the person's own moral standards. If this level of reasoning develops at all, it is found among adolescents and adults (see Table 5.1).

Information Processing: Learning, Remembering, Problem Solving

Key elements in children's information processing include the following (Pressley & Hilden, 2006):

- Development of selective attention;
- Development of the capacity of memory and of the understanding of the processes of memory; and
- Development of the ability to solve problems, as, for example, by finding the correct formula and applying it.

Development of Selective Attention

The ability to focus one's attention and screen out distractions advances steadily through middle childhood (Rubia et al., 2006). Preoperational children engaged in problem solving tend to focus (or center) their attention on one element of the problem at a time, which is a major reason they lack conservation. Concrete-operational children can attend to multiple aspects of the problem at once, permitting them to conserve number and volume.

An experiment (Strutt et al., 1975) illustrated how selective attention and the ability to ignore distraction develop during middle childhood. The researchers

conventional level According to Kohlberg, a period during which moral judgments largely reflect social rules and conventions.

postconventional level According to Kohlberg, a period during which moral judgments are derived from moral principles, and people look to themselves to set moral standards.

sensory memory The structure of memory first encountered by sensory input; information is maintained in sensory memory for only a fraction of a second.

asked children between 6 and 12 years of age to sort a deck of cards as quickly as possible on the basis of the figures depicted on each card (e.g., circle versus square). In one condition, only the relevant dimension (i.e., form) was shown on each card. In another condition, a dimension not relevant to the sorting also was present (e.g., a horizontal or vertical line in the figure). In a third condition, two irrelevant dimensions were present (e.g., a star above or below the figure, in addition to a horizontal or vertical line in the figure). As seen in Figure 5.6, the irrelevant information interfered with sorting ability for all age groups, but older children were much less affected than younger children.

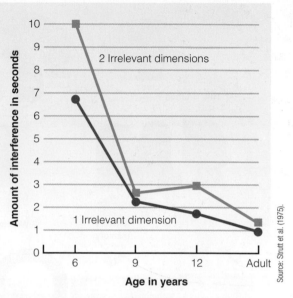

Figure 5.6 Development of the Ability to Ignore Distractions
Irrelevant information interfered with sorting ability for all age groups, but older children were less affected than younger ones.

Developments in the Storage and Retrieval of Information

Psychologists use the term *memory* to refer to the processes of storing and retrieving information. Many psychologists divide memory functioning into three major processes or structures: sensory memory, working memory, and long-term memory (see Figure 5.7).

Sensory Memory

When we look at an object and then blink our eyes, the visual impression of the object lasts for a fraction of a second in what is called **sensory memory** or the *sensory register*. Then the "trace" of the stimulus decays. The concept of sensory memory applies to all the senses. For example, when we are introduced to somebody, the trace of the sound of the name also decays, but we can remember the name by focusing on it.

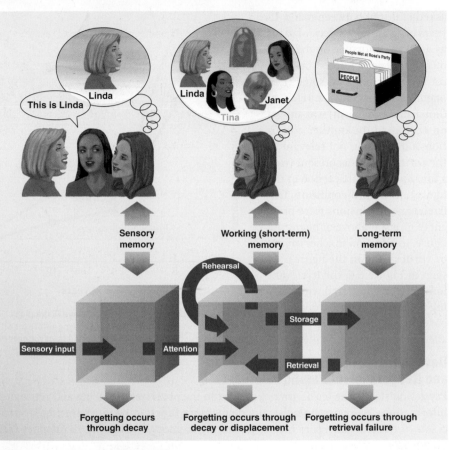

working memory The structure of memory that can hold a sensory stimulus for up to 30 seconds after the trace decays.

encode To transform sensory input into a form that is more readily processed.

rehearse To repeat.

long-term memory The structure of memory capable of relatively permanent storage of information.

elaborative strategy A method for increasing retention of new information by relating it to well-known information.

Figure 5.7 The Structure of Memory Many psychologists divide memory into three processes or "structures." Sensory information enters sensory memory, where memory traces are held briefly before decaying. If we attend to the information, much of it is transferred to working memory (also called short-term memory), where it may decay or be displaced if it is not transferred to long-term memory. We may use rehearsal (repetition) or elaborative strategies to transfer memories to long-term memory, from which they can be retrieved with the proper cues.

© 2012 Cengage Learning

Working Memory (Short-Term Memory)

When children focus on a stimulus in the sensory register, it tends to be retained in **working memory** (also called *short-term memory*) for up to 30 seconds after the trace of the stimulus decays. The ability to maintain information in short-term memory depends on cognitive strategies and on the capacity to continue to perceive a vanished stimulus. Memory function in middle childhood seems largely adult in organization and strategies and shows only quantitative improvement through early adolescence (Alloway et al., 2004; Archibald & Gathercole, 2006).

Auditory stimuli can be maintained longer in short-term memory than can visual stimuli. For this reason, one strategy for promoting memory is to **encode** visual stimuli as sounds. Then the sounds can be repeated out loud or mentally. In Figure 5.7, mentally repeating or **rehearsing** the sound of Linda's name helps the woman remember it.

Long-Term Memory

Think of **long-term memory** as a vast storehouse of information containing names, dates, places, what Johnny did to you in second grade, what Alyssa said about you when you were 12. Long-term memories may last days, years, or, for practical purposes, a lifetime.

There is no known limit to the amount of information that can be stored in long-term memory. From time to time, it may seem that we have forgotten, or lost, a long-term memory, such as the names of elementary- or high-school classmates. But it is more likely that we cannot find the right cues to retrieve it. It is lost in the same way we misplace an object but know it is still in the house.

Older children are more likely than younger children to use rote rehearsal, or repetition, to try to remember information (Saito & Miyake, 2004; Towse & Cowan, 2005). A more effective method than rote rehearsal is purposefully relating new material to well-known information, making it meaningful. Relating new material to known material is called an **elaborative strategy**. English teachers use an elaborative strategy when they have children use new words in sentences to help remember them.

Organization in Long-Term Memory

As children's knowledge of concepts advances, the storehouse of their long-term memory becomes organized according to categories. Preschoolers tend to organize their memories by grouping objects that share the same function (Lucariello et al., 2004; Towse, 2003). "Toast" may be grouped with "peanut butter sandwich" because both are edible. In middle childhood "toast" and "peanut butter" are likely to be joined as foods.

The Structure of Memory

Learn more about the three processes involved in memory.

Working Memory and Mathematics

Is there a link between differences in math achievement and working memory?

When items are correctly categorized in long-term memory, children are more likely to recall accurate information about them. For instance, do you "remember" whether whales breathe underwater? If you did not know that whales are mammals or if you knew nothing about mammals, a correct answer might depend on an instance of rote learning. If children have incorrectly classified whales as fish, they might search their "memories" and construct the wrong answer.

Knowledge in a particular area increases the capacity to store and retrieve related information. Chess experts are superior to amateurs at remembering where chess pieces have been placed on the board. In one particular study (Gobert & Simon, 2000), the experts were 8- to 12-year-old children and the amateurs were adults!

Development of Recall Memory

Children's memory is a good overall indicator of their cognitive ability (Gathercole et al., 2004a, 2004b; Towse & Cowan, 2005). In an experiment on categorization and memory, researchers placed objects that fell into four categories (furniture, clothing, tools, fruit) on a table before second and fourth graders (Hasselhorn, 1992). The children were allowed 3 minutes to arrange the pictures as they wished and to remember as many as they could. Fourth graders were more likely to categorize and recall the pictures than second graders.

Children's Eyewitness Testimony

Jean Piaget distinctly "remembered" an attempt to kidnap him from his baby carriage as he was being wheeled along the Champs-Élysées. He recalled the excited throng, the abrasions on the face of the nurse who rescued him, the police officer's white baton, and the flight of the assailant. But although they were graphic, Piaget's memories were false. Years later, the nurse admitted that she had made up the tale.

A child witness is typically asked questions to prompt information. But such questions may be leading; that is, they may suggest an answer. The

How reliable is children's eyewitness testimony? By age 10 or 11, children may be no more suggestible than adults. The findings for younger children are inconsistent, however.

metacognition Awareness of and control of one's cognitive abilities.

metamemory Knowledge of the functions and processes involved in one's storage and retrieval of information.

authorities or Piaget's nurse may have asked him leading questions that supported her false tale. For example, "What happened at school?" is not a leading question, but "Did your teacher touch you?" is. Can children's testimony be distorted by leading questions? It appears that by the age of 10 or 11, children are no more suggestible than adults, but younger children are more likely to be misled (Bruck et al., 2006; Krackow & Lynn, 2003). Research also indicates that repeated questioning may lead children to make up events that never happened to them (Roebers & Schneider, 2002).

What, then, are investigators to do when the only witnesses to criminal events are children? Maggie Bruck and her colleagues (2006) recommended that interviewers avoid leading or suggestive questions to minimize influencing the child's response.

Development of Metacognition and Metamemory

Children's knowledge and control of their cognitive abilities is termed **metacognition**. The development of metacognition is shown by the presence of the ability to formulate problems, awareness of the processes required to solve a problem, activation of cognitive strategies, maintenance of focus on the problem, and checking of answers.

As a sixth grader decides which homework assignments to do first, memorizes the state capitals for tomorrow's test, and then tests herself to see which she needs to study more, she is displaying metacognition (Flavell et al., 2002; Stright et al., 2001). **Metamemory** is an aspect of metacognition that refers to children's awareness of the functioning memory. Older students are more likely to accurately assess their knowledge; so they store and retrieve information more effectively (Towse & Cowan, 2005).

Older children also show more knowledge of strategies that can be used to facilitate memory. Preschoolers will usually use rehearsal if someone suggests they do, but not until about the age of 6 or 7 do children use it on their own (Flavell et al., 2002). As children develop, they are more likely to use selective rehearsal to remember important information.

Language Development and Literacy

Children's language ability grows more sophisticated in middle childhood. During this time, children learn to read as well. Many children are exposed to a variety of linguistic experiences, and these experiences affect cognitive development.

False Memories and Suggestibility

Watch and learn how children are susceptible to creating false memories when asked leading questions.

▶ **LO12** Describe language development in middle childhood.

▶ **LO13** Describe the skills that are involved in reading.

Vocabulary and Grammar

By the age of 6, the child's vocabulary has expanded to nearly 10,000 words. By 7–9 years of age, most children realize that words can have different meanings, so riddles and jokes that require some semantic sophistication entertain them. (Remember the joke at the beginning of this module.) By the age of 8 or 9, children are able to form tag questions, in which the question is tagged on to the end of a declarative sentence, such as "You want more ice cream, don't you?" and "You're sick, aren't you?" (Weckerly et al., 2004).

Children make subtle advances in articulation and in the capacity to use complex grammar. Preschoolers have difficulty understanding passive sentences such as "The truck was hit by the car," but children in the middle years have less difficulty interpreting them (Aschermann et al., 2004).

During these years, children develop the ability to use connectives, as illustrated by the sentence "I'll eat my spinach, but I don't want to." They also learn to form constructions with indirect objects and direct objects (e.g., "She showed her sister the toy").

Reading Skills and Literacy

Millions of people around the world are not literate and therefore cannot access contemporary knowledge. Even in the United States, some people cannot read or write, and the problem is most severe among recent immigrants.

Reading involves perceptual, cognitive, and linguistic processes (Smolka & Eviatar, 2006). It relies on the integration of visual and auditory information. Children must accurately perceive the sounds in their language and make basic visual discriminations (Levinthal & Lleras, 2007). Children must perceive the visual differences between letters such as *b* and *d* and *p* and *q*.

How do children become familiar with their own written languages? TV programs, such as *Sesame Street*, books, street signs, names of stores and restaurants, and the writing on packages all expose chidren to written language. Children from homes where books and other sources of stimulation are plentiful learn to read more readily. Reading storybooks with parents in the preschool years helps prepare a child for reading (Raikes et al., 2006).

Methods of Teaching Reading

Children read by integrating visual and auditory information (they associate what they see with sounds), whether they use the word-recognition method or the phonetic method. The **word-recognition method** associates visual stimuli such as *cat* and *Robert* with

word-recognition method A method for learning to read in which children come to recognize words through repeated exposure to them.

phonetic method A method for learning to read in which children decode the sounds of words based on their knowledge of the sounds of letters and letter combinations.

sight vocabulary Words that are immediately recognized on the basis of familiarity with their overall shapes, rather than decoded.

bilingual Using or capable of using two languages with nearly equal or equal facility.

the sound combinations that produce the spoken words. This capacity is usually acquired by rote learning, or extensive repetition.

In the **phonetic method**, children learn to associate written letters and letter combinations (such as *ph* or *sh*) with the sounds they indicate. Then they sound out words. The phonetic method provides skills children can use to decode new words, but some children learn more rapidly at early ages through the word-recognition method. The phonetic method can slow them down with familiar words. Most children and adults read familiar words by word recognition and make some effort to sound out new words.

Some English words can be read only by recognition, such as *one* and *two*. This method is useful when it comes to words such as *danger*, *stop*, *poison*, and a child's name, because it provides children with a basic **sight vocabulary**. But decoding skills help children read new words on their own.

Reading. Children who read at home during the school years show better reading skills in school and more positive attitudes toward reading.

Bilingualism: Linguistic Perspectives on the World

In 2000, approximately 47 million Americans spoke a language other than English at home (Shin & Bruno, 2003). Languages such as Spanish, Chinese, Korean, or Russian are spoken in the home, and perhaps in the neighborhood.

Compared to children who speak only one language, **bilingual** children do not have more academic problems. But a century ago, it was widely believed that children reared in bilingual homes were retarded in their cognitive development. The theory was that mental capacity is limited, so people who store two linguistic systems are crowding their mental abilities. Bilingual children "mix" languages (Gonzalez, 2006), but they can generally separate the two languages from an early age. At least half the children in the United States who speak Spanish in the home are proficient in both languages (Shin & Bruno, 2003).

Today most linguists consider it advantageous for children to be bilingual because knowledge of more than one language contributes to the complexity of the child's cognitive processes (Bialystok & Craik, 2007). For example, bilingual children are more likely to understand that the symbols used in language are arbitrary. Monolingual children are more likely to think erroneously that the word *dog* is an inherent part of the animal rather than an arbitrary label. A bilingual child from a Hispanic background would know that the animal is also called a *perro* in Spanish, and would thus be more likely to understand that labels for the same object can differ.

Check Your Learning Quiz 5.2

Go to **login.cengagebrain.com** and take the online quiz.

▶ **LO14** Define *intelligence*.

▶ **LO15** Discuss various theories of intelligence.

Did you know that—

- Researchers do not agree on what intelligence is?
- One psychologist includes "street smarts" as an aspect of intelligence?
- Two children can answer exactly the same items on an intelligence test correctly, yet one can be above average in intelligence and the other below average?
- Highly intelligent children are not necessarily creative?
- Highly creative children are not necessarily all that intelligent?
- Some researchers believe that intelligence is mainly determined by heredity?
- Other researchers believe that intelligence is mainly determined by environmental factors?
- Still other researchers believe that heredity and environmental factors are so deeply entangled in contributing to intelligence that it is all but impossible to say which, if either, is more important?

▼

In early childhood, children begin to develop a sense of whether or not they are good at things. In middle childhood, that sense of being good at things—or not so good at things—has much to do with schoolwork. Children gain impressions of how intelligent they are compared with other family members and schoolmates.

We tend to associate **intelligence** with academic success, advancement on the job, and appropriate social behavior. Despite our sense of familiarity with the concept of intelligence, intelligence cannot be seen, touched, or measured physically. For this reason, it is subject to various interpretations. As noted by Alfred Binet, the founder of modern intelligence testing, many people assume that intelligence is a fixed quantity, something like a knob on the head that's bigger in some people than in others. Binet challenged that notion, and the extent to which intelligence is biologi-

intelligence According to Wechsler, the "capacity … to understand the world [and the] resourcefulness to cope with its challenges."

achievement That which is attained by one's efforts and presumed to be made possible by one's abilities.

What is intelligence? Where does it come from?

© Mike Kemp/Rubberball/Corbis

cally determined, environmentally determined, or both remains something of an open question.

Regardless of its origins, intelligence is usually perceived as a child's underlying competence or *learning ability*. **Achievement**, by contrast, involves a child's acquired competencies or *performance*. Achievement is made possible, at least in part, by intelligence. Most psychologists would agree that many of the competencies underlying achievement are seen during middle childhood, when most children are first exposed to formal schooling.

Theories of Intelligence

Let's consider some theoretical approaches to intelligence. Then we will see how researchers and practitioners assess intellectual functioning.

Factor Theories

Many investigators view intelligence as consisting of one or more major mental abilities, or factors. In 1904, Charles Spearman suggested that the behaviors we consider intelligent have a common underlying factor *g*—"general intelligence"—that represents broad reasoning and problem-solving abilities, and that specific capacities, or *s* factors, account for certain individual abilities, like music or poetry (Lubinski, 2004).

Psychologist Louis Thurstone (1938) believed that intelligence consists of several specific factors, or *primary mental abilities*, such as the ability to learn the meaning of words and visuospatial abilities (see Table 5.2). Thurstone's research suggested that these factors were somewhat independent.

Table 5.2
Primary Mental Abilities, According to Thurstone

Ability	Definition
Visual and spatial abilities	Visualizing forms and spatial relationships
Perceptual speed	Grasping perceptual details rapidly, perceiving similarities and differences between stimuli
Numerical ability	Computing numbers
Verbal meaning	Knowing the meanings of words
Memory	Recalling information (words, sentences, etc.)
Word fluency	Thinking of words quickly (rhyming, doing crossword puzzles, etc.)
Deductive reasoning	Deriving examples from general rules
Inductive reasoning	Inferring general rules from examples

Sternberg's Theory of Intelligence

Psychologist Robert Sternberg (2011) constructed a three-part, or "triarchic," theory of intelligence. The parts are analytical intelligence, creative intelligence, and practical intelligence (see Figure 5.8). Analytical intelligence is academic ability. Creative intelligence is defined by the abilities to cope with novel situations and to profit from experience. Practical intelligence, or "street smarts," enables people to adapt to the demands of their environment, including the social environment.

Gardner's Theory of Multiple Intelligences

Psychologist Howard Gardner (1983, 2006), like Sternberg, believes that intelligence—or intelligences—reflects more than academic ability. Gardner referred to each kind of intelligence in his theory as "an intelligence" because each differs in quality (see Figure 5.9).

Three of Gardner's intelligences are verbal ability, logical–mathematical reasoning, and spatial intelligence (visuospatial skills). Others include bodily–kinesthetic intelligence (as shown by dancers and gymnasts), musical intelligence, inter-

© 2012 Cengage Learning

Analytical intelligence
(academic ability)
Abilities to solve problems,
compare and contrast, judge,
evaluate, and criticize

Creative intelligence
(creativity and insight)
Abilities to invent, discover,
suppose, and theorize

Practical intelligence
("street smarts")
Abilities to adapt to the demands
of one's environment and apply
knowledge in practical situations

Figure 5.8 Sternberg's Triarchic Theory of Intelligence Robert Sternberg views intelligence as three pronged, with analytical, creative, and practical aspects.

Figure 5.9 Gardner's Theory of Multiple Intelligences Gardner argued that there are many intelligences, and that each has its neurological bases in its own parts of the brain.

personal intelligence (as shown by empathy and ability to relate to others), and interpersonal knowledge (self-insight). Individuals may show great intelligence in one area without notable abilities in others. Critics agree that many people have special talents, as in music, but they question whether such talents are intelligences (Neisser et al., 1996).

Emotional and Social Intelligence

Read and expand your knowledge of emotional and social intelligence.

▶ **LO16** Describe tests used to measure intelligence.

▶ **LO17** Discuss cultural bias in intelligence testing.

There are thus many views of what intelligence is and how many kinds of intelligence there may be. We do not yet have the final word on the nature of intelligence, but I would like to share Linda Gottfredson's definition:

> [Intelligence is] a very general mental capability that, among other things, involves the ability to reason, plan, solve problems, think abstractly, comprehend complex ideas, learn quickly and learn from experience. It is not merely book learning, a narrow academic skill, or test-taking smarts. Rather it reflects a broader and deeper capability for comprehending our surroundings—"catching on," "making sense," of things, or "figuring out what to do." (Linda Gottfredson in Nisbett, 2009, p. 4)

Measurement of Intellectual Development

There may be disagreements about the nature of intelligence, but thousands of intelligence tests are administered by psychologists and educators every day.

The Stanford-Binet Intelligence Scales (SBIS) and the Wechsler scales for children and adults are the most widely used and well-respected intelligence tests. The SBIS and Wechsler scales yield scores called **intelligence quotients (IQs)**. The concept of intelligence per se is more difficult to define. The SBIS and Wechsler scales have been carefully developed and revised over the years. Each of them has been used to make vital educational decisions about children. In many cases, children whose test scores fall below or above certain scores are placed in special classes for intellectually deficient or gifted children.

intelligence quotient (IQ) (1) A ratio obtained by dividing a child's mental age on an intelligence test by his or her chronological age; (2) a score on an intelligence test.

mental age (MA) The intellectual level at which a child is functioning, as assessed according to the typical mental functioning for a child of a given age.

chronological age (CA) A person's age.

The Stanford-Binet Intelligence Scales

The SBIS originated in the work of Frenchmen Alfred Binet and Theodore Simon about a century ago for the French public school system. Binet assumed that intelligence increased with age. Therefore, older children should get more items right. Thus, Binet arranged a series of questions in order of difficulty, from easier to harder. It has since undergone revision and refinement.

The Binet–Simon scale yielded a score called a **mental age (MA)**. The MA shows the intellectual level at which a child is functioning. A child with an MA of 6 is functioning, intellectually, like the average 6-year-old child.

The Stanford-Binet Intelligence Scales. In 1905, Alfred Binet and Theodore Simon in France introduced the idea of measuring intelligence. This version of the test was produced in 1937 by Lewis Terman and Maude Merrill in the United States and was specifically designed for younger children.

© SSPL/The Image Works

Lewis Terman published an adaptation of the Binet–Simon scale for use with American children in 1916. Because Terman carried out his work at Stanford University, it is now named the Stanford-Binet Intelligence Scales. The SBIS yields an intelligence quotient, or IQ, rather than an MA. The SBIS today can be used with children from the age of 2 up to adults. Table 5.3 shows the kinds of items answered correctly by half the respondents at the given ages.

The IQ states the relationship between a child's mental age and his or her actual or chronological age (CA). An MA of 8 is an above-average score for a 6-year-old but a below-average score for a 10-year-old.

Alfred Binet

Read and learn more about Alfred Binet.

Table 5.3
Items Similar to Those on the Stanford-Binet Intelligence Scales

Level (Years)	Item
2	1. Children show knowledge of basic vocabulary words by identifying parts of a doll, such as the mouth, ears, and hair. 2. Children show counting and spatial skills along with visual–motor coordination by building a tower of four blocks to match a model.
4	1. Children show word fluency and categorical thinking by filling in the missing words when they are asked questions such as "Father is a man; mother is a _____?" or "Hamburgers are hot; ice cream is _____?" 2. Children show comprehension by answering correctly when they are asked questions such as "Why do people have automobiles?" or "Why do people have medicine?"
9	1. Children can point out verbal absurdities, as in this question: "In an old cemetery, scientists unearthed a skull which they think was that of George Washington when he was only 5 years of age. What is silly about that?" 2. Children display fluency with words, as shown by answering questions such as "Can you tell me a number that rhymes with *snore*?" or "Can you tell me a color that rhymes with *glue*?"
Adult	1. Adults show knowledge of the meanings of words and conceptual thinking by correctly explaining the differences between word pairs like *sickness* and *misery*, *house* and *home*, and *integrity* and *prestige*. 2. Adults show spatial skills by correctly answering questions such as "If a car turned to the right to head north, in what direction was it heading before it turned?"

© 2012 Cengage Learning

The IQ is computed by the formula

$$IQ = \frac{\text{Mental Age (MA)}}{\text{Chronological Age (CA)}} \times 100$$

According to this formula, a child with an MA of 6 and a CA of 6 would have an IQ of 100. Furthermore, because of the factor of chronological age in the formula, children of different ages might answer the same items on a test the same but end up receiving different IQ scores.

Today, IQ scores on the SBIS are derived by comparing children's and adults' performances with those of other people of the same age. People who get more items correct than average attain IQ scores above 100, and people who answer fewer items correctly attain scores below 100.

The Wechsler Scales

David Wechsler (1975) developed a series of scales for use with school-age children (Wechsler Intelligence Scale for Children), younger children (Wechsler Preschool and Primary Scale of Intelligence), and adults (Wechsler Adult Intelligence Scale).

The Wechsler scales group test questions into subtests, such as those shown below, that measure different intellectual tasks. For this reason, subtests compare a person's performance on one type of task (such as defining words) with another (such as using blocks to construct geometric designs). The Wechsler scales thus suggest children's strengths and weaknesses as well as provide overall measures of intellectual-functioning.

Wechsler described some subtests as measuring verbal tasks and others as assessing performance tasks (see sample items below). In general, verbal subtests require knowledge of verbal concepts, whereas performance subtests (see Figure 5.10) require familiarity with spatial-relations concepts. Wechsler's scales permit the computation of verbal and performance IQs.

Verbal Items

- *Information:* "What is the capital of the United States?," "Who was Shakespeare?"

- *Comprehension:* "Why do we have ZIP codes?," "What does 'A stitch in time saves nine' mean?"

- *Arithmetic:* "If three candy bars cost 25 cents, how much will 18 candy bars cost?"

- *Similarities:* "How are good and bad alike?," "How are peanut butter and jelly alike?"

Nonverbal/Performance Items

- *Picture completion:* Pointing to the missing part of a picture.

- *Picture arrangement:* Arranging cartoon pictures in sequence so that they tell a meaningful story.

- *Block design:* Copying pictures of geometric designs using multicolored blocks.

- *Object assembly:* Putting pieces of a puzzle together so that they form a meaningful object.

Measures of IQ

Watch and learn more about how intelligence is measured.

Picture arrangement

These pictures tell a story, but they are in the wrong order. Put them in the right order so that they tell a story.

Picture completion

What part is missing from this picture?

Block design

Put the blocks together to make this picture.

Object assembly

Put the pieces together as quickly as you can.

© 2012 Cengage Learning

Figure 5.10 Performance Items on an Intelligence Test This figure shows items that resemble those found on the Wechsler Intelligence Scale for Children.

Verbal Items (Continued)
- *Vocabulary:* "What does *canal* mean?"
- *Digit span*: Repeating a series of numbers, presented by the examiner, forward and backward.

Nonverbal/Performance Items (Continued)
- *Coding:* Rapid scanning and drawing of symbols that are associated with numbers.
- *Mazes:* Using a pencil to trace the correct route from a starting point to home.

Figure 5.11 indicates the labels that Wechsler assigned to various IQ scores and the approximate percentages of the population who attain IQ scores at those levels. Most children's IQ scores cluster around the average. Only about 5% of the population have IQ scores above 130 or below 70.

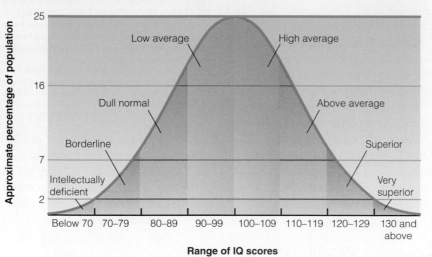

Figure 5.11 Variations in IQ Scores IQ scores vary according to a bell-shaped, or "normal," curve. Scores tend to cluster around the central score (defined as 100) and then to decrease in frequency as they move upward or downward.

IQ Test Items

Interact with performance items from an IQ test.

▸ **LO18** Describe patterns in the development of intelligence.

The Testing Controversy

Most psychologists and educational specialists consider intelligence tests to be at least somewhat biased against African Americans and members of lower social classes (Snyderman & Rothman, 1990). If scoring well on intelligence tests requires a certain type of cultural experience, the tests are said to have a **cultural bias**. For this reason, psychologists have tried to construct **culture-free intelligence tests**, or *culture-fair intelligence tests*.

Some tests do not rely on expressive language at all. For example, Raymond Cattell's (1949) Culture Fair Intelligence Test evaluates reasoning ability through the child's comprehension of the rules that govern a progression of geometric designs, as shown in Figure 5.12.

But culture-free tests have not lived up to their promise. First, middle-class children still outperform lower-class children on them (Rushton et al., 2003). Middle-class children, for example, are more likely to have basic familiarity with materials used in the testing, such as blocks and pencils and paper. They are more likely to have played with blocks (a practice relevant to the Cattell test). Second, culture-free tests do not predict academic success as well as other intelligence tests, and scholastic aptitude remains the central concern of educators (Keogh & Whyte, 2006).

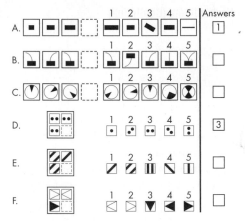

Figure 5.12 Examples of Types of Items Found on Cattell's Culture Fair Intelligence Test Culture-fair tests attempt to use items that do not discriminate against ethnic groups on the basis of cultural background. For each item, which answer (1, 2, 3, 4, or 5) completes the series? Answers are shown below.

Source: Sample items from Cattell's Culture-Fair Intelligence Test. Copyright © 1949, 1960. Reproduced with permission from the publishers, Hogrefe Ltd., from Culture Fair Scale 2, Test A by R. B. Cattell and A. K. S. Cattell. The UK version of the test is soon to be updated and restandardized.

Answers: 1, X, 3, X, X

cultural bias A factor hypothesized to be present in intelligence tests that provides an advantage for test takers from certain cultural backgrounds.

culture-free test A test from which cultural biases have been removed.

Patterns of Intellectual Development

Intellectual growth seems to occur in at least two major spurts. The first occurs at about the age of 6; it coincides with entry into school and also with the shift from preoperational to concrete-operational thought. School may help crystallize intellectual functioning at this time. The second spurt occurs at about age 10 or 11.

But once they reach middle childhood, children appear to undergo relatively more stable patterns of gains in intellectual functioning, although there are still spurts (Deary et al., 2004). As a result, intelligence tests gain greater predictive power. In a classic study by Marjorie Honzik and her colleagues (1948), intelligence test scores taken at the age of 9 correlated strongly (+0.90) with scores at the age of 10 and more moderately (+0.76) with scores at the age of 18. Testing at age 11 even showed a moderate to high relationship with scores at the age of 77 (Deary et al., 2004).

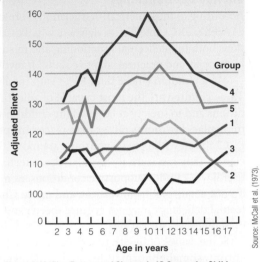

Figure 5.13 Five Patterns of Change in IQ Scores for Children in the Fels Longitudinal Study In the Fels Longitudinal Study, IQ scores remained stable between the ages of 2½ and 17 for only one of five groups, Group 1.

Despite the increased predictive power of intelligence tests during middle childhood, individual differences exist. In the classic Fels Longitudinal Study (see Figure 5.13), two groups of children (Groups 1 and 3) made reasonably consistent gains in intelligence-test scores between the ages of 10 and 17, whereas three groups declined. Group 4, children who had shown the most intellectual promise at age 10, went on to show the most precipitous decline, although they still wound up in the highest 2%–3% of the population (McCall et al., 1973). Many factors influence changes in IQ scores, including changes in the home, socioeconomic circumstances, and education (Deary et al., 2004).

Differences in Intellectual Development

The average IQ score in the United States is close to 100. About half the children in the United States attain IQ scores in the broad average range from 90 to 110. Nearly 95% attain scores between 70 and 130. Children who attain IQ scores below 70 are generally labeled "intellectually deficient" or "mentally retarded." Children who attain scores of 130 or above are usually labeled "gifted."

▶ **LO19** Discuss intellectual deficiency and giftedness.

▶ **LO20** Discuss socioeconomic and ethnic differences in intelligence.

▶ **LO21** Discuss the relationship between creativity and intelligence.

Intellectual Deficiency

According to the American Association on Intellectual and Developmental Disabilities (AAIDD, 2007), intellectual deficiency "is a disability characterized by significant limitations both in intellectual functioning and in adaptive behavior as expressed in conceptual, social, and practical adaptive skills." It involves an IQ score of no more than 70–75.

Most children (more than 80%) with intellectual deficiency have mild deficiency. These children are the most capable of adjusting to the demands of educational institutions and to society at large. Many children with mild deficiency are mainstreamed in regular classrooms rather than placed in special-needs classes.

Children with Down syndrome are most likely to have moderate intellectual deficiency. They can learn to speak, to dress, feed, and clean themselves, and to engage in useful work under supportive conditions, as in a sheltered workshop, but they usually do not acquire skills in reading and math. Children with severe and profound intellectual deficiency may not acquire speech and self-help skills and may remain dependent on others for survival.

Some causes of intellectual deficiency are biological. The deficiency can stem from chromosomal abnormalities such as Down syndrome; genetic disorders such as phenylketonuria; and brain damage (AAIDD, 2007). Brain damage can have many origins, including childhood accidents and problems during pregnancy. For example, maternal alcohol abuse, malnutrition, or diseases can damage the fetus. In **cultural-familial intellectual deficiency**, children are biologically normal but do not develop age-appropriate behavior at the normal pace because of an impoverished home environment. They may have little opportunity to interact with adults or play with stimulating toys.

Giftedness

Giftedness involves more than excellence on the tasks provided by standard intelligence tests. In determining who is gifted, most educators include children who have outstanding abilities; are capable of high performance in a specific academic area, such as language or mathematics; or show creativity, leadership, distinction in the visual or performing arts, or bodily talents, as in gymnastics and dancing.

Socioeconomic and Ethnic Differences

Research has found differences in IQ scores between socioeconomic and ethnic groups. Lower-class American children attain IQ scores some 10–15 points lower than those attained by middle- and upper-class children. African American, Latin American, and

cultural-familial intellectual deficiency Substandard intellectual performance stemming from lack of opportunity to acquire knowledge and skills.

creativity A mental trait characterized by flexibility, ingenuity, and originality.

convergent thinking A thought process that attempts to focus on the single best solution to a problem.

divergent thinking Free and fluent association to the elements of a problem.

Native American children all tend to score below the norms for European Americans (Neisser et al., 1996). Youth of Asian descent frequently outscore youth of European backgrounds on achievement tests in math and science, including the math portion of the SAT (Dandy & Nettelbeck, 2002; Stevenson et al., 1993).

Asian students and their mothers tend to attribute academic success to hard work (Randel et al., 2000), whereas American mothers are more likely to attribute academic success to natural ability (Basic Behavioral Science Task Force, 1996). Thus Asian students may work harder.

Creativity and Intellectual Development

Asian children and Asian American children frequently outscore other American children on intelligence tests. Can we attribute the difference to genetic factors or to Asian parents' emphasis on aquiring cognitive skills?

Creativity is the ability to do things that are novel and useful (Sternberg, 2006b). Creative children and adults can solve problems to which there are no preexisting solutions, no tried and tested formulas (Simonton, 2006a, b). Creative children take chances (R. M. Milgram & Livne, 2006; Sternberg, 2006a): They refuse to accept limitations. They appreciate art and music. They challenge social norms. They examine ideas that other people accept at face value.

Some scientists have argued that creativity and innovation require high levels of general intelligence (Heilman et al., 2003), but the tests we use to measure intelligence and creativity tend to show only a moderate relationship between IQ scores and measures of creativity (Sternberg & Williams, 1997). Some children who obtain average IQ scores excel in creative areas such as music or art.

Children mainly use convergent thinking to arrive at the correct answers on intelligence tests. In **convergent thinking**, thought is limited to present facts; the problem solver narrows his or her thinking to find the best solution. A child uses convergent thinking to arrive at the right answer to a multiple-choice question or to a question on an intelligence test.

Creative thinking tends to be divergent rather than convergent (O. Vartanian et al., 2003). In **divergent thinking**, the child associates freely to the elements of the problem. (We use divergent thinking when we are trying to generate ideas to answer an essay question or to find keywords to search on the Internet.) Tests of creativity determine how flexible, fluent, and original a person's thinking is. A mea-

Closing the Achievement Gap

Watch and learn how one school addressed the academic achievement gap.

Bias in Intelligence Testing

Learn more about intelligence, Gardner's multiple intelligences, and the idea of cultural and social biases in intelligence testing.

▶ **LO22** Discuss the roles of nature and nurture in the development of intelligence.

sure of creativity might ask you how many ways you can classify the following group of names:

| Martha | Paul | Jeffry | Sally | Pablo | Joan |

Other measures of creativity include suggesting improvements or unusual uses for a familiar toy or object, naming things that belong in the same class, producing words similar in meaning, and writing different endings for a story.

Determinants of Intellectual Development

If heredity is involved in human intelligence, closely related people ought to have more similar IQs than distantly related or unrelated people, even when they are reared separately. Figure 5.14 shows the averaged results of more than 100 studies of IQ and heredity (Bouchard et al., 1990). The IQ scores of identical (monozygotic, or MZ) twins are more alike than the scores for any other pairs, even when the twins have been reared apart. The average correlation for MZ twins reared together is +0.85; for those reared apart, it is +0.67. Correlations between the IQ scores of fraternal (dizygotic, DZ) twins, siblings, and parents and children are generally comparable, as is their degree of genetic relationship. The correlations tend to vary from about +0.40 to +0.59.

Overall, studies suggest that the **heritability** of intelligence is between 40% and 60% (Bouchard et al., 1990; Neisser et al., 1996). That is, about half of the difference between your IQ score and those of other people can be explained in terms of genetic factors.

Let's return to Figure 5.14. Note that genetic pairs (such as MZ twins) reared together show higher correlations between IQ scores than similar genetic pairs (such as other MZ twins) who lived apart. This finding holds for MZ twins, siblings, parents, children, and unrelated people. For this reason, the same group of studies that suggests that heredity plays a role in determining IQ scores also suggests that the environment plays a role.

Classic projects involving adopted children in Colorado, Texas, and Minnesota (Coon et al., 1990; Scarr, 1993; Turkheimer, 1991) found a stronger relationship between the IQ scores of adopted children and their biological parents than between the IQ scores of adopted children and their adoptive parents.

Studies of environmental influences on IQ use several research strategies, including discovering situational factors that affect IQ scores, exploring children's abilities to rebound from early deprivation, and exploring the effects of positive early environ-

heritability The degree to which the variations in a trait from one person to another can be attributed to genetic factors.

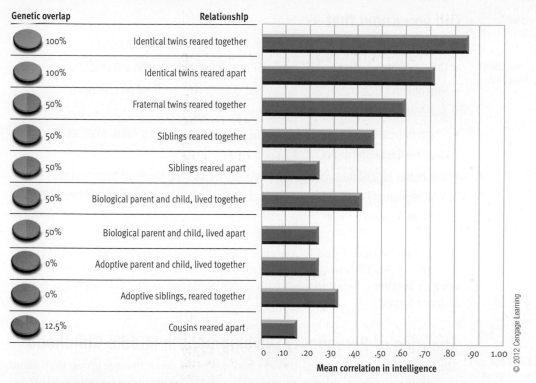

Genetic overlap	Relationship
100%	Identical twins reared together
100%	Identical twins reared apart
50%	Fraternal twins reared together
50%	Siblings reared together
50%	Siblings reared apart
50%	Biological parent and child, lived together
50%	Biological parent and child, lived apart
0%	Adoptive parent and child, lived together
0%	Adoptive siblings, reared together
12.5%	Cousins reared apart

Mean correlation in intelligence

© 2012 Cengage Learning

Figure 5.14 Findings of Studies of the Relationship between IQ Scores and Heredity. The data represent a composite of several studies. By and large, correlations are higher between people who are more closely related, yet people who are reared together have more similar IQ scores than people who are reared apart. Such findings suggest that both genetic and environmental factors contribute to IQ scores.

ments. Children whose parents are responsive and provide appropriate play materials and varied experiences during the early years attain higher IQ and achievement-test scores (Bradley, 2006). Graduates of Head Start and other preschool programs also show significant gains in IQ and other test scores (D. A. Phillips & Styfco, 2007).

Many psychologists believe that heredity and environment interact to influence intelligence (Lubinski & Benbow, 2000; Winner, 2000). An impoverished environment may prevent some children from living up to their potential. An enriched environment may encourage others to realize their potential.

Check Your Learning Quiz 5.3

Go to **login.cengagebrain.com** and take the online quiz.

▶ **LO23** Describe personality development in middle childhood.

▶ **LO24** Explain the relationship between social cognition and perspective taking.

Did you know that—

- Children's self-esteem tends to decline throughout middle childhood?
- Children with a favorable self-image tend to have parents who are strict?
- Parents and classmates tend to have an equally strong effect on children's self-esteem in middle childhood?
- Some children blame themselves for all the problems in their lives, whether they deserve the blame or not?
- It is better for children with school phobia to be pushed to return to school rather than remain at home until the origins of the problem are uncovered and resolved?

▼

In the years between 6 and 12, the child's social world expands. Peers take on greater importance and friendships deepen. Entry into school exposes the child to the influence of teachers. Relationships with parents change as children develop greater independence.

Theories of Personality Development in Middle Childhood

latency stage In psychoanalytic theory, the fourth stage of psychosexual development, characterized by repression of sexual impulses and development of skills.

industry versus inferiority A stage of psychosocial development in Erikson's theory occurring in middle childhood; mastery of tasks leads to a sense of industry, whereas failure produces feelings of inferiority.

social cognition The development of children's understanding of the relationship between the self and others.

The major theories of personality have had less to say about this age group than about the other periods of childhood and adolescence. Nevertheless, common threads emerge.

Psychodynamic Theory

According to Freud, children in the middle years are in the **latency stage**. Freud believed that sexual feelings remain repressed (unconscious) during this period. Children use this period to focus on developing intellectual, social, and other culturally valued skills.

The acquisition of cognitive and social skills is the major developmental task of middle childhood, according to Erik Erikson and Freud. Erikson labeled this stage **industry versus inferiority**. Children who are able to master the challenges of the middle years develop a sense of industry or competence. Children who have difficulties in school or with peer relationships may develop a sense of inferiority.

Social Cognitive Theory

Social cognitive theory focuses on the importance of rewards and modeling in middle childhood. During these years, children depend less on external rewards and punishments and increasingly regulate their own behavior. They are exposed to an increasing variety of models. Not only parents but also teachers, other adults, peers, and symbolic models (such as TV characters or the heroine in a story) serve as influential models (Anderson et al., 2007; Oates & Messer, 2007).

Cognitive-Developmental Theory and Social Cognition

According to Piaget, middle childhood coincides with the stage of concrete operations and is partly characterized by a decline in egocentrism and an expansion of the capacity to view the world and oneself from other people's perspectives. This cognitive advance affects the child's social relationships (Mischo, 2004; Zan & Hildebrandt, 2003).

Social cognition refers to perception of the social world; our concern is the development of children's perspective-taking skills. Robert Selman and his colleagues (Selman, 1980; Selman & Dray, 2006) studied the development of these skills by presenting children with a social dilemma such as the following:

> Holly is an 8-year-old girl who likes to climb trees. She is the best tree climber in the neighborhood. One day while climbing down from a tall tree, she falls off the bottom branch but does not hurt herself. Her father sees her fall. He is upset and asks her to promise not to climb trees any more. Holly promises. Later that day, Holly and her friends meet Sean. Sean's kitten is caught up in a tree and can't get down. Something has to be done right away, or the kitten may fall. Holly is the only one who climbs trees well enough to reach the kitten and get it down, but she remembers her promise to her father. (Selman, 1980, p. 36)

Children in Selman's studies were then asked questions such as "How will Holly's father feel if he finds out she climbed the tree?" Based on the children's responses, Selman (1976) described five levels of perspective-taking skills in childhood (see below).

Social-Emotional Learning

Watch children learn to model appropriate social behavior in school.

▶ **LO25** Describe how the self-concept develops during middle childhood.

▶ **LO26** Discuss the development of learned helplessness.

Table 5.3
Levels of Perspective Taking

Children with better perspective-taking skills tend to have better peer relationships (Selman & Dray, 2006).	
Selman's Perspective-Taking Skill Levels	
Level 0, Ages 3–6	Children are egocentric and do not realize that other people have perspectives different from their own. A child of this age will typically say that Holly will save the kitten because she likes kittens and that her father will be happy because he likes kittens too. The child assumes that everyone feels as she does.
Level 1, Ages 5–9[a]	Children understand that people in different situations may have different perspectives. The child still assumes that only one perspective is "right." A child might say that Holly's father would be angry if he did not know why she climbed the tree. But if she told him why, he would understand. The child recognizes that the father's perspective may differ from Holly's because of lack of information. But once he has the information, he will assume the "right" (i.e., Holly's) perspective.
Level 2, Ages 7–12[a]	The child understands that people may think or feel differently because they have different values or ideas. The child also recognizes that others are capable of understanding the child's own perspective. Therefore, the child is better able to anticipate reactions of others. The typical child of this age might say that Holly knows that her father will understand why she climbed the tree and that he therefore will not punish her.
Level 3, Ages 10–15[a]	The child finally realizes that both she and another person can consider each other's point of view at the same time. The child may reason along these lines: Holly's father will think that Holly shouldn't have climbed the tree. But now that he has heard her side of the story, he would feel that she was doing what she thought was right. Holly realizes that her father will consider how she felt.
Level 4, Ages 12+	The child realizes that mutual perspective taking does not always lead to agreement. The perspectives of the larger social group also must be considered. A child of this age might say that society expects children to obey their parents and therefore that Holly should realize why her father might punish her.

[a]Ages may overlap.
Source: Selman (1976).

Development of the Self-Concept in Middle Childhood

In early childhood, children's self-concept focuses on concrete external traits, such as appearance, activities, and living situations. But as children undergo the cognitive developments of middle childhood, more abstract internal traits, or personality traits, begin to play a role. Social relationships and group memberships take on significance (Harter, 2006; R. A. Thompson, 2006).

An investigative method called the Twenty Statements Test bears out this progression. Children are given a sheet of paper with the question "Who am I?" and 20 spaces in which to write answers. Consider the answers of a 9-year-old boy and an 11-year-old girl (Montemayor & Eisen, 1977, pp. 317–318):

> The nine-year-old boy: My name is Bruce C. I have brown eyes. I have brown hair. I have brown eyebrows. I'm 9 years old. I LOVE? sports. I have 7 people in my family. I have great? eye site. I have lots! of friends. I live on 1923 Pinecrest Drive. I'm going on 10 in September. I'm a boy. I have a uncle that is almost 7 feet tall. My school is Pinecrest. My teacher is Mrs. V. I play hockey! I'm also the smartest boy in the class. I LOVE! food. I love fresh air. I LOVE school.

> The eleven-year-old girl: My name is A. I'm a human being. I'm a girl. I'm a truthful person. I'm not pretty. I do so-so in my studies. I'm a very good cellist. I'm a very good pianist. I'm a little bit tall for my age. I like several boys. I like several girls. … I play tennis. I am a very good musician. … I'm always ready to be friends with anybody. Mostly I'm good, but I lose my temper. I'm not well liked by some girls and boys. I don't know if boys like me or not.

Only the 9-year-old lists his age and address, discusses his family, and focuses on physical traits, such as eye color, in his self-definition. The 9-year-old mentions his likes, which can be considered rudimentary psychological traits, but they are tied to the concrete, as would be expected of a concrete-operational child. The 9- and 11-year-olds list their competencies. The 11-year-old's struggle to bolster her self-esteem—her insistence on her musical abilities despite her qualms about her attractiveness—shows a greater concern with psychological traits and social relationships.

Self-Concept

Discover the differences between self-concept in early childhood and self-concept in middle childhood.

Self-Esteem

Explore to learn more about self esteem in middle childhood, and learned helplessness

Self-Esteem

As children enter middle childhood, they evaluate their self-worth in many different areas (Tassi et al., 2001). Preschoolers tend to see themselves as generally good at doing things or not. But by 5–7 years of age, children are able to judge their performance in seven different areas: physical ability, physical appearance, peer relationships, parent relationships, reading, math, and general school performance. They also report a general self-concept (Harter, 2006).

Children's self-esteem declines throughout middle childhood, reaching a low ebb at 12 or 13. Then it increases during adolescence (Harter, 2006). What accounts for the decline? Because preschoolers are egocentric, their self-concepts may be unrealistic. By middle childhood, children can compare themselves with other children and arrive at a more honest and critical self-appraisal. Girls tend to have more positive self-concepts than boys regarding reading, general academics, and helping others. Boys tend to have more positive self-concepts in math, physical ability, and physical appearance (J. E. Jacobs et al., 2005; L. Wang, 2005).

Authoritative parenting apparently contributes to children's self-esteem (Baumrind, 1991a, 1991b; Supple & Small, 2006). Children with a favorable self-image tend to have parents who are restrictive, involved, and loving. Children with low self-esteem are more likely to have authoritarian or rejecting–neglecting parents.

Social acceptance by peers is related to self-perceived competence in academic, social, and athletic domains (Nesdale & Lambert, 2007). Parents and classmates have an equally strong effect on children's self-esteem in middle childhood. Friends and teachers have relatively less influence but also matter (Harter, 2006).

Learned Helplessness

learned helplessness An acquired (hence, learned) belief that one is unable to obtain the rewards one would wish to obtain.

conduct disorder A disorder marked by persistent breaking of the rules and violations of the rights of others.

One outcome of low self-esteem in academics is known as **learned helplessness**. Learned helplessness is the acquired belief that one is unable to obtain the rewards that one seeks. "Helpless" children tend to quit following failure, whereas children who believe in their own ability tend to persist or change their strategies (B. J. Zimmerman, 2000). One reason for this difference is that "helpless" children believe that success is due more to ability than effort and that they have little ability in a particular area. Consequently, persistence seems futile (Bandura et al., 2001). Helpless children typically obtain lower grades and lower scores on IQ and achievement tests (S. Goldstein & Brooks, 2005).

A gender difference emerges in mathematics (Simpkins et al., 2006). Researchers have found that even when girls are performing as well as boys in math and science, they have less confidence in their ability (Anderman et al., 2001). Why? Many parents and teachers hold the stereotype that girls have less math ability than boys despite their daughter's and female students' demonstrated skills.

Behavioral Problems That Tend to Arise in Middle Childhood

Millions of children in the United States suffer from emotional or behavioral problems and could profit from professional treatment, but most of them are unlikely to receive it. Here we focus on conduct disorders, depression, and anxiety.

Conduct Disorders

Children with **conduct disorders** persistently break rules or violate the rights of others. They exhibit behaviors such as lying, stealing, fire setting, truancy, cruelty to animals, and fighting (American Psychiatric Association, 2000). Conduct disorders typically emerge by 8 years of age and are much more common in boys than girls (Nock et al., 2006).

Children with conduct disorders are often involved in sexual activity before puberty and smoke, drink, and abuse other substances. They have a low tolerance for frustration and may have temper flare-ups. They tend to blame other people for their scrapes. Academic achievement is usually below grade level, but intelligence is usually at least average. Many children with conduct disorders also are diagnosed with ADHD (Chronis et al., 2007).

Origins of Conduct Disorders

Conduct disorders may have a genetic component (Scourfield et al., 2004). Other contributors include antisocial family members, deviant peers, inconsistent discipline, parental insensitivity to the child's behavior, physical punishment, and family stress (Black, 2007).

Treatment of Conduct Disorders

The treatment of conduct disorders is challenging, but it seems that cognitive-behavioral techniques involving parent training hold promise (Kazdin, 2000; Sukhodolsky et al., 2005). Children profit from interventions in which their behavior is monitored closely, there are consequences (such as time-outs) for unacceptable behavior, physical punishment is avoided, and positive social behavior is rewarded (Cavell, 2001).

Childhood Depression

Monkey Business Images/Veer

Kristin, age 11, feels "nothing is working out for me." For the past year, she has been failing in school, although she previously had been a B student. She has trouble sleeping, feels tired all the time, and has started refusing to go to school. She cries easily and thinks her peers are making fun of her because she is "ugly and stupid." Her mother recently found a note written by Kristin that said she wanted to jump in front of a car "to end my misery."
—Adapted from Weller & Weller, 1991, p. 655

Although childhood is supposed to be the best time of life, many children are depressed.

Many children, like Kristin, are depressed. Depressed children may feel sad, blue, down in the dumps. They may show poor appetite, insomnia, lack of energy and inactivity, loss of self-esteem, difficulty concentrating, loss of interest in people and activities they usually enjoy, crying, feelings of hopelessness and helplessness, and thoughts of suicide (American Psychiatric Association, 2000).

But many children do not recognize depression in themselves until the age of 7 or so. When children cannot report their feelings, depression is inferred from behavior, such as withdrawal from social activity. In some cases, childhood depression is masked by conduct disorders, physical complaints, academic problems, and anxiety.

It has been estimated that between 5% and 9% of children are seriously depressed in any given year. Depression occurs equally often in girls and boys.

Origins of Depression

attributional style The way in which one is disposed toward interpreting outcomes (successes or failures), as in tending to place blame or responsibility on oneself or on external factors.

The origins of depression are complex and varied. Psychological and biological explanations have been proposed. Some social cognitive theorists explain depression in terms of relationships between competencies (knowledge and skills) and feelings of

Table 5.4
John and the Math Quiz: "Why Did I Get All Those Questions Wrong?"

Attributional Style	
If John interprets his poor performance on the math quiz according to internal, stable, and global factors, he's likely to feel depressed. If he sees the quiz result according to external, unstable, and specific factors, he's likely to avoid excessive self-blame and be better prepared for the next quiz.	
Internal: "It's all my fault"	External: "This is a ridiculous test"
Stable: "This happens to me all the time," "There's nothing I can do"	Unstable: "Ms. Keech told us the wrong stuff that would be on the test"
Global: "I'm just no good in math," "I never understand anything in this class"	Specific: "I'll do better on the next test," "This one doesn't mean anything"

© 2012 Cengage Learning

self-esteem. Children who gain academic, social, and other competencies usually have high self-esteem. Perceived low levels of competence are linked to helplessness, low self-esteem, and depression. Longitudinal studies have found that problems in academics, socializing, physical appearance, and sports can predict feelings of depression (Kistner, 2006). Some competent children might not credit themselves because of excessive parental expectations. Or children may be perfectionistic themselves. Perfectionistic children may be depressed because they cannot meet their own standards.

A tendency to blame oneself (an internal attribution) or others (an external attribution) is called a child's **attributional style**. Certain attributional styles can contribute to helplessness and hopelessness and hence to depression (L. J. Kagan et al., 2004; Runyon & Kenny, 2002).

Some children blame themselves for all the problems in their lives, whether they deserve the blame or not. Research shows that children who are depressed are more likely to attribute the causes of their failures to internal, stable, and global factors, factors they are relatively helpless to change (Lewinsohn, Rohde, et al., 2000; see Table 5.4). Helplessness triggers depression. Consider the case of two children who do poorly on a math test. John thinks, "I'm a jerk! I'm just no good in math! I'll never learn." Jim thinks, "That test was tougher than I thought it would be. I'll have to work harder next time." John is perceiving the problem as global (he's "a jerk") and stable (he'll "never learn"). Jim perceives the problem as specific rather than global (related to the type of math test the teacher makes up) and as unstable rather than stable (he can change the results by working harder). In effect, John thinks "It's me" (an internal attribution). By contrast, Jim thinks "It's the test" (an external attribution).

There is also evidence of genetic factors in depression (Kendler, Gardner, et al., 2007). A Norwegian study of 2,794 twins estimated that the heritability of depression in females was 49% and 25% in males (Orstavik et al., 2007). On a neurological level, evidence suggests that depressed children (and adults) underutilize the neurotransmitter **serotonin** (Vitiello, 2006).

Treatment of Depression

Parents and teachers can do a good deal to alleviate relatively mild feelings of depression among children—involve children in enjoyable activities, encourage them to develop skills, praise them when appropriate, and point out when they are being too hard on themselves. But if feelings of depression persist, treatment is called for.

Psychotherapy for depression tends to be cognitive-behavioral today. Children (and adolescents) are encouraged to do enjoyable things and build social skills. They are made aware of their tendencies to minimize their accomplishments, exaggerate their problems, and overly blame themselves for shortcomings (see, for example, A. Ellis & Dryden, 1996).

Because depressed children may underutilize serotonin, drugs that increase the action of serotonin in the brain (selective serotonin reuptake inhibitors, such as Luvox, Prozac, and Zoloft) are sometimes used to treat childhood depression. Although these drugs are often effective, the Food and Drug Administration has warned that there may be a link between their use and suicidal thinking in children (G. Harris, 2004).

Childhood Anxiety

Children show many kinds of anxiety disorders, and they are accompanied by depression in 50%–60% of children (Kendler et al., 2007). Yet many children show anxiety disorders, such as **generalized anxiety disorder**, in the absence of depression

serotonin A neurotransmitter that is involved in mood disorders such as depression.

generalized anxiety disorder An anxiety disorder in which anxiety appears to be present continuously and is unrelated to the situation.

phobia An irrational, excessive fear that interferes with one's functioning.

separation anxiety disorder (SAD) An extreme form of otherwise normal separation anxiety that is characterized by anxiety about separating from parents; often takes the form of refusal to go to school.

school phobia Fear of attending school, marked by extreme anxiety at leaving parents.

(Kearney & Bensaheb, 2007). Other anxiety disorders shown by children include **phobias**, such as **separation anxiety disorder (SAD)**, and stage fright. (Beidel & Turner, 2007).

Separation Anxiety Disorder

It is normal for children to show anxiety when they are separated from their caregivers. Separation anxiety is normal and begins during the first year. But the sense of security that is usually provided by bonds of attachment encourages children to explore their environment and become progressively independent.

Separation anxiety disorder (SAD) is an extreme form of separation anxiety that affects an estimated 4%–5% of children and young adolescents (American Psychiatric Association, 2000; Shear et al., 2006). It occurs more often in girls and is often associated with school refusal. The disorder may persist into adulthood, leading to an exaggerated concern about the well-being of one's children and spouse and difficulty tolerating separation from them.

SAD is diagnosed when separation anxiety is persistent and excessive, when it is inappropriate for the child's developmental level, and when it interferes with activities or development tasks, such as attending school. Six-year-olds ought to be able to enter first grade without nausea and vomiting and without dread that they or their parents will come to harm. Children with SAD tend to cling to their parents and follow them around the house. They may voice concerns about death and dying and insist that someone stay with them at bedtime. They may complain of nightmares and have stomachaches on school days. They may throw tantrums or plead with their parents not to leave the house.

SAD may occur before middle childhood, preventing adjustment to day care or nursery school. SAD usually becomes a significant problem in middle childhood because that is when children are expected to adjust to school.

Separation Anxiety Disorder, School Phobia, and School Refusal

SAD is characterized by anxiety about separating from parents and may be expressed as **school phobia**—fear of school—or refusal to go to school (which can be based on fear or other factors). Separation anxiety is not behind all instances of school refusal. Some children refuse school because they perceive it as unpleasant, unsatisfying, or hostile, and it may be. Some children are concerned about

Separation Anxiety Disorder

Read "Alison—A Case of Separation Anxiety Disorder."

Selective Mutism in Children

Watch and learn about selective mutism, a form of social phobia which is caused by severe anxiety in children.

doing poorly in school or being asked questions in class (in which case they may have stage fright). High parental expectations may heighten concern, as may problems with classmates.

Treatment of School Phobia or School Refusal

It is usually not better for children with school phobia to remain at home until the origins of the problem are uncovered and resolved. Most professionals agree that the first rule in the treatment of school phobia is: Get the child back into school. The second rule is: Get the child back into school. And the third rule... You get the idea. The disorder often disappears once the child is back in school on a regular basis.

Jake Wyman/Getty Images

School phobia is often a form of separation anxiety. This boy is afraid to be separated from his mother. He imagines that something terrible will happen to her (or to him) when they are apart. Many mornings he complains of a tummy ache or of being too tired to go to school.

There is nothing wrong with trying to understand why a child refuses to attend school. Knowledge of the reasons for refusal can help parents and educators devise strategies for assisting the child. But perhaps such understanding need not precede insistence that the child return to school. Things that parents can do to get a child back into school include:

- Do not accede to the child's demands to stay home.
- Secure the cooperation of the child's teacher, principal, and school nurse.
- If there is a specific school-related problem, such as an overly strict teacher, help the child—and teacher—find ways to handle the situation.
- Reward the child for attending school.

Antidepressant medication has been used—often in conjunction with cognitive-behavioral methods—with much success (D. S. Pine et al., 2001; Walkup et al., 2001). However, drugs do not teach children how to cope. Many health professionals suggest that the drugs are best used only when psychological treatments have proven to be ineffective (Masi, Mucci, et al., 2001).

In spite of these social and emotional issues that can affect children, most children in developed nations come through middle childhood quite well, in good shape for the challenges and dramas of adolescence.   ·

Check Your Learning Quiz 5.4

Go to **login.cengagebrain.com** and take the online quiz.

▶ **LO30** Describe familial influences during middle childhood.

▶ **LO31** Discuss the effects of maternal employment on children.

▶ **LO32** Discuss the effects of having lesbian or gay parents.

Did you know that—

- At the ages of 10 to 12, children tend to evaluate their parents more harshly than they did in early childhood?
- Being reared by lesbian or gay parents has not been shown to influence children's adjustment or their sexual orientation?
- Divorce is harder on the children than on the parents?
- It is not necessarily better for bickering parents to remain together "for the sake of the children"?
- In middle childhood, friends are generally viewed as children who do things for one another?
- The daughters of employed women are more achievement oriented and set higher career goals for themselves than the daughters of unemployed women?
- In middle childhood, children who are popular tend to be relatively attractive and mature for their age?

▼

A college student taking a child development course had a conversation with a 9-year-old girl named Karen (adapted from Rowen, 1973):

> **Student:** *Karen, how was school today?*
> **Karen:** *Oh, it was all right. I don't like it a lot.*
> **Student:** *How come?*
> **Karen:** *Sara and Becky won't talk to me. I told Sara I thought her dress was very pretty, and she pushed me out of the way. That made me so mad.*
> **Student:** *That wasn't nice of them.*
> **Karen:** *No one is nice except for Amy. At least she talks to me.*

coregulation A gradual transferring of control from parent to child, beginning in middle childhood.

Here is part of a conversation between a different college student and her 9-year-old cousin, Sue:

Sue: My girlfriend Heather in school has the same glasses as you. My girlfriend—no, not my girlfriend, my friend—my friend picked them up yesterday from the doctor, and she wore them today.

Student: What do you mean—not your girlfriend, but your friend? Is there a difference?

Sue: Yeah, my friend. 'Cause Wendy is my girlfriend.

Student: But what's the difference between Heather, your friend, and Wendy, your girlfriend?

Sue: Well, Wendy is my best friend, so she's my girlfriend. Heather isn't my best friend, so she's just a friend.

In the years between 6 and 12, the child's social world expands. Peers take on greater importance and friendships deepen. Entry into school exposes the child to the influence of teachers. Relationships with parents change as children develop greater independence.

The Family

In middle childhood, the family continues to play a key role in socializing the child, although peers, teachers, and other outsiders begin to play a greater role (Harter, 2006).

Parent–Child Relationships

Parent–child interactions focus on some new concerns during middle childhood, including school-related matters, assignment of chores, and peer activities (W. A. Collins et al., 2000). Parents do less monitoring of children's activities and provide less direct feedback than they did in the preschool years. Control is gradually transferred from parent to child in a process known as **coregulation** (Maccoby, 2002; Wahler et al., 2001). Children begin to internalize the standards of their parents.

Children and parents spend less time together in middle childhood than in the preschool years. Children spend more time with their mothers than with their fathers. Mothers' interactions with school-age children continue to revolve around caregiving; fathers are relatively more involved in recreation (Wolfenden & Holt, 2005).

Because of their developing cognitive ability, 10- to 12-year-olds evaluate their parents more harshly than they did in early childhood (Selman & Dray, 2006). But throughout middle childhood, children rate their parents as their best source of emotional support (Cowan & Cowan, 2005; Katz et al., 2005).

▶ **L033** Discuss the effects of divorce and unhappily married parents on children.

The Effects of Maternal Employment

Why is this section labeled "The Effects of Maternal Employment"? Why not "Parental Employment" or "Paternal Employment"? Perhaps because of the traditional role of women as homemakers. A half century ago, most women remained in the home, but today, nearly 3 out of 4 married mothers of children under age 18 are employed, as are 4 out of 5 divorced, separated, or widowed mothers (U.S. Bureau of the Census, 2007).

Many commentators have been concerned about the effects of maternal employment on children. In part, this has been based on more traditional values that argue that the mother ought to remain in the home. But concern has also been based on research findings that suggest that maternal employment and nonmaternal care have some negative effects on children (Belsky, 2006b).

One common belief is that Mom's being in the workforce rather than in the home leads to delinquency. Researchers using data on 707 adolescents, aged 12–14, from the National Longitudinal Survey of Youth examined whether the occupational status of a mother was connected with delinquent behavior (Vander Ven & Cullen, 2004). They found that maternal employment per se made no difference, but delinquency was connected with lack of supervision.

There are benefits of maternal employment. Daughters of employed women are more achievement oriented and set higher career goals for themselves than daughters of nonworking women (Hangal & Aminabhavi, 2007). Children of working mothers tend to be more prosocial, less anxious, and more flexible in their gender-role stereotypes (Nomaguchi, 2006; D. W. Wright & Young, 1998).

transsexual A person who wishes to be a person of the other gender and who may undergo hormone treatments, cosmetic surgery, or both to achieve the appearance of being a member of the other gender.

Lesbian and Gay Parents

"Where did you get that beautiful necklace?" I asked the little girl in the pediatrician's office. "From my moms," she answered. It turned out that her family

Gen Nishino/Getty Images

What are the effects of maternal employment on children? Why did we not ask, "What are the effects of parental employment on children"?

Being reared by lesbian or gay parents has not been shown to influence children's adjustment or their sexual orientation.

consisted of two women, each of whom had a biological child, one girl and one boy.

Research on lesbian and gay parenting has fallen into two general categories: the general adjustment of the children and the likelihood of children of lesbian and gay parents to be lesbian or gay themselves. Research by Charlotte Patterson (2006) has generally found that the psychological adjustment of children of lesbian and gay parents is comparable to that of children of heterosexual parents. Despite the stigma attached to homosexuality, lesbians and gay men are as likely as heterosexual parents to sustain positive family relationships (Wainright et al., 2004).

What of the sexual orientation of the children of lesbian and gay parents? Richard Green (1978) observed 37 children and young adults, aged 3–20, who were being reared—or had been reared—by lesbians or **transsexuals**. All but one of the children reported or recalled preferences for toys, clothing, and friends (male or female) that were typical for their gender and age. All the 13 older children who reported sexual fantasies or sexual behavior were heterosexually oriented.

Generation X or Generation Ex? What Happens to Children Whose Parents Get Divorced?

Is this the time of "Generation Ex"—a generation characterized by ex-wives and ex-husbands? More than one million American children each year experience the divorce of their parents. Nearly 40% of European American children and 75% of African American children in the United States who are born to married parents will spend at least part of their childhoods in single-parent families as a result of divorce (Marsiglio, 2004).

Divorce may be tough on parents; it can be even tougher on children (Amato, 2006). No longer do children eat with both parents. No longer do they go to ball games, movies, or Disneyland with both of them. The parents are now often supporting two households, resulting in fewer resources for the children (Tashiro et al., 2006). Many children who live with their mothers scrape by—or fail to scrape by—in poverty. The mother who was once available may become an occasional visitor, spending more time at work and placing the kids in day care for extended periods.

Most children live with their mothers after a divorce (Amato, 2006). Some fathers remain devoted to their children despite the split, but others tend to spend less time with their children as time goes on. Not only does the drop-off in paternal attention deprive children of activities and social interactions, but it also saps their self-esteem: "Why doesn't Daddy love me anymore? What's wrong with me?"

The children of divorce are more likely to have conduct disorders, drug abuse, and poor grades in school (Amato, 2006). Their physical health may decline (Troxel & Matthews, 2004). By and large, the fallout for children is worst during the first year after the breakup. Children tend to rebound after a couple of years or so (Malone et al., 2004).

Talking to Children About Divorce

Talking to children about a divorce is difficult. The following tips can help both the children and parents with the challenge and stress of these conversations (American Academy of Child & Adolescent Psychiatry, 2008. Copyright © 2008 by the Academy of Child & Adolescent Psychiatry. Reprinted by permission.)

- Do not keep it a secret or wait until the last minute.
- Tell your children together with your spouse.
- Keep things simple and straightforward.
- Tell them the divorce is not their fault.

- Admit that this will be sad and upsetting for everyone.
- Reassure your children that you both still love them and will always be their parents.
- Do not discuss each other's faults or problems with the children.

Should Parents Remain Married "For the Sake of the Children"?

Many people believe—for moral reasons—that marriage and family life must be permanent, no matter what. People must consider the moral aspects of divorce in the light of their own value systems. But—from a perspective based purely on the research evidence—what should bickering, unhappily married parents do? The answer seems to depend largely on how they behave in front of the children. Research has shown that severe parental bickering is linked to the same kinds of problems that children experience when their parents get separated or divorced (Troxel & Matthews, 2004). When children are exposed to adult or marital conflict, they display a biological "alarm reaction": their heart rate, blood pressure, and sweating rise sharply (El-Sheikh et al., 2009). Therefore, Hetherington and her colleagues have suggested that divorce can be a positive alternative to family conflict (Hetherington, 1989; Wallerstein et al., 2005).

Life in Stepfamilies: His, Hers, Theirs, and...

Most divorced people remarry, usually while the children are young. More than 1 in 3 American children will spend part of their childhood in a stepfamily (U.S. Bureau of the Census, 2004).

The rule of thumb about the effects of living in stepfamilies is that there is no rule of thumb (Coleman et al., 2000). Many stepparents treat stepchildren as though they were biologically their own (Marsiglio, 2004), but there are also some risks to living in stepfamilies, such as the greater risk of being physically abused by stepparents than by biological parents (Adler-Baeder, 2006). There is also a significantly higher incidence—by a factor of 8—of sexual abuse by stepparents than by natural parents.

Why do we find these risks in stepfamilies? According to evolutionary psychologists, people often behave as though they want their genes to flourish in the next generation. Thus, it could be that stepparents are less devoted to rearing other people's children.

▶ **L034** Discuss peer influences during middle childhood.

▶ **L035** Describe the development of children's concepts of friendship.

Peer Relationships

Families exert the most powerful influence on a child during his or her first few years. But as children move into middle childhood, peers take on more importance.

Peers as Socialization Influences

Parents can provide children only with experience relating to adults. Children profit from experience with peers because peers have interests and skills that reflect the child's generation (Molinari & Corsaro, 2000).

Peers afford children practice in cooperating, relating to leaders, and coping with aggressive impulses, including their own. Peers can be important confidants (Dunn & Hughes, 2001; Hanlon et al., 2004). Peers, like parents, help children learn what types of impulses—affectionate, aggressive, and so on—they can safely express. Children who are at odds with their parents can turn to peers as sounding boards. They can compare feelings and experiences. When children share troubling ideas and experiences with peers, they realize they are normal and not alone (Barry & Wentzel, 2006).

Peer Acceptance and Rejection

Acceptance or rejection by peers is important in childhood because problems with peers affect adjustment later on (Wentzel et al., 2004). Popular children tend to be attractive, mature for their age, and successful in sports or academics, although attractiveness seems to be more important for girls than boys (Langlois et al., 2000). Socially speaking, popular children are friendly, nurturant, cooperative, helpful, and socially skillful (H. L. Xie et al., 2006). They also have high self-esteem.

Children who are aggressive and disrupt group activities are more likely to be rejected by peers (Boivin et al., 2005). Most rejected children do not learn to conform. Instead, they remain on the fringes of the group and may find aggressive friends (A. J. Rose et al., 2004).

Development of Friendships

In the preschool years and early years of middle childhood, friendships are based on geographic closeness or proximity. Friendships are superficial: quickly formed, easily broken. What matters are shared activities and who has the swing set or sandbox (Berndt, 2004; T. R. Gleason, Gower, et al., 2005).

Between 8 and 11, children recognize the importance of friends' meeting each other's needs and possessing desirable traits (Zarbatany et al., 2004). They are more likely to say that friends are nice and share their interests. They increasingly pick friends who are similar in behavior and personality. Trustworthiness, mutual understanding, and a willingness to disclose personal information characterize friendships in middle childhood and beyond (Hamm, 2000; Rotenberg et al., 2004). Compared with boys, girls tend to develop closer friendships and seek confidants (Zarbatany et al., 2000).

Robert Selman (1980) described five stages in children's changing concepts of friendship (see Table 5.5). The stages correspond to the levels of perspective-taking skills discussed earlier.

Friends behave differently with each other than with other children. School-age friends are more verbal, attentive, relaxed, and responsive to each other during play than are mere acquaintances (Cleary et al., 2002). Conflicts can occur among friends, but when they do, they tend to be less intense and get resolved in positive ways (Wojslawowicz Bowker et al., 2006).

Children in middle childhood will typically say they have more than one "best" friend (Berndt et al., 1989). Nine-year-olds report an average of four best friends (M. Lewis & Feiring, 1989). Best friends tend to be more alike than other friends.

In middle childhood, boys tend to play in larger groups than girls. Children's friendships are almost exclusively with others of the same gender, continuing the trend of gender segregation (Hartup, 1983).

The School

The school exerts a powerful influence on many aspects of the child's development. Schools, like parents, set limits on behavior, make demands for mature behavior, attempt to communicate, and are oriented toward nurturing positive physical, social, and cognitive development. Schools influence children's IQ scores, achievement motivation, and career aspirations (Aber et al., 2007; Woolfolk, 2008). Schools also influence social and moral development (Killen & Smetana, 2006).

Schools are also competitive environments, and children who do too well—and students who do not do well enough—may incur the resentment or ridicule of others.

Peer Acceptance

Watch and learn about peer acceptance and popularity in middle childhood.

▶ **LO36** Discuss the effects of the school on social and emotional development.

▶ **LO37** Describe the characteristics of a good school.

Table 5.5
Stages in Children's Concepts Of Friendship

Stage	Name	Approximate Age (Years)[a]	What Happens
0	Momentary physical interaction	3–6	Children remain egocentric. Their concept of a friend is one who likes to play with the same things and lives nearby.
1	One-way assistance	5–9	Children are less egocentric but view a friend as someone who does what they want.
2	Fair-weather cooperation	7–12	Friends are viewed as doing things for one another, but the focus remains on self-interest.
3	Intimate and mutual sharing	10–15	The focus is on the relationship rather than on the individuals separately. Friendship is viewed as providing mutual support over a long period of time.
4	Autonomous interdependence	12 and above	Children (and adolescents and adults) understand that friendships grow and change as people change and that they may need different friends to satisfy different needs.

[a]Ages may overlap
Source: Selman (1980).

Entry Into School

Children must master many new tasks when they start school—conquering new academic challenges, meeting new school and teacher expectations, fitting into a new peer group, coping with extended separation from parents, and developing increased self-control and self-help skills.

How well prepared are children to enter school? School readiness involves at least three critical factors:

1. The diversity and inequity of children's early life experiences
2. Individual differences in young children's development and learning
3. The degree to which schools establish reasonable and appropriate expectations of children's capabilities when they enter school

Some children enter school less well prepared than others. Kindergarten teachers report that many students begin school unprepared to learn (Slavin, 2006; Woolfolk, 2010). Most teachers say that children often lack the language skills needed to succeed. Poor health care and nutrition and lack of adequate parental stimulation and support place many children at risk for academic failure before they enter school.

Bullying

Nine-year-old Stephanie did not want to go to school. As with many other children who refuse school, she showed anxiety at the thought of leaving home. But Stephanie was not experiencing separation anxiety from her family. It turns out that she had gotten into a disagreement with Susan, and Susan had told her she would beat her mercilessly if she showed up at school again. To highlight her warning, Susan had shoved Stephanie across the hall.

Stephanie was a victim of bullying. Susan was a bully. Stephanie did not know it, but, ironically, Susan was also bullied from time to time by a couple of other girls at school.

Was there something unusual about all this? Not really. Boys are more likely than girls to be bullies, but many girls engage in bullying (Perren & Alsaker, 2006). All in all, it is estimated that 10% of students in the United States have been exposed to extreme bullying, and that 70%–75% of students overall have been bullied (Q. Li, 2007).

Bullying has devastating effects on the school atmosphere. It transforms the perception of school from a safe place into one of a violent place (Batsche & Porter, 2006). Bullying also impairs adjustment to middle school, where it is sometimes carried out by older children against younger children (Perren & Alsaker, 2006; Scheithauer et al., 2006).

Many but not all bullies have some things in common. For one thing, their achievement tends to be lower than average, such that peer approval (or deference from peers) might be more important to them than academics (Batsche & Porter, 2006; Perren & Alsaker, 2006). Bullies are more likely to come from homes of lower socioeconomic status (Perren & Alsaker, 2006; Pereira et al., 2004). Many of these homes are characterized by violence between parents.

Numerous studies have also investigated the personalities of bullies (Baldry, 2003; Pereira et al., 2004). Bullying is associated with more frequent diagnoses of conduct disorder, oppositional defiant disorder, attention deficit/hyperactivity disorder, and

Emotional Bullying

Watch and learn about the complexities of emotional bullying.

depression. Bullies are also more likely to have personality problems, such as assuming that others are predisposed to harm them. Not surprisingly, they also show more problems with impulse control.

The School Environment: Setting the Stage for Success or…

Research summaries (Slavin, 2006; Woolfolk, 2008) indicate that an effective school has the following characteristics:

- An active, energetic principal
- An orderly but not oppressive atmosphere
- Empowerment of teachers; that is, teachers participating in decision making
- Teachers with high expectations that children will learn
- A curriculum that emphasizes academics
- Frequent assessment of student performance
- Empowerment of students; that is, students participating in setting goals, making decisions, and engaging in cooperative learning activities

Certain aspects of the school environment are important as well. One key factor is class size. Smaller classes permit students to receive more individual attention and are particularly useful in teaching the "basics"—reading, writing, and arithmetic—to students at risk for academic failure (Slavin, 2006; Woolfolk, 2008).

Teachers

Teachers, like parents, set limits, make demands, communicate values, and foster development. They are powerful role models and dispensers of reinforcement. After all, children spend several hours each weekday with teachers.

Teacher Influences on Student Performance

Pygmalion effect A positive self-fulfilling prophecy in which an individual comes to display improved performance because of the positive expectation of the people with whom he or she interacts.

self-fulfilling prophecy An event that occurs because of the behavior of those who expect it to occur.

Achievement is enhanced when teachers expect students to master the curriculum, allocate most of the available time to academic activities, and manage the classroom effectively. Students learn more in classes when they are actively instructed or supervised by teachers than when they are working on their own. The most effective teachers ask questions, give personalized feedback, and provide opportunities for drill and practice (Slavin, 2006).

Student achievement also is linked to the emotional climate of the classroom (Slavin, 2006; Woolfolk, 2008). Students do not do as well when teachers rely heavily on criticism, ridicule, threats, or punishment. Achievement is high in classrooms with a pleasant, friendly—but not overly warm—atmosphere.

Teacher Expectations

There is a saying that "you find what you're looking for." Consider the so-called **Pygmalion effect** in education. In Greek mythology, the amorous sculptor Pygmalion breathed life into a beautiful statue he had carved. Teachers also try to bring out positive traits they believe dwell within their students. A classic experiment by Robert Rosenthal and Lenore Jacobson (1968) suggested that teacher expectations can become **self-fulfilling prophecies**. Rosenthal and Jacobson first gave students a battery of psychological tests. Then they informed teachers that a handful of the students, although average in performance to date, were about to blossom forth intellectually in the current school year.

In fact, the tests indicated nothing about the chosen children. These children had been selected at random. The purpose of the experiment was to determine whether enhancing teacher expectations could affect student performance. It did; the identified children made significant gains in IQ scores.

In subsequent research, however, results have been mixed. Some studies have found support for the Pygmalion effect (Madon et al., 2001; Sarrazin et al., 2005a, 2005b). Others have not. But these findings have serious implications for children from ethnic-minority and low-income families, because there is some indication that teachers expect less from children in these groups (Slavin, 2006; Woolfolk, 2008). Teachers who expect less may spend less time encouraging and working with children.

What are some of the ways that teachers can help motivate all students to do their best? Anita Woolfolk (2008) suggested the following:

- Make the classroom and the lesson interesting and inviting.
- Ensure that students can profit from social interaction.
- Make the classroom a safe and pleasant place.
- Recognize that students' backgrounds can give rise to diverse patterns of needs.
- Help students take appropriate responsibility for their successes and failures.
- Encourage students to perceive the links between their own efforts and their achievements.
- Help students set attainable short-term goals.

Self-Fulfilling Prophecies

Watch and learn how teacher beliefs about student academic abilities actually affect children's performance.

According to research, teachers motivate high student achievement by creating a safe learning environment, setting attainable goals, and making the classroom atmosphere interesting and engaging.

Sexism in the Classroom

Although girls were systematically excluded from formal education for centuries, today we might not expect to find **sexism** among teachers. Teachers, after all, are generally well educated. They are also trained to be fair minded and sensitive to the needs of their young charges in today's changing society.

However, we may not have heard the last of sexism in our schools. According to a classic review of more than 1,000 research publications about girls and education, girls are treated unequally by their teachers, their male peers, and the school curriculum (American Association of University Women, 1992). The reviewers concluded that:

sexism Discrimination or bias against people based on their gender.

sexual harassment Unwelcome verbal or physical conduct of a sexual nature.

- Many teachers pay less attention to girls than boys, especially in math, science, and technology classes.
- Many girls are subjected to **sexual harassment**—unwelcome verbal or physical conduct of a sexual nature—from male classmates, and many teachers ignore it.

- Some textbooks still stereotype or ignore women, portraying males as the movers and shakers in the world.

In a widely cited study, Myra Sadker and David Sadker (in D. M. Sadker & Silber, 2007) observed students in fourth-, sixth-, and eighth-grade classes in four states and the District of Columbia. Teachers and students were European American and African American, urban, suburban, and rural. In almost all cases, the findings were depressingly similar: Boys generally dominated classroom communication, whether the subject was math (a traditionally "masculine" area) or language arts (a traditionally "feminine" area). Despite the stereotype that girls are more likely to talk, boys were 8 times more likely than girls to call out answers without raising their hands. Teachers were less than impartial in responding to boys and girls when they called out. Teachers, both male and female, were more likely to accept calling out from boys. Girls were more likely to be reminded that they should raise their hands and wait to be called on. Boys, it appears, are expected to be impetuous, but girls are reprimanded for "unladylike behavior." Until they saw videotapes of themselves, the teachers were largely unaware they were treating girls and boys differently.

Check Your Learning Quiz 5.5

Go to **login.cengagebrain.com** and take the online quiz.

GO to your Psychology CourseMate at login.cengagebrain.com and take the Chapter Post-Test to see which Learning Objectives you've mastered and which need more review. Use the chapter review guide below and the online activities—including flashcards to review key terms—to measure your learning.

Measure
>Your Learning

Online Activities

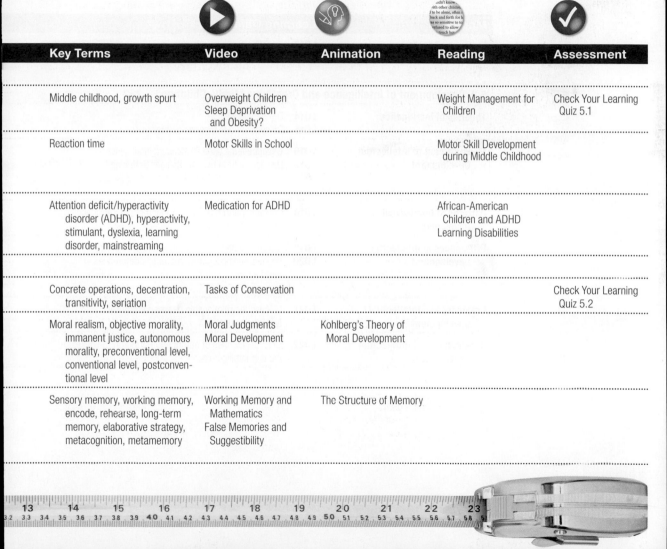

Key Terms	Video	Animation	Reading	Assessment
Middle childhood, growth spurt	Overweight Children Sleep Deprivation and Obesity?		Weight Management for Children	Check Your Learning Quiz 5.1
Reaction time	Motor Skills in School		Motor Skill Development during Middle Childhood	
Attention deficit/hyperactivity disorder (ADHD), hyperactivity, stimulant, dyslexia, learning disorder, mainstreaming	Medication for ADHD		African-American Children and ADHD Learning Disabilities	
Concrete operations, decentration, transitivity, seriation	Tasks of Conservation			Check Your Learning Quiz 5.2
Moral realism, objective morality, immanent justice, autonomous morality, preconventional level, conventional level, postconventional level	Moral Judgments Moral Development	Kohlberg's Theory of Moral Development		
Sensory memory, working memory, encode, rehearse, long-term memory, elaborative strategy, metacognition, metamemory	Working Memory and Mathematics False Memories and Suggestibility	The Structure of Memory		

Online Activities

Key Terms	Video	Animation	Reading	Assessment
Word-recognition method, phonetic method, sight vocabulary, bilingual				
Intelligence, achievement			Emotional and Social Intelligence	Check Your Learning Quiz 5.3
Intelligence quotient (IQ), mental age (MA), chronological age (CA), cultural bias, culture-free test	Measures of IQ	IQ Test Items	Alfred Binet	
Cultural-familial intellectual deficiency	Closing the Achievement Gap Bias in Intelligence Testing			
Creativity, convergent thinking, divergent thinking				
Heritability				

Measure >Your Learning

Online Activities

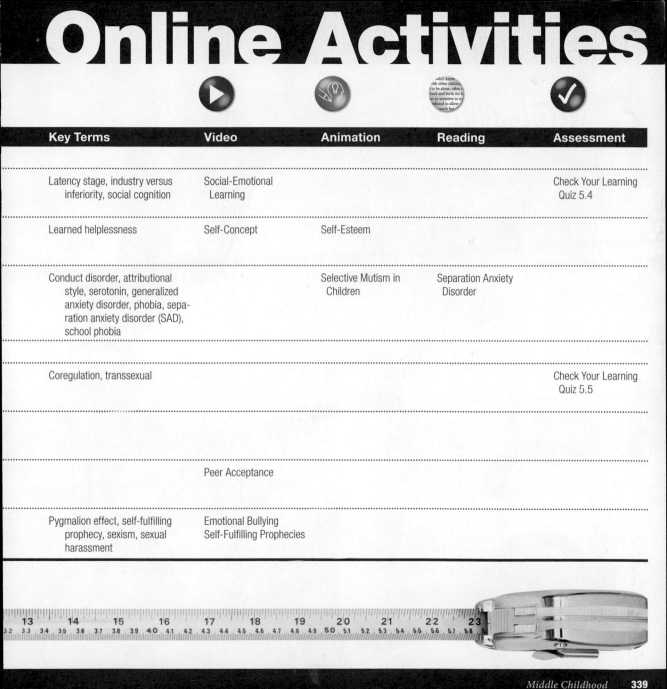

Key Terms	Video	Animation	Reading	Assessment
Latency stage, industry versus inferiority, social cognition	Social-Emotional Learning			Check Your Learning Quiz 5.4
Learned helplessness	Self-Concept	Self-Esteem		
Conduct disorder, attributional style, serotonin, generalized anxiety disorder, phobia, separation anxiety disorder (SAD), school phobia		Selective Mutism in Children	Separation Anxiety Disorder	
Coregulation, transsexual				Check Your Learning Quiz 5.5
	Peer Acceptance			
Pygmalion effect, self-fulfilling prophecy, sexism, sexual harassment	Emotional Bullying Self-Fulfilling Prophecies			

Adolescence

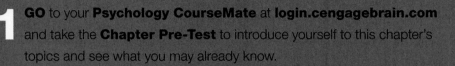

Prepare to Learn

1 **GO** to your **Psychology CourseMate** at **login.cengagebrain.com** and take the **Chapter Pre-Test** to introduce yourself to this chapter's topics and see what you may already know.

2 **READ** the **Learning Objectives** (LOs, in the left sidebars) and begin the chapter.

3 **COMPLETE** the **Online Activities** (in the right sidebars) *as you read each module.* Activities include **videos, animations, readings,** and **quizzes.**

4 **CHECK Your Learning** by going online to take the quiz at the end of each module and review material as necessary.

5 **MEASURE Your Learning** after reading the chapter by taking the online **Chapter Post-Test.** Use the chapter review guide at the end of the chapter as needed.

WATCH for these **Online Activities** icons as you read:

Video

Animation

Reading

Assessment

Online Activities

These online activities are essential to mastering this chapter. Go to login.cengagebrain.com:

 Videos Watch the following videos:

- Premature Puberty
- Puberty and Body Image
- Adolescents and Risk-Taking
- Exercise Bulimia
- Hypothetical Propositions in Teenagers
- Teens and Moral Development
- Prescription Drugs and Teens
- Teen Depression

 Animations Interact with and visualize important processes, timelines, and concepts:

- Puberty
- Visual-Spatial Test Items
- Identity Formation

 Readings Delve deeper into key content:

- Rachel: A Case of Anorexia
- Nicole: A Case of Bulimia
- How Adolescents Solve the Puzzle and the Pendulum Problem
- How Parents Can Help Early Adolescents In School
- Ethnic Identity and Gender in Career Self-Efficacy Expectancies
- Ethnicity and Development of Identity
- Facebook Behavior of College Students
- Sexting: One More Way for Adolescents to Stay in Touch
- What Parents Want From Sex-Education Courses
- Does Sex on TV Encourage Sexual Behavior in Teenagers?
- Warning Signs of Suicide

 Assessment Measure your mastery:

- Chapter Pre-Test
- Check Your Learning Quizzes
- Chapter Post-Test

▶ **LO1** Define *adolescence*.

▶ **LO2** Describe the developments of puberty.

▶ **LO3** Discuss the effects of early and late maturation on adolescents.

▶ **LO4** Discuss body image in adolescence.

Did you know that—

- American adolescents are no longer growing taller than their parents?

- Girls are not usually fertile right after they begin to menstruate?

- Girls who mature early tend to have lower self-esteem than girls who mature late?

- Practicing a musical instrument makes changes in the brain?

- Accidents are the leading cause of death among adolescents?

- Adolescents need more sleep than adults do?

- Girls with anorexia nervosa may believe that they're fat even when everybody around them tells them they look like all skin and bones?

▼

adolescence A transitional period between childhood and adulthood, usually seen as being bounded by puberty at the lower end and the assumption of adult responsibilities at the upper end.

puberty The biological stage of development characterized by changes that lead to reproductive capacity.

feedback loop A system in which glands regulate each other's functioning through a series of hormonal messages.

primary sex characteristics The structures that make reproduction possible.

secondary sex characteristics Physical indicators of sexual maturation—such as changes to the voice and growth of bodily hair—that do not directly involve reproductive structures.

Perhaps no other period of life is as exciting—and bewildering—as **adolescence**, bounded at the lower end by the age of 11 or 12 and at the upper end by the age of 18 or 19. Except for infancy, more changes occur during adolescence than any other time of life. In our society, adolescents are "neither fish nor fowl," as the saying goes, neither children nor adults. Adolescents may be old enough to reproduce and be as large as their parents, yet they may not be allowed to get drivers' licenses until they are 16 or 17, and they cannot attend R-rated films unless accompanied by an adult. Given the restrictions placed on them, their growing yearning for independence, and a sex drive heightened by increased levels of sex hormones, it is not surprising that adolescents are occasionally in conflict with their parents.

The idea that adolescence is an important and separate developmental stage was proposed by G. Stanley Hall (1904). Hall believed that adolescence is marked by turmoil and used the German term *Sturm und Drang* ("storm and stress") to refer to the conflicts of adolescence. Contemporary theorists no longer see adolescent storm and stress as inevitable (Smetana, 2005). Instead, they see adolescence as a period when biological, cognitive, social, and emotional functioning are reorganized. Nevertheless, adolescents need to adapt to numerous changes.

Puberty: The Biological Eruption

Puberty is a stage of development characterized by reaching sexual maturity and the ability to reproduce. The onset of adolescence coincides with the advent of puberty. Puberty is controlled by a **feedback loop** involving the hypothalamus, pituitary gland, gonads—the ovaries in females and the testes in males—and hormones. The hypothalamus signals the pituitary gland, which in turn releases hormones that control physical growth and the gonads. The gonads respond to pituitary hormones by increasing their production of sex hormones (androgens and estrogens). The sex hormones further stimulate the hypothalamus, perpetuating the feedback loop.

The sex hormones also trigger the development of primary and secondary sex characteristics. The **primary sex characteristics** are the structures that make reproduction possible. In girls, these are the ovaries, vagina, uterus, and fallopian tubes. In boys, they are the penis, testes, prostate gland, and seminal vesicles. The **secondary sex characteristics** are physical indicators of sexual maturation that are not directly involved in reproduction. They include breast development, deepening of the voice, and the appearance of facial, pubic, and underarm hair.

The Adolescent Growth Spurt

The stable growth patterns in height and weight that characterize early and middle childhood end abruptly with the adolescent growth spurt. Girls start to spurt in height sooner than boys, at an average age of a little more than 10. Boys start to spurt about 2 years later. Girls and boys reach their peak growth in height about 2 years after the growth spurt begins, at about 12 and 14 years, respectively (see Figure 6.1). The spurt in height for both girls and boys continues for about another 2 years at a gradually declining pace. Boys add nearly 4 inches per year during the fastest year of the spurt, compared with slightly more than 3 inches per year for girls. Overall, boys add an average of 14½ inches during the spurt and girls add a little more than 13 inches (Tanner, 1991a).

Adolescents begin to spurt in weight about half a year after they begin to spurt in height. The period of peak growth in weight occurs about a year and a half after the onset of the spurt. As with height, the growth spurt in weight then continues for a little more than 2 years. Because the spurt in weight lags the spurt in height, many adolescents are relatively slender compared with their preadolescent stature. However, adolescents tend to eat enormous quantities of food to fuel their growth spurts.

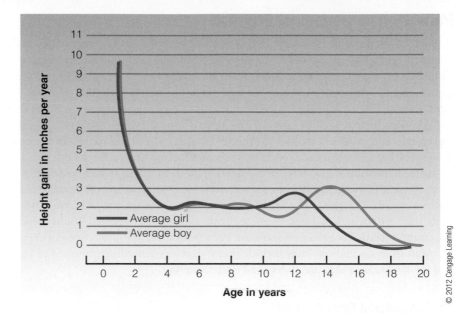

Figure 6.1 Spurts in Growth Girls begin the adolescent growth spurt about 2 years earlier than boys. Girls and boys reach their periods of peak growth about 2 years after the spurt begins.

Active 14- and 15-year-old boys may consume 3,000–4,000 calories a day without becoming obese.

Girls' and boys' body shapes begin to differ in adolescence. Girls develop relatively broader hips compared with their shoulders, whereas the opposite is true for boys. A girl's body shape is more rounded than a boy's because girls gain almost twice as much fatty tissue as boys. Boys gain twice as much muscle tissue as girls.

Asynchronous Growth

asynchronous growth Unbalanced growth, such as the growth that occurs during the early part of adolescence and causes many adolescents to appear gawky.

secular trend A historical trend toward increasing adult height and earlier puberty.

Adolescents may be awkward and gawky due to **asynchronous growth**; different parts of the body grow at different rates. The hands and feet mature before the arms and legs do. As a consequence, adolescent girls and boys may complain of big hands or feet. Legs reach their peak growth before the shoulders and chest. Boys stop growing out of their pants about a year before they stop growing out of their jackets (Tanner, 1989).

The Secular Trend

During the twentieth century, children in the Western world grew dramatically more rapidly and wound up taller than children from earlier times (S. S. Sun et al., 2005). This historical trend toward increasing adult height was also accompanied by an earlier onset of puberty, and is known as the **secular trend**. Figure 6.2 shows that Swedish boys and girls grew more rapidly in 1938 and 1968 than they did in 1883 and ended up several inches taller. At the age of 15, boys were more than 6 inches taller and girls were more than 3 inches taller, on average, than their counterparts from the previous century (Tanner, 1989). The occurrence of a secular trend in height and weight has been documented in nearly all European countries and the United States.

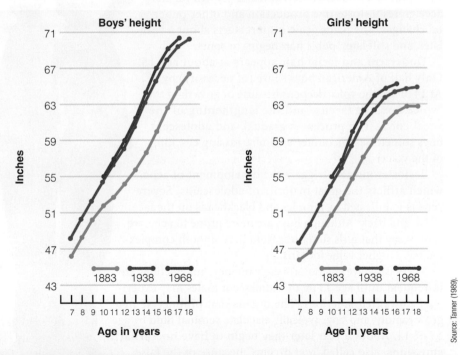

Source: Tanner (1989).

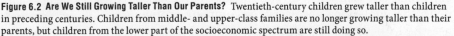

Figure 6.2 Are We Still Growing Taller Than Our Parents? Twentieth-century children grew taller than children in preceding centuries. Children from middle- and upper-class families are no longer growing taller than their parents, but children from the lower part of the socioeconomic spectrum are still doing so.

Today, children from middle- and upper-class families in developed nations, including the United States, no longer grow taller than their parents, whereas their poorer counterparts continue to gain in height from generation to generation (Tanner, 1989). Improved nutrition would appear to play a key role.

Changes in Boys

At puberty, the pituitary gland stimulates the testes to increase their output of testosterone, leading to further development of the male genitals. The first visible sign of puberty is accelerated growth of the testes, which begins at an average age of about 11½, plus or minus 2 years. Testicular growth further accelerates testosterone production and other pubertal changes. The penis growth spurt starts about a year later, and still later, pubic hair begins to spurt.

Underarm and facial hair appears at about age 15. Only half of American boys shave (of necessity) by 17. At 14 or 15, the voice deepens because of growth of the "voice box," or larynx, and the lengthening of the vocal cords. The process is gradual, and adolescent boys sometimes encounter an embarrassing cracking of the voice.

Testosterone also triggers the development of acne, which afflicts the great majority of adolescents. Severe acne is manifested by pimples and blackheads on the face, chest, and back. Although boys are more prone to acne, we cannot say that girls suffer less from it. A smooth complexion has a higher value for girls.

Males can have erections in early infancy, but erections are infrequent until age 13 or 14. Adolescent males may experience unwanted erections. The organs that produce **semen** grow rapidly, and boys typically ejaculate seminal fluid by age 13 or 14. About a year later they begin to have **nocturnal emissions**, also called "wet dreams" because of the false myth that emissions necessarily accompany erotic

semen The fluid that contains sperm and substances that nourish and help transport sperm.

nocturnal emission Emission of seminal fluid while asleep.

gynecomastia Enlargement of breast tissue in males.

epiphyseal closure The process by which the cartilage that separates the long end of a bone from the main part of the bone turns to bone.

menarche The onset of menstruation.

© Rubberball Photography/Veer

dreams. Mature sperm are found in ejaculatory emissions by about the age of 15.

Nearly half of all boys experience enlargement of the breasts, or **gynecomastia**, which usually declines in a year or two. Gynecomastia stems from the small amount of female sex hormones secreted by the testes.

At age 20 or 21, men stop growing taller because testosterone causes **epiphyseal closure**, which prevents the long bones from making further gains in length. Puberty for males draws to a close.

Changes in Girls

In girls, the pituitary gland signals the ovaries to boost estrogen production at puberty. Estrogen may

Girls and boys start their growth spurts at slightly different times, but once they spurt, the gains are swift.

stimulate the growth of breast tissue (breast buds) as early as the age of 8 or 9, but the breasts usually begin to enlarge during the 10th year. The development of fatty tissue and ducts elevates the areas of the breasts surrounding the nipples and causes the nipples to protrude. The breasts typically reach full size in about 3 years, but the *mammary glands* do not mature fully until a woman has a baby. Estrogen also promotes the growth of the fatty and supporting tissue in the hips and buttocks, which, along with the widening of the pelvis, causes the hips to round. Beginning at about age 11, girls develop pubic and underarm hair.

Estrogen causes the *labia*, vagina, and uterus to develop during puberty, and androgens cause the *clitoris* to develop. The vaginal lining varies in thickness according to the amount of estrogen in the bloodstream. Estrogen typically brakes the female growth spurt some years before testosterone brakes that of males.

Menarche

Menarche (first menstruation) commonly occurs between the ages of 11 and 14, plus or minus 2 years (Capron et al., 2007; Mendle et al., 2006). During the past 150 years, menarche has occurred at progressively earlier ages in Western nations, another example of the secular trend (see Figure 6.3; Tanner, 1991b).

Premature Puberty

Discover some of the problems associated with the early onset of puberty in girls.

Puberty

Interact to learn more about the physical and emotional changes of puberty.

What accounts for the earlier age of puberty? One hypothesis is that girls must reach a certain body weight to trigger pubertal changes such as menarche. Body fat could trigger the changes because fat cells secrete a protein that signals the brain to secrete hormones that raise estrogen levels. Menarche comes later to girls who have a lower percentage of body fat, such as those with eating disorders or athletes (Angier, 1997; Bosi & de Oliveira, 2006). The average body weight for triggering menarche depends on the girl's height (Frisch, 1994). Today's girls are larger than those of the early twentieth century because of improved nutrition and health care.

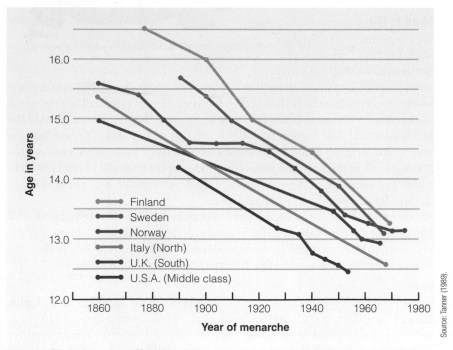

Figure 6.3 The Decline in Age at Menarche The age at menarche has been declining since the mid-1800s among girls in Western nations, apparently because of improved nutrition and health care.

Regulation of the Menstrual Cycle

Testosterone levels remain fairly stable in boys throughout adulthood, but estrogen and progesterone levels in girls vary markedly and regulate the menstrual cycle. Following menstruation—the sloughing off of the endometrium—estrogen levels increase, leading once more to the growth of endometrial tissue. Girls usually begin to ovulate 12–18 months after menarche. After the ovum is released, if it is not fertilized, estrogen and progesterone levels drop suddenly, triggering menstruation once again.

The average menstrual cycle is 28 days, but variations are common. Girls' cycles are often irregular for a few years after menarche but later become more regular. Most cycles during the first 12–18 months after menarche occur without ovulation.

Early Versus Late Maturers

Early-maturing boys tend to be more popular than their late-maturing peers and more likely to be leaders in school (Graber et al., 2004). They are more poised, relaxed, and good-natured. Their edge in sports and the admiration of their peers heighten their sense of worth. On the negative side, early maturation is associated with greater risks of aggression and delinquency (Lynne et al., 2007) and abuse of alcohol and other drugs (Costello et al., 2007). Coaches may expect too much of them in sports, and peers may want them to fight their battles. Sexual opportunities may create demands before they know how to respond (T. H. Lam et al., 2002).

Late maturers have the "advantage" of not being rushed into maturity. On the other hand, late-maturing boys often feel dominated by early-maturing boys. They have been found to be more dependent and insecure and may be more likely to get involved in substance abuse (Ge et al., 2003).

Although boys who mature early usually have higher self-esteem than those who mature late, early-maturing girls may feel awkward because they are among the first of their peers to begin the physical changes of puberty. They become conspicuous with their height and their developing breasts. Boys of their age may tease them. Tall girls of dating age frequently find that shorter boys are reluctant to approach them or be seen with them. All in all, early-maturing girls are at greater risk for psychological problems and substance abuse than girls who mature later on (Ge et al., 2003; Lynne et al., 2007). Many girls who mature early obtain lower grades in school and initiate sexual activity earlier (T. H. Lam et al., 2002). For reasons such as these, the parents of early-maturing girls may increase their vigilance and restrictiveness, leading to new parent–child conflicts.

Puberty and Body Image

Watch and learn how the dramatic changes of puberty and age of onset affect body image.

▶ **LO5** Describe brain development during adolescence.

Body Image

Adolescents are quite concerned about their physical appearance, particularly in early adolescence during the rapid physical changes of puberty (D. C. Jones & Crawford, 2006). By age 18, girls and boys are more satisfied with their bodies (M. E. Eisenberg et al., 2006). Adolescent females in our society tend to be more preoccupied with body weight and slimness than adolescent males (Paxton et al., 2006). Many adolescent males want to gain weight to build their muscle mass (Stanford & McCabe, 2005).

Brain Development

Unlike infants whose brain activity is completely determined by their parents and environment, [adolescents] may actually be able to control how their own brains are wired and sculpted. … This argues for doing a lot of things as a teenager. … You are hard-wiring your brain in adolescence. Do you want to hard-wire it for sports and playing music and doing mathematics or for lying on the couch in front of the television?

—Neuroscientist Jay Giedd (2002) of the National Institute of Mental Health

What happens to the brains of adolescents who spend hours a day practicing the piano or the violin? Their learning translates physically into increases in the thickness of the parts of the cerebral cortex that are being used (Bermudez et al., 2009; Johnson et al., 2008; also see Figure 6.4). The gains in thickness of the cerebral cortex represent increases in gray matter, which consists of associative neurons that transmit messages back and forth in the brain when we are engaged in thought and sensorimotor activities. The neurons sprout new axon tips and dendrites, creating new synapses and increasing the flow of information.

Brain-imaging studies reveal a general pattern of brain development into the teenage years related both to maturation and to the use of brain regions (Giedd et al., 2009).

Yes, she's practicing the violin, but what is she doing to her brain?

But even while parts of the brain gain in processing ability, there is also a pruning process that seems to follow the principle "Use it or lose it." Neural connections, or synapses, that are used are retained, but those that lie unused are lost.

Many adolescents show poor judgment, at least from time to time, and take risks that most adults would avoid, such as excessive drinking, substance abuse, reckless driving, violence, disordered eating behavior, and unprotected sexual activity (Berten & Rossem, 2009). It seems that brain development or immaturity may play a role. Deborah Yurgelun-Todd and her colleagues (Sava & Yurgelun-Todd, 2008) showed pictures of people with fearful expressions to adolescents ranging in age from 11 to 17 while the adolescents' brains were scanned by functional magnetic resonance imaging. Compared to adults, the adolescents' frontal lobes (the seat of executive functioning) were less active and their amygdalas (a part of the limbic system that is involved in discriminating emotions, including fear) were more active. The adolescents often misread the facial expressions, with those younger than 14 more often inferring sadness, anger, or confusion rather than fear. The older adolescents responded correctly more often and also showed the more adult pattern of less activity in the amygdala and more in the frontal lobes. One reason many adolescents fail to show the judgment, insight, and reasoning ability of adults may be immaturity of the frontal lobes (Yurgelun-Todd, 2007).

Both genes (heredity) and the environment play major roles in shaping early brain development (Lenroot et al., 2009), but there is an interaction between heredity and the environment. Adolescents' experiences affect which parts of the cortex thicken and which are "pruned."

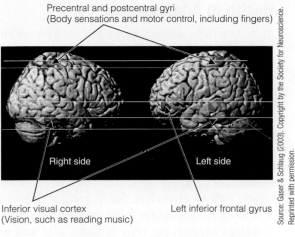

Precentral and postcentral gyri
(Body sensations and motor control, including fingers)

Right side   Left side

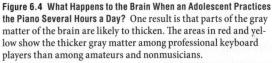

Inferior visual cortex
(Vision, such as reading music)

Left inferior frontal gyrus

Source: Gaser & Schlaug (2003). Copyright by the Society for Neuroscience. Reprinted with permission.

Figure 6.4 What Happens to the Brain When an Adolescent Practices the Piano Several Hours a Day? One result is that parts of the gray matter of the brain are likely to thicken. The areas in red and yellow show the thicker gray matter among professional keyboard players than among amateurs and nonmusicians.

Health in Adolescence

Most American adolescents are healthy. Few are chronically ill or miss school. Injuries tend to heal quickly. Yet about 18% of the nation's adolescents have at least one serious health problem (B. Bloom et al., 2006).

Causes of Death

Death rates are low in adolescence, but they are nearly twice as great for male adolescents as female adolescents. A major reason for this discrepancy is that males take more risks that end in death as a result of accidents, suicide, or homicide. These three causes of death account for most adolescent deaths (Federal Interagency Forum on Child and Family Statistics [Federal Forum], 2007). Nearly 80% of adolescent deaths are due to injuries, and motor-vehicle and firearm injuries account for more than half of those injuries (Federal Forum, 2007). Firearms account for 80% of homicides and nearly 50% of suicides (Federal Forum, 2007).

Nutrition

Physical growth occurs more rapidly in the adolescent years than at any other time after birth, with the exception of the first year of infancy. To fuel the adolescent growth spurt, the typical girl needs 1,800–2,400 calories per day and the typical boy needs 2,200–3,200 calories (U.S. Department of Agriculture, 2005). The nutritional needs of adolescents vary according to their activity level and stage of pubertal development. At the peak of the growth spurt, adolescents use twice as much calcium, iron, zinc, magnesium, and nitrogen as during other years of adolescence (U.S. Department of Agriculture, 2005). Calcium intake is particularly important for females to build bone density and help prevent **osteoporosis** later in life, but most teenagers do not consume enough calcium. Adolescents are also likely to obtain less vitamin A, thiamine, and iron than recommended, but more fat, sugar, and sodium (U.S. Department of Agriculture, 2005).

One reason for adolescents' nutritional deficits is irregular eating patterns. Breakfast is often skipped, especially by dieters (Niemeier et al., 2006). Teenagers may rely on fast food and junk food, which are high in fat and calories. Junk food is connected with being overweight, and being overweight in adolescence can lead to chronic illness and premature death in adulthood (Niemeier et al., 2006).

osteoporosis A condition involving progressive loss of bone tissue.

Sleep

It might seem that adolescents sleep around the clock, especially on weekends, but adolescents need about 8½–9¼ hours of sleep per night (National Sleep Foundation, 2009a). On weekends, therefore, many adolescents are trying to catch up on their sleep.

Research shows that many if not most American adolescents experience sleep deprivation—defined as obtaining 6 or fewer hours of sleep per night (Hagenauer et al., 2009; R. E. Roberts et al., 2009). Getting enough sleep is a biological need, important to coping with the rapid biological changes of puberty, but surveys show that most teenagers average less than 7 hours of sleep per school night and report feeling tired at school and during extracurricular activities (National Sleep Foundation, 2009). Teenagers find it difficult to obtain enough sleep due to hectic schedules with after-school jobs and activities, homework, family obligations, and evening (or late-night!) e-mailing, texting, and chatting with friends. Changes in the

Adolescents need 8½–9¼ hours of sleep a night, but American adolescents average less than 7 hours and are sleep deprived.

brain also tend to push back the clock for adolescents—a change called a *phase delay*—so that they would preferably go to bed later than they did as children. However, school usually begins early in the morning, so parents may push the adolescent to get to bed early. Ironically, the typical adolescent's natural time to go to asleep might be 11 p.m. or even later. Teenagers may thus feel wide awake at an imposed bedtime, even if they are exhausted. Moreover, they are compelled to wake up when their bodies are arguing that it is the middle of the night and they have not had enough sleep to feel rested and alert. As a result, many adolescents have trouble paying attention in school, solving problems, retaining information, and coping with stress. Sleep deprivation also poses a heightened risk for automobile accidents, irritability, depression, and poor impulse control.

Eating Disorders: When Dieting Turns Deadly

The American ideal has slimmed down to where most American females of normal weight are dissatisfied with the size and shape of their bodies (Paxton et al., 2005). In Module 6.2 we will see that adolescents also tend to think that others are paying a great deal of attention to their appearance. Because of cultural emphasis on slimness

Risk-Taking

Watch and learn more about risk-taking in adolescence.

▶ **LO9** Discuss eating disorders.

and adolescents' psychology, they are highly vulnerable to eating disorders, which are characterized by gross disturbances in patterns of eating.

Anorexia Nervosa

Anorexia nervosa is a life-threatening eating disorder characterized by extreme fear of being heavy, dramatic weight loss, a distorted body image, and resistance to eating enough to maintain a healthful weight. Anorexia nervosa afflicts males as well as females, but most studies put the female-to-male ratio at 10 to 1 or greater (Kjelsås et al., 2004). By and large, anorexia nervosa afflicts women during adolescence and young adulthood (Polivy et al., 2005). The typical person with anorexia is a young European American female of higher socioeconomic status (Striegel-Moore et al, 2003). Affluent females are more likely to read the magazines that idealize slender bodies and shop in the boutiques that cater to females with svelte figures (Forbush et al., 2007).

Females with anorexia nervosa can drop 25% or more of their weight within a year. Severe weight loss triggers abnormalities in the endocrine system (i.e., with hormones) that prevent ovulation (S. Nielsen & Palmer, 2003). General health declines. Problems arise in the respiratory system (Forman-Hoffman et al., 2006) and the cardiovascular system (Katzman, 2005). Females with anorexia are at risk for premature development of osteoporosis (Katzman, 2005). The mortality rate for anorexic females is about 4%–5%.

Girls often develop anorexia nervosa to lose weight after gains from menarche (Shroff et al., 2006). Dieting and exercise continue well after the weight has been lost, and even after others say things are going too far. Denial is a major factor of anorexia nervosa. Distortion of the body image is also a major feature of the disorder.

anorexia nervosa An eating disorder characterized by irrational fear of weight gain, distorted body image, and severe weight loss.

bulimia nervosa An eating disorder characterized by cycles of binge eating and purging as a means of controlling weight gain.

Bulimia Nervosa

Bulimia nervosa is characterized by recurrent cycles of binge eating and purging. Binge eating often follows on the heels of dieting (Williams, 2004). There are various methods of purging. Vomiting is common. Other avenues include strict dieting or fasting, laxatives, and fol-

Anorexia nervosa is a life-threatening eating disorder in which an individual—most often an adolescent or young adult female—has a distorted body image and consequently refuses to eat. She may lose 25% of her body weight in a year and impair the health of nearly all her bodily systems.

lowing demanding exercise regimes. Individuals with eating disorders will not settle for less than their idealized body shape and weight (Kaye et al., 2004). Bulimia, like anorexia, is connected with irregular menstrual cycles (Edler et al., 2007) and tends to afflict women during adolescence and young adulthood (Nolen-Hoeksema et al., 2007). Eating disorders are upsetting and dangerous in themselves, but are also connected with depression (Nolen-Hoeksema et al., 2007).

Perspectives on Eating Disorders

Psychoanalytic theory suggests that anorexia nervosa may help young women cope with sexual fears, especially fear of pregnancy. Their breasts and hips flatten, and perhaps, in adolescents' fantasies, they remain asexual children. Anorexia prevents some adolescents from separating from their families and assuming adult responsibilities.

A particularly disturbing risk factor for eating disorders in adolescent females is a history of child abuse, especially sexual abuse (Corstorphine et al., 2007). One study found a history of childhood sexual abuse in about half of women with bulimia nervosa, as opposed to a rate of about 7% among women without the disorder (Deep et al., 1999).

Certainly young women have a very slender social ideal set before them in women such as Paris Hilton. As the cultural ideal slenderizes, women with normal body weight according to health charts feel fat, and heavy women feel huge (Winzelberg et al., 2000).

Eating disorders tend to run in families, which raises the possibility of genetic involvement. Genetic factors would not directly cause eating disorders, but might involve obsessive and perfectionistic personality traits (Wade et al., 2000).

Treatment

Eating disorders are connected with serious health problems, and the low weight of individuals with anorexia can be life threatening. Some adolescent girls are admitted to the hospital for treatment against their will (Brunner et al., 2005). When the individual with anorexia does not—or cannot—eat adequately through the mouth, measures such as tube feeding may be used. Antidepressants (selective serotonin reuptake inhibitors) are often used to treat eating disorders because they stir the appetite of anorexic individuals and decrease binge eating in bulimic individuals (Grilo et al., 2005; Walsh et al., 2006). Cognitive-behavioral therapy has been used to help anorexic and bulimic individuals challenge their perfectionism and distorted body images.

Exercise Bulimia

Watch and learn about a form of bulimia which focuses on the ritual of exercise, a method of purging.

Anorexia Case Study

Read "Rachel: A Case of Anorexia."

Bulimia Case Study

Read "Nicole: A Case of Bulimia."

Check Your Learning Quiz 6.1

Go to **login.cengagebrain.com** and take the online quiz.

Did you know that—

- Many adolescents see themselves as being on stage?
- It is normal for male adolescents to think of themselves as action heroes and to act as though they are made of steel?
- Adolescent boys as a group do not outperform adolescent girls in mathematics?
- Most adolescents make moral decisions based on their own ethical principles and may choose to disobey the laws of the land if they conflict with those principles?
- The transition from elementary school is more difficult for boys than for girls?
- It is probably not helpful for parents to help adolescents complete their homework?
- Adolescents who work after school obtain lower grades?

▼

I am a college student of extremely modest means. Some crazy psychologist interested in something called "formal operational thought" has just promised to pay me $20 if I can make a coherent logical argument for the proposition that the federal government should under no circumstances ever give or lend more to needy college students. Now what could people who believe that possibly say by way of supporting that argument? Well, I suppose they could offer this line of reasoning. ...
—Flavell et al., 2002

This "college student of extremely modest means" is thinking like an adolescent. Concrete-operational children are bound by the facts as they are, but the adolescent (and the adult) can ponder abstract ideas and see the world as it could be. Our college student recognizes that a person can find arguments for causes in which he or she does not believe.

formal operations The fourth stage in Piaget's cognitive-developmental theory, characterized by the capacity for flexible, reversible operations concerning abstract ideas and concepts, such as symbols, statements, and theories.

The Adolescent in Thought: My, My, How Formal

The stage of **formal operations** is the top level in Jean Piaget's theory. Adolescents in this stage have reached cognitive maturity, even if rough edges remain. For many children in developed nations, the stage of formal operations can begin at about the time of puberty, 11 or 12 years old. But some reach this stage somewhat later, and some not at all. Piaget describes the accomplishments of the stage of formal operations in terms of the individual's increased ability to classify objects and ideas, engage in logical thought, and hypothesize, just as researchers make hypotheses in their investigations. The adolescent can group and classify symbols, statements, and even theories. Adolescents can follow and formulate arguments from premises to conclusions and back once more, even if they do not believe the arguments. Hypothetical thinking, the use of symbols to represent other symbols, and deductive reasoning allow the adolescent to more fully comprehend the real world and to play with the world that dwells within the mind alone.

Hypothetical Thinking

In formal-operational thought, adolescents discover the concept of what might be. They can project themselves into situations that transcend their immediate experience and become wrapped up in fantasies. Adolescents can think ahead, systematically trying out various possibilities in their minds. They "conduct research" to see whether their hypotheses about themselves and their friends and teachers are correct, for example, trying on different clothes and attitudes to see which work best for them.

In terms of career decisions, the wealth of possible directions leads some adolescents to experience anxiety about whether they will pick the career that is the best fit for them and to experience a sense of loss because they may be able to choose only one.

Sophisticated Use of Symbols

Children in elementary school can understand what is meant by abstract symbols such as 1 and 2. They can also perform operations in which numbers are added, subtracted, and so on. But consider x, the primary algebraic symbol for variables. Children up to the age of 11 or 12 or so usually cannot fully understand the symbolic meaning of this concept, even if they can be taught the mechanics of solving for x in simple equations. But formal-operational children can grasp intuitively what is meant by x. Formal-operational children, or adolescents, can perform mental operations with symbols that stand for nothing in their own experience.

These symbols include those used in geometry. Adolescents work with points that have no dimensions, lines that have no width and are infinite in length, and circles

Hypothetical Propositions in Teenagers

Observe how abstract and hypothetical thinking change during adolescence.

▸ **LO12** Discuss gender differences in cognitive abilities.

that are perfectly round, even though such things are not found in nature. The ability to manipulate these symbols will permit them to work in theoretical physics or math or to obtain jobs in engineering or architecture.

Formal-operational individuals can understand, appreciate, and sometimes produce metaphors—figures of speech in which words or phrases that ordinarily signify one thing are applied to another. We find metaphors in literature, but consider how everyday figures of speech enhance our experience: *squeezing* out a living, *basking in the sunshine* of fame or glory, *hanging by a thread*, or *jumping* to conclusions.

Enhanced cognitive abilities can backfire when adolescents adamantly advance their religious, political, and social ideas without recognition of the subtleties and practical issues that might give pause to adults. For example, let's begin with the premise, "Industries should not be allowed to pollute the environment." If Industry A pollutes the environment, an adolescent may argue to shut down Industry A, at least until it stops polluting. The logic is reasonable and the goal is noble, but Industry A may be indispensable to the nation, or many thousands of people may be put out of work if it is shut down. More experienced people might prefer to seek a compromise.

Adolescent Egocentrism

Adolescents show a new egocentrism, in which they comprehend the ideas of other people but have difficulty sorting out those things that concern other people from the things that concern themselves.

The Imaginary Audience

Many adolescents fantasize about becoming rock stars or movie stars adored by millions. The concept of the **imaginary audience** achieves part of that fantasy, in a way. It places the adolescent on stage, but surrounded by critics more than by admirers. Adolescents assume that other people are concerned with their appearance and behavior, more so than they really are (Elkind, 1967, 1985). The self-perception of adolescents as being on stage may account for their intense desire for privacy and their preoccupation with their appearance.

imaginary audience The belief that others around us are as concerned with our thoughts and behaviors as we are; one aspect of adolescent egocentrism.

personal fable The belief that our feelings and ideas are special and unique and that we are invulnerable; one aspect of adolescent egocentrism.

The Personal Fable

Spider-Man and the Fantastic Four, stand aside! Because of the **personal fable**, many adolescents become action heroes, at least in their own minds. In the personal fable, one believes that one's thoughts and emotions are special and unique (Aalsma et al.,

2006). It also refers to the common adolescent belief that one is invulnerable.

The personal fable is connected with such behaviors as showing off and risk taking (Omori & Ingersoll, 2005). Many adolescents assume that they can smoke with impunity. Cancer? "It can't happen to me." They drive recklessly. They engage in spontaneous, unprotected sexual activity, assuming that sexually transmitted infections (STIs) and unwanted pregnancies happen to other people, not to them.

Many adolescents believe that their parents and other adults— even their peers—could never feel what they are feeling or know the depth of their passions. "You just don't understand me!" claims the adolescent. But, at least often enough, we do.

It is typically during adolescence that young people become capable of understanding what is meant by algebraic symbols and working with them to solve problems.

Gender Differences in Cognitive Abilities

Although females and males do not differ noticeably in overall intelligence, beginning in childhood, gender differences appear in certain cognitive abilities (Johnson & Bouchard, 2007). Females are somewhat superior to males in verbal ability. Males seem somewhat superior in visuospatial skills. The picture for mathematics is more complex, with females excelling in some areas and males in others.

Verbal Ability

Verbal abilities include reading, spelling, grammar, oral comprehension, and word fluency. As a group, females surpass males in verbal ability throughout their lives (D. F. Halpern, 2003, 2004). These differences show up early. Girls seem to acquire language faster than boys. They make more prelinguistic vocalizations, utter their first word sooner, and develop larger vocabularies. Boys in the United States are more likely than girls to be dyslexic and read below grade level (D. F. Halpern, 2003, 2004).

Why do females excel in verbal abilities? Biological factors such as the organization of the brain may play a role, but do not discount cultural factors—whether a culture stamps a skill as gender neutral, masculine, or feminine (E. B. Goldstein, 2005). In Nigeria and England, reading is looked on as a masculine activity, and boys traditionally surpass girls in reading ability. But in the United States and Canada, reading tends to be stereotyped as feminine, and girls tend to excel.

Solving the Puzzle and the Pendulum

Read how children of different ages, including adolescents, solve problems like "The Puzzle and Pendulum."

Visuospatial Ability

Visuospatial ability refers to the ability to visualize objects or shapes and to mentally manipulate and rotate them. This ability is important in such fields as art, architecture, and engineering. Boys begin to outperform girls on many types of visuospatial tasks starting at age 8 or 9, and the difference persists into adulthood (Johnson & Bouchard, 2007). The gender difference is particularly notable on tasks which require imagining how objects will look if they are rotated in space (A. R. Delgado & Prieto, 2004) (see Figure 6.5).

Some researchers link visuospatial performance to evolutionary theory and sex hormones. It may be related to a genetic tendency to create and defend a territory (Ecuyer-Dab & Robert, 2004). High levels of prenatal androgens have also been linked to better performance on visuospatial and arithmetic tasks among 4- and 6-year-old girls (Finegan et al., 1992; Jacklin et al., 1988).

One environmental theory is that gender stereotypes

postconventional level A period during which moral judgments are derived from moral principles and people look to themselves to set moral standards.

a. Spatial visualization
Embedded-figure test. Study the figure on the left. Then cover it up and try to find where it is hidden in the figure on the right. The left-hand figure may need to be shifted in order to locate it in the right-hand figure.

b. Spatial perception
Water-level test. Examine the glass of water on the left. Now imagine that it is slightly tilted, as on the right. Draw in a line to indicate the location of the water level.

c. Mental rotation
Mental-rotation test. If you mentally rotate the figure on the left, which of the five figures on the right would you obtain?

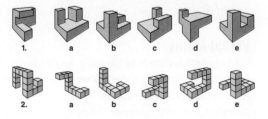

Answers: a. 1: Orient the pattern as if it were a tilted capital M, with the left portion along the top of the white triangle. 2: This pattern fits along the right sides of the two black triangles on the left. 3: Rotate this figure about 100° to the right, so that it forms a Z, with the top line coinciding with the top of the top white triangle. **b.** The line should be horizontal, not tilted. **c.** 1: c; 2: d.

Figure 6.5 Examples of Tests Used to Measure Visuospatial Ability No gender differences are found on the spatial visualization tasks in part a. Boys do somewhat better than girls on the tasks measuring spatial perception in part b. The gender difference is greatest on the mental rotation tasks in part c. What are some possible reasons for these differences?

influence the spatial experiences of children. Gender-stereotyped "boys' toys," such as blocks, Legos, and Erector sets, provide more practice with spatial skills than gender-stereotyped "girls' toys." Boys are also more likely to engage in sports, which involve moving balls and other objects through space (D. F. Halpern, 2004).

Mathematical Ability

For half a century or more, it has been believed that male adolescents generally outperform females in mathematics, and research has tended to support that belief (Collaer & Hill, 2006; D. F. Halpern, 2004). For example, in a review of 100 studies involving more than three million individuals, Janet Hyde and her colleagues (Hyde, Fennema, et al., 1990) found a slight superiority for girls in computational skills in the elementary and middle-school years, but boys began to perform better in word problems in high school and college. There were no gender differences in understanding math concepts at any age. However, a more recent study by Hyde and her colleagues (Hyde, Lindberg, et al., 2008) of some seven million second through eleventh graders found no gender differences for performance in mathematics on standardized tests. The complexity of the test items apparently made no difference. Nevertheless, most Americans have different expectations for boys and girls, and these expectations may still dissuade girls from entering fields in science and math (Hyde, Lindberg, et al., 2008).

The Adolescent in Judgment: Moral Development

Children in early childhood tend to view right and wrong in terms of rewards and punishments. Lawrence Kohlberg referred to such judgments as *preconventional*. In middle childhood, *conventional* thought tends to emerge, and children usually begin to judge right and wrong in terms of social conventions, rules, and laws. In adolescence, many—not all—individuals become capable of formal-operational thinking, which allows them to derive conclusions about what they should do in various situations by reasoning from ethical principles. And many of these individuals engage in *postconventional* moral reasoning. They *deduce* proper behavior.

The Postconventional Level

In the **postconventional level**, moral reasoning is based on the person's own moral standards. Consider once more the case of Heinz that was introduced in Module 5.2. Moral judgments are derived from personal values, not from conventional standards

Visual-Spatial Test Items

Interact with the test items seen in Figure 6.5.

▶ **LO13** Discuss Kohlberg's views on moral reasoning in adolescence.

or authority figures. In the contractual, legalistic orientation of Stage 5, it is recognized that laws stem from agreed-on procedures and that many rights have great value and should not be violated (see Table 6.1). But under exceptional circumstances, such as in the case of Heinz, laws cannot bind the individual. A Stage 5 reason for stealing the drug might be that it is the right thing to do, even though it is illegal. Conversely, it could be argued that if everyone in need broke the law, the legal system and the social contract would be destroyed.

Stage 6 thinking relies on supposed universal ethical principles, such as those of human life, individual dignity, justice, and *reciprocity*. Behavior that is consistent with these principles is considered right. If a law is seen as unjust or contradicts the right of the individual, it is wrong to obey it.

In the case of Heinz, it could be argued from the perspective of Stage 6 that the principle of preserving life takes precedence over laws prohibiting stealing. Therefore, it is morally necessary for Heinz to steal the drug, even if he must go to jail. It could also be asserted, from the principled orientation, that if Heinz finds the social contract or the law to be the highest principle, he must remain within the law, despite the consequences.

Stage 5 and 6 moral judgments were virtually absent among the 7- and 10-year-olds in Kohlberg's (1963) sample of American children. They increased in frequency

Table 6.1
Kohlberg's Postconventional Level of Moral Development

Stage	Moral Reasoning That Support Heinz's Stealing the Drug	Moral Reasoning That Oppose Heinz's Stealing the Drug
Stage 5: Contractual, legalistic orientation—one must weigh pressing human needs against society's need to maintain social order	This thing is complicated because society has a right to maintain law and order, but Heinz has to take the drug to save his wife.	I can see why Heinz feels he has to take the drug, but laws exist for the benefit of society as a whole and cannot simply be cast aside.
Stage 6: Universal ethical-principles orientation—people must follow universal ethical principles and their own consciences, even if it breaks the law	In this case, the law conflicts with the principle of the sanctity of human life. Heinz must take the drug because his wife's life is more important than the law.	If Heinz truly believes that stealing the drug is worse than letting his wife die, he should not take it. People have to make sacrifices to do what they think is right.

during the early and middle teens. By age 16, Stage 5 reasoning was shown by about 20% of adolescents and Stage 6 reasoning was demonstrated by about 5% of adolescents. However, Stage 3 and 4 judgments were made more frequently at all ages—7 through 16—studied by Kohlberg and other investigators (Commons et al., 2006; Rest, 1983) (see Figure 6.6).

Gender Differences in Moral Development

Do males reason at higher levels of moral development than females? Kohlberg and Kramer (1969) reported that the average stage of moral development for men was Stage 4, which emphasizes justice, law, and order. The average stage for women was reported to be Stage 3, which emphasizes caring and concern for others.

Carol Gilligan (1982) argued that this gender difference reflects patterns of socialization: 11-year-old Jake views Heinz's dilemma as a math problem. He sets up an equation showing that life has greater value than property. Heinz should thus steal the drug. But 11-year-old Amy notes that stealing the drug and letting Heinz's wife die are both wrong. She searches for alternatives, such as getting a loan, saying that it wouldn't be wise for Heinz to go to jail and no longer be around to help his wife.

Although Gilligan saw Amy's reasoning as being as sophisticated as Jake's, Kohlberg's system considers Amy to be reasoning at a lower level of moral development. Gilligan and other researchers (G. Jorgensen, 2006) agree that Amy, like other girls, has been socialized into caring about the needs of others and foregoing simplistic judgments of right and wrong. But to Jake, clear-cut conclusions are to be derived from a set of premises.

But is Amy really reasoning at a lower level than Jake? Is she incapable of following his logic, or is she brining additional concerns into consideration?

Moral Behavior and Moral Reasoning

Are individuals with mature moral judgments more likely to engage in moral behavior? The answer seems to be yes (Emler et al., 2007). Adolescents with higher levels of moral reasoning are more likely to exhibit moral behavior (Maclean et al., 2004). Studies have

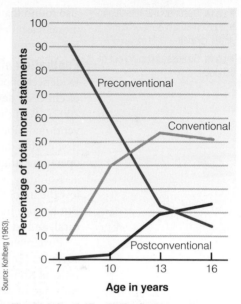

Source: Kohlberg (1963).

Figure 6.6 Age and Type of Moral Judgment The incidence of preconventional reasoning declines from more than 90% of moral statements at age 7 to less than 20% of statements at age 16. Conventional moral statements increase with age between the ages of 7 and 13 but then level off to account for 50%–60% of statements at ages 13 and 16. Postconventional moral statements are all but absent at ages 7 and 10 but account for about 20%–25% of statements at ages 13 and 16.

Adolescents and Moral Development

Watch adolescents explain what they would do in the Heinz example.

▶ **LO14** Describe the transition from elementary school to the upper grades.

▶ **LO15** Discuss dropping out of school.

also found that group discussion of moral dilemmas elevates delinquents' levels of moral reasoning (Smetana, 1990).

Evaluation of Kohlberg's Theory

Evidence supports Kohlberg's view that the moral judgments of children develop in an upward sequence (Boom et al., 2007), even though most children do not reach postconventional thought. Postconventional thought, when found, first occurs during adolescence, apparently because formal-operational thinking is a prerequisite for it (Patenaude et al., 2003).

Kohlberg believed that the stages of moral development follow the unfolding of innate sequences and are therefore universal. But he may have underestimated the influence of social, cultural, and educational institutions (Dawson, 2002).

Postconventional thinking is all but absent in developing societies (Snarey, 1994). Perhaps postconventional reasoning reflects Kohlberg's personal ideals and not a natural, universal stage of development (Helwig, 2006). In his later years, Kohlberg (1985) dropped Stage 6 reasoning from his theory in recognition of this possibility.

Whose reasoning is more mature? Eleven-year-old Jake sees Heinz's dilemma as a math problem and argues that because life has greater value than property, Heinz should thus steal the drug to save his wife. But 11-year-old Amy believes that stealing the drug and letting Heinz's wife die are both wrong, so she searches for alternatives, such as getting a loan, because Heinz can't do his wife much good if he winds up in jail for stealing.

The Adolescent in School

How can we emphasize the importance of the school to the development of the adolescent? Adolescents are highly influenced by the opinions of their peers and their teachers. Their self-esteem rises or falls with the pillars of their skills.

The transition to middle, junior high, or high school generally involves a shift from a smaller neighborhood elementary school to a larger, more impersonal setting with more students and different teachers for different classes. These changes may not fit the developmental needs of early adolescents. For example, adolescents express a desire for increased autonomy, yet teachers in junior high typically allow less student input and exert more control than teachers in elementary school (Tobbell, 2003).

The transition to the new school setting is often accompanied by a decline in grades and participation in school activities. Students may also experience a drop in self-esteem and an increase in stress (Rudolph & Flynn, 2007).

The transition from elementary school appears to be more difficult for girls than boys. Girls are more likely to be undergoing puberty and to earn the attention of boys in higher grades, whereas younger boys are not likely to be of interest to older girls. Girls experience major life changes, and children who experience many life changes at once find it more difficult to adjust (Tobbell, 2003).

But the transition need not be that stressful (Rudolph et al., 2001). Elementary and middle schools can help ease the transition. Some middle schools create a more intimate, caring atmosphere by establishing smaller schools within the school building. Others have "bridge programs" during the summer that introduce students to the new school culture and strengthen their academic skills.

Dropping Out

Completing high school is a critical developmental task. The consequences of dropping out can be grim. Dropouts are more likely to be unemployed or have low incomes (Wald & Losen, 2007). They are more likely to develop delinquency, criminal behavior, and substance abuse (D. M. Donovan & Wells, 2007).

Excessive school absence and reading below grade level are two predictors of school dropout (N. Lever et al., 2004). Other risk factors include low grades, low self-esteem, problems with teachers, substance abuse, being old for one's grade level, and being male (South et al., 2007). Adolescents who adopt adult roles early, especially marrying at a young age or becoming a parent, are also more likely to drop out (Bohon et al., 2007). Students from low-income households or large urban areas are also at greater risk (National Center for Education Statistics, 2007). Table 6.2 shows demographic factors and the risk of dropping out of school.

Preventing Dropping Out

Many programs have been developed to prevent dropping out of school. Successful programs have some common characteristics (Bost & Riccomini, 2006; Reschly & Christenson, 2006): early preschool interventions (such as Head Start); identification and monitoring of high-risk students; small class size, individualized instruction, and counseling; vocational components that link learning and community work experiences; involvement of families or community organizations; and clear and reasonable educational goals. Unfortunately, most intervention efforts are usually not introduced until students are on the verge of dropping out—when it is usually too late.

Helping Teens in School

Read "How Parents Can Help Early Adolescents in School."

▶**LO16** Explain how adolescents make career choices.

▶**LO17** Discuss the pros and cons of adolescent employment.

Table 6.2
Characteristics of 15- Through 24-Year-Olds Who Dropped Out of Grades 10–12

Characteristic	Dropout rate (%)	Number of dropouts (thousands)	Population enrolled (thousands)	% of all dropouts
Total	3.8	414	10,870	100.0
Gender				
Male	4.2	233	5,515	56.3
Female	3.4	181	5,355	43.7
Race/ethnicity				
European American	2.8	196	6,897	47.3
African American	7.3	112	1,538	27.2
Latin American	5.0	86	1,717	20.8
Asian/Pacific Islander	1.6	6	411	1.5
More than one race	4.9	12	241	2.9
Family income				
Low income	8.9	137	1,544	33.1
Middle income	3.8	228	5,990	55.2
High income	1.5	49	3,326	11.7
Age				
15–16	2.1	72	3,347	17.4
17	2.4	93	3,797	22.5
18	3.9	105	2,693	25.3
19	9.1	64	702	15.4
20–24	24.4	81	331	19.5

Source: Adapted from National Center for Education Statistics (2007, Table 1).

The Adolescent at Work: Career Development and Work Experience

Deciding what job or career to pursue after the completion of school is one of the most important choices we make.

Career Development

Children do not have a clear understanding of the kinds of jobs that are necessary in a society, or how jobs might relate to their personal abilities and talents. Maturation and experience lead them to become more realistic and practical as they head into adolescence. In adolescence, ideas about the kind of work one wants to do tend to become more firmly established, but a particular occupation may not be chosen until the college years or later (Rottinghaus et al., 2003).

Holland's Career Typology

High-school guidance counselors often help students match their interests, abilities, and personalities with the types of careers that are available. They also use a variety of career tests to help adolescents make practical and potentially fulfilling choices. A number of these tests are based on John Holland's (J. L. Holland, 1997) RIASEC model of vocational types (see Figure 6.7). Holland theorized that there are six basic personality types that can be matched with various kinds of careers: realistic, investigative, artistic, social, enterprising, and conventional. Within each of the six types, some careers require more education and certain kinds of talents than others do. For example, social people may find careers as child-care workers, as teachers, or even as psychologists. Working in child care might require only a high-school education; psychology requires a doctoral degree.

- Realistic people are concrete in thinking and mechanically oriented. They tend to be best adjusted in occupations that involve motor activity, such as attending gas stations, farming, auto repair, or construction work.
- Investigative people are abstract in their thinking, creative, and open to experience. They tend to do well in higher-level education and in research.
- Artistic people also tend to be creative and open to experience. They are emotional and intuitive. They tend to be content in the visual and performing arts.
- Social people tend to be outgoing (extroverted) and concerned for social welfare. They gravitate toward occupations in teaching (kindergarten through high school), counseling, and social work.

- Enterprising people tend to be adventurous, outgoing, and dominant. They gravitate toward leadership roles in industry and organizations.
- Conventional people thrive on routine and have needs for order, self-control, and social approval. They gravitate toward occupations in banking, accounting, clerical work, and the military.

C

These people have clerical or numerical skills. They like to work with data, to carry out other people's directions, or to carry things out in detail.

R

These people have mechanical or athletic abilities. They like to work with machines and tools, to be outdoors, or to work with animals or plants.

I

These people like to learn new things. They enjoy investigating and solving problems and advancing knowledge.

E

These people like to work with people. They like to lead and influence others for economic or organizational gains.

S

This group enjoys working with people. They like to help others, including the sick. They enjoy informing and enlightening people.

A

This group is highly imaginative and creative. They enjoy working in unstructured situations. They are artistic and innovative.

Figure 6.7 John Holland's Vocational Personality Types Psychologists have found that people are better adjusted in careers that fit their personality types. Where do you think you fit in Holland's types? Does one type describe you, or a combination of two or more?

Many people combine several vocational types (Nauta, 2007). A copywriter in an advertising agency, for instance, might be both artistic and enterprising. Holland's Vocational Preference Inventory assesses these personality types, as do various vocational tests that are used in high schools and colleges.

All in all, more than 20,000 occupations are found in the *Dictionary of Occupational Titles*, compiled by the U.S. Department of Labor. But most young people choose from a relatively small range of occupations on the basis of their personalities, experiences, and opportunities (Nauta, 2007).

Adolescents in the Workforce

Life experiences help shape vocational development. One life experience that is common among American teenagers is holding a job.

Prevalence of Adolescent Employment

About half of all high-school sophomores, two thirds of juniors, and almost three fourths of seniors have a job during the school year (Bachman et al., 2003). Girls and boys are equally likely to be employed, but boys work more hours (Staff et al., 2004).

Although millions of adolescents between the ages of 14 and 18 are legally employed, another two to three million work illegally (J. H. Holloway, 2004). Others work too many hours, work late hours on school nights, or hold hazardous jobs. Middle-class teenagers are twice as likely to be employed as lower-income teenagers, but employed lower-income adolescents work longer hours (Bachman et al., 2003).

Pros and Cons of Adolescent Employment

The potential benefits of adolescent employment include developing a sense of responsibility, self-reliance, and discipline; learning to appreciate the value of money and education; acquiring positive work habits and values; and enhancing occupational aspirations (Porfeli, 2007). On the other hand, most working adolescents are in jobs with low pay, high turnover, little authority, and little chance for advancement (Staff et al., 2004). Some question the benefits of such jobs. Students who work lengthy hours—more than 11–13 hours per week—report lower grades, higher rates of drug and alcohol use, more delinquent behavior, lower self-esteem, and higher levels of psychological problems than students who do not work or who work only a few hours (Brandstätter & Farthofer, 2003). Perhaps the most prudent course is for parents and educators to limit the number of hours adolescents work, particularly during the school year.

Ethnic Identity and Career Choices

Read and learn how our ethnic identity and attitudes may our affect early career decisions.

Check Your Learning Quiz 6.2

Go to **login.cengagebrain.com** and take the online quiz.

Did you know that—

- Adolescents often imitate their peers' clothing, speech, hairstyles, and ideals?
- Most American adolescent females are as concerned about occupational choices as American adolescent males are?
- Most adolescents are not in a state of rebellion against their parents?
- Most adolescents' friends are not "bad influences"?
- Petting is practically universal among American adolescents?
- About three quarters of a million American teenagers become pregnant each year?
- Children who show aggressive, antisocial, and hyperactive behavior at an early age are more likely to show delinquent behavior in adolescence?
- More adolescent girls than boys attempt suicide, but more boys succeed?

▼

ego identity versus role diffusion Erikson's fifth life crisis, during which adolescents develop a firm sense of who they are and what they stand for (ego identity), or they do not develop a sense of who they are and instead tend to be subject to the whims of others (role diffusion).

psychological moratorium A period when adolescents experiment with different roles, values, beliefs, and relationships.

identity crisis A turning point in development during which one examines one's values and makes decisions about life roles.

identity diffusion An identity status that characterizes those who have no commitments and who are not in the process of exploring alternatives.

What am I like as a person? Complicated! I'm sensitive, friendly and outgoing, though I can also be shy, self-conscious, and even obnoxious. … I'm responsible, even studious every now and then, but on the other hand I'm a goof-off too, because if you're too studious, you won't be popular. … Sometimes I feel phony, especially around boys. … I'll be flirtatious and fun-loving. And then everybody else is looking at me. … Then I get self-conscious and embarrassed and become radically introverted, and I don't know who I really am! I can be my true self with my close friends. I can't be my real self with my parents. They don't understand me. They treat me like I'm still a kid. That gets confusing, though. I mean, which am I, a kid or an adult?

—Adapted from Harter, 1990, pp. 352–353

These thoughts of a 15-year-old girl illustrate a key aspect of adolescence: the search for an answer to the question "Who am I?" She is struggling to reconcile contradictory traits and behaviors to determine the "real me." Adolescents are preoccupied not only with their present selves but also with what they want to become.

Development of Identity: "Who Am I?"

In this module, we explore social and emotional development in adolescence. We begin with the formation of identity.

Erikson and Identity Development

Erik Erikson's fifth stage of psychosocial development is called **ego identity versus role diffusion**. The primary task is for adolescents to develop ego identity: a sense of who they are and what they stand for. They are faced with choices about their future occupations, political and religious beliefs, gender roles, and more. Formal-operational thinking enables adolescents to consider the hypothetical costs and benefits of pursuing various life paths (Roeser et al., 2006).

One aspect of identity development is a **psychological moratorium** during which adolescents experiment with different roles, values, beliefs, and relationships (Erikson, 1968). During this time, adolescents undergo an **identity crisis** in which they examine their values and make decisions about their life roles. Should they attend college? What career should they pursue? Should they become sexually active? With whom?

In their search for identity, many—not all—adolescents join "in" groups, slavishly imitating their peers' clothing, speech, hairstyles, and ideals (Erikson, 1963). Those who successfully resolve their identity crises develop a strong sense of who they are and what they stand for. Those who do not may be intolerant of people who are different and may blindly follow people who adhere to convention.

Identity Statuses

James Marcia built on Erikson's approach. He theorized four *identity statuses* (1991) that represent combinations of the dimensions of exploration and commitment that Erikson believed were critical to the development of identity (S. J. Schwartz, 2001) (see Table 6.3). *Exploration* involves active questioning and searching among alternatives to establish goals, values, or beliefs. *Commitment* is a stable investment in one's goals, values, or beliefs.

Identity diffusion is least advanced and includes adolescents who neither have commitments nor are trying to form them (Berzonsky, 2005). This stage is characteristic of younger adolescents and of older adolescents who drift through life or become alienated and rebellious (Snarey & Bell, 2003).

Identity Formation

Explore and learn more about the concept of identity formation, including the four statuses, healthy identity formation and the role of ethnicity.

Table 6.3
The Four Identity Statuses of James Marcia

		Exploration	
		Yes	**No**
		Identity Achievement	**Foreclosure**
Commitment	**Yes**	• Most developed in terms of identity • Has experienced a period of exploration • Has developed commitments • Has a sense of personal well-being, high self-esteem, and self-acceptance • Cognitively flexible • Sets goals and works toward achieving them	• Has commitments without considering alternatives • Commitments based on identification with parents, teachers, or other authority figures • Often authoritarian and inflexible
		Moratorium	**Identity Diffusion**
	No	• Actively exploring alternatives • Attempting to make choices with regard to occupation, ideological beliefs, and so on • Often anxious and intense • Ambivalent feelings toward parents and authority figures	• Least developed in terms of identity • Lacks commitments • Not trying to form commitments • May be carefree and uninvolved or unhappy and lonely • May be angry, alienated, rebellious

© 2012 Cengage Learning

foreclosure An identity status that characterizes those who have made commitments without considering alternatives.

moratorium An identity status that characterizes those who are actively exploring alternatives in an attempt to form an identity.

identity achievement An identity status that characterizes those who have explored alternatives and have developed commitments.

In the **foreclosure** status, individuals make commitments without considering alternatives. These commitments are usually established early in life and are often based on identification with parents, teachers, or religious leaders who have made a strong impression (Saroglou & Galand, 2004).

The **moratorium** status describes a person who is actively exploring alternatives in an attempt to make choices (Akman, 2007). Such individuals are often anxious and intense.

Identity achievement describes those who have explored alternatives and developed relatively firm commitments. They generally have high self-esteem and self-acceptance (Adams et al., 2006).

Development of Identity Statuses

Before high school, children show little interest in questions of identity. Most are in either identity diffusion or foreclosure statuses. During the high-school and college years, adolescents increasingly move from the diffusion and foreclosure statuses to the moratorium and achievement statuses (Snarey & Bell, 2003). The greatest gains in identity formation occur in college (Berzonsky & Kuk, 2005). College students are exposed to a variety of lifestyles, beliefs, and career choices, which spur consideration of identity issues. Are you a student who has changed majors once or twice (or more)? If so, you have most likely experienced the moratorium identity status, which is common among college students. College seniors have a stronger sense of identity than first-year students as a result of resolving identity crises (H. L. Lewis, 2003).

Gender and Development of Identity

Erikson believed that there were gender differences in the development of identity, and his views reflected the times and culture in which he wrote. Identity development relates to relationships and occupational choice, among other matters. Erikson (1968, 1975) assumed that relationships were more important to women's development of identity, while occupational and ideological matters were relatively more important to men's. He believed that a young woman's identity was intimately bound up with her roles as wife and mother. Studies today show that both adolescent females and males are concerned about occupational choices, even though females are more likely to expect that they will have to balance the demands of a career and a family (Berzonsky, 2004). This gender difference may persist because females continue to assume primary responsibility for child rearing, even though most women are employed outside the home (Anthis et al., 2004).

Development of the Self-Concept

Before adolescence, children describe themselves primarily in terms of their physical characteristics and their actions. As they approach adolescence, children begin to incorporate psychological characteristics and social relationships into their self-descriptions (Damon, 1991).

Adolescents' self-perceptions are more complex than those of younger children. Many factors come into play, as seen in Susan Harter's Self-Perception Profile for Adolescents. Items similar to those from Harter's assessment method include:

1. I'm good-looking. (Factor: General attractiveness)
2. I get good grades. (Scholastic competence)

Achieving Ethnic Identity

Read "Ethnicity and Development of Identity."

   3. I have a lot of friends. (Peer support)

   4. I do well at sports. (Athletic competence)

   5. I'm ready to do well in a job. (Job competence)

   6. I don't get into trouble. (Conduct)

   7. I date the people to whom I'm attracted. (Romantic appeal)

(Source: Worrell (1997).)

Furthermore, adolescents may describe themselves as anxious or sarcastic with parents but talkative and cheerful with friends. Such contradictions and conflicts in self-description reach their peak at about age 14 and then decline (Harter & Monsour, 1992). The advanced formal-operational skills of older adolescents allow them to integrate contradictory aspects of the self. The older adolescent might say, "I'm very adaptable. When I'm around my friends, who think that what I say is important, I'm very talkative; but around my family, I'm quiet because they're not interested enough to really listen to me" (Damon, 1991, p. 988).

Self-Esteem

Self-esteem tends to decline as the child progresses from middle childhood to the age of about 12 or 13 (Harter & Whitesell, 2003). The growing cognitive maturity of young adolescents makes them increasingly aware of the disparity between their ideal selves and their real selves, especially in terms of physical appearance (Durkin et al., 2007; Seidah & Bouffard, 2007). Boys might fantasize that they would like to have the physiques of the warriors they see in video games or in the media (Konijn et al., 2007). Most girls want to be thin, thin, thin (O'Dea, 2006).

After hitting a low point at about age 12 or 13, self-esteem gradually improves (Harter & Whitesell, 2003). Perhaps adolescents adjust their ideal selves to better reflect reality. Also, as adolescents develop academic, physical, and social skills, they may grow less self-critical (Shirk et al., 2003).

For most adolescents, low self-esteem produces temporary discomfort (Harter & Whitesell, 2003). For others, low self-esteem has serious consequences. For example, low self-esteem is often found in teenagers who are depressed or suicidal (Shirk et al., 2003).

Emotional support from parents and peers is important in self-esteem. Adolescents who feel highly regarded by family and friends are more likely to feel positive about themselves (Costigan et al., 2007).

Relationships With Parents and Peers

Adolescents, coping with the task of establishing a sense of identity and direction in their lives, are heavily influenced both by parents and by peers.

Relationships With Parents

Although most adolescents get along well with their parents, they spend less time with their parents than they did in childhood (Larson & Richards, 1991). Adolescents continue to interact more with their mothers than their fathers. Teenagers have more conflicts with their mothers, but they also view their mothers as being more supportive and knowing them better (Costigan et al., 2007). Adverse relationships with fathers are often associated with depression in adolescents (Sheeber et al., 2007), but good relations with fathers contribute to psychological well-being (Flouri & Buchanan, 2003).

The decrease in time spent with family may reflect the adolescents' striving for independence. A certain degree of distancing from parents may be adaptive as adolescents form relationships outside the family. However, adolescents continue to maintain love, loyalty, and respect for their parents (W. A. Collins & Laursen, 2006). And adolescents who feel close to their parents have more self-reliance and self-esteem, better school performance, and fewer adjustment problems (Costigan et al., 2007).

The relationship between parents and teens is not always rosy, of course. Early adolescence, in particular, is characterized by increased bickering and a decrease in shared activities and expressions of affection (Smetana, Campione-Barr, et al., 2006). Conflicts typically center on the everyday details of family life, such as chores, homework, curfews, personal appearance, finances, and dating—often because adolescents believe that they should manage matters that were previously controlled by parents (Costigan

What happens to relationships with parents during adolescence? Parent–child relationships are redefined during adolescence, as most adolescents strive for independence. There are often conflicts about choices of friends and clothing and how and where adolescents spend their time. But despite conflict, most adolescents continue to love and respect their parents.

▶ **LO21** Explain how relationships with parents change during adolescence.

▶ **LO22** Discuss adolescents' peer relationships.

et al., 2007). But parents, especially mothers, continue to believe that they should retain control in most areas, for example, encouraging adolescents to do their homework and clean their rooms. As adolescents get older, they and their parents are more likely to compromise (Smetana, Campione-Barr, et al., 2006). On the other hand, parents and adolescents are usually quite similar in their values and beliefs regarding social, political, religious, and economic issues (W. A. Collins & Laursen, 2006). Even though the notion of a generation gap between adolescents and their parents may persist as a stereotype, there is little evidence of one.

As adolescents grow older, parents are more likely to relax controls and less likely to use punishment (Smetana, Campione-Barr, et al., 2006). Although parent–child relationships change, most adolescents feel that they are close to and get along with their parents, even though they may develop a less idealized view of them (W. A. Collins & Laursen, 2006).

Parenting Styles

Differences in parenting styles continue to influence the development of adolescents (Costigan et al., 2007). Adolescents from authoritative homes—whose parents are willing to exert control and explain the reasons for doing so—show the most competent behavior. They are more self-reliant, do better in school, have better mental health, and show the lowest incidence of psychological problems and misconduct, including drug use.

Relationships With Peers

The transition from childhood to adolescence is accompanied by a shift in the relative importance of parents and peers. Although relationships with parents generally remain positive, the role of peers as a source of activities, influence, and support increases. Parents are perceived as the most frequent providers of social and emotional support by fourth graders—by seventh grade, friends of the same gender are seen to be as supportive as parents. By 10th grade, same-gender friends are viewed as providing more support than parents (Furman & Buhrmester, 1992).

Friendships in Adolescence

Adolescents have more friends than younger children do (Feiring & Lewis, 1991). Most adolescents have one or two "best friends" and several good friends. Teenagers see their friends frequently, usually several hours a day (Hartup, 1983). And

Monkey Business Images/Shutterstock.com

Development of Friendship in Adolescence Adolescents tend to spend more time with their friends than with their families. They look for one or more close friends, or confidants. They also tend to belong to cliques and crowds. All these relationships serve different but overlapping functions.

when teenagers are not with their friends, you can often find them talking on the phone, texting, or instant messaging.

Friendships in adolescence differ from the friendships of childhood. Adolescents are more likely to stress acceptance, intimate self-disclosure, and mutual understanding (González et al., 2004). One eighth-grade girl described her best friend this way: "I can tell her things and she helps me talk. And she doesn't laugh at me if I do something weird—she accepts me for who I am" (Berndt & Perry, 1990, p. 269). Second, adolescents stress loyalty and trustworthiness (Rotenberg et al., 2004). They may say that a friend will "stick up for you in a fight" and will not "talk about you behind your back." Finally, adolescents are more likely than younger children to share with friends and less likely to compete with them.

Adolescents and their friends are similar in many respects. They typically are the same age and race. They almost always are the same gender. Even though romantic attachments increase during the teen years, most adolescents still choose members of their own gender as best friends (Hartup, 1993). Friends are often alike in school attitudes, educational aspirations, and grades. Friends also tend to have similar attitudes about drinking, drug use, and sexual activity (Youniss & Haynie, 1992).

Facebook and Adolescents

Read about the Facebook behavior of college students.

Friendship contributes to psychological adjustment. Adolescents who have a close friend have higher self-esteem than adolescents who do not (Berndt, 1992).

Intimacy and closeness appear to be more central to the friendships of girls than of boys (Schraf & Hertz-Lazarowitz, 2003). Adolescent and adult females also are generally more likely than males to disclose secrets, personal problems, thoughts, and feelings to their friends (Dindia & Allen, 1992).

Friendship networks among girls are smaller and more exclusive than networks among boys (Schraf & Hertz-Lazarowitz, 2003). Girls tend to have one or two close friends, whereas boys tend to congregate in larger, less intimate groups. The activities of girls' and boys' friendship networks differ as well. Girls are more likely to engage in unstructured activities such as talking and listening to music. Boys are more likely to engage in organized group activities, games, and sports.

Peer Groups

Most adolescents belong to one or more peer groups: *cliques* and *crowds* (Henzi et al., 2007). **Cliques** consist of five to 10 individuals who hang around together, sharing activities and confidences. **Crowds** are larger groups who may or may not spend much time together and are identified by their activities or attitudes. Crowds are usually given labels by other adolescents—"jocks," "brains," "druggies," or "nerds." The most negatively labeled groups ("druggies," "rejects") show higher levels of alcohol and drug abuse, delinquency, and depression.

Adolescent peer groups function with less adult guidance or control than childhood peer groups (Staff et al., 2004). Adolescent peer groups may include members of the other gender, sharply contrasting with the gender segregation of childhood peer groups. Such associations may lead to dating and romantic relationships.

Dating and Romantic Relationships

Romantic relationships usually begin during early and middle adolescence, and most adolescents start dating or going out by the time they graduate from high school (Florsheim, 2003). For heterosexuals, the development of dating typically takes the following sequence: putting oneself in situations where peers of the other gender probably will be present (e.g., hanging out at the mall), group activities including peers of the other gender (e.g., school dances or parties), group dating (e.g., joining a mixed-gender group at the movies), and then traditional two-person dating (Connolly, Craig, et al., 2004).

clique A group of five to 10 individuals who hang around together and who share activities and confidences.

crowd A large, loosely organized group of people who may or may not spend much time together and who are identified by the activities of the group.

Dating serves a number of functions. First and foremost, people date to have fun. Dating, especially in early adolescence, also serves to enhance prestige with peers. It gives adolescents additional experiences in learning to relate to people. Finally, dating prepares adolescents for adult courtship (Florsheim, 2003).

Dating relationships tend to be casual and short-lived in early adolescence. In late adolescence, relationships tend to become more stable and committed (Connolly, Furman, et al., 2000). Eighteen-year-olds are more likely than 15-year-olds to mention love, trust, and commitment when they describe romantic relationships (Feiring, 1993).

Peer Influence

Peer pressure is fairly weak in early adolescence. It peaks during mid-adolescence and declines after about age 17 (Reis & Youniss, 2004). Peer influence may increase during adolescence because peers provide a standard by which adolescents measure their own behavior as they develop independence from the family (Foster-Clark & Blyth, 1991). Peers also provide support in times of trouble (Kirchler et al., 1991).

Parents often worry that their teenage children will fall in with the wrong crowd and be persuaded to engage in self-destructive behavior. There is a widespread assumption that peer and parental influences will be in conflict, with peers exerting pressure on adolescents to engage in negative behaviors such as alcohol and drug abuse. However, parents and peers are usually complementary rather than competing influences (Reis & Youniss, 2004).

Parents and peers also seem to exert influence in different domains. Adolescents are more likely to conform to peer standards in matters of style and taste, such as clothing, hairstyles, speech patterns, and music (Camarena, 1991). They are more likely to agree with their parents on moral principles and educational and career goals (Savin-Williams & Berndt, 1990).

Adolescents influence each other positively and negatively. In many cases, peer pressure to finish high school and achieve academically can be stronger than pressures to engage in misconduct (B. B. Brown et al., 1993; Steinberg, 1996). Yet many times adolescents discourage one another from doing well or from doing too well in school. Adolescents who smoke, drink, use drugs, and engage in sexual activity also often have friends who engage in these behaviors, but adolescents tend to choose friends and peers who are like them to begin with.

▶ **LO23** Discuss sexual behavior in adolescence.

Sexuality

My first sexual experience occurred in a car after the high school junior prom. We were both virgins, very uncertain but very much in love. We had been going together since eighth grade. The experience was somewhat painful. I remember wondering if I would look different to my mother the next day. I guess I didn't because nothing was said.

Because of the flood of sex hormones, adolescents tend to experience a powerful sex drive. In addition, they are bombarded with sexual messages in the media, including scantily clad, hip-grinding, crotch-grabbing pop stars; print ads for barely-there underwear; and countless articles on "How to tell if your boyfriend has been [whatever]" and "The 10 things that will drive your girlfriend wild." Teenagers are strongly motivated to follow the crowd, yet they are also influenced by the views of their parents and teachers. So what is a teen to do?

Sexual activity in adolescence can take many forms. In this section, we consider sexual identity, sexual behavior, and teenage pregnancy.

Gender Identity

Most people, including a majority of adolescents, have a heterosexual gender identity. They are sexually attracted to and interested in forming romantic relationships with people of the other gender. However, some people have a **homosexual** identity or orientation. They are attracted to and interested in forming romantic relationships with people of their own gender. Males with a homosexual orientation are referred to as *gay males*. Females with a homosexual orientation are referred to as *lesbians*. However, males and females with a homosexual orientation are sometimes categorized together as gay people or gays. *Bisexual* people are attracted to both females and males.

According to Ritch Savin-Williams and Lisa Diamond (2004; Savin-Williams, 2007), the development of gender identity in gay males and lesbians involves several steps: attraction to members of the same gender, self-labeling as gay or lesbian, sexual contact with members of the same gender, and eventual disclosure of one's sexual orientation to other people. There is generally a gap of about 10 years between initial attraction to members of the same gender, which tends to occur at about the age of 8 or 9, and disclosure of one's orientation to other people, which usually occurs at about age 18. But some gay males and lesbians never disclose their sexual orientations to anyone or to certain people, such as their parents.

homosexual Referring to an erotic orientation toward members of one's own gender.

masturbation Sexual self-stimulation.

petting Kissing and touching the breasts and genitals.

The process of "coming out"—that is, accepting one's homosexual orientation and declaring it to others—may be a long and painful struggle (Bagley & D'Augelli, 2000). Gay adolescents may be ostracized and rejected by family and friends. Depression and suicide rates are higher among gay youth than among heterosexual adolescents. As many as 1 in 3 gay, lesbian, or bisexual adolescents has attempted suicide (Hershberger & D'Augelli, 2000). Homosexual adolescents often engage in substance abuse, run away from home, and do poorly in school (S. T. Russell, 2006).

Masturbation

Masturbation, or sexual self-stimulation, is the most common sexual outlet in adolescence. Surveys indicate that most adolescents masturbate at some time. The Kinsey studies, published in the mid-twentieth century (Kinsey et al., 1948, 1953), suggested that masturbation was nearly universal among male adolescents but less common among adolescent females. This gender difference is confirmed in nearly every survey (Herbenick et al., 2010; Reece et al., 2010). Boys who masturbate do so more often than girls who masturbate. It is unclear whether this gender difference reflects a stronger sex drive in boys, greater social constraints on girls, or both. Beliefs that masturbation is harmful and guilt about it lessen the incidence (Ortega et al., 2005), although masturbation has not been shown to be physically harmful.

Male–Female Sexual Behavior

Adolescents today start dating and going out earlier than in past generations. Teens who date earlier are more likely to engage in sexual activity during high school (Guttmacher Institute, 2007). Teens who initiate sexual activity earlier are also less likely to use contraception and more likely to become pregnant. But early dating does not always lead to early sex, and early sex does not always lead to unwanted pregnancies.

Petting is practically universal among American adolescents and has been for many generations. Adolescents use petting to express affection, satisfy their curiosities, heighten their sexual arousal, and reach orgasm while avoiding pregnancy and maintaining virginity. Many adolescents do not see themselves as having sex if they stop short of vaginal intercourse (Guttmacher Institute, 2007). Girls are more likely than boys to be coerced into petting and to feel guilty about it (Larsson & Svedin, 2002).

Sexting and Adolescents

Is sexting one more way for teens to stay in touch?

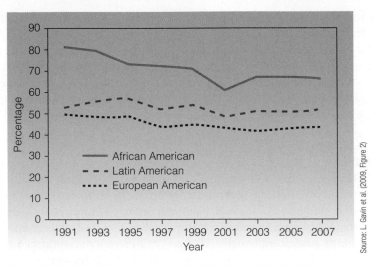

Source: L. Gavin et al. (2009, Figure 2)

Figure 6.8 Percentage of Students in Grades 9–12 Who Report Having Had Sexual Intercourse

Surveys show that African American high-school students have been more likely to engage in sexual intercourse than Latin American and European American students (see Figure 6.8). The incidences of kissing, petting, oral sex, and sexual intercourse all increase with age. For example, according to a survey by the Centers for Disease Control and Prevention, 42% of girls of aged 15–17 reported engaging in oral sex, compared with 72% of girls aged 18 or 19 (Mosher et al., 2005).

Effects of Puberty

The hormonal changes of puberty probably are partly responsible for the onset of sexual activity. In boys, levels of testosterone are associated with sexual behavior. In girls, however, testosterone levels are linked to sexual interests but not to sexual behavior. Social factors may therefore play a greater role in regulating sexual behavior in girls than boys (Browning et al., 2000; O'Donnell et al., 2003).

The physical changes associated with puberty also may trigger the onset of sexual activity. For example, the development of secondary sex characteristics such as breasts in girls and muscles and deep voices in boys may make them more sexually attractive. Early-maturing girls are more likely to have older friends, who may draw them into sexual relationships.

Parental Influences

Teenagers who have close relationships with their parents are less likely to initiate sexual activity at an early age (Bynum, 2007). Adolescents who communicate well with their parents also delay the onset of sexual activity (Aspy et al., 2007). If these youngsters do have sexual intercourse, they are more likely to use birth control and have fewer partners.

Peer Influences

A good predictor of sexual activity for adolescents is the sexual activity of their best friends (Dishion & Stormshak, 2007). When teenagers are asked why they do not wait to have sex until they are older, the main reason reported is usually peer pressure (O'Donnell et al., 2003). Peers, especially those of the same gender, also serve as a key source of sex education for adolescents. Adolescents report that they are somewhat more likely to receive information about sex from friends and media sources— TV shows, films, magazines, and the Internet—than from sex-education classes or their parents (Kaiser Family Foundation et al., 2003).

Teenage Pregnancy

In the United States today, 9 in 10 adolescents who become pregnant do so accidentally and without committed partners (America's Children, 2007). Most young women in developed nations defer pregnancy until after they have completed some or all of their education. Many do so until they are well into their careers and in their late 20s, their 30s, even their 40s. Why do adolescents get pregnant? For one thing, adolescent girls typically get little advice in school or at home about how to deal with boys' sexual advances. Another reason is failure to use contraception. Some initiate sex at very early ages, when they are least likely to use contraception (Buston et al., 2007). Many adolescent girls, especially younger adolescents, do not have access to contraceptive devices. Among those who do, fewer than half use them reliably (Buston et al., 2007).

Some teenage girls purposefully get pregnant to try to force their partners to make a commitment to them. Some are rebelling against their parents or the moral standards of their communities. But most girls become pregnant because they and their partners miscalculate the odds of getting pregnant (Buston et al., 2007).

Parents and Sex Ed

Read "What Parents Want from Sex-Education Courses."

Sexy TV Shows and Teens

Does sex on TV encourage sexual behavior in teenagers and lead to teenage pregnancy?

▶ **LO24** Discuss juvenile delinquency.

For all these reasons, about 750,000–800,000 teenage girls in the United States are impregnated each year. The pregnancies result in about half a million births. However large this number may sound, 10–20 years ago about one million girls were getting pregnant each year. The drop-off may reflect findings that sexual activity among teenagers has leveled off and that relatively more adolescents are using contraception consistently. Researchers at the Centers for Disease Control and Prevention attribute the drop-off in careless sex to educational efforts by schools, the media, religious institutions, and communities (America's Children, 2007).

Consequences of Teenage Pregnancy

Actually, the outcome of teenage pregnancies for young women who want their babies and have the resources to nurture them are generally good (S. A. Rathus, Fichner-Rathus, et al., 2011). Females tend to be healthy in late adolescence. However, the medical, social, and economic costs of *unplanned* or *unwanted* pregnancies among adolescents are enormous both to the mothers and to the children. Adolescent mothers are more likely to experience medical complications during the months of pregnancy and their labor is likely to be prolonged. The babies are at greater risk of being premature and of having low birth weight (Mathews & MacDorman, 2007). These medical problems are not necessarily because of the age of the mother, but rather because teenage mothers—especially poor teenage mothers—are less likely to have access to prenatal care or to obtain adequate nutrition.

The teenage mother is less likely than her peers to graduate from high school or move on to postsecondary education. Therefore, she will earn less and be in greater need of public assistance. Few teenage mothers obtain assistance from the babies' fathers. The fathers typically cannot support themselves, much less a family.

Preventing Teenage Pregnancy

The past several decades have seen a dramatic increase in programs to help prevent teenage pregnancies. Prevention efforts include educating teenagers about sexuality and contraception and providing family planning services (Santelli et al., 2003). An overwhelming majority of American parents want their children's schools to have sex education.

How successful are sex-education programs? The better programs increase students' knowledge about sexuality. Despite fears that sex education will increase sex-

juvenile delinquency Conduct in a child or adolescent characterized by illegal activities.

ual activity in teenagers, some programs seem to delay the onset of sexual activity (S. E. Bennett & Assefi, 2005; Santelli et al., 2003). Among teenagers who already are sexually active, sex education is associated with the increased use of effective contraception.

Juvenile Delinquency

The term **juvenile delinquency** refers to the behavior of children or adolescents who engage in illegal activities and come into contact with the criminal-justice system. At the most extreme end, juvenile delinquency includes serious behaviors such as homicide, rape, and robbery. Less serious offenses, such as truancy, underage drinking, running away from home, and sexual promiscuity, are considered illegal only when performed by minors. Hence, these activities are termed *status offenses*.

Antisocial and criminal behaviors show a dramatic increase in many societies during adolescence and then taper off during adulthood. For example, about 4 in 10 serious crimes in the United States are committed by individuals under the age of 21, and about 3 in 10 are committed by adolescents under 18 (Snyder & Sickmund, 2006).

Many delinquent acts do not result in arrest or conviction. And when adolescents are arrested, their cases may be disposed of informally, as by referral to a mental-health agency (Snyder & Sickmund, 2006).

Ethnicity, Gender, and Juvenile Delinquency

African American adolescents are more likely to be arrested than European American adolescents. For example, African American youths constitute about 13% of the adolescent population in the United States but about one fourth of juvenile arrests in general and about one half of those for violent crimes (Snyder & Sickmund, 2006). Figure 6.9 shows that in recent years the delinquency case rate for African American youngsters has been more than twice that for European American youngsters.

Criminologist Donna Bishop (2005) noted a couple of possible explanations for the difference regarding European Americans and African Americans. The *differential offending hypothesis* suggests that there are actual racial differences in the incidence and seriousness of delinquent behavior. The *differential treatment hypothesis* suggests that African American and European American youth probably do not

Prescription Drugs and Teens

Watch teens talk about their addictions to prescription drugs and the illegal ways they obtain them.

▶ **LO25** Discuss adolescent suicide.

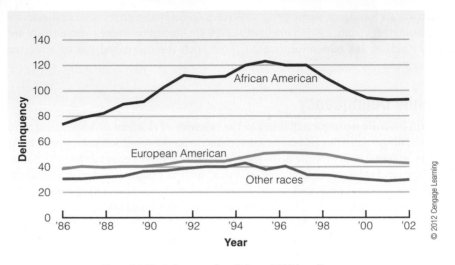

Figure 6.9 **The Delinquency Case Rate per 1,000 Juveniles**

© 2012 Cengage Learning

behave differently but are treated differently—intentionally or accidentally—by the juvenile justice system. That is, "the system" expects worse behavior from African American youngsters, so it polices them more actively and cracks down on them more harshly. One result of differential treatment is that African American adolescents have more interaction with the juvenile justice system and are more likely to think of themselves as criminals.

Economic and family factors are also connected with racial and ethnic differences in juvenile offending. African American (and Latin American) children and adolescents are 3 times as likely as European American youth to be living in poverty (Snyder & Sickmund, 2006). Moreover, African American children are less likely than European American (or Latin American) children to be living with both of their biological parents, regardless of whether or not their parents are married (Snyder & Sickmund, 2006). We cannot say that poverty *causes* delinquency or that a broken family *causes* delinquency, but poverty and broken families appear to be risk factors.

Boys are much more likely than girls to engage in delinquent behavior, especially crimes of violence. On the other hand, girls are more likely to commit status offenses such as truancy or running away (Snyder & Sickmund, 2006).

Who Are the Delinquents?

Even if the causal paths are less than clear, a number of factors are associated with delinquency. Children who show aggressive, antisocial, and hyperactive behavior at an early age are more likely to show delinquent behavior in adolescence (S. W. Baron et al., 2007). Delinquency also is associated with having a lower verbal IQ, immature moral reasoning, low self-esteem, feelings of alienation, and impulsivity (Lynam et al., 2007). Other personal factors include little interest in school, early substance abuse, early sexuality, and delinquent friends (Ruchkin & Vermeiren, 2006).

The families of juvenile delinquents are often characterized by lax and ineffective discipline, low levels of affection, and high levels of family conflict, physical abuse, severe parental punishment, and neglect (Vermeiren et al., 2004). The parents and siblings of juvenile delinquents frequently have engaged in antisocial, deviant, or criminal behavior themselves (Snyder & Sickmund, 2006).

Suicide: When the Adolescent Has Nothing— Except Everything—to Lose

Adolescence is an exciting time of life. For many, the future is filled with promise. Many count the days until they graduate high school, until they enter college. Many enjoy thrilling fantasies of what might be. And then there are those who take their own lives. Suicide is the third leading cause of death among adolescents (National Center for Injury Prevention and Control, 2007b). Since 1960, the suicide rate has more than tripled for young people aged 15–24. About 1–2 American adolescents in 10,000 commit suicide each year. About 1 in 10 has attempted suicide.

Risk Factors in Suicide

Most suicides among adolescents and adults are linked to feelings of depression and hopelessness (S.-T. Cheng & Chan, 2007). Jill

BananaStock/Jupiterimages

Teen Depression

Watch and learn how often adolescents should be screened for depression, which may be a precursor to suicide.

Warning Signs of Suicide

Read and learn how to recognize the warning signs of suicide.

Rathus and her colleagues (J. H. Rathus & Miller, 2002) found that suicidal adolescents experience four areas of psychological problems: (1) confusion about the self, (2) impulsiveness, (3) emotional instability, and (4) interpersonal problems. Some suicidal teenagers are highly achieving, rigid perfectionists who have set impossibly high expectations for themselves (A. L. Miller, Wyman, et al., 2000). Many teenagers throw themselves into feelings of depression and hopelessness by comparing themselves negatively with others, even when the comparisons are inappropriate. ("True, you didn't get into Harvard, but you did get into the University of California at Irvine, and it's a great school.")

Adolescent suicide attempts are more common after stressful life events, especially events that entail loss of social support, as in the death of a parent or friend, breaking up with a boyfriend or girlfriend, or a family member's leaving home (J. Cooper et al., 2002). Other contributors to suicidal behavior include concerns over sexuality, school grades, problems at home, and substance abuse (Conner & Goldston, 2007; Cuellar & Curry, 2007). It is not always a stressful event itself that precipitates suicide, but the adolescent's anxiety or fear of being "found out" for something, such as failing a course or getting arrested.

Suicide tends to run in families (National Center for Injury Prevention and Control, 2007b). Do genetic factors play a role, possibly leading to psychological disorders, such as depression, that are connected with suicide? Could it be that a socially impoverished family environment infuses several family members with feelings of hopelessness? Or does the suicide of one family member simply give others the idea that suicide is the way to manage problems?

Researchers have found the following warning signs of suicide among adolescents: belief that it is acceptable to kill oneself, drug abuse and other kinds of delinquency, victimization by bullying, extensive body piercing, stress, hostility, depression and other psychological disorders, heavy smoking, and low self-esteem.

Why do you think that extensive body piercing is a warning sign of possible suicide among adolescents? Can you find teenagers in the news who have committed suicide because they were bullied? Why do you think that heavy smoking is a warning sign?

Ethnicity, Gender, and Suicide

Rates of suicide and suicide attempts vary among different ethnic groups. Native American and Latin American teenagers have the highest suicide rates, in part because of the stresses to which they are exposed, in part because of their lack of access to health care (Duarté-Vélez & Bernal, 2007). European Americans are next. African American teens are least likely to attempt suicide or to think about it (Freedenthal, 2007).

About three times as many adolescent females as males attempt suicide, but about four times as many males complete a suicide (National Center for Injury Prevention and Control, 2007b). Males are apparently more likely to "succeed" at suicide because males are more likely to use more rapid and lethal methods, such as shooting themselves, whereas females are more likely to overdose on drugs like tranquilizers or sleeping pills (National Center for Injury Prevention & Control, 2007b). Females often do not take enough of these chemicals to kill themselves. It also takes time for them to work, providing other people the chance to intervene before they die.

Check Your Learning Quiz 6.3

Go to **login.cengagebrain.com** and take the online quiz.

▸ **LO26** Discuss the definition of adulthood.

▸ **LO27** Explain social and cultural conditions that set the stage for emerging adulthood.

Did you know that—

- Many researchers argue that during the past half century, a new stage of development has arisen that encompasses the ages of 18 to 25?

- Traditionally speaking, getting married and holding a job have been considered two of the criteria for reaching adulthood?

- Over the past 50 years or so, the average age for getting married (the first time!) in the United States has risen from 20 to 26 for women and from 22 to 28 for men?

- Fifty years ago, couples tended to have their first child about a year after getting married?

- Although most women did not attend college 50–60 years ago, today the majority of college undergraduates are women?

- The typical American will hold about seven different jobs between the ages of 20 and 29?

▼

When our mothers were our age, they were engaged. They at least had some idea what they were going to do with their lives. I, on the other hand, will have a dual degree in majors that are ambiguous at best and impractical at worst (English and political science), no ring on my finger and no idea who I am, much less what I want to do. Under duress, I will admit that this is a pretty exciting time. Sometimes, when I look out across the wide expanse that is my future, I can see beyond the void. I realize that having nothing ahead to count on means I now have to count on myself; that having no direction means forging one of my own.
—Kristen, age 22 (Page, 1999, pp. 18, 20)

Well, Kristen has some work to do; she needs to forge her own direction. Just think: What if Kristen had been born into the caste system of old England or India, into a traditional Islamic society, or into the United States of the 1950s, when the TV sitcom *Father Knows Best* was perennially in the top 10? Kristen would have had a sense of direction, that's certain. But of course, it would have been the sense of direction society or tradition had created for her, not her own.

emerging adulthood Period of development, spanning the ages of 18 to 25, in which young people engage in extended role exploration.

But Kristen was not born into any of these societies. She was born into the open and challenging United States of the current generation. She has the freedom to become whatever the interaction of her genetic heritage and her educational and social opportunities will enable her to become—and the opportunities are many. With freedom comes the need to make choices. When we need to make choices, we profit from information. Kristen is in the process of accumulating

"Emerging adulthood" is a new stage of development in developed nations. Some researchers suggest that affluent societies like ours have spawned a new stage of development, emerging adulthood, that involves an extended period of self-exploration during which one remains financially dependent.

information about herself and about the world outside. According to psychologist Jeffrey Arnett (2007), she is in **emerging adulthood**. In earlier days, adolescents made a transition, for better or worse, directly into adulthood. Now many of them—especially those in affluent nations with abundant opportunities—spend time in what some theorists think of as a new period of development roughly spanning the ages of 18 to 25, although we also see the age of 29 mentioned as the upper limit.

Adulthood itself has been divided into stages, and the first of these, young adulthood, has been seen largely as the period of life when people focus on establishing their careers or pathways in life. It has been acknowledged that the transition to adulthood could be slow or piecemeal, with many individuals in their late teens and early 20s remaining dependent on their parents and reluctant or unable to make enduring commitments, in terms of either identity formation or the development of intimate relationships. The question is whether another stage of development exists, one that bridges adolescence and young adulthood. A number of developmental theorists, including Arnett (2011) and Labouvie-Vief (2006), believe there is another stage.

The Meaning of Adulthood

Let us consider what the term *adulthood* means. Legally, adulthood has many ages, depending on what you want to do. The age of consent to marry varies from state to state, but in general, marriage is permitted in the teens. The age for drinking legally is 21.

The age for driving varies. By and large, however, adulthood is usually defined in terms of what people do rather than how old they are. Over the years, marriage has been a key criterion for adulthood, according to people who write about human development (J. S. Carroll et al., 2007). Other criteria include holding a full-time job and living independently (not with one's parents). Today, the transition to adulthood is mainly marked by adjustment issues, such as deciding on one's values and beliefs, accepting self-responsibility, becoming financially independent, and establishing an equal relationship with one's parents (Arnett, 2011; B. H. Gottlieb et al., 2007). Marriage is no longer necessarily a crucial marker for entering adulthood (B. H. Gottlieb et al., 2007).

An End to Traditional Gender Roles

Traditional guidelines have been shattered. Half a century ago, most young people, by their late teens or by their early twenties, had begun reasonably stable adult lives in terms of romantic relationships and work. Not too many undertook advanced training or education beyond the level of high school. In 1960, the median age for marriage for women was 20. For men, it was 22. A decade later, by 1970, the ages had risen to 21 for women and 23 for men. But by the year 2000, there was a dramatic 4-year rise, to 25 for women and 27 for men. And now the median ages are 26 for women and 28 for men. Something has changed.

One factor is sex—sexual behavior, that is. Because of the advent of the birth-control pill, sex, for millions, became separated from pregnancy—despite the fact that many adolescents become pregnant because they do not use birth control reliably. The sexual revolution of the 1960s and 1970s was another reason that most young people decided that they did not have to wait until marriage to enter into sexual relationships. On the other hand, most young people are not promiscuous. They tend to enter into a series of sexually monogamous relationships—termed *serial monogamy*—until they are ready to form more lasting unions. There is also wide acceptance today of multiple premarital sexual relationships—for women as well as men—so long as they occur within the context of committed relationships.

Fifty year ago, couples tended to have their first child about a year after getting married. Nowadays, many couples delay childbearing due to college and graduate school and in order to devote much of their twenties to establishing a career. Today, as noted by Arnett (2011), many emerging adults do not see having children as an achievement to be sought, but rather as a pitfall, or worse, a threat to the good life that is to be avoided—at least through much or all of the twenties.

Gender roles have also changed over the past half century. Fifty to 60 years ago, very few women entered college. The occupations open to women were secretarial work, waiting tables, cleaning, and, at the professional level, teaching and nursing. Even these were largely viewed as temporary positions until a woman could find a husband and have children. Today, however, women occupy about 56% of the undergraduate seats in colleges across the nation (National Center for Education Statistics, 2010). Women today also enter careers once considered the preserve of men, such as law and medicine—even the so-called STEM fields of science, technology, engineering, and math. It takes time to prepare for and become established in these fields. Once there, women are unlikely to leave them for a family. Many women do take maternity leaves when necessary, but men are also becoming likely to take paternity leaves.

Table 6.4 shows the percentages of bachelor's and doctoral degrees that were awarded to women during three periods of time: 1990–1991, 1995–1996, and 2005–2006. At the bachelor's-degree level, women have been advancing steadily in

Table 6.4
Percentage of Bachelor's and Doctoral Degrees Women Earned, by Field Of Study

	1990–1991	1995–1996	2005–2006
Bachelor's Degrees			
Health professions & related clinical sciences	83.9	81.5	86.0
Biological & biomedical sciences	50.8	52.6	61.5
Physical sciences & science technologies	31.6	36.0	41.8
Mathematics & statistics	47.3	46.1	45.1
Engineering & engineering technologies	14.1	16.2	17.9
Doctoral Degrees			
Health professions & related clinical sciences	57.7	60.3	72.5
Biological & biomedical sciences	36.9	41.8	49.2
Physical sciences & science technologies	19.6	22.9	30.0
Mathematics & statistics	19.2	20.6	29.5
Engineering & engineering technologies	9.3	12.6	20.2

Source: U.S. Department of Education, National Center for Education Statistics (NCES). Digest of Education Statistics, 2007 *(NCES 2008-022), tables 258, 286, 288, 290–294, 296, 299–301, 303, 305, and 307, data from U.S. Department of Education, NCES, 1990–91, 1995–96, and 2005–06 Integrated Postsecondary Education Data System, "Completions Survey" (IPEDS-C:91–96), and IPEDS, Fall 2006. Table 27.1.*

▶ **LO28** Discuss the factors involved in defining emerging adulthood.

the biological and biomedical sciences, physical sciences, and engineering. They have dominated the reception of bachelor's degrees in the health professions and related clinical sciences, receiving 6 of 7 bachelor's degrees in 2005–2006. Women appear to have leveled off at close to half the bachelor's degrees in math and statistics, and are obtaining a dramatically increasing percentage of doctoral degrees in all STEM fields. Although it is not shown in Table 6.4, women now obtain the majority of graduate degrees overall, including doctoral degrees.

For both women and men, the changes from a manufacturing-based economy to an information-based economy increased the need for advanced education and training over the past half century (Arnett, 2007, 2011). Now about 60% of young people undergo advanced training and education to prepare themselves (National Center for Education Statistics, 2010).

Features of Emerging Adulthood

Emerging adulthood is theorized as a distinct period of development found in societies that allow young people an extended opportunity to explore their roles in life. These tend to be affluent societies, such as those found in industrialized nations—our own among them. Many parents in the United States are affluent enough to continue to support their children throughout college and in graduate school. When parents cannot do the job, the government often steps in to help—for example, through student loans. These supports allow young people the luxury of sorting out identity issues and creating meaningful life plans—even if some still do not know where they are going after they graduate from college. Should they know who they are and what they are doing by the age of 21 or 22? Are they spoiled? These are value judgments that may or may not be on the mark. But let us note that many adults change their careers several times, partly because they did not sort out who they were and where they were going at an early age. On the other hand, even in the United States, many people lack the supports needed for successfully emerging into adulthood.

Jeffrey Arnett (2007, 2011) has hypothesized that five features distinguish the stage of emerging adulthood that is sandwiched between the stages of adolescence, which precedes it, and young adulthood, which follows it:

The Age of Identity Explorations

Many people of the ages discussed by Arnett and Labouvie-Vief—from 18 or 20 to about 25 or 30—are on the path to making vital choices in terms of their love lives and their career lives. As noted in the following section, they are experimenting with romantic partners and career possibilities.

The Age of Instability

In times gone past, it might have been the case that adolescents would obtain jobs fresh out of high school—if they completed high school—and keep them for many years, sometimes a lifetime. Today, Arnett notes, Americans have an average of about seven different jobs during the years between 20 and 29. Over this period they also frequently change their romantic partners—sometimes by choice, sometimes because the partner decides to move on. They also switch their living arrangements, often moving from place to place with little if any furniture. And they frequently change educational directions, finding what they like, finding what they can actually do, finding what is available to them.

The Age of Self-Focus

People are exceptionally self-focused during emerging adulthood. This does not mean that they are egocentric as in childhood or adolescence, or selfish (Arnett, 2011; Labouvie-Vief, 2006). It means, simply, that they are freer to make decisions than they are as children or adolescents; they are more mature, more independent from parental influences, and they usually have more resources. They are also free of the constraints of trying to mesh their lives with those of life partners.

Oliver Rossi/Getty Images

Emerging adults tend to be self-focused, meaning that they are freer to make decisions than they were as children and adults.

The Age of Feeling In-Between

Emerging adults are similar to adolescents in one way: Whereas adolescents may feel that they exist somewhere between childhood and

▶ **LO29** Discuss Erikson's views on an extended adolescence.

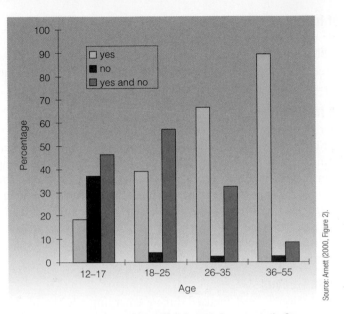

Source: Arnett (2000, Figure 2).

Figure 6.10 Subjective Conceptions of Adult Status in Response to the Question "Do You Feel That You Have Reached Adulthood?"

adulthood, emerging adults are likely to think that they are swimming between adolescence and "real" adulthood. They are likely to be out of school—that is, high school or undergraduate college—but obtaining further training or education. They are beyond the sometimes silly flirtations of adolescence but not yet in long-term, or at least permanent, relationships. They may not be completely dependent on caregivers, but they are just as unlikely to be self-supporting. They may be between roommates or apartments.

Where are they? In transit. Emerging adults seem to be well aware of the issues involved in defining the transition from adolescence to adulthood. Arnett (2000) reported what people say when they are asked whether they think they have become adults. The most common answer of 18- to 25-year-olds was something like "In some respects yes and in other respects no" (see Figure 6.10). Many think that they have developed beyond the conflicts and exploratory voyages of adolescence, but they may not yet have the ability—or desire—to assume the financial and interpersonal responsibilities they associate with adulthood.

The Age of Possibilities

Human beings are the only creatures on earth that allow their children to come back home.

—Bill Cosby

I take a very practical view of raising children. I put a sign in each of their rooms: "Checkout Time is 18 years."

—Erma Bombeck

Emerging adults typically feel that the world lies open before them. Like the majority of adults, they have what Arnett (2011) and Labouvie-Vief (2006) have termed an *optimistic bias*. The majority believe that things will work out.

In this age of possibilities, emerging adults have the feeling that they have the opportunity to make dramatic changes in their lives. Unlike children and adolescents, they are, to a large degree, independent of their parents. Many of them leave home for good; others return home for financial reasons. Some have a "revolving door" existence: leave home and then come back, according to the ebb and flow of financial and emotional resources..

Erik Erikson's Views

Erik Erikson (1968) did not use the term *emerging adulthood*, but he did recognize that developed nations tend to elongate the period of adolescence. Erikson used the term *moratorium* to describe the extended quest for identity among people who dwell in adolescence. Erikson and other theorists also believed that it was more meaningful for the individual to take the voyage to identity rather than foreclose it by adopting the viewpoints of other people. Although there are pluses in taking time to formulate one's identity, there are also downsides. For example, remaining dependent on parents can compromise an individual's self-esteem. Taking out loans for graduate school means that there is more to pay back; many individuals mortgage their own lives as they invest in their futures. Women who focus on their educations and their careers may bear children later. Although many people appreciate children more when they bear them later in life, they also become less fertile as the years wend their way, and they may find themselves in a race with their "biological clock."

And then, of course, there are those who remain adolescents forever.

Check Your Learning Quiz 6.4

Go to **login.cengagebrain.com** and take the online quiz.

GO to your Psychology CourseMate at login.cengagebrain.com and take the Chapter Post-Test to see which Learning Objectives you've mastered and which need more review. Use the chapter review guide below and the online activities—including flashcards to review key terms—to measure your learning.

Online Activities

Key Terms	Video	Animation	Reading	Assessment
Adolescence, puberty, feedback loop, primary sex characteristics, secondary sex characteristics, asynchronous growth, secular trend, semen, nocturnal emission, gynecomastia, epiphyseal closure, menarche	Premature Puberty Puberty and Body Image	Puberty		Check Your Learning Quiz 6.1
Osteoporosis	Risk-Taking			
Anorexia nervosa, bulimia nervosa	Exercise Bulimia		Anorexia Case Study Bulimia Case Study	
Formal operations, imaginary audience, personal fable	Hypothetical Propositions in Teenagers			Check Your Learning Quiz 6.2
			Solving the Puzzle and the Pendulum	
Postconventional level	Adolescents and Moral Development	Visual-Spatial Test Items		
			Helping Teens in School	

Measure
^Your Learning

Online Activities

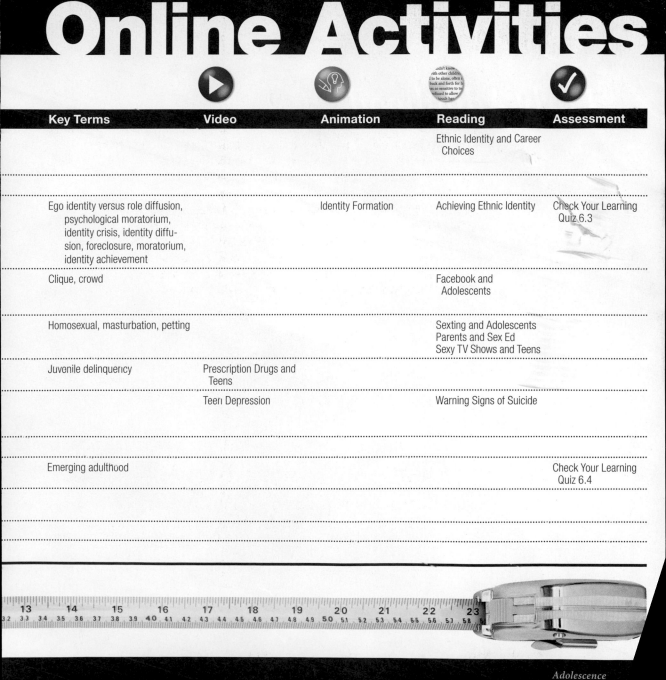

Key Terms	Video	Animation	Reading	Assessment
			Ethnic Identity and Career Choices	
Ego identity versus role diffusion, psychological moratorium, identity crisis, identity diffusion, foreclosure, moratorium, identity achievement		Identity Formation	Achieving Ethnic Identity	Check Your Learning Quiz 6.3
Clique, crowd			Facebook and Adolescents	
Homosexual, masturbation, petting			Sexting and Adolescents Parents and Sex Ed Sexy TV Shows and Teens	
Juvenile delinquency	Prescription Drugs and Teens			
	Teen Depression		Warning Signs of Suicide	
Emerging adulthood				Check Your Learning Quiz 6.4

Early Adulthood

7

CHAPTER

Image Source/Getty Images

Prepare ^ to Learn

1 **GO** to your **Psychology CourseMate** at **login.cengagebrain.com** and take the **Chapter Pre-Test** to introduce yourself to this chapter's topics and see what you may already know.

2 **READ** the **Learning Objectives** (LOs, in the left sidebars) and begin the chapter.

3 **COMPLETE** the **Online Activities** (in the right sidebars) *as you read each module.* Activities include **videos, animations, readings,** and **quizzes.**

4 **CHECK Your Learning** by going online to take the quiz at the end of each module and review material as necessary.

5 **MEASURE Your Learning** after reading the chapter by taking the online **Chapter Post-Test.** Use the chapter review guide at the end of the chapter as needed.

WATCH for these **Online Activities** icons as you read:

Video   Animation   Reading   Assessment

These online activities are essential to mastering this chapter. Go to login.cengagebrain.com:

Videos Watch the following videos:

- Ringtones and the Cochlea
- Substance Abuse Disorder
- Why Is Nicotine So Addictive?
- Women and Stress
- Debunking Myths about HPV
- Decision Making
- Dancing and Attraction
- Rules of Attraction
- Social Exclusion
- Commitment Phobia
- Cohabitation
- Same Sex Marriage
- Happy to Be Child-Free
- Deciding on How Many Children
- Motherhood: Finding Time
- Divorce Ceremonies?

Animations Interact with and visualize important processes, timelines, and concepts:

- Cognitive Changes in Early Adulthood
- Erikson and Levinson's Theories about Early Adulthood

Readings Delve deeper into key content:

- The Skinny on Weight Control
- The Body Mass Index (BMI) Chart
- Questionnaire: Do You Have a Problem With Alcohol?
- Preventing and Coping with Stress
- Preventing Sexually Transmitted Infections
- How to Handle Menstrual Discomfort
- The Cultural Myths That Create a Climate That Supports Rape
- How to Resist Sexual Harassment

Assessment Measure your mastery:

- Chapter Pre-Test
- Check Your Learning Quizzes
- Chapter Post-Test

Did you know that—

- Sensory sharpness, muscle strength, and cardiovascular fitness all peak in early adulthood?
- You need at least 30 minutes of vigorous physical activity 5 or more days a week?
- You may have a problem with alcohol if people have annoyed you by criticizing your drinking?
- Overdose of cocaine can cause cardiovascular and respiratory collapse?
- Your sexual orientation—as heterosexual or homosexual—may have to do with your exposure to sex hormones in the womb?
- The most common mode of transmission of HIV worldwide is male–female sex?
- Some women are raped because of a widespread cultural myth that women "deep down inside" want to be overpowered by men?

▼

Adulthood has been divided into stages. The first of these, early adulthood, is usually considered to range from the ages of 20 to 40, although, as we saw in Module 6.4, the years from 18 to 25, or even to 30, have also been seen as a stage of emerging adulthood. Early adulthood is usually seen as the period when people focus on establishing careers or pathways in life. Of course, many people continue to explore what they will be doing through much of early adulthood, and some never attempt to establish pathways in life.

Reaching the Zenith

Physical development peaks in early adulthood. Most people are at their heights of sensory sharpness, strength, reaction time, and cardiovascular fitness. Young adults are at their tallest, and height remains stable through middle adulthood, declining somewhat in late adulthood. A higher percentage of men's body mass is made of muscle, and men are normally stronger than women. Physical strength in both men and women peaks in the 20s and early 30s, then slowly declines (Markham, 2006).

Sensory sharpness also peaks in the early 20s (Fozard & Gordon-Salant, 2001). Visual acuity remains stable until middle adulthood, when a gradual decline leads to farsightedness and, in many people, a need for reading glasses. Hearing tends to decline once people reach their late 20s and early 30s, particularly for high-pitched tones.

Cardiovascular, respiratory, and immune changes due to aging begin in early adulthood, but they are gradual. The heart muscle becomes more rigid, decreasing the maximum heart rate and reducing the ability of the heart to pump enough blood to provide oxygen for stressful exercise. But regular exercise increases cardiovascular and respiratory capacity from what they would otherwise be at any age. As people age, the immune system produces fewer white blood cells and the disease-fighting ability of those that remain declines.

Fertility in both sexes declines as early adulthood progresses, and after age 35, women are usually advised to have their fetuses checked for Down syndrome and other chromosomal abnormalities. Older men's sperm may also contribute to chromosomal abnormalities. A major problem in women is the decline in the quality and reduced number of ova (egg cells). But because of advances in reproductive technology, today it is not unusual for women to have healthy children, including their first children, in their 30s and 40s.

Both sexes may find their hair thinning and graying by the end of early adulthood. Toward the end of early adulthood, and almost certainly in middle adulthood, the skin begins to loosen, grow less elastic, and wrinkle, more so in women than in men.

Health and Fitness

As a group, young adults tend to be healthy. Their immune systems are generally functioning well. Table 7.1 shows the leading causes of death for 15- to 44-year-olds in 2006. The National Center for Health Statistics, which accumulated the data, did not distinguish between 15- to 19-year-olds, who are late adolescents, and 20- to 24-year-olds, who are early adults (and possibly, according to some views, emerging adults). The leading cause of death for late teenagers and early adults in the United States in 2006 clearly was accidents. Because 15- to 24-year-olds tend to

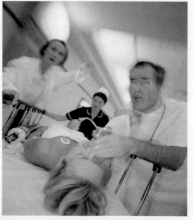

Accidents are the leading cause of death among young adults.

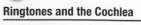

Ringtones and the Cochlea

Watch and learn about a ringtone that is inaudible to adults.

Table 7.1
Leading Causes of Death for Early Adults

15–24 year olds	25–44 year olds
• Accidents 46.5%	• Accidents 25.8%
• Homicide 16.4%	• Cancer 13.9%
• Suicide 12.0%	• Heart disease 12.4%
• Cancer 4.7%	• Suicide 9.1%
• Heart disease 3.1%	• Homicide 6.1%
• Congenital problems 1.3%	• HIV/AIDS 4.1%
• Stroke 0.6%	• Liver disease 2.3%
• HIV/AIDS 0.6%	• Diabetes 2.2%
• Influenza & pneumonia 0.5%	• Stroke 2.2%
• Complications of childbirth 0.5%	• Influenza & pneumonia 0.9%

Source: National Center for Health Statistics Health, United States, 2009: With special feature on medical technology. Hyattsville, MD. Table 29.

be healthy, the next two leading causes of death were violence—by others (homicide) and self-inflicted (suicide). Homicide does not disappear as one of the top ten leading causes of death until middle age (which is bounded by the ages of 40–45 at the lower end and 60–65 at the upper end). Cancer and heart disease kill a much larger percentage of people aged 25–44 than aged 15–24, although they still take second and third place, behind accidents, among 25- to 44-year-olds. HIV/AIDS becomes a much more prominent cause of death among 25- to 44-year-olds because it takes many years for the condition to overwhelm the body's immune system, even if the infection occurred during the teenage years or early 20s.

Given that so many young adults are in excellent or good health, it is ironic that many are careless about their health or put it on the "back burner." Many are concerned about their careers or college or their social lives and think of health issues—diet, smoking, sedentary lives, excessive drinking—as something they can get to later on.

Consider the results of a poll by the Centers for Disease Control and Prevention (CDC) that reported on the health-related behavior patterns of a nationally representative sample of more than 18,000 young adults aged 18–24 (McCracken et al., 2007). More than 3 respondents in 4 (78%) ate fewer than the recommended five servings of fruits and vegetables each day. Forty-three percent reported either no physical activ-

adaptive thermogenesis The process by which the body converts food energy (calories) to heat at a lower rate when a person eats less, because of, for example, famine or dieting.

ity or insufficient physical activity. More than 1 in 4 (29%) were smokers, and 30% reported binge drinking—having five drinks in a row on single occasions. About one respondent in four (26%) was *overweight* (having a body mass index [BMI] of 25.0–29.9), and another 14% were *obese* (having a BMI of 30.0 or above).

You can calculate your body mass index as follows: Write down your weight in pounds. Multiply it by 703. Divide the product by the square of your height in inches. For example, if you weigh 160 pounds and are 5 feet 8 inches tall, your BMI is (160 × 703)/4,624, or 24.33. A BMI of 25 or higher is defined as overweight. A BMI of 30 or higher is defined as obese.

Diet and Weight

In general, mankind, since the improvement of cookery, eats twice as much as nature requires.

—Benjamin Franklin

The "good news" in the CDC survey (McCracken et al., 2007) is that the 40% of 18- to 24-year-olds reported as being overweight or obese is lower than the 67.3% (more than two thirds!) reported in the general adult population, aged 20–74 (B. Marsh, 2011). Overweight and obese young women were more likely than young men to report dieting. The sex difference in dieting is found among the entire adult population (Bish et al., 2005). Americans have been ballooning in weight over the past half century or so. In the 1960s, 31.5% of adults aged 20–74 were overweight and another 13.3% were obese, totaling 44.8%. As of the middle 2000s, the numbers had swelled to 32.1% overweight and 35.2% obese, adding up to that 67.3%.

Why are so many young adults overweight and obese? Many biological and psychological factors are involved. Being overweight runs in families. Studies of monkeys (Kavanagh et al., 2007) and of human twins (Silventoinen et al., 2007) have suggested strong roles for heredity. Efforts by overweight and obese people to maintain a slender profile may be sabotaged by a mechanism that helps preserve life in times of famine—**adaptive thermogenesis**. This mechanism causes the body to produce less energy (burn fewer calories) when the person goes on a diet (Major et al., 2007). This does not mean that overweight people will not lose weight by dieting; it means that it will take longer than expected.

The Skinny on Weight Control

Read about the most effective ways to manage weight.

Body Mass Index Chart

Explore the BMI chart and calculate your body mass index.

Fatty tissue in the body also metabolizes (burns) food more slowly than muscle. For this reason, a person with a high fat-to-muscle ratio metabolizes food more slowly than a person of the same weight with more muscle. Psychological factors, such as observational learning, stress, and emotional states, also contribute to obesity.

Exercise

Adults 18 and older need at least 30 minutes of vigorous physical activity five or more days a week to be healthy (Physical Activity Fact Sheet, 2005). Significant benefits can be reaped from a moderate amount of activity, such as 30 minutes of brisk walking or raking leaves, 15 minutes of running, or 45 minutes of volleyball. You can break 30–60 minutes of physical activity into smaller segments of 10 or 15 minutes through the day.

This amount of activity can substantially reduce the risk of developing or dying from cardiovascular disease, type 2 diabetes, and certain cancers, such as colon cancer. Exercise also benefits the brain and cognitive performance (Stein et al., 2007). Exercise may even help with psychological disorders such as anxiety and depression (Stein et al., 2007). The "trick" for most young adults is to integrate exercise into their daily routines, perhaps by means of moderately vigorous activities for 15 minutes two times a day or for 10 minutes three times a day.

Substance Abuse and Dependence

substance abuse A persistent pattern of use of a substance characterized by frequent intoxication and impairment of physical, social, or emotional well-being.

substance dependence A persistent pattern of use of a substance that is accompanied by physiological addiction.

tolerance Habituation to a drug such that increasingly higher doses are needed to achieve similar effects.

abstinence syndrome A characteristic cluster of symptoms that results from a sudden decrease in the level of usage of a substance.

People use drugs not only to cope with medical problems but also to deal with daily tensions, social anxiety, run-of-the-mill depression, and even boredom. Where does the use of a drug or substance end and substance abuse begin? According to the American Psychiatric Association (2000), **substance abuse** is the ongoing use of a substance despite the social, occupational, psychological, or physical problems it causes. When young adults miss school or work because they are intoxicated or "sleeping it off," they are abusing alcohol.

A person who is dependent on a substance loses control over using it. **Substance dependence** means that having it in the body becomes the norm. **Tolerance** develops as the body becomes habituated to the substance; as a result, one may need more of the substance to achieve the same effects. A number of substances are physically addictive, so when the dosage is lowered, withdrawal symptoms, also known as **abstinence syndrome**, occur. When addicted individuals lower their intake of alcohol, they may experience symptoms such as tremors (shakes), high blood pressure, rapid heart and pulse rate, anxiety, restlessness, and weakness. Three of the most common types of abused substances are depressants, stimulants, and hallucinogenics.

Effects of Depressants

Depressants slow the activity of the nervous system. They include alcohol, narcotics derived from the opium poppy (such as heroin, morphine, and codeine), and sedatives (such as barbiturates and methaqualone).

Alcohol lessens inhibitions, so that drinkers may do things when drinking that they might otherwise resist (K. F. Donohue et al., 2007). Alcohol is also an intoxicant: It distorts perceptions, impairs concentration, hinders coordination, and slurs the speech. Alcohol use is most prevalent among 21- to 34-year-olds. More than one million students between the ages of 18 and 24 are accidentally injured each year while under the influence, assaulted by other students who have been drinking, or raped by college men who have been drinking.

Women have less of an enzyme—aldehyde dehydrogenase—that metabolizes alcohol in the stomach than men do. Therefore, alcohol "goes to their heads" more quickly. Asians also have less of the enzyme than Europeans do, placing them at increased risk of a "flushing response" when they drink.

The major medical use of heroin, morphine, and other opioids is relief from pain. But they also can provide a euphoric "rush." Heroin is addictive, and regular users develop tolerance. *Barbiturates* are depressants with various legitimate medical uses, such as relief from pain, anxiety, and tension, but people can become rapidly dependent on them.

Effects of Stimulants

Stimulants speed up the heartbeat and other bodily functions. Nicotine, cocaine, and amphetamines are the most common stimulants; nicotine is the addictive chemical in tobacco (Nonnemaker & Homsi, 2007). Nearly 450,000 Americans die from

Alcohol Dependent?

Take the questionnaire "Do You Have a Problem With Alcohol?"

Substance Abuse Disorder

Watch one man describe his experiences with alcohol addiction and withdrawal.

Nicotine Addiction

Watch and learn why nicotine is so addictive.

▶ **LO6** Discuss the effects of stress on health.

smoking-related problems each year (American Lung Association, 2007). Cigarette smoke contains carbon monoxide, which causes shortness of breath, and hydrocarbons ("tars"). Smoking is responsible for most respiratory diseases and lung cancer.

Cocaine accelerates the heart rate, spikes the blood pressure, constricts the arteries of the heart, and thickens the blood, a combination that can cause cardiovascular and respiratory collapse (A. L. Mitchell, 2006). Overdoses can cause restlessness, insomnia, tremors, and even death. Amphetamines can keep users awake for long periods and reduce their appetites. Tolerance for amphetamines develops rapidly. The powerful amphetamine called methamphetamine may be physically addictive (Jonkman, 2006). Methamphetamine abuse can cause brain damage, leading to problems in learning and memory.

Effects of Hallucinogenics

Hallucinogenics give rise to perceptual distortions called hallucinations, which sometimes can be so strong as to be confused with reality. Marijuana, Ecstasy, LSD, and PCP are hallucinogenic drugs. Marijuana, which is typically smoked, helps users relax, elevates their mood, increases sensory awareness, and can induce visual hallucinations,

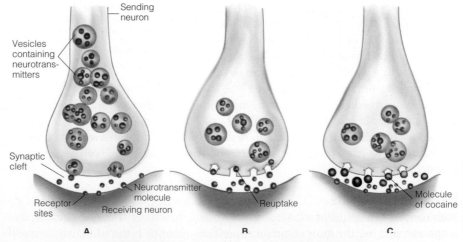

hallucinogenic A drug that gives rise to hallucinations.

© 2012 Cengage Learning

Figure 7.1 How Cocaine Produces Euphoria and Why People "Crash"

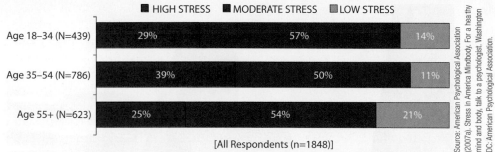

■ HIGH STRESS ■ MODERATE STRESS ▢ LOW STRESS

Age 18–34 (N=439): 29% | 57% | 14%

Age 35–54 (N=786): 39% | 50% | 11%

Age 55+ (N=623): 25% | 54% | 21%

[All Respondents (n=1848)]

Source: American Psychological Association (2007a). Stress in America Mindbody. For a healthy mind and body, talk to a psychologist. Washington DC: American Psychological Association.

Figure 7.2 Evaluation of Amount of Stress Experienced, According to Age In a poll by the American Psychological Association, 86% of emerging adults (mean age = 18.34) were either moderately or highly stressed, and 89% of young adults in their 30s (mean age = 35.54) were moderately or highly stressed. Middle-aged adults, aged 35–54, were most likely to be highly stressed (39% of them), and older adults, aged 55 and above, reported experiencing somewhat less stress (only 25% of them said they are highly stressed).

for example, time seeming to slow down. Marijuana carries health risks such as impairing perceptual–motor coordination and short-term memory (Egerton et al., 2006; Lamers et al., 2006). Research suggests that regular users may experience withdrawal, which is a sign of addiction (Budney et al., 2007).

Ecstasy, a popular "party" drug, provides the boost of a stimulant and mild hallucinogenic effects. The combination appears to free users from inhibitions and awareness of the consequences of risky behavior, such as unprotected sex. Ecstasy can also impair working memory, increase anxiety, and lead to depression (Lamers et al., 2006). LSD is the acronym for lysergic acid diethylamide, another hallucinogenic drug. High doses of hallucinogenics can impair coordination and judgment (driving while using hallucinogenic drugs poses grave risks), change the mood, and cause paranoid delusions.

Stress and Health

According to a national poll taken by the American Psychological Association (2007a), one third of Americans report that they are living with "extreme stress." Stress has a negative impact on people's psychological and physical health and on their social, academic, and vocational lives.

As you can see in Figure 7.2, overall, Americans in middle adulthood were most highly stressed, and older Americans were least highly stressed. On the other hand,

Women and Stress

Are women more prone to the effects of chronic stress? Watch and learn.

Preventing and Coping with Stress

Read about ways adults can relieve and prevent stress.

▶ **LO7** Discuss sexual activity during early adulthood.

▶ **LO8** Discuss sexual orientation.

▶ **LO9** Discuss sexually transmitted infections.

▶ **LO10** Discuss menstrual problems.

▶ **LO11** Discuss sexual coercion.

© Masterfile Royalty Free

Daily hassles are notable conditions and experiences that are threatening or harmful to a person's well-being. This person is apparently overworked. Perhaps he works so hard because of financial hassles. He probably has time-pressure hassles and health hassles—or, given his diet, health hassles may be forthcoming. His work environment also seems to be crashing in on him.

young adults were more likely than older adults to respond to stress in unhealthful ways, such as lying awake at night and skipping meals (American Psychological Association, 2007a).

Stress-Management Tips

Here are some suggestions for managing stress more effectively (American Psychological Association, 2007b):

- Get in touch with the ways in which you experience stress.
- Identify the situations and people that are stressing you out.
- Get in touch with how you handle—or don't handle—stress.
- Develop better ways to cope with stress.
- Take care of your health.
- Obtain social support.

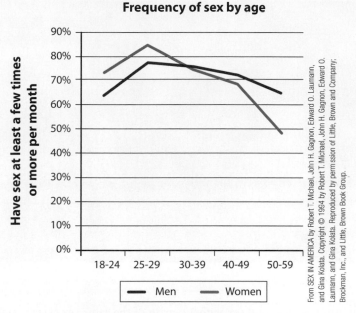

Figure 7.3 Frequency of Sex by Age

Sexuality

Sexual activity with a partner usually peaks in the 20s. The results reported in Figure 7.3 represent the percentages of men and women in a nationally representative survey who said that they had sex at least a few times each month.

Why does this age group have sex most frequently? The answer is a combination of youth and opportunity. Men and women in this age group are still to some degree experiencing the flood of sex hormones that affected them as adolescents. Now, however, they are of an age at which they are likely to be in sexual relationships.

Sexual Orientation

About 7% of American women and men define themselves as being "other than heterosexual," but the behavior of the other 93% doesn't exactly match up with the way in which people label themselves. For example, nearly twice as many people—about

ULTRA.F/Digital Vision/Jupiterimages

14%—say they have had oral sex with a person of the same sex (Herbenick, Reece, Sanders, et al., 2010; Herbenick, Reece, Schick, et al., 2010a, 2010b; Reece et al., 2010). Is sexuality a continuum, with heterosexuals on one end and homosexuals on the other? What exactly causes sexual orientation?

Theories of the origins of sexual orientation look at both nature and nurture—the biological makeup of the individual and environmental influences. Learning theorists look for the roles of factors such as reinforcement, which may come in the form of sexual behavior with members of one's own sex or childhood sexual abuse by someone of the same sex. But critics note that most people become aware of their sexual orientation before they have sexual contacts with either sex (Laumann, et al., 1994).

There is some evidence for genetic factors in sexual orientation (J. V. Kohl, 2007; Sefcek et al., 2007). Twin studies have indicated that about 52% of identical (monozygotic, MZ) twin pairs are concordant (in agreement) for a gay male sexual orientation, compared with 22% for fraternal (dizygotic, DZ) twins (Bailey & Pillard,

1991). MZ twins fully share their genetic heritage, whereas DZ twins, like other pairs of siblings, have a 50% overlap.

Evolutionary psychologists have also endeavored to explain gay and lesbian sexual orientations, even though it may be difficult, at first, to see how gay and lesbian sexual orientations confer any evolutionary advantage. Kirkpatrick (2000) suggested that male–male and female–female sexual behavior derive from individual selection for reciprocal *altruism*. That is, strong male–male and female–female alliances have advantages for group survival in that they bind group members together emotionally. Other researchers have compared the family trees of lesbians and gay men with those of heterosexuals and found that women related to lesbians and gay men have more children (Iemmola & Ciani, 2009). Therefore, genetic factors linked to the X sex chromosome that might influence homosexual orientation in males are not eliminated by natural selection because they also increase fertility in women who carry the genes.

In addition to promoting the development of male and female sex organs and regulating the menstrual cycle, sex hormones also fuel the sex drive and may influence *whom* one will find sexually attractive (Huang, 2007).

Sexually Transmitted Infections (STIs)

Each year, millions of young American adults contract a sexually transmitted infection (STI) (Centers for Disease Control and Prevention, 2006). Chlamydia, a bacterial infection of the vagina or urinary tract that can result in sterility, is the most commonly occurring STI in young adults, followed by gonorrhea, HPV/genital warts, genital herpes, syphilis, and HIV/AIDS. Because of its lethality, HIV/AIDS tends to capture most of the headlines. However, other STIs are more widespread, and some of them can also be deadly.

Nearly 2.8 million new chlamydia infections occur each year (Centers for Disease Control and Prevention, 2006). The incidence of chlamydia is especially high among college students. Chlamydia is a major cause of pelvic inflammatory disease, which can lead to infertility.

Each year in the United States, there are about one million new infections with the human papilloma virus (HPV) (Centers for Disease Control and Prevention, 2006), which causes genital warts and is associated with cervical cancer. A vaccine is available that prevents most young women from being infected with HPV; it is most effective if administered before they become sexually active (Pichichero, 2006).

HIV/AIDS

HIV/AIDS is the most devastating STI. If left untreated, it is lethal, and the long-term prospects of those who do receive treatment remain unknown. HIV—the virus that causes AIDS—is spreading rapidly around the world; by the end of the twentieth century it had infected nearly 39 million people (UNAIDS, 2006). The primary mode of HIV transmission worldwide is male–female sex. Anal intercourse is another mode of HIV transmission and is often practiced by gay males. Injecting drugs is another way in which HIV is spread, because sharing needles with infected individuals can transmit HIV. Other major risk factors include having sex with multiple partners, failing to use condoms, and abusing drugs and alcohol (UNAIDS, 2006).

Women account for a minority of cases of HIV/AIDS in the United States, but in many places around the world they are more likely than men to be infected with HIV. A United Nations study in Europe, Africa, and Southeast Asia found that sexually active teenage girls have higher rates of HIV infection than older women or young men in these regions (UNAIDS, 2006).

Although knowledge about HIV/AIDS is widespread among U.S. adolescents, only about half modify their sexual practices as a result (Santelli, Lindberg, et al., 2000). The causes, methods of transmission, symptoms, and treatment—where it exists—of HIV/AIDS and other STIs are described in Table 7.2.

Menstrual Problems

Fifty percent to 75% of women experience at least some discomfort prior to or during menstruation, including *dysmenorrhea*, menstrual migraines, *amenorrhea*, *premenstrual syndrome (PMS)*, and *premenstrual dysphoric disorder (PMDD)* (Sommerfeld, 2003). **Dysmenorrhea** is the most common menstrual problem, and pelvic cramps are the most common symptom. Cramps are most often brought about by high amounts of hormones called **prostaglandins**, which cause muscles in the uterine wall to contract, as during labor. Fluid retention in the pelvic region may cause bloating.

Amenorrhea is the absence of menstruation, and a sign of infertility. **Premenstrual syndrome (PMS)** is the combination of biological and psychological symptoms that may affect women during the 4- to 6-day interval preceding their menses each month. The most common premenstrual symptoms are minor psychological discomfort, muscular tension, and aches or pains, but only a small minority of women

dysmenorrhea Painful menstruation.

prostaglandins Hormones that cause muscles in the uterine wall to contract, as during labor.

amenorrhea The absence of menstruation.

premenstrual syndrome (PMS) The discomforting symptoms that affect many women during the 4- to 6-day interval preceding their periods.

premenstrual dysphoric disorder (PMDD) A condition similar to but more severe than PMS.

Many women find that vigorous exercise helps them manage premenstrual problems.

report symptoms severe enough to impair their social, academic, or occupational functioning. The causes of PMS may involve the body's responses to changing levels of sex hormones. PMS also appears to be linked with imbalances in neurotransmitters such as serotonin and GABA, which are connected with the appetite, anxiety, and mood changes (Bäckström et al., 2003). There are many treatment options for PMS: exercise, dietary control, hormone treatments, and medications that reduce anxiety or increase the activity of serotonin in the nervous system.

Premenstrual dysphoric disorder (PMDD) is more severe than PMS, and is a diagnostic category by the American Psychiatric Association (2000). According to the American Psychiatric Association, a diagnosis of PMDD requires that several of the following symptoms be present most of the time during the week before the period and ending within a few days after the period begins: tension, mood changes, irritability and anger, difficulty concentrating, fatigue, changes in appetite, sleeping too much or too little, feeling overwhelmed, and physical discomfort.

HPV Myths

Watch and learn important facts and myths about HPV.

Preventing STIs

Read and explore how to prevent sexually transmitted infections.

Menstrual Discomfort

Read "How to Handle Menstrual Discomfort."

Table 7.2
Overview of Sexually Transmitted Infections (STIs)

STI and Cause	Transmission	Symptoms
Chlamydia and nongonococcal urethritis: *Chlamydia trachomatis* bacterium in women	Vaginal, oral, or anal sex; passage through the birth canal of an infected mother	Women and men may be symptom free or experience frequent and painful urination and a discharge
Genital herpes: Herpes simplex virus type 2 (HSV-2)	Vaginal, oral, or anal sex	Painful, reddish bumps around the genitals, thighs, or buttocks that blister, fill with pus, and break, shedding viral particles; possible fever, aches, and pains
Gonorrhea ("clap," "drip"): Gonococcus bacterium (*Neisseria gonorrhoeae*)	Vaginal, oral, or anal sex; passage through the birth canal of an infected mother	In men, yellowish, thick discharge, and burning urination; women may be symptom free or have vaginal discharge, burning urination, or irregular menstruation
HIV/AIDS: Acronym for *human immunodeficiency virus* and *acquired immunodeficiency syndrome*	Vaginal or anal sex; infusion of contaminated blood by needle sharing or from mother to baby during childbirth; breast-feeding	Usually none for many years; swollen lymph nodes, fever, weight loss, fatigue, diarrhea; deadly "opportunistic infections"
HPV/Genital warts: Human papillomavirus (HPV)	Sexual contact; contact with infested towels or clothing	Painless warts resembling cauliflowers on the genitals or anus or in the rectum; associated with cervical cancer
Pubic lice ("crabs"): *Pthirus pubis* (an insect, not a crab)	Sexual contact; contact with an infested towel, sheet, or toilet seat	Intense itching in pubic area and other hairy regions to which lice can attach
Syphilis: *Treponema pallidum*	Vaginal, oral, or anal sex; touching an infectious chancre	Hard, painless chancre that appears at the site of the infection within 2–4 weeks; may progress through additional stages if untreated

Rape: The Most Intimate Crime of Violence

Half a million American women each year are victimized by the crime of violence called rape. All in all, the weight of the evidence suggests that about 1 in 4 women in the United States is raped during her lifetime (R. Campbell & Wasco, 2005). Women aged 16–24 are 2 to 3 times more likely to be raped than girls or older women (Quinsey et al., 2006).

Rape has its sexual aspects, but it is also the subjugation of women by men (Malamuth et al., 2005). The definition of rape varies from state to state, but is usually defined as sex with a nonconsenting person by the use of force or the threat of

Diagnosis	Treatment
Analysis of cervical smear in women; analysis of penile fluid in men	Antibiotics
Clinical inspection of sores; culture and examination of fluid drawn from sores	Antiviral drugs may provide relief and help with healing, but are not cures
Clinical inspection; culture of discharge	Antibiotics
Blood, saliva, or urine tests detect HIV antibodies; other tests confirm the presence of HIV itself	There is no cure; a "cocktail" of highly active antiretroviral therapy prolongs life in many people living with HIV/AIDS
Clinical inspection	A vaccine can prevent infection in most young women; warts may be removed by freezing, topical drugs, burning, or surgery
Clinical inspection	Topical drugs containing pyrethrins or piperonal butoxide
Clinical inspection or examination of fluid from a chancre; blood test	Antibiotics

© 2012 Cengage Learning

force. Penile vaginal penetration is usually not necessary to fit the definition. Most states permit the prosecution of husbands who rape their wives.

The government's National Crime Victimization Survey (U.S. Department of Justice, 2006) estimated that 191,000 women were sexually assaulted in 2004. This figure included some 72,000 rapes and another 40,000 attempted rapes. About 10% of rape victims are men, and their assailants are also generally men. But about two thirds of victims do not report rapes, because of concern that they will be humiliated by the criminal justice system or fear of reprisal from their families or the rapist (U. S. Department of Justice, 2006).

Types of Rape

According to the U.S. Department of Justice (2006), about 5 rapes in 6 are committed by acquaintances of the victim, including classmates, coworkers, dates, and family friends. Acquaintance rapes are less likely than stranger rapes to be reported to the police (Fisher et al., 2003), because rape survivors may not perceive sexual assaults by acquaintances as rapes. Even when acquaintance rapes are reported to police, they may be treated as "misunderstandings" or lovers' quarrels rather than crimes (R. Campbell, 2006). Date rape is a form of acquaintance rape; it is more likely to occur when the couple has too much to drink and then parks in the man's car or goes to his residence (Cole, 2006; Locke & Mahalik, 2005).

Social Attitudes, Myths, and Cultural Factors That Encourage Rape

Many people believe a number of myths about rape, such as "Women say no when they mean yes" and "The way women dress, they are just asking to be raped" (Maxwell et al., 2003). Yet another myth is that deep down inside, women want to be overpowered and forced into sex by men. These myths have the effect of justifying rape in assailants' and the public's minds.

Males are also often reinforced from childhood for aggressive and competitive behavior, as in sports. Gender typing may lead men to reject "feminine" traits such as tenderness and empathy that might restrain aggression (Yost & Zurbriggen, 2006).

Sexual Harassment

Sexual harassment occurs everywhere: in colleges, in the workplace, in the military, and online. It victimizes 40%–60% of working women and similar percentages of female students in colleges and universities (American Psychological Association, 1998).

For legal purposes, sexual harassment in the workplace is usually defined as deliberate or repeated unwanted comments, gestures, or physical contact. Sexual harassment makes the workplace or other setting a hostile place. Examples include unwelcome sexual jokes, suggestive comments, verbal abuse, leering at or ogling a person's body, unwelcome physical contact, outright sexual assault, and demands for sex accompanied by threats concerning one's job or student status.

Charges of sexual harassment are often ignored or trivialized by coworkers and employers. The victim may hear, "Why make a big deal out of it? It's not like you were

sexual harassment Deliberate or repeated unwanted comments, gestures, or physical contact.

attacked in the street." Yet evidence shows that people who are sexually harassed suffer from it. Some become physically ill (Rospenda et al., 2005). Some find harassment on the job so unbearable that they resign (Sims et al., 2005). College women have dropped courses and switched majors, and medical residents have even left their programs to avoid it (Stratton et al., 2005).

One reason that sexual harassment is so stressful is that blame tends to fall on the victim. Some harassers argue that charges of harassment are exaggerated. In our society, women are often demonized if they assert themselves, but they remain victimized if they don't (Witkowska & Gådin, 2005).

Sexual harassment sometimes has more to do with the abuse of power than sexual desire (Finkelman, 2005). This is especially so in work settings that are traditionally male dominated, such as the firehouse, the construction site, or the military academy (Stratton et al., 2005). The U.S. Supreme Court has recognized sexual harassment as a form of sex discrimination and held that employers are accountable if harassment creates a hostile or abusive work environment.

Rape Myths

Read about the cultural myths that create a climate that supports rape.

Sexual Harrassment

Read and explore how to resist sexual harassment.

Check Your Learning Quiz 7.1

Go to **login.cengagebrain.com** and take the online quiz.

Did you know that—

- People are generally at the height of their cognitive powers in early adulthood?
- Late adolescents are likely to have the broadest knowledge of science?
- College students are likely to exchange black-and-white thinking for recognition that judgments of good and bad are derived within certain belief systems?
- Young adults find it easier to harbor both positive and negative feelings about their goals and about people than adolescents do?
- Young adults are less egocentric than adolescents are?
- Within a year after cashing their checks, million-dollar lottery winners often feel aimless and dissatisfied if they quit their jobs after striking it rich?

▼

As with physical development, people are at the height of their cognitive powers during early adulthood. Some aspects of cognitive development, such as memory, show a general decline as people age, yet people typically retain their verbal skills and may even show improvement in vocabulary and general knowledge (Fair, 2007). Performance on tasks that require reasoning or problem-solving speed and visuospatial skills, such as piecing puzzles together, tends to decline in middle and late adulthood.

Consider the difference between crystallized intelligence and fluid intelligence. **Crystallized intelligence** represents one's lifetime of intellectual attainments, which generally increases with age. **Fluid intelligence**—the ability to process information, such as solving a math problem, rapidly—is more susceptible to the effects of aging (Lachman, 2004). Therefore, it is fluid intelligence that peaks in early adulthood.

What other cognitive developments take place in early adulthood? After all, Piaget did not propose a fifth stage of cognitive development, beyond formal-operational thought. And postconventional thought, the final stage in Kohlberg's theory of moral development, often develops in adolescence. Nevertheless, we will see that the cognitive processes of early adults can differ markedly from those of adolescents.

crystallized intelligence One's intellectual attainments, as shown, for example, by vocabulary and accumulated knowledge.

fluid intelligence Mental flexibility; the ability to process information rapidly.

epistemic cognition Thought processes directed at considering how we arrive at our beliefs, facts, and ideas.

Cognition and the Sociocultural Setting

In terms of brain development, most verbal and quantitative capacities of the sort measured by the SAT and the ACT probably develop by late adolescence and early adulthood. However, adolescence carries with it a certain egocentrism that can impair judgment, problem solving, and other areas of cognition. The experiences of early adulthood within a given sociocultural setting can lead to further cognitive developments. Many people, on the other hand, become set in their cognitive ways long before the arrival of early adulthood.

K. Warner Schaie (2002; Schaie & Zanjani, 2006) studied cognitive development of adolescents and young adults in our sociocultural setting—one in which a high-school education is more or less universal and many high-school graduates continue with higher education. He found, for example, that late adolescents are likely to have the broadest general knowledge of the sciences. Their high-school curricula are likely to have included some biology, chemistry, physics, earth sciences, and mathematics. Early adults actually begin to lose some of their general scientific knowledge, but those who continue with their education or training tend to develop more focused, deeper knowledge in specific scientific areas. It is also in late adolescence—in high school—that girls, now more than ever, remain with boys and keep pace with them in these classes. But once in college, where there are choices as to major and minor fields of interest, we are more likely to find divergences based on personal preferences. Later we will see that males are somewhat more likely than females to decide to continue in the sciences and mathematics.

Perry's Theory of Epistemic Cognition

William Perry's (1970/1998, 1981) theory of **epistemic cognition** concerns our ideas about how we arrive at our beliefs, facts, and our ideas. Early adults may wonder why their beliefs differ from those of others and may seek to justify or revise their thinking and their conclusions. College students' views on what they know—and on how they come to know what they know—become more complex as they are exposed to the kinds of arguments and discussions that take place on campus (P. M. King & Kitchener, 2004; Magolda, 2004). Cognitive development in college life doesn't just rest on exposure to "great books"; it is also fostered by being challenged by students from different backgrounds and by professors who have views that differ from one's own (Moshman, 2005).

Cognitive Changes in Early Adulthood

Interact and learn about how thinking changes as we enter adulthood.

Students often enter college or adult life assuming that there are right and wrong answers for everything, and that the world can be divided easily into black versus white, good versus bad, and us versus them. This type of thinking is termed **dualistic thinking**. After a while, in a multicultural society or on a college campus, students may realize that judgments of good or bad are often made from a certain belief system, such as a specific religion or cultural background, so that such judgments actually represent **relativistic thinking** rather than absolute judgments (Vukman, 2005). For example, some world cultures may believe that they put women "on pedestals" by restricting their activities outside the home. The newly relativistic college student may be hard-pressed to take issue with this argument, but as thought deepens, adults may become capable of what Perry refers to as *commitment within relativistic thinking*. That is, the more cognitively mature person can say, "Yes, I understand where you're coming from when you say you're putting women on pedestals by preventing them from going out-doors unless they are chaperoned, but my bottom line is that you're treating them like second-class citizens and would never allow them to do the same to you."

Labouvie-Vief's Theory of Pragmatic Thought

Gisela Labouvie-Vief's (2006) theory of **pragmatic thought** notes that adults must typically narrow possibilities into choices, whether these are choices about careers or graduate school or life partners. The "cognitively healthy" adult is more willing than the egocentric adolescent to compromise and cope within the world as it is, not the world as she or he would like it to be. In order to deal with the real world, adults need to be able to accept living with mixed feelings about their goals. As people mature, Labouvie-Vief found, they tend to develop a **cognitive–affective complexity** that enables them to harbor both positive and negative feelings about their career choices ("I may never get rich, but when I wake up in the morning, I'll look forward to what I'm doing that day") and their partners ("Okay, he may not be a hunk, but he's stable and kind"). Adults function best when they accept reality but choose goals that allow them to experience positive feelings (Labouvie-Vief & González, 2004).

Postformal Thinking

Most developmentalists agree that the cognitive processes of early adults are in many ways more advanced than the cognitive processes of adolescents—at least in our cultural setting (Commons, 2004; Gurba, 2005). Early adults maintain most of the ben-

dualistic thinking Dividing the cognitive world into opposites, such as good versus bad or us versus them.

relativistic thinking The process by which certain belief systems or cultural backgrounds are seen as influencing judgments.

pragmatic thought Decision making characterized by willingness to accept reality and compromise.

cognitive–affective complexity A mature form of thinking that permits people to harbor positive and negative feelings about their career choices and other matters.

Table 7.3
Age-Relevance per Age Decade: Most-Attributed Characteristics

Decade	Characteristics
0+	Innocent (94.8), unruly (86.2), adorable (86.2), naive (84.5), endearing (81.0), cute (81.0), curious (81.0)
10+	Impolite (91.4), mannerless (89.7), disruptive (87.9), insolent (86.2), complex (86.2), young (84.5), aggressive (84.5)
20+	In love (93.1), ambitious (93.1), sexy (93.1), young (91.4), romantic (91.4), daring (89.7), attractive (89.7)
30+	Competitive (93.1), hard-working (93.1), enterprising (91.4), impressive (91.4), capable (89.7), efficient (89.7), strong (87.9)
40+	Hard-working (86.2), slogger (86.2), organized (86.2), capable (84.5), efficient (84.5), punctual (84.5), tempered (84.5)
50+	Respectful (86.2), cultured (86.2), hard-working (82.8), organized (82.8), provident (82.8), methodical (81.0), rational (81.0)
60+	Respectful (82.8), cultured (82.8), beneficent (79.3), humane (77.6), benevolent (77.6), conciliatory (75.9), honorable (75.9)
70+	Nostalgic (86.2), tired (77.6), cultured (75.9), humane (74.1), peace-loving (72.4), nice (72.4), honorable (70.7)
80+	Isolated (87.9), nostalgic (84.5), tired (84.5), mourning (84.5), sick (82.8), unwell (82.8), solitary (82.8)
90+	Dying (93.1), isolated (89.7), old (89.7), alone (87.9), sick (86.2), solitary (84.5)

Note. Scores indicate the percentage of the total sample who said that the given attribute is typical for this age category.
Source: Gruhn, D., Gilet, A-L., Studer, J., & Labouvie-Vief, G. (2010, December 13). Age-Relevance of Person Characteristics: Persons' Beliefs About Developmental Change Across the Lifespan. Developmental Psychology, doi: 10.1037/a00213151-12.

efits of their general secondary educations, and, as noted earlier, some may have gathered specialized knowledge and skills through opportunities in higher education. Many have gained knowledge and expertise in the career world as well.

Decision Making
Watch and learn about decision-making, an aspect of pragmatic thought in adulthood.

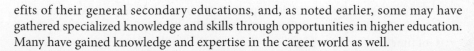

What developmentalists do not agree on is whether they should consider the cognitive abilities of young adults to be a fifth stage of cognitive development, called, perhaps, a *postformal* stage, that would extend beyond Piaget's stage of formal operations. Such a postformal stage would highlight the lessened egocentrism of young adults and their capacity to view the world more relativistically.

College and Cognitive Development

Emily, 22, was in her senior year at a college in Massachusetts, and she was describing her semester abroad in South Africa. Her face lit up as she painted a picture—not at all rosy—of her experiences working on HIV/AIDS education programs. She discussed the conditions of the South African poor and the "insanely deplorable" treatment of workers in the diamond mines. Little if any of Emily's experiences would improve her scores on standardized tests, and they would have little impact on graduate admissions exams like the Law School Admission Test. Nonetheless, it is safe to say that these experiences had a major impact on Emily's cognitive development.

In her semester abroad, Emily took full advantage of the diversity students can experience in college. Some students attend colleges that are close to home, culturally if not necessarily geographically. Others attend colleges that are more diverse. Diversity speaks to the differences we find among groups of people: ethnic and cultural diversity (race, religion, country of origin, language), socioeconomic level, gender, age, and sexual orientation. Many students find more kinds of people on campus than they dreamt of before they began college. They meet people from other backgrounds, places, and walks of life—among them, their professors.

Here are some ideas adapted from the Association of American Colleges & Universities (2007) on how you can benefit from diversity on your campus to achieve cognitive growth:

- Recognize that your way of looking at the world is not universal.
- Embrace opportunities for encountering people who are different.
- Recognize that your initial reaction to cultural difference may be defensive.
- Understand what makes other people's cultural views and traits valuable to them.
- Listen carefully to others' descriptions of cultural differences and concerns.
- Immerse yourself in a different culture (as Emily did) for an extended period of time.

- Commit yourself to understanding a given situation from another point of view.

Colleges also tend to encourage the development of writing skills, speaking skills, and critical thinking (Bensley et al., 2010; Noblitt et al., 2010). Nearly all colleges have first-year writing requirements that require students to express their ideas through the written word and, frequently, orally. In teaching critical thinking, many professors challenge students to take nothing for granted—not to believe things just because they are in print or because they were uttered by authority figures or celebrities. Critical thinking refers to a process of thoughtfully analyzing and probing the questions, statements, and arguments of others, which is likely to be taught in the sciences, the humanities—literally all across the curriculum. Critical thinking means examining definitions of terms, examining the premises or assumptions behind arguments, and then scrutinizing the logic with which arguments are developed. Students are encouraged to:

- Be skeptical—keep an open mind.
- Examine definitions of terms.
- Examine the assumptions or premises of arguments.
- Be cautious in drawing conclusions from evidence.
- Consider alternative interpretations of research evidence.
- Do not oversimplify.
- Do not overgeneralize.
- Apply critical thinking to all areas of life— a skeptical attitude and a demand for evidence are useful not only in college but in all areas of life.

Discrepancies in STEM Fields

Recent research suggests that men and women are about equal overall in math ability (Hyde & Mertz, 2009), but higher percentages of men enter so-called STEM fields (science, technology, engineering, and mathematics) than women do. Why? According to psy-

Winston Davidian/Jupiterimages

▶ **LO18** Discuss the value of work.

▶ **LO19** Describe career development.

chologists Stephen Ceci, Wendy Williams, and Susan Barnett (2009), who have studied the issue extensively, the reasons are likely as follows:

1. Women who are proficient in math are more likely than math-proficient men to prefer careers that do not require skills in math.
2. More males than females obtain extremely high scores on the SAT math test and the quantitative reasoning sections of the Graduate Record Exam.
3. Women who are proficient in math are more likely than men with this proficiency to have high verbal competence as well, which encourages many such women to choose other careers.

Career Development

Work is a major part of life, and early adulthood is the time when most of us become established in our careers. We will consider how this happens, but before this, let's ask what motivates people to work in the first place.

The first reason people work is obvious: Earning a living, fringe benefits, and ensuring future security all inspire people to pursue careers and employment. These external benefits of working are called *extrinsic motives*; however, extrinsic motives alone do not explain why people work. Work can also satisfy many internal or *intrinsic motives*, including the opportunities to engage in stimulating and satisfying activities and to develop one's talents (Ryan & Deci, 2000). Many million-dollar lottery winners who quit their jobs felt aimlessness and dissatisfaction afterward (Corliss, 2003). Moreover, within a year of cashing their checks, lottery winners generally reported happiness (or unhappiness) levels corresponding to their prewinning levels (Corliss, 2003). Despite folk wisdom, money does not always buy happiness; many people seek more in life than extrinsic rewards such as a paycheck and financial security. They also want the intrinsic rewards gained through engaging in challenging activities, broadening their social contacts, and filling their days with meaningful activity.

Intrinsic reasons for working include (Duffy & Sedlacek, 2007):

- *The work ethic:* Many people hold the view that we are morally obligated to avoid idleness.

- *Self-identity:* Our occupational identity can become intertwined with our self-identity.
- *Self-fulfillment:* We often express our personal needs and interests through our work.
- *Self-worth:* Recognition and respect for a job well done contribute to self-esteem.
- *Socialization:* The workplace extends our social contacts.
- *Public roles:* Work roles help define our functions in the community.

Choosing a Career and Stages of Career Development

For most of us, career development has a number of stages. We now discuss how we choose a career, based on David Super's traditional theory of career development and more contemporary views.

The first or *fantasy stage* involves the child's unrealistic conception of self-potential and of the world of work, which dominates from early childhood until about age 11. Young children focus on glamour professions, such as acting, medicine, sports, and law enforcement (Auger et al., 2005). They show little regard for the fit between these occupations and their abilities. During the second or *tentative choice stage*, from about age 11 through high school, children base their choices on their interests, abilities, and limitations, as well as glamour.

Beyond age 17 or so, in the *realistic choice stage*, choices become narrowed as students weigh job requirements and rewards against their interests, abilities, and values (Nauta, 2007). They may direct their educational plans to ensure they obtain the knowledge and skills they need to enter their intended occupations. Some follow the paths of role models such as parents or respected members of the community (Auger et al., 2005). Many "fall into" careers not because of particular skills and interests, but because of what is available at the time, family pressures, or the lure of high income or a certain lifestyle. Others may "job hop" through several different career paths before finally finding one that fits well.

During the *maintenance stage*, a person begins "settling" into career roles, which often happens in the second half of the thirties. Although a person may change positions within a company or within a career, as in moving from marketing to management, there is often a sense of continuing development of the career, a feeling of forward motion. Of course, people can also get "trapped" in dead-end jobs during this stage (Savickas, 2005).

Here is where we diverge from Super's traditional view of career development. Because of corporate downsizing, mergers, acquisitions, fewer benefits, and layoffs, many employees no longer feel the loyalty to their employers that workers once did. Thus they are more likely to job hop when the opportunity arises. People are also living longer, healthier lives in rapidly changing times. They are staying in school longer and returning to school for education, training, and retraining. Today it is the norm, rather than the exception, for people to switch jobs more than once. That said, vocational interests tend to be stable over the life course (Rottinghaus, Coon, et al., 2007). Though people may switch jobs, they generally seek jobs that reflect stable interests.

The final stage in Super's scheme is the *retirement stage*, during which the individual severs bonds with the workplace. In Chapter 9 we will see that retirement today is far from final. Retirees often become restless and undertake second or third careers.

One of the developmental tasks in beginning a career is finding a sponsor or mentor who can help you learn how to carry out the job tasks.

Hemera Technologies/Photos.com/Jupiterimages

Developmental Tasks in Beginning a Career

One of the challenges of early adulthood is becoming established in the career world. Different careers hold different challenges, but a number of challenges are common enough. They include (Bozionelos & Wang, 2006; Quigley & Tymon, 2006):

- Learning how to carry out the job tasks;
- Accepting your subordinate status within the organization or profession;
- Learning how to get along with your coworkers and supervisor;
- Showing that you can maintain the job, make improvements, and show progress;
- Finding a sponsor or mentor to "show you the ropes";
- Defining the boundaries between the job and other areas of life; trying not to bring home your troubles on the job;
- Evaluating your occupational choice in the light of measurable outcomes of your work; and
- Learning to cope with daily hassles on the job, frustrations, successes, and failures.

Check Your Learning Quiz 7.2

Go to **login.cengagebrain.com** and take the online quiz.

▶ **LO20** Examine separating from one's family of origin.

Did you know that—

- People are considered more attractive when they are smiling?

- People look more attractive when they are "decked out" in red?

- It is not true that "opposites attract"—it's more likely that "birds of a feather flock together"?

- Couples can remain in love after passion fades?

- Jealousy can lessen feelings of affection and heighten feelings of insecurity and depression, leading to a breakup?

- Many people remain lonely because they fear being rejected by others?

▼

Early adulthood spans the decades from ages 20 to 40. Some theorists begin at 17 or 18, however, and others extend the period to age 44 or 45. The traditional view of development in early adulthood was laid down by developmental psychologist Robert Havighurst (1972) 40 years ago. He believed that each stage of development involved accomplishing certain "tasks"; the tasks he described for early adulthood include the following:

1. Getting started in an occupation;
2. Selecting and courting a mate;
3. Learning to live contentedly with one's partner;
4. Starting a family and becoming a parent;
5. Assuming the responsibilities of managing a home;
6. Assuming civic responsibilities; and
7. Finding a congenial social group.

Many modern early adults will laugh at this list of tasks. Others will think that it doesn't sound too bad at all. I bring it to your attention simply because it is a traditional view of young adulthood from past generations that ignores some realities of human diversity and contemporary life. For example, many early adults (and older adults) remain single today. Many never assume civic responsibilities. Many married couples choose not to have children, and some others are infertile. Gay men and lesbians may have partners, but many do not become parents—and Havighurst was certainly not including them. Nor did Havighurst list *separation* from one's family of origin as a task involved in young-adulthood. We consider this task next.

Separation and Individuation

Young adults leave home at different ages and for different reasons, and some never have a traditional home life to begin with. The typical developmental milestones seem distant to young adults who have spent years in orphanages, bounced about from one foster home to another, or spent time in detention or in the homes of grandparents or other relatives because their parents could not provide a home (Minkler & Fuller-Thomson, 2005).

Young adults who enter the job market out of high school, or without completing high school, may live at home for a while to save some money before venturing out on their own. When they do, they may move in with roommates or to a poorer neighborhood than that of their parents so that they can afford independent living. Even so, parents may contribute cash.

Other young adults may leave home to go to college or enlist in the military. If students are attending a local college, they may stay at home or move in with roommates so they can afford it. Young adults who attend college away from home do leave, but very often a room is kept for them at home and is relatively untouched. Psychologically, the "nest" remains for if and when they need it. Highly traditional or insecure parents may find a son's or daughter's leaving for college to be so stressful that departure damages the parent–child relationship (Steele, 2005b). The departure tends to be more stressful when the child is a daughter, perhaps because women appear to be more vulnerable than men "out there" in the world.

Those who enlist in the military have their housing needs taken care of. Their rupture from home and neighborhood is sudden and complete, although they can return when they are on leave or their service is finished.

If young adults are working within commuting distance of their homes of origin, even after graduating college, they may return home to live for financial reasons. Entry-level jobs often do not pay well, or the young adult may want to try to save enough to place a down payment on a house or accumulate apartment rent in advance. It is not uncommon for young adults to get married and then move in with

▸ **LO21** Describe Erikson's life crisis of intimacy versus isolation.

▸ **LO22** Discuss Levinson's seasons of life, focusing on early adulthood.

individuation The young adult's process of becoming an individual by means of integrating his or her own values and beliefs with those of his or her parents and society at large.

intimacy versus isolation According to Erik Erikson, the central conflict or life crisis of early adulthood, in which a person develops an intimate relationship with a significant other or risks heading down a path toward social isolation.

life structure In Levinson's theory, the underlying pattern of a person's life at a given stage, as defined by relationships, career, race, religion, economic status, and the like.

the dream According to Levinson and his colleagues, the drive to become someone, to leave one's mark on history, which serves as a tentative blueprint for the young adult.

a set of parents. And sometimes a couple who are living together without being married move in with a set of tolerant parents.

Whether or not young adults leave the nest, it is time for them to separate from their parents psychologically. Psychologists and educators refer to the relevant processes as *separation* and **individuation**—that is, becoming an individual by means of integrating one's own values and beliefs with those of one's parents and one's society.

Most men in our society consider separation and individuation to be key goals of personality development in early adulthood (Blazina et al., 2007). But many psychologists have argued that things are somewhat different for women—that for women, the establishment and maintenance of social relationships are also of primary importance (Gilligan, 1990; Jordan et al., 1991). Nevertheless, many young women work on becoming their own people in the sense of separating their values and patterns of behavior from those of their mothers (Brockman, 2003). When young men's views differ from those of their parents, they are more likely to engage in an active struggle or a fight for independence (Levpušcek, 2006).

The transition to college or to the workplace can play a role in separation and individuation. Employment and financial independence can lessen feelings of connectedness with parents, whereas college or university can maintain these feelings (Buhl et al., 2003). Feelings of connectedness are related to the amount of financial and emotional support students receive from parents (J. L. Tanner, 2006).

Intimacy Versus Isolation

Erik Erikson was aware that young adults often have problems separating from their parents. He was a psychoanalyst, and many of the young women who opened their hearts to him complained of difficulties with disappointing mothers whose values were different from and usually more traditional than their own. However, Erikson focused on one central conflict for each stage of life, and the core conflict he identified for early adulthood was **intimacy versus isolation**.

Erikson (1963) saw the establishment of intimate relationships as the key "crisis" of early adulthood. Young adults who have evolved a firm sense of identity during adolescence are now ready to "fuse" their identities with those of other people through marriage and abiding friendships. Erikson's clinical experience led him to believe that young adults who had not achieved ego identity—a firm sense of who they are and what they stand for—may not be ready to commit themselves to others.

They may not be able to gauge the extent to which their developing values may conflict with those of a potential intimate partner. He suggested that in our society, which values compatibility in relationships, an absent or fluctuating ego identity is connected with the high divorce rate in teenage marriages. Once passion fades a bit, conflicting ways of looking at the world may be too abrasive to bear. Erikson argued that young adults who do not reach out to develop intimate relationships risk retreating into isolation and loneliness.

Is it "normal" and psychologically healthy to develop intimate relationships in early adulthood? Or is it merely an option?

Erikson, like Havighurst, has been criticized for suggesting that young adults who choose to remain celibate or single are not developing normally (Hayslip et al., 2006). Erikson believed that it was normal, and psychologically healthy, for people to develop intimate relationships and bear children within a generally stable and nurturing environment during early adulthood.

Seasons of Life

In 1978, psychologist Daniel Levinson—who had worked with Erik Erikson at Harvard University—and his colleagues published an influential book on development called *Seasons of a Man's Life*. Levinson later followed it with *Seasons of a Woman's Life* (1996). These books explained Levinson's view, compatible with Erikson's, that adults go through certain periods of life, dubbed *seasons*, in which their progress and psychological well-being are shaped by common social and physical demands and crises, such as developing relationships, rearing children, establishing and developing a career, and coming to terms with one's successes and failures. At any given moment, the underlying pattern of a person's life is his or her **life structure**. One's religion, race, and socioeconomic status also influence life structure and life satisfaction. Many young adults also adopt what Levinson calls **the dream**—the drive to become someone, to leave his or her mark on history—which serves as a tentative blueprint for life. Levinson (1996) found that women undergo somewhat similar developments, but experience more social constraints, both from their families of origin and from society in general. Thus it may take women longer to leave home, and there may

Erikson and Levinson's Theories about Early Adulthood

Interact and learn about social and emotional theories of early adulthood.

▶ **LO23** Discuss interpersonal attraction.

▶ **LO24** Discuss different types of love.

be more pressure on them to go from one home (their parents') to another (their husbands').

Levinson labeled the ages of 28–33 the *age-30 transition.* For men and women, he found that the late 20s and early 30s are commonly characterized by reassessment: "Where is my life going?" "Why am I doing this?"

Levinson and his colleagues also found that the later 30s were often characterized by settling down or planting roots. At this time, many people felt a need to make a financial and emotional investment in their homes. Their concerns became focused on promotion or tenure, career advancement, mortgages, and, in many or most cases, raising their own families.

Striving for success? According to Levinson, the 20s are fueled by ambition.

Erik Isakson/Blend Images/Jupiterimages

Today, Levinson's views already sound rather archaic, at least when they are applied to young women (Hayslip et al., 2006). It has become acceptable and widespread for women to lead independent, single lives, for as long as they wish. And, truth be told, the great majority of career women in sizeable American cities simply would not care what anyone thinks about their marital status or living arrangements. And given the mobility young adults have in the United States today, many will not live in places where people frown upon their styles of life.

Attraction and Love: Forces That Bind?

Young adults separate from their families of origin and (often) join with others. In developed nations, they are free to choose the people with whom they will associate and develop friendships and romantic relationships. The emotional forces that fuel these associations are *attraction* and *love*.

Attraction

Investigators define feelings of attraction as psychological forces that draw people together. Some researchers find that physical appearance is the key factor in consideration of partners for dates, sex, and long-term relationships (J. M. B. Wilson et al., 2005). We might like to claim that sensitivity, warmth, and intelligence are more important to us, but we may never learn about other people's personalities if they do not meet minimal standards for attractiveness (Langlois et al., 2000; Strassberg & Holty, 2003).

Is Beauty in the Eye of the Beholder?

Are our standards of beauty subjective, or is there broad agreement on what is attractive? In certain African tribes, long necks and round, disklike lips are signs of feminine beauty. Women thus stretch their necks and lips to make themselves more appealing (Ford & Beach, 1951).

In our society, tallness is an asset for men (Furnham, 2009; Kurzban & Weeden, 2005). Although women may be less demanding than men concerning a variety of physical features, height—that is, tallness—is more important to women in the selection of dates and mates than it is to men.

Although preferences for facial features may transcend time and culture, preferences for body weight and shape may be more culturally determined. For example, plumpness has been valued in many cultures.

Grandmothers who worry that their granddaughters are starving themselves often come from cultures in which stoutness is acceptable or desirable. In contemporary Western society, there is pressure on both males and females to be slender, especially women (Furnham, 2009). Women generally favor men with a V-taper—broad shoulders and a narrow waist.

An examination of 5,810 Yahoo personal ads—Internet dating profiles—showed that "thin" was more "in" in the expressed preferences for partners of European Americans and males (Glasser et al., 2009). European American males were more likely than African American and Latino American males to want to date slender and buffed women. African American and Latino American men were significantly more likely to be interested in women with large or thick bodies.

Why did they deck her out in red? Cultural conditioning and the human biological heritage provide two good answers.

© Fancy Photography/Veer

Andrew Elliot and Daniela Niesta (2008) ran a series of experiments in which men rated the same woman as being more attractive when her photograph was shown against a red background than against white, gray, and a variety of other background colors. The link between red and physical attraction may also be rooted in our biological heritage. Many nonhuman female primates, including baboons, chimpanzees, gorillas, and rhesus monkeys, show reddened genital regions and sometimes chests and faces when they are nearing ovulation—the time when they are fertile (Barelli et al., 2008).

The Effect of Nonphysical Traits on Perceptions of Physical Beauty

Although there are physical standards for beauty in our culture, nonphysical traits also affect our perceptions. For example, the attractiveness of a partner is likely to be enhanced by traits such as familiarity, liking, respect, and sharing of values and goals (Kniffin & Wilson, 2004). People also rate the attractiveness of faces higher when the faces are smiling than when they are not smiling (O'Doherty et al., 2003).

Sex Differences in Perceptions of Attractiveness

Gender-role expectations may affect perceptions of attractiveness. For example, women are more likely to be attracted to socially dominant men than men are to be attracted to socially dom-

attraction–similarity hypothesis The view that people tend to develop romantic relationships with people who are similar to themselves in physical attractiveness and other traits.

Table 7.4
Sex Differences in Preferences for a Mate

How Willing Would You Be to Marry Someone Who—	Men	Women
Was not "good-looking"?	3.41	4.42
Was older than you by 6 or more years?	4.15	5.29
Was younger than you by 6 or more years?	4.54	2.80
Was not likely to hold a steady job?	2.73	1.62
Would earn much less than you?	4.60	3.76
Would earn much more than you?	5.19	5.93
Had more education than you?	5.22	5.82
Had less education than you?	4.67	4.08
Had been married before?	3.35	3.44
Already had children?	2.84	3.11
Was of a different religion?	4.24	4.31
Was of a different race?	3.08	2.84

Note: Answers were given on a 7-point scale, with 1 meaning *not at all* and 7 meaning *very willing*.
Source: Based on the information in Susan Sprecher, Quintin Sullivan, & Elaine Hatfield (1994). Mate Selection Preferences: Gender Differences Examined in a National Sample. Journal of Personality and Social Psychology, 66(6), 1074–1080.

inant women (Buunk et al., 2002). Women who viewed videos of prospective dates found men who acted outgoing and self-expressive more appealing than men who were passive (Riggio & Woll, 1984). Yet men who viewed videos in the Riggio and Woll (1984) study were put off by outgoing, self-expressive behavior in women.

Susan Sprecher and her colleagues (1994) surveyed a nationally representative sample of more than 13,000 English- or Spanish-speaking adults living in the United States. In one section of their questionnaire, they asked respondents how willing they would be to marry someone who was older, younger, of a different religion, not likely to hold a steady job, not good-looking, and so forth. Each item was followed by a 7-point scale in which 1 meant *not at all* and 7 meant *very willing*. As shown in Table 7.4, women were more willing than men to marry someone who was not good-looking. On the other hand, women were less willing to marry someone not likely to hold a steady job.

Are Preferences Concerning Attractiveness Inborn?

Evolutionary psychologists believe that evolutionary forces favor the continuation of gender differences in preferences for mates because certain preferred traits provide reproductive advantages (Buss, 2005). Some physical features, like cleanliness, good complexion, clear eyes, good teeth, good hair, firm muscle tone, and a steady gait, are universally appealing to both females and males. Perhaps they are markers of reproductive potential (Buss, 2005). Age and health may be relatively more important to a woman's appeal, because these characteristics tend to be associated with her reproductive capacity: The "biological clock" limits her reproductive potential. Physical characteristics associated with a woman's youthfulness, such as smooth skin, firm muscle tone, and lustrous hair, may thus have become more closely linked to a woman's appeal (Buss, 2005). A man's reproductive value, however, may depend more on how well he can provide for his family than on his age or physical appeal. The value of men as reproducers, therefore, is more intertwined with factors that contribute to a stable environment for child rearing—such as economic status and reliability. Evolutionary psychologists argue that these gender differences in mate preferences may have been passed down through the generations as part of our genetic heritage (Buss, 2005).

The Attraction–Similarity Hypothesis: Do "Opposites Attract" or Do "Birds of a Feather Flock Together"?

Do not despair if you are less than exquisite in appearance, along with most of us mere mortals. You may be saved from permanently blending in with the wallpaper by the effects of the **attraction–similarity hypothesis**. This hypothesis holds that

Dancing and Attraction

Are men who dance well more attractive to women? Watch and learn.

The Rules of Attraction

How does shallowness affect dating and attraction?

people tend to develop romantic relationships with people who are similar to themselves in attractiveness and other traits (Klohnen & Luo, 2003; Morry & Gaines, 2005).

Researchers have found that people who are involved in committed relationships are most likely to be similar to their partners in their attitudes and cultural attributes (Amodio & Showers, 2005). Our partners tend to be like us in race and ethnicity, age, level of education, and religion.

A nationally representative survey (Michael et al., 1994) found that:

- The sex partners of nearly 94% of single European American men were European American women.
- About 2% of single European American men were partnered with Latina American women, 2% with Asian American women, and fewer than 1% with African American women.
- The sex partners of nearly 82% of African American men were African American women.
- Nearly 8% of African American men were partnered with European American women. Under 5% were partnered with Latina American women.
- About 83% of women and men chose partners within 5 years of their own age and of the same or a similar religion.
- Of all the women in the study, not one with a graduate college degree had a partner who had not finished high school.
- Men with a college degree almost never had sexual relationships with women with much more or much less education than they had.

reciprocity The tendency to respond in kind when we feel admired and complimented.

romantic love A form of love fueled by passion and feelings of intimacy.

Michael Keller/Corbis and Andrew Lichtenstein / The Image Works

Do opposites attract, or do we tend to pair off with people who are similar to us in level of physical attractiveness, attitudes, and tastes? From looking at these couples, it seems that similarity often runs at least skin deep.

Reciprocity: If You Like Me, You Must Have Excellent Judgment

Has anyone told you that you are good-looking, brilliant, and emotionally mature to boot? That your taste is elegant? Ah, what superb judgment! When we feel admired and complimented, we tend to return these feelings and behaviors. This is called **reciprocity**. Reciprocity is a potent determinant of attraction (Levine, 2000; Sprecher, 1998). Perhaps the power of reciprocity has enabled many couples to become happy with one another and reasonably well adjusted.

Attraction can lead to feelings of love. Let us now turn to that most fascinating topic.

Love

The experience of **romantic love**, as opposed to attachment or sexual arousal, occurs within a cultural context in which the concept is idealized (Berscheid, 2003, 2006). Western culture has a long tradition of idealizing the concept of romantic love, as represented, for instance, in romantic fairy tales that have been passed down through the generations. In fact, our exposure to the concept of romantic love may begin with hearing those fairy tales, and later, perhaps, continue to blossom through exposure to romantic novels, television and film scripts, and the heady tales of friends and relatives.

Researchers have found that love is a complex concept, involving many areas of experience (Berscheid, 2003, 2006). Let us consider two psychological perspectives on love, both of which involve emotional arousal.

Love as Appraisal of Arousal

Social psychologists Ellen Berscheid and Elaine Hatfield (Berscheid, 2003, 2006; Hatfield & Rapson, 2002) have defined romantic love in terms of a state of intense physiological arousal and the cognitive appraisal of that arousal as love. The arousal may be experienced as a pounding heart, sweaty palms, and butterflies in the stomach when one is in the presence of, or thinking about, one's love interest. Cognitive appraisal of the arousal means attributing the arousal to some cause, such as fear or love. The perception that one has fallen in love is thus derived from: (1) a state of intense arousal that is connected with an appropriate love object (that is, a person, not an event like a rock concert), (2) a cultural setting that idealizes romantic love, and (3) the attribution of the arousal to feelings of love for the person.

Sternberg's Triangular Theory of Love

Robert Sternberg's (2006a) "triangular theory" of love includes three building blocks, or components, of loving experiences:

1. *Intimacy*: The experience of warmth toward another person that arises from feelings of closeness and connectedness, and the desire to share one's innermost thoughts.
2. *Passion*: Intense romantic or sexual desire, accompanied by physiological arousal.
3. *Commitment*: Commitment to maintain the relationship through good times and bad.

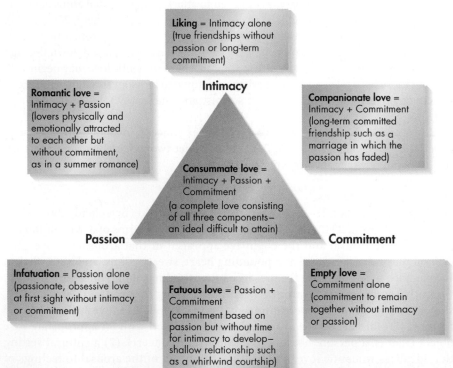

Liking = Intimacy alone (true friendships without passion or long-term commitment)

Romantic love = Intimacy + Passion (lovers physically and emotionally attracted to each other but without commitment, as in a summer romance)

Companionate love = Intimacy + Commitment (long-term committed friendship such as a marriage in which the passion has faded)

Consummate love = Intimacy + Passion + Commitment (a complete love consisting of all three components— an ideal difficult to attain)

Infatuation = Passion alone (passionate, obsessive love at first sight without intimacy or commitment)

Fatuous love = Passion + Commitment (commitment based on passion but without time for intimacy to develop— shallow relationship such as a whirlwind courtship)

Empty love = Commitment alone (commitment to remain together without intimacy or passion)

Figure 7.4 Sternberg's Triangular Theory of Love

Sternberg's model is triangular in that various kinds of love can be conceptualized in terms of a triangle in which each vertex represents one of the building blocks (see Figure 7.4). In Sternberg's model, couples are well matched if they possess corresponding levels of passion, intimacy, and commitment (Drigotas et al., 1999; Sternberg, 2006). According to the model, various combinations of the building blocks of love characterize different types of love relationships. For example, infatuation (passionate love) is typified by sexual desire but not by intimacy or commitment.

"Being in love" can refer to states of passion or infatuation, whereas friendship is usually based on shared interests, liking, and respect. Friendship and passionate love do not necessarily overlap. There is nothing that prevents people in love from becoming good friends, however—perhaps even the best of friends. Sternberg's model recognizes that the intimacy we find in true friendships and the passion we find in love are blended in two forms of love—romantic love and consummate love. These love types differ along the dimension of commitment, however.

Romantic love has both passion and intimacy but lacks commitment. It may burn brightly and then flicker out or it may develop into a more complete love, called *consummate love*, in which all three components flower. Consummate love is an ideal toward which many Westerners strive. Sometimes a love relationship has both passion and commitment but lacks intimacy. Sternberg calls this *fatuous* (foolish) *love*. Fatuous love is associated with whirlwind courtships that burn brightly but briefly as the partners realize that they are not well matched. In companionate love, intimacy and commitment are strong, but passion is lacking. Companionate love typifies long-term relationships and marriages in which passion has ebbed but a deep and abiding friendship remains (Hatfield & Rapson, 2002).

Jealousy

> O! beware, my lord, of jealousy;
> It is the green-ey'd monster …
> —William Shakespeare, *Othello*

Thus was Othello, the Moor of Venice, warned of jealousy in the Shakespearean play that bears his name. Yet Othello could not control his feelings and wound up killing his beloved (and innocent) wife, Desdemona. Partners can become jealous, for example,

▶ **LO25** Discuss loneliness and what people can do about it.

when others show sexual interest in their partners or when their partners show interest in another.

Jealousy can lead to loss of feelings of affection, feelings of insecurity and rejection, anxiety, loss of self-esteem, and feelings of mistrust. Jealousy, therefore, can be one reason that relationships fail. In extreme cases jealousy can cause depression or give rise to spouse abuse, suicide, or, as with Othello, murder (Puente & Cohen, 2003; Vandello & Cohen, 2003).

Some young adults—including college students—play jealousy games. They let their partners know that they are attracted to other people. They flirt openly or manufacture tales to make their partners pay more attention to them, to test the relationship, to inflict pain, or to take revenge for a partner's disloyalty.

What are the effects of jealousy on a relationship?

Loneliness

Loneliness increases from childhood to adolescence, when peer relationships are beginning to supplant family ties and individuals are becoming—often—painfully aware of how other adolescents may be more successful at making friends and earning the admiration of others (H. Cheng & Furnham, 2002). But young adults are also likely to encounter feelings of loneliness because of life changes such as entering college or graduate school or moving to a new city to take advantage of job prospects (Cacioppo & Patrick, 2008). They often leave behind childhood friends and neighbors with whom they had lengthy relationships (J. Kagan, 2009).

Some young adults feel lonely even when they are in relationships. A study of 101 dating couples with a mean age of 21 found that poor relationships contributed to feelings of loneliness and depression—even though the individuals had partners (Segrin et al., 2003). Loneliness also means that the individual feels that she or he is lacking in social support. Stress can lead to a host of health problems, such as obesity and high blood pressure, and social support helps people cope with stress (Hawkley et al., 2003; Pressman et al., 2005). Therefore, it is not surprising that feelings of loneliness are connected with such health problems as well as depression.

The causes of loneliness are many and complex. Lonely people tend to have several of the following characteristics: lack of social skills, lack of interest in other people, and lack of empathy (Cramer, 2003). Fear of rejection is often connected with self-criticism of social skills and expectations of failure in relating to others (Vorauer et al., 2003). Lonely people also fail to disclose personal information to potential friends (Solano et al., 1982), are cynical about human nature (for example, seeing people as only out for themselves), and demand too much too soon.

Coping With Loneliness

What can you do to deal with loneliness in your own life? Here are some suggestions:

1. Challenge your feelings of pessimism. Adopt the attitude that things happen when you make them happen.
2. Challenge your cynicism about human nature. Yes, lots of people are selfish and not worth knowing, but your task is to find people who possess the qualities you value.
3. Challenge the idea that failure in social relationships is unbearable and is therefore a valid reason for giving up on them. We must all learn to live with some rejection. Keep looking for people who possess the qualities you value and who will find things of value in you.
4. Get out among people. Sit down at a table with people in the cafeteria, not off in a corner by yourself. Smile and say hi to people who interest you.
5. Make numerous social contacts. Join committees, intramural sports, social-action groups, the photography club, or the ski club.
6. Become a good listener. Ask people for opinions and actually listen to what they have to say. Tolerate diverse opinions.
7. Give people the chance to know you. Seek common ground by exchanging opinions and talking about your interests.
8. Remember that you're worthy of friends—warts and all. None of us is perfect.
9. Use your college counseling center. You might even ask whether there's a group at the center for students seeking to improve their dating or social skills.

Social Exclusion

Watch and learn about research on social exclusion and the ways people who have been rejected respond.

Check Your Learning Quiz 7.3

Go to **login.cengagebrain.com** and take the online quiz.

▶ **LO26** Discuss the lifestyle of being single.

Did you know that—

- Being single has become a more common U.S. lifestyle over the past few decades?
- In the United States, more than half of people who get married live together first?
- Marriage remains the most common lifestyle for people aged 35–44?
- Two out of three Americans now support either marriage equality or civil unions for same-sex couples?
- Having a child is no way to help save a marriage that is in trouble?
- More than 1 child in 4 is being reared by a single parent?

▼

The Single Life

Being single, not married, is now the most common lifestyle of people in their early 20s. By 2000, 1 woman in 4 and 3 men in 10 in the United States aged 15 or older had never married. Half a century earlier, in 1950, 1 woman in 5 and about 1 man in 4 aged 15 or older had never been married. In 2000, more than 4 men in 5 (84%) in the 20–24 age range were unmarried, up from 55% in 1970 (U.S. Bureau of the Census, 2006). The number of single women in this age group doubled to 73% from 36% in 1970.

Several factors contribute to the increased proportion of singles. More young adults are postponing marriage to pursue educational and career goals. As we'll discuss in a bit, many are also deciding to live together (cohabit), at least for a while, rather than get married. People are also getting married later, as shown in Table 7.5. The

Mike Kemp/Getty Images

There is no single "singles scene." Although some singles meet in singles' bars, many meet in more casual settings, such as the neighborhood laundromat. Some singles advertise online or in newspapers or magazines.

serial monogamy A series of exclusive sexual relationships.

celibacy Abstention from sexual activity, whether from choice or lack of opportunity.

typical man in the United States gets married at about age 27 today, compared with age 23 fifty years ago (U.S. Bureau of the Census, 2006). The typical woman gets married today at about age 25; fifty years ago, she got married at age 20.

Families headed by single mothers have doubled to more than one quarter of all families, as compared with three decades ago (U.S. Bureau of the Census, 2010). About one third as many children live with single fathers. Some single mothers started their families as single, but the increased prevalence of divorce also swells their ranks. Most single fathers were previously married or cohabiting.

Single people encounter less social stigma today. They are less likely to be perceived as socially inadequate or as failures. Many young adults do not choose to be single. Some have not yet found Mr. or Ms. Right. On the other hand, many young adults see being single as an alternative, open-ended way of life—not a temporary stage that precedes marriage. As career options for women have expanded, women are not as financially dependent on men as their mothers and grandmothers were.

Being single has its problems. Many single people are lonely (Soons & Liefbroer, 2008). Some singles would prefer to have a steady, committed relationship. Other single people, usually women, worry about their physical safety living alone or being out on dates with new people. Some young adults who are living alone find it difficult to satisfy their needs for intimacy, companionship, and sex. Despite these concerns, most singles are well adjusted.

Single people differ in their sexual interests and lifestyles. Many achieve emotional and psychological security through a network of intimate relationships with friends. Many are sexually active and practice **serial monogamy** (Kulick, 2006). Others have a primary sexual relationship with one steady partner but occasional flings. A few pursue casual sexual encounters. By contrast, some singles remain celibate, either by choice or from lack of opportunity. Some choose **celibacy** for religious reasons, to focus on work or another cause, because they find sex unalluring, or because of fear of STIs (Laumann, Gagnon, et al., 1994).

Cohabitation

> There is nothing I would not do
> If you would be my POSSLQ.
>
> —Charles Osgood

Table 7.5
Estimated Median Age at First Marriage

Year	Males	Females
2010	28.2	26.1
2000	26.8	25.1
1990	26.1	23.9
1980	24.7	22.0
1970	23.2	20.8
1960	22.8	20.3
1950	22.8	20.3

Source: U.S. Census Bureau, November 10, 2010. U.S. Census Bureau reports men and women wait longer to marry. http://www.census.gov/newsroom/releases/archives/families_households/cb10-174.html. Accessed April 25, 2011.

Commitment Phobia

Are men more "commitment phobic" than women? Watch and learn theories.

▶**LO27** Describe the practice of cohabitation.

POSSLQ? POSSLQ is the unromantic abbreviation used by the U.S. Bureau of the Census to refer to **cohabitation**. It stands for Person(s) of the Opposite Sex Sharing Living Quarters and applies to unmarried heterosexual couples who live together.

Some social scientists believe that cohabitation has become accepted within the social mainstream. Whether or not this is so, society in general has become more tolerant (Laumann, Mahay et al., 2007). We seldom hear cohabitation referred to as "living in sin" as we once did. People today are more likely to refer to cohabitation with value-free expressions such as "living together."

The numbers of households in the United States consisting of an unmarried adult male and female living together has increased more than tenfold since 1960, from fewer than half a million couples to around five million couples today (Whitehead & Popenoe, 2006). The rate is about twice as high among African American couples as European American couples (Laumann, Mahay, et al., 2007). Another half million households consist of same-sex couples who live together (Simons & O'Connell, 2003).

Cohabitation was once referred to as "living in sin," but it has become an increasingly common lifestyle. Some sociologists predict that cohabitation will replace marriage as the nation's most popular lifestyle sometime during the next few decades.

Fuse/Getty Images

More than half (56%) of the marriages that took place in the 1990s were preceded by the couple living together (Bramlett & Mosher, 2002). There is a 75% probability that a cohabiting European American woman will marry her partner if the couple cohabit for 5 years (Bramlett & Mosher, 2002). The probabilities drop to 61% for Latina American women and 48% for African American women. Some social scientists see cohabitation as a new stage of courtship. As you can see in Table 7.6, more than half of today's high-school seniors believe that it is a good idea for couples to live together before getting married, to test their compatibility. Even so, about 40% of these couples get divorced later on, so "trial marriages" may not provide couples with accurate information.

cohabitation Living together with a romantic partner without being married.

Young adults cohabit for many reasons. Cohabitation, like marriage, is an alternative to living alone. Romantic partners may have deep feelings for each other but not be ready to get married. Some couples prefer cohabitation because it provides an abiding relationship without the legal entanglements of marriage (Hussain, 2002; Marquis, 2003).

Willingness to cohabit is related to less traditional views of marriage and gender roles (Hussain, 2002; Marquis, 2003). For example, divorced people are more likely to cohabit than people who have never been married. Perhaps the experience of divorce leaves some people more willing to share their lives than their bank accounts. Cohabitants are also less likely than noncohabitants to say that religion is very important to them (Bramlett & Mosher, 2002). Tradition aside, many cohabitants are simply less committed to their relationships than married people are (Hussain, 2002; Marquis, 2003). It is more often the man who is unwilling to make a commitment, because men are typically more interested in sexual variety, at least in the short term (D. L. Cohen & Belsky, 2008). In the long term, however, both men and women may seek a heavy investment in a relationship, feelings of love, companionship, and a sharing of resources (Njus & Bane, 2009).

Economic factors also come into play. Young adults may decide to cohabit because of the economic advantages of sharing household expenses. Cohabiting individuals who receive public assistance risk losing support if they get married (Hussain, 2002; Marquis, 2003). College students may cohabit secretly to maintain parental support that they might lose if they were to reveal their living arrangements.

Cohabiting couples may believe that cohabitation will strengthen eventual marriage by helping them iron out the kinks in their relationship. But some studies have suggested that the likelihood of divorce within 10 years of marriage is nearly twice as great among married couples who cohabited before marriage (Smock, 2000). Why?

We cannot conclude that cohabitation necessarily causes divorce. We must be cautious about drawing causal conclusions from correlational data. Selection factors—the factors that led some couples to cohabit and others not to cohabit— may explain the results (see Figure 7.5). For example, as noted earlier, cohabitant tend to be less traditional and less religious than noncohabitants (Hussain, 2002; Marquis, 2003), and thus tend to be less committed to the values and interests traditionally associated with the institution of marriage. Therefore, the attitudes of

Table 7.6
Percentage of U.S. High-School Seniors Who Agreed or Mostly Agreed With the Statement "It Is Usually a Good Idea for a Couple to Live Together Before Getting Married in Order to Find Out Whether They Really Get along"

Period	Boys	Girls
1976–1980	44.9	32.3
1981–1985	47.4	36.5
1986–1990	57.8	45.2
1991–1995	60.5	51.3
1996–2000	65.7	59.1
2001–2004	64.1	57.0

Note: Number of respondents for each sex for each period is about 6,000, except for 2001–2004, for which it is about 4,500.
Source: *Whitehead & Popenoe (2006)*
http://www.census.gov/compendia/ statab/cats/population/marital_status_ and_living_arrangements.html.

Cohabitation Pros and Cons

Watch and learn about research on cohabitation.

▶ **LO28** Discuss various kinds of marriage.

▶ **LO29** Discuss marital satisfaction.

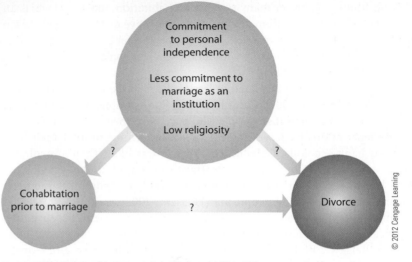

Commitment to personal independence

Less commitment to marriage as an institution

Low religiosity

Cohabitation prior to marriage

Divorce

© 2012 Cengage Learning

Figure 7.5 The Relationship Between Cohabitation and Risk of Divorce Does living together before marriage heighten the risk of divorce later on, or do factors that encourage cohabitation also heighten the risk of divorce?

cohabitants, and not necessarily cohabitation itself, are likely to be responsible for higher rates of divorce.

Households with cohabiting couples often include children (U.S. Bureau of the Census, 2010). One third of cohabiting couples who have never been married have children. And almost half of divorced people who are cohabiting with new partners have children.

monogamy Marriage between one person and one other person.

polygamy Marriage in which a person has more than one spouse and is permitted sexual access to each of them.

polygyny Marriage between one man and more than one woman (a form of *polygamy*).

polyandry Marriage between one woman and more than one man (a form of *polygamy*).

Marriage: Tying the Knot

It is a truth universally acknowledged that a single man in possession of a good fortune must be in want of a wife.
—Jane Austen, *Pride and Prejudice*

My wife and I were happy for 20 years. Then we met.
—Rodney Dangerfield

Marriage is still the most common lifestyle among adults aged 35–44 (see Table 7.7). These are young adults and adults entering into middle adulthood. They are mature enough to have completed graduate school or to have established careers. Although the overall percentage of American households made up of married couples has been decreasing, most recently from 52% in 2000 to 49% in 2010 (U.S. Bureau of the Census, 2011), more than two thirds of American men and women aged 35–44 are married.

Why Do People Get Married?

Even in this era of serial monogamy and cohabitation, people get married. Marriage meets many personal and cultural needs. For traditionalists, marriage legitimizes sexual relations. It provides an institution in which children can be supported and socialized. Marriage (theoretically) restricts sexual relations so that a man can be assured—or assume—that his wife's children are his. Unless one has signed a prenuptial agreement to the contrary, marriage permits the orderly transmission of wealth from one family to another and one generation to another.

Today, because more people believe that premarital sex is acceptable between two people who feel affectionate toward each other, the desire for sex is less likely to motivate marriage. But marriage provides a sense of security and opportunities to share feelings, experiences, and ideas with someone with whom one forms a special attachment. Most young adults agree that marriage is important for people who plan to spend the rest of their lives together (Jayson, 2008).

Broadly speaking, many people in the United States today want to get married because they believe that they will be happier. A University of Chicago poll (see Table 7.8) suggested that the majority of them are correct, even if the percentages have deteriorated since the 1970s.

Types of Marriage

Among male and female couples, we have two types of marriage: monogamy and polygamy. In **monogamy**, one person is married to one other person. In **polygamy**, a person has more than one spouse and is permitted sexual access to each of them.

Polygyny has been the most prevalent form of polygamy among the world's preliterate societies (Ford & Beach, 1951; Frayser, 1985). In polygynous societies, including some Islamic societies, men are permitted to have multiple wives. **Polyandry** is relatively rare.

**Table 7.7
Married Percentage of
U.S. Persons Aged 35–44**

Year	Males	Females
1960	88.0	87.4
1970	89.3	86.9
1980	84.2	81.4
1990	74.1	73.0
2000	69.0	71.6
2010	68.4	71.5

Source: U.S. Bureau of the Census (2011).

**Table 7.8
Percentage of U.S. Married
Persons Aged 18 and Older
Who Said Their Marriages Were
"Very Happy"**

Period	Men	Women
1973–1976	69.6	68.6
1977–1981	68.3	64.2
1982–1986	62.9	61.7
1987–1991	66.4	59.6
1993–1996	63.2	59.7
1998–2004	64.4	60.4

Source: 2010 State of Our Unions. Copyright © 2010 by the National Marriage Project at the University of Virginia. Republished by permission. http://www.virginia.edu/marriageproject/pdfs/Union_11_12_10.pdf

Arranged Marriage

In the Broadway musical *Fiddler on the Roof*, Tevye, the Jewish father of three girls of marriageable age in 1905 Russia, demands that his daughters marry Jewish men to perpetuate their family's religious and cultural traditions. Today, traditional societies such as those of India (Myers et al., 2005) and Pakistan (Zaidi & Shuraydi, 2002) frequently use arranged marriages, in which the families of the bride and groom more or less arrange for the union.

As in *Fiddler*, one of the purposes of arranged marriage ensures that the bride and groom share similar backgrounds so that they will carry on family traditions. Supporters of arranged marriage also argue that it is wiser to follow family wisdom than one's own heart, especially since the attraction couples feel is often infatuation and not a deep, abiding love. Proponents also claim a lower divorce rate for arranged marriages than for "self-arranged marriages" (but it must be noted that couples who enter arranged marriages are generally more traditional to begin with). In Hong Kong, for example, as arranged marriage declines and couples marry whom they wish, the divorce rate is increasing (Fan & Lui, 2008).

Marriage Equality and Civil Unions

In churches and in politics, the debate about homosexuality has focused recently on marriage equality—that is, whether gay men and lesbians should be allowed to get married. Nationwide, support for gay marriage is on the upswing. According to the results of nationally representative *New York Times*/CBS News polls (2009), in 2004 only a little over one fifth of respondents (22%) supported marriage equality; 33% supported civil unions, but 2 people in 5 (40%) wanted no legal recognition of gay relationships. In 2009, the percentage of people supporting marriage equality almost doubled to 42%, and another 25% supported civil unions. Only 28%, down from 40% in 2004, favored no legal recognition of unions. A Gallup Poll published in 2011 show that for the first time, a majority of Americans (53%) favored legal same-sex marriage. Forty-five percent opposed it.

© Rubberball/Veer

homogamy The practice of people getting married to people who are similar to them.

Several countries, as diverse as the Netherlands, Spain, Canada, and South Africa, and several states, including Massachusetts, Connecticut, Iowa, and New York, have extended full marriage rights to same-sex couples. Committed gay and lesbian couples who cannot legally get married may enter into civil unions, domestic partnerships, or registered partnerships in various places. These unions offer varying degrees of the benefits of marriage.

Whom Do We Marry: Are Marriages Made in Heaven or in the Neighborhood?

Although the selection of a mate is (officially) free in our society, factors such as race, social class, and religion often determine the categories of people within which we seek mates (Laumann, Mahay, et al., 2007). Young adults tend to marry others from the same area and social class. Since neighborhoods are often made up of people from a similar social class, storybook marriages like Cinderella's are the exception to the rule.

Despite fairy tales like Cinderella, we tend to marry people who are similar to us in physical appearance and attitudes. We also tend to be similar in height and weight, intelligence, even the use of alcohol and other drugs.

Young adults tend to marry people who are similar to themselves in physical attractiveness, attitudes, background, and interests (Blackwell & Lichter, 2004). More often than not, young adults are similar to their mates in height, weight, personality traits, intelligence, educational level, religion, and even in use of alcohol and tobacco (Myers, 2006; Reynolds et al., 2006). Yet more than one third of Asian Americans and Latino and Latina Americans marry outside their racial or ethnic groups, along with about 13% of African Americans and 7% of European Americans (Carey, 2005). The concept of "like marrying like" is termed **homogamy**. Research shows that marriages between people from similar backgrounds tend to be more stable (Myers, 2006), perhaps because partners are more likely to share values and attitudes (Willetts, 2006).

Most people also tend to follow *age homogamy*—to select a partner who falls in their own age range, with husbands 2 to 5 years older than wives (Buss, 1994; Michael et al., 1994). But age homogamy reflects the tendency to marry in early adulthood. Persons who marry late or who remarry tend not to select partners so close in age, because they are out in the world—rather than in school or fresh out of school—and tend to work with or otherwise meet people from different age groups.

Same Sex Marriage

Watch and learn about one couple's civil union.

▶ **LO30** Discuss parenthood.

Marital Satisfaction

The nature of romantic relationships and the satisfaction of the partners strongly affect the well-being of each member of the couple at various stages throughout adulthood (Bertoni et al., 2007). An Italian study of married couples found that the partners' confidence in their abilities to influence their relationship for the better contributed to the quality of the marriage (Bertoni et al., 2007). In turn, the quality of the marital relationship appeared to positively affect individuals' physical and psychological health. Another study found that intimacy, which is fueled by trust, honesty, and the sharing of innermost feelings, is strongly connected with marital satisfaction (Patrick et al., 2007). So is psychologically supporting one's spouse.

Satisfaction with one's career is positively correlated with marital satisfaction, and both of them are related to general life satisfaction (Perrone et al., 2007). Perhaps general tendencies toward happiness (or depression) manifest themselves in various segments of life, including vocational life and romantic relationships. Or perhaps doing very well in one arena can cast a positive glow on other parts of life.

Researchers in one study investigated the effects of infants' sleep patterns and crying on marital satisfaction in 107 first-time parent couples during the first year following birth. In general, marital satisfaction decreased as the year wore on, and the baby's crying was apparently the main source of the problem (Meijer & van den Wittenboer, 2007). Parental loss of sleep compounded the difficulties.

Satisfaction in the Relationships of Heterosexual and Homosexual Couples

Numerous researchers have studied the factors that predict satisfaction in a relationship or the deterioration and ending of a relationship. Much of this research has sought to determine whether there are differences in the factors that satisfy heterosexual and homosexual couples, and the interesting finding is that we are hardpressed to find differences. Both heterosexual and homosexual couples are more satisfied when they receive social support from their partners, when there is sharing of power in the relationship, when they fight fair, and when they perceive their partners to be committed to the relationship (Matthews et al., 2006; Twist, 2005). One difference that stands out favors the stability of homosexual couples: They tend to distribute household chores evenly and not in terms of gender-role stereotypes (Kurdek, 2005, 2006). But there are a couple of differences that favor stability in the relationships of the heterosexual couples: They are more likely to have the support of their families and less likely to be stigmatized by society at large.

Parenthood

Just as people are getting married in their later 20s in the United States today, so are they delaying parenthood into their later 20s (Arnett, 2007; Whitehead & Popenoe, 2006). Many women do not bear children until they are in their 30s, some in their 40s. But bearing children in developed nations is generally seen as something that ideally occurs in early adulthood, although a few hundred thousand teenage girls bear children in the United States each year. Becoming a parent is a major life event that requires changes in nearly every sphere of life: personal, social, and financial (Redshaw & van den Akker, 2007). In fact, many individuals and couples in contemporary developed nations no longer think of parenthood as a necessary part of marriage or a relationship (Doherty et al., 2007).

Why do people have children? Reflect on the fact that reliable birth-control methods have separated sex acts from reproduction. Except for women living under the most "traditional" circumstances or for couples who accidentally get pregnant, becoming pregnant is a choice. In developed nations, most couples report that they choose to have children for personal happiness or well-being (Dyer, 2007). In more traditional societies people report having children to strengthen marital bonds, provide social security, assist with labor (as in having more farmhands), provide social status, maintain the family name and lineage, secure property rights and inheritance, and in some places, improve the odds of—yes—reincarnation (Dyer, 2007). Of these reasons, having children to care for one in one's old age ("social security") looms large. In the United States, the federal Social Security program helps support older people, but how many middle-aged people (typically daughters) are running in one direction to rear their children and in another to provide emotional and other support for elderly parents and other relatives?

It is actually unlikely that having a child will save a marriage. Numerous studies have shown that with the added stress of caring for a new baby, the quality of a couple's adjustment often declines significantly throughout the year following delivery (e.g., E. Lawrence et al., 2007; Simonelli, et al., 2007).

Happy to be Child-Free

Watch and learn why some married couples chose to be childless.

Deciding on How Many Children

What are the factors in deciding how many children to have? Watch and learn.

Parenthood and Role Overload

Some research has focused on the effects of newborns' entering the lives of working-class families, especially when the mother must return to work shortly after the birth (e.g., Perry-Jenkins et al., 2007). In such cases, the parents are frequently depressed, and conflict often emerges. Although fathers in such cases may give lip service to helping with the baby and do a few things to help out here and there, the mother is almost always the primary caregiver (G. Wall & Arnold, 2007) and thus encounters role overload. That is, the mother suffers from playing roles as both primary caregiver and, in our demanding economy, one of two primary breadwinners.

Yet a longitudinal study of 45 couples expecting their first child showed that family life does not have to be this stressful (J. P. McHale & Rotman, 2007). The couples were assessed during pregnancy and from infancy through toddlerhood—at 3, 12, and 30 months after birth. When the parents generally agreed on their beliefs about parenting, and who should do what, their postnatal adjustment was largely solid and remained stable. In other words, if each member of the couple believed they should share caregiving equally and they lived up to it, their adjustment was good. If they believed that one parent should be primarily responsible for caregiving and abided by that scenario, adjustment was also good. Consistency between their expressed beliefs and their behavior predicted adjustment.

Parenthood in Dual-Earner Families

The financial realities of contemporary life, along with the women's movement, have made women in the workplace the norm in American society. Thus young married or cohabiting adults with children more often than not are dual-earner families.

European and American studies have found that the mothers in dual-earner families encounter more stress than the fathers do (Schneewind & Kupsch, 2007; A. Wall, 2007). Evidence of a powerful sex difference in dual-earner families is also found in an analysis of longitudinal survey data on 884 dual-earner couples (Chesley & Moen, 2006). Caring for children was connected with declines in well-being for dual-earner women, but, ironically, with increases in well-being for dual-earner men. Perhaps the men were relieved of much stress by the second income. Dual-earner women with flexible work schedules encountered less stress than women with fixed schedules, apparently because they were more capable of managing their role overload.

What happens in the workplace doesn't necessarily stay in the workplace. A study of 113 dual-earner couples found that problems in the workplace contributed to tension in the couples, health problems, and dissatisfaction with the relationship (R. A. Matthews et al., 2006).

Sometimes a dual-worker couple decides that one of them needs to spend more time in the home for the benefit of the children. Because of problems balancing work and family life, it is usually the mother and not the father who cuts back on work or drops out of the workforce altogether (A. Wall, 2007). Because of experience with dual-earner families around them, a sample of 194 adolescents from dual-earner families generally expected that they (if they were female) or their partners (if they were male) would be the ones to cut back or quit work in the future, at least temporarily, if the couple had a child (Weinshenker, 2006). The responses showed little insight into the problems raised by interrupting careers. On the other hand, the fact that their mothers work did encourage the adolescents—female and male—to say they believed in gender egalitarianism.

Single Parenthood

The public image of the single parent is probably quite distorted. In many ways, single parents have a great deal in common with cohabiting or married parents.

There are nearly 17 million single parents in the United States today, and they are rearing about 25 million children—more than 1 child in 4 (Grall, 2009). Five of six single parents are mothers, and one of six is a father. Nearly half are separated or divorced, and about one third have never been married. Four single mothers out of five are in the workforce, and half of them work full time. Ninety percent of single fathers also work. Only 1 single mother in 4 or 5 receives public assistance, such as Medicaid or food stamps.

Single parents must usually survive on one income. When it comes down to getting to work and getting the children to school, they learn quickly that if something needs to get done, they have to do it for themselves. Children in single-parent families tend to learn to assume responsibilities earlier than children in two-parent families. The upside is that they develop maturity more quickly.

Motherhood: Finding the Time

Watch women discuss the challenges and rewards of being a mother.

▶ **L031** Discuss divorce and its repercussions.

Divorce: Breaking Bonds

Whenever I date a guy, I think, is this the man I want my children to spend their weekends with?

—Rita Rudner

Between 40% and 50% of the marriages in the United States end in divorce (U.S. Bureau of the Census, 2011). The divorce rate in the United States rose steadily through much of the twentieth century before leveling off in the 1980s. Divorced women outnumber divorced men, in part because men are more likely to remarry.

Why the increase in divorce? Until the mid-1960s, adultery was the only legal grounds for divorce in most states. But no-fault divorce laws have been enacted in nearly every state, allowing a divorce to be granted without a finding of marital misconduct. The increased economic independence of women has also contributed to the divorce rate. More women today have the economic means of breaking away from a troubled marriage. Also, today more people consider marriage an alterable condition than in prior generations.

Americans today also want more from marriage than did their grandparents. They expect marriage to be personally fulfilling as well as an institution for family life and rearing children. The most common reasons given for a divorce today are problems in communication and a lack of understanding. Key complaints include a husband's criticism, defensiveness, contempt, and stonewalling—not lack of financial support (Carrère et al., 2000; Gottman et al., 1998).

The Cost of Divorce

Divorce is usually connected with financial and emotional problems. When a household splits, the resources often cannot maintain the earlier standard of living for each partner. Divorce hits women in the pocketbook harder than men. According to a Population Reference Bureau report, a woman's household income drops by about 24% (Bianchi & Spain, 1997). A man's declines by about 6%. Women who have not pursued a career may have to struggle to compete with younger, more experienced workers. Divorced mothers often face the combined stress of the sole responsibility for child rearing and the need to increase their incomes. Divorced fathers may find it difficult to pay alimony and child support while establishing a new lifestyle.

Divorce can also prompt feelings of failure as a spouse and parent, loneliness and uncertainty about the future, and depression. Married people appear to be better able to cope with the stresses and strains of life, perhaps because they can lend each other emotional support. Divorced and separated people have the highest rates of physical and mental illness (Carrère et al., 2000; F. O. Lorenz et al., 2006). They also have high rates of suicide (Donald et al., 2006; Lorant et al., 2005). As noted in Chapter 5, children are often the biggest losers when parents get a divorce, yet chronic marital conflict is also connected with psychological distress in children (Amato & Cheadle, 2008). Researchers attribute children's problems after divorce not only to the

Divorced people, like other singles, go on dates. Some have been "burned" by a past relationship and might not be ready to "hook up" quickly. They appreciate all the trappings of a real date—dinner, getting dressed up, a movie, and flowers.

divorce itself but also to a consequent decline in the quality of parenting. Children's adjustment is enhanced when both parents maintain parenting responsibilities and set aside their differences long enough to agree on child-rearing practices (Hetherington, 2006a). Children of divorce also benefit when their parents avoid saying negative things about each other in the children's presence (Amato & Cheadle, 2008; Hetherington, 2006a).

Despite the difficulties in adjustment, most divorced people eventually bounce back. Most remarry. Indeed, divorce may permit personal growth and renewal and the opportunity to take stock of oneself and establish a new, more rewarding life.

As we see in the next chapter, middle adulthood presents challenges that continue from early adulthood, as well as a number of new challenges. Issues of parenting continue, and sometimes they move in two directions—toward children and toward one's own parents.

Divorce Ceremonies

Watch and learn about the divorce ceremony, a surprising new trend in Japan.

Check Your Learning Quiz 7.4

Go to **login.cengagebrain.com** and take the online quiz.

GO to your Psychology CourseMate at login.cengagebrain.com and take the Chapter Post-Test to see which Learning Objectives you've mastered and which need more review. Use the chapter review guide below and the online activities—including flashcards to review key terms—to measure your learning.

Module		Learning Objectives
7.1 Physical Development: Early Adulthood 408		
Reaching the Zenith	LO1	Describe physical development during early adulthood.
Health and Fitness	LO2	Discuss the leading causes of death in early adulthood.
	LO3	Discuss weight and weight control in early adulthood.
	LO4	Discuss exercise in early adulthood.
Substance Abuse and Dependence	LO5	Discuss substance abuse and dependence.
Stress and Health	LO6	Discuss the effects of stress on health.
Sexuality	LO7	Discuss sexual activity during early adulthood.
	LO8	Discuss sexual orientation.
	LO9	Discuss sexually transmitted infections.
	LO10	Discuss menstrual problems.
	LO11	Discuss sexual coercion.
7.2 Cognitive Development: Early Adulthood 426		
Cognition and the Sociocultural Setting	LO12	Explain how social and scientific developments affect cognitive development.
Perry's Theory of Epistemic Cognition	LO13	Explain how ideas about how we know what we know change in early adulthood.
	LO14	Define *dualistic thinking* and *relativistic thinking*.
Labouvie-Vief's Theory of Pragmatic Thought	LO15	Explain how thinking becomes more pragmatic in early adulthood.
Postformal Thinking	LO16	Explain what is meant by *postformal thinking*.
College and Cognitive Development	LO17	Explain how college can contribute to cognitive development.

Online Activities

Key Terms	Video	Animation	Reading	Assessment
	Ringtones and the Cochlea			Check Your Learning Quiz 7.1
Adaptive thermogenesis			The Skinny on Weight Control Body Mass Index Chart	
Substance abuse, substance dependence, tolerance, abstinence syndrome, hallucinogenic	Substance Abuse Disorder Nicotine Addiction		Alcohol Dependent?	
	Women and Stress		Preventing and Coping with Stress	
Dysmenorrhea, prostaglandins, amenorrhea, premenstrual syndrome (PMS), premenstrual dysphoric disorder (PMDD), sexual harassment	HPV Myths		Preventing STIs Menstrual Discomfort Rape Myths Sexual Harrassment	
Crystallized intelligence, fluid intelligence				Check Your Learning Quiz 7.2
Epistemic cognition, dualistic thinking, relativistic thinking		Cognitive Changes in Early Adulthood		
Pragmatic thought, cognitive–affective complexity	Decision Making			

Measure ∧ Your Learning

Online Activities

Key Terms	Video	Animation	Reading	Assessment
Individuation				Check Your Learning Quiz 7.3
Intimacy versus isolation				
Life structure, the dream		Erikson and Levinson's Theories about Early Adulthood		
Attraction–similarity hypothesis, reciprocity, romantic love	Dancing and Attraction The Rules of Attraction			
	Social Exclusion			
Serial monogamy, celibacy	Commitment Phobia			Check Your Learning Quiz 7.4
Cohabitation	Cohabitation Pros and Cons			
Monogamy, polygamy, polygyny, polyandry, homogamy	Same Sex Marriage			
	Happy to Be Child-Free Deciding on How Many Children Motherhood: Finding Time			
	Divorce Ceremonies			

Middle Adulthood

8

PNC/Brand X Pictures/Jupiterimages

1 **GO** to your **Psychology CourseMate** at **login.cengagebrain.com** and take the **Chapter Pre-Test** to introduce yourself to this chapter's topics and see what you may already know.

2 **READ** the **Learning Objectives** (LOs, in the left sidebars) and begin the chapter.

3 **COMPLETE** the **Online Activities** (in the right sidebars) *as you read each module.* Activities include **videos, animations, readings,** and **quizzes.**

4 **CHECK Your Learning** by going online to take the quiz at the end of each module and review material as necessary.

5 **MEASURE Your Learning** after reading the chapter by taking the online **Chapter Post-Test.** Use the chapter review guide at the end of the chapter as needed.

WATCH for these **Online Activities** icons as you read:

Video

Animation

Reading

Assessment

Online Activities

These online activities are essential to mastering this chapter. Go to login.cengagebrain.com:

 Videos Watch the following videos:

- Atherosclerosis
- Erectile Dysfunction
- A Drug to Increase Sexual Desire in Women
- Male Menopause?
- The Brain and Memory
- Midlife Memory Declines
- Women Over 40 with Eating Disorders
- Failure to Launch
- Work and Flextime
- Grandfamilies
- The Sandwich Generation: Middle-Aged Adults Caring for Their Aging Parents

 Animations Interact with and visualize important processes, timelines, and concepts:

- Cognitive Changes in Middle Age
- Developmental Tasks of Middle Age
- The Big Five: The Five-Factor Model of Personality

 Readings Delve deeper into key content:

- Aging, Gender, and Ethnicity
- Who Is Having a (Midlife) Crisis?
- Parent-Child Relationships
- Adult Children and Aging Parents

 Assessment Measure your mastery:

- Chapter Pre-Test
- Check Your Learning Quizzes
- Chapter Post-Test

▶ **LO1** Describe physical development in middle adulthood.

Did you know that—

- Many people in the United States do not profit from having the best health care in the world?
- Cancer is the leading cause of death in middle adulthood?
- A man's lifetime risk for contracting cancer is 1 in 2, and a woman's is 1 in 3?
- Fatty deposits may be building up in your arteries even though you don't feel them?
- Stress impairs the functioning of the immune system?
- Beyond early adulthood, the frequency of sex declines with age?
- Sexual dysfunctions are quite common?

▼

Back in 1992, when the American Board of Family Practice asked 1,200 Americans when middle age begins, 46% said it occurred when you realize you don't know who the new music groups are (Beck, 1992). If they had been polled today, perhaps they would have said that middle age begins when you don't know who won *American Idol* or *Dancing With the Stars*. In chrono-logical terms, developmentalists con-sider **middle adulthood** to span the years from 40 to 65, with 60–65 as a transition period to late adulthood. But we might also note that some develop-mentalists are beginning to assert that we are truly becoming only as old as we feel, that 65 is the new 55, and so on.

Some theorists view middle age as a time of peak performance, and others have portrayed it as a time of crisis or decline (Lachman, 2004). Physically speaking, we peak in early adulthood, but those who eat right and exercise may undergo only a gradual and rela-

In middle adulthood, many of us become grandparents.

middle adulthood The stage of adulthood between early adulthood and late adulthood, beginning at 40–45 and ending at 60–65.

interindividual variability The fact that people do not age in the same way or at the same rate.

presbyopia Loss of elasticity in the lens, which makes it harder to focus on nearby objects.

tively minor physical decline in middle adulthood. As people age, they become more vulnerable to a variety of illnesses, but they also become less prone to irresponsible behavior that may result in injury or death. On the other hand, some sensory and sexual changes might well become major issues. Cognitively speaking, we are at our peak for many intellectual functions in middle adulthood, but there may be some loss of processing speed and some lapses in memory. Even so, these are often counterbalanced by expertise.

Physical Development

No two people age in the same way or at the same rate. This phenomenon is called **interindividual variability**. But whatever individual differences may exist, physiological aging is defined by changes in the body's integumentary system (the skin, hair, and nails), senses, reaction time, and lung capacity. These changes may well be unavoidable. Other changes that often occur during middle adulthood—in metabolism, muscle mass, strength, bone density, aerobic capacity, blood-sugar tolerance, and ability to regulate body temperature—may be moderated and sometimes reversed through exercise and diet.

Skin and Hair

Hair usually begins to gray in middle adulthood as the production of *melanin*, the pigment responsible for hair color, decreases. Hair loss also accelerates with aging, especially in men. Much of the wrinkling associated with aging is actually caused by exposure to ultraviolet rays.

Beginning gradually in early adulthood, the body produces fewer proteins that give the skin its elasticity. The body also produces fewer *keratinocytes*—the cells in the outer layer of the skin that are regularly shed and renewed—leaving the skin dryer and more brittle.

Sensory Functioning

Normal age-related changes in vision begin to appear by the mid-30s and assert themselves as significant problems in middle adulthood. **Presbyopia** (Latin for "old vision") refers to loss of elasticity in the lens, which makes it harder to focus on, or accommodate to, nearby objects or fine print. Cataracts, glaucoma, and hearing loss are other sensory problems associated with late adulthood.

Aging, Gender, and Ethnicity

Read about the gender and ethnic differences in aging and life expantancy.

Reaction Time

Reaction time—the amount of time it takes to respond to a stimulus—increases with age, mainly because of changes in the nervous system. Starting at around age 25, we begin to lose neurons, which are responsible for sensing signals such as sights and sounds, and coordinating muscular responses to them. It may take longer to respond to changes in traffic lights and to click the keys required to read text messages.

Lung Capacity

Lung tissue stiffens with age, diminishing its capacity to expand, such that breathing capacity may decline by half between early and late adulthood. Regular exercise can offset much of this loss, and beginning to exercise regularly in middle adulthood can expand breathing capacity beyond what it was earlier in life.

In middle adulthood, the lenses of the eyes become stiffer, making it more difficult to focus on small print. Many people begin to use reading glasses during this stage of life.

Diane Macdonald/Getty Images

Lean-Body Mass and Body Fat

Beginning at age 20, we lose nearly 7 pounds of lean-body mass (which includes muscle) with each decade. The rate of loss accelerates after the age of 45. Fat replaces lean-body mass; consequently, the average person's body mass index rises, meaning that there may be weight gain without dietary changes. And there may be loss of strength, as noted later.

Muscle Strength

Loss of muscle lessens strength. However, the change is gradual, and in middle adulthood, exercise can readily compensate by increasing the size of remaining muscle cells. Exercise will not regain the prowess of the athlete in early adulthood, but it will contribute to vigor, health, and a desirable body shape.

Metabolism

Metabolism is the rate at which the body processes or "burns" food to produce energy. The resting metabolic rate—also called the *basal metabolic rate*—declines as we age. Fatty tissue burns fewer calories than muscle, and the decline in basal metabolic rate is largely attributable to the loss of muscle tissue and the corresponding increase in fatty tissue. Since we require fewer calories to maintain our weight as we age, middle-aged people (and older adults) are likely to gain weight if they eat as much as they did as young adults.

Bone Density

Bone, which consists largely of calcium, begins to lose density and strength at around the age of 40. As bones lose density, they become more brittle and prone to fracture. Bones in the spine, hip, thigh (femur), and forearm are the most prone to density loss as we age. We discuss osteoporosis, a disorder affecting the strength of bones, in Chapter 9.

Comstock Images/Jupiter Images

▶ **LO2** Discuss the major health concerns of middle adulthood.

Aerobic Capacity

As we age, the cardiovascular system becomes less efficient. Heart and lung muscles shrink. Aerobic capacity declines as less oxygen is taken into the lungs and the heart pumps less blood. The maximum heart rate declines, but exercise expands aerobic capacity at *any* age.

Blood-Sugar Tolerance

Blood sugar, or glucose, is the basic fuel and energy source for cells. The energy from glucose supports cell activities and maintains body temperature. Glucose circulates in the bloodstream and enters cells with the help of insulin, a hormone secreted by the pancreas.

As we age, the tissues in our body become less capable of taking up glucose from the bloodstream. Body tissues lose their sensitivity to insulin; the pancreas must thus produce more of it to achieve the same effect. Therefore, blood sugar levels rise, increasing the risk of adult-onset diabetes. Eating cereal with a large amount of added sugar might have a minimal effect on glucose levels in childhood, but it can become problematic in middle age.

Health

The health of people aged 40–65 in developed nations such as ours is better than it has ever been. Nearly everyone has been vaccinated for preventable diseases. Many, perhaps the majority, practice preventive health care. Once people reach 40, they are advised to have annual physical checkups. More is known today about curing or treating illnesses than has ever been known.

Yet there are racial, ethnic, and gender differences in the incidence and treatment of various diseases. People from certain groups appear to be more likely to develop certain chronic conditions such as hypertension and specific types of cancer. The statement that people in the United States profit from having the best health care in the world is too broad to be considered true. The "best" health care has not reached everyone. Some socioeconomic groups and racial and ethnic minority groups lack access to health care. Moreover, men, more so than women, often resist seeking health care when symptoms arise.

As we consider the health of people in middle adulthood, we focus on many things that can go wrong. But for most of us, things go quite right if we get regular medical checkups, pay attention to our diets, get some exercise, avoid smoking, drink in moderation if at all, regulate stress, and—we hope—have some supportive relationships.

Leading Causes of Death

In early adulthood, the three leading causes of death screamed out their preventability: accidents, homicide, and suicide. In middle adulthood (see Table 8.1), diseases come to the fore. Cancer and heart disease are numbers 1 and 2, and accidents now show up in third place. Cancer and heart disease are also preventable to some degree, of course. According to the American Cancer Society (2007), people should start getting screened for prostate cancer (men around age 50), breast cancer (women around age 40), and cancer of the colon and rectum (men and women around age 50). Most men should have digital rectal exams (in which the doctor uses a gloved finger to feel the prostate gland) and blood

Table 8.1
Leading Causes of Death in Middle Adulthood

	45–54	55–64
Cancer	119.0	333.4
Heart disease	90.2	218.8
Accidents	40.7	33.2
Chronic liver disease	18.0	22.6
Suicide	16.6	13.8
Stroke and other cerebrovascular disease	14.9	34.3
Diabetes	13.4	37.1
Chronic respiratory disease	8.4	40.4
Blood poisoning	5.4	12.9
Kidney disease	5.0	13.6
Homicide	4.8	3.0
Influenza and pneumonia	4.6	10.8

Note: Annual deaths per 100,000 people.
Source: Arialdi M. Minino, Melanie P. Heron, Sherry L. Murphy, & Kenneth D. Kochanek. (2007, October 10). Deaths: Final data for 2004. National vital statistics reports, 55(19). Adapted from Table 9, pp. 27–29, http://www.cdc.gov/nchs/data/nvsr/nvsr55/nvsr55_19.pdf.

tests for prostate-specific antigen at 50. However, African American men are at greater risk of developing prostate cancer and are advised to start screening at age 45. The society recommends that women begin having mammograms to screen for breast cancer at age 40. A baseline electrocardiogram, which is one measure of the health of the heart, is usually done around the age of 50 and repeated every 2 or 3 years.

Cancer

Although heart disease is the nation's number one cause of death, cancer is the overall leading cause of death in middle adulthood, and cancer eventually causes nearly 1 of every 4 deaths in the United States (see Table 8.2). Table 8.2 does *not* reveal the fact that women have a sharply increased incidence of death due to heart disease following menopause. In many cases, cancer can be controlled or cured, especially when detected early.

Table 8.2
Annual Deaths Due to Cancer and Heart Disease in Middle Adulthood and Late Adulthood, per 100,000 People

Cause	45–54	55–64	65–74	75–84	85 and over
Cancer	119.0	333.4	755.1	1,280.4	1,653.3
Heart disease	90.2	218.8	541.6	1,506.3	4,895.9

Source: Arialdi M. Minino, Melanie P. Heron, Sherry L. Murphy, & Kenneth D. Kochanek. (2007, October 10). Deaths: Final data for 2004. National vital statistics reports, 55(19). Adapted from Table 9, pp. 27–29, http://www.cdc.gov/nchs/data/nvsr/nvsr55/nvsr55_19.pdf.

Cancer is a chronic, noncommunicable disease characterized by uncontrolled growth of cells, forming masses of excess tissue called *tumors*. Tumors can be *benign* (noncancerous) or *malignant* (cancerous). Benign tumors do not spread and rarely pose a threat to life. Malignant tumors invade and destroy surrounding tissue. Cancerous cells in malignant tumors may also break away from the primary tumor and travel through the bloodstream or lymphatic system to form new tumors, called **metastases**, elsewhere in the body. Metastases damage vital body organs and systems and in many cases lead to death. The incidence of cancer increases dramatically with age (see Table 8.2). Table 8.3 shows the lifetime risk of being diagnosed with various kinds of cancer.

Cancer begins when a cell's DNA, its genetic material, changes such that the cell divides indefinitely. The change is triggered by mutations in the DNA, which can be caused by internal or external factors. Internal factors include heredity, problems in the immune system, and hormonal factors. External agents are called carcinogens and include some viruses, chemical compounds in tobacco and elsewhere, and ultraviolet solar radiation.

metastasis The development of malignant or cancerous cells in parts of the body other than where they originated.

About 1 man in 2 and 1 woman in 3 in the United States will eventually develop cancer if they live long enough (Fay, 2004). The incidence of death from cancer almost triples between ages 55 and 64, as compared with ages 45 to 54 (see Table 8.2).

Although cancer cuts across all racial and ethnic groups, African Americans have higher than average colorectal cancer incidence and death rates (Centers for Disease Control and Prevention, 2011). African Americans have twice the average death rate from prostate cancer. The incidence of cervical cancer in Latina American women is higher than that in other demographic groups. Only 52% of American Indian and Alaska Native women age 40 years and over have had a recent mammogram. American Indian and Alaska Natives have the poorest survival rate from cancer.

Much of the difference in mortality rates can be attributed to lack of early detection and treatment (Centers for Disease Control and Prevention, 2011). One reason for late diagnosis is that many minority groups lack health insurance or access to health-care facilities. Members of minority groups may also avoid screening by the health-care system, which they see as impersonal, insensitive, and racist.

Though there are many causes of cancer (see Table 8.3) and risk factors vary among population groups, 2 out of 3 cancer deaths in the United States are the result

Table 8.3
Lifetime Risk of Being Diagnosed with Cancer

Type	Men	Women
All	1 in 2	1 in 3
Prostate	1 in 6	—
Breast	1 in 909	1 in 7
Lung and bronchus	1 in 13	1 in 18
Colon/rectum	1 in 17	1 in 18
Melanoma	1 in 53	1 in 78
Urinary bladder	1 in 28	1 in 88
Non-Hodgkin's lymphoma	1 in 46	1 in 56
Leukemia	1 in 68	1 in 96
Kidney and renal pelvis	1 in 68	1 in 114
Cervix	—	1 in 125
Ovary	—	1 in 58
Pancreas	1 in 80	1 in 80
Oral cavity and pharynx	1 in 71	1 in 147

Source: Adapted from Fay, M. P. (2004). Estimating Age-Conditional Probability of Developing Cancer Using a Piecewise Mid-Age Joinpoint Model to the Rates. Statistical Research and Applications Branch, NCI, Technical Report # 2003-03, 2004.

of two controllable factors: smoking and diet (Willett, 2005). Cigarette smoking causes 87% of lung-cancer deaths in the United States and is responsible for most cancers of the mouth, larynx, pharynx, esophagus, and bladder. Secondhand smoking also accounts for several thousand cancer deaths per year. Diet may account for about 30% of all cancers in Western cultures. However, many cases of cancer also involve family history, or heredity (Kauff & Offit, 2007).

Traditional methods for treating cancer are surgery (surgical removal of cancerous tissue), radiation (high-dose X-rays or other sources of high-energy radiation to kill cancerous cells and shrink tumors), chemotherapy (drugs that kill cancer cells or shrink tumors), and hormonal therapy (hormones that stop tumor growth). These methods have their limitations. Anticancer drugs and radiation kill healthy tissue as well as malignant tissue. They also have side effects such as nausea, vomiting, loss of appetite, loss of hair, and weakening of the immune system.

Heart Disease

Heart disease kills 28% of Americans, whereas cancer kills 24% (Miniño et al., 2007). In heart disease, the flow of blood to the heart is insufficient to supply the heart with the oxygen it needs. Heart disease most commonly results from **arteriosclerosis** or *hardening of the arteries*, which impairs circulation and increases the risk of a blood clot (thrombus). The most common form of arteriosclerosis is **atherosclerosis**—the buildup of fatty deposits called *plaque* in the lining of arteries (see Figure 8.1). Plaque results in the heart's receiving insufficient blood and can cause a heart attack.

The risk factors for heart disease are shown in Figure 8.2. One's age, race or ethnicity, and gender also affect the likelihood of incurring heart disease and, of

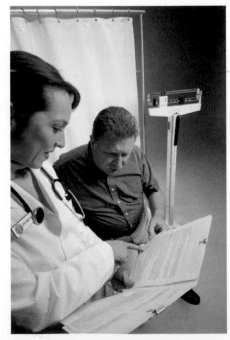

Creatas/Jupiterimages

arteriosclerosis Hardening of the arteries.

atherosclerosis The buildup of fatty deposits (plaque) on the lining of arteries.

leukocyte White blood cell.

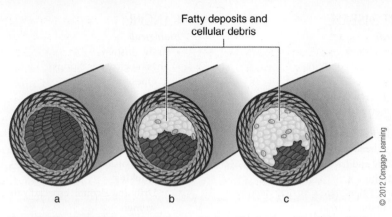

Fatty deposits and cellular debris

© 2012 Cengage Learning

Figure 8.1 Atherosclerosis. In atherosclerosis, (a) the walls of open arteries receive (b) fatty deposits called plaque. (c) As arteries narrow, blood flow becomes constricted, setting the stage for heart attacks or strokes.

course, are beyond one's control. However, people can exert control over many factors shown in Figure 8.2. They can stop smoking; they can exercise; they can eat wisely; and they can go for regular medical checkups.

The Immune System

The immune system is the body's defense against infections and some other sources of disease. It combats disease in several ways. One is the production of white blood cells, which engulf and kill pathogens such as bacteria, fungi, and viruses, and worn-out and cancerous body cells. The technical term for white blood cells is **leukocytes**.

Leukocytes recognize foreign substances by their shapes. The foreign substances are termed *antigens* because the body reacts to them by generating specialized proteins, or *antibodies*. Antibodies attach themselves to the foreign substances, deactivating them and marking them for destruction. The immune system "remembers" how to battle antigens by maintaining their antibodies in the bloodstream, often for years.

Inflammation is another function of the immune system. When injury occurs, blood vessels in the area first contract (to stem bleeding) and then dilate. Dilation

Atherosclerosis

Watch and learn more about the causes of artery hardening, including current research on prevention.

▶**LO3** Discuss the functioning of the immune system.

▶**LO4** Discuss sexuality in middle adulthood.

HEART DISEASE

Biological:
- Family history
- Physiological conditions:
    Obesity
    High serum cholesterol
    Hypertension

Psychological (personality and behavior):
- Type A behavior
- Hostility and holding in feelings of anger
- Job strain
- Chronic fatigue, stress, anxiety, depression, and emotional strain
- Patterns of consumption:
    Heavy drinking (but a drink a day may be helpful with heart disease)
    Smoking
    Overeating
- Sudden stressors
- Physical inactivity

Sociocultural:
- African Americans are more prone to hypertension and heart disease than European Americans are.
- Access to health care
- Timing of diagnosis and treatment

CANCER

Biological:
- Family history
- Physiological conditions:
    Obesity

Psychological (personality and behavior):
- Patterns of consumption:
    Smoking
    Drinking alcohol, especially in women
    Eating animal fats
    Sunbathing (skin cancer)
    Prolonged depression
    Prolonged stress may increase vulnerability to cancer by depressing activity of the immune system.

Sociocultural:
- Socioeconomic status
- Access to health care
- Timing of diagnosis and treatment
- Higher death rates are found in nations with higher rates of fat intake.

Figure 8.2 Factors in Heart Disease and Cancer

increases the flow of blood, cells, and natural chemicals to the damaged area, causing redness, swelling, and warmth. The increased blood supply floods the region with white blood cells to combat invading microscopic life forms such as bacteria, which otherwise might use the local damage as a port of entry into the body.

John Lund/Heather Hryciw/JupiterImages

Stress and the Immune System

Stress suppresses the immune system, as measured by the presence of substances in the blood that make up the immune system (Arranz et al., 2007; Thornton et al., 2007). Stress thus leaves us more vulnerable to infections such as the common cold (Barnard et al., 2005; S. Cohen, 2003).

The stress hormones connected with anger—steroids, epinephrine, and norepinephrine—can constrict the blood vessels to the heart, leading to a heart attack in people who are vulnerable (Monat et al., 2007). The stress of chronic hostility and anger is connected with higher cholesterol levels and a greater risk of heart disease (Richards et al., 2000).

Sexuality

Most people in middle adulthood lead rich sex lives (Duplassie & Daniluk, 2007; Vares et al., 2007). Table 8.4 compares the frequency of sex in early adulthood with that in middle adulthood. Generally, the frequency of sexual activity tends to decline in middle adulthood (Michael et al., 1994), but the decline is gradual. Note that a significant percentage of 50- to 59-year-old women become sexually inactive. This drop-off may in part reflect lack of opportunity. Women in this age group are increasingly likely to be widowed, and as divorced women grow older, they are also increasingly less likely to remarry.

Erectile Dysfunction

Is there a connection between depression in men and erectile dysfunction? Watch and learn about one man's case.

Viagra for Women?

Watch and learn about an experimental drug that increases sexual desire in women.

Table 8.4
Frequency of Sex in the Past 12 Months According to Age (%)

	Not at All	A Few Times per Year	A Few Times per Month	2 or 3 Times per Week	4 or More Times per Week
Men					
25–29	7	15	31	36	11
30–39	8	15	37	33	6
40–49	9	18	40	27	6
50–59	11	22	43	20	3
Women					
25–29	5	10	38	37	10
30–39	9	16	36	33	6
40–49	15	16	44	20	5
50–59	30	22	35	12	2

Note: Percentages for 18- to 24-year-olds are excluded because they are likely to reflect sexual opportunity as well as sexual interest and biological factors.
From SEX IN AMERICA by Robert T. Michael, John H. Gagnon, Edward O. Laumann, and Gina Kolata. Copyright © 1994 by Robert T. Michael, John H. Gagnon, Edward O. Laumann, and Gina Kolata. Reproduced by permission of Little, Brown and Company; Brockman, Inc., and Little, Brown Book Group.

menopause The cessation of menstruation.

perimenopause The beginning of menopause, usually characterized by 3–11 months of amenorrhea or irregular periods.

climacteric The gradual decline in reproductive capacity of the ovaries, generally lasting about 15 years.

In the latter part of middle adulthood, the years of 57 to 64, nearly three quarters of adults remain sexually active (Lindau et al., 2007), but sexual problems are often working their way into relationships. The most common problems among women are lack of sexual desire and difficulty becoming sexually aroused (I. Goldstein et al., 2006; Lindau et al., 2007). The most common problem among men is erectile dysfunction (Johannes et al., 2000).

But it is misleading to focus on the negative. Even women in middle adulthood whose partners use Viagra to obtain erections generally report heightened sexual satisfaction as a result and often have an increase in sexual desire (Vares et al., 2007).

Many middle-aged women who have chosen to remain single also report satisfying sex lives (A. J. Bridges, 2007).

Menopause, Perimenopause, and the Climacteric

Menopause, or the "change of life," is the cessation of menstruation. Menopause is a normal process that most commonly occurs between the ages of 46 and 50 and lasts for about 2 years. **Perimenopause** refers to the beginning of menopause and is usually characterized by 3–11 months of amenorrhea (lack of menstruation) or irregular periods.

© Paul Burns/Corbis

Menopause is a specific event in a longer-term process known as the **climacteric** ("critical period"), which is the gradual decline in the reproductive capacity of the ovaries due to a decline in production of estrogen. The climacteric generally lasts about 15 years, from about 45 to 60. After 35 or so, the menstrual cycles of many women shorten, from an average of 28 days to 25 days at age 40 and 23 days by the mid-40s. By the end of her 40s, a woman's cycles may become erratic, with some periods shortened and others missed.

The estrogen deficit may lead to unpleasant perimenopausal sensations, such as night sweats and hot flashes (suddenly feeling hot) and hot flushes (suddenly reddened skin). Hot flashes and flushes may alternate with cold sweats, in which a woman feels suddenly cold and clammy. All of these sensations reflect *vasomotor instability*, disruptions in the body mechanisms that dilate or constrict the blood vessels to maintain an even body temperature. Additional signs of estrogen deficiency include dizziness, headaches, joint pain, tingling in the hands or feet, burning or itchy skin, and heart palpitations. The skin usually becomes drier. There is some loss of breast tissue and decreased vaginal lubrication during sexual arousal. However, menopause does not signal an end to women's sexual appetite. Some women actually feel liberated because of the separation of sex from reproduction.

Male Menopause?

Do men experience a menopause-like condition in middle adulthood?

Long-term estrogen deficiency has been linked to brittleness and porosity of the bones—osteoporosis. Osteoporosis can be handicapping, even life threatening. The brittleness of the bones increases the risk of serious fractures, especially of the hip, which many older women never recover from (Marwick, 2000). Estrogen deficiency also can impair cognitive functioning and feelings of psychological well-being (J. L. Ross et al., 2000; Yaffe et al., 2000).

Hormone Replacement Therapy

Some women with severe physical symptoms due to menopause have been helped by hormone replacement therapy (HRT), which typically consists of synthetic estrogen and progesterone. HRT may reduce the hot flushes and other symptoms brought about by hormonal deficiencies (den Tonkelaar & Oddens, 2000). Estrogen replacement also lowers the risks of osteoporosis (Grady, 2003a, 2003b) and colon cancer (Solomon & Dluhy, 2003).

Yet HRT is controversial. A Women's Health Initiative study of some 16,600 postmenopausal women aged 50–79 found that exposure to a combination of estrogen and progestin appeared to significantly increase the risk of breast cancer, strokes, and blood clots (Chlebowski et al., 2003).

Because of the Chlebowski study and studies with similar findings, the number of women using HRT has dropped significantly over the past few years (Rabin, 2007), and many women are considering alternatives. Breast-cancer specialist Larry Norton (cited in Duenwald, 2002) noted that progestin alone prevents or lessens hot flashes in about 70% of women. Selective serotonin reuptake inhibitors are also of help (Stearns et al., 2003).

Gender Differences in Sex Hormones and Fertility

For women, menopause is a time of relatively distinct age-related declines in sex hormones and fertility. In men, the decline in the production of male sex hormones and fertility is more gradual (Tan & Culberson, 2003). It is therefore not surprising to find a man in his 70s or older fathering a child. However, many men in their 50s experience problems in achieving and maintaining erections (Conrad, 2007), which may reflect circulatory problems, hormone deficiencies, or other factors (Charlton, 2004).

To help with these symptoms, physicians in the United States write more than one million prescriptions for testosterone and related drugs each year, but the benefits are not fully proven, and the risks, including heightened risks of prostate cancer and heart disease, should inspire caution (Tan, 2002; Vastag, 2003).

sexual dysfunction A persistent or recurrent problem in becoming sexually aroused or reaching orgasm.

Sexual Dysfunctions

Sexual dysfunctions are persistent or recurrent problems in becoming sexually aroused or reaching orgasm. Many of us have sexual problems on occasion, but sexual dysfunctions are chronic and cause significant distress.

We do not have precise figures on the occurrence of sexual dysfunctions. The most accurate information may be based on the National Health and Social Life Survey (Laumann, Gagnon et al., 1994; see Table 8.5), in which the researchers found that sexual dysfunctions are quite common. Women more often reported painful sex, lack of pleasure, inability to reach orgasm, and lack of desire. Men were more likely to report reaching orgasm too soon ("premature ejaculation") and performance anxiety. Premature ejaculation is most likely to affect men in early adulthood. Dysfunctions that tend to begin or be prominent in middle adulthood include erectile dysfunction and lack of interest in sex.

Lack of desire is more common among women than men (I. Goldstein et al., 2006). Nevertheless, the belief that men are always eager for sex is only a myth. The lack of desire is often limited to one partner. When one member of a couple is more interested in sex than the other, sex therapists often recommend that couples try to compromise and try to resolve problems in the relationship that may dampen sexual ardor (Moore & Heiman, 2006). Couples usually find that sex is no better than other facets of their relationship (A. K. Matthews et al., 2006).

Repeated erectile problems, characterized by persistent difficulty in achieving or maintaining an erection during the course of sexual activity, may make men anxious when sexual opportunities arise, because they expect failure rather than pleasure. As a result, they may avoid sex (Bancroft, Carnes, & Janssen, 2005; Bancroft, Carnes, Janssen, et al., 2005). Their partners may also avoid sexual contact because of their own frustration. The incidence of erectile dysfunction increases with age. A study of men aged 40–69 in Massachusetts found that nearly half reported problems in obtaining and maintaining erections, with men in the 50- to 59-year-old age group reporting erectile problems two thirds as frequently as men in the 60- to 69-year-old age group (Johannes et al., 2000).

The reduction in testosterone levels that occurs in middle and later adulthood may in part explain a gradual loss of sexual desire in men—along with some loss of muscle mass and strength (Janssen, 2006). But women's sexual desire may also decline with age because of physical and psychological changes (I. Goldstein et al., 2006; Hayes & Dennerstein, 2005). Some medications, especially those used to control anxiety, depression, or hypertension, may also reduce desire. Viagra has helped a number of women whose sexual response has been hindered by antidepressants (Nurnberg et al., 2008).

Fatigue may lead to erectile disorder in men, and inadequate lubrication and, consequently, painful sex in women. But these will be isolated incidents unless the person attaches too much meaning to them and becomes concerned about future performances. Painful sex, however, can also reflect underlying infections or medical conditions.

Table 8.5
Sexual Dysfunctions Reported Within the Previous Year (%)

	Men (%)	Women (%)
Pain during sex	3.0	14.4
Lack of pleasure in sex	8.1	21.2
Inability to reach orgasm	8.3	24.1
Lack of interest in sex	15.8	33.4
Anxiety about performance*	17.0	11.5
Reaching climax too early	28.5	10.3
Inability to maintain an erection**	10.4	—
Trouble lubricating	—	18.8

*Anxiety about performance is not itself a sexual dysfunction but it figures prominently in sexual dysfunctions.
**Incidence increases with age; survey figures may be an underestimate.
Source: Adapted from Tables 10.8A and 10.8B, pages 370 and 371, in Laumann, E. O., Gagnon, J. H., Michael, R. T., & Michaels, S. (1994). The social organization of sexuality: Sexual practices in the United States. Chicago: University of Chicago Press.

Biological causes of erectile disorder affect the flow of blood to and through the penis, a problem that becomes more common as men age or experience damage to nerves involved in erection (I. Goldstein, 1998, 2000). Erectile problems can arise when clogged or narrow arteries leading to the penis deprive the penis of blood and oxygen (I. M. Thompson et al., 2005).

Similarly, aging can affect the sexual response of women. Perimenopausal and postmenopausal women usually produce less vaginal lubrication than younger women, and the vaginal walls thin, which can render sex painful (Dennerstein & Goldstein, 2005) and create performance anxiety (McCabe, 2005; W. W. Schultz et al., 2005). Artificial lubrication can supplement the woman's own production, and estrogen replacement may halt or reverse some of the sexual changes of aging (I. Goldstein & Alexander, 2005). But partners also need to have realistic expectations and consider enjoyable sexual activities they can engage in without discomfort or high demands (McCarthy & Fucito, 2005).

Middle-aged and older men might try weight control and regular exercise to ward off erectile dysfunction (Derby, 2000). Exercise seems to lessen clogging of arteries, keeping them clear for the flow of blood into the penis. Oral medications—Viagra, Levitra, and Cialis—are commonly used to treat erectile disorder.

Check Your Learning Quiz 8.1

Go to **login.cengagebrain.com** and take the online quiz.

▶**LO5** Explain how cognitive development in adulthood shows multidirectionality, inter-individual variability, and plasticity.

Did you know that—

• Throughout much of adulthood, some people make gains in intelligence and other people experience losses?

• The average IQ score in the United States increased over the past half century?

• Scores on the verbal subtests of standardized intelligence tests can increase throughout the life span?

• Long-term memory and general knowledge often increase with age?

• Many middle-aged people are as creative as they were in early adulthood?

▼

Cognitive development continues through middle adulthood, but in various directions (Schaie, 2005; Willis & Schaie, 2006). For example, the overall Wechsler Adult Intelligence Scale score of a 53-year-old farmer in Kansas may start to decrease around age 27. His "verbal intelligence," as measured mainly by his knowledge of the meaning of words, remains pretty much the same, but his "performance subtest" scores, or his ability to perform on timed spatially related subtests, declines. A woman in her mid-40s may have gone to business school and climbed the corporate ladder during her mid- to late 20s but then decided to change her life at the age of 40 and become extremely knowledgeable in art history and opera. A 55-year-old family practitioner is "lost" when he tries to understand the science behind a new medical test presented at a professional meeting in San Francisco; nevertheless, he learns how to interpret a report based on results from the test and he discovers, to his relief, that most of his peers are in the same boat. A 47-year-old woman returns to college to complete her B.A. At first she is fearful of competing with the "kids," but she finds out quickly enough that her sense of purpose more than compensates for what she thinks of as any "loss in brainpower."

multidirectionality In the context of cognitive development, the fact that some aspects of intellectual functioning may improve while others remain stable or decline.

plasticity The fact that intellectual abilities are not absolutely fixed but can be modified.

Changes in Intellectual Abilities

In middle adulthood, intellectual development is multidirectional, varies interindividually, and has plasticity. **Multidirectionality** refers to how cognition improves in some ways but remains stable or declines in other ways. Intellect, according to multidirectionality, is measured by degreess but also explained and affected by heredity, environment, and increasing intellectual areas by furthering study.

We discussed interindividual variability in terms of physical development, and we find it in cognitive development as well. People mature in different cultural settings. Some still frown on education for women. Some areas have better schools than others. Some youth find themselves in subcultures in which their peers disapprove of them if they earn high grades or seek approval from teachers. We also find interindividual variability in middle adulthood. Some people find themselves or allow themselves to be in "ruts" in which they gain little if any new knowledge. Others are hungry for new perspectives, so they read, and travel and visit museums in any spare moment they can find.

Plasticity refers to the fact that people's intellectual abilities are not absolutely fixed but can be modified under certain conditions at almost any time in life. The ideal period for language learning may be childhood, but you can pick up a new language in your 40s, 50s, or even later. You learn the meanings of new words for a lifetime (unless you lock yourself in a closet).

The Flynn Effect and Cohort Effects

Then there is the so-called Flynn effect. Philosopher and researcher James Flynn (2003) found that the average IQ score increased some 18 points in the United States between the years of 1947 and 2002. Psychologist Richard Nisbett (2007) argued that our genetic codes could not possibly have changed enough in half a century to account for this enormous difference, and concluded that social and cultural factors such as the penetration of better educational systems and mass media must be the reasons for the change. IQ scores in the United States have actually risen over the past couple of generations.

The people who were middle-aged in 1947 and those who were middle-aged in 2002 belong to different cohorts. Figure 8.3 shows some cohort effects from the Seattle Longitudinal Study, begun in 1956 by K. Warner Schaie. Participants were tested every 7 years, and Schaie and his colleagues were able to assess cohort effects as well as longitudinal effects on intellectual functioning. The figure shows that groups of adults born more recently were superior to those born at earlier times in four of five mental abilities assessed: inductive reasoning, verbal meaning, spatial orientation, and word fluency (Schaie, 1994). The cohorts born earlier per-

▶ **LO6** Discuss crystallized and fluid intelligence in middle adulthood.

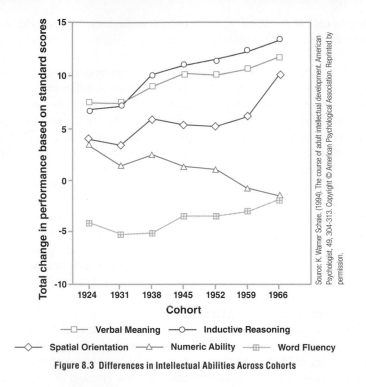

Source: K. Warner Schaie. (1994). The course of adult intellectual development. American Psychologist, 49, 304-313. Copyright © American Psychological Association. Reprinted by permission.

Figure 8.3 Differences in Intellectual Abilities Across Cohorts

formed better in numeric ability. Schaie noted that the intellectual functioning of the members of a society reflects their education and the technology of the day (Charness & Schaie, 2003). The results also suggest that the younger cohorts might actually have been exposed to a better educational system—one that encouraged them to think abstractly (*inductive reasoning*), learn the meaning of words (*verbal meaning, word fluency*), and interact with geometric figures (*spatial orientation*).

crystallized intelligence A cluster of knowledge and skills that depends on accumulated information and experience, awareness of social conventions, and good judgment.

fluid intelligence A person's skills at processing information.

Crystallized Intelligence Versus Fluid Intelligence

Some might ask whether math ability and vocabulary size are really measures of intelligence, when these are merely the types of items we find on intelligence tests and people's scores on intelligence tests can change as a result of experience. But John

Horn came up with a useful distinction: crystallized intelligence versus fluid intelligence.

Crystallized intelligence is defined as a cluster of knowledge and skills that depends on accumulated information and experience, awareness of social conventions, and the capacity to make good decisions and judgments. Crystallized intelligence includes knowledge of the specialized vocabulary in a field; in English, for example, one might know the meanings of the terms *iambic pentameter, rhetoric,* and *onomatopoeia.* We know that it is socially desirable to look a business associate in the eye in the United States, but did you know that this behavior is considered hostile in Japan? Choosing to eat healthful foods could also be considered a sign of crystallized intelligence.

Fluid intelligence involves a person's skills at processing information. Let's do a quick comparison to a computer. Your crystallized intelligence is like the amount of information you have in storage. Your fluid intelligence is more like the sizes of your processor and your memory (meaning *working memory*—how much you can keep in mind at once), which work together to access and manipulate information and arrive at answers quickly and accurately. According to researchers, environmental factors play a powerful role in the formation of crystallized intelligence, whereas neurological factors strongly influence fluid intelligence (Horn & Noll, 1997; Salthouse & Davis, 2006).

Studies have shown that crystallized intelligence tends to increase with age through middle adulthood. In the absence of senile dementias, crystallized intelligence commonly increases throughout the life span, along with the verbal-subtest scores of standardized intelligence tests. The same studies that indicate that crystallized intelligence tends to increase throughout adulthood have tended to show a decline for fluid intelligence (Escorial et al., 2003; Salthouse, 2001). K. Warner Schaie's Longitudinal data (see Figure 8.4) shows that the intellectual factor of perceptual speed—the rate at which individuals solve problems related to the senses of vision, hearing, and so on, which is most strongly related to fluid intelligence—is also the one that drops off most dramatically from early adulthood to late adulthood (Schaie, 1994). Spatial orientation and numeric ability, both related to fluid intelligence, also decline dramatically in late adulthood. Verbal ability and inductive reasoning are more related to crystallized intelligence, and these show gains through middle adulthood and hold up in late adulthood.

Cognitive Changes in Middle Age

Interact and learn more about how cognition changes after early adulthood.

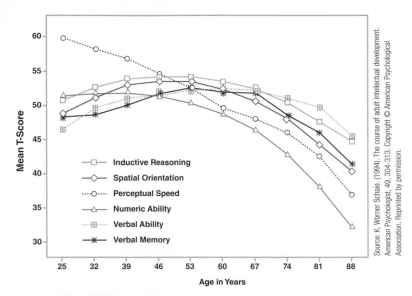

Source: K. Warner Schaie. (1994). The course of adult intellectual development. American Psychologist, 49, 304-313. Copyright © American Psychological Association. Reprinted by permission.

Figure 8.4 Longitudinal Changes in Six Intellectual Abilities, Ages 25–88

Figure 8.4 reveals group trends; there are interindividual variations. Schaie and his colleagues (2004) found that circumstances such as the following tend to lessen cognitive decline in advanced late adulthood:

- Maintaining good physical health;
- Experiencing favorable environmental conditions, such as decent housing;
- Remaining intellectually active through reading and keeping up with current events;
- Being open to new ideas and new styles of life;
- Living with a partner who is intellectually active; and
- Being satisfied with one's achievements.

When these factors are present, they help individuals maximize their potential at any age.

Information Processing

One of the interesting things about aging is that it can become more difficult to keep new information in working memory even when long-term memory remains relatively intact. It sometimes seems that information goes "in one ear and out the other."

Speed of Information Processing

There are several ways to measure the speed of information processing. One is simply physical: *reaction time*. That is the amount of time it takes to respond to a stimulus. If you touch a hot stove, how long does it take you to pull your hand away? In one assessment of reaction time, people pushed a button when a light was flashed. People in middle adulthood responded to the light more slowly—their reaction time was greater—than young adults (Hartley, 2006). The difference in reaction time is only a fraction of a second, but it is enough to keep the typical middle-aged adult out of the firing line in the military and on the sidelines of professional sports (Salthouse & Berish, 2005). It can also make a difference when avoiding a collision on the freeway.

Reaction time is only one aspect of processing speed. Perceptual speed is a broad cognitive aspect intertwined with fluid intelligence. As with reaction time, the changes in perceptual speed in middle adulthood are not that dramatic, but they are measurable. Because of continuous experience with reading and writing, an educated person in middle adulthood may be better than ever at doing crossword puzzles (largely dependent on crystallized intelligence), but she might find it somewhat more difficult to navigate new cities than she did in early adulthood (largely dependent on fluid intelligence) (Salthouse & Siedlecki, 2007).

Most researchers believe that the decline in processing speed reflects changes in the integrity of the nervous system. Having said that, hypotheses on the mechanism run rampant, from the death of neurons in the brain to changes in specific parts of the brain and in the secretion of neurotransmitters (Hartley, 2006).

Memory

Memory is one of the intellectual factors that showed improvement through most of the years of middle adulthood and stability from 53 to 60, according to longitudinal research by K. Warner Schaie (1994). Not all researchers agree. Researchers use several kinds of memory tasks, and they do not necessarily find the same results with all of them (Salthouse et al., 2006). By and large, despite Schaie's results, most researchers have concluded that people in middle adulthood and late adulthood perform less well than young adults at memorizing lists of words, numbers, or passages of prose (Salthouse & Davis, 2006).

The main strategies for memorization are *rote rehearsal* and *elaborative rehearsal*. In the latter part of middle adulthood, learning new information by rote repetition is less efficient than it was in early adulthood (Salthouse & Babcock, 1991). We are also apparently less capable of screening out distractions (Radvansky et al., 2005). Elaborative rehearsal—that is, relating new information to things we already know—may suffer somewhat, since we are also apparently somewhat less capable of rapid classification or categorization (Hultsch et al., 1998).

We have been speaking of working, or short-term, memory. Let's look at storage, or long-term, memory. Not all memory functions decline in middle adulthood. By and large, we are more likely to retain or expand our general knowledge in middle adulthood (Prull et al., 2000; Zacks et al., 2000), for instance, by learning more about something of which we have little knowledge or experience.

Then there is the matter of *procedural memory*, a kind of motor memory of how to do things—how to ride a bicycle, how to use a keyboard, how to write with a pen, how to drive a car. One of my favorite photos is of the older Jean Piaget riding a bicycle. The student of children looks childlike, but the message for the student of psychology or education is that we can maintain procedural memories for a lifetime. Long-term memory and general knowledge often improve with age.

Expertise and Practical Problem Solving

Someone in middle adulthood would be the ideal new hire for any employer. Middle-aged people have the verbal abilities of younger people and perhaps some more, have lost very little in the way of fluid intelligence, and have a greater store of expertise and practical problem-solving skills (Leclerc & Hess, 2007). Although, again, there is always interindividual variation, as a group middle-aged people show this every day in every way.

Over the years, they have also acquired social skills that enable them to deal better with subordinates and with supervisors. They have a better feel for other people's limitations and potentials, and they have a better understanding of how to motivate them. They may also have experience that will help them be calmer in stressful situations.

The parent who was so distraught when the first child cried may now be relaxed when the grandchildren cry. Part of the difference may be the "distance"—the generation of removal. But part of it is also the years of learning that the children will survive and develop into normal human beings (whatever that means) whether or not they cry as children.

In terms of vocations, the initial training or education of middle-aged people has now had the benefits of years of experience. People in middle adulthood have learned what works and what does not work for them. In the cases of the professions, for instance, "book learning" and perhaps internships have been supplemented by years of experience in the real world. Pianist Arthur Rubinstein became so accomplished as the years wore on that he often practiced "mentally"—he needed the physical keyboard only intermittently. Although he lost some speed when playing rapid passages, he compensated by slowing before entering them, and he created drama when he escalated his pacing.

Creativity and Learning

Middle adulthood offers numerous opportunities for exercising creativity, expanding knowledge, and gaining intellectual experience.

The Brain and Memory

Watch and learn about research on declarative memory, the memory that helps us recall facts and events.

Midlife Memory Declines

Watch and learn about the possible causes of midlife memory declines.

▶ **LO7** Discuss creativity in middle adulthood.

▶ **LO8** Discuss the experiences of middle-aged returning students.

Creativity

People in middle adulthood can be creative, and in fact, many middle adults are at the height of their creativity. Artist Pablo Picasso painted *Guernica*, which protested the Spanish civil war and is one of the best known images in art, at the age of 56. Author Toni Morrison wrote the Pulitzer Prize–winning novel *Beloved* at the age of 56. Inventor Thomas Edison built the kinetoscope, an early peephole method for watching films, at the age of 44. Yet researchers have found some differences in creativity among young adults and middle-aged people. Aspects of creativity that are more likely to be found among young adults include creativity in music, mathematics, and physics (Norton et al., 2005; Simonton, 2006a). Wolfgang Amadeus Mozart, considered by many critics to be the greatest composer in history, died at the age of 35. Albert Einstein published his general theory of relativity at the age of 36.

Research suggests that younger students as well as returning students and instructors benefit from the variety of viewpoints in a classroom that includes students from different generations.

Writers and visual artists often continue to improve into middle adulthood, although their most emotional and fervent works may be produced at younger ages. The most emotionally charged works of poets tend to be penned in early adulthood (Simonton, 2007). However, it is simply wrong to attempt to generalize that middle-aged people are no longer as creative as they were in early adulthood.

Mature Learners

For most adults, learning is a perpetual process. We learn when new people move into the neighborhood or when we watch or listen to the media. We learn when we hear what is happening with a family member, or observe a pet. But when psychologists and educators use the term "adult learning," they are usually speaking of learning as it occurs within some formal educational setting.

Even when we limit our discussion to educational settings, we find vast diversity and interindividual variation. But research on mature learners suggests that they are likely to have some things in common: They are apt to be highly motivated, and they are more likely than younger learners to find the subject matter interesting for its own sake (Bye et al., 2007).

Women make up about 63% of postsecondary students aged 35 and above in the United States (U.S. Department of Education, 2005). Among those with families, you might assume that those who returned to college would be the ones with the least exacting combinations of family and work demands. Actually, it's the other way around (Hostetler et al., 2007): Women with the greatest demands on them from family and work are the ones most likely to return to school. But once they're back, their major source of stress is time constraints; those who receive the emotional support of their families and employers experience the least stress and do best (Kirby et al., 2004).

The percentage of returning students in postsecondary institutions has increased markedly since 1970, from about 10% to 17% of the student population (U.S. Department of Education, 2005). When returning students come to campus, they often feel a bit on the periphery of things because rules, regulations, and activities are generally designed for younger students (Brady, 2007). They are often not sure whether or not they should share their thoughts or perspectives with the class; perhaps, they may think, their ideas will be out of date. Then again, some returning students achieved commanding positions at work or in social roles, and it may be difficult for them to accept their subordinate status in the teacher–student relationship (Marron & Rayman, 2002). However, all in all, research suggests that students, both younger and returning, and their instructors benefit from the mix of views in a classroom that includes returning students (Brady, 2007).

Check Your Learning Quiz 8.2

Go to **login.cengagebrain.com** and take the online quiz.

▶ **LO9** Dispute Havighurst's tasks of middle adulthood.

Did you know that—

- There is no evidence confirming that most people experience a midlife crisis in middle adulthood?
- Most mothers do not experience empty-nest syndrome when the last child leaves home?
- People's personalities tend to remain stable throughout middle adulthood?
- College-educated women show less personal distress as they advance from middle adulthood to late adulthood?
- Job satisfaction increases throughout middle adulthood?

▼

Havighurst's Developmental Tasks of Middle Adulthood

In the 1950s there was a TV sitcom called *Father Knows Best* (don't laugh), with upright Jim Anderson as the title character. He was an insurance agent who was apparently born in a suit and wore it 24 hours a day. His wife was apparently born in an apron and wore it proudly all day long. The series caught them in middle age, with three children, presumably because they could not have the average 2.4 children. The older two, teenagers, were called Bud and Princess. They lived in a spacious, clean, suburban house and had a spacious, clean, suburban car.

It was with the vision, perhaps, of such a "fine," "typical" American family in mind that Robert Havighurst proposed his "developmental tasks" of middle adulthood in the 1970s. There is no room in Havighurst's vision of normalcy for gay men and lesbians, for people who cannot have or choose not to have children, for people who choose the single life, or for people who do not undertake "meaningful" social and civic responsibilities. Having said that, we must admit that Havighurst did arrive at a list of issues that affect many of us at midlife, many of which we will be discussing in this chapter.

Many of us do "launch" our children into the outside world during our middle adulthood, and we do help them establish themselves—sometimes for much longer than we might have anticipated. We may find that our preferences in leisure activities have changed over the years, or we may be continuing them—athletic, cultural, or social. Some of us are establishing deeper relationships with life partners, but the fact is that some are living alone, never partnered or divorced, and some are living with stepfamilies and possibly struggling along. Some of us are involved in meaningful social or civic activities, but some of us are loners, and, as we will see, going it alone can have negative consequences for our mental and physical well-being.

Havighurst sounds pessimistic about work—keeping our performance at a satisfactory level. Many of us are reaching peak performance in middle adulthood. We have gained expertise, and our abilities remain generally intact.

Yes, there may be issues in adjusting to physical aging. Our bodies will be changing. We may encounter illnesses we really weren't thinking all that much about during young adulthood. We may have to come to the aid of aging parents. On the other hand, we may also find new rewards in our relationships with our aging parents once we are both quite "grown up."

Robert Havighurst's Developmental Tasks of Middle Adulthood

✓ Helping our children establish themselves in the outside world
✓ Developing a range of enjoyable leisure activities
✓ Establishing a deeper relationship with our life partner
✓ Becoming involved in meaningful social and civic responsibilities
✓ Keeping our performance at work at a satisfactory level
✓ Adjusting to the physical changes that accompany aging through the midlife period
✓ Adjusting to the demands and responsibilities of caring for aging parents

© Image Source

Theories of Development in Middle Adulthood

Is middle adulthood a distinct stage or phase of life? Theories of development in middle adulthood largely deal with this question. According to Erikson's theory of psychosocial development, middle adulthood is characterized by a particular life crisis. We shall describe that crisis and consider the evidence, pro and con. Daniel Levinson spoke of a specific midlife transition and a midlife crisis (not to be confused with Erikson's *life crises*). Again we shall consider the evidence. Then we will look at the

Developmental Tasks of Middle Adulthood

Interact and learn more about Havighurst's list of tasks every normal adult encounters at middle age.

▶ **LO10** Discuss Erikson's and Levinson's theories of development in middle adulthood.

ways in which personality appears to change—or not to change—during middle adulthood.

Erik Erikson's Theory of Psychosocial Development

The major psychological challenge of the middle years, according to Erikson, is **generativity versus stagnation**. Generativity is the ability to generate or produce. Psychosocial generativity is an instinctual drive toward procreation—that is, bearing and rearing children—in Erikson's view (1980). To Erikson, the negative counterpart of generativity meant rejection or suppression of this natural drive and would lead to stagnation. He did recognize that some people did not have children of their own due to physical, social, or interpersonal conditions. Under such circumstances, substitutes were possible that might not be as naturally or as fully satisfying but that might work for the individual. For example, a person or couple without children (or even with children) might contribute to the teaching or welfare of other people's children, or might contribute to charity or to civic works. Erikson and others (e.g., Thiele & Whelan, 2006) also noted that grandparenthood provides additional opportunities for satisfying generativity in middle adulthood. Today, environmentalists are acting in a generative manner when they take steps to care for future generations (de St. Aubin et al., 2004). Generativity not only contributes to future generations, it also enhances one's self-esteem and sense of meaning in life (Marushima, 2000).

Erikson argued that people who do not engage in generative behavior risk stagnating and falling into routines that can strip their lives of meaning and purpose. This particular point remains murky. For example, Van Hiel and colleagues (2006) administered a battery of psychological tests to nearly 200 middle-aged adults, many of whom were identified as high in generativity and many of whom were identified as high in stagnation. The more generative group scored significantly higher in the personality variable of conscientiousness, and the more stagnating group scored significantly higher on the personality variable of neuroticism. Neuroticism is defined as emotional instability—an enduring tendency to experience negative feelings such as anxiety, anger, guilt, and depression. So the first question we might ask is whether some people stagnate because of less generative behavior or whether their lower generativity is related to personality traits such as neuroticism. The Van Hiel group also found, with a group of 457 middle-aged adults, that

generativity versus stagnation Erikson's seventh stage of psychosocial development, in which the life crisis is the dichotomy between generativity and stagnation.

midlife transition A psychological shift into middle adulthood theorized to occur between the ages of 40 and 45 as people begin to believe they have more to look back upon than forward to.

midlife crisis A time of dramatic self-doubt and anxiety during which people sense the passing of their youth and become concerned with their own aging and mortality.

generativity and stagnation are independent dimensions rather than opposites. In other words, middle-aged people can be low in generativity and also be low in stagnation. Other researchers will doubtlessly replicate or challenge this research.

Amy Eckert/Getty Images

Daniel Levinson's Seasons

According to Daniel Levinson and his colleagues, the ages 40–45 comprise a **midlife transition**—a psychological shift into middle adulthood that is often accompanied by a crisis during which people fear they have more to look back upon than forward to. This crisis is termed a **midlife crisis** and is defined as a time of dramatic self-doubt and anxiety during which people sense the passing of their youth and become preoccupied with concern about the imminence of their own mortality. Levinson believed that marker events such as menopause, the death of a parent or a friend, or a child's "leaving the nest" could trigger the crisis.

Once beset by the crisis, individuals could attempt to deny the realities of aging, such as by having an extramarital affair to prove to themselves they are still sexually attractive, buying a sports car (red, of course), or suddenly shifting careers. Many people, however, view the years from age 45 onward as a type of second adulthood, filled with opportunities for new directions and fulfillment.

For many people today, a midlife crisis is imposed from the outside in the form of a career crash resulting from corporate and government *downsizing*—the thinning of the ranks of employees. But people who are flexible enough to make the transition to other careers can find increased satisfaction.

The 50s are often more relaxed and productive than the 40s. Yet many people in their fifties need to adjust to the children leaving home (the "empty nest"), the effects of aging, and competition from younger workers. But we will also see that the last child's leaving home can more often than not be a positive event.

▶ **LO11** Explain why the age of 35 has had particular significance for women.

▶ **LO12** Explain the life-events approach to thinking about middle adulthood.

Entering Midlife: Crisis, Turning Point, or Prime of Life?

Theorists have made much of turning 35 or 40, or of entering midlife. I mention the age of 35 because it was crucial to journalist Gail Sheehy in her popular book *Passages*, published in 1976. Sheehy interviewed a number of adult women and men and reported that the women seemed to enter middle age about 5 years earlier than the men, at about the age of 35. Why 35? In the 1970s, 35 was the age at which women were usually advised to stop using the birth-control pill for fear of side effects and to start using amniocentesis to check for chromosomal abnormalities in the fetus if they were pregnant. At this age, their "biological clocks" were also running out. Today we could say that 40 or so is the new 30 or 35 and that most women at 35 can still safely use "the pill"; and many women do become pregnant in their late 30s and early 40s. However, amniocentesis is still usually recommended for women who become pregnant at 35 or later.

With people nowadays more likely to live into their late 70s or 80s, 40 has become a much more realistic halfway point than 35—or, as some might label it, a turning point (Wethington et al., 2004). As noted earlier, Daniel Levinson and his colleagues (1978) considered the transition to midlife at about the age of 40 a crisis, a midlife crisis, characterized by taking stock and often recognizing that one has fallen short of

Dick Makin/Getty Images

one's dream or dreams: The once promising ballerina who has never danced *The Nutcracker* at Lincoln Center. The Wharton business major who never sat at the *Fortune* 500 merger that brought in $25,000,000. The Naval Academy graduate at the top of her class who never made admiral.

These portraits are negative, to say the least. While some theorists present portraits of middle-aged people suddenly focusing on tragedy, loss, or doom, other human-development theorists have found people to be in or entering the prime of life (Almeida & Horn, 2004; Lachman, 2004). People can develop certain illnesses at almost any time of life, but as described earlier, most people in middle adulthood encounter little decline in physical prowess. Only professionals who rely on peak performance, such as athletes and dancers, will find the loss compelling enough to shuttle them into new life directions. Intellectually, moreover, there is little if any loss in fluid intelligence, and crystallized intelligence is growing—especially among professionals who are continuing to develop skills in their chosen fields.

Middle-aged adults, especially professionals, are also often earning more money than young adults. They are more likely to be settled geographically and vocationally, although there can certainly be midlife career changes and movement from one organization or business to another. By now they may have built systems of social support and may be involved in enduring romantic and social relationships and have children. The flip side of all this, as we will see, may be overwhelming responsibility, such as caring for children, a spouse, and aging parents and remaining in the workplace all at once—quite a juggling act! But many in middle adulthood are at the height of their productivity and resilience, despite all challenges.

The Life-Events Approach

The life-events approach focuses on the challenges and changes rather than phases or stages of life that people encounter during middle age. Numerous researchers have found that the most stressful life challenges and changes of middle adulthood tend to include:

- the death of a spouse or a child
- the death of a parent or a sibling
- marital divorce or separation, or separation from a cohabitant
- hospitalization or change in the health status of oneself, one's child, one's parent, or one's sibling
- the need to care for one's parents
- a change in the relationship with one's children
- financial difficulties
- concern about one's appearance, weight, or aging
- moving
- change or loss of employment
- a change in a relationship with an important friend
- or a change in responsibilities at work

(Etaugh & Bridges, 2006; F. O. Lorenz et al., 2006).

Women Over 40 with Eating Disorders

Watch and learn how specific life events are triggers for anorexia in middle-aged women.

Midlife Crisis

Who is having a (Midlife) crisis?

▶ **LO13** Discuss stability and change in social and emotional development in middle adulthood.

One common change in middle adulthood takes place when the last child leaves the home. Though it was once assumed that women without children in the home would experience a painful **empty-nest syndrome**, this can just as often be a positive event (Etaugh & Bridges, 2006). Today, many middle-aged women in developed nations can keep themselves "as young as they feel." Most of them are in the workforce and find life satisfaction in activities other than child rearing and home-making. We should also note

What will their personalities be like in 20 years?

STABILITY   CHANGE

Stuart Mcclymont/Getty Images

that some children fail to leave home by 18 or 21, or—in a syndrome that has been referred to as *failure to launch*—even by age 30. Other adult children, because of financial problems or just for convenience, are in and out of their parents' home in what has been dubbed the *revolving-door syndrome*.

Negative life events, including physical illness and depression, are stressful and have been shown to be harmful to people's health in middle adulthood (F. O. Lorenz et al., 2006; Ryff et al., 2002). An accumulation of stressful life events may even accelerate age-related declines in memory functioning (VonDras et al., 2005).

Nevertheless, middle-aged people's situations—such as having understanding and helpful family members or friends—and attitudes can have moderating effects on stressors (Etaugh & Bridges, 2006). A sense of control has been shown to mitigate the effects of stress and foster feelings of well-being among midlife adults (Windsor et al., 2008). Middle-aged adults who perceive negative life events as specific rather than global problems and who believe that those events can be changed are less likely to be depressed by them (Adler et al., 2006).

empty-nest syndrome A feeling of loneliness or loss of purpose that parents, and especially mothers, are theorized to experience when the youngest child leaves home.

"big five" personality traits Basic personality traits derived from contemporary statistical methods: extraversion, agreeableness, conscientiousness, neuroticism (emotional instability), and openness to experience.

Stability and Change in Middle Adulthood

The **"big five" personality traits**—or the five basic factors of personality isolated by Robert McCrae, Paul Costa, and their colleagues—are used by a number of researchers to study stability and change in the personality development of adults over several decades (McCrae & Costa, 2006; Terracciano et al., 2006). These factors are extraversion, agreeableness, conscientiousness, neuroticism (emotional instability), and openness to experience (see Table 8.6). Cross-cultural research has found that these five factors appear to define the personality structure of many people, including American, German, Portuguese, Israeli, Chinese, Korean, and Japanese people (McCrae & Costa, 1997). A study of more than 5,000 German, British, Spanish, Czech, and Turkish people suggested that the factors are related to people's basic temperaments, which are considered to be largely inborn (McCrae et al., 2000). The researchers interpreted the results to suggest that our personalities tend to mature rather than be shaped by environmental conditions, although the expression of personality traits is certainly affected by culture. (For example, a person who is "basically" open to new experiences is likely to behave less openly in a traditional, fundamentalist society than in an open society.)

Table 8.6
The "Big Five": The Five-Factor Model of Personality

Factor	Name	Traits
I	Extraversion	Contrasts talkativeness, assertiveness, and activity with silence, passivity, and reserve
II	Agreeableness	Contrasts kindness, trust, and warmth with hostility, selfishness, and distrust
III	Conscientiousness	Contrasts organization, thoroughness, and reliability with carelessness, negligence, and unreliability
IV	Neuroticism	Contrasts nervousness, moodiness, and sensitivity to negative stimuli with coping ability
V	Openness to experience	Contrasts imagination, curiosity, and creativity with shallowness and lack of perceptiveness

Failure to Launch

Learn about preventing the failure-to-launch scenario of grown children living with parents.

The Big Five: The Five-Factor Model of Personality

Interact with the five-factor model of personality.

© 2012 Cengage Learning

Are There Sudden Shifts in Personality?

The notions of crises or turning points in emotional development also suggest that people undergo rather sudden changes or shifts in personality. As pointed out by Robert McCrae and Paul Costa Jr. (2006), it has also been widely assumed that adult life events such as getting married, working one's way up in a vocation, and having and rearing children would deeply affect people's personality. However, at least after the age of 30, two decades of longitudinal research found that the big five personality traits tend to show a good deal of stability over time (B. W. Roberts & DelVecchio, 2000). McCrae and Costa, in fact, suggested that this stability brings into question whether it makes sense for any developmentalists, such as the Levinson group (1978), to suggest that there are predictable phases or stages of adult development.

Longitudinal and cross-sectional research has shown that there are some consistent trends of group personality change over the years but, by and large, those who are most extroverted in young adulthood will remain most extroverted in middle adulthood (B. W. Roberts & DelVecchio, 2000; B. W. Roberts et al., 2006). However, for adults as a group, male and female, the traits of agreeableness and conscientiousness increase somewhat from young adulthood to middle adulthood. Neuroticism declines throughout the same period, meaning that people become more emotionally stable. Extraver-

Table 8.7
Themes Used on Scales to Assess Development of Personality in Women From Young Adulthood Through Late Adulthood

Theme	Sample Feelings Assessed
Identity certainty	Feeling that I am my own person; believing that I will seize my opportunities; being of a clear mind about what I can accomplish
Confident power	Having self-confidence; having a sense of authority and power; believing that others respect me
Concern with aging	Looking old; thinking about death a great deal; feeling less attractive than I used to be; feeling that men are no longer interested in me
Generativity	Having a sense of being needed; helping younger people learn and develop; trying to make positive changes in society; having interests beyond my immediate family
Personal distress	Feeling depressed or disillusioned; feeling angry at men or women; having feelings of incompetence; feeling alone; feeling exploited

Source: Stewart, A.J., Ostrove, J.M., & Helson, R. (2001). Middle aging in women: Patterns of personality change from the 30s to the 50s. Journal of Adult Development, 8, 23–37.

sion and openness to new experience either remain the same or tend to decline slightly in middle adulthood, suggesting again greater stability in personality, or "maturity." The trait of being open to new experience decreases once more in late adulthood.

Personality Themes Among College-Educated Women

Cohorts of college-educated women in their 20s, 40s, and 60s were assessed by researchers to determine personality themes. Several researchers developed the scales used for this assessment—see Table 8.7 (A. J. Stewart et al., 2001). As you can see in Figure 8.5, scores on three of the scales were higher for women in their 40s than women in their 20s, and then higher again for women in their 60s: identity certainty, confident power, and concern with aging. Generativity was higher in the 40s than in the 20s, but the generativity of the cohort in their 60s was much the same as in the 40s. Despite increasing concern with aging, personal distress was lower among older women, suggesting, perhaps, that older women are more settled. Remember, however, that these samples were of college-educated women, so they were less likely to incur certain financial and health problems in late adulthood than people on the lower rung of the socioeconomic ladder.

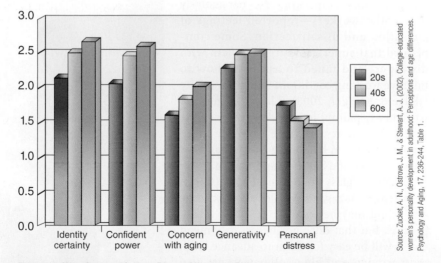

Source: Zucket, A. N., Ostrove, J. M., & Stewart, A. J. (2002). College-educated women's personality development in adulthood: Perceptions and age differences. Psychology and Aging, 17, 236-244, Table 1.

Figure 8.5 Mean Scores of College-Educated Women of Different Ages According to Five Personality Themes

▶ **LO14** Discuss career developments typical of middle
adulthood.

Work in Middle Adulthood

As suggested by Erikson and Levinson, many workers are at their peak in middle adulthood. They have had years to "learn the ropes," and many have advanced into the highest ranks of their trades or professions. One's work can continue to provide social benefits, a sense of identity, and self-esteem.

Job Satisfaction

Only 45% of American workers are satisfied with their jobs, according to a Conference Board survey (2010) of 5,000 households. Some 10% were unemployed, but others were unhappy with their pay, recognition, or health or retirement benefits. Job satisfaction is also associated with such factors as the opportunity to engage in interesting work and the availability of child-care facilities (J. E. A. Russell, 2008).

A study of more than 2,000 university employees found that job satisfaction increased steadily throughout middle adulthood (Hochwarter et al., 2001). The gains were greatest for men, and especially for men who were white-collar workers, for example, professors. Some workers—particularly blue-collar workers—reported feelings of alienation and dissatisfaction. Some complained that supervisors treated them with disrespect and failed to ask them how to improve working conditions and productivity (Judge & Klinger, 2008). These feelings are particularly painful for middle-aged workers when the supervisors are young adults. Women are often balancing the demands of the workplace and a family, and they may still experience a "glass ceiling" on the job (Casini & Sanchez-Mazas, 2005). People in middle adulthood may be sought out in the hiring process, but that does not necessarily mean that it will be easy for them to advance. Still, most women and blue-collar workers also

reported more satisfaction on the job throughout middle age—although not as much as white-collar men.

The growing job satisfaction throughout middle age can be linked to factors such as increased expertise and income. Workers in middle adulthood may also have more realistic perceptions of their career goals. They may have come to terms with recognition that (most of them) will never be the CEO of Apple, the governor of California, or the first person to set foot on Mars.

Career Change in Middle Adulthood

People change careers for many reasons, such as more money, more job security, more prestige, and more stimulation (Jepsen & Choudhuri, 2001; Sullivan et al., 2003). Most people who change their careers do so in young adulthood. People tend to have greater responsibilities in middle adulthood and to have become more entrenched in their pursuits. They may also wonder whether they still have the time and ability to start over.

For reasons such as these, most career changes in midlife involve shifts into related fields (Shultz & Adams, 2007). In the entertainment world, an actor might become a director or a producer. In the field of education, a teacher or professor might move into educational administration. More radical shifts can occur as well, and they can be successful (D. T. Hall, 2004). A laboratory chemist who has spent 20 years working for a pharmaceutical company might decide she wishes to work with people and have more time for herself, so she might move into teaching high-school chemistry and traveling during the summers. I know of a social worker who decided to become a rabbi at the age of 43 and undertook several years of study. She said that from her perspective she wasn't really changing much at all, just getting better at Hebrew.

These are all voluntary, planned changes. Some middle-aged people change careers following a personal crisis such as a divorce, conflict with coworkers, or being fired. In such cases, middle-aged people sometimes pick up whatever work they can to sustain themselves (Shultz & Adams, 2007).

Unemployment

My friend lost her executive position in her late 40s when her company was bought out and a new management team came in. She knew she was in a vulnerable position because the company taking over usually "chops off the head" of the acquired

Work and Flextime

What are the pros and cons of on-the-job flextime programs? Watch and learn.

company; still, she thought she might be low enough on the totem pole to escape notice. Not so. New management cut in half the number of professionals at her level. At first she focused on the fact that her severance package was good. She thought she would take a month off to relax and then use the headhunting firm hired by the company to relocate. However, she soon found that hers was a relatively small industry and that there were very few openings that approximated her level. Former friends from work clustered around her at first, but began to drift away. After 4 months she had sunk into a deep clinical depression.

The effects of unemployment on the health of young and middle-aged adults was studied by a group of researchers (McKee-Ryan et al., 2005) using meta-analysis to average out the findings of 104 studies. Unemployed adults had lower physical and psychological well-being than employed adults, and unemployed middle-aged adults had lower well-being than unemployed young adults. Within the samples of unemployed middle-aged adults, those who fared worst were those who considered work more important, had fewer financial resources and less social support, and tended to blame themselves for losing their jobs. Those who had emotional and financial resources and social support, who could structure their time, and who had realistic strategies for job hunting or finding substitutes for jobs fared best.

A study of small samples of unemployed men, twenty-two 15- to 30-year-olds and eleven 40- to 62-year-olds, paralleled the findings of the McKee-Ryan group (Broomhall & Winefield, 1990). The groups had been out of work for an average of 18–20 months. The men in the middle-aged group were significantly less satisfied with their lives and in poorer psychological health than the younger men.

Age influences how hard women search for a job and how willing they are to accept certain kinds of jobs. In a study of married women in four age groups, post-adolescents (up to age 21) spent more time trying to find employment than did women aged 22–35, 36–49, or 50–62 (Kulik, 2000). (As in the Broomhall and Winefield study, the groupings do not perfectly fit the definitions of young adulthood and middle adulthood.) The women aged 50–62 were most likely to accept jobs low in pay, as long as they liked the work, and those aged 22–49 were most likely to reject jobs because they conflicted with family life or because of work conditions. As in the study by McKee-Ryan and her colleagues (2005), the older women in the study were more likely to experience declines in their well-being following the loss of employment. On the other hand, the older women were least likely to suffer financial strain. We certainly cannot generalize this finding to single women who, as a group, would presumably have fewer financial resources.

Check Your Learning Quiz 8.3

Go to **login.cengagebrain.com** and take the online quiz.

▶ **LO15** Explain how relationships with parents change in middle adulthood.

▶ **LO16** Discuss the challenges of grandparenting.

▶ **LO17** Explain what is meant by the *sandwich generation*.

▶ **LO18** Explain the development of relationships with siblings and friends in middle adulthood.

Did you know that—

- In traditional societies, young adults usually do not leave their home of origin until they get married or some other key event takes place?

- Grandchildren tend to spend more time in activities with their grandmothers than their grandfathers?

- The majority of aging parents live near a child?

- Middle-aged people tend to have fewer friends than young adults do, but they have more in common with the friends who remain?

▼

The term *middle adulthood* is a convenient way of describing people whose ages lie between young adulthood and late adulthood. In terms of their family relationships, their generation is in the middle in another way: It is "sandwiched" in between their own children (and grandchildren) and their parents.

Evolving Parent–Child Relationships

Infants are completely dependent on their parents. Children are also dependent. Adolescents strive for independence, and as they mature and gain experience, parents generally begin to share control with them. As a matter of fact, it is stressful for parents when adolescents do not exert self-control, and when parents must direct them in many areas of life—getting them up in time for school, urging them to maintain their personal hygiene, fighting with them over their choice of clothing, and coaxing them to complete their homework.

Once their children become emerging adults or young adults, most parents in the United States are content to "launch" their children into the world to live on their own or with roommates. In many cases, the children remain at least partly financially dependent, sometimes for several years (Aquilino, 2005). If they have been close to their parents, they may also remain somewhat emotionally dependent once they are out on their own as well—or at the very least, it may hurt when their parents disapprove of their personal choices.

Parents are usually satisfied with their children's living away from home if they call or e-mail regularly and drop by (or allow the parents to drop by) with some sort of reasonable frequency. Parents often try to find a balance between staying in touch and "interfering," especially once their children have partners or children of their own.

In some traditional societies, young adults do not usually leave the home of origin until they are married or some other key event takes place. Alessandra Rusconi (2004) compared Germany and Italy and found that Germans normally left home to set up independent homes prior to marriage. In Italy, however, the picture was mixed. In large industrial cities, young adults tended to follow the German model, whereas more rural and southern Italians tended to remain in the home until they got married. Similarly, parents in some traditional societies assume that their adult children will live nearby; moving to another part of the country is not only painful but also something of an embarrassment for them among their extended family and community.

When the children of middle-aged adults find a partner or get married, new challenges can emerge. First of all, it may seem that nobody is "good enough" for their child. The parents must then deal with the issues of whether, and how, they express their feelings about it. Regardless of the partner or spouse chosen by their child, there are also in-laws and the extended family of the in-laws. Sometimes there is a good match between the families of both partners, but more often the families would not have chosen each other as friends. Still, for the sake of the children, the parents usually try to act friendly on the occasions when the families are together. But the new relationships can be another source of stress.

And then the children may have children.

Grandparenting

Let's begin this section by selecting one of the following two statements. Which of them will you live by (or forever destroy your relationship with your child by)?

1. As a grandparent, you have the right to tell your son or daughter how to raise your grandchild.
2. As a grandparent, you have to keep your mouth tightly shut when you see your son-in-law or daughter-in-law doing the wrong thing with your grandchild.

As you can see, one of the most challenging jobs of the newly minted grandparent is to navigate carefully between the treacherous rocks of reckless interference and painful neglect.

Young adulthood is the time of life when most of those who will bear children do so, and middle adulthood is the time of life when most of us who will become grandparents begin that role. Having and relating to grandchildren, like having and relating to one's own children, has its pluses and its minuses. But research generally finds that the balance is more positive in the case of having grandchildren. For example, a study of grandparenting conducted in China, Greece, and Poland found that having grandchildren was viewed as an overwhelmingly positive event in each culture and that it was beneficial to grandparents both socially and psychologically (Filus, 2006). The study also found that grandparents, like parents, participated in the care of grandchildren and in their recreational and educational activities. But the balance differed, as it does in the United States. Parents spend a higher proportion of their time taking care of the basic needs of their children, whereas grandparents spend relatively more time in recreational and educational activities. We are speaking, of course, of situations in which the grandparents do not live in the same household with the grandchildren.

Creatas Images/Jupiterimages

Studies in the United States, Poland, Greece, Germany, and China have all found that grandchildren through adolescence spend more time involved in activities with their grandmothers than with their grandfathers (Filus, 2006; Höpflinger & Hummel, 2006). Grandchildren are also relatively more involved with their mother's parents than their father's parents. It may come as a surprise, but the gender of the grandchild has little effect on these overall findings. Even male grandchildren tend to generally gravitate more toward contacts with grandmothers than with grandfathers. Despite the greater involvement with grandmothers, grandchildren say they value their grandfathers just as highly—but researchers are not about to devise an experiment that would put children's lip service to the test!

One of the "hyped" advantages of being a grandparent is that one is able to play with one's grandchildren but then go home, leaving the "work" to the children's parents. In many cases, however, this mind-set assumes plentiful sources of money and leisure time. It hardly addresses all the complications of family separations or divorce, or loss of identity as a family unit, which are so common today (L. J. Bridges et al., 2007; Soliz, 2007). It doesn't address the fact that some grandparents hardly get to see—or never get to see—their grandchildren because of geographical separation or because of harsh feelings following family conflict.

The notion of grandparents enjoying the best of the grandchild while escaping responsibility also ignores the fact that in thousands of cases grandparents bear the primary responsibility for rearing grandchildren (C. G. Goodman, 2007a; Hayslip & Kaminski, 2006).

Grandparents in Charge

One or both parents typically determine how their children will be raised. But sometimes grandparents play a major role—or *the* major role (C. G. Goodman, 2007a). For example, an Israeli study of immigrants from Ethiopia and Eastern European countries found that grandparents who lived with single parents and their grandchildren had a strong influence on their grandchildren and contributed to the overall adjustment of the family (Doron & Markovitzky, 2007).

When grandparents live with couples and their grandchildren, they have less influence on child rearing, according to many studies (e.g., Doron & Markovitzky, 2007; C. G. Goodman, 2007b); under these circumstances, they are less likely to contribute to the adjustment of the family. Rather than "filling a hole," they frequently become a

Grandfamilies

Millions of children are being raised by grandparents. Watch one family talk about raising their granddaughter as their own.

source of discord between their son or daughter and their son- or daughter-in-law.

In some cases grandparents are the sole caregivers of their grandchildren. These arrangements typically begin when the grandchild has a single parent (Hayslip & Kaminski, 2006; H.-O. H. Park & Greenberg, 2007). The single parent may die. The single parent may be in the military and be sent on a tour of duty. The parent may place the child with grandparents while she or he tries living in another location, with or without a new job, and the time extends. The parent may run off, perhaps involved with drugs or prostitution.

Regardless of the reasons why grandparents—usually grandmothers—assume the responsibility for parenting grandchildren, becoming a parent again in middle adulthood can be particularly stressful (Gerard et al., 2006; Leder et al., 2007). Do they attend

Grandparents must sometimes play the major role in the rearing of grandchildren. Grandparents are more likely to have to assume this role when grandchildren have a single parent.

school meetings with young parents and continually make explanations? If they are at the height of their careers, where do they find the time for all the chores (F. M. Ludwig et al., 2007)? Do they have to become current with the new crop of children's TV programs? It's a far cry from playing with the grandchildren, or taking them to a museum, and then going home—leaving the work to the parents!

But let us not forget that most grandparents do enjoy their roles in their grandchildren's lives. Their grandchildren value them deeply, even when they do not see them as often as they might wish (L. J. Bridges et al., 2007). Grandparents' greater fund of child-rearing experience often allows them to relate to their grandchildren in a more relaxed way than parents can.

Lesbians and Bisexual Women as Grandparents

One study that relied on extensive interviews of lesbian and bisexual grandmothers found that the experiences of these women were in some ways similar to those of heterosexual people, and in other ways quite different (Orel, 2006). Like most heterosexual grandparents, the lesbian and bisexual grandmothers believed that they were important sources of emotional support for their grandchildren. They also reported that their children either helped (facilitated) or hindered (discouraged) their relationships with their grandchildren, and that the pattern might shift from time to time. On the other hand, all of the grandmothers in the study were concerned about whether or not they should disclose their sexual orientations to their grandchildren and exactly how they should go about it.

Middle-Aged Children and Aging Parents

Because of increasing life expectancy, more than half of the middle-aged people in developed nations have at least one living parent, and the generations frequently go on to experience late adulthood together (Callahan, 2007; U.S. Bureau of the Census, 2008). In East Asian nations such as China, Japan, and Korea, older parents tend to live with their children and their grandchildren, but not so in the United States (H.-K. Kwok, 2006).

You might think that most aging American parents move to Sunbelt locations such as Florida and Arizona, but it isn't so. Nearly two thirds of them live near a child (U.S. Bureau of the Census, 2008) and frequently visit and call. The relationships between

© 2008 Eric Lowenbach/Getty Images

People in middle adulthood who are responsible for meeting the needs of their children yet also burdened by the needs of aging parents.

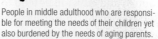

Parent-Child Relationships

Read "Reciprocity in Parent–Child Relations Over the Adult Life Course."

Adult Children and Aging Parents

Read "Children of Aging Parents."

middle-aged adults and older parents can grow quite close, especially as tensions and expectations from earlier years tend to slip into history. If an older mother had been disappointed in her now middle-aged daughter's choice of a husband, now the marriage may have ended or worked out, or there might be grandchildren to focus on. The years and other events place things in perspective.

If the aging parents require assistance, in the United States and Canada the task usually falls to a middle-aged daughter, who then becomes part of the **sandwich generation**. She is "sandwiched" between several generations, caring for or contributing to the support of her own children at the same time she is caring for one or two parents (Grundy & Henretta, 2006). She may also be helping out with grandchildren. If she is fortunate, there is a sibling living in the vicinity to share the task. Given that she is also likely to be in the workforce, her role overload is multiplied (Gans & Silverstein, 2006).

In other societies—such as Hong Kong in China, where aging parents usually live with a son's family—it is more often than not the son who assumes the major responsibility for caring for his parents, emotionally and financially (H.-K. Kwok, 2007). In this patriarchal society, the son's priorities often run like this: first, his own children; second, his parents; third, his wife.

Siblings

Sibling relationships continue into late adulthood for most adults in the United States. The majority of people in middle adulthood have at least one living brother or sister. Most adult sibling relationships are close, but they tend to reflect the nature of sibling relationships in childhood. Then, too, sisters tend to have more intimate relationships than brothers (Bedford & Avioli, 2006). Yet now and then sibling relationships that were antagonistic or competitive in childhood or adolescence grow closer in middle adulthood if the siblings cooperate in caring for a disabled parent (Leone, 2000). Conversely, a sibling relationship that had been close can grow distant if one sibling allows another to do all the work in caring for a parent.

Friends

Adolescents are often parts of cliques and crowds, and young adults often have large numbers of friends. In middle adulthood, the number of friends tends to dwindle, and couples and individuals tend to place more value on the friends they keep (R. G. Adams & Ueno, 2006). In midlife, people become less willing to spend their time with "just anybody"; therefore, their remaining friends are still more likely to be close matches in

sandwich generation The term given to middle-aged people who need to meet the demands of their own children and of aging parents.

terms of interests, activities, and, often, years of mutual experience. For this reason, the loss of a friend is felt more deeply. But as in earlier years, there are gender differences. Male friends are more likely to be competitive and less likely to be intimate than female friends (R. G. Adams & Ueno, 2006; Muhlbauer & Chrisler, 2007).

Social isolation is connected with poorer physical and psychological health and with mortality. Compared to women, men are more likely to lack friends and other close social relationships. In a survey of 1,421 Detroit men ranging in age from 20 to 93, Toni Antonucci and Kira Birditt (2004) found that men without close social ties were significantly more depressed than men with solid relationships.

In the next chapter, we'll turn our attention to the developments that occur in late adulthood.

Midlife friends tend to be close matches in terms of background and interests.

The Sandwich Generation

Watch and learn more about adult children caring for their aging parents.

Check Your Learning Quiz 8.4

Go to **login.cengagebrain.com** and take the online quiz.

GO to your Psychology CourseMate at login.cengagebrain.com and take the Chapter Post-Test to see which Learning Objectives you've mastered and which need more review. Use the chapter review guide below and the online activities—including flashcards to review key terms—to measure your learning.

Measure ^ **Your Learning**

Online Activities

Key Terms	Video	Animation	Reading	Assessment
Middle adulthood, interindividual variability, presbyopia			Aging, Gender and Ethnicity	Check Your Learning Quiz 8.1
Metastasis, arteriosclerosis, atherosclerosis	Atherosclerosis			
Leukocyte				
Menopause, perimenopause, climacteric, sexual dysfunction	Erectile Dysfunction Viagra for Women? Male Menopause?			
Multidirectionality, plasticity, crystallized intelligence, fluid intelligence	The Brain and Memory Midlife Memory Declines			Check Your Learning Quiz 8.2
		Cognitive Changes in Middle Age		
		Developmental Tasks in Middle Age		
Generativity versus stagnation, midlife transition, midlife crisis				Check Your Learning Quiz 8.3

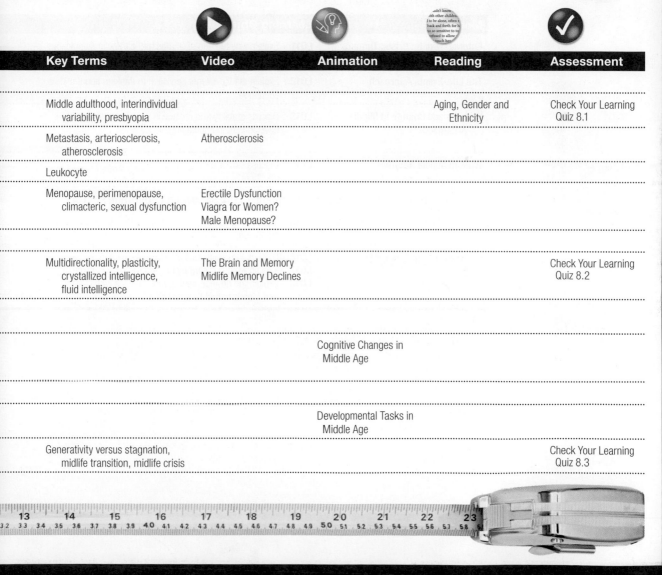

Module	Learning Objectives	
Entering Midlife: Crisis, Turning Point, or Prime of Life?	LO11	Explain why the age of 35 has had particular significance for women.
The Life-Events Approach	LO12	Explain the life-events approach to thinking about middle adulthood.
Stability and Change in Middle Adulthood	LO13	Discuss stability and change in social and emotional development in middle adulthood.
Work in Middle Adulthood	LO14	Discuss career developments typical of middle adulthood.

8.4 Social Development in Middle Adulthood: In the Sandwich Generation? 514

Evolving Parent–Child Relationships	LO15	Explain how relationships with parents change in middle adulthood.
Grandparenting	LO16	Discuss the challenges of grandparenting.
	LO17	Explain what is meant by the *sandwich generation*.
	LO18	Explain the development of relationships with siblings and friends in middle adulthood.

Online Activities

Key Terms	Video	Animation	Reading	Assessment
	Women Over 40 with Eating Disorders		Midlife Crisis	
Empty-nest syndrome	Failure to Launch			
"Big five" personality traits		The Big Five: The Five-Factor Model of Personality		
	Work and Flextime			
Sandwich generation	Grandfamilies The Sandwich Generation		Parents-Child Relationships Adult Children and Aging Parents	Check Your Learning Quiz 8.4

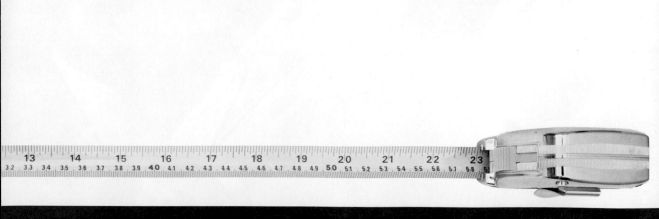

Late Adulthood

CHAPTER

9

© Juice Images/Alamy

Chapter Outline and Learning Objectives

1 GO to your **Psychology CourseMate** at **login.cengagebrain.com** and take the **Chapter Pre-Test** to introduce yourself to this chapter's topics and see what you may already know.

2 READ the **Learning Objectives** (LOs, in the left sidebars) and begin the chapter.

3 COMPLETE the **Online Activities** (in the right sidebars) *as you read each module.* Activities include **videos, animations, readings,** and **quizzes.**

4 CHECK Your Learning by going online to take the quiz at the end of each module and review material as necessary.

5 MEASURE Your Learning after reading the chapter by taking the online **Chapter Post-Test.** Use the chapter review guide at the end of the chapter as needed.

WATCH for these **Online Activities** icons as you read:

Video   Animation   Reading   Assessment

These online activities are essential to mastering this chapter. Go to login.cengagebrain.com:

Videos Watch the following videos:

- Senior Sexuality
- Cognitive Models of Aging
- Dementia and Cognition
- Pick's Disease
- Alzheimer's Disease
- Alzheimer's Test
- Assisted Living and the Social Model of Care
- Child and Adult Day Care
- Caring for Aging Parents
- Technology and Caring for the Elderly
- Delaying Retirement
- Active Elderly
- Enjoying Retirement

Animations Interact with and visualize important processes, timelines, and concepts:

- The Aging Brain
- Problem Solving
- Depression and Anxiety in Older Adults
- Keys to Successful Aging

Readings Delve deeper into key content:

- 10 Ways to Recognize Hearing Loss: A Questionnaire
- Osteoporosis
- Sleep Apnea
- Programmed Theories of Aging
- Planning for Retirement

Assessment Measure your mastery:

- Chapter Pre-Test
- Check Your Learning Quizzes
- Chapter Post-Test

▶ **LO1** Discuss physical development in late adulthood.

Did you know that—

- In Colonial America, aging was viewed so positively that men often claimed to be older than they actually were?
- Women can maintain the ability to reach orgasm for a lifetime?
- Most older adults remain independent in their living arrangements?
- Substance abuse is quite common in late adulthood?

▼

An agequake is on the horizon. People who are currently age 65 and above—those who are in **late adulthood**—are the most rapidly growing segment of the American population. So many people are living longer that we are in the midst of a "graying of America," an aging of the population that is having significant effects on many aspects of society.

Physical Development

In 1900, only 1 person in 25 was over the age of 65. Today, that figure has more than tripled, to 1 in 8. By midcentury, more than 1 in 5 Americans will be 65 years of age or older, and we expect to see the percentage of Americans over the age of 75 double (Kawas & Brookmeyer, 2001). To put these numbers in historical context, consider that through virtually all of human history, until the beginning of the nineteenth century, only a small fraction of humans lived to the age of 50.

Longevity and Life Expectancy

late adulthood The final stage of development, beginning at age 65.

life span The maximum amount of time a person can live under optimal conditions. Also called *longevity*.

life expectancy The amount of time a person can actually be expected to live in a given setting.

One's **life span**, or *longevity*, is the length of time one can live under the best of circumstances. The life span of a species, including humans, depends on its genetic programming. With the right genes and environment, and with the good fortune to avoid serious injuries or illnesses, people have a maximum life span of about 115 years.

Life expectancy refers to the number of years a person in a given population group can actually expect to live. The average European American child born 100 years ago in the United States could expect to live 47 years. The average African

American could expect a shorter life of 35.5 years (Andersen & Taylor, 2009). Since then, great strides have been made in increasing life expectancy. High infant mortality rates due to diseases such as German measles, smallpox, polio, and diphtheria contributed to the lower life expectancies of a century ago. These diseases have been brought under control or eradicated. Other major killers, including bacterial infections such as tuberculosis, are now largely controlled by antibiotics. Factors that contribute to longevity include public health measures such as safer water supplies, improved dietary habits, and health care. Table 9.1 shows the life expectancy of males and females born today in various regions and countries of the world.

Gender Differences in Life Expectancy

Life expectancy among men in the United States trails that among women by about 5 years (76 years for men vs. 81 years for women) (CIA, 2011). Why the gap? For one thing, heart disease typically develops later in life in women than in men, as estrogen provides some protection against it. Also, men are more likely to die from accidents, cirrhosis of the liver, strokes, suicide, homicide, HIV/AIDS, and some forms of cancer. Many of these causes of death reflect unhealthful habits that are more typical of men, such as drinking, reckless behavior, and smoking.

Table 9.1
Life Expectancy at Birth (in Years) by Region, Country, and Gender

	Males	Females
Africa		
Egypt	70	75
Mozambique	51	53
Asia		
Afghanistan	45	45
China	73	77
India	66	68
Japan	79	86
South Korea	76	82
Latin America		
Brazil	69	76
Cuba	75	80
Jamaica	72	75
Mexico	74	79
Europe		
France	78	85
Germany	78	82
Italy	79	85
Poland	72	80
Russia	60	73
Sweden	79	84
United Kingdom	78	82
North America		
Canada	79	84
United States	76	81

Source: Central Intelligence Agency ([CIA], 2011).

Many men are also reluctant to have regular physical examinations or to talk over health problems with their doctors. Many men avoid medical attention until problems that could have been easily prevented or treated become serious or life threatening. For example, women are more likely to examine themselves for signs of breast cancer than men are to examine their testicles for unusual lumps.

Physical Changes

After we reach our physical peak in our 20s, our biological functions begin a gradual decline. Aging also involves adapting to changing physical and social realities. "Young Turks" in the workplace eventually become the "old guard." One-time newlyweds come to celebrate their silver and golden anniversaries. Yet aging can involve more than adjustment; it can bring about personal growth and exciting changes in direction as well. With advanced age many of us become more harmonious with others and within ourselves. However, we must learn to adapt to changes in our mental skills and abilities. Though older people's memories and fluid intelligence may not be as keen as they once were, maturity and experience frequently make people founts of wisdom.

Aging also has social aspects. Our self-concepts and behavior as "young," "middle-aged," or "old" stem in large measure from cultural beliefs. In Colonial times, "mature" people had great prestige, and men routinely claimed to be older than they were. Women, among whom reproductive capacity was valued, did not do so. By contrast, the modern era has been marked by **ageism**—prejudice against people because of their age. Stereotypes that paint older people as crotchety, sluggish, forgetful, and fixed in their ways shape the way people respond to older people and actually impair their performance (Horton, 2008).

In Chapter 8 we reviewed a number of physical changes that occur as people advance from early adulthood to middle adulthood and, in a number of cases, to late adulthood (changes in the skin, hair, and nails; senses; reaction time; lung capacity; metabolism; muscle strength; bone density; aerobic capacity; blood-sugar toler-

ageism Prejudice against people because of their age.

cataract A condition characterized by clouding of the lens of the eye.

glaucoma A condition involving abnormally high fluid pressure in the eye.

presbycusis Loss of acuteness of hearing due to age-related degenerative changes in the ear.

osteoporosis A disorder in which bones become more porous, brittle, and subject to fracture, due to loss of calcium and other minerals.

Dave & Les Jacobs/Blend Images/Jupiterimages

ance; and ability to regulate body temperature). Here we revisit and highlight changes in sensory functioning and bone density as they apply to late adulthood.

Changes in Sensory Functioning

Beginning in middle age, the lenses of the eyes become stiffer, leading to presbyopia, as discussed in Module 8.1 (Chapter 8). Chemical changes of aging can lead to vision disorders such as **cataracts** and **glaucoma**. Cataracts cloud the lenses of the eyes, reducing vision. Today, outpatient surgery for correcting cataracts is routine. If the surgery is performed before the condition progresses too far, the outcome for regained sight is excellent. Glaucoma is a buildup of fluid pressure inside the eyeball. It can lead to tunnel vision (lack of peripheral vision) or blindness. Glaucoma rarely occurs before age 40, and affects about 1 in 250 people over the age of 40, and 1 in 25 people over 80. Rates are higher among African Americans than European Americans, and among diabetics than nondiabetics. Glaucoma is treated with medication or surgery.

After we reach our physical peak in our 20s, our biological functions begin a gradual decline.

The sense of hearing, especially the ability to hear higher frequencies, also declines with age. **Presbycusis** is age-related hearing loss that affects about 1 person in 3 over the age of 65 (Sommers, 2008). Hearing ability tends to decline more quickly in men than in women. Hearing aids magnify sound and can compensate for hearing loss.

Taste and smell become less acute as we age. Our sense of smell decreases almost ninefold from youth to advanced late adulthood. We also lose taste buds in the tongue with aging. As a result, foods must be more strongly spiced to yield the same flavor.

Bone Density

Bones begin to lose density in middle adulthood, becoming more brittle and vulnerable to fracture. Bones in the spine, hip, thigh, and forearm lose the most density as we age. **Osteoporosis** is a disorder in which bones lose so much calcium that they become dangerously prone to breakage. An estimated 10 million people in the United States over the age of 50 have osteoporosis of the hip (United States Department of Health and Human Services [USDHHS], 2005). Osteoporosis results in

Hearing Loss

Read "The NIDCD's 10 Ways to Recognize Hearing Loss: A Questionnaire."

Osteoporosis

Read and learn more about osteoporosis.

more than one million bone fractures a year in the United States, the most serious of which are hip fractures (that is, breaks in the thigh bone just below the hip joint). Hip fractures often result in hospitalization, loss of mobility, and, as is often the case in people in advanced late adulthood, death from complications. Fifteen to twenty percent of the people who sustain a hip fracture die within a year (L. C. Brunner et al., 2003).

Osteoporosis can shorten one's stature by inches and deform one's posture, causing the curvature in the spine known as *dowager's hump*. Both men and women are at risk of osteoporosis, but it poses a greater threat to women. Men typically have a larger bone mass, which provides them with more protection against the disorder. Following the decline in bone density that women experience after menopause, women stand about twice the risk of hip fractures and about eight times the risk of spine fractures that men do. But older women who engage in walking as a form of regular exercise are less likely than their sedentary counterparts to suffer hip fractures (USDHHS, 2004a). To prevent osteoporosis and promote their own bone health, the U.S. Surgeon General recommends, beginning in childhood and continuing into late adulthood, individuals:

- Eat a well-balanced diet.
- Get the recommended daily requirements for calcium. Three 8-ounce glasses of low-fat milk each day, combined with the calcium from the rest of a normal diet, is enough for most individuals.
- Get enough vitamin D from sunshine—but if not possible, changes in diet and vitamin supplements can help make up the difference.
- Meet recommended guidelines for physical activity, which includes at least 30 minutes a day for adults and 60 minutes for children, and specific strength and weight-bearing activities that help build and maintain bone mass thoughout life.

Sleep

Older people need about 7 hours of sleep per night, yet sleep disorders such as insomnia and **sleep apnea** become more common in later adulthood (Wickwire et al., 2008). People experiencing sleep apnea stop breathing repeatedly during the night, causing them to wake. Apnea may be more than a sleep problem. For reasons that are not entirely clear, it is linked to increased risk of heart attacks and strokes.

sleep apnea Temporary suspension of breathing while asleep.

Sleep problems in late adulthood may involve physical changes that bring discomfort. Sometimes they symptomize psychological disorders such as depression, anxiety, or dementia. Men with enlarged prostate glands commonly need to urinate during the night, causing awakening. Other contributing factors include loneliness, especially after the death of a close friend, spouse, or life partner.

Sleep medications are the most common treatment for insomnia (Wickwire et al., 2008). Alternatives may include keeping a regular sleep schedule, challenging exaggerated worries about the consequences of remaining awake, using relaxation techniques, and exercising. Sleep apnea may be treated with surgery to widen the upper airways that block breathing or with devices such as a nose mask that maintains air pressure to keep airways open during sleep (Wickwire et al., 2008).

Sexuality

Even in the aftermath of the sexual revolution of the 1960s, many people still tie sex to reproduction. Therefore, they assume that sex is appropriate only for the young. There are unfounded cultural myths that suggest that older people are sexless and that older men with sexual interests are "dirty old men." If older people believe these myths, they may renounce sex or feel guilty if they remain sexually active. Older women are handicapped by a double standard of greater tolerance of continued sexuality among men.

People do not lose their sexuality as they age, however (Laumann et al., 2006). Sexual daydreaming, sex drive, and sexual activity all tend to decline with age, but sexual satisfaction may remain high (Barnett & Dunning, 2003). Older people with partners usually remain sexually active (Laumann et al., 2006). Most older people report that they like sex. Sexual activity among older people, as among other groups, is influenced not only by physical structures and

Stockbyte/JupiterImages

Sleep Apnea

Read and learn more about sleep apnea.

Senior Sex

Explore "Senior Sexuality."

changes, but also by psychological well-being, feelings of intimacy, and cultural expectations (Laumann et al., 2006).

Although many older people retain the capacity to respond sexually, physical changes do occur. But if older people fine-tune their expectations, they may find themselves leading some of their most sexually fulfilling years (Trudel et al., 2007).

Changes in Women

Many of the physical changes in older women stem from a decline in estrogen production. The vaginal walls lose much of their elasticity and grow paler and thinner. Thus, sexual activity may become painful. The thinning of the walls may also place greater pressure against the bladder and urethra during sex, sometimes leading to urinary urgency and a burning sensation during urination.

The vagina shrinks. The labia majora lose much of their fatty deposits and become thinner. The vaginal opening constricts, and penile entry may become difficult. Following menopause, women also produce less vaginal lubrication, and what they do produce may take minutes, not seconds, to appear. Lack of adequate lubrication is a key reason for painful sex. Women's nipples still become erect as they are sexually aroused, but orgasmic spasms become less powerful and fewer in number. Thus, orgasms may feel less intense, even though the experience of orgasm may remain just as satisfying. The uterine contractions that occur during orgasm may become discouragingly painful for some older women. Despite these changes, women can retain their ability to reach orgasm well into their advanced years.

Changes in Men

Age-related changes tend to occur more gradually in men than in women and are not clearly connected with any one biological event (Barnett & Dunning, 2003). Male adolescents may achieve erection in seconds. After about age 50, men take progressively longer to achieve erection. Erections become less firm, perhaps because of lowered testosterone levels (Laumann et al., 2006).

Testosterone production usually declines gradually from about age 40 to age 60, and then begins to level off. However, the decline is not inevitable and may be related to a man's general health. Sperm production tends to decline, but viable sperm may be produced by men in their 70s, 80s, and 90s.

Nocturnal erections diminish in intensity, duration, and frequency as men age, but they do not normally disappear altogether (P. J. Perry et al., 2001). An adolescent

programmed theories of aging Views of aging based on the concept that the processes of aging are governed, at least in part, by genetic factors.

may require but a few minutes to regain erection and ejaculate again after a first orgasm, whereas a man in his 30s may require half an hour. Past age 50, regaining erection may require several hours.

Older men produce less ejaculate, and the contractions of orgasm become weaker and fewer. Still, an older male may enjoy orgasm as thoroughly as he did at a younger age. Following orgasm, erection subsides more rapidly than in a younger man.

Patterns of Sexual Activity

Despite decline in physical functions, older people can lead fulfilling sex lives. Years of sexual experience may more than compensate for any lessening of physical response (Laumann et al., 2006). Frequency of sexual activity tends to decline with age because of hormonal changes, physical problems, boredom, and cultural attitudes. Yet sexuality among older people is variable (Laumann et al., 2006). Many older people engage in sexual activity as often as or more often than when younger; some develop an aversion to sex; others lose interest.

Couples may adapt to the physical changes of aging by broadening their sexual repertoire to include more diverse forms of stimulation. The availability of a sexually interested and supportive partner may be the most important determinant of continued sexual activity (Laumann et al., 2006).

Theories of Aging

So far, everyone who has lived has aged—which may not be a bad fate, considering the alternative. Although we can make lengthy lists of the things that happen as we age, we don't know exactly why they happen. Theories of aging fall into two broad categories:

- *Programmed theories* see aging as the result of genetic instructions.
- *Cellular-damage theories* propose that aging results from damage to cells.

Programmed Theories of Aging

Programmed theories of aging propose that aging and longevity are determined by a biological clock that ticks at a rate governed by genes. That is, the seeds of our own demise are carried in our genes. Evidence supporting a genetic link to aging comes in part from studies showing that longevity tends to run in families (Perls, 2005). For example, the siblings of centenarians are more likely than members of the general population to live to be 100 themselves (Perls et al., 2002).

Theories of Aging

Read and learn more about programmed theories of aging.

▶ **LO3** Compare programmed and cellular-damage theories of aging.

cellular-clock theory Aging theory focusing on the limits of cell division.

telomere A protective segment of DNA located at the tip of a chromosome.

hormonal-stress theory Aging theory that hypothesizes that stress hormones, left at elevated levels, make the body more vulnerable to chronic conditions.

immunological theory Aging theory that holds that the immune system is preset to decline by an internal biological clock.

cellular-damage theories of aging Views of aging based on the concept that internal bodily changes and external environmental insults cause cells and organ systems to malfunction, leading to death.

wear-and-tear theory Aging theory that suggests that over time our bodies become less capable of repairing themselves.

free-radical theory Aging theory that attributes aging to damage caused by the accumulation of free radicals.

cross-linking theory Aging theory that suggests stiffening of body proteins eventually breaks down bodily processes, leading to aging.

But why should organisms carry "suicidal" genes? Programmed-aging theorists believe that it would be adaptive for species to survive long enough to reproduce and transmit their genes to future generations. From the evolutionary perspective, there would be no advantage to the species (and probably a disadvantage, given limited food supplies) to repair cell machinery and body tissues to maintain life indefinitely.

Cellular-clock theory focuses on the built-in limits of cell division. After dividing about 50 times, human cells cease dividing and eventually die (Hayflick, 1996). Researchers find clues to the limits of cell division in **telomeres**, the protective segments of DNA at the tips of chromosomes. Telomeres shrink each time cells divide. When the loss of telomeres reaches a critical point after a number of cell divisions, the cell may no longer be able to function (Epel et al., 2006). The length of the telomeres for a species may determine the number of times a cell can divide and survive.

Hormonal-stress theory focuses on the endocrine system, which releases hormones into the bloodstream. Hormonal changes foster age-related changes such as puberty and menopause. As we age, stress hormones including corticosteroids and adrenaline are left at elevated levels after illnesses, making the body more vulnerable to chronic conditions such as diabetes, osteoporosis, and heart disease. The changes in production of stress hormones over time may be preprogrammed by genes.

Immunological theory holds that the immune system is preset to decline by an internal biological clock. For example, the production of antibodies declines with age, rendering the body less able to fight off infections. Age-related changes in the immune system also increase the risk of cancer and may contribute to general deterioration.

Twins Gin Kanie (left) and Kin Narita lived to the ages of 108 and 107.

©Yoshida-Fujifotos/The Image Works

Cellular-Damage Theories of Aging

Programmed theories assume that internal bodily processes are preset to age by genes. **Cellular-damage theories of aging** propose that internal bodily changes and external environmental assaults (such as carcinogens and toxins) cause cells and organ systems to malfunction, leading to death. For example, the **wear-and-tear theory** suggests that over the years our bodies—as machines that wear out through use—become less capable of repairing themselves.

Do you think exposure to ultraviolet light, extreme heat, and air pollution contribute to cellular damage and aging?

© Tim Pannell/Corbis

The **free-radical theory** attributes aging to damage caused by the accumulation of unstable molecules called *free radicals*. Free radicals are produced during metabolism by oxidation, possibly damaging cell proteins, membranes, and DNA (Sierra, 2006). Most free radicals are naturally disarmed by nutrients and enzymes called *antioxidants*. Most antioxidants are either made by the body or found in food. As we age, our bodies produce fewer antioxidants (Rattan et al., 2006). People whose diets are rich in antioxidants are less likely to develop heart disease and some cancers.

As we age, cell proteins bind to one another in a process called *cross-linking*, thereby toughening tissues. Cross-linking stiffens collagen—the connective tissue supporting tendons, ligaments, cartilage, bone, and skin. One result is coarse, dry skin. (Flavored animal collagen, or gelatin, is better known by the brand name Jell-O.) **Cross-linking theory** holds that the stiffening of body proteins accelerates and eventually breaks down bodily processes, leading to some of the effects of aging (Rattan et al., 2006). The immune system combats cross-linking, but becomes less able to do so as we age.

In considering the many theories of aging, we should note that aging is an extremely complex biological process that may not be explained by any single theory or cause. Aging may involve a combination of these and other factors.

Is Calorie Restriction the Fountain of Youth?

Restricting calories by approximately 30% may trigger antiaging responses that evolved to increase the chances of survival when food is scarce. For example, calorie restriction in humans, nonhuman primates, and other mammals lowers blood

▶ **LO4** Identify common health concerns of late adulthood.

pressure, cholesterol, and blood-sugar and insulin levels. It strengthens the immune system and lowers the fat mass (Roth et al., 2004). Calorie restriction also fends off Alzheimer's-like symptoms in rhesus monkeys.

In laboratory experiments, mice were fed a diet that was 30% to 40% lower in calories than normal but contained all necessary nutrients. The development of chronic diseases and cancers was retarded, and the mice lived 50% beyond their normal life spans (Hursting et al., 2003).

Calorie restriction may raise levels of dehydroepiandrosterone sulfate (DHEAS), a hormone that reduces the risk of cancer and improves immune-system functioning. DHEAS production usually begins to decline after approximately age 30, dipping to as low as 5% to 15% of peak levels by age 60. DHEAS levels are higher than normal in long-lived men and in rhesus monkeys with calorie-restricted diets (Chong et al., 2004).

It remains to be seen whether, and by how much, calorie restriction extends the life span of people who have access to modern health care. Moreover, it is difficult enough for many people to keep their weight within normal limits. How willing would we be to lower our calorie intake further? Researchers are therefore also seeking alternate ways of triggering the antiaging responses caused by calorie restriction.

Health Concerns and Aging

Though aging takes a toll on our bodies, many gerontologists believe that disease is not inevitable. They distinguish between *normal aging* and *pathological aging*. In **normal aging**, physiological processes decline slowly with age and the person is able to enjoy many years of health and vitality into late adulthood. In **pathological aging**, chronic diseases or degenerative processes, such as heart disease, diabetes, and cancer, lead to disability or premature death. Older people typically need more health care than younger people. Though people over the age of 65 make up about 12% of the population, they occupy 25% of the hospital beds. As the numbers of older people increase in the twenty-first century, so will the cost of health care.

normal aging Processes of aging that undergo a gradual decline, enabling people to enjoy health and vitality well into late adulthood.

pathological aging Aging in which chronic diseases or degenerative processes, such as heart disease, diabetes, and cancer, lead to disability or premature death.

Medicare, a federally controlled health insurance program for older Americans and the disabled, only partially subsidizes the health-care needs of these groups. Another government program, Medicaid, covers a portion of the health-care costs of people of all ages who are otherwise unable to afford coverage. Many older adults use both programs.

Most older adults do not require institutional care, such as nursing homes or residential care facilities. More than 2 of 3 adults age 65 and older live in their own homes. Less than 10% of older adults live in nursing homes or other long-term care facilities. The population of nursing homes is made up largely of people age 80 and older. Yet if older adults live long enough, nearly half will eventually require some form of nursing or home health care.

It is also untrue that most older Americans spend their later years in a retirement community. The majority of older adults remain in their own communities after retirement. Moreover, despite beliefs that most older people are impoverished, Americans aged 65 and above are actually less likely than the general population to live under the poverty level.

In 1900, older people were more likely to die from infectious diseases such as influenza and pneumonia than they are today. Today, older people are at greater risk of dying from chronic diseases such as heart disease and cancer. More than 4 out of 5 people over the age of 65 have at least one chronic health problem (Heron, 2007). Some of these problems, like varicose veins, are minor. Others, like heart disease, pose serious health risks. Figure 9.1 shows the percentages of people aged 65 and older who are affected by

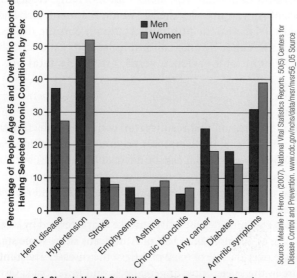

Source: Melanie P. Heron. (2007). National Vital Statistics Reports, 50(5) Centers for Disease Control and Prevention. www.cdc.gov/nchs/data/nvsr/nvsr56_05 Source Rathus/HDEV 2e, Figure 17.2, page 318.

Figure 9.1 Chronic Health Conditions Among People Age 65 and Over The leading chronic health conditions affecting people in late adulthood are hypertension, heart disease, and arthritis.

common chronic health conditions. While longevity is increasing, so too are the number of years older people are living with one or more chronic health problems.

Heart Disease, Cancer, and Stroke

The three major causes of death of Americans aged 65 and older are heart disease, cancer, and stroke (see Table 9.2). Cancer is the leading cause of death in women between the ages of 40 and 79, and men between the ages of 60 and 79, but heart disease is the nation's leading cause of death among both men and women beyond the age of 80.

The risk of most cancers rises as we age because the immune system becomes less able to rid the body of precancerous and cancerous cells. Many older people are not adequately screened or treated for cancer or heart disease. One reason for the gap in diagnosis and treatment is *elder bias* (Ludwick & Silva, 2003), or discrimination against the elderly on the part of some health professionals.

Among the top chronic conditions listed in Figure 9.1, several are also leading causes of death or pose significant risk factors for mortality. Hypertension, which affects about 50% of Americans over the age of 65, is a major risk factor for heart attacks and strokes. Diabetes, the fifth most common chronic illness, is the sixth leading cause of death. Other chronic conditions, such as cataracts, chronic sinusitis, visual impairment, and varicose veins, are rarely fatal but can lead to disability.

Arthritis

Arthritis is joint inflammation that results from conditions affecting the structures inside and surrounding the joints. Symptoms progress from swelling, pain, and stiffness to loss of function. Children can also be affected by arthritis, but it is more common with advancing age. Arthritis is more common in women than men and in African Americans than European Americans. *Osteoarthritis* and *rheumatoid arthritis* are the two most common forms of arthritis.

Osteoarthritis is a painful, degenerative disease characterized by wear and tear on the joints. By the age of 60, more than half of Americans show some signs of the disease. Among people over the age of 65, 2 of 3 have the disease. The joints most commonly affected are in the knees, hips, fingers, neck, and lower back. Osteoarthritis is caused by erosion of cartilage, the pads of fibrous tissue that cushion the ends of bones. As cartilage wears down, bones grind together, causing pain (Axford et al.,

arthritis Inflammation of the joints.

osteoarthritis A painful, degenerative disease characterized by wear and tear on the joints.

2008). Osteoarthritis is more common among obese people because excess weight adds to the load on the hip and knee joints. Health professionals use over-the-counter anti-inflammatory drugs (aspirin, acetaminophen, ibuprofen, naproxen) and prescription anti-inflammatory drugs to help relieve pain and discomfort (Axford et al., 2008). In severe cases, joint-replacement surgery may be needed. Many older people report that they are mobile and pain free within a few months after joint replacement. Physical therapy and certain exercises may also be prescribed.

Table 9.2
10 Leading Causes of Death Among Men and Women
65 Years and Over of All Races

Cause of Death	Percentage of Total Deaths (Male)	Percentage of Total Deaths (Female)
Heart disease	29.4%	28.7%
Cancer	25.4%	19.3%
Chronic respiratory diseases	6.4%	5.3%
Stroke	5.5%	7.6%
Diabetes	3.1%	2.9%
Influenza and pneumonia	2.7%	2.9%
Alzheimer's disease	2.6%	5.2%
Accidents	2.3%	1.9%
Kidney disease	2.2%	2.0%
Blood poisoning	1.4%	1.5%

Source: Melanie P. Heron. (2010). National Vital Statistics Reports, 58(14). Centers for Disease Control and Prevention. http://www.cdc.gov/nchs/data/nvsr/ncsr58/nvsr58_14.pdf

Rheumatoid arthritis is characterized by chronic inflammation of the membranes that line the joints, caused by the body's immune system attacking its own tissues. The condition affects the entire body. It can produce unrelenting pain and eventually lead to severe disability. Bones and cartilage may also be affected. Onset of the disease usually occurs between the ages of 40 and 60. Anti-inflammatory drugs are used to treat it.

Substance Abuse

Abuse or misuse of medication (prescription and over-the-counter drugs), much of which is unintentional, poses a serious health threat to older Americans. Forty percent of all prescription drugs in the United States are taken by people age 60 and older, and more than half of people in that age group take two to five medications daily (Johnson-Greene & Inscore, 2005). Among the most commonly used drugs are blood-pressure medication, tranquilizers, sleeping pills, and antidepressants. Taken correctly, prescription drugs can be of help. If used incorrectly, they can be harmful.

Substance abuse is far from rare in late adulthood, although it has a different flavor from substance abuse among young people. Millions of older adults are addicted to, or risk becoming addicted to, prescription drugs, especially tranquilizers. About a quarter of a million older adults are hospitalized each year because of adverse drug reactions. Reasons include the following (Johnson-Greene & Inscore, 2005; Pawaskar & Sansgiry, 2006):

1. *The dosage of drugs is too high.* Because bodily functions slow with age (such as the ability of the liver and kidneys to clear drugs out of the body), the same amount of a drug can have stronger effects and last longer in older people.
2. *Some people may misunderstand directions or be unable to keep track of their usage.*
3. *Many older people have more than one doctor, and treatment plans may not be coordinated.*

rheumatoid arthritis A painful, degenerative disease characterized by chronic inflammation of the membranes that line the joints.

Although alcohol consumption is lower overall among older people than among younger adults, many older adults suffer from long-term alcoholism, and the health risks of alcohol abuse increase with age. The slowdown in the metabolic rate reduces the body's ability to metabolize alcohol, increasing the likelihood of intoxication. The combination of alcohol and other drugs, including prescription drugs, can be dangerous or even lethal. Alcohol can also lessen or intensify the effects of prescription drugs.

Accidents

Though accidents can occur at any age, older people face greater risks of unintentional injuries from falls, motor-vehicle accidents, residential fires, and nonfatal poisoning. Accidents are the eighth leading cause of death among older men, and the ninth leading cause of death among older women in the United States. Falls are especially dangerous for older adults with osteoporosis, because of the increased risks of fractures (Facts about Falling, 2008).

Many accidents involving older adults could be prevented by equipping the home with safety features such as railings and nonskid floors. Wearing proper glasses and using hearing aids can reduce the risk of accidents resulting from vision or hearing problems, including many motor-vehicle accidents. Adherence to safe driving speeds is especially important among older drivers because they have slower reaction times than do younger drivers.

Sean Murphy/Getty Images

Check Your Learning Quiz 9.1

Go to **login.cengagebrain.com** and take the online quiz.

▶ **LO5** Discuss developments in memory in late adulthood.

Did you know that—

- People who had graduated 50 years earlier recognized photos of high-school classmates 75% of the time?
- Senior citizens have more difficulty remembering people's names than younger adults?
- Seniors show almost no decline in implicit memory—such as riding a bicycle or using basic multiplication tables?
- Long-term memory has no known limits?
- Senior citizens recall events from the second and third decades of life in greatest detail?
- Age-related declines in processing speed and working memory may explain why many seniors forget things they were planning to do?
- Seniors may retain their receptive vocabularies even as they develop problems in the number of words they can use in expressing themselves?
- Senior citizens often show more wisdom than younger adults?
- Dementia and Alzheimer's disease are not a consequence of normal aging but rather of disease processes?

▼

My wife studied the work of artist Jack Tworkov. When he was in his 30s, his paintings were realistic. In his 50s, his works were abstract expressionistic, like those of Jackson Pollock. In his 60s, his paintings remained abstract and became hard-edged with geometric precision. At the age of 79, a year before his death, he was experimenting with a loosely flowing calligraphic style that he never showed to the public.

Although Tworkov's body was in decline, he told my wife, "Every morning I go to the easel in a fever." He wore a T-shirt and blue jeans, and something about him reminded me of the self I had projected as a teenager. But Tworkov seemed more at ease in his attire at 79 than I had been at 16.

Tworkov was fortunate in that his cognitive processes were clear. Given the scores of new works he showed us, it also appeared that his processing speed had remained good—or at least good enough. His visual and motor memory and his capacity to rivet his attention to a task all remained superb. All these skills are part of what we have labeled *fluid intelligence*, and they are most vulnerable to decline in late adulthood (Saggino et al., 2006). We had no personal way of comparing these skills to what they were 20 or 40 years earlier, but based simply on what we saw, we were stunned at his ability.

Crystallized intelligence can continue to improve throughout much of late adulthood (Mangina & Sokolov, 2006). However, if you have another look at Figure 8.4, you will see that all cognitive skills, on average, tend to decline in advanced age.

Memory: Remembrance of Things Past—and Future

In a classic study of memory, Harry Bahrick and his colleagues (1975) sought to find out how well high-school graduates would recognize photographs of their classmates. Some of their subjects had graduated 15 years earlier, and others had been out of school for some 50 years. The experimenters interspersed photos of actual classmates with 4 times as many photos of strangers. People who had graduated 15 years earlier correctly recognized people who were former schoolmates 90% of the time. But those who had graduated about 50 years earlier still recognized former classmates 75% of the time. A chance level of recognition would have been only 20% (1 photo in 5 was of an actual classmate). Thus, the visual-recognition memories had lasted half a century in people who were now in late adulthood.

Developmentalists speak of various kinds of memories. First, we can distinguish between *retrospective* and *prospective* memories—memories of the past ("retro") and memories of the things we plan to do in the future (we'll discuss both later in the chapter). We can then divide retrospective memories into *explicit* and *implicit*

How long do memories last? What images flood these senior citizens' minds as they look through a photo album going back 40 or 50 years?

memories. **Explicit memories** are of specific information, such as things we did or things that happened to us (called *episodic* or *autobiographical memories*) and general knowledge, such as the author of *Hamlet* (*semantic memory*). **Implicit memories** are more automatic and recall the performance of tasks such as reciting the alphabet or multiplication tables, riding a bicycle, or using a doorknob.

Older adults often complain that they struggle to remember the names of people they know, even people they know very well. They are frustrated by the awareness that they knew the name yesterday, perhaps even a half hour ago, but now it is gone. When they do recall it, or another person reminds them of the name, they think, "Of course!" and perhaps belittle themselves for forgetting. An experiment with young adults and adults in their 70s found that the older adults did have a disproportionate difficulty naming pictures of public figures, but not of uncommon objects (Rendell et al., 2005). It seems that the working memories of older adults hold less information simultaneously than the working memories of young adults. Perhaps, then, when they are picturing the person whose name they forget, or thinking about that person engaged in some activity, the picture or activity momentarily displaces the name (Braver & West, 2008).

The temporal memory of older adults—that is, their recall of the order in which events have occurred—may become confused (Dumas & Hartman, 2003; Hartman & Warren, 2005). Older adults may have difficulty discriminating actual events from illusory events (Rybash & Hrubi-Bopp, 2000).

Older adults usually do not fare as well as younger adults in tasks that measure explicit memory, but they tend to do as well, or nearly as well, in tasks that assess implicit memory (D. D. Mitchell & Bruss, 2003). Implicit-memory tasks tend to be automatic and do not require any conscious effort. They may reflect years of learning and repetition. Examples include memory of multiplication tables or the alphabet. I could ask you to name which letter comes after P or to recite the alphabet. The second task would be easier because that is the way in which you learned, and overlearned, the 26 letters of the alphabet. It is said that you never forget how to ride a bicycle or to use a keyboard; these are also implicit memories—in these cases, sensorimotor habits.

Daniel Schacter (1992) illustrated implicit memory with the story of a woman with amnesia who was found wandering the streets. The police picked her up and found that she could not remember who she was or anything else about her life, and she had no identification. After extensive fruitless questioning, the police hit on the

explicit memory Memory for specific information, including autobiographical information, such as what you had for breakfast, and general knowledge, such as state capitals.

implicit memory Automatic memory based on repetition and apparently not requiring any conscious effort to retrieve.

idea of asking her to dial phone numbers—any number at all. Although the woman did not "know" what she was doing, she dialed her mother's number. She could not make her mother's number explicit, but dialing it was a habit, and she remembered it *implicitly*.

Associative Memory

We use associative learning, and associative memory, to remember that the written letter A has the sound of an A. We also use associative memory to develop a sight vocabulary; that is, we associate the written word *the* with the sound of the word; we do not decode it as we read. In these cases we usually learn by rote rehearsal, or repetition. But we also often use elaborative rehearsal, which is a more complex strategy that makes learning meaningful, to retrieve the associated spellings for spoken words. For example, we may remember to recall the rule "I before E except after C" to retrieve the correct spelling of *retrieve*.

Aging has a detrimental effect on associative memory (Naveh-Benjamin, Brav, et al., 2007). Consider the digit-symbol subscale of the Wechsler Intelligence Scales. While looking back and forth between the answer key and the test items, the individual is asked to fill in as many numbers as possible within a certain amount of time. The abilities to look back and forth and to write efficiently play roles in performance, but so does the ability to associate—or memorize—which symbols correspond with which number. After going back and forth a few times, someone who can associate the square with the number 2 will get more items correct than someone who has to keep on looking. Older adults generally have more difficulty making the associations than early adults do.

In research into age and associative memory, older adults also have been found to have greater difficulty discriminating between new combinations of items on an associative-recognition task and those they have already seen or heard. That is, they find it more difficult to recognize pairs of words that have been presented before than to recognize which individual items they have seen or heard before and which are new (Light et al., 2004).

Various explanations have been hypothesized for the age-related deficit in associative memory. One is difficulty in the initial binding or learning phase of individual pieces of information, when the individual is attempting to encode them (Naveh-Benjamin, Hussain, et al., 2003). Older adults may have more difficulty than younger people in learning that a square is associated with the number 2 or that a triangle is associated

The Aging Brain

Interact to learn more about the brain in late adulthood.

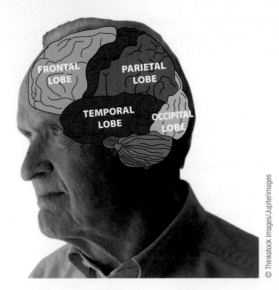

Figure 9.2 The Aging Brain In the aging brain, atrophy in the frontal lobe and in the middle (medial) part of the temporal lobe may account for deficits in associative memory.

© Thinkstock Images/Jupiterimages

with a 3. Yet they would presumably have little difficulty remembering what symbols they had used in the task (e.g, the square and the triangle) and what symbols they had not used (Cohn et al., 2008). A second hypothesis suggests that the associative learning itself is not the problem, but that older adults have more difficulty retrieving the information they have learned (Yonelinas, 2002), which may reflect binding that decays, poor use of strategies to retrieve the associations, or both.

Research by Melanie Cohn and her colleagues (2008) suggests that impairments in associative memory among older adults represent problems in the initial binding of information and the use of effective strategies for retrieval (such as creating sentences which use both members of a pair of words as they are presented). For example, if one member of a pair of words is "man," and another is "cigarette," an elaborative strategy for recollecting the pair could be to rapidly construct the sentence, "The man refuses to smoke a cigarette." Cohn and her colleagues believe that these cognitive developments "are consistent with neurobiological models" of memory that focus on the frontal and medial temporal lobes of the brain (see Figure 9.2). The frontal regions—the executive center of the brain—are involved in directing attention and organizing information and strategic processes. The medial temporal lobe binds elements to form memory traces, recovers information in response to use of proper memory cues, and is therefore a key to recollection. Neurological research shows that deterioration is evident in aging in the frontal lobes and to a lesser degree in the medial temporal lobe, thus logically impairing binding and the use of effective strategies for the retrieval of information.

Long-Term Memory

Long-term memory has no known limits. Memories may reside there for a lifetime, to be recalled with the proper cues. But long-term memories are also subject to distortion, bias, and even decay.

Harry Bahrick and his colleagues (2008) administered questionnaires to 267 alumni of Ohio Wesleyan University, who had graduated anywhere from 1 to 50 years earlier. Subjects thus ranged in age from early adulthood to late adulthood. They were asked to recall their college grades, and their recollections were checked against their actual grades. Of 3,967 grades, 3,025 were recalled correctly. Figure 9.3 relates correct responses to the age of the

Will he remember these grades in 50 years? The likely answer might surprise you.

respondent. The number of correct recollections fell off with the age of the respondent, due generally to errors of omission—that is, leaving items blank rather than entering the wrong grade. As a matter of fact, graduates who were out of school more

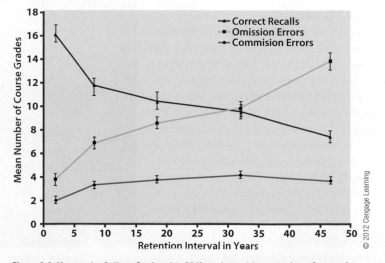

Figure 9.3 Memory for College Grades, 1 to 50 Years Later Mean number of correctly recalled grades, omission errors, and commission errors as a function of retention interval.

▶ **LO6** Discuss language development in late adulthood.

▶ **LO7** Discuss developments in problem solving in late adulthood.

than 40 years entered no more wrong grades, on average, than those who were out of school 8 years or so. The researchers found a grade-inflation bias: 81% of entries of the wrong grade inflated the true grade.

In typical studies of long-term memory, researchers present older adults with timelines that list ages from early childhood to the present day and ask them to fill in key events and to indicate how old they were at the time. Using this technique, people seem to recall events from the second and third decades of life in greatest detail and with the most emotional intensity (Glück & Bluck, 2007). These include early romances (or their absence), high-school days, music groups and public figures, sports heroes, life dreams, and early disappointments. Many psychologists look to psychological explanations for these findings, and considering that coming of age and the development of identity are common characteristics of the second and third decades of life, they may be correct in their pursuit. But note that sex hormones also have their strongest effects in adolescence and early adulthood, and the secretion of these hormones is connected with the release of neurotransmitters that are involved in memory formation (Lupien et al., 2007).

Prospective Memory

Why do we need electronic organizers, desk calendars, and shopping lists? To help us remember the things we have planned to do. As noted earlier, **retrospective memory** helps us retrieve information from the past. **Prospective memory** aids us in remembering things we have planned to do in the future, despite the passage of time and despite the occurrence of interfering events. In order for prospective memory to succeed, we need to have foolproof strategies, such as alarm reminders on our cell phones, or we need to focus our attention and keep it focused. Distractibility will prevent us from reaching the goal.

retrospective memory Memory of past events and general knowledge.

prospective memory Memory of things one has planned for the future.

A Swiss study (Zeintl et al., 2007) examined the relationships between processing speed, working memory (the amount of information a person can keep in mind at once), prospective memory,

Comstock/Jupiterimages

Loud enough? Many older adults have problems understanding the spoken language due to declines in both hearing ability and working memory.

and retrospective memory among 361 people between the ages of 65 and 80. It was found that age-related declines in processing speed and working memory—aspects of fluid intelligence—had important effects on retrospective memory. However, there were age-related declines in prospective memory that appeared to be independent of processing speed and working memory. In other words, even if fluid intelligence remained intact, prospective memory might decline, suggesting powerful roles for attention and distractibility.

Age-related decline in prospective memory is greatest when the task to be completed is not crucial and the cues used to jog the memory are not very prominent, according to another study (Kliegel et al., 2008). When the task is important and older adults use conspicuous cues to remind them, age-related declines in prospective memory tend to disappear. However, the adults have to be cognitively intact enough to plan the strategy.

Language Development

People aged 75 and above tend to show a decline in reading comprehension that is related to a decrease in the scope of working memory (De Beni et al., 2007). Because of the decline in working memory and because of impairments in hearing, many older adults find it more difficult to understand the spoken language (Burke & Shafto, 2008). However, when the speaker slows down and articulates more clearly, comprehension increases (Gordon-Salant et al., 2007).

Older adults may also show deficiencies in language production. Although they may retain their receptive vocabularies, they often show a gradual decline in their expressive vocabularies—that is, the number of words they produce (Hough, 2007). It appears that declines in associative memory and working memory decrease the likelihood that words will "be there" when older people try to summon up ideas (Burke & Shafto, 2008). Similarly, older people are more likely to experience the frustrating "tip of the tongue" phenomenon, in which they are certain that they know a word but temporarily cannot produce it (Shafto et al., 2007).

Problem Solving

Figure 9.4 shows the so-called Duncker candle problem, which is sometimes used to challenge problem-solving skills. The goal is to attach the candle to the wall, using only the objects shown, so that it will burn properly. Rather than be concerned about

Problem Solving

Watch and learn more about problem solving in late adulthood.

▸ **LO8** Discuss the development of wisdom in late adulthood.

▸ **LO9** Discuss dementia in late adulthood, including Alzheimer's disease.

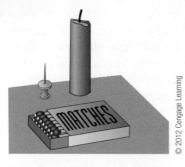

© 2012 Cengage Learning

Figure 9.4 The Duncker Candle Problem
Can you use the objects shown on the table to attach the candle to the wall of the room so that it will burn properly? You can find the answer in Figure 9.7.

whether or not you solve the problem, notice the types of thoughts you have already had as you have surveyed the objects in the figure. Even if you haven't arrived at a solution yet, you have probably used mental trial and error to visualize what might work. (You will find the answer to the Duncker candle problem in Figure 9.7.)

These standard problem-solving methods require executive functioning to select strategies, working memory to hold the elements of the problem in mind, and processing speed to accomplish the task while the elements remain in mind, all of which have fluid components that tend to decline with age (Hassing & Johansson, 2005). Experiments with young and older adults have consistently shown that the older adults use fewer strategies and display slower processing speed in solving complex math problems (Allain et al., 2007; Lemaire & Arnaud, 2008).

How important, you might wonder, is it for older people to solve complex math problems or "teasers" like the Duncker candle roblem? The answer depends on what people are attempting to accomplish in life. However, research suggests that for the vast majority of older adults, abstract problem-solving ability, as in complex math problems, is not related to their quality of life. "Real-world" or everyday problem-solving skills are usually of greater concern (Gilhooly et al., 2007).

Moreover, when older adults encounter interpersonal conflicts, they tend to regulate their emotional responses differently from young and middle-aged adults. Whereas the younger groups are relatively more likely to express feelings of anger or frustration, to seek support from other people, or to solve interpersonal problems, the older adults are more likely to focus on remaining calm and unperturbed (Coats & Blanchard-Fields, 2008). The difference appears to be partially due to older adults' decreased tendency to express anger and increased priority on regulating emotion. Perhaps the older adults do not wish to be "jarred," but it also sounds a bit like wisdom.

dementia A condition characterized by deterioration of cognitive functioning.

Wisdom

We may seek athletes who are in their 20s, but we prefer coaches who are decades older. It may be desirable to hire science teachers and college professors who have recently graduated and can be presumed to be up to date in their knowledge of their disciplines, but we may prefer school principals and department chairpersons who are somewhat older. It is helpful to have 18-year-olds who are bursting with energy knocking on doors to get out the vote, but we require our presidential candidates to be older. Why? Because we associate age with *wisdom*.

Distractability is one cognitive hazard of aging. Developmental psychologist Lynn Hasher suggested that distractibility can enable older adults to take a broader view of various situations: Shifting one's attention from item to item "may enable older adults to ultimately know more about a situation and … what's going on than their younger peers. … [This] characteristic may play a significant role in why we think of older people as wiser" (2008).

Kunzmann and Baltes (2005) noted that wise people approach life's problems in a way that addresses the meaning of life. They consider not only the present, but also the past and the future, as well as the contexts in which the problems arise. They tend to be tolerant of other people's value systems and to acknowledge that there are uncertainties in life and that one can only attempt to find workable solutions in an imperfect world. Ardelt (2008a, 2008b) added emotional and philosophical dimensions to the definition of wisdom. She suggested that wise people tend to possess an unselfish love for others and tend to be less afraid of death. In the following module we explore social and emotional developments of late adulthood. We see that most senior citizens can continue to lead rich, satisfying lives.

In the following section we see that memory, language, problem solving, and wisdom can all be lost if people develop dementia.

Dementia and Alzheimer's Disease

Dementia is a condition characterized by dramatic deterioration of cognitive abilities involving thinking, memory, judgment, and reasoning. It is a consequence not of normal aging, but of disease processes that damage brain tissue. Some causes of dementia include brain infections such as meningitis, HIV, and encephalitis; and

Dementia and Cognition

Watch and learn how cognition is affected by dementia.

Pick's Disease: A Form of Dementia

Watch and learn more about a form of dementia called Pick's Disease.

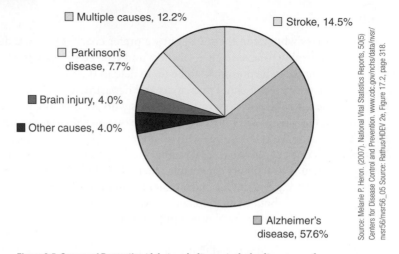

Figure 9.5 **Causes of Dementia** Alzheimer's disease is the leading cause of dementia.

chronic alcoholism, infections, strokes, and tumors (Heron, 2007; see Figure 9.5). The most common form of dementia is **Alzheimer's disease (AD)**, a progressive brain disease affecting four to five million Americans.

The risk of AD increases dramatically with age (see Figure 9.6). About 1 in 10 Americans over the age of 65 has AD, jumping to more than 1 in 2 among those 75–84 years old. AD is rare in people under the age of 65. Although some dementias may be reversible, especially those caused by tumors and treatable infections and those that result from depression or substance abuse, the dementia resulting from AD is progressive and irreversible.

AD is the fifth leading killer of older Americans. It progresses in several stages. At first there are subtle cognitive and personality changes in which people with AD have trouble managing finances and recalling recent events. As AD progresses, people find it harder to manage daily tasks, select clothes, recall names and addresses, and drive. Later, they have trouble using the bathroom and maintaining hygiene. They no longer recognize family and friends or speak in full sentences. They may become restless, agitated, confused, and aggressive. They may get lost in stores, parking lots, even their own homes. They may experience hallucinations or paranoid delusions, believ-

Alzheimer's disease (AD) A severe form of dementia characterized by memory lapses, confusion, emotional instability, and progressive loss of cognitive functioning.

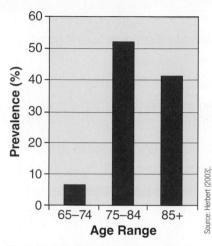

Figure 9.6 **Rates of Alzheimer's Disease Among Older Adults** The risk of Alzheimer's disease is greatest among people in the 75- to 84-year age range.

Source: Herbert (2003).

© 2012 Cengage Learning

Figure 9.7 **Answer to the Duncker Candle Problem**

ing that others are attempting to harm them. People with AD may eventually become unable to walk or communicate and may become completely dependent on others.

Although the cause or causes of AD remain a mystery, scientists believe that both environmental and genetic factors are involved (Goldman et al., 2008; Tomiyama et al., 2008). It is possible that the accumulation of plaque in the brain causes the memory loss and other symptoms of AD; however, experiments with nonhumans have suggested that memory deficits may precede the formation of significant deposits of plaque (Jacobsen et al., 2006).

Medicines can help improve memory functions in people with AD, but their effects are modest. Researchers are investigating whether regular use of anti-inflammatory drugs and antioxidants may lower the risk of developing AD by preventing the brain inflammation associated with the disease (S. L. Gray et al., 2008; Meinert & Breitner, 2008). Calorie restriction may prevent the accumulation of plaque (Qin et al., 2006). Researchers are also investigating whether cognitive training that focuses on the enhancement of memory and processing speed can delay or prevent the development of AD (Acevedo & Loewenstein, 2007; Vellas et al., 2008).

Alzheimer's Disease

Where is the best place to care for those with dementia and Alzheimer's? Watch and learn.

Alzheimer's Test

Watch and learn how AD may be predicted before its onset.

Check Your Learning Quiz 9.2

Go to **login.cengagebrain.com** and take the online quiz.

Did you know that—

- The majority of people aged 65 and older consider themselves to be in good or excellent health compared to other people of their age?

- Physical activity in late adulthood is associated with a lower mortality rate?

- It is normal for older people to be depressed when their friends and partners are dying?

- African Americans who attend church more than once a week live more than 13 years longer than African Americans who never attend?

- Older married couples argue more than younger married couples do?

▼

For many people, the later years are the best years—especially when they are filled with meaningful activity. The stresses involved in building and maintaining a career, selecting a mate, and rearing children are mostly gone. Questions of identity, typically, are settled.

Troubling emotions such as depression and anxiety tend to decline as we age, whereas positive emotions remain fairly steady (Charles et al., 2001). On the whole, older Americans are at least as happy as younger people. According to the National Health Interview Survey, the majority of people 65 and older consider themselves to be in excellent, very good, or good overall health when compared with other people of their age (Centers for Disease Control and Prevention, 2009).

Yet, as we will see, aging has its challenges. Older people are more likely to be bereaved by the loss of spouses and close friends. Older people may need to cope with declining health, retirement, and relocation.

Theories of Social and Emotional Development in Late Adulthood

ego integrity versus despair Erikson's eighth life crisis, defined by maintenance of the belief that life is meaningful and worthwhile despite physical decline and the inevitability of death versus depression and hopelessness.

Late adulthood differs from the phases of life that come before it. Previous phases or stages focus on growth and gains, or at least on stability, in most areas. In late adulthood, we must also cope with decline and death. Theories of development in late adulthood deal with the ways in which we can approach our relationships with our changing bodies, our mental capacities, transitions in intimate relationships, our families, society at large, and voluntary and involuntary relocations.

Erik Erikson's Psychosocial Theory and Offshoots

Erikson labeled his eighth or final stage of life the stage of **ego integrity versus despair**. As a perennial optimist, Erikson believed that people who achieved positive outcomes to earlier life crises—for example, generativity rather than stagnation in middle adulthood—would be more likely to obtain ego integrity than despair in late adulthood.

Ego Integrity Versus Despair

The basic challenge in the crisis of ego integrity versus despair is to maintain the belief that life is meaningful and worthwhile despite physical decline and the inevitability of death. Ego integrity derives from wisdom, as well as from the acceptance that one's life span is limited and occurs at a certain point in the sweep of history. We spend most of our lives accumulating things and relationships; Erikson also argues that adjustment in the later years requires the wisdom to let go.

Robert Peck's Developmental Tasks

Robert Peck (1968) amplified Erikson's stage of ego integrity versus despair by outlining three developmental tasks that people face in late adulthood:

Ego differentiation versus work-role preoccupation. After retirement, people need to find new ways of defining their self-worth outside of their achievements in the workplace, perhaps in terms of roles in the community, activities with friends and family, or spiritual undertakings.

Body transcendence versus body preoccupation. At some point in late adulthood, people face inevitable physical decline, and it is in their best interests to come to terms with it by placing more value on cognitive activities and social relationships. Some people, of course, run into chronic illnesses or disabilities years earlier and must face the need to transcend body preoccupation prior to late adulthood.

Ego transcendence versus ego preoccupation. Ego transcendence means preparing in some way to go beyond the physical limitations of one's own life span. As death comes nearer, some prepare to transcend death by helping secure the futures of their children or grandchildren. Others work more broadly to benefit a church, synagogue, or mosque, or to leave planet Earth in "better shape" than they found it.

Based on extensive interviews with small samples, Monika Ardelt (2008a) wrote that ego transcendence grows out of self-reflection and willingness to learn from experience. She believes ego transcendence—which she also called *the quieting of the ego*—is characterized by a concern for the well-being of humankind in general, not only for the self and close loved ones.

The Life Review

Daniel Levinson theorized that one aspect of the "midlife crisis" was that people realized they had more to look back on than forward to. The existence of the midlife crisis may now be in dispute, but no one can argue that people in late adulthood have more to look back on than forward to. In fact, one of the complaints younger people sometimes level at older relatives is that they too often engage in reminiscence—that is, relating stories from the distant past. At times, it may seem that some older people live in the past, possibly in denial of current decline and the approach of death.

Reminiscence was once considered a symptom of dementia, but contemporary researchers consider it to be a normal aspect of aging (Kunz, 2007). In working with healthy older volunteers as individuals and in groups, Robert Butler (2002) found that **life reviews** can be complex and nuanced, incoherent and self-contradictory, or even replete with irony, tragedy, and comedy. Butler believes that older people engage in life reviews to attempt to make life meaningful, to move on with new relationships as contemporaries pass on, and to help find ego integrity and accept the end of life.

Butler (2002) also argued that health-care professionals rely far too much on drugs to ease the discomforts of older adults. Pilot programs have suggested that therapists may be able to relieve depression and other psychological problems in older adults by helping them reminisce about their lives (Bohlmeijer et al., 2005).

Disengagement Theory

According to **disengagement theory**, older people and society mutually withdraw from one another as older people approach death (E. Cumming & Henry, 1961). People in late adulthood focus more on their inner lives, preparing for the inevitable. Because of retirement, government or industry now supports them through pensions or charity rather than vice versa. Family members expect less from them.

How accurate is this theory? Probably not very. It seems that well-being among older adults generally increases when they pursue goals rather than withdraw from society

life review Looking back on the events of one's life in late adulthood, often in an effort to construct a meaningful narrative.

disengagement theory The view that older adults and society withdraw from one another as older adults approach death.

activity theory The view that older adults fare better when they engage in physical and social activities.

socioemotional selectivity theory The view that we place increasing emphasis on emotional experience as we age but limit our social contacts to regulate our emotions.

(Frazier et al., 2007). Goals might have to be adjusted so that they are consistent with the person's physical and cognitive abilities, but disengagement does not appear to be the path to adjustment. Moreover, relationships between children and parents change as parents travel the years of late adulthood, but children—who are now middle-aged—often maintain close, supportive ties with aging parents, and despite some diminished capacities, aging parents may become founts of wisdom.

Activity Theory

In contrast to disengagement theory, **activity theory** states that older adults are better adjusted when they are more active and involved in physical and social activities. Barriers to activity among older adults include societal beliefs that older people should "take it easy" and structural matters such as forced retirement based purely on a worker's age rather than his or her actual capacities.

Research shows that physical activity is associated with a lower mortality rate in late adulthood (Talbot et al., 2007). Leisure and informal social activities contribute to life satisfaction among retired people (Joung & Miller, 2007). An Israeli study found particular benefits for life satisfaction in activities involving the next generation, the visual and performing arts, and spiritual and religious matters (Nimrod, 2007). However, there was also value in independent activities in the home.

According to activity theory, senior citizens are better adjusted when they are more active and are involved in social activities.

Socioemotional Selectivity Theory

Socioemotional selectivity theory addresses the development of older adults' social networks. Laura Carstensen (Charles & Carstensen, 2007) hypothesized that increasing emphasis is placed on emotional experience as we age. As a result, we are more focused on emotionally fulfilling experiences. Figure 9.8 shows the results of an experiment by Carstensen and her colleagues (1999) in which research participants aged 20–83 read two pages from a popular novel. Then the subjects spent an hour on meaningless activities before being asked to recall everything they could about the pages they had read. Their recollections were classified as emotional or nonemotional. The proportion of emotional material recalled increased by age group, showing a greater emotional response of the older subjects.

Assisted Living and the Social Model of Care

Watch and learn about a home that meets the social needs of senior citizens.

▸ **LO14** Discuss self-esteem in late adulthood.

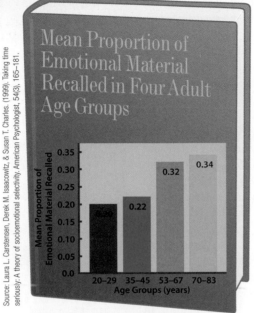

Source: Laura L. Carstensen, Derek M. Isaacowitz, & Susan T. Charles. (1999). Taking time seriously: A theory of socioemotional selectivity. American Psychologist, 54(3), 165–181.

Figure 9.8 Mean Proportion of Emotional Material Recalled in Four Adult Age Groups

In order to regulate their emotional lives as they grow older, people limit their social contacts to a few individuals who are of major importance to them. By the time older adults reach their 80s, they are likely to have whittled their social networks down to a few family members and friends. This does not mean that older adults are antisocial. It means, rather, that they see themselves as having less time to waste and that they are more risk averse; that is, they do not want to involve themselves in painful social interactions.

Carstensen and her colleagues (Ersner-Hershfield et al., 2008) also noted that older people's perceived limitation on future time increases their appreciation for life, which brings about positive emotions. On the other hand, the same constraints on future time heighten awareness that such positive experiences will be drawing to a close, thus giving rise to mixed emotional states that have a poignant quality.

Psychological Development

Various psychological issues affect older adults, including self-esteem and the factors that contribute to self-esteem in late adulthood. Self-esteem, as we will see, is tied into independence and dependence. Also, the psychological problems of depression and anxiety can affect us at any age, but they warrant special focus in late adulthood.

Self-Esteem

To study the life-span development of self-esteem, Richard Robins and his colleagues (2002) recruited more than 300,000 individuals to complete an extensive on-line questionnaire that provided demographic information (age, gender, ethnic back-

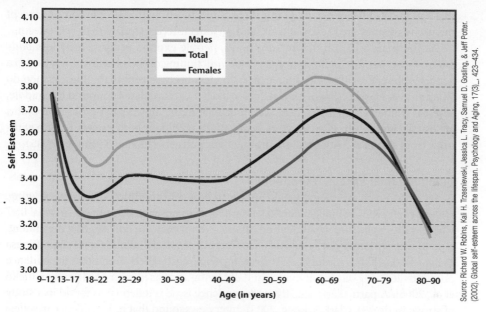

Figure 9.9 Mean Level of Self-Esteem as a Function of Age

Source: Richard W. Robins, Kali H. Trzesniewski, Jessica L. Tracy, Samuel D. Gosling, & Jeff Potter. (2002). Global self-esteem across the lifespan. Psychology and Aging, 17(3), 423–434.

ground, and so forth) and measures of self-esteem. Two thirds of the respondents were from the United States, and 57% were female. Results are shown in Figure 9.9. Generally, the self-esteem of males was higher than that of females. Self-esteem was high in childhood (likely an inflated estimate) and dipped precipitously with entry into adolescence. It then rose gradually throughout middle adulthood and declined in late adulthood, with most of the decline occurring between the ages of 70 and 85. However, this is all relative. Even for people in their 80s, self-esteem levels were above the midpoint of the questionnaire.

Robins and Trzesniewski (2005) suggested a couple of possible reasons for the drop in self-esteem they found among people in their 70s and 80s. The first is that life changes such as retirement, loss of a spouse or partner, lessened social support, declining health, and downward movement in socioeconomic status account for the drop in self-esteem. The other hypothesis is more optimistic, namely that older people are wiser and more content. Erikson (1968) and other theorists have suggested the possibility that ego transcendence occurs in this stage of life, meaning that people come to accept themselves as they are, "warts and all," and no longer need to inflate their self-esteem.

As the years wear on in late adulthood, people express progressively less *body esteem*—that is, pride in the appearance and functioning of their bodies. There is also a gender difference, with older men expressing less body esteem than older women do (Kaminski & Hayslip, 2006). Men are more likely to accumulate fat around the middle, whereas women are more likely to accumulate fat in the hips. Sexual-arousal problems are usually more distressing for men. Older adults with poor body esteem tend to withdraw from sexual activity, often frustrating their partners (Mohan & Bhugra, 2005).

Independence Versus Dependence

Being able to care for oneself would appear to be a core condition of successful aging. Older people who are independent tend to think of themselves as leading a "normal life," whereas those who are dependent on others, even if they are only slightly dependent, tend to worry more about aging and encountering physical disabilities and stress (Sousa & Figueiredo, 2002). A study of 441 healthy people aged 65–95 found that dependence on others to carry out the activities of daily living increased with age (Perrig-Chiello et al., 2006). A particularly sensitive independence issue is toileting, as found in a study of stroke victims (J. Clark & Rugg, 2005). Interviews found that independence in toileting is especially important in enabling older people to avoid slippage in self-esteem.

Socioemotional Adjustment of Older Lesbian, Gay, and Bisexual Adults

A survey of 416 lesbian, gay, and bisexual adults aged 60–91 years found that the great majority reported high levels of self-esteem and good or excellent mental health. Three participants in four (75%) indicated that their physical health was also good or excellent. Most of the older adults in the study reported having developed resilience to prejudice against sexual minorities and related sources of stress; nevertheless, there remained a number of suggestions of distress. For example, as shown in Figure 9.10, 27% of respondents reported feeling lonely; 10% reported that at times they had considered suicide; and 17% reported that they wished they were heterosexual.

Psychological Problems

Problems in coping with aging are associated with psychological problems, including depression and anxiety.

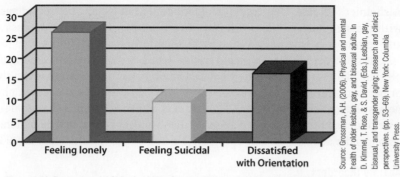

Source: Grossman, A.H. (2006). Physical and mental health of older lesbian, gay, and bisexual adults. In D. Kimmel, T. Rose, & S. David. (Eds.) Lesbian, gay, bisexual, and transgender aging: Research and clinical perspectives. (pp. 53–69). New York: Columbia University Press.

Figure 9.10 Percentage of Older Lesbian, Gay, and Bisexual Adults Who Feel Lonely or Suicidal or Wish They Were Heterosexual

Depression

Depression affects some 10% of people aged 65 and above (Kvaal et al., 2008). Depression in older people can be a continuation of depression from earlier periods of life, or it can be a new development (Fiske, 2006). It can be connected with the personality factor of neuroticism (Duberstein et al., 2008), possible structural changes in the brain (Ballmaier et al., 2008), or a possible genetic predisposition to imbalances of the neurotransmitter norepinephrine (Togsverd et al., 2008). Researchers are also investigating links between depression and physical illnesses such as Alzheimer's disease, heart disease, stroke, Parkinson's disease, and cancer. Depression is also connected with the loss of friends and loved ones, but it is a mental disorder that goes beyond sadness or bereavement. The loss of companions and friends will cause profound sadness, but mentally healthy people bounce back within approximately a year and find new sources of pleasure and support. Inability to bounce back is a symptom of depression.

Depression goes undetected and untreated in older people much of the time (Cochran, 2005). It may be overlooked because its symptoms are masked by physical complaints such as low energy, loss of appetite, and insomnia, and because health-care providers tend to focus more on older people's physical health than their mental health. Many older people are reluctant to admit to depression because psychological problems carried more of a stigma when they were young. Depression is also connected with memory lapses and other cognitive impairment, such as difficulty concentrating (Ballmaier et al., 2008), so some cases of depression are attributed simply to the effects of aging or are misdiagnosed as dementia or

Depression and Anxiety in Older Adults

Interact and learn more about psychological issues that affect people in late adulthood.

▶ **LO15** Explain issues surrounding independence and dependence in late adulthood.

▶ **LO16** Discuss psychological problems such as depression and anxiety in late adulthood.

Alzheimer's disease. Depression in older people can usually be treated successfully with the same means that work in younger people, such as antidepressant drugs and cognitive-behavioral psychotherapy (Schuurmans et al., 2006).

Untreated depression can lead to suicide, which is most common among older people. The highest rates of suicide are found among older men who have lost their wives or partners, have lost their social networks, or fear the consequences of physical illnesses and loss of freedom (J. G. Johnson et al., 2008; Schmidtke et al., 2008). Though fewer older adults suffer from depression than younger adults, suicide is more frequent among older adults, especially European American men (Eddleston et al., 2006).

Anxiety Disorders

Anxiety disorders affect at least 3% of people aged 65 and older, but coexist with depression in about 8%–9% of older adults (Kvaal et al., 2008). Older women are approximately twice as likely to be affected as older men (Stanley & Beck, 2000). The most common anxiety disorders among older adults are **generalized anxiety disorder** and **phobic disorders**. **Panic disorder** is rare. Most cases of **agoraphobia** affecting older adults tend to be of recent origin and may involve the loss of social support systems due to the death of a life partner or close friends. Then again, some older individuals who are frail may have realistic fears of falling on the street and may be misdiagnosed as agoraphobic if they refuse to leave the house alone. Generalized anxiety disorder may arise from the perception that one lacks control over one's life.

generalized anxiety disorder General feelings of dread and foreboding.

phobic disorder Irrational, exaggerated fear of an object or situation.

panic disorder Recurrent experiencing of attacks of extreme anxiety in the absence of external stimuli that usually evoke anxiety.

agoraphobia Fear of open, crowded places.

Anxiety disorders can be harmful to older people's physical health. When older adults with anxiety disorders are subjected to stress, their levels of cortisol (a stress hormone) rise, and it takes a good deal of time for them to subside (Chaudieu et al., 2008). Cortisol suppresses the functioning of the immune system, making people more vulnerable to illness.

Mild tranquilizers (Valium is one) are commonly used to quell anxiety in older adults. Psy-

Some older adults develop agoraphobia as a result of loss of social support due to the death of a partner or friends.

Golden Pixels LLC./Shutterstock.com

chological interventions, such as cognitive-behavioral therapy, have proven beneficial and do not carry the risk of side effects or potential dependence (Caudle et al., 2007).

Social Contexts of Aging

People do not age within a vacuum, but within social and communal contexts, including their living arrangements, facilities and services within their communities, religious affiliations, and family and social relationships.

Communities and Housing for Older People

There's no place like home. According to surveys, older Americans consistently report that they prefer to remain in their homes as long as their physical and mental conditions allow them to do so (Sabia, 2008). Older people with plentiful financial resources, large amounts of equity in their homes, and strong ties to their communities are more likely to remain in their homes. Conversely, older people with declining health conditions, changes in their family composition, and significant increases in property taxes and costs of utilities are likely to need to consider residing elsewhere (Sabia, 2008). In many suburban communities, for example, property taxes have been skyrocketing to keep pace with the costs of public education. Older people no longer have children in the schools or—most crucially—sufficient income to pay the increased taxes, and so they often sell their homes.

Older people who live in urban areas (especially inner cities) are often highly concerned about exposure to crime, particularly crimes of violence. Ironically, people aged 80 and older are significantly less likely to be victimized than people in other age groups (Beaulieu et al., 2008). Social support helps older people cope with their concerns about victimization (Beaulieu et al., 2008). And if older adults are victimized, social support may help them avoid symptoms of stress disorders, such as intrusive thoughts and nightmares (Sexton, 2008).

When older people can no longer manage living on their own, they may consider utilizing the services of home health aides and visiting nurses to help them remain in the home. More affluent older people can afford to hire live-in help. Others may move in with adult children. Still others may move into assisted-living residences, in which they have their own apartments, community dining rooms, 24-hour nursing aid, and on-call physician care.

Child and Adult Day Care

Watch and learn about a growing trend that aims to bring two generations together to address quality day care for children and elders.

Caring for Aging Parents

Watch adult children discuss how they take care of aging parents.

Technology and Caring for the Elderly

Watch how home-based high-tech gadgetry is used to ensure the health and safety of seniors.

If older adults do relocate to residences for the elderly, their existing social networks tend to be disrupted and they are challenged to find new friends and create new networks (Dupuis-Blanchard, 2008). It is valuable for such residences to have communal dining facilities and organized activities, including transportation to nearby shopping and entertainment. Residents typically take time in engaging other people socially and are selective in forming new relationships (Dupuis-Blanchard, 2008).

Older adults may be reluctant to relocate to nursing homes because nursing homes signify the loss of independence. Surveys have indicated that older adults are relatively more willing to enter nursing homes when they perceive themselves to be in poor health and when one or more close family members live near the nursing home (Jang et al., 2008).

There are frightening stories of what happens in nursing homes, but there are heartening stories, as well. Occasionally, cases of **elder abuse** occur, with staff acting harshly toward residents, sometimes in response to cognitively impaired residents' acting aggressively toward the staff (Rosen et al., 2008). However, a well-selected and well-trained staff can deal well with impaired residents, many of whom are disoriented and frightened (Kazui et al., 2008).

Religion

Religion involves beliefs and practices centered on claims about the nature of reality and moral behavior, usually codified as rituals, religious laws, and prayers. Religions also usually encompass cultural traditions and myths, faith, spiritual experience, and communal as well as private worship. Nearly half the people in the world identify with one of the "Abrahamic" religions: Judaism, Christianity, and Islam. These religions, and many others, teach that there is a life after death and that moral living will enable one to experience the benefits of the afterlife.

We discuss religion as part of the social context in which older adults (and others) dwell, because religion often involves participating in the social, educational, and charitable activities of a congregation, as well as worshiping. Therefore, religion and religious activities provide older adults a vast arena for social networking.

Religion also has a special allure as people approach the end of life. As people undergo physical decline, religion asks them to focus instead on moral conduct and spiritual "substance" such as the soul. People who experience physical suffering in this world are advised to look forward to relief in the next.

elder abuse The abuse or neglect of senior citizens, particularly in nursing homes.

Therefore, it is not surprising that studies have found that religious involvement in late adulthood is usually associated with less depression (Braam et al., 2008) and more life satisfaction (Korff, 2006). Frequent churchgoing has also been shown to be associated with fewer problems in the activities of daily living among older people (N. S. Park et al., 2008). Here, of course, we can assume that there are benefits for social networking as well as for church attendance per se.

Consider some of the benefits of frequent churchgoing found in studies of older African Americans. Older African Americans who attended services more than once a week lived 13.7 years longer, on average, than their counterparts who *never* attended church (Marks et al., 2005). In-depth interviews with the churchgoers found several reasons for their relative longevity, including avoidance of negative coping methods such as aggressive behavior and drinking alcohol, success in evading victimization by violence, a sense of hopefulness, and social support.

In addition to their cognitive and spiritual values, religion and religious activities provide older adults with an arena for social networking.

Family and Social Relationships

Family and social relationships provide some of the most obvious—and most important—elements in the social lives of older adults.

Marriage

While approximately half the marriages in the United States end in divorce, it is important to note that 20%–25% of them last half a century or more, ending only with the death of one of the spouses. Married people face very different life tasks as young adults, middle-aged adults, and older adults (P. B. Baltes, 1997), and the qualities in relationships that help them fulfill these tasks may also vary from stage to stage. Core issues in early adulthood are the selection of a partner, the development of a shared life, and emotional intimacy. Given these needs, similarity in personality may foster feelings of attachment and intimacy and provide a sense of equity in contributing to the relationship (Shiota & Levenson, 2007).

By middle adulthood, the partners' concerns appear to shift toward meeting shared and individual responsibilities (Moen, Kim, et al., 2001). The partnership needs to handle tasks such as finances, household chores, and parenting. Conflicts may easily arise over a division of labor unless the couple can divide the tasks readily (Hatch & Bulcroft, 2004; Shiota & Levenson, 2007).

When couples reach their 60s, many midlife responsibilities such as child rearing and work have declined, allowing the partners to spend more time together, and intimacy becomes a central issue once more. In this stage, couples report less disagreement over finances, household chores, and parenting (or grandparenting), but may have concerns about emotional expression and companionship (Hatch & Bulcroft, 2004). As compared with couples in midlife, older couples show more affectionate behavior when they discuss conflicts, and they disagree with one another less in general (Carstensen, Gottman, et al., 1995).

On the other hand, older couples may complain they spend too much time together, especially women whose husbands have just retired (Shiota & Levenson, 2007). If similarity in personality is a problem in this stage of life, perhaps it is because highly similar spouses are getting bored with one another (Amato & Previti, 2003).

In a study of 120 older Israeli couples, Kulik (2004) found that sharing power in the relationship and dividing household tasks contributed to satisfaction in the relationships. Past assistance from one's spouse in a time of need also affected the quality of the marriage and life satisfaction for both partners in the relationship.

Divorce, Cohabitation, and Remarriage

Having worked out most of the problems in their relationships and learned to live with those that remain, older adults are less likely than younger adults to seek divorce. The ideal of lifelong marriage retains its strength (Amato et al., 2007). Because of fear of loss of assets, family disruption, and relocation, older adults do not undertake divorce lightly. When they do, it is often because they belong to an aberrant marriage, which is particularly punitive, or because one of the partners has taken up a relationship with an outsider (Bengtson et al., 2005).

Older people are increasingly likely to cohabit today, making up about 4% of the unmarried population (S. L. Brown, Lee, et al., 2006). Nearly 90% of older people who cohabit have been married, and they are less likely than younger people to wish to remarry (Mahay & Lewin, 2007). Although they are less likely than younger cohabitants to marry their partners, older cohabitants report being in more intimate, stable relationships (V. King & Scott, 2005). Whereas younger cohabitants often see their lifestyle as a prelude to marriage, older cohabitants are more likely to see their relationship as an alternate lifestyle. As reasons for avoiding remarriage, they cite such concerns as ramifications for pensions and disapproval of adult children, who may be worried about their inheritance (King & Scott, 2005). Yet when older partners do remarry, as when they decide to cohabit, they usually make a strong commitment to one another and form a stable relationship (E. A. Kemp & Kemp, 2002).

Gay and Lesbian Relationships

Most of the research on gay men and lesbians has focused on adolescents and young adults (A. H. Grossman et al., 2003). However, a growing body of information about older gay men and lesbians has shown that, as with heterosexuals, gay men and lesbians in long-term partnerships tend to enjoy higher self-esteem, less depression, fewer suicidal urges, and less alcohol and drug abuse (D'Augelli et al., 2001). Gay men in long-term partnerships are also less likely to incur sexually transmitted infections (Wierzalis et al., 2006).

Senior citizens are increasingly likely to cohabit today, and divorced seniors are less likely to remarry than younger people are. Even so, older cohabitants are more likely than their younger counterparts to report that they are in stable relationships.

An interesting pattern has emerged in which gay men or lesbians sometimes form long-term intimate relationships with straight people of the other gender (Muraco, 2006). These relationships do not involve sexual activity, but the couples consider themselves to be "family" and are confidants.

Widowhood

Losing one's spouse in late adulthood is certainly one of the most traumatic experiences—if not the most traumatic—of one's life. The couple may have been together for half a century or more, and most of the rough edges of the relationship will likely have been smoothed. Men in their 70s seem to have the most difficulty coping, especially when they have retired and have been expecting to spend more time with their wives during the coming years (Lund & Caserta, 2001). In contrast, middle-aged widowers are relatively more capable of dealing with their loss (Lund & Caserta, 2001).

Once widowed, men and women both need to engage in the activities of daily living by taking care of their personal hygiene, assuming the responsibilities that had been handled by their spouse, and remaining connected to the larger social community, whether that community mostly involves kin, friends, or people at a place of worship (Caserta & Lund, 2007). Yet the involuntary nature of being widowed is much more likely to lead to social isolation than is marital separation (Glaser et al., 2006). The reasons for isolation are physical, cognitive, and emotional. Widowhood leads to a decline in physical and mental health, including increased mortality and deterioration in memory functioning (Aartsen et al., 2005). Loss of a spouse also heightens the risks of depression and suicide among older adults, more so among men than women (Ajdacic-Gross et al., 2008).

Men who are widowed are more likely than women to remarry, or at least to form new relationships with the other gender. One reason is simply that women tend to outlive men, so there are more older women who are available. Another is that women, more so than men, make use of the web of kinship relations and close friendships available to them. Men may also be less adept than women at various aspects of self and household care, and therefore seek that help from a new partner.

Singles and Older People Without Children

Single, never-married, noncohabiting adults without children make up a small minority of the adult American population. According to data from the United States, Japan, Europe, Australia, and Israel, single older adults without children are just as likely as people who have had children—married or not—to be socially active and involved in volunteer work (Wenger et al., 2007). They also tend to maintain close relationships with siblings and long-time friends. Very old (mean age = 93) mothers and women who have not had children reported equally positive levels of well-being (Hoppmann & Smith, 2007).

On the other hand, married older men without children appear to be especially dependent on their spouses (Wenger et al., 2007). Older adults with children also seem to be more likely than people without children to have a social network that permits them to avoid nursing homes or other residential care upon physical decline (Wenger et al., 2007).

Siblings

By and large, older sibling pairs tend to shore each other up with emotional support (M. F. Taylor et al., 2008). This is especially true among sisters (as women are more likely than men to talk about feelings) who are close in age and geographically near one another. Siblings (and children) of the widowed tend to ramp up their social contacts and emotional support (Guiaux et al., 2007). A widowed person's sibling, especially a sister, often takes the place of the spouse as a confidant (Wenger & Jerrome, 1999).

A life-span developmental study of twin relationships found that, compared with other sibling relationships, the twin relationships were more intense in terms of frequency of contacts, intimacy, conflict, and emotional support (Neyer, 2002). Frequency of contact and emotional closeness declined from early to middle adulthood, but increased again in late adulthood (mean age at time of study = 71.5 years).

Friendships

You can't pick your relatives—at least not your blood relatives—but you can choose your friends. Older people have often narrowed their friendships to friends who are most like them and enjoy the same kinds of activities. As a way of regulating their emotions, they tend to avoid "friends" with whom they have had conflict over the years. Friends serve many functions in the lives of older adults, including providing social networks, acting as confidants, and offering emotional closeness and support, especially when a family member or another friend dies.

Adult Children and Grandchildren

It is when one is in late adulthood that one's grandchildren also typically reach adulthood. The generation of removal that grandparents had from their grandchildren in middle adulthood continues to provide a perspective on the grandchildren's behavior and achievements that the grandparents might not have had with their own children. Although there is great variation in relationships between grandparents and adult grandchildren, research has suggested that both cohorts view each other in a positive light and see their ties as deep and meaningful (C. L. Kemp, 2005). They conceptualize their relationships as distinct family connections that involve unconditional love, emotional support, obligation, and respect. Grandparents and adult grandchildren often act as friends and confidants. As they experience life events together, their relationships can seem precious and capable of being cut short at any time.

Check Your Learning Quiz 9.3

Go to **login.cengagebrain.com** and take the online quiz.

▶ **LO19** Explain how people plan for retirement.

▶ **LO20** Discuss factors that contribute to adjustment to retirement.

Did you know that—

• Couples usually make their retirement plans collaboratively?

• Older adults who are better adjusted to retirement are involved in a variety of activities?

• The people who are best adjusted to retirement are in stable relationships, in good health, and financially secure? (What a surprise!)

• Leisure activities are important for retirees' physical and psychological health?

• Nonsmoking contributes to successful aging?

• Successful agers tend to let go of things they no longer do well, and compensate by engaging in other satisfying activities?

▼

Bernice, a woman in her 70s, said, "I failed retirement." What she meant was that she tried to retire but found herself bored and returned to work. Her work is not that common— she runs a successful art gallery. She supervises her staff, meets people, including curators of museums, and talks about art throughout much of the day. To understand what most people face at retirement age (whatever that is), let's view the meaning of work.

Once upon a time, it was assumed that people retired as soon as they could afford to do so, usually at age 65. But according to the *National Vital Statistics Reports* (Arias, 2007), the average person has two decades of life in front of him or her at the age of 65. That number has been increasing and is likely to continue to increase. Moreover, with medical advances, that person is more and more likely to be robust. Therefore, many people, especially professionals, are working beyond the age of 65.

Yet for most people, a time of retirement does eventually arrive. Let us see how retirement planning may pave the way for a successful retirement, how people adjust to retirement, and what kinds of activities they engage in after retiring. We'll also discuss the broader question: Just what is meant by "successful aging," and how do we do it?

Retirement Planning

One of the keys to a successful retirement is planning (Reitzes & Mutran, 2004). Retirement planning may include regularly putting money aside in plans such as IRAs, Keoghs, and various pension plans in the workplace; investing in stocks, bonds, or a second home; and, perhaps, investigating the kinds of health care, cultural activities, weather (including effects on allergies), and crime statistics in the town or city being considered for retirement.

People who live alone may do their retirement planning as individuals. However, couples—including married and cohabiting heterosexuals and gay and lesbian couples—usually make their retirement plans collaboratively (Mock et al., 2006; Moen, Huang, et al., 2006). By and large, the greater the satisfaction in the relationship, the more likely the partners are to make their retirement plans together (Mock & Cornelius, 2007). Phyllis Moen and her colleagues (2006) found that in married couples, husbands more often than wives tended to be in control of the plans, although control was also related to the partner's workload and income level. Men in same-gender couples are more likely than women in same-gender couples to do retirement planning, but women who do such planning are more likely to do it collaboratively.

When planning for retirement, many retirees can assume they will live at least another two decades. How can they maximize their enjoyment of retirement?

Adjustment to Retirement

Let's begin this section with two questions: Is the key to retirement doing as little as possible? And does adjustment to retirement begin with retirement? The answer to both questions is no.

Research has consistently shown that older adults who are best adjusted to retirement are highly involved in a variety of activities, such as community activities and organizations (Kloep & Hendry, 2007). In the case of community activities, the experience and devotion of retirees renders their participation an important asset for the community, and the activities promote the adjustment of older adults into retirement.

Pinquart and Schindler (2007) found in a retirement study that retirees could be divided into three groups according to their satisfaction with retirement and various other factors. The group that was most satisfied with retirement maintained leisure activities and other activities not related to work as sources of life satisfaction, or replaced work with more satisfying activities. They retired at a typical retirement age and had a wealth of resources to compensate for the loss of work: They were married,

Planning for Retirement

Read and explore retirement planning.

Delaying Retirement

Watch and learn why many Americans continue to work well past age 65.

▶ **LO21** Describe leisure activities after retirement.

in good health, and of high socioeconomic status. The majority of the second group retired at a later age and tended to be female; the majority of the third group retired at a younger age and tended to be male. The second and third groups were not as satisfied with retirement. They were in poorer health, less likely to be married, and lower in socioeconomic status than the first group. The third group had a spotty employment record. Another way to look at this data is to suggest that retirement per se didn't change these people's lives in major ways.

A 2-year longitudinal study found that the adjustment of older retirees was affected by their preretirement work identities (Reitzes & Mutran, 2006). For example, upscale professional workers continued to be well-adjusted and had high self-esteem. They weren't simply "retirees"; they were retired professors or retired doctors or retired lawyers and the like. On the other hand, hourly-wage earners and other blue-collar workers had somewhat lower self-esteem and were more likely to think of themselves as simply "retirees."

Certain factors impeded adjustment to retirement: a lengthy attachment to work, lack of control over the transition to retirement (e.g., forced retirement at age 65), worrying prior to retirement about what retirement would bring, and lack of self-confidence (Reitzes & Mutran, 2004; van Solinge & Henkens, 2005). Nevertheless, a wide range of feelings about giving up work surface just before retirement. Some people are relieved; others are worried—about finances, about surrendering their work roles, or both. Even so, most retirees report that their well-being has increased a year after they have retired, and that much of the stress they felt before retiring has diminished (Nuttman-Shwartz, 2007).

Leisure Activities and Retirement

Most retirees are involved in some form of leisure activity. A British study of adults with an average age of 72 (Ball et al., 2007) reported that nearly 3 in 4 (73%) engaged in leisure activities; 23% in "active leisure" (sailing, walking); 18% in "passive leisure" (listening to music, watching television); 24% in social activities; 20% in hobbies; and 15% in other activities. The key motives for leisure activity were pleasure and relaxation.

What are leisure activities for retirees? Another study, by Jo-Ida Hansen and her colleagues (Hansen et al., 2008), surveyed 194 retirees, with an average age of 72, about leisure activities. The respondents had been employed at a Midwestern university. Their self-reported leisure activities fell into three clusters or factors, as shown in Table 9.3. Factor I included athletic, competitive, and outdoor activities. Factor II involved artistic, cultural, and self-expressive activities. Partying was the sole activity that defined Factor III. Partying isn't just for youngsters.

Research has shown that engaging in leisure activities is essential for retirees' physical and psychological health (Hansen et al., 2008). A recent Japanese study found that older men's failure to engage in leisure activities with neighbors, social organizations, and friends was strongly associated with feelings of depression (Arai et al., 2007). Similarly, older women appeared to need to engage in leisure activities with social groups, children, and grandchildren in order to avoid depression.

Shared leisure activities also contribute to the satisfaction of marital and other intimate partners and to family well-being (Ton & Hansen, 2001). They reduce stress (Melamed et al., 1995) and help retirees avert boredom (Sonnentag, 2003). Contributing to civic activities or volunteering at hospitals and the like also enhances retirees' self-esteem and fosters feelings of self-efficacy (Siegrist et al., 2004).

A model of leisure development proposed by Kleiber and Kelly (1980) featured retirement and aging as the final period. Leisure takes on special importance after retirement and may become central to the retiree's identity and self-acceptance. If the retiree's health remains robust, leisure activities tend to carry over from working days and may ease the transition to retirement. On the other hand, the physical aspects of aging and the death of companions can force changes in the choice of activities and diminish the level of satisfaction derived from them.

Table 9.3
Factor Analysis of Leisure Activities of Retirees

Factor	Name	Items
I	Athletic–Competitive–Outdoors	Adventure sports, team sports, hunting and fishing, individual sports, camping and outdoors, building and repair, cards and games, computer activities, collecting
II	Artistic–Cultural–Self-Expressive	Shopping, arts and crafts, entertaining and culinary arts, cultural arts, dancing, literature and writing, socializing, gardening and nature, community involvement, travel
III	Social	Partying

Source: Jo-Ida C. Hansen, Bryan J. Dik, & Shuangmei Zhou. (2008). An examination of the structure of leisure interests of college students, working-age adults, and retirees. Journal of Counseling Psychology, 55(2), 133–145.

Active Elderly
Watch and learn how one retiree retired successfully.

Enjoying Retirement
Watch one retiree describe the importance of leisure activities during retirement.

Successful Aging

Despite the changes that accompany aging, the majority of Americans in their 70s reported being generally satisfied with their lives (Volz, 2000). In a national poll of some 1,600 adults by the *Los Angeles Times*, 75% of older people said they feel younger than their years (J. Y. Stewart & Armet, 2000). If we look at those poll results from another perspective, we can probably say that most people have more negative expectations about aging than are warranted by the evidence.

There have been many definitions of successful aging. One journal article identified 28 studies with 29 definitions of the concept (Depp & Jeste, 2006). By and large, the definitions included physical activity, social contacts, self-rated good health, absence of cognitive impairment and depression, nonsmoking, and absence of disabilities and chronic diseases such as arthritis and diabetes. According to these common criteria, 35% of the older people sampled in these studies could be said to be aging successfully.

Selective Optimization With Compensation

Successful aging also involves determining the best fit between person and environment within the scope of physical, cognitive, and social changes of late adulthood (see, e.g., P. B. Baltes & Baltes, 1990). From this point of view, often referred to as **selective optimization with compensation**, older people manage to maximize their gains while minimizing their losses.

Most research by developmentalists has focused on decline and loss as major themes associated with late adulthood, noted Margaret Baltes and Laura Carstensen (2003), and therefore most research has tended to direct attention away from the fact that many older people experience late adulthood as a satisfying and productive stage of life. The concept of selective optimization with compensation is related to socioemotional selectivity theory, and is a key theme in adaptive aging (now also known as successful aging). In keeping with socioemotional selectivity theory, successful agers tend to seek emotional fulfillment by reshaping their lives to concentrate on what they find to be important and meaningful. Baltes and Carstensen (2003) defined the process of selection as a narrowing of the array of goals and arenas to which older people direct their resources. In fact, they went so far as to consider

selective optimization with compensation Reshaping of one's life to concentrate on what one finds to be important and meaningful in the face of physical decline and possible cognitive impairment.

Brand X Pictures/JupiterImages

selective optimization with compensation the "cardinal principle of life-span development" (2003).

Research about people aged 70 and older has revealed that successful agers form emotional goals that bring them satisfaction (Löckenhoff & Carstensen, 2004). In applying the principle of selective optimization with compensation, successful agers may no longer compete in certain athletic or business activities (Bajor & Baltes, 2003; Freund & Baltes, 2002). Instead, they focus on matters that allow them to maintain a sense of control over their own lives.

Successful agers also tend to be optimistic. Such an outlook may be derived from transcendence of the ego, from spirituality, or sometimes from one's genetic heritage. (Yes, there is a genetic component to happiness—see Lykken & Csikszentmihalyi, 2001.) However, retaining social contacts and building new ones also contributes to a positive outlook, as does continuing with one's athletic activities, when possible, and one's artistic and cultural activities.

Though late adulthood is often viewed as a time to sit back and rest, it is an excellent opportunity to engage in new challenges and activities, such as going back to school.

The stereotype is that retirees look forward to late adulthood as a time when they can rest from life's challenges. But sitting back and allowing the world to pass by is a prescription for depression, not for living life to its fullest. In one experiment, Sandman and Crinella (1995) randomly assigned people (average age = 72) either to a foster-grandparent program with neurologically impaired children or to a control group. They followed both groups for 10 years. The foster grandparents carried out physical challenges, such as walking a few miles each day, and also engaged in new kinds of social interactions. Those in the control group did not engage in these activities. After 10 years, the foster grandparents showed superior overall cognitive functioning, including memory functioning, and better sleep patterns, as compared with the controls.

In the more normal course of events, many successful agers challenge themselves by taking up new pursuits such as painting, photography, or writing. Some travel to new destinations. Others return to school, taking special courses for older students, sitting in on regular college classes, or participating in seminars on special topics of interest.

Although senior citizens are living longer and leading richer lives than they did in past generations, in one way or another life does draw to a close. The following modules discuss "life's final chapter."

Keys to Successful Aging

Interact and learn more about successfully getting older.

Check Your Learning Quiz 9.4

Go to **login.cengagebrain.com** and take the online quiz.

GO to your Psychology CourseMate at login.cengagebrain.com and take the Chapter Post-Test to see which Learning Objectives you've mastered and which need more review. Use the chapter review guide below and the online activities—including flashcards to review key terms—to measure your learning.

Module		Learning Objectives
9.1 Physical Development in Late Adulthood: What Happens and Why? 530		
Physical Development	LO1	Discuss physical development in late adulthood.
Sexuality	LO2	Discuss changes in sexuality in late adulthood.
Theories of Aging	LO3	Compare programmed and cellular-damage theories of aging.
Health Concerns and Aging	LO4	Identify common health concerns of late adulthood.
9.2 Cognitive Development in Late Adulthood: On Memories and Wisdom 546		
Memory: Remembrance of Things Past—and Future	LO5	Discuss developments in memory in late adulthood.
Language Development	LO6	Discuss language development in late adulthood.
Problem Solving	LO7	Discuss developments in problem solving in late adulthood.

Measure Your Learning

Online Activities

Key Terms	Video	Animation	Reading	Assessment
Late adulthood, life span, life expectancy, ageism, cataract, glaucoma, prcsbycusis, osteoporosis, sleep apnea			Hearing Loss Osteoporosis Sleep Apnea	Check Your Learning Quiz 9.1
	Senior Sex			
Programmed theories of aging, cellular-clock theory, telomere, hormonal-stress theory, immunological theory, cellular-damage theories of aging, wear-and-tear theory, free-radical theory, cross-linking theory			Theories of Aging	
Normal aging, pathological aging, arthritis, osteoarthritis, rheumatoid arthritis				
Explicit memory, implicit memory, retrospective memory, prospective memory		The Aging Brain		Check Your Learning Quiz 9.2
		Problem Solving		

Measure ˄ **Your Learning**

Online Activities

Key Terms	Video	Animation	Reading	Assessment
Dementia, Alzheimer's disease (AD)	Dementia and Cognition Pick's Disease: A Form of Dementia Alzheimer's Disease Alzheimer's Test			
Ego integrity versus despair, life review, disengagement theory, activity theory, socioemotional selectivity theory	Assisted Living and the Social Model of Care			Check Your Learning Quiz 9.3
Generalized anxiety disorder, phobic disorder, panic disorder, agoraphobia		Depression and Anxiety in Older Adults		
Elder abuse	Child and Adult Day Care Caring for Aging Parents Technology and Caring for the Elderly			
	Delaying Retirement		Planning for Retirement	Check Your Learning Quiz 9.4
	Active Elderly Enjoying Retirement			
Selective optimization with compensation		Keys to Successful Aging		

Life's Final Chapter

10

Prepare to Learn 586

 Measure Your Learning 610

^ Prepare to Learn

1 **GO** to your **Psychology CourseMate** at **login.cengagebrain.com** and take the **Chapter Pre-Test** to introduce yourself to this chapter's topics and see what you may already know.

2 **READ** the **Learning Objectives** (LOs, in the left sidebars) and begin the chapter.

3 **COMPLETE** the **Online Activities** (in the right sidebars) *as you read each module.* Activities include **videos, animations, readings,** and **quizzes.**

4 **CHECK Your Learning** by going online to take the quiz at the end of each module and review material as necessary.

5 **MEASURE Your Learning** after reading the chapter by taking the online **Chapter Post-Test.** Use the chapter review guide at the end of the chapter as needed.

WATCH for these **Online Activities** icons as you read:

Video

Animation

Reading

Assessment

These online activities are essential to mastering this chapter. Go to login.cengagebrain.com:

 Videos Watch the following videos:

- The Last Lectures: How a College Professor Copes With His Terminal Cancer Diagnosis
- Hospice Workers Prepare Families and Help Patients Live Until They Die
- A Daughter Grieves
- The Loss of a Child

 Animations Interact with and visualize important processes, timelines, and concepts:

- Stages of Dying
- Aspects of Euthanasia

 Readings Delve deeper into key content:

- The Legal Standards of Death: The Terri Schiavo Case
- Organ Donation: The Gift of Life

 Assessment Measure your mastery:

- Chapter Pre-Test
- Check Your Learning Quizzes
- Chapter Post-Test

▶ **L01** Define *death* and *dying*, and evaluate views on stages of dying.

Did you know that—

- People who are brain-dead may continue to breathe?

- The hospice considers the entire family, not just the dying person, to be the focus of care?

- The more religious a physician is, the more likely she or he is to object to physician-assisted suicide?

- The wishes of people with living wills may not be carried out if they become unable to speak for themselves?

▼

When we are young and our bodies are supple and strong, it may seem that we will live forever. All we have to do is eat right and exercise, and avoid smoking, reckless driving, and hanging around with the wrong people in the wrong neighborhoods. We may have but a dim awareness of our own mortality. We parcel thoughts about death and dying into a mental file cabinet to be opened later in life, along with items like retirement, Social Security, and varicose veins. But death can occur at any age—by accident, violence, or illness. Death can also affect us deeply at any stage of life through the loss of others.

The denial of death is deeply embedded in our culture. Many people prefer not to think about death or plan ahead for their eventual demise, as though thinking about it or planning for it might magically bring it about sooner. Elisabeth Kübler-Ross wrote, "We use euphemisms, we make the dead look as if they were asleep, we ship the children off to protect them from the anxiety and turmoil around the house if the [person] is fortunate enough to die at home, [and] we don't allow children to visit their dying parents in the hospitals" (1969, p. 21). When we consider death and dying, a number of questions arise:

death The irreversible cessation of vital life functions.

dying The end stage of life, in which bodily processes decline, leading to death.

brain death Cessation of activity of the cerebral cortex.

whole brain death Cessation of activity of the cerebral cortex and brain stem.

- How do we know when a person has died?
- Are there stages of dying?
- What is meant by the "right to die"? Do people have a right to die?
- What is a living will?

- Is there a proper way to mourn? Are there stages of grieving?

This chapter addresses these questions and many more.

Understanding Death and Dying

Death is commonly defined as the cessation of life. Many people think of death as a part of life, but death is the termination of life rather than a part of it. **Dying**, though, is a part of life. It is the end stage of life, in which bodily processes decline, leading to death. Yet life can still hold significance and meaning even in the face of impending death.

altrendo images/Getty Images

Charting the Boundaries Between Life and Death

How do we know that a person has died? Is it the stoppage of the heart? Of breathing? Of brain activity?

Medical authorities generally use **brain death** as the basis for determining that a person has died (Appel, 2005). The most widely used criteria for establishing brain death include absence of activity of the cerebral cortex, as shown by a flat EEG recording. When there is no activity in the cortex, consciousness—the sense of self and all psychological functioning—has ceased. The broader concept of **whole brain death** includes death of the brain stem, which is responsible for certain automatic functions, such as reflexes like breathing. Thus a person who is brain-dead can continue to breathe. On the other hand, in some cases people have been kept "alive," even though they were whole-brain-dead, by life-support equipment that took over their breathing and circulation.

Death is also a legal matter. Most states rely on some combination of these criteria in establishing the legal standard of death. In most states, a person is considered legally dead if there is an irreversible cessation of breathing and circulation or if there is an irreversible cessation of brain activity, including activity in the brain stem, which controls breathing (Appel, 2005). People whose hearts and lungs have ceased functioning can often be revived with cardiopulmonary resuscitation (CPR).

The Case of Terri Schiavo

Expand your knowledge of the legal standards of death by reading about the Terri Schiavo case.

▶ **LO2** Identify settings in which people die.

Are There Stages of Dying?

Our overview of the process of dying has been influenced by the work of Elisabeth Kübler-Ross (1969). From her observations of terminally ill patients, Kübler-Ross found some common responses to news of impending death. She hypothesized that there are five stages of dying through which many dying patients pass. She has suggested that older people who suspect that death may be near may undergo similar responses:

1. *Denial.* In this stage, people think, "It can't be me. The diagnosis must be wrong." Denial can be flat and absolute, or it can fluctuate so that one minute the patient accepts the medical verdict, and the next, the patient starts chatting animatedly about distant plans.
2. *Anger.* Denial usually gives way to anger and resentment toward the young and healthy, and, sometimes, toward the medical establishment: "It's unfair. Why me?" or "They didn't catch it in time."
3. *Bargaining.* People may bargain with God to postpone death, promising, for example, to do good deeds if they are given another 6 months, or another year.
4. *Depression.* With depression come feelings of grief, loss, and hopelessness—grief at the prospect of leaving loved ones and life itself.
5. *Final acceptance.* Ultimately, inner peace may come as a quiet acceptance of the inevitable. This "peace" is not contentment; it is nearly devoid of feeling. The patient may still fear death, but comes to accept it with a sense of peace and dignity.

Much current "death education" suggests that hospital staff and family members can support dying people by understanding the stages they are going through, by not imposing their own expectations on patients, and by helping patients achieve final acceptance when the patients are ready to do so. But critics note that staff may be imposing Kübler-Ross's expectations on dying patients.

There are other critiques of the views of Kübler-Ross. For example, Joan Retsinas (1988) noted that Kübler-Ross's stages are limited to cases in which people receive a diagnosis of a terminal illness. Retsinas pointed out that most people die because of advanced years with no specific terminal diagnosis, and Kübler-Ross's approach may not be of much use in helping us understand reactions under circumstances other than terminal illness.

Edwin Shneidman (1977) acknowledged the presence of feelings such as those described by Kübler-Ross in dying people, but his research showed that individuals

hospice An organization that treats dying patients by focusing on palliative care rather than curative treatment.

palliative care Treatment focused on the relief of pain and suffering rather than cure.

behave in dying more or less as they behaved during earlier periods when they experienced stress, failure, and threat. A gamut of emotional responses and psychological defenses emerges, especially denial; they can be observed in every death. However, the process of dying does not necessarily follow any progression of stages, as suggested by Kübler-Ross. The key factors that appear to affect the adjustment of the dying individual include the nature and extent of possible biological cognitive impairment, pain and weakness, the time or phase of the person's life, the person's philosophy of life (and death), and prior experiences with crises.

Where People Die

A hundred years ago, most people died in their homes, surrounded by family members. Today, only a small minority of Americans—typically those who are in advanced old age or are gravely or terminally ill—die in their own homes. The growing exception, as we will see, concerns those terminally ill patients who receive hospice care at home. According to the National Hospice and Palliative Care Organization ([NHPCO], 2007), 74% of hospice patients die in a private residence, nursing home, or other residential facility. Many people, of course, die suddenly wherever they happen to be at the time, because of accidents, heart attacks, or other unanticipated events.

In the Hospital

Today, about half of the deaths that occur in the United States do so in hospitals, and another 1 in 5 occur in nursing homes (NHPCO, 2007). Yet hospitals are impersonal places to die. Hospitals function to treat diseases, not to help prepare patients and their families for death. Instead of dying in familiar surroundings, comforted by family and friends, patients in hospitals often face death alone, cut off from their usual supports. On the other hand, patients and their families may assume that going to the hospital gives them the best chance of averting death.

Under Hospice Care

Increasing numbers of dying people and their families are turning to **hospices**, which provide **palliative care**, to help make their final days as meaningful and pain-free as possible. About 1.3 million Americans received hospice care in 2006, an increase of 162% over the previous 10 years (NHPCO, 2007). Of these, about 44% died of cancer

Stages of Dying

Interact and learn more about Kübler-Ross's theory about the process of dying.

The Last Lectures

Watch the last lectures given by a professor diagnosed with terminal cancer.

▶ **L03** Discuss euthanasia and the controversies surrounding it.

The hospice considers the entire family, not just the patient, to be the unit of care.

euthanasia The purposeful taking of life to relieve suffering.

active euthanasia The administration of a lethal treatment (usually a drug) to cause a quick and painless death.

voluntary active euthanasia The intentional administration of lethal drugs or other means of producing a painless death with the person's informed consent.

(NHPCO, 2007). The word *hospice* derives from the Latin *hospitium*, meaning "hospitality," the same root of the words *hospital* and *hospitable*. The derivation is fitting, as hospices provide a homelike atmosphere to help terminally ill patients approach death with a maximum of dignity and a minimum of pain and discomfort. When necessary, hospices can provide care in inpatient settings such as hospitals, nursing facilities, or hospice centers, but most hospice care is provided in the patient's home.

Hospice workers typically work in teams that include physicians, nurses, social workers, mental-health or pastoral counselors, and home health aides. Members provide physical, medical, spiritual, and emotional support to the entire family, not just the patient. Bereavement specialists assist the family in preparing for the loss and help them through grieving after the death. In contrast to hospitals, hospices provide the patient and family with as much control over decision making as possible. The patient's wishes not to be resuscitated or kept alive on life-support equipment are honored. Patients are given ample amounts of painkilling narcotics to alleviate suffering.

Hospices not only provide a more supportive environment for the patient and family, but they are less costly than hospital treatment, especially home-based care. Though the patient may be required to pay some of the costs, most of the costs are borne by insurance plans.

Supporting a Dying Person

Hospice workers are trained in what to do to help people who are dying. Following are some things you can do. First of all, you must be there for the person. Put yourself at the same eye level and don't withhold touching. Be available to listen, to talk, and to share experiences. Give the person the opportunity to talk about death and to grieve, but don't be afraid to also talk about the ongoing lives of mutual acquaintances. People who are dying often need to focus on other things than impending death, and some enjoy humorous events. They may be comforted to hear about your life experiences—your concerns and worries as well as your joys, hopes, and dreams. But be aware of the person's emotional state on any given day. Some days are better than others. Don't attempt to minimize the person's emotional pain or need to grieve by changing the subject or refusing to acknowledge it. Be sensitive to the person's feelings, and offer consolation and support. People with cognitive impairment may repeat certain thoughts many times; you can go with it or gently guide the conversation in another direction. They may repeatedly ask whether certain tasks have been taken care of, and a simple yes may do each time (Kelly et al., 2009).

Euthanasia: Is There a Right to Die?

The word **euthanasia**, literally meaning "good death," is derived from the Greek roots *eu* ("good") and *thanatos* ("death"). Also called *mercy killing*, it refers to the purposeful taking of a person's life through gentle or painless means to relieve pain or suffering.

Active Euthanasia: Mercy Killing or Murder?

In **active euthanasia**, a lethal treatment (usually a drug) is administered to cause a quick and painless death. Usually a spouse or family member administers it.

Voluntary Active Euthanasia

When euthanasia is carried out with the patient's consent, it is called **voluntary active euthanasia**. Voluntary active euthanasia remains illegal throughout most of the United States, although legal challenges to state laws are working their way through the courts. It is not illegal in some other countries, such as the Netherlands.

Aspects of Euthanasia

Interact and learn more about euthanasia.

Hospice Care

Watch and learn how hospice workers help families and patients.

Physician-Assisted Suicide

In some cases of voluntary active euthanasia, physicians have assisted patients with terminal or incapacitating illnesses who wished to die by providing them with lethal doses of drugs and sometimes by administering the drugs when the patients were too ill to administer them themselves. The best-known cases of such physician-assisted suicides have involved Dr. Jack Kevorkian, a retired pathologist dubbed "Dr. Death" by the

Dr. Jack Kevorkian

press for having assisted in more than 35 patient suicides. Following an assisted suicide that was aired on *60 Minutes* in 1998, Kevorkian was convicted of second-degree homicide in Michigan and served 8 years of a 10-to-25-year prison sentence. Unlike Kevorkian, most physicians who assist in patient suicides do so without publicity, for fear of legal prosecution and sanctions by medical societies, which remain ethically opposed to the practice.

Involuntary Active Euthanasia

Involuntary active euthanasia stands on shakier moral, ethical, and legal ground than voluntary euthanasia. In involuntary active euthanasia, a person causes the death of another person without the second person's informed consent. Cases of involuntary euthanasia usually involve patients who are comatose or otherwise incapacitated and whose guardians believe they would have wanted to die if they had retained the capacity to make the decision. Still, in the eyes of the law, it is considered homicide.

Terminal Sedation

involuntary active euthanasia
The intentional administration of lethal drugs or other means of producing a painless death without the person's informed consent.

Terminal sedation is an alternative to euthanasia. It is the practice of relieving distress in a terminally ill patient in the last hours or days of his or her life, usually by means of a continuous intravenous infusion of a sedative drug, such as a tranquilizer. Terminal sedation is not intended to hasten death, although there is some debate as to whether it has that effect (Cellarius, 2008).

Attitudes Toward Physician-Assisted Suicide

The issue of physician-assisted suicide continues to be debated among physicians and in the lay community, even though the American Medical Association stands strongly against it. Physicians themselves are split on the question of whether this form of active euthanasia is ever justified. Physicians opposing assisted suicides often cite the belief that it goes against thousands of years of medical tradition of treating patients.

Euthanasia is legal in the Netherlands, but that does not mean that it is undertaken lightly. For example, when a patient or a patient's family requests euthanasia to relieve a terminally ill patient's suffering, about half of the physicians try to avoid the issue because their values oppose it or it is emotionally burdensome (Georges et al., 2008). Many of these physicians suggest that it is often possible to lessen patients' suffering without hastening their death (Rietjens et al., 2008). Physicians who were open to euthanasia explained that patients' suffering sometimes could not be lessened with medicine.

Euthanasia, defined as performance of the death-inducing act by another person (such as a physician), is illegal nearly everywhere in the United States. Oregon and Washington enacted Death With Dignity Acts (in 1997 and 2008, respectively), which enable terminally ill patients to ask physicians to prescribe lethal doses of medication. The medication is then administered by patients themselves (Facts About the Death With Dignity Act, 2007).

A nationally representative survey of American physicians found that 69% object to physician-assisted suicide, 18% object to terminal sedation, but only 5% object to withdrawal of artificial life support (Curlin et al., 2008). Religion played a role in the physicians' attitudes, as is illustrated in Figure 10.1: Among highly religious physicians, 84% objected to physician-assisted suicide, as compared with 55% of physicians who were not particularly religious; 25% of highly religious physicians objected to terminal sedation, as compared with 12% of less religious physicians.

A survey of 988 terminally ill patients (Emanuel et al., 2000) found that 60.2% said they supported euthanasia or physician-assisted suicide in general, but only 10.6% reported seriously considering it for themselves. Patients who were 65 and older and who felt more appreciated by others were less likely to consider euthanasia and suicide. Not surprisingly, depression, pain, and substantial caregiving needs all contributed to consideration of suicide.

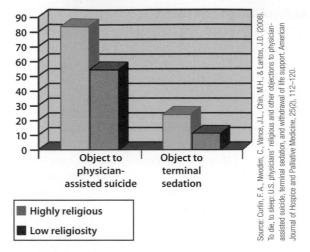

Source: Curlin, F. A., Nwodim, C., Vance, J.L., Chin, M.H., & Lantos, J.D. (2008). To die, to sleep: U.S. physicians' religious and other objections to physician-assisted suicide, terminal sedation, and withdrawal of life support. American Journal of Hospice and Palliative Medicine, 25(2), 112–120.

Figure 10.1 Percentage of Physicians Who Object to Physician-Assisted Suicide or Terminal Sedation, by Religiosity

Passive Euthanasia

Passive euthanasia involves actions that hasten death by means of withholding potentially life-saving treatments, such as failing to resuscitate a terminally ill patient who stops breathing, or withdrawing medicine, food, or life-support equipment (such as a respirator) from a comatose patient. The legal status of passive euthanasia varies with the circumstances. One form of passive euthanasia that is legal throughout the United States and Canada is the withholding or withdrawing of life-sustaining equipment or techniques from terminally ill people who clearly specify their wish not to be kept alive by aggressive or heroic treatment. The declaration of these wishes may be in the form of a *living will* (discussed next), which specifies the conditions under which the person desires to have life-sustaining treatment withdrawn or withheld.

passive euthanasia The withholding or withdrawal of life-sustaining treatment to hasten death.

living will A document prepared when a person is well, directing medical-care providers to terminate life-sustaining treatment in the event that the person becomes incapacitated and unable to speak.

The Living Will

Carlos suffers a tragic accident that leaves him in an irreversible coma and dependent on artificial life support—a respirator to maintain his breathing and feeding tubes to supply his body with nutrients. Would Carlos want his life to be maintained by whatever means were at the disposal of modern medicine, or would he prefer doctors to withdraw life support, allowing him to die naturally?

Keisha has been in pain day after day. She suffers from a terminal disease and her heart suddenly stops due to cardiac arrest. Would she want the doctors to resuscitate her by whatever means necessary in order to prolong her life for another few days or weeks? Who is to decide when it is time for her to die—Keisha or the doctors managing her care?

In 1990, the U.S. Supreme Court ruled that individuals have a right to end life-sustaining treatment. The decision provided the legal basis for the **living will**, a legal document that a person drafts when well to direct health-care workers not to use aggres-

sive medical procedures or life-support equipment to prolong vegetative functioning in the event that the person becomes permanently incapacitated and unable to communicate his or her wishes. Terminally ill patients can insist, for example, that "Do Not Resuscitate" orders be included in their charts, directing doctors not to use CPR in the event of cardiac arrest.

The withdrawal of life-sustaining treatment is a form of passive euthanasia. Unlike active euthanasia, death is not induced by administering a drug or assisting in the patient's suicide. More than 90% of the American public approves of living wills.

Living wills must be drafted in accordance with state laws. The living will only takes effect if people are unable to speak for themselves. For this reason, living wills usually identify a proxy such as the next of kin to make decisions in the event that the signer cannot communicate.

Still, many living wills are ignored. Some are disregarded by proxies, often because they don't judge the patient's wishes accurately, or if they do, because they can't bear the emotional burden of "pulling the plug." Physicians, too, may not comply with advance directives, perhaps because they weren't available when needed or they weren't clear. Physicians are more likely to follow specific advance directives (e.g., "Do not resuscitate") than general guidelines.

The Gift of Life

Read "Organ Donation: The Gift of Life."

▶ **LO4** Discuss the ways in which people of different ages view death.

Life-Span Perspectives on Death

Psychologists have found interesting developments in people's understanding of and reactions to death.

Children

Younger children lack the cognitive ability to understand the permanent nature of death (Slaughter & Griffiths, 2007). Preschoolers may think that death is reversible or temporary, a belief reinforced by cartoon characters who die and come back to life again (Poltorak & Glazer, 2006). Nevertheless, their thinking becomes increasingly realistic as they progress through the ages of 4, 5, and 6 (Li-qi & Fu-xi, 2006). It appears that children's understanding of death is increased as they learn about the biology of the human body and how various organs contribute to the processes of life (Slaughter & Griffiths, 2007).

Loss is often most difficult to bear for children, especially the loss of a parent (Greidanus, 2007). Death of a loved one strikes at the core of a child's sense of security and well-being. Older children may feel guilty because of the mistaken belief that they brought about the death by once wishing for the person to die. The loss of security may lead to anger, which may be directed toward surviving family or expressed in aggressive play. They also may show regressive or infantile behaviors, such as talking "baby talk" or becoming more demanding of food or attention. Some children may persist for several weeks in maintaining the belief that the deceased person is still alive. Though child psychiatrists believe this is normal, prolonged denial can be a harbinger of the development of more severe problems (Crenshaw, 2007).

When children learn about death, it is normal for them to fear it. But children in various cultures are also taught that it is possible to survive death, either through reincarnation, as in some Eastern religions, or as in the transcendence of the soul, as in Christianity. Children in the United States are sometimes told things like "Your father is now in heaven and you will see him there again. Meanwhile, he is watching over you." The concept of surviving death renders death less permanent and less frightening to many children—and adults (Lattanzi-Licht, 2007).

How can you help a child cope with grief? First of all, don't force a frightened child to attend a funeral. Another kind of service or observance may be more appropriate, such as lighting a candle, saying a prayer, or visiting a grave site at another time. Many helping professionals suggest avoiding the use of euphemisms that deny the reality the children face—euphemisms such as "Aunt Jane is sleeping comfortably now." They also suggest responding to children's questions and worries as honestly and openly as possible, but in a way that reassures them that you are available to help them cope with their loss. But here, of course, we again run into the issue of what the reality of death is; the person who believes in an afterlife, the agnostic, and the atheist all have different versions.

It is generally advised to let children know that they can express their feelings openly and freely without fear of criticism. Spend time with them, providing emotional support and reassurance. Also, be aware of danger signals— such as loss of sleep or appetite, depressed mood for several weeks, the development of excessive fears (such as fear of being alone), withdrawal from friends, a sharp decline in school performance, or refusal to attend school—that indicate that the child may need professional help.

There has been debate as to whether it is best to encourage children to let go of their ties to the person who has died, reach some sort of "closure," and "move on" with their own lives (Greidanus, 2007). Research suggests that it is possible for children to maintain their bond with the deceased person even while they continue to grieve, invest in other relationships and new activities, and learn to live under the changed circumstances (Sasaki, 2007).

Adolescents

Adolescents are "in between" in many ways. They know full well that when life functions come to an end in a particular body, they cannot be restored, yet they are not beyond constructing magical, spiritual, or pseudoscientific theories as to how some form of life or thought might survive (Balk et al., 2007). Adolescents also speak of death in terms of concepts such as light, darkness, transition, and nothingness (Oltjenbruns & Balk, 2007).

Adolescents become increasingly exposed to death among older family members such as grandparents, and even among fellow adolescents, some of whom have died of illness but others from accidents, suicide, or foul play. Adolescents are more likely than young children to attend funerals, including funerals with open caskets. These experiences challenge the adolescent sense of immortality that is connected with the personal fable (Noppe & Noppe, 2004). Even though adolescents come to recognize that the concept of death applies to them, they continue to engage in

A Daughter Grieves

Watch and learn how a young girl copes with her mother's death.

riskier behavior than adults do. On the other hand, those adolescents who perceive certain behaviors to be highly risky are less likely to engage in them (Mills et al., 2008).

Adults

Most young adults in developed nations need not spend much time thinking about the possibility of their deaths. The leading causes of death in early adulthood are accidents, suicide, and homicide. Except for those living in high-risk environments such as war zones, some inner cities, or, in the case of women, places where there are high rates of maternal death during pregnancy and childbirth, young adults do not often die. Heart disease, cancer, HIV/AIDS, and, for women, complications of pregnancy remain less common causes of death in the United States.

In middle adulthood, heart disease and cancer have become the leading causes of death. People are advised to become proactive by screening for cardiovascular problems and several kinds of cancer. There are some gender differences with kinds of cancer, but educated women and men become aware that age is a risk factor for both heart disease and cancer, and they are likely to become aware of middle-aged people who died "untimely" deaths from them.

Heart disease and cancer remain the leading causes of death in late adulthood. Table 10.1 breaks the figures down by age group, showing, for example, the highly dramatic advances of heart disease, accidents, and Alzheimer's disease with the years. As people move into advanced old age, many should no longer be driving, due to loss of sensory acuity and slowed reaction time. They are also more prone to falls. Alzheimer's disease and other dementias increase greatly. Some older people come to fear disability and discomfort nearly as much as death.

Theorists of social and emotional development in late adulthood suggest that ego transcendence, or concern for the well-being of humankind in general, enables some people to begin to face death with an inner calm (Ardelt, 2008a). On the other hand, continued physical, leisure, and informal social activities are all associated with greater life satisfaction among older, retired people (Joung & Miller, 2007; Talbot et al., 2007). There is no single formula for coping with physical decline and the approach of death.

Table 10.1
Leading Causes of Death in Late Adulthood, by Age Group

	65–74	75–84	85 and older
Heart disease	462.9[a]	1,315.0	4,267.7
Cancer	715.5	1,256.3	1,590.2
Strokes and other cerebrovascular disease	93.0	322.3	1,015.5
Chronic respiratory disease	148.1	368.9	596.1
Accidents	45.2	105.5	286.7
Diabetes	78.1	162.7	276.2
Alzheimer's disease	20.6	176.7	849.1
Influenza and pneumonia	28.7	114.1	463.2
Kidney disease	40.1	113.0	290.6
Blood poisoning	32.8	79.9	174.4
Suicide	12.6	16.3	15.6
Chronic liver disease	26.7	28.4	19.8
High blood pressure	16.2	49.5	191.1
Parkinson's disease	11.9	71.9	143.5
Homicide	2.1	2.1	1.5

[a]Annual deaths per 100,000 people.
Source: Xu JQ, Kochanek KD, Murphy SL, Tejada-Vera B. Deaths: Final data for 2007. National vital statistics reports; vol 58 no 19. Hyattsville, MD: National Center for Health Statistics. 2010. Adapted from Table 9, pp. 29–31. (Accessed April 29, 2011). Available at http://www.cdc.gov/nchs/data/nvsr/nvsr58/nvsr58_19.pdf

Check Your Learning Quiz 10.1

Go to **login.cengagebrain.com** and take the online quiz.

▶ **LO5** Discuss issues in making funeral arrangements.

Did you know that—

- If you are present at a death, you should call the family doctor or the police, or dial 911?

- It is a good idea to bring a friend when making arrangements at a funeral home so that you don't spend too much out of feelings of guilt?

- Different cultures prescribe different periods of mourning and different rituals for expressing grief?

- There is no right way to grieve, nor a fixed period of time that grief should last?

- Research suggests that there might be five stages of grief?

- Just spending time with a bereaved person helps?

▼

For most of us, coping with death is at best complicated, and at worst painful and disorienting. Losing a spouse or life partner is generally considered to be the most stressful life change we can endure.

What to Do When Someone Dies

If you are present at someone's death, call the family doctor, the police, or 911. A doctor is needed to complete the death certificate and indicate the cause of death. If the cause of death cannot be readily determined, a coroner or medical examiner may become involved to determine it. Once the body has been examined by the doctor and the death certificate has been completed, a funeral director may be contacted to remove the body from the home or the hospital, and arrangements may be made for burial, cremation, or placement in a mausoleum. If death occurs unexpectedly or foul play is involved or suspected, an autopsy may be performed to determine the cause and circumstances of death. Sometimes an autopsy is performed, with the family's consent, if the knowledge gained from the procedure could benefit medical science.

Different cultures often have very different approaches to funerary traditions. Compare these musicians, for example, who are part of a cremation ceremony in Bali, Indonesia, to the mourners in black on page 604.

Funeral Arrangements

Funerals provide an organized way of responding to death according to religious customs and cultural traditions. They offer family and community a ritual that allows them to grieve publicly and say farewell to the person who died. Funerals grant a kind of closure that can help observers begin to move on with their lives.

Family members of the deceased decide how simple or elaborate they prefer the funeral to be, whether they want embalming (treating a dead body with chemicals in order to preserve it), and whether the deceased's body should be buried or cremated (reducing a dead body to ashes by burning, usually as a funeral rite). Sometimes these matters are spelled out by religious or family custom. Sometimes family members fight over them.

After their homes, automobiles, and children's educations, funerals may be American families' largest expense. Consider these guidelines to arrange a funeral that meets your needs and remains in your budget:

- Have a good friend go with you to arrange the funeral. Bring someone who will be able to make decisions based on reason and good sense, rather than emotions of guilt.

▶**LO6** Discuss grief and bereavement.

▶**LO7** Discuss cross-cultural differences in response to death.

▶**LO8** Discuss research concerning stages of grieving.

- If a funeral home has not yet been selected, shop around; you can and should ask about services and costs.
- Be aware that some cemeteries offer the plot for free but then make their profits from charging exorbitant maintenance fees, opening and closing fees, charges for monuments, and other fees.
- Veterans are entitled to a free burial plot in a national cemetery, but the family will incur the costs of transporting the body.
- Caskets are often the major burial expense, ranging from $500 to $50,000 and more! Recognize that the type of casket you choose makes no difference to the deceased person, and tell the funeral director to show you models that fall within the price range that you are comfortable paying.

Legal and Financial Matters

Many legal and financial matters usually require attention after a death. There may be issues concerning estates, inheritance, outstanding debts, insurance, and amounts owed for funeral expenses. It can be difficult for family members to focus on these matters during a time of grief. They should seek legal counsel if they have questions about how to handle the deceased person's affairs and protect their own financial interests. Usually an attorney is needed to settle the estate, especially if the estate is sizeable or if complex matters arise in sorting through the deceased person's affairs.

Grief and Bereavement

bereavement A state of intense grief following the loss of a loved one.

grief Emotional suffering resulting from a death.

mourning A period of time after the death of a loved one during which a person expresses grief and may follow rituals such as the wearing of black clothing.

The death of a close friend or family member can be a traumatic experience. It typically leads to a state of **bereavement**, an emotional state of longing and deprivation that is characterized by feelings of **grief** and a deep sense of loss. **Mourning** is synonymous with grief over the death of a person, but also describes culturally prescribed ways of displaying grief. Different cultures prescribe different periods of mourning and different rituals for expressing grief.

Russell Underwood/Photolibrary/Getty Images

The tradition of wearing unadorned black clothing for mourning dates at least to the Roman Empire. In rural parts of Mexico, Italy, and Greece, widows are often still expected to wear black for the remainder of their lives. In England and the United States, the wearing of black is on the decline.

Coping with loss requires time and the ability to come to terms with the loss and move ahead with one's life. Having a supportive social network also helps.

Grieving

There is no one right way to grieve, nor a fixed period of time that grief should last. In some cases, especially for parents who have lost a child, grief never ends, although it does tend to lessen over time. People grieve in different ways. Some grieve more publicly, while others reveal their feelings only in private. You may not always know when someone is grieving.

Special *pan de muertos* (bread of the dead) is sold during the Day of the Dead in Mexico.

Death Around the Globe: Festivals for the Dead?

Around the globe, there are those who depart the world and those who are left behind to remember them and, often, to celebrate them. Many cultures have festivals or holidays during which they celebrate the dead:

- In Latin America and Spain, people build altars to the departed on the Day of the Dead (*Dia de los Muertos*), using skulls made of sugar, marigolds, and the favorite foods of the deceased. Mexicans visit cemeteries in an attempt to communicate with the souls of the dead. They build altars and offer food, drink—tequila, mescal, pulque, and the like—and photographs to encourage the souls to visit.
- In many other European countries, Roman Catholics take off from work on All Saints' Day and All Souls' Day, visit cemeteries with flowers and candles, and shower children with candy and toys.

Losing a Child

Watch how one family grieves the loss of a child.

▶ **LO9** Discuss ways of coping with death.

- In Japan, Buddhists celebrate the Bon Festival to honor the departed spirits of their ancestors. Bon is a time for visiting one's hometown, reuniting with family, cleaning graves, and—yes—dancing.
- On the holiday of Chuseok, Koreans visit shrines for the spirits of their more distant ancestors and worship them. They bring offerings of food and drink to the graves of their more immediate ancestors.
- Chinese who observe the traditional Qing Ming Festival tend the graves of their departed in the spring. The seventh month of the Chinese calendar is Ghost Month, when many Chinese believe that the spirits of the dead visit Earth from the underworld.
- During the holiday of Araw ng mga Patay (Day of the Dead), bereaved families in the Philippines may camp out near grave sites for a night or two, bringing flowers, repairing tombs, and lighting candles. Families eat, drink, sing and dance, and play cards.

Are There Stages of Grieving?

John Bowlby (1961), the attachment theorist, was the first to propose a stage theory of grief for coping with bereavement. It included four stages: shock–numbness, yearning–searching, disorganization–despair, and reorganization. The stage theory of grief has become generally accepted when applied to various kinds of losses, including children's responses to parental separation, adults' responses to marital separation (C. Gray et al., 1991), and hospital staffs' responses to the death of an inpatient.

S. Jacobs (1993) modified the stage theory of grief to include the following stages: numbness–disbelief, separation distress (yearning–anger–anxiety), depression–mourning, and recovery. Jacobs's stage theory, like those that have come before, is largely based on anecdotes and case studies.

In order to test Jacobs' theory, Paul Maciejewski and his colleagues (2007) administered five items measuring disbelief, yearning, anger, depression, and acceptance of death to 233 bereaved individuals from 1 to 24 months following their losses. The researchers found that disbelief was highest just after the loss and gradually waned over the course of 2 years. Acceptance of the loss showed the opposite course, being nonexistent at the outset, growing gradually, and peaking 2 years later. Yearning, anger, and depression rose suddenly in the predicted order and then each waned gradually.

Maciejewski and his colleagues (2007) believed they found support for the theory, and to some degree they did. The predicted feelings were present and arose in the predicted order. However, others reviewing the same data noted that these five emotions were the only ones for which the investigators tested; ones they neglected could have been more powerful (Bonanno & Boerner, 2007; Silver & Wortman, 2007).

Advice for Coping

What can you do if you are faced with the death of someone who is close to you? Consider some combination of the following: First, take care of yourself. People who are grieving can become so absorbed with their loss that they fail to attend to their own personal needs. They may not eat or bathe. They may feel guilty doing things for themselves and avoid any pleasurable experiences. One can grieve without withdrawing from life.

Allow yourself to feel your loss. Some people prefer to bottle up their feelings, but covering up feelings or trying to erase them with tranquilizers may prolong grieving. When you feel the time is right, turning to a trusted friend or a counselor may help you get in touch with your feelings.

David Harry Stewart/Getty Images

Don't reject offers of help from friends and family. If they don't know how they can help, tell them what you need.

Don't command yourself to get over it. Give yourself time. There is no fixed timetable for grief to run its course. Don't let other people push you into moving on to "the next stage" unless you are prepared to do so.

Join a bereavement support group. You will find that you are not alone in your suffering. Sharing experiences can help you cope better and work through your grief in a supportive environment (Reif et al, 1995).

Advice for Helping a Bereaved Friend or Relative Cope

When someone you know has lost a loved one, it is natural to want to reach out to her or him. Yet you may not know how to help, or you may fear that you'll say the wrong thing. *Don't worry about what to say.* Just spending time with the bereaved person can help. Nor should you expect to have all the answers; sometimes there are no answers. Sometimes what matters is simply being a good listener. Don't be afraid to talk about the deceased person. Take your cue from the bereaved person. Not talking about the departed person brings down a curtain of silence that can make it more difficult for the bereaved person to work through feelings of grief. By the same token, don't force bereaved people to talk about their feelings. Keep in touch regularly, but don't assume that because you don't get a call, the person doesn't want to talk. The bereaved person may be too depressed or lack the energy to reach out. Offer to help with chores like shopping, running errands, and babysitting (Benkel et al., 2009; S. L. Brown, Brown, et al., 2008).

Don't minimize the loss, and avoid clichés like "You're young, you can have more children" or "It was for the best." Also recognize that there is no fixed timetable for grief to run its course.

Lying Down to Pleasant Dreams…

The American poet William Cullen Bryant is best known for his poem "Thanatopsis," which he composed at the age of 18. "Thanatopsis" expresses Erik Erikson's goal of ego integrity—optimism that we can maintain a sense of trust through life. By meeting squarely the challenges of our adult lives, perhaps we can take our leave with dignity. When our time comes to "join the innumerable caravan"—the billions who have died before us— perhaps we can depart life with integrity.

So live that when thy summons comes to join
The innumerable caravan, which moves
To that mysterious realm, where each shall take
His chamber in the silent halls of death,
Thou go not, like the quarry-slave at night,
Scourged to his dungeon, but, sustained and soothed
By an unfaltering trust, approach thy grave
Like one who wraps the drapery of his couch
About him, and lies down to pleasant dreams.

Bryant, of course, wrote "Thanatopsis" at age 18, not at 85, the age at which he died. At that advanced age, his feelings—and his verse—might have differed. But literature and poetry, unlike science, need not reflect reality. They can serve to inspire and warm us.

Check Your Learning Quiz 10.2

Go to **login.cengagebrain.com**
and take the online quiz.

GO to your Psychology CourseMate at login.cengagebrain.com and take the Chapter Post-Test to see which Learning Objectives you've mastered and which need more review. Use the chapter review guide below and the online activities—including flashcards to review key terms—to measure your learning.

Online Activities

Key Terms	Video	Animation	Reading	Assessment
Death, dying, brain death, whole brain death	The Last Lectures	Stages of Dying	The Case of Terri Schiavo	Check Your Learning Quiz 10.1
Hospice, palliative care	Hospice Care			
Euthanasia, active euthanasia, voluntary active euthanasia, involuntary active euthanasia, passive euthanasia, living will		Aspects of Euthanasia		
	A Daughter Grieves		The Gift of Life	
				Check Your Learning Quiz 10.2
Bereavement, grief, mourning	Losing a Child			

abstinence syndrome A characteristic cluster of symptoms that results from a sudden decrease in the level of usage of a substance.

accommodation The modification of existing schemes to permit the incorporation of new events or knowledge.

achievement That which is attained by one's efforts and presumed to be made possible by one's abilities.

active euthanasia The administration of a lethal treatment (usually a drug) to cause a quick and painless death.

activity theory The view that older adults fare better when they engage in physical and social activities.

adaptation The interaction between the organism and the environment, consisting of assimilation and accommodation.

adaptive thermogenesis The process by which the body converts food energy (calories) to heat at a lower rate when a person eats less, because of, for example, famine or dieting.

adolescence A transitional period between childhood and adulthood, usually seen as being bounded by puberty at the lower end and the assumption of adult responsibilities at the upper end.

ageism Prejudice against people because of their age.

agoraphobia Fear of open, crowded places.

allele A member of a pair of genes.

alpha-fetoprotein assay A blood test that assesses the mother's blood level of alpha-fetoprotein, a substance linked with fetal neural-tube defects.

Alzheimer's disease (AD) A severe form of dementia characterized by memory lapses, confusion, emotional instability, and progressive loss of cognitive functioning.

ambivalent/resistant attachment A type of insecure attachment characterized by severe distress at leave-takings from and ambivalent behavior at reunions.

amenorrhea The absence of menstruation.

amniocentesis A procedure for drawing and examining fetal cells sloughed off into amniotic fluid to determine the presence of various disorders.

amniotic fluid Fluid within the amniotic sac that suspends and protects the fetus.

amniotic sac Sac containing fetus.

amplitude Loudness (of sound).

androgens Male sex hormones.

anesthetics Agents that lessen pain.

animism The attribution of life and intentionality to inanimate objects.

anorexia nervosa An eating disorder characterized by irrational fear of weight gain, distorted body image, and severe weight loss.

A-not-B error The error made when an infant selects a familiar hiding place (A) for an object rather than a new hiding place (B), even after the infant has seen the object hidden in the new place.

anoxia Absence of oxygen.

Apgar scale A measure of a newborn's health that assesses appearance, pulse, grimace, activity level, and respiratory effort.

aphasia A disruption in the ability to understand or produce language.

appearance–reality distinction The difference between real events, on the one hand, and mental events, fantasies, and misleading appearances, on the other hand.

arteriosclerosis Hardening of the arteries.

arthritis Inflammation of the joints.

artificial insemination Injection of sperm into the uterus to fertilize an ovum.

artificialism The belief that environmental features were made by people.

assimilation The incorporation of new events or knowledge into existing schemes.

asynchronous growth Unbalanced growth, such as the growth that occurs during the early part of adolescence and causes many adolescents to appear gawky.

atherosclerosis The buildup of fatty deposits (plaque) on the lining of arteries.

attachment An affectional bond characterized by seeking closeness with another and distress upon separation.

attachment-in-the-making phase The second phase in the development of attachment, characterized by preference for familiar figures.

attention deficit/hyperactivity disorder (ADHD) A disorder characterized by excessive inattention, impulsiveness, and hyperactivity.

attraction–similarity hypothesis The view that people tend to develop romantic relationships with people who are similar to themselves in physical attractiveness and other traits.

attraction–similarity hypothesis The view that people tend to develop romantic relationships with people who are similar to themselves in physical attractiveness and other traits.

attributional style The way in which one is disposed toward interpreting outcomes (successes or failures), as in tending to place blame or responsibility on oneself or on external factors.

authoritarian A child-rearing style in which parents demand submission and obedience.

authoritative A child-rearing style in which parents are restrictive and demanding yet communicative and warm.

autism A developmental disorder characterized by failure to relate to others, communication problems, intolerance of change, and ritualistic behavior.

autism spectrum disorders (ASDs) Developmental disorders characterized by impairment in communication and social skills and by repetitive, stereotyped behavior.

autobiographical memory The memory of specific episodes or events.

autonomous morality The second stage in Piaget's cognitive-developmental theory of moral development, in which children base moral judgments on the intentions of the wrongdoer and on the amount of damage done.

autosome A member of a pair of chromosomes (with the exception of sex chromosomes).

avoidant attachment A type of insecure attachment characterized by apparent indifference to leave-takings from and reunions with an attachment figure.

axon A long, thin part of a neuron that transmits impulses to other neurons through branching structures called *axon terminals*.

babbling The child's first vocalizations that have the sounds of speech.

Babinski reflex Fanning the toes when the soles of the feet are stroked.

bed-wetting Failure to control the bladder during the night.

behaviorism Watson's view that science must study observable behavior only and investigate relationships between stimuli and responses.

bereavement A state of intense grief following the loss of a loved one.

"big five" personality traits Basic personality traits derived from contemporary statistical methods: extraversion, agreeableness, conscientiousness, neuroticism (emotional instability), and openness to experience.

bilingual Using or capable of using two languages with nearly equal or equal facility.

blastocyst A stage within the germinal period of prenatal development in which the zygote has the form of a sphere of cells surrounding a cavity of fluid.

bonding The formation of parent–infant attachment.

brain death Cessation of activity of the cerebral cortex.

Braxton-Hicks contractions The first, usually painless, contractions of childbirth.

Brazelton Neonatal Behavioral Assessment Scale A measure of a newborn's motor behavior, response to stress, adaptive behavior, and control over physiological state.

breech (bottom-first) presentation Buttocks-first childbirth.

Broca's aphasia An aphasia caused by damage to Broca's area and characterized by difficulty speaking.

bulimia nervosa An eating disorder characterized by cycles of binge eating and purging as a means of controlling weight gain.

canalization The tendency of growth rates to return to normal after undergoing environmentally induced change.

carrier A person who carries and transmits characteristics but does not exhibit them.

case study A carefully drawn biography of the life of an individual.

cataract A condition characterized by clouding of the lens of the eye.

categorical self Definitions of the self that refer to external traits.

celibacy Abstention from sexual activity, whether from choice or lack of opportunity.

cellular-clock theory Aging theory focusing on the limits of cell division.

cellular-damage theories of aging Views of aging based on the concept that internal bodily changes and external environmental insults cause cells and organ systems to malfunction, leading to death.

centration Focusing on an aspect or characteristic of a situation or problem.

cephalocaudal From head to tail.

cerebellum The part of the brain stem involved in coordination and balance.

cerebrum The part of the brain responsible for learning, thought, memory, and language.

cervix The narrow lower end of the uterus, through which a baby passes to reach the vagina.

cesarean section Delivery of a baby by abdominal surgery.

chorionic villus sampling (CVS) A method for the prenatal detection of genetic abnormalities that samples the membrane enveloping the amniotic sac and fetus.

chromosome A rod-shaped structure, composed of genes, found within the nuclei of cells.

chronological age (CA) A person's age.

chronosystem The environmental changes that occur over time and have an effect on the child.

class inclusion Categorizing a new object or concept as belonging to a broader group of objects or concepts.

classical conditioning A simple form of learning in which one stimulus comes to bring forth the response usually brought forth by a second stimulus by being paired repeatedly with the second stimulus.

clear-cut-attachment phase The third phase in the development of attachment, characterized by intensified dependence on the primary caregiver.

climacteric The gradual decline in reproductive capacity of the ovaries, generally lasting about 15 years.

clique A group of five to 10 individuals who hang around together and who share activities and confidences.

cognitive–affective complexity A mature form of thinking that permits people to harbor positive and negative feelings about their career choices and other matters.

cognitive-developmental theory The stage theory that holds that the child's abilities to mentally represent the world and solve problems unfold as a result of the interaction of experience and the maturation of neurological structures.

cohabitation Living together with a romantic partner without being married.

cohort effect Similarities in behavior among a group of peers that stem from the fact that group members were born at the same time in history.

conception The union of a sperm cell and an ovum that occurs when the chromosomes of each of these cells combine to form 23 new pairs.

concrete operations The third stage in Piaget's scheme, characterized by flexible, reversible thought concerning tangible objects and events.

conduct disorder A disorder marked by persistent breaking of the rules and violations of the rights of others.

congenital Present at birth and resulting from genetic or chromosomal abnormalities or exposure to the prenatal environment.

conservation In cognitive psychology, the principle that properties of substances such as weight and mass remain the same (are conserved) when superficial characteristics such as their shapes or arrangement are changed.

contact comfort The pleasure derived from physical contact with another.

contrast assumption The assumption that objects have only one label.

control group A group made up of participants in an experiment who do not receive the treatment but for whom all other conditions are comparable to those of participants in the experimental group.

conventional level According to Kohlberg, a period during which moral judgments largely reflect social rules and conventions.

convergence Inward movement of the eyes to focus on an object that is drawing nearer.

convergent thinking A thought process that attempts to focus on the single best solution to a problem.

cooing Prelinguistic vowel-like sounds that reflect feelings of positive excitement.

coregulation A gradual transferring of control from parent to child, beginning in middle childhood.

corpus callosum The thick bundle of nerve fibers that connects the left and right hemispheres of the brain.

correlation coefficient A number ranging from +1.00 to −1.00 that expresses the direction (positive or negative) and strength of the relationship between two variables.

creativity A mental trait characterized by flexibility, ingenuity, and originality.

critical period A period during which an embryo is particularly vulnerable to a certain teratogen; during this period, imprinting can occur.

cross-linking theory Aging theory that suggests that the stiffening of body proteins eventually breaks down bodily processes, leading to aging.

cross-sectional research The study of developmental processes by taking measures of participants of different age groups at the same time.

cross-sequential research An approach that combines the longitudinal and cross-sectional methods by following individuals of different ages for abbreviated periods of time.

crowd A large, loosely organized group of people who may or may not spend much time together and who are identified by the activities of the group.

crystallized intelligence A cluster of knowledge and skills that depends on accumulated information and experience, awareness of social conventions, and good judgment.

cultural bias A factor hypothesized to be present in intelligence tests that provides an advantage for test takers from certain cultural backgrounds.

cultural-familial intellectual deficiency Substandard intellectual performance stemming from lack of opportunity to acquire knowledge and skills.

culture-free test A test from which cultural biases have been removed.

cystic fibrosis A fatal genetic disorder in which mucus obstructs the lungs and pancreas.

death The irreversible cessation of vital life functions.

decentration Simultaneous focusing on more than one aspect or dimension of a problem or situation.

deep structure The underlying meanings in a language.

deferred imitation The imitation of people and events that occurred in the past.

dementia A condition characterized by deterioration of cognitive functioning.

dendrite A rootlike part of a neuron that receives impulses from other neurons.

deoxyribonucleic acid (DNA) Genetic material that takes the form of a double helix composed of phosphates, sugars, and bases.

dependent variable A measure of an assumed effect of an independent variable.

DES Diethylstilbestrol, a synthetic estrogen that has been linked to cancer in the reproductive organs of children of women who used it when pregnant.

developmental psychology The discipline that studies the physical, cognitive, social, and emotional development of humans.

differentiation The processes by which behaviors and physical structures become specialized.

dilate To widen.

disengagement theory The view that older adults and society withdraw from one another as older adults approach death.

disinhibit To encourage a response that has been previously suppressed.

divergent thinking Free and fluent association to the elements of a problem.

dizygotic (DZ) twins Twins that derive from two zygotes; fraternal twins.

dominant trait A trait that is expressed.

donor IVF The transfer of a donor's ovum, fertilized in a laboratory dish, to the uterus of another woman.

Down syndrome A chromosomal abnormality characterized by mental retardation and caused by an extra chromosome in the 21st pair.

dramatic play Play in which children enact social roles.

dualistic thinking Dividing the cognitive world into opposites, such as good versus bad or us versus them.

dying The end stage of life, in which bodily processes decline, leading to death.

dyslexia A reading disorder characterized by letter reversals, mirror reading, slow reading, and reduced comprehension.

dysmenorrhea Painful menstruation.

early childhood The period of childhood from the ages of 2 to 6, roughly following infancy and ending with entry into first grade.

echolalia The automatic repetition of sounds or words.

ecological systems theory The view that explains child development in terms of the reciprocal influences between children and environmental settings.

ecology The branch of biology that deals with the relationships between living organisms and their environment.

ectoderm The outermost cell layer of the newly formed embryo from which the skin and nervous system develop.

efface To become thin.

ego identity versus role diffusion Erikson's fifth life crisis, during which adolescents develop a firm sense of who they are and what they stand for (ego identity), or they do not develop a sense of who they are and instead tend to be subject to the whims of others (role diffusion).

ego integrity versus despair Erikson's eighth life crisis, defined by maintenance of the belief that life is meaningful and worthwhile despite physical decline and the inevitability of death versus depression and hopelessness.

egocentrism Putting oneself at the center of things such that one is unable to perceive the world from another person's point of view.

elaborative strategy A method for increasing retention of new information by relating it to well-known information.

elder abuse The abuse or neglect of senior citizens, particularly in nursing homes.

embryonic disk The platelike inner part of the blastocyst that differentiates into the ectoderm, mesoderm, and endoderm of the embryo.

embryonic stage The stage of prenatal development that lasts from implantation through the eighth week of pregnancy; it is characterized by the development of the major organ systems.

emerging adulthood Period of development, spanning the ages of 18 to 25, in which young people engage in extended role exploration.

emotional regulation Techniques for controlling one's emotional states.

empty-nest syndrome A feeling of loneliness or loss of purpose that parents, and especially mothers, are theorized to experience when the youngest child leaves home.

encode To transform sensory input into a form that is more readily processed.

encopresis Failure to control the bowels once the normal age for bowel control has been reached. Also called *soiling*.

endoderm The inner layer of the embryo from which the lungs and digestive system develop.

endometriosis Inflammation of endometrial tissue sloughed off into the abdominal cavity rather than out of the body during menstruation; the condition is characterized by abdominal pain and sometimes infertility.

endometrium The inner lining of the uterus.

enuresis Failure to control the bladder (urination) once the normal age for control has been reached.

epiphyseal closure The process by which the cartilage that separates the long end of a bone from the main part of the bone turns to bone.

episiotomy A surgical incision between the birth canal and anus that widens the vaginal opening.

epistemic cognition Thought processes directed at considering how we arrive at our beliefs, facts, and ideas.

equilibration The creation of an equilibrium, or balance, between assimilation and accommodation.

estrogen A female sex hormone produced mainly by the ovaries.

ethologist A scientist who studies the behavior patterns characteristic of various species.

ethology The study of behaviors that are specific to a species.

euthanasia The purposeful taking of life to relieve suffering.

evolutionary psychology The branch of psychology that deals with the ways in which the history of human adaptation to the environment influences behavior and mental processes, with special focus on aggressive behavior and mating strategies.

exosystem Community institutions and settings that indirectly influence the child, such as the school board and the parents' workplaces.

experiment A method of scientific investigation that seeks to discover cause-and-effect relationships by introducing independent variables and observing their effects on dependent variables.

experimental group A group made up of participants who receive a treatment in an experiment.

explicit memory Memory for specific information, including autobiographical information, such as what you had for breakfast, and general knowledge, such as state capitals.

expressive language style The use of language primarily as a means for engaging in social interaction.

expressive vocabulary The number of words one can use in the production of language.

extinction Decrease in frequency of a response due to absence of reinforcement.

failure to thrive (FTT) A disorder of infancy and early childhood characterized by variable eating and inadequate gains in weight.

fast mapping A process of quickly determining a word's meaning, which facilitates children's vocabulary development.

feedback loop A system in which glands regulate each other's functioning through a series of hormonal messages.

fetal alcohol syndrome (FAS) A cluster of symptoms shown by children of women who drank heavily during pregnancy, including characteristic facial features and mental retardation.

fetal stage The stage of development that lasts from the beginning of the ninth week of pregnancy through birth; it is characterized by gains in size and weight and by maturation of the organ systems.

fine motor skills Skills employing the small muscles used in manipulation, such as those in the fingers.

fixed action pattern A stereotyped pattern of behavior that is evoked by a "releasing stimulus"; an instinct.

fluid intelligence A person's skills at processing information.

fluid intelligence Mental flexibility; the ability to process information rapidly.

foreclosure An identity status that characterizes those who have made commitments without considering alternatives.

formal operations The fourth stage in Piaget's cognitive-developmental theory, characterized by the capacity for flexible, reversible operations concerning abstract ideas and concepts, such as symbols, statements, and theories.

free-radical theory Aging theory that attributes aging to damage caused by the accumulation of free radicals.

gender constancy The concept that one's gender remains the same despite changes in appearance or behavior.

gender identity The knowledge that one is female or male.

gender role A cluster of traits and behaviors that are considered stereotypical of females or males.

gender stability The concept that one's gender is unchanging.

gender-schema theory The view that one's knowledge of the gender schema in one's society guides one's assumption of gender-typed preferences and behavior patterns.

gene The basic unit of heredity. Genes are composed of deoxyribonucleic acid (DNA).

general anesthesia Elimination of pain by putting a person to sleep.

generalized anxiety disorder An anxiety disorder in which anxiety appears to be present continuously and is unrelated to the situation.

generalized anxiety disorder General feelings of dread and foreboding.

generativity versus stagnation Erikson's seventh stage of psychosocial development, in which the life crisis is the dichotomy between generativity and stagnation.

genetic counselor A health worker who compiles information about a couple's genetic heritage to advise them as to whether their children might develop genetic abnormalities.

genetics The branch of biology that studies heredity.

genotype The genetic form or constitution of a person as determined by heredity.

germinal stage The period of development between conception and the implantation of the embryo.

glaucoma A condition involving abnormally high fluid pressure in the eye.

goodness of fit An agreement between the parents' expectations of a child and the child's temperament.

grasping reflex Grasping objects that touch the palms.

grief Emotional suffering resulting from a death.

gross motor skills Skills employing the large muscles used in locomotion.

growth spurt A period during which growth advances at a dramatically rapid rate compared with other periods.

gynecomastia Enlargement of breast tissue in males.

habituation The process of becoming used to a stimulus such that one discontinues responding to it.

hallucinogenic A drug that gives rise to hallucinations.

hemophilia A genetic disorder in which blood does not clot properly.

heritability The degree to which the variations in a trait from one person to another can be attributed to genetic factors.

heterozygous Having two different alleles.

HIV/AIDS Human immunodeficiency virus cripples the body's immune system; Acquired Immunodeficiency Syndrome weakens the immune system and leaves it vulnerable to diseases it would otherwise fight off.

holophrase A single word that is used to express complex meanings.

homogamy The practice of people getting married to people who are similar to them.

homosexual Referring to an erotic orientation toward members of one's own gender.

homozygous Having two identical alleles.

hormonal-stress theory Aging theory that hypothesizes that stress hormones, left at elevated levels, make the body more vulnerable to chronic conditions.

hospice An organization that treats dying patients by focusing on palliative care rather than curative treatment.

Huntington's disease A fatal genetic neurologic disorder with onset in middle age.

hyperactivity Excessive restlessness and overactivity; a characteristic of ADHD.

hypothesis A proposition to be tested.

hypoxia Less oxygen than required.

identity achievement An identity status that characterizes those who have explored alternatives and have developed commitments.

identity crisis A turning point in development during which one examines one's values and makes decisions about life roles.

identity diffusion An identity status that characterizes those who have no commitments and who are not in the process of exploring alternatives.

imaginary audience The belief that others around us are as concerned with our thoughts and behaviors as we are; one aspect of adolescent egocentrism.

immanent justice The view that retribution for wrongdoing is a direct consequence of the wrongdoing.

immunological theory Aging theory that holds that the immune system is preset to decline by an internal biological clock.

implicit memory Automatic memory based on repetition and apparently not requiring any conscious effort to retrieve.

imprinting The process by which waterfowl become attached to the first moving object they follow.

in vitro fertilization (IVF) Fertilization of an ovum in a laboratory dish.

incubator A heated, protective container for premature infants.

independent variable A condition in a scientific study that is manipulated so that its effects can be observed.

indiscriminate attachment The display of attachment behaviors toward any person.

individuation The young adult's process of becoming an individual by means of integrating his or her own values and beliefs with those of his or her parents and society at large.

inductive Characteristic of disciplinary methods, such as reasoning, that attempt to foster understanding of the principles behind parental demands.

industry versus inferiority A stage of psychosocial development in Erikson's theory occurring in middle childhood; mastery of tasks leads to a sense of industry, whereas failure produces feelings of inferiority.

infancy The period of very early childhood, characterized by lack of complex speech; the first 2 years after birth.

information-processing approach The view of cognitive development that focuses on how children manipulate sensory information or information stored in memory.

initial-preattachment phase The first phase in the development of attachment, characterized by indiscriminate attachment.

inner speech Vygotsky's concept of the ultimate binding of language and thought; originates in vocalizations that may regulate the child's behavior and become internalized by age 6 or 7.

insecure attachment A type of attachment characterized by avoiding the caregiver, excessive clinging, or inconsistency.

intelligence According to Wechsler, the "capacity … to understand the world [and the] resourcefulness to cope with its challenges."

intelligence quotient (IQ) (1) A ratio obtained by dividing a child's mental age on an intelligence test by his or her chronological age; (2) a score on an intelligence test.

interindividual variability The fact that people do not age in the same way or at the same rate.

intimacy versus isolation According to Erik Erikson, the central conflict or life crisis of early adulthood, in which a person develops an intimate relationship with a significant other or risks heading down a path toward social isolation.

intonation The use of pitches of varying levels to help communicate meaning.

involuntary active euthanasia The intentional administration of lethal drugs or other means of producing a painless death without the person's informed consent.

juvenile delinquency Conduct in a child or adolescent characterized by illegal activities.

Klinefelter syndrome A chromosomal disorder found among males that is caused by an extra X sex chromosome and characterized by infertility and mild mental retardation.

Lamaze method A childbirth method in which women are educated about childbirth, breathe in patterns that lessen pain during birth, and have a coach present.

language acquisition device Neural prewiring that eases the child's learning of grammar.

lanugo Fine, downy hair on premature babies.

late adulthood The final stage of development, beginning at age 65.

latency stage In psychoanalytic theory, the fourth stage of psychosexual development, characterized by repression of sexual impulses and development of skills.

learned helplessness An acquired (hence, learned) belief that one is unable to obtain the rewards one would wish to obtain.

learning disorder A disorder characterized by inadequate development of specific academic, language, and speech skills.

leukocyte White blood cell.

life crisis An internal conflict that attends each stage of psychosocial development.

life expectancy The amount of time a person can actually be expected to live in a given setting.

life review Looking back on the events of one's life in late adulthood, often in an effort to construct a meaningful narrative.

life span The maximum amount of time a person can live under optimal conditions. Also called *longevity*.

life structure In Levinson's theory, the underlying pattern of a person's life at a given stage, as defined by relationships, career, race, religion, economic status, and the like.

life-span perspective The perspective in which psychologists study the biological, cognitive, social, and emotional changes across the life span.

living will A document prepared when a person is well, directing medical-care providers to terminate life-sustaining treatment in the event that the person becomes incapacitated and unable to speak.

local anesthetic Reduction of pain in an area of the body.

locomotion Movement from one place to another.

longitudinal research The study of developmental processes by taking repeated measures of the same group of participants at various stages of development.

long-term memory The structure of memory capable of relatively permanent storage of information.

macrosystem The basic institutions and ideologies that influence the child.

mainstreaming Placing disabled children in classrooms with nondisabled children.

masturbation Sexual self-stimulation.

maturation The unfolding of genetically determined traits, structures, and functions.

mean length of utterance (MLU) The average number of morphemes used in an utterance.

medulla A part of the brain stem that regulates vital and automatic functions such as breathing and the sleep–wake cycle.

meiosis The form of cell division in which each pair of chromosomes splits so that one member of each pair moves to the new cell. As a result, each new cell has 23 chromosomes.

menarche The onset of menstruation.

menopause The cessation of menstruation.

mental age (MA) The intellectual level at which a child is functioning, as assessed according to the typical mental functioning for a child of a given age.

mesoderm The central layer of the embryo from which the bones and muscles develop.

mesosystem The interlocking settings that influence the child, such as the interaction of the school and the larger community.

metacognition Awareness of and control of one's cognitive abilities.

metamemory Knowledge of the functions and processes involved in one's storage and retrieval of information.

metastasis The development of malignant or cancerous cells in parts of the body other than where they originated.

microsystem The immediate settings with which the child interacts, such as the home, the school, and peers.

middle adulthood The stage of adulthood between early adulthood and late adulthood, beginning at 40–45 and ending at 60–65.

middle childhood The years between 6 and 12, sometimes called "the school years" and defining the period between early childhood and the onset of adolescence.

midlife crisis A time of dramatic self-doubt and anxiety during which people sense the passing of their youth and become concerned with their own aging and mortality.

midlife transition A psychological shift into middle adulthood theorized to occur between the ages of 40 and 45 as people begin to believe they have more to look back upon than forward to.

midwife An individual who helps women in childbirth.

miscarriage The expulsion of an embryo or fetus before it can sustain life on its own, most often due to defective development.

mitosis The form of cell division in which each chromosome splits lengthwise to double in number. Half of each chromosome combines with chemicals to retake its original form and then moves to the new cell.

model In learning theory, a person whose behaviors are imitated by others.

monogamy Marriage between one person and one other person.

monozygotic (MZ) twins Twins that derive from a single zygote that has split into two; identical twins. Each MZ twin carries the same genetic code.

moral realism The first stage in Piaget's cognitive-developmental theory of moral development, in which the child judges acts as moral when they conform to authority or to the rules of the game.

moratorium An identity status that characterizes those who are actively exploring alternatives in an attempt to form an identity.

Moro reflex Arching the back, flinging out the arms and legs, and drawing them back to the chest in response to a sudden change in position.

morpheme The smallest unit of meaning in a language.

motility Self-propulsion.

mourning A period of time after the death of a loved one during which a person expresses grief and may follow rituals such as the wearing of black clothing.

multidirectionality In the context of cognitive development, the fact that some aspects of intellectual functioning may improve while others remain stable or decline.

multifactorial problems Problems that stem from the interaction of heredity and environmental factors.

multiple sclerosis A disorder in which hard fibrous tissue replaces myelin, impeding neural transmission.

muscular dystrophy A chronic disease characterized by a progressive wasting away of the muscles.

mutation A sudden variation in a heritable characteristic, as by an accident that affects the composition of genes.

mutism Refusal to speak.

myelin sheath A fatty, whitish substance that encases and insulates axons.

myelination The coating of axons with myelin.

natural childbirth Childbirth without anesthesia.

naturalistic observation A scientific method in which organisms are observed in their natural environments.

nature The processes within an organism that guide it to develop according to its genetic code.

negative correlation A relationship between two variables in which one variable increases as the other decreases.

negative reinforcer A reinforcer that, when removed, increases the frequency of a response.

neonate A newborn infant, especially during the first 4 weeks.

nerve A bundle of axons from many neurons.

neural tube A hollowed-out area in the blastocyst from which the nervous system develops.

neuron A cell in the nervous system that transmits messages.

neurotransmitter A chemical that transmits a neural impulse across a synapse from one neuron to another.

nocturnal emission Emission of seminal fluid while asleep.

non-rapid-eye-movement (non-REM) sleep A sleep period when dreams are unlikely.

nonsocial play Forms of play in which children do not interact with other children.

normal aging Processes of aging that undergo a gradual decline, enabling people to enjoy health and vitality well into late adulthood.

nurture Environmental factors that influence development.

object permanence Recognition that objects continue to exist when they are not in view.

objective morality The perception of morality as objective, that is, as existing outside the cognitive functioning of people.

operant conditioning A simple form of learning in which an organism learns to engage in behavior that is reinforced.

osteoarthritis A painful, degenerative disease characterized by wear and tear on the joints.

osteoporosis A disorder involving progressive loss of bone tissue; this condition causes the bones to become more porous, brittle, and subject to fracture, due to loss of calcium and other minerals.

overextension The use of words in situations in which their meanings become extended.

overregularization The application of regular grammatical rules for forming inflections to irregular verbs and nouns.

ovulation The releasing of an ovum from an ovary.

oxytocin A hormone that stimulates labor contractions.

pacifier A device such as an artificial nipple or teething ring that soothes babies when it is sucked.

palliative care Treatment focused on the relief of pain and suffering rather than cure.

panic disorder Recurrent experiencing of attacks of extreme anxiety in the absence of external stimuli that usually evoke anxiety.

passive euthanasia The withholding or withdrawal of life-sustaining treatment to hasten death.

pathological aging Aging in which chronic diseases or degenerative processes, such as heart disease, diabetes, and cancer, lead to disability or premature death.

pelvic inflammatory disease (PID) An infection of the abdominal region that may have various causes and that may impair fertility.

perceptual constancy Perceiving objects as maintaining their identity although sensations from them change as their positions change.

perimenopause The beginning of menopause, usually characterized by 3–11 months of amenorrhea or irregular periods.

permissive–indulgent A child-rearing style in which parents are warm and not restrictive.

personal fable The belief that our feelings and ideas are special and unique and that we are invulnerable; one aspect of adolescent egocentrism.

petting Kissing and touching the breasts and genitals.

phenotype The actual form or constitution of a person as determined by heredity and environmental factors.

phenylketonuria (PKU) A genetic abnormality in which phenylalanine builds up and causes mental retardation.

phobia An irrational, excessive fear that interferes with one's functioning.

phobic disorder Irrational, exaggerated fear of an object or situation.

phonetic method A method for learning to read in which children decode the sounds of words based on their knowledge of the sounds of letters and letter combinations.

pincer grasp Grasping objects between the fingers and the thumb.

pitch Highness or lowness (of a sound), as determined by the frequency of sound waves.

placenta An organ connected to the uterine wall and to the fetus by the umbilical cord. The placenta serves as a relay station between mother and fetus for the exchange of nutrients and wastes.

plasticity The fact that intellectual abilities are not absolutely fixed but can be modified.

plasticity The tendency of other parts of the brain to take up the functions of injured parts.

polyandry Marriage between one woman and more than one man (a form of *polygamy*).

polygamy Marriage in which a person has more than one spouse and is permitted sexual access to each of them.

polygenic Resulting from many genes.

polygyny Marriage between one man and more than one woman (a form of *polygamy*).

positive correlation A relationship between two variables in which one variable increases as the other increases.

positive reinforcer A reinforcer that, when applied, increases the frequency of a response.

postconventional level A period during which moral judgments are derived from moral principles, and people look to themselves to set moral standards.

postconventional level According to Kohlberg, a period during which moral judgments are derived from moral principles and people look to themselves to set moral standards.

postpartum depression (PPD) Serious maternal depression following delivery, characterized by sadness, apathy, and feelings of worthlessness.

postpartum period The period immediately following childbirth.

pragmatic thought Decision making characterized by willingness to accept reality and compromise.

pragmatics The practical aspects of communication, such as adaptation of language to fit the social situation.

precausal A type of thought in which natural cause-and-effect relationships are attributed to will and other preoperational concepts.

preconventional level According to Kohlberg, a period during which moral judgments are based largely on expectations of rewards or punishments.

prelinguistic vocalization A vocalization made by an infant before the use of language.

premature Born before the full term gestation. Also referred to as *preterm*.

premenstrual dysphoric disorder (PMDD) A condition similar to but more severe than PMS.

premenstrual syndrome (PMS) The discomforting symptoms that affect many women during the 4- to 6-day interval preceding their periods.

prenatal Before birth.

preoperational stage The second stage in Piaget's scheme, characterized by inflexible and irreversible mental manipulation of symbols.

presbycusis Loss of acuteness of hearing due to age-related degenerative changes in the ear.

presbyopia Loss of elasticity in the lens, which makes it harder to focus on nearby objects.

preterm Born prior to 37 weeks of gestation.

primary circular reactions The repetition of actions that first occurred by chance and that focus on the infant's own body.

primary sex characteristics The structures that make reproduction possible.

progestin A synthetic hormone used to maintain pregnancy that can cause masculinization of the fetus.

programmed theories of aging Views of aging based on the concept that the processes of aging are governed, at least in part, by genetic factors.

prosocial behavior Behavior that benefits other people, generally without expectation of reward.

prospective memory Memory of things one has planned for the future.

prostaglandins Hormones that cause muscles in the uterine wall to contract, as during labor.

proximodistal From the inner part (or axis) of the body outward.

psycholinguistic theory The view that language learning involves an interaction between environmental influences and an inborn tendency to acquire language.

psychological moratorium A period when adolescents experiment with different roles, values, beliefs, and relationships.

psychosexual development The process by which libidinal energy is expressed through different erogenous zones during different stages of development.

psychosocial development Erikson's theory emphasizing the importance of social relationships and conscious choice throughout eight stages of development.

puberty The biological stage of development characterized by changes that lead to reproductive capacity.

Pygmalion effect A positive self-fulfilling prophecy in which an individual comes to display improved performance because of the positive expectation of the people with whom he or she interacts.

rapid-eye-movement (REM) sleep A sleep period when dreams are likely, as suggested by rapid eye movements.

reaction time The amount of time required to respond to a stimulus.

receptive vocabulary The number of words one understands.

recessive trait A trait that is not expressed when the gene or genes involved have been paired with dominant genes.

reciprocity The tendency to respond in kind when we feel admired and complimented.

referential language style The use of language primarily as a means for labeling objects.

reflex An unlearned, stereotypical response to a stimulus.

regression A return to behavior characteristic of earlier stages of development.

rehearsal Repetition.

rehearse To repeat.

reinforcement The process of providing stimuli following responses to increase the frequency of the responses.

rejecting–neglecting A child-rearing style in which parents are neither restrictive and controlling nor supportive and responsive.

relativistic thinking The process by which certain belief systems or cultural backgrounds are seen as influencing judgments.

respiratory distress syndrome Weak and irregular breathing, typical of preterm babies.

retrospective memory Memory of past events and general knowledge.

Rh incompatibility A condition in which antibodies produced by the mother are transmitted to the child, possibly causing brain damage or death.

rheumatoid arthritis A painful, degenerative disease characterized by chronic inflammation of the membranes that line the joints.

romantic love A form of love fueled by passion and feelings of intimacy.

rooting reflex Turning the mouth and head toward stroking of the cheek or the corner of the mouth.

rubella A viral infection that can cause retardation and heart disease in the embryo. Also called German measles.

sandwich generation The term given to middle-aged people who need to meet the demands of their own children and of aging parents.

scaffolding Vygotsky's term for temporary cognitive structures or methods of solving problems that help the child as he or she learns to function independently.

scheme An action pattern or mental structure that is involved in the acquisition and organization of knowledge.

school phobia Fear of attending school, marked by extreme anxiety at leaving parents.

script An abstract, generalized account of a familiar, repeated event.

secondary circular reactions The repetition of actions that produce an effect on the environment.

secondary sex characteristics Physical indicators of sexual maturation—such as changes to the voice and growth of bodily hair—that do not directly involve reproductive structures.

secular trend A historical trend toward increasing adult height and earlier puberty.

secure attachment A type of attachment characterized by being mildly distressed at leave-takings and readily soothed by reunion.

selective optimization with compensation Reshaping of one's life to concentrate on what one finds to be important and meaningful in the face of physical decline and possible cognitive impairment.

self-concept One's self-description and self-evaluation according to various categories, such as child, adolescent, or adult, one's gender, and one's skills.

self-fulfilling prophecy An event that occurs because of the behavior of those who expect it to occur.

semen The fluid that contains sperm and substances that nourish and help transport sperm.

sensitive period The period from about 18 months of age to puberty when the brain is especially capable of learning language.

sensorimotor stage Piaget's first stage of cognitive development, which lasts through infancy and is generally characterized by increasingly complex coordination of sensory experiences with motor activity.

sensory memory The structure of memory first encountered by sensory input; information is maintained in sensory memory for only a fraction of a second.

separation anxiety Fear of separation from a target of attachment.

separation anxiety disorder (SAD) An extreme form of otherwise normal separation anxiety that is characterized by anxiety about separating from parents; often takes the form of refusal to go to school.

separation–individuation The process of becoming separate from and independent of the mother.

serial monogamy A series of exclusive sexual relationships.

seriation Placing objects in an order or series according to a property or trait.

serotonin A neurotransmitter that is involved in mood disorders such as depression.

sex chromosome A chromosome in the shape of a Y (male) or X (female) that determines the gender of a child.

sexism Discrimination or bias against people based on their gender.

sex-linked chromosomal abnormality An abnormality that is transmitted from generation to generation and carried by a sex chromosome.

sex-linked genetic abnormality An abnormality resulting from genes that are found on the X sex chromosome; more likely to be shown by male offspring (who do not have an opposing gene from a second X chromosome) than by female offspring.

sexual dysfunction A persistent or recurrent problem in becoming sexually aroused or reaching orgasm.

sexual harassment Deliberate or repeated unwanted comments, gestures, or physical contact.

shaping Gradual building of complex behavior through reinforcement of successive approximations to the target behavior.

sickle-cell anemia A genetic disorder that decreases the blood's capacity to carry oxygen.

sight vocabulary Words that are immediately recognized on the basis of familiarity with their overall shapes, rather than decoded.

sleep apnea Temporary suspension of breathing while asleep.

sleep terrors Frightening dreamlike experiences that occur during the deepest stage of non-REM sleep, shortly after the child has gone to sleep.

small for gestational age Descriptive of neonates who are small for their age.

social cognition The development of children's understanding of the relationship between the self and others.

social cognitive theory A cognitively oriented learning theory that emphasizes observational learning.

social play Play in which children interact with and are influenced by others.

social referencing Using another person's reaction to a situation to form one's own response.

social smile A smile that occurs in response to a human voice or face.

socioemotional selectivity theory The view that we place increasing emphasis on emotional experience as we age but limit our social contacts to regulate our emotions.

somnambulism Sleepwalking.

sonogram A procedure for using ultrasonic sound waves to create a picture of an embryo or fetus.

stage theory A theory of development characterized by distinct periods of life.

standardized test A test in which an individual's score is compared to the scores of a group of similar individuals.

stepping reflex Taking steps when held under the arms and leaned forward so the feet press the ground.

stereotype A fixed, conventional idea about a group.

stillbirth The birth of a dead fetus.

stimulant A drug that increases the activity of the nervous system.

substance abuse A persistent pattern of use of a substance characterized by frequent intoxication and impairment of physical, social, or emotional well-being.

substance dependence A persistent pattern of use of a substance that is accompanied by physiological addiction.

sudden infant death syndrome (SIDS) The death, while sleeping, of apparently healthy babies who stop breathing.

surface structure The superficial grammatical constructions in a language.

symbolic play Play in which children make believe that objects and toys are other than what they are. Also called *pretend play*.

syntax The rules in a language for placing words in order to form sentences.

syphilis A sexually transmitted infection that attacks major organ systems.

Tay-Sachs disease A fatal genetic neurological disorder.

telegraphic speech A type of speech in which only the essential words are used.

telomere A protective segment of DNA located at the tip of a chromosome.

temperament An individual difference in style of reaction that is present early in life.

teratogens Environmental influences or agents that can damage the embryo or fetus.

term The typical 9-month period from conception to childbirth.

tertiary circular reactions The purposeful adaptation of established schemes to new situations.

testosterone A male sex hormone produced mainly by the testes.

thalidomide A sedative used in the 1960s that has been linked to birth defects, especially deformed or absent limbs.

the dream According to Levinson and his colleagues, the drive to become someone, to leave one's mark on history, which serves as a tentative blueprint for the young adult.

theory of mind A commonsense understanding of how the mind works.

time lag The study of developmental processes by taking measures of participants of the same age group at different times.

toddler A child who walks with short, uncertain steps.

tolerance Habituation to a drug such that increasingly higher doses are needed to achieve similar effects.

tonic-neck reflex Turning the head to one side, extending the arm and leg on that side, and flexing the limbs on the opposite side.

toxemia (or pre-eclampsia) A life-threatening disease that can afflict pregnant women; characterized by high blood pressure.

transductive reasoning Reasoning from the specific to the specific.

transition Movement of the head of the fetus into the vagina.

transitivity The principle that if A is greater than B and B is greater than C, then A is greater than C.

transsexual A person who wishes to be a person of the other gender and who may undergo hormone treatments, cosmetic surgery, or both to achieve the appearance of being a member of the other gender.

trophoblast The outer part of the blastocyst from which the amniotic sac, placenta, and umbilical cord develop.

Turner syndrome A chromosomal disorder found among females that is caused by having a single X sex chromosome and characterized by infertility.

ulnar grasp Grasping objects between the fingers and the palm.

ultrasound Sound waves too high in pitch to be sensed by the human ear.

umbilical cord A tube that connects the fetus to the placenta.

uterus The hollow organ within females in which the embryo and fetus develop.

vernix Oily white substance on the skin of premature babies.

visual accommodation Automatic adjustments of the lenses to focus on objects.

visual recognition memory The kind of memory shown in an infant's ability to discriminate previously seen objects from novel objects.

voluntary active euthanasia The intentional administration of lethal drugs or other means of producing a painless death with the person's informed consent.

wear-and-tear theory Aging theory that suggests that over time our bodies become less capable of repairing themselves.

Wernicke's aphasia An aphasia caused by damage to Wernicke's area and characterized by impaired comprehension of speech and difficulty producing the right word.

whole brain death Cessation of activity of the cerebral cortex and brain stem.

whole-object assumption The assumption that words refer to whole objects and not to their component parts or characteristics.

word-recognition method A method for learning to read in which children come to recognize words through repeated exposure to them.

working memory The structure of memory that can hold a sensory stimulus for up to 30 seconds after the trace decays.

zone of proximal development Vygotsky's term for the situation in which a child carries out tasks with the help of someone who is more skilled.

AAIDD. (2007). American Association on Intellectual and Developmental Disabilities. Available at http://www.aaidd.org.

Aalsma, M. C., Lapsley, D. K., & Flannery, D. J. (2006). Personal fables, narcissism, and adolescent adjustment. *Psychology in the Schools, 43*(4), 481–491.

Aartsen, M. J., et al. (2005). Does widowhood affect memory performance of older persons? *Psychological Medicine, 35*(2), 217–226.

Abdelaziz, Y. E., Harb, A. H., & Hisham, N. (2001). *Textbook of clinical pediatrics.* Philadelphia: Lippincott Williams & Wilkins.

Aber, J. L., Bishop-Josef, S. J., Jones, S. M., McLearn, K. T., & Phillips, D. A. (Eds.). (2007). *Child development and social policy: Knowledge for action. APA Decade of Behavior volumes.* Washington, DC: American Psychological Association.

Acevedo, A., & Loewenstein, D. A. (2007). Non-pharmacological cognitive interventions in aging and dementia. *Journal of Geriatric Psychiatry and Neurology, 20*(4), 239–249.

Adams, G. R., Berzonsky, M. D., & Keating, L. (2006). Psychosocial resources in first-year university students: The role of identity processes and social relationships. *Journal of Youth and Adolescence, 35*(1), 81–91.

Adams, R. G., & Ueno, K. (2006). Middle-aged and older adult men's friendships. In V. H. Bedford & B. Formaniak Turner (Eds.), *Men in relationships: A new look from a life course perspective* (pp. 103–124). New York: Springer.

Adler, J. M., Kissel, E. C., & McAdams, D. P. (2006). Emerging from the CAVE: Attributional style and the narrative study of identity in midlife adults. *Cognitive Therapy and Research, 30*(1), 39–51.

Adler-Baeder, F. (2006). What do we know about the physical abuse of stepchildren? A review of the literature. *Journal of Divorce & Remarriage, 44*(3–4), 67–81.

Adolph, K. E., & Berger, S. E. (2005). Physical and motor development. In M. H. Bornstein & M. E. Lamb (Eds.), *Developmental science: An advanced textbook* (5th ed., pp. 223–281). Hillsdale, NJ: Erlbaum.

Agency for Healthcare Research and Quality. (2004, April). Chronic illnesses. In *Child health research findings,* Program Brief, AHRQ Publication 04-P011. Rockville, MD: Author. Available at http://www.ahrq.gov/research/childfind/chfchrn.htm

Aguiar, A., & Baillargeon, R. (2002). Developments in young infants' reasoning about occluded objects. *Cognitive Psychology, 45*(2), 267–336.

Ainsworth, M. D. S. (1967). *Infancy in Uganda: Infant care and the growth of love.* Baltimore: Johns Hopkins University Press.

Ainsworth, M. D. S. (1989). Attachments beyond infancy. *American Psychologist, 44,* 709–716.

Ainsworth, M. D. S., Blehar, M. C., Waters, E., & Wall, S. (1978). *Patterns of attachment: A psychological study of the Strange Situation.* Hillsdale, NJ: Erlbaum.

Ainsworth, M. D. S., & Bowlby, J. (1991). An ethological approach to personality development. *American Psychologist, 46*(4), 333–341.

Ajdacic-Gross, V., et al. (2008). Suicide after bereavement. *Psychological Medicine, 38*(5), 673–676.

Akman, Y. (2007). Identity status of Turkish university students in relation to their evaluation of family problems. *Social Behavior and Personality, 35*(1), 79–88.

Alexander, G. M. (2003). An evolutionary perspective of sex-typed toy preferences: Pink, blue, and the brain. *Archives of Sexual Behavior, 32*(1), 7–14.

Alexander, G. M., Wilcox, T., & Woods, R. (2009). Sex differences in infants' visual interest in toys. *Archives of Sexual Behavior, 38*(3), 427–433.

Alfirevic, Z., Sundberg, K., & Brigham, S. (2003). Amniocentesis and chorionic villus sampling for prenatal diagnosis. Retrieved from Cochrane Database of Systematic Reviews. DOI·10.1002/14651858.CD003252

Allain, P., Kauffmann, M., Dubas, F., Berrut, G., & Le Gall, D. (2007). Executive functioning and normal aging: A study of arithmetic word-problem-solving. *Psychologie & Neuro-Psychiatrie du Vieillissement, 5*(4), 315–325.

Alloway, T. P., Gathercole, S. E., Willis, C., & Adams, A. (2004). A structural analysis of working memory and related cognitive skills in young children. *Journal of Experimental Child Psychology, 87*(2), 85–106.

Almeida, D. M., & Horn, M. C. (2004). Is daily life more stressful during middle adulthood? In O. G. Brim, C. D. Ryff, & R. C. Kessler (Eds.), *How healthy are we?: A national study of well-being at midlife* (pp. 425–451). The John D. and Catherine T. MacArthur Foundation series on mental health and development. Studies on successful midlife development. Chicago: University of Chicago Press.

Aloi, J. A. (2009). Nursing the disenfranchised: Women who have relinquished an infant for adoption. *Journal of Psychiatric and Mental Health Nursing, 16*(1), 27–31.

Amanatullah, E. T., & Morris, M. W. (2010). Negotiating gender roles: Gender differences in assertive negotiating are mediated by women's fear of backlash and attenuated when negotiating on behalf of others. *Journal of Personality and Social Psychology, 98*(2), 256-267.

Amato, P. R. (2006). Marital discord, divorce, and children's well-being: Results from a 20-year longitudinal study of two generations. In A. Clarke-Stewart & J. Dunn (Eds.), *Families count: Effects on child and adolescent development* (pp. 179–202). The Jacobs Foundation series on adolescence. New York: Cambridge University Press.

Amato, P. R., Booth, A., Johnson, D. R., & Rogers, S. J. (2007). *Alone together: How marriage in America is changing.* Cambridge, MA: Harvard University Press.

Amato, P. R., & Cheadle, J. E. (2008). Parental divorce, marital conflict and children's behavior problems: A comparison of adopted and biological children. *Social Forces, 86*(3), 1139–1161.

Amato, P. R., & Previti, D. (2003). People's reasons for divorcing. *Journal of Family Issues, 24,* 602–626.

American Academy of Child & Adolescent Psychiatry. (2008). Children and divorce. Available at http://www.aacap.org/cs/root/facts_for_families/children_and_divorce

American Academy of Family Physicians. (2006). Nutrition in toddlers. *American Family Physician, 74*(9), 1527–1532. Available at http://www.aafp.org/afp/20061101/1527.html

American Academy of Pediatrics. (2007, February 7). *A woman's guide to breastfeeding.* Available at http://www.aap.org/family/brstguid.htm

American Association of University Women. (1992). *How schools shortchange women: The AAUW report.* Washington, DC: AAUW Educational Foundation.

American Cancer Society. (2007). Available at http://www.cancer.org

American Fertility Association. (2007). Available at http://www.theafa.org/fertility/malefactor/index .html. Accessed October 20, 2010.

American Heart Association. (2007). Overweight in children. Available at http://www .americanheart.org/presenter.jhtml?identifier =4670

American Heart Association. (2009). Available at http://www.americanheart.org/presenter .jhtml?identifier=1200000

American Lung Association. (2007). Various fact sheets. Available at http://www.lungusa.org

American Psychiatric Association. (2000). *Diagnostic and statistical manual of mental disorders (DSM–IV–TR)*. Washington, DC: Author.

American Psychological Association (1998, March 16). Sexual harassment: Myths and realities. Available at www.apa.org

American Psychological Association. (2007a). *Stress in America: Mind/body health: For a healthy mind and body, talk to a psychologist.* Washington, DC: Author.

American Psychological Association. (2007b). Stress tip sheet. Available at http://www.apa .org/helpcenter/stress-tips.aspx

America's Children. (2007). Centers for Disease Control and Prevention. National Center for Health Statistics. Childstats.gov. *America's children: Key national indicators of well-being, 2007.* Adolescent children. Indicator Fam6: Birth Rates for Females Ages 15–17 by Race and Hispanic Origin, 1980–2005. Available at http://www.childstats .gov/americaschildren/famsoc6.asp

Ammaniti, M., Speranza, A. M., & Fedele, S. (2005). Attachment in infancy and in early and late childhood: A longitudinal study. In K. A Kerns & R. A. Richardson (Eds.), *Attachment in middle childhood* (pp. 115–136). New York: Guilford.

Amodio, D. M., & Showers, C. J. (2005). "Similarity breeds liking" revisited: The moderating role of commitment. *Journal of Social and Personal Relationships, 22*(6), 817–836.

Anderman, E. M., et al. (2001). Learning to value mathematics and reading: Relations to mastery and performance-oriented instructional practices. *Contemporary Educational Psychology, 26*(1), 76–95.

Andersen, M. L., & Taylor, H. H. (2009). *Sociology: The essentials* (5th ed.). Belmont, CA: Wadsworth.

Anderson, C. A., Gentile, D. A., & Buckley, K. E. (2007). *Violent video game effects on children*

and adolescents: Theory, research, and public policy. New York: Oxford University Press.

Andreou, G., Krommydas, G., Gourgoulianis, K. I., Karapetsas, A., & Molyvdas, P. A. (2002). Handedness, asthma, and allergic disorders: Is there an association? *Psychology, Health, and Medicine, 7*(1), 53–60.

Angier, N. (1997, January 7). Chemical tied to fat control could help trigger puberty. *New York Times*, pp. C1, C3.

Angier, N. (2007, June 12). Sleek, fast, and focused: The cells that make Dad Dad. *New York Times*, pp. F1, F6.

Annett, M. (1999). Left-handedness as a function of sex, maternal versus paternal inheritance, and report bias. *Behavior Genetics, 29*(2), 103–114.

Annett, M., & Moran, P. (2006). Schizotypy is increased in mixed-handers, especially right-handed writers who use the left hand for primary actions. *Schizophrenia Research, 81*(2–3), 239–246.

Anthis, K. S., Dunkel, C. S., & Anderson, B. (2004). Gender and identity status differences in late adolescents' possible selves. *Journal of Adolescence, 27*(2), 147–152.

Antonucci, T. C., & Birditt, K. S. (2004, July). Lack of close relationships and well-being across the life span. Paper presented at the meeting of the American Psychological Association, Honolulu, HI.

Appel, J. M. (2005). Defining death. *Journal of Medical Ethics, 31*(11), 641–642.

Aquilino, W. S. (2005). Impact of family structure on parental attitudes toward the economic support of adult children over the transition to adulthood. *Journal of Family Issues, 26*(2), 143–167.

Arai, A., et al. (2007). Association between lifestyle activity and depressed mood among home-dwelling older people. *Aging & Mental Health, 11*(5), 547–555.

Archer, J. (2006). Testosterone and human aggression: An evaluation of the challenge hypothesis. *Neuroscience & Biobehavioral Reviews, 30*(3), 319–345.

Archibald, L. M. D., & Gathercole, S. E. (2006). Short-term memory and working memory in specific language impairment. In T. P. Alloway & S. E. Gathercole (Eds.), *Working memory and neurodevelopmental disorders* (pp. 139–160). New York: Psychology Press.

Ardelt, M. (2008a). Self-development through selflessness: The paradoxical process of growing wiser. In H. A. Wayment & J. J. Bauer (Eds.), *Transcending self-interest: Psychological explorations of the quiet ego. Decade of behavior* (pp. 221–233). Washington, DC: American Psychological Association.

Ardelt, M. (2008b). Wisdom, religiosity, purpose in life, and death attitudes of aging adults. In A. Tomer, G. T. Eliason, T. Grafton, & P. T. P. Wong (Eds.), *Existential and spiritual issues in death attitudes* (pp. 139–158). Hillsdale, NJ: Erlbaum.

Arias, E. (2007, March 28). United States Life Tables. *National Vital Statistics Reports, 54*(14), Table 11. Available at http://www.cdc.gov/nchs/ data/nvsr/nvsr54/nvsr54_14.pdf

Arija, V., et al. (2006). Nutritional status and performance in test of verbal and non-verbal intelligence in 6-year-old children. *Intelligence, 34*(2), 141–149.

Arnett, J. J. (2000). Emerging adulthood. *American Psychologist, 55*(5), 469–480.

Arnett, J. J. (2007). Socialization in emerging adulthood: From the family to the wider world, from socialization to self-socialization. In J. E. Grusec & P. D. Hastings (Eds.), *Handbook of socialization: Theory and research* (pp. 208–231). New York: Guilford.

Arnett, J. J. (2011). Emerging adulthood. In L. A. Jensen (Ed.), *Bridging cultural and developmental approaches to psychology: New syntheses in theory, research and policy* (pp. 255–275). New York: Oxford University Press.

Arnon, S., et al. (2006). Live music is beneficial to preterm infants in the neonatal intensive care unit environment. *Birth: Issues in Perinatal Care, 33*(2), 131–136.

Arranz, L., Guayerbas, N., & De la Fuente, M. (2007). Impairment of several immune functions in anxious women. *Journal of Psychosomatic Research, 62*(1), 1–8.

Aschermann, E., Gülzow, I., & Wendt, D. (2004). Differences in the comprehension of passive voice in German- and English-speaking children. *Swiss Journal of Psychology, 63*(4), 235–245.

Ash, D. (2004). Reflective scientific sense-making dialogue in two languages: The science in the dialogue and the dialogue in the science. *Science Education, 88*(6), 855–884.

Aslin, R. N., & Schlaggar, B. L. (2006). Is myelination the precipitating neural event for language development in infants and toddlers? *Neurology, 66*(3), 304–305.

Aspy, C. B., et al. (2007). Parental communication and youth sexual behaviour. *Journal of Adolescence, 30*(3), 449–466.

Association of American Colleges & Universities. (2007). Case Study Facilitation Guidelines: February Fifth Forum: Cultivating Community.

Available at http://www.diversityweb.org/diversity_innovations/institutional_leadership/institutional_statements_plans/knox.cfm

Atkinson, G., & Davenne, D. (2007). Relationships between sleep, physical activity and human health. *Physiology & Behavior, 90*(2–3), 229–235.

Auger, R. W., Blackhurst, A. E., & Wahl, K. H. (2005). The development of elementary-aged children's career aspirations and expectations. *Professional School Counseling, 8*(4), 322–329.

August, D., Carlo, M., Dressler, C., & Snow, C. (2005). The critical role of vocabulary development for English language learners. *Learning Disabilities Research & Practice, 20*(1), 50–57.

Auyeung, B., et al. (2009). Fetal testosterone predicts sexually differentiated childhood behavior in girls and in boys. *Psychological Science, 20*(2), 144–148.

Axford, J., Heron, C., Ross, F., & Victor, C. R. (2008). Management of knee osteoarthritis in primary care: Pain and depression are the major obstacles. *Journal of Psychosomatic Research, 64*(5), 461–467.

Bachman, J. G., Safron, D. J., Sy, S. R., & Schulenberg, J. E. (2003). Wishing to work: New perspectives on how adolescents' part-time work intensity is linked to educational disengagement, substance use, and other problem behaviours. *International Journal of Behavioral Development, 27*(4), 301–315.

Bäckström T., et al. (2003). The role of hormones and hormonal treatments in premenstrual syndrome. *CNS Drugs, 17*(5), 325–342.

Bagley, C., & D'Augelli, A. R. (2000). Suicidal behaviour in gay, lesbian, and bisexual youth. *British Medical Journal, 320*(7250), 1617–1618.

Bahrick, H. P., Bahrick, P. O., & Wittlinger, R. P. (1975). Fifty years of memory for names and faces: A cross-sectional approach. *Journal of Experimental Psychology: General, 104*(1), 54–75.

Bahrick, H. P., Hall, L. K., & Da Costa, L.A. (2008). Fifty years of memory of college grades: Accuracy and distortions. *Emotion, 8*(1), 13–22.

Bailey, J. M., & Pillard, R. C. (1991). A genetic study of male sexual orientation. *Archives of General Psychiatry, 48*(12), 1089–1096.

Bajor, J. K., & Baltes, P. B. (2003). The relationship between selection optimization with compensation, conscientiousness, motivation, and performance. *Journal of Vocational Behavior, 63*(3), 347–367.

Bakalar, N. (2005, November 22). Premature births increase along with C–sections. *New York Times*, p. F8.

Bakker, D. J. (2006). Treatment of developmental dyslexia: A review. *Pediatric Rehabilitation, 9*(1), 3–13.

Baldry, A. C. (2003). Bullying in schools and exposure to domestic violence. *Child Abuse and Neglect, 27*(7), 713–732.

Balk, D., Wogrin, C., Thornton, G., & Meagher, D. (2007). *Handbook of thanatology*. New York: Routledge/Taylor & Francis Group.

Ball, V., Corr, S., Knight, J., & Lowis, M. J. (2007). An investigation into the leisure occupations of older adults. *British Journal of Occupational Therapy, 70*(9), 393–400.

Ballmaier, M., et al. (2008). Hippocampal morphology and distinguishing late-onset from early-onset elderly depression. *American Journal of Psychiatry, 165*(2), 229–237.

Baltes, M., & Carstensen, L. L. (2003). The process of successful aging: Selection, optimization and compensation. In U. M. Staudinger & U. Lindenberger (Eds.), *Understanding human development: Dialogues with lifespan psychology* (pp. 81–104). Dordrecht, Netherlands: Kluwer Academic Publishers.

Baltes, P. B. (1997). On the incomplete architecture of human ontogeny: Selection, optimization, and compensation as foundation of developmental theory. *American Psychologist, 52*(4), 366–380.

Baltes, P. B., & Baltes, M. M. (1990). Psychological perspectives on successful aging: The model of selective optimization with compensation. In P. B. Baltes & M. M. Baltes (Eds.), *Successful aging: Perspectives from the behavioral sciences* (pp. 1–34). New York: Cambridge University Press.

Bancroft, J., Carnes, L., & Janssen, E. (2005). Unprotected anal intercourse in HIV-positive and HIV-negative gay men: The relevance of sexual arousability, mood, sensation seeking, and erectile problems. *Archives of Sexual Behavior, 34*(3), 299–305.

Bancroft, J., Carnes, L., Janssen, E., Goodrich, D., & Long, J. S. (2005). Erectile and ejaculatory problems in gay and heterosexual men. *Archives of Sexual Behavior, 34*(3), 285–297.

Bandura, A. (1986). *Social foundations of thought and action: A social-cognitive theory*. Englewood Cliffs, NJ: Prentice Hall.

Bandura, A. (2006a). Going global with social cognitive theory: From prospect to paydirt. In S. I. Donaldson, D. E. Berger, & K. Pezdek (Eds.), *Applied psychology: New frontiers and rewarding careers* (pp. 53–79). Hillsdale, NJ: Erlbaum.

Bandura, A. (2006b). Toward a psychology of human agency. *Perspectives on Psychological Science, 1*(2), 164–180.

Bandura, A., Barbaranelli, C., Vittorio Caprara, G., & Pastorelli, C. (2001). Self-efficacy beliefs as shapers of children's aspirations and career trajectories. *Child Development, 72*(1), 187–206.

Bandura, A., Ross, S. A., & Ross, D. (1963). Imitation of film-mediated aggressive models. *Journal of Abnormal and Social Psychology, 66*(1), 3–11.

Barelli, C., Heistermann, M., Boesch, C., & Reichard, U. H. (2008). Mating patterns and sexual swellings in pair-living and multiple groups of wild white-handed gibbons, *Hylobates lar*. *Animal Behaviour, 75*(3), 991–1001.

Barnard, C. J., Collins, S. A., Daisley, J. N., & Behnke, J. M. (2005). Maze performance and immunity costs in mice. *Behaviour, 142*(2), 241–263.

Barnett, J. E., & Dunning, C. (2003). Clinical perspectives on elderly sexuality. *Archives of Sexual Behavior, 32*(3), 295–296.

Baron, S. W., Forde, D. R., & Kay, F. M. (2007). Self-control, risky lifestyles, and situation: The role of opportunity and context in the general theory. *Journal of Criminal Justice, 35*(2), 119–136.

Barr, R. G., Paterson, J. A., MacMartin, L. M., Lehtonen, L., & Young, S. N. (2005). Prolonged and unsoothable crying bouts in infants with and without colic. *Journal of Developmental & Behavioral Pediatrics, 26*(1), 14–23.

Barr, R., Rovee-Collier, C., & Campanella, J. (2005). Retrieval protracts deferred imitation by 6-month-olds. *Infancy, 7*(3), 263–283.

Barry, C. M., & Wentzel, K. R. (2006). Friend influence on prosocial behavior: The role of motivational factors and friendship characteristics. *Developmental Psychology, 42*(1), 153–163.

Basic Behavioral Science Task Force of the National Advisory Mental Health Council. (1996). Basic behavioral science research for mental health: Sociocultural and environmental practices. *American Psychologist, 51*(7), 722–731.

Batsche, G. M., & Porter, L. J. (2006). Bullying. In G. G. Bear & K. M. Minke (Eds.), *Children's needs III: Development, prevention, and intervention* (pp. 135–148). Washington, DC: National Association of School Psychologists.

Bauer, K. W., Yang, Y. W., & Austin, S. B. (2004). "How can we stay healthy when you're throwing all of this in front of us?": Findings from focus groups and interviews in middle schools on environmental influences on nutrition and physical activity. *Health Education and Behavior, 31*(1), 33–46.

Bauman, M. L., Anderson, G., Perry, E., & Ray, M. (2006). Neuroanatomical and neurochemical studies of the autistic brain: Current thought and future directions. In S. O. Moldin & J. L. R. Rubenstein (Eds.), *Understanding autism: From basic neuroscience to treatment* (pp. 303–322). Boca Raton, FL: CRC Press.

Baumrind, D. (1989). Rearing competent children. In W. Damon (Ed.), *Child development today and tomorrow* (pp. 349–378). San Francisco: Jossey-Bass.

Baumrind, D. (1991a). The influence of parenting style on adolescent competence and substance use. *Journal of Early Adolescence, 11*(1), 56–95.

Baumrind, D. (1991b). Parenting styles and adolescent development. In J. Brooks-Gunn, R. Lerner, & A. C. Petersen (Eds.), *Encyclopedia of adolescence* (pp. 746–758). New York: Garland.

Baumrind, D. (2005). Taking a stand in a morally pluralistic society: Constructive obedience and responsible dissent in moral/character education. In L. Nucci (Ed.), *Conflict, contradiction, and contrarian elements in moral development and education* (pp. 21–50). Hillsdale, NJ: Erlbaum.

Beaulieu, M.-D., et al. (2008). When is knowledge ripe for primary care? *Evaluation & the Health Professions, 31*(1), 22–42.

Beck, E., Burnet, K. L., & Vosper, J. (2006). Birth-order effects on facets of extraversion. *Personality and Individual Differences, 40*(5), 953–959.

Beck, M. (1992, December 7). The new middle age. *Newsweek*, 50–56.

Bedford, V. H., & Avioli, P. S. (2006). "Shooting the bull": Cohort comparisons of fraternal intimacy in midlife and old age. In V. H. Bedford & B. Formaniak Turner (Eds.), *Men in relationships: A new look from a life course perspective* (pp. 81–101). New York: Springer.

Beidel, D. C., & Turner, S. M. (2007). Clinical presentation of social anxiety disorder in children and adolescents. In D. C. Beidel & S. M. Turner (Eds.), *Shy children, phobic adults: Nature and treatment of social anxiety disorders* (2nd ed., pp. 47–80). Washington, DC: American Psychological Association.

Beilei, L., Lei, L., Qi, D., & von Hofsten, C. (2002). The development of fine motor skills and their relations to children's academic achievement. *Acta Psychologica Sinica, 34*(5), 494–499.

Belmonte, M. K., & Carper, R. A. (2006). Monozygotic twins with Asperger syndrome: Differences in behaviour reflect variations in brain structure and function. *Brain and Cognition, 61*(1), 110–121.

Belsky, J. (2006a). Determinants and consequences of infant–parent attachment. In L. Balter & C. S. Tamis-LeMonda (Eds.), *Child psychology: A handbook of contemporary issues* (2nd ed., pp. 53–77). New York: Psychology Press.

Belsky, J. (2006b). Early child care and early child development: Major findings of the NICHD Study of Early Child Care. *European Journal of Developmental Psychology, 3*(1), 95–110.

Belsky, J., et al. (2007). Are there long-term effects of early child care? *Child Development, 78*(2), 681–701.

Bender, H. L., et al. (2007). Use of harsh physical discipline and developmental outcomes in adolescence. *Development and Psychopathology, 19*(1), 227–242.

Bengtson, V. L., et al. (Eds.). (2005). *Sourcebook of family theory and research*. Thousand Oaks, CA: Sage.

Benkel, I., Wijk, H., & Molander, U. (2009). Managing grief and relationship roles influence which forms of social support the bereaved needs. *American Journal of Hospice and Palliative Medicine, 26*(4), 241–245.

Bennett, S. E., & Assefi, N. P. (2005). School-based teenage pregnancy prevention programs: A systematic review of randomized controlled trials. *Journal of Adolescent Health, 36*(1), 72–81.

Bensley, A., et al. (2010). Teaching and assessing critical thinking skills for argument analysis in psychology. *Teaching of Psychology, 37*(2), 91–96.

Berg, C. J., Chang, J., Callaghan, W. M., & Whitehead, S. J. (2003). Pregnancy-related mortality in the United States, 1991–1997. *Obstetrics and Gynecology, 101*(2), 289–296.

Bermudez, P., Lerch, J. P., Evans, A. C., & Zatorre, R. J. (2009). Neuroanatomical correlates of musicianship as revealed by cortical thickness and voxel-based morphometry. *Cerebral Cortex, 19*(7), 1583–1596.

Berndt, T. J. (1992). Friendship and friends' influence in adolescence. *Current Directions in Psychological Science, 1*(5), 156–159.

Berndt, T. J. (2004). Friendship and three A's (aggression, adjustment, and attachment). *Journal of Experimental Child Psychology, 88*(1), 1–4.

Berndt, T. J., Miller, K. E., & Park, K. E. (1989). Adolescents' perceptions of friends and parents' influence on aspects of their school adjustment. *Journal of Early Adolescence, 9*(4), 419–435.

Berndt, T. J., & Perry, T. B. (1990). Distinctive features and effects of early adolescent friendships. In R. Montemayor, G. R. Adams, & T. P. Gullotta (Eds.), *From childhood to adolescence: A transitional period?* (pp. 269–287). Newbury Park, CA: Sage.

Bernstein, I. M., et al. (2005). Maternal smoking and its association with birth weight. *Obstetrics & Gynecology, 106*(5), 986–991.

Berscheid, E. (2003). On stepping on land mines. In Sternberg, R. J. (Ed.), *Psychologists defying the crowd: Stories of those who battled the establishment and won* (pp. 33–44). Washington, DC: American Psychological Association.

Berscheid, E. (2006). Searching for the meaning of "love." In R. J. Sternberg & K. Weis (Eds.), *The new psychology of love* (pp. 171–183). New Haven, CT: Yale University Press.

Berten, H., & Rossem, R. V. (2009). Doing worse but knowing better: An exploration of the relationship between HIV/AIDS knowledge and sexual behavior among adolescents in Flemish secondary schools. *Journal of Adolescence, 32*(5), 1303–1319.

Bertoni, A., et al. (2007). Stress communication, dyadic coping and couple satisfaction: A cross-sectional and cross-cultural study. *Età Evolutiva, 86*(Feb), 58–66.

Berzonsky, M. D. (2004). Identity style, parental authority, and identity commitment. *Journal of Youth and Adolescence, 33*(3), 213–220.

Berzonsky, M. D. (2005). Ego identity: A personal standpoint in a postmodern world. *Identity, 5*(2), 125–136.

Berzonsky, M. D., & Kuk, L. S. (2005). Identity style, psychosocial maturity, and academic performance. *Personality and Individual Differences, 39*(1), 235–247.

Bialystok, E., & Craik, F. I. M. (2007). Bilingualism and naming: Implications for cognitive assessment. *Journal of the International Neuropsychological Society, 13*(2), 209–211.

Bialystok, E., & Senman, L. (2004). Executive processes in appearance–reality tasks: The role of inhibition of attention and symbolic representation. *Child Development, 75*(2), 562–579.

Bianchi, S. M., & Spain, D. (1996). Women, work and family in America. *Population Bulletin, 51*(3). 2–46.

Bird, A., Reese, E., & Tripp, G. (2006). Parent–child talk about past emotional events: Associations with child temperament and goodness-of-fit. *Journal of Cognition and Development, 7*(2), 189–210.

Bish, C. L., et al. (2005). Diet and physical activity behaviors among Americans trying to lose weight. *Obesity Research, 13*(3), 596–607.

Bishop, D. M. (2005). The role of race and ethnicity in juvenile justice processing. In D. F. Hawkins & K. Kempf-Leonard (Eds.), *Our children, their children: Confronting racial and ethnic differences in American juvenile justice* (pp. 23–82). The John D. and Catherine T. MacArthur Foundation series on mental health and development. Research network on adolescent development and juvenile justice. Chicago: University of Chicago Press.

Black, D. W. (2007). Antisocial personality disorder, conduct disorder, and psychopathy. In J. E. Grant & M. N. Potenza. (Eds.), *Textbook of men's mental health* (pp. 143–170). Washington, DC: American Psychiatric Publishing.

Blackwell, D. L., & Lichter, D. T. (2004). Homogamy among dating, cohabiting, and married couples. *Sociological Quarterly, 45*(4), 719–737.

Blass, E. M., & Camp, C. A. (2003). Changing determinants in 6- to 12-week-old human infants. *Developmental Psychobiology, 42*(3), 312–316.

Blazina, C., Eddins, R., Burridge, A., & Settle, A. G. (2007). The relationship between masculinity ideology, loneliness, and separation-individuation difficulties. *The Journal of Men's Studies, 15*(1), 101–109.

Bloom, B., Dey, A. N., & Freeman, G. (2006). Summary health statistics for U.S. children: National Health Interview Survey, 2005. National Center for Health Statistics. *Vital Health Stat 10*(231), 2006.

Bloom, L. (1998). Language acquisition in its developmental context. In W. Damon (Ed.), *Handbook of child psychology, Volume 2: Cognition, perception, and language* (pp. 309–370). Hoboken, NJ: Wiley.

Bloom, P. (2002). Mind reading, communication, and the learning of names for things. *Mind and Language, 17*(1–2), 37–54.

Boccia, M., & Campos, J. J. (1989). Maternal emotional signals, social referencing, and infants' reactions to strangers. In N. Eisenberg (Ed.), *New directions for child development, Volume 44: Empathy and related emotional responses* (pp. 25–49). San Francisco: Jossey-Bass.

Bohlmeijer, E., Valenkamp, M., Westerhof, G., Smith, F., & Cuijpers, P. (2005). Creative reminiscence as an early intervention for depression. *Aging & Mental Health, 9*(4), 302–304.

Bohon, C., Garber, J., & Horowitz, J. L. (2007). Predicting school dropout and adolescent sexual behavior in offspring of depressed and nondepressed mothers. *Journal of the American Academy of Child & Adolescent Psychiatry, 46*(1), 15–24.

Boivin, M., Vitaro, F., & Poulin, F. (2005). Peer relationships and the development of aggressive behavior in early childhood. In R. E. Tremblay, W. W. Hartup, & J. Archer (Eds.), *Developmental origins of aggression* (pp. 376–397). New York: Guilford.

Bone health and osteoporosis: a report of the Surgeon General. Rockville, Md: U.S. Dept. of Health and Human Services, Public Health Service, Office of the Surgeon General; Washington, D.C., 2005. p.436

Bonanno, G. A., & Boerner, K. (2007). The stage theory of grief. *Journal of the American Medical Association, 297*(24), 2693.

Boom, J., Wouters, H., & Keller, M. (2007). A cross-cultural validation of stage development: A Rasch re-analysis of longitudinal socio-moral reasoning data. *Cognitive Development, 22*(2), 213–229.

Booth-LaForce, C., et al. (2006). Attachment, self-worth, and peer-group functioning in middle childhood. *Attachment & Human Development, 8*(4), 309–325.

Bosi, M. L., & de Oliveira, F. P. (2006). Bulimic behavior in adolescent athletes. In P. I. Swain (Ed.), *New developments in eating disorders research* (pp. 123–133). Hauppauge, NY: Nova Science Publishers.

Bost, L. W., & Riccomini, P. J (2006). Effective instruction: An inconspicuous strategy for dropout prevention. *Remedial and Special Education, 27*(5), 301–311.

Bouchard, T. J., Jr., & Loehlin, J. C. (2001). Genes, evolution, and personality. *Behavior Genetics, 31*(3), 243–273.

Bouchard, T. J., Jr., Lykken, D. T., McGue, M., Segal, N. L., & Tellegen, A. (1990). Sources of human psychological differences: The Minnesota study of twins reared apart. *Science, 250*(4978), 223–228.

Bower, T. G. R. (1974). *Development in infancy.* San Francisco: W. H. Freeman.

Bowlby, J. (1961). Processes of mourning. *International Journal of Psychoanalysis, 42*(4–5), 317–339.

Bowlby, J. (1988). *A secure base.* New York: Basic Books.

Bozionelos, N., & Wang, L. (2006). The relationship of mentoring and network resources with career success in the Chinese organizational environment. *International Journal of Human Resource Management, 17*(9), 1531–1546.

Braam, A. W., et al. (2008). God image and mood in old age. *Mental Health, Religion, & Culture, 11*(2), 221–237.

Bradley, R. H. (2006). The home environment. In N. F. Watt et al. (Eds.), *The crisis in youth mental health: Critical issues and effective programs, Volume 4: Early intervention programs and policies: Child psychology and mental health* (pp. 89–120). Westport, CT: Praeger/Greenwood.

Bradley, R. H., Caldwell, B. M., & Corwyn, R. F. (2003). The child care HOME inventories: Assessing the quality of family child care homes. *Early Childhood Research Quarterly, 18*(3), 294–309.

Brady, E. M. (2007). Review of adulthood: New terrain. *Educational Gerontology, 33*(1), 85–86.

Bramlett, M. D., & Mosher, W. D. (2002). Cohabitation, marriage, divorce, and remarriage. *Vital and Health Statistics, 23*(22). Available at http://www.cdc.gov/nchs/data/series/sr_23/sr23_022.pdf

Branco, J. C., & Lourenço, O. (2004). Cognitive and linguistic aspects in 5- to 6-year-olds' class-inclusion reasoning. *Psicologia Educação Cultura, 8*(2), 427–445.

Brandstätter, H., & Farthofer, A. (2003). Influence of part-time work on university students' academic performance. *Zeitschrift für Arbeits- und Organisationspsychologie, 47*(3), 134–145.

Brandtjen, H., & Verny, T (2001). Short and long term effects on infants and toddlers in full time daycare centers. *Journal of Prenatal & Perinatal Psychology & Health, 15*(4), 239–286.

Braver, T. S., & West, R. (2008). Working memory, executive control, and aging. In F. I. M. Craik & T. A. Salthouse (Eds.), *The handbook of aging and cognition* (3rd ed., pp. 311–372). New York: Psychology Press.

Brazier, A., & Rowlands, C. (2006). PKU in the family: Working together. *Clinical Child Psychology and Psychiatry, 11*(3), 483–488.

Breastfeeding. (2006). Centers for Disease Control and Prevention. Available at http://www.cdc.gov/breastfeeding/faq/index.htm

Bridges, A. J. (2007). Successful living as a (single) woman. *Psychology of Women Quarterly, 31*(3), 327–328.

Bridges, L. J., Roe, A. E. C., Dunn, J., & O'Connor, T. G. (2007). Children's perspectives on their relationships with grandparents following parental separation: A longitudinal study. *Social Development, 16*(3), 539–554.

Briones, T. L., Klintsova, A. Y., & Greenough, W. T. (2004). Stability of synaptic plasticity in the adult rat visual cortex induced by complex environment exposure. *Brain Research, 1018*(1), 130–135.

Brockman, D. D. (2003). *From late adolescence to young adulthood.* Madison, CT: International Universities Press.

Brody, L. R., Zelazo, P. R., & Chaika, H. (1984). Habituation–dishabituation to speech in the neonate. *Developmental Psychology, 20*(1), 114–119.

Bronfenbrenner, U., & Morris, P. A. (2006). The bioecological model of human development. In R. M. Lerner & W. Damon (Eds.), *Handbook of child psychology* (6th ed.), *Volume 1: Theoretical models of human development* (pp. 793–828). Hoboken, NJ: Wiley.

Bronson, G. W. (1990). Changes in infants' visual scanning across the 2- to 14-week age period. *Journal of Experimental Child Psychology, 49*(1), 101–125.

Bronson, G. W. (1991). Infant differences in rate of visual encoding. *Child Development, 62*(1), 44–54.

Bronson, G. W. (1997). The growth of visual capacity: Evidence from infant scanning patterns. *Advances in Infancy Research, 11*(1), 109–141.

Broomhall, H. S., & Winefield, A. H. (1990). A comparison of the affective well-being of young and middle-aged unemployed men matched for length of unemployment. *British Journal of Medical Psychology, 63*(1), 43–52.

Brown, B. B., Mounts, N., Lamborn, S. D., & Steinberg, L. (1993). Parenting practices and peer group affiliation in adolescence. *Child Development, 64*(2), 467–482.

Brown, R. (1973). *A first language: The early stages.* Cambridge, MA: Harvard University Press.

Brown, R. (1977). Introduction. In C. A. Snow & C. Ferguson (Eds.), *Talking to children.* New York: Cambridge University Press.

Brown, S. L., Brown, R. M., House, J. S., & Smith, D. M. (2008). Coping with spousal loss: Potential buffering effects of self-reported helping behavior. *Personality and Social Psychology Bulletin, 34*(6), 849-861.

Brown, S. L., Lee, G. R., & Bulanda, J. R. (2006). Cohabitation among older adults. *Journals of Gerontology: Series B: Psychological Sciences and Social Sciences, 61B*(2), S71–S79.

Brownell, C. A., & Carriger, M. S. (1990). Changes in cooperation and self-other differentiation during the second year. *Child Development, 61*(4), 1164–1174.

Browning, J. R., Hatfield, E., Kessler, D., & Levine, T. (2000). Sexual motives, gender, and sexual behavior. *Archives of Sexual Behavior, 29*(2), 135–153.

Bruck, M., Ceci, S. J., & Principe, G. F. (2006). The child and the law. In K. Renninger, I. E. Sigel, W. Damon, & R. M. Lerner (Eds.), *Handbook of child psychology* (6th ed.), *Volume 4: Child psychology in practice* (pp. 776–816). Hoboken, NJ: Wiley.

Brugger, P., et al. (2009). Semantic, perceptual and number space. *Neuroscience Letters, 418*(2), 133–137.

Brunner, L. C., Eshilian-Oates, L., & Kuo, T. Y. (2003). Hip fractures in adults. *American Family Physician, 67*(3), 537–542.

Brunner, R., Parzer, P., & Resch, F. (2005). Involuntary hospitalization of patients with anorexia nervosa: Clinical issues and empirical findings. *Fortschritte der Neurologie, Psychiatrie, 73*(1), 9–15.

Bryden, P. J., Bruyn, J., & Fletcher, P. (2005). Handedness and health: An examination of the association between different handedness classifications and health disorders. *Laterality: Asymmetries of Body, Brain and Cognition, 10*(5), 429–440.

Budney, A. J., Vandrey, R. G., Hughes, J. R., Moore, B. A., & Bahrenburg, B. (2007). Oral delta-9-tetrahydrocannabinol suppresses cannabis withdrawal symptoms. *Drug and Alcohol Dependence, 86*(1), 22–29.

Buela-Casal, G., Olivas-Avila, J. A., Musi-Lechuga, B., & Zych, I. (2011). The h index of presidents of the American Psychological Association through journal articles included in the Web of Science database. *International Journal of Clinical and Health Psychology, 11*(1), 95–107.

Bugental, D. B., & Happaney, K. (2004). Predicting infant maltreatment in low-income families: The interactive effects of maternal attributions and child status at birth. *Developmental Psychology, 40*(2), 234–243.

Buhl, H. M., Wittmann, S., & Noack, P. (2003). Child–parent relationship of university students and young employed adults. *Zeitschrift für Entwicklungspsychologie und Pädagogische Psychologie, 35*(3), 144–152.

Bunikowski, R., et al. (1998). Neurodevelopmental outcome after prenatal exposure to opiates. *European Journal of Pediatrics, 157*(9), 724–730.

Burke, D. M., & Shafto, M. A. (2008). Language and aging. In F. I. M. Craik & T. A. Salthouse (Eds.), *The handbook of aging and cognition* (3rd ed., pp. 373–443). New York: Psychology Press.

Bushman, B. J. (1998). Priming effects of media violence on the accessibility of aggressive constructs in memory. *Personality and Social Psychology Bulletin, 24*(5), 537–545.

Bushnell, E. W. (1993, June). *A dual-processing approach to cross-modal matching: Implications for development.* Paper presented at the meeting of the Society for Research in Child Development, New Orleans, LA.

Bushnell, I. W. R. (2001). Mother's face recognition in newborn infants: Learning and memory. *Infant and Child Development, 10*(1–2), 67–74.

Buss, D. M. (1994). *The evolution of desire: Strategies of human mating.* New York: Basic Books.

Buss, D. M. (Ed.). (2005). *The handbook of evolutionary psychology.* Hoboken, NJ: Wiley.

Buss, D. M. (2009). How can evolutionary psychology successfully explain personality and individual differences? *Perspectives on Psychological Science, 4*(4), 359–366.

Buss, D. M., & Duntley, J. D. (2006). The evolution of aggression. In M. Schaller, J. A. Simpson, & D. T. Kenrick (Eds.), *Evolution and social psychology: Frontiers of social psychology* (pp. 263–285). Madison, CT: Psychosocial Press.

Bussey, K., & Bandura, A. (1999). Social cognitive theory of gender development and differentiation. *Psychological Review, 106*(4), 676–713.

Buston, K., Williamson, L., & Hart, G. (2007). Young women under 16 years with experience of sexual intercourse: Who becomes pregnant? *Journal of Epidemiology & Community Health, 61*(3), 221–225.

Butterfield, S. A., & Loovis, E. M. (1993). Influence of age, sex, balance, and sport participation on development of throwing by children in grades K–8. *Perceptual and Motor Skills, 76*(2), 459–464.

Butler, R. N. (2002). The life review. *Journal of Geriatric Psychology, 35*(1), 7–10.

Buunk, B. P., et al. (2002). Age and gender differences in mate selection criteria for various involvement levels. *Personal Relationships, 9*(3), 271–278.

Bye, D., Pushkar, D., & Conway, M. (2007). Motivation, interest, and positive affect in traditional and nontraditional undergraduate students. *Adult Education Quarterly, 57*(2), 141–158.

Bynum, M. S. (2007). African American mother–daughter communication about sex and daughters' sexual behavior: Does college racial composition make a difference? *Cultural Diversity & Ethnic Minority Psychology, 13*(2), 151–160.

Cacioppo, J. T., & Patrick, W. (2008). *Loneliness: Human nature and the need for social connection.* New York: Norton.

Callahan, J. J. (2007). Sandwich anyone? *Gerontologist, 47*(4), 569–571.

Callan, M. J., Ellard, J. H., & Nicol, J. E. (2006). The belief in a just world and immanent justice reasoning in adults. *Personality and Social Psychology Bulletin, 32*(12), 1646–1658.

Calvert, S. L., & Kotler, J. A. (2003). Lessons from children's television: The impact of the Children's Television Act on children's learning. *Journal of Applied Developmental Psychology, 24*(3), 275–335.

Camarena, P. M. (1991). Conformity in adolescence. In R. M. Lerner, A. C. Petersen, & J. Brooks-Gunn (Eds.), *Encyclopedia of adolescence* (pp. 232–236). New York: Garland.

Campanella, J., & Rovee-Collier, C. (2005). Latent learning and deferred imitation at 3 months. *Infancy, 7*(3), 243–262.

Campbell, A., Shirley, L., & Caygill, L. (2002). Sex-typed preferences in three domains: Do two-year-olds need cognitive variables? *British Journal of Psychology, 93*(2), 203–217.

Campbell, A., Shirley, L., Heywood, C., & Crook, C. (2000). Infants' visual preference for sex-congruent babies, children, toys and activities: A longitudinal study. *British Journal of Developmental Psychology, 18*(4), 479–498.

Campbell, D. A., Lake, M. F., Falk, M., & Backstrand, J. R. (2006). A randomized control trial of continuous support in labor by a lay doula. *Journal of Obstetric, Gynecologic, and Neonatal Nursing, 35*(4), 456–464.

Campbell, D. W., Eaton, W. O., & McKeen, N. A. (2002). Motor activity level and behavioural control in young children. *International Journal of Behavioral Development, 26*(4), 289–296.

Campbell, R. (2006). Rape survivors' experiences with the legal and medical systems. *Violence Against Women, 12*(1), 30–45.

Campbell, R., & Wasco, S. M. (2005). Understanding rape and sexual assault. *Journal of Interpersonal Violence, 20*(1), 127–131.

Campbell, S. B., et al. (2004). The course of maternal depressive symptoms and maternal sensitivity as predictors of attachment security at 36 months. *Development and Psychopathology, 16*(2), 231–252.

Campos, J. J., Hiatt, S., Ramsey, D., Henderson, C., & Svejda, M. (1978). The emergence of fear on the visual cliff. In M. Lewis & L. Rosenblum (Eds.), *The origins of affect* (pp. 149–182). New York: Plenum.

Campos, J. J., Langer, A., & Krowitz, A. (1970). Cardiac responses on the visual cliff in prelocomotor human infants. *Science, 170*(3954), 196–197.

Camras, L. A., et al. (2007). Do infants show distinct negative facial expressions for fear and anger? Emotional expression in 11-month-old European American, Chinese, and Japanese Infants. *Infancy, 11*(2), 131–155.

Candy, T. R., Crowell, J. A., & Banks, M. S. (1998). Optical, receptoral, and retinal constraints on foveal and peripheral vision in the human neonate. *Vision Research, 38*(24), 3857–3870.

Canitano, R. (2007). Epilepsy in autism spectrum disorders. *European Child & Adolescent Psychiatry, 16*(1), 61–66.

Caplan, M., Vespo, J., Pedersen, J., & Hale, D. F. (1991). Conflict and its resolution in small groups of one- and two-year-olds. *Child Development, 62*(6), 1513–1524.

Caplan, P. J., & Larkin, J. (1991). The anatomy of dominance and self-protection. *American Psychologist, 46*(5), 536.

Capron, C., Thérond, C., & Duyme, M. (2007). Brief report: Effect of menarcheal status and family structure on depressive symptoms and emotional/behavioural problems in young adolescent girls. *Journal of Adolescence, 30*(1), 175–179.

Carey, B. (2007a, March 26). Poor behavior is linked to time in day care. *New York Times.* Available at http://www.nytimes.com

Carey, B. (2007b, June 22). Research finds firstborns gain the higher I.Q. *New York Times.* Available at http://www.nytimes.com

Carrère, S., Buehlman, K. T., Gottman, J. M., Coan, J. A., & Ruckstuhl, L. (2000). Predicting marital stability and divorce in newlywed couples. *Journal of Family Psychology, 14*(1), 42–58.

Carroll, J. S., et al. (2007). So close, yet so far away: The impact of varying marital horizons on emerging adulthood. *Journal of Adolescent Research, 22*(3), 219–247.

Carstensen, L. L., Gottman, J. M., & Levenson, R. W. (1995). Emotional behavior in long-term marriage. *Psychology and Aging, 10*(1), 140–149.

Carstensen, L. L., Isaacowitz, D. M., & Charles, S. T. (1999). Taking time seriously: A theory of so-

cioemotional selectivity. *American Psychologist, 54*(3), 165–181.

Carver, L. J., & Vaccaro, B. G. (2007). 12-month-old infants allocate increased neural resources to stimuli associated with negative adult emotion. *Developmental Psychology, 43*(1), 54–69.

Casas, J. F., et al. (2006). Early parenting and children's relational and physical aggression in the preschool and home contexts. *Journal of Applied Developmental Psychology, 27*(3), 209–227.

Caserta, M. S., & Lund, D. A. (2007). Toward the development of an Inventory of Daily Widowed Life (IDWL). *Death Studies, 31*(6), 505–534.

Casini, A., & Sanchez-Mazas, M. (2005). "This job is not for me!": The impact of the gender norm and the organizational culture on professional upward mobility. *Cahiers Internationaux de Psychologie Sociale, 67–68*(Sep–Dec), 101–112.

Cassia, V. M., Simion, F., & Umilta, C. (2001). Face preference at birth: The role of an orienting mechanism. *Developmental Science, 4*(1), 101–108.

Caton, D., et al. (2002). Anesthesia for childbirth: Controversy and change. *American Journal of Obstetrics & Gynecology, 186*(5), S25–S30.

Cattell, R. B. (1949). *The culture fair intelligence test.* Champaign, IL: Institute for Personality and Ability Testing.

Caudle, D. D., et al. (2007). Cognitive errors, symptom severity, and response to cognitive behavior therapy in older adults with generalized anxiety disorder. *American Journal of Geriatric Psychiatry, 15*(8), 680–689.

Caulfield, R. (2000). Beneficial effects of tactile stimulation on early development. *Early Childhood Education Journal, 27*(4), 255–257.

Cavallini, A., et al. (2002). Visual acuity in the first two years of life in healthy term newborns: An experience with the Teller Acuity Cards. *Functional Neurology: New Trends in Adaptive and Behavioral Disorders, 17*(2), 87–92.

Cavell, T. A. (2001). Updating our approach to parent training. I. The case against targeting noncompliance. *Clinical Psychology: Science and Practice, 8*(3), 299–318.

Cellarius, V. (2008). Terminal sedation and the "imminence condition." *Journal of Medical Ethics, 34*(2), 69–72.

Centers for Disease Control and Prevention. (2006). *HIV/AIDS Surveillance Report, 2005, v. 17.* Atlanta: U.S. Department of Health and Human Services, Centers for Disease Control and Prevention. Available at http://www.cdc.gov/hiv/topics/surveillance/resources/reports

Centers for Disease Control and Prevention. (2011). Cancer Prevention and Control, Factors that contribute to health disparities in cancer. Available at http://www.cdc.gov/cancer/healthdisparities/basic_info/challenges.htm

Centers for Disease Control and Prevention. National Center for Health Statistics. (2009). Early release of selected estimates based on data from the 2008 National Health Interview Survey. Available at http://www.cdc.gov/nchs/nhis/released200906.htm

Central Intelligence Agency. (2004, September 17). The World Factbook. Available at http://www.cia.gov/cia/publications/factbook

Central Intelligence Agency. (2011). The World Factbook. Available at http://www.cia.gov/cia/publications/factbook

Cernoch, J., & Porter, R. (1985). Recognition of maternal axillary odors by infants. *Child Development, 56,* 1593–1598.

Chapman, M., & McBride, M. C. (1992). Beyond competence and performance: Children's class inclusion strategies, superordinate class cues, and verbal justifications. *Developmental Psychology, 28*(2), 319–327.

Charles, S. T., & Carstensen, L. L. (2007). Emotion regulation and aging. In J. J. Gross (Ed.), *Handbook of emotion regulation* (pp. 307–327). New York: Guilford.

Charles, S. T., Reynolds, C. A., & Gatz, M. (2001). Age-related differences and change in positive and negative affect over 23 years. *Journal of Personality and Social Psychology, 80*(1), 136–151.

Charlton, R. (2004). Ageing male syndrome, andropause, androgen decline or mid-life crisis? *Journal of Men's Health & Gender, 1*(1), 55–59.

Charness, N., & Schaie, K. W. (2003). *Impact of technology on successful aging.* New York: Springer.

Chaudieu, I., et al. (2008). Abnormal reactions to environmental stress in elderly persons with anxiety disorders. *Journal of Affective Disorders, 106*(3), 307–313.

Cheng, H., & Furnham, A. (2002). Personality, peer relations, and self-confidence as predictors of happiness and loneliness. *Journal of Adolescence, 25*(3), 327–339.

Cheng, S.-T., & Chan, A. C. M. (2007). Multiple pathways from stress to suicidality and the protective effect of social support in Hong Kong adolescents. *Suicide and Life-Threatening Behavior, 37*(2), 187–196.

Cherney, I. D., Harper, H. J., & Winter, J. A. (2006). Nouveaux jouets: Ce que les enfants identifient comme "jouets de garcons" et "jouets de filles." *Enfance, 58*(3), 266–282.

Chesley, N., & Moen, P. (2006). When workers care: Dual-earner couples' caregiving strategies, benefit use, and psychological well-being. *American Behavioral Scientist, 49*(9), 1248–1269.

Chess, S., & Thomas, A. (1991). Temperament. In M. Lewis (Ed.), *Child and adolescent psychiatry: A comprehensive textbook* (pp. 772–801). Baltimore: Williams & Wilkins.

Chlebowski, R. T., et al. (2003). Influence of estrogen plus progestin on breast cancer and mammography in healthy postmenopausal women: The Women's Health Initiative Randomized Trial. *Journal of the American Medical Association, 289,* 3243–3253.

Chomsky, N. (1988). *Language and problems of knowledge.* Cambridge, MA: MIT Press.

Chomsky, N. (1990). On the nature, use, and acquisition of language. In W. G. Lycan (Ed.), *Mind and cognition* (pp. 627–646). Oxford: Blackwell.

Chong, L., McDonald, H., & Strauss, E. (2004). Deconstructing aging. *Science, 305*(5689), 1419.

Chou, T.-L., et al. (2006). Developmental and skill effects on the neural correlates of semantic processing to visually presented words. *Human Brain Mapping, 27*(11), 915–924.

Christian, P., et al. (2003). Effects of alternative maternal micronutrient supplements on low birth weight in rural Nepal: Double blind randomised community trial. *British Medical Journal, 326*(7389), 571.

Christophersen, E. R., & Mortweet, S. L. (2003). Establishing bedtime. In E. R. Christophersen & S. L. Mortweet (Eds.), *Parenting that works: Building skills that last a lifetime* (pp. 209–228). Washington, DC: American Psychological Association.

Chronis, A. M., et al. (2007). Maternal depression and early positive parenting predict future conduct problems in young children with attention-deficit/hyperactivity disorder. *Developmental Psychology, 43*(1), 70–82.

Clancy, B., & Finlay, B. (2001). Neural correlates of early language learning. In M. Tomasello & E. Bates (Eds.), *Language development: The essential readings* (pp. 307–330). Malden, MA: Blackwell.

Clark, E. V. (1973). What's in a word? On the child's acquisition of semantics in his first language. In E. Moore (Ed.), *Cognitive development and the acquisition of language.* New York: Academic Press.

Clark, E. V. (1975). Knowledge, context, and strategy in the acquisition of meaning. In D. P. Dato (Ed.), *Georgetown University roundtable on language and linguistics* (pp. 77–98). Washington, DC: Georgetown University Press.

Clark, J. (2005). Sibling relationships: Theory and issues for practice. *Child & Family Social Work, 10*(1), 90–91.

Clark, J., & Rugg, S. (2005). The importance of independence in toileting. *British Journal of Occupational Therapy, 68*(4), 165–171.

Clarke-Stewart, K. A., & Beck, R. J. (1999). Maternal scaffolding and children's narrative retelling of a movie story. *Early Childhood Research Quarterly, 14*(3), 409–434.

Clayton, R., & Crosby, R. A. (2006) Measurement in health promotion. In R. A. Crosby, R. J. DiClemente, & L. F. Salazar (Eds.), *Research methods in health promotion* (pp. 229–259). San Francisco: Jossey-Bass.

Cleary, D. J., Ray, G. E., LoBello, S. G., & Zachar, P. (2002). Children's perceptions of close peer relationships: Quality, congruence and meta-perceptions. *Child Study Journal, 32*(3), 179–192.

Clode, D. (2006). Review of *A left-hand turn around the world: Chasing the mystery and meaning of all things southpaw. Laterality: Asymmetries of Body, Brain and Cognition, 11*(6), 580–581.

Cnattingius, S. (2004). The epidemiology of smoking during pregnancy: Smoking prevalence, maternal characteristics, and pregnancy outcomes. *Nicotine & Tobacco Research, 6*(Supp. l2), S125–S140.

Coats, A. H., & Blanchard-Fields, F. (2008). Emotion regulation in interpersonal problems: The role of cognitive-emotional complexity, emotion regulation goals, and expressivity. *Psychology and Aging, 23*(1), 39–51.

Cochran, S. V. (2005). Assessing and treating depression in men. In G. E. Good & G. R. Brooks (Eds.), *The new handbook of psychotherapy and counseling with men* (pp. 121–133). San Francisco: Jossey-Bass.

Cohen, D. L., & Belsky, J. (2008). Individual differences in female mate preferences as a function of attachment and hypothetical ecological conditions. *Journal of Evolutionary Psychology, 6*(1), 25–42.

Cohen, L. S., et al. (2006). Relapse of major depression during pregnancy in women who maintain or discontinue antidepressant treatment. *Journal of the American Medical Association, 295*(5), 499–507.

Cohen, S. (2003). Psychosocial models of the role of social support in the etiology of physical disease. In P. Salovey & A. J. Rothman (Eds.), *Social psychology of health* (pp. 227–244). New York: Psychology Press.

Cohen-Bendahan, C. C. C., van de Beek, C., & Berenbaum, S. A. (2005). Prenatal sex hormone effects on child and adult sex-typed behavior: Methods and findings. *Neuroscience and Biobehavioral Reviews, 29*(2), 353–384.

Cohn, M., Emrich, S. M., & Moscovitch, M. (2008). Age-related deficits in associative memory. *Psychology and Aging, 23*(1), 93–103.

Cole, T. B. (2006). Rape at U.S. colleges often fueled by alcohol. *Journal of the American Medical Association, 296*(5), 504–505.

Coleman, M., Ganong, L. H., & Fine, M. (2000). Reinvestigating remarriage: Another decade of progress. *Journal of Marriage & the Family, 62*(4), 1288–1307.

Coleman, P. K. (2003). Perceptions of parent–child attachment, social self-efficacy, and peer relationships in middle childhood. *Infant and Child Development, 12*(4), 351–368.

Collaer, M. L., & Hill, E. M. (2006). Large sex difference in adolescents on a timed line judgment task: Attentional contributors and task relationship to mathematics. *Perception, 35*(4), 561–572.

Collins, W. A., & Laursen, B. (2006). Parent–adolescent relationships. In P. Noller & J. A. Feeney (Eds.), *Close relationships: Functions, forms and processes* (pp. 111–125). Hove, England: Psychology Press/Taylor & Francis.

Collins, W. A., Maccoby, E. E., Steinberg, L., Hetherington, E. M., & Bornstein, M. H. (2000). Contemporary research on parenting: The case for nature and nurture. *American Psychologist, 55*(2), 218–232.

Colombo, J. (1993). *Infant cognition.* Newbury Park, CA: Sage.

Commons, M. L. (2004). The state of the art on Perry and epistemological development? *Journal of Adult Development, 11*(2), 59–60.

Commons, M. L., Galaz-Fontes, J. F., & Morse, S. J. (2006). Leadership, cross-cultural contact, socio-economic status, and formal operational reasoning about moral dilemmas among Mexican non-literate adults and high school students. *Journal of Moral Education, 35*(2), 247–267

Conel, J. L. (1959). *The postnatal development of the human cerebral cortex, 5.* Cambridge, MA: Harvard University Press.

Confer, J. C., et al. (2010). Evolutionary psychology: Controversies, questions, prospects, and limitations. *American Psychologist, 65*(2), 110–126.

Conference Board. (2010). I can't get no . . . job satisfaction. Available at http://www.conferenceboard.org/publications/publicationdetail.cfm?publicationid=1727

Conner, K. R., & Goldston, D. B. (2007). Rates of suicide among males increase steadily from age 11 to 21: Developmental framework and outline for prevention. *Aggression and Violent Behavior, 12*(2), 193–207.

Connolly, J., Craig, W., Goldberg, A., & Pepler, D. (2004). Mixed-gender groups, dating, and romantic relationships in early adolescence. *Journal of Research on Adolescence, 14*(2), 185–207.

Connolly, J., Furman, W., & Konarski, R. (2000). The role of peers in the emergence of heterosexual romantic relationships in adolescence. *Child Development, 71*(5), 1395–1408.

Connor, P. D., Sampson, P. D., Streissguth, A. P., Bookstein, F. L., & Barr, H. M. (2006). Effects of prenatal alcohol exposure on fine motor coordination and balance: A study of two adult samples. *Neuropsychologia, 44*(5), 744–751.

Conrad, P. (2007). *The medicalization of society: On the transformation of human conditions into treatable disorders.* Baltimore: Johns Hopkins University Press.

Constantino, J. N., et al. (2006). Autistic social impairment in the siblings of children with pervasive developmental disorders. *American Journal of Psychiatry, 163*(2), 294–296.

Cooke, B. M., Breedlove, S. M., & Jordan, C. L. (2003). Both estrogen receptors and androgen receptors contribute to testosterone-induced changes in the morphology of the medial amygdala and sexual arousal in male rats. *Hormones & Behavior, 43*(2), 336–346.

Coon, H., Fulker, D. W., DeFries, J. C., & Plomin, R. (1990). Home environment and cognitive ability of 7-year-old children in the Colorado adoption project: Genetic and environmental etiologies. *Developmental Psychology, 26*(3), 459–468.

Cooper, J., Appleby, L., & Amos, T. (2002). Life events preceding suicide by young people. *Social Psychiatry and Psychiatric Epidemiology, 37*(6), 271–275.

Coovadia, H. (2004). Antiretroviral agents. How best to protect infants from HIV and save their mothers from AIDS. *New England Journal of Medicine, 351*(3), 289–292.

Coplan, R. J., Rubin, K. H., Fox, N. A., Calkins, S. D., et al. (1994). Being alone, playing alone, and acting alone: Distinguishing among reticence,

and passive and active solitude in young children. *Child Development, 65*(1), 129–137.

Coren, S. (1992). *The left-hander syndrome.* New York: Free Press.

Corliss, R. (2003, August 12). Bollywood: Frequently questioned answers. *Time Magazine.* Available at http://www.time.com/time/columnist/corliss/article/0,9565,475407,00.html

Cornwell, A. C., & Feigenbaum, P. (2006). Sleep biological rhythms in normal infants and those at high risk for SIDS. *Chronobiology International, 23*(5), 935–961.

Corstorphine, E., Waller, G., Lawson, R., & Ganis, C. (2007). Trauma and self-impulsivity in the eating disorders. *Eating Behaviors, 8*(1), 23–30.

Costello, E. J., Sung, M., Worthman, C., & Angold, A. (2007). Pubertal maturation and the development of alcohol use and abuse. *Drug and Alcohol Dependence, 88*(1001), S50–S59.

Costigan, C. L., Cauce, A. M., & Etchison, K. (2007). Changes in African American mother–daughter relationships during adolescence: Conflict, autonomy, and warmth. In B. J. R. Leadbeater & N. Way (Eds.), *Urban girls revisited: Building strengths* (pp. 177–201). New York: New York University Press.

Courage, M. L., Howe, M. L., & Squires, S. E. (2004). Individual differences in 3.5-month olds' visual attention: What do they predict at 1 year? *Infant Behavior and Development, 27*(1), 19–30.

Cowan, P. A., & Cowan, C. P. (2005). Five-domain models: Putting it all together. In P. A. Cowan, C. P. Cowan, J. C. Ablow, V. K. Johnson, & J. R. Measelle (Eds.), *The family context of parenting in children's adaptation to elementary school* (pp. 315–333). Monographs in parenting series. Hillsdale, NJ: Erlbaum.

Cramer, D. (2003). Facilitativeness, conflict, demand for approval, self-esteem, and satisfaction with romantic relationships. *Journal of Psychology, 137*(1), 85–98.

Crenshaw, D. A. (2007). Life span issues and assessment and intervention. In D. Balk et al. (Eds.), *Handbook of thanatology* (pp. 227–234). New York: Routledge/Taylor & Francis Group.

Crombie, G., & Desjardins, M. J. (1993, March). *Predictors of gender: The relative importance of children's play, games, and personality characteristics.* Paper presented at the meeting of the Society for Research in Child Development, New Orleans, LA.

Crook, C. K., & Lipsitt, L. P. (1976). Neonatal nutritive sucking: Effects of taste stimulation upon sucking rhythm and heart rate. *Child Development, 47*(2), 518–522.

Crowther, C., et al. (2006). Neonatal respiratory distress syndrome after repeat exposure to antenatal corticosteroids: A randomised control trial. *Lancet, 367*(9526), 1913–1919.

Cruz, N. V., & Bahna, S. L. (2006). Do foods or additives cause behavior disorders? *Psychiatric Annals, 36*(10), 724–732.

Cuellar, J., & Curry, T. R. (2007). The prevalence and comorbidity between delinquency, drug abuse, suicide attempts, physical and sexual abuse, and self-mutilation among delinquent Hispanic females. *Hispanic Journal of Behavioral Sciences, 29*(1), 68–82.

Cumming, E., & Henry, W. E. (1961). *Growing old: The process of disengagement.* New York: Basic Books.

Cumming, S. P., Eisenmann, J. C., Smoll, F. L., Smith, R. E., & Malina, R. M. (2005). Body size and perceptions of coaching behaviors by adolescent female athletes. *Psychology of Sport and Exercise, 6*(6), 693–705.

Cunningham, R. L., & McGinnis, M. Y. (2007). Factors influencing aggression toward females by male rats exposed to anabolic androgenic steroids during puberty. *Hormones and Behavior, 51*(1), 135–141.

Curlin, F. A., Nwodim, C., Vance, J. L., Chin, M. H., & Lantos, J. D. (2008). To die, to sleep: U.S. physicians' religious and other objections to physician-assisted suicide, terminal sedation, and withdrawal of life support. *American Journal of Hospice and Palliative Medicine, 25*(2), 112–120.

Cystic Fibrosis Foundation. (2007). Available at http://www.cff.org

Daman-Wasserman, M., Brennan, B., Radcliffe, F., Prigot, J., & Fagen, J. (2006). Auditory-visual context and memory retrieval in 3-month-old infants. *Infancy, 10*(3), 201–220.

Damon, W. (1991). Adolescent self-concept. In R. M. Lerner, A. C. Petersen, & J. Brooks-Gunn (Eds.), *Encyclopedia of adolescence* (pp. 1018–1021). New York: Garland.

Dandy, J., & Nettelbeck, T. (2002). The relationship between IQ, homework, aspirations and academic achievement for Chinese, Vietnamese and Anglo-Celtic Australian school children. *Educational Psychology, 22*(3), 267–276.

Dane, S., & Erzurumluoglu, A. (2003). Sex and handedness differences in eye–hand visual reaction times in handball players. *International Journal of Neuroscience, 113*(7), 923–929.

Dang-Vu, T. T., Desseilles, M., Peigneux, P., & Maquet, P. (2006). A role for sleep in brain plasticity. *Pediatric Rehabilitation, 19*(2), 98–118.

Daniels, S. R. (2006). The consequences of childhood overweight and obesity. *The Future of Children, 16*(1), 47–67.

D'Augelli, A. R., Grossman, A. H., Hershberger, S. L., & O'Connell, T. S. (2001). Aspects of mental health among older lesbian, gay, and bisexual adults. *Aging & Mental Health, 5*(2), 149–158.

Davis, L., Edwards, H., Mohay, H., & Wollin, J. (2003). The impact of very premature birth on the psychological health of mothers. *Early Human Development, 73*(1–2), 61–70.

Davis, S. R., Davison, S. L., Donath, S., & Bell, R. J. (2005). Circulating androgen levels and self-reported sexual function in women. *Journal of the American Medical Association, 294*(1), 91–96.

Dawson, T. L. (2002). New tools, new insights: Kohlberg's moral judgement stages revisited. *International Journal of Behavioral Development, 26*(2), 154–166.

Deary, I. J., Whiteman, M. C., Starr, J. M., Whalley, L. J., & Fox, H. C. (2004). The impact of childhood intelligence on later life: Following up the Scottish mental surveys of 1932 and 1947. *Journal of Personality and Social Psychology, 86*(1), 130–147.

De Beni, R., Borella, E., & Carretti, B. (2007). Reading comprehension in aging: The role of working memory and metacomprehension. *Aging, Neuropsychology, and Cognition, 14*(2), 189–212.

DeCasper, A. J., & Fifer, W. P. (1980). Of human bonding: Newborns prefer their mothers' voices. *Science, 208*(4448), 1174–1176.

DeCasper, A. J., & Prescott, P. A. (1984). Human newborns' perception of male voices: Preference, discrimination, and reinforcing value. *Developmental Psychobiology, 17*(5), 481–491.

DeCasper, A. J., & Spence, M. J. (1991). Auditorially mediated behavior during the perinatal period: A cognitive view. In M. J. Weiss & P. R. Zelazo (Eds.), *Infant attention* (pp. 142–176). Norwood, NJ: Ablex.

Deep, A. L., et al. (1999). Sexual abuse in eating disorder subtypes and control women: The role of comorbid substance dependence in bulimia nervosa. *International Journal of Eating Disorders, 25*(1), 1–10.

de Haan, M., & Groen, M. (2006). Neural bases of infants' processing of social information in faces. In P. J. Marshall & N. A. Fox (Eds.), *The development of social engagement: Neurobiological perspectives* (pp. 46–80).

Series in affective science. New York: Oxford University Press.

Dehaene-Lambertz, G., Pena, M., Christophe, A., & Landrieu, P. (2004). Phoneme perception in a neonate with a left sylvian infarct. *Brain and Language, 88*(1), 26–38.

Delgado, A. R., & Prieto, G. (2004). Cognitive mediators and sex-related differences in mathematics. *Intelligence, 32*(1), 25–32.

Dennerstein, L., & Goldstein, I. (2005). Postmenopausal female sexual dysfunction: At a crossroads. *Journal of Sexual Medicine, 2*(Supp. 3), 116–117.

Dennis, W. (1960). Causes of retardation among institutional children: Iran. *Journal of Genetic Psychology, 96*(Mar), 47–59.

Dennis, W., & Dennis, M. G. (1940). The effect of cradling practices upon the onset of walking in Hopi children. *Journal of Genetic Psychology, 56*, 77–86.

den Tonkelaar, I. & Oddens, B. J. (2000). Determinants of long-term hormone replacement therapy and reasons for early discontinuation. *Obstetrics & Gynecology, 95*(4), 507–512.

Depp, C. A., & Jeste, D. V. (2006). Definitions and predictors of successful aging: A comprehensive review of larger quantitative studies. *American Journal of Geriatric Psychiatry, 14*(1), 6–20.

Derby, C. A. (2000, October 2). Cited in Associated Press (2000, October 2). Study finds exercise reduces the risk of impotence.

de St. Aubin, E., McAdams, D. P., & Kim, T.-C. (Eds.). (2004). *The generative society: Caring for future generations* (pp. 429–448). Washington, DC: American Psychological Association.

de Villiers, J. G., & de Villiers, P. A. (1999). Language development. In M. H. Bornstein & M. E. Lamb (Eds.), *Developmental psychology: An advanced textbook* (4th ed., pp. 313–373). Hillsdale, NJ: Erlbaum.

Dezoete, J. A., MacArthur, B. A., & Tuck, B. (2003). Prediction of Bayley and Stanford–Binet scores with a group of very low birthweight children. *Child: Care, Health and Development, 29*(5), 367–372.

DiLalla, D. L., Gottesman, I. I., Carey, G., & Bouchard, T. J., Jr. (1999). Heritability of MMPI Harris–Lingoes and Subtle–Obvious subscales in twins reared apart. *Assessment, 6*(4), 353–366.

Dindia, K., & Allen, M. (1992). Sex differences in self-disclosure: A meta-analysis. *Psychological Bulletin, 112*(1), 106–124.

Dishion, T. J., & Stormshak, E. A. (2007b). Family and peer social interaction. In T. J. Dishion & E. A. Stormshak. (Eds.), *Intervening in children's lives: An ecological, family-centered approach to mental health care* (pp. 31–48). Washington, DC: American Psychological Association.

Doherty, W. J., Carroll, J. S., & Waite, L. J. (2007). Supporting the institution of marriage: Ideological, research, and ecological perspectives. In A. S. Loveless & T. B. Holman (Eds.), *The family in the new millennium: World voices supporting the "natural" clan, Volume 2: Marriage and human dignity* (pp. 21–51). Praeger perspectives. Westport, CT: Praeger/Greenwood.

Dollfus, S., et al. (2005). Atypical hemispheric specialization for language in right-handed schizophrenia patients. *Biological Psychiatry, 57*(9), 1020–1028.

Dombrowski, M. A. S., et al. (2000). Kangaroo skin-to-skin care for premature twins and their adolescent parents. *American Journal of Maternal/Child Nursing, 25*(2), 92–94.

Donald, M. et al. (2006). Risk and protective factors for medically serious suicide attempts. *Australian and New Zealand Journal of Psychiatry, 40*(1), 87–96.

Donohue, K. F., Curtin, J. J., Patrick, C. J., & Lang, A. R. (2007). Intoxication level and emotional response. *Emotion, 7*(1), 103–112.

Donovan, D. M., & Wells, E. A. (2007). "Tweaking 12-step": The potential role of 12-step self-help group involvement in methamphetamine recovery. *Addiction, 102*(Supp. 1), 121–129 .

Dorling, J., et al. (2006). Data collection from very low birthweight infants in a geographical region: Methods, costs, and trends in mortality, admission rates, and resource utilisation over a five-year period. *Early Human Development, 82*(2), 117–124.

Doron, H., & Markovitzky, G. (2007). Family structure and patterns and psychological adjustment to immigration in Israel. *Journal of Ethnic & Cultural Diversity in Social Work, 15*(1–2), 215–235.

Drasgow, E., Halle, J. W., & Phillips, B. (2001). Effects of different social partners on the discriminated requesting of a young child with autism and severe language delays. *Research in Developmental Disabilities, 22*(2), 125–139.

Drewett, R., Blair, P., Emmett, P., Emond, A., & the ALSPAC Study Team. (2004). Failure to thrive in the term and preterm infants of mothers depressed in the postnatal period: A population-based birth cohort study. *Journal of Child Psychology and Psychiatry and Allied Disciplines, 45*(2), 359–366.

Drigotas, S. M., Rusbult, C. E., & Verette, J. (1999). Level of commitment, mutuality of commitment, and couple well-being. *Personal Relationships, 6*(3), 389–409.

Duarté-Vélez, Y. M., & Bernal, G. (2007). Suicide behavior among Latino and Latina adolescents: Conceptual and methodological issues. *Death Studies, 31*(5), 425–455.

Duberstein, P. R., Pálsson, S. P., Waern, M., & Skoog, I. (2008). Personality and risk for depression in a birth cohort of 70-year-olds followed for 15 years. *Psychological Medicine, 38*(5), 663–671.

Duenwald, M. (2002, July 16). Hormone therapy: One size, clearly, no longer fits all. *New York Times,* p. F6.

Duffy, R. D., & Sedlacek, W. E. (2007). What is most important to students' long-term career choices. *Journal of Career Development, 34*(2), 149–163.

Duggan, A., et al. (2004). Evaluating a statewide home visiting program to prevent child abuse in at-risk families of newborns: Fathers' participation and outcomes. *Child Maltreatment: Journal of the American Professional Society on the Abuse of Children, 9*(1), 3–17.

Dumas, J. A., & Hartman, M. (2003). Adult age differences in temporal and item memory. *Psychology and Aging, 18*(3), 573–586.

Dunn, J., Davies, L. C., O'Connor, T. G., & Sturgess, W. (2001). Family lives and friendships: The perspectives of children in step-, single-parent, and nonstep families. *Journal of Family Psychology, 15*(2), 272–287.

Dunn, J., & Hughes, C. (2001). "I got some swords and you're dead!": Violent fantasy, antisocial behavior, friendship, and moral sensibility in young children. *Child Development, 72*(2), 491–505.

Duplassie, D., & Daniluk, J. C. (2007). Sexuality: Young and middle adulthood. In M S. Tepper & A. F. Owens (Eds.), *Sexual health, Volume 1: Psychological foundations* (pp. 263–289). Praeger perspectives: Sex, love, and psychology. Westport, CT: Praeger/Greenwood.

Dupuis-Blanchard, S. M. (2008). Social engagement in relocated older adults. *Dissertation Abstracts International: Section B: The Sciences and Engineering. 68*(7-B), 4387.

Durkin, S. J., Paxton, S. J., & Sorbello, M. (2007). An integrative model of the impact of exposure to idealized female images on adolescent girls' body satisfaction. *Journal of Applied Social Psychology, 37*(5), 1092–1117.

Dyer, S., & Moneta, G. B. (2006). Frequency of parallel, associative, and cooperative play in British children of different socioeconomic status. *Social Behavior and Personality, 34*(5), 587–592.

Dyer, S. J. (2007). The value of children in African countries: Insights from studies on infertility. *Journal of Psychosomatic Obstetrics & Gynecology, 28*(2), 69–77.

Dykman, R. A., Casey, P. H., Ackerman, P. T., & McPherson, W. B. (2001). Behavioral and cognitive status in school-aged children with a history of failure to thrive during early childhood. *Clinical Pediatrics, 40*(2), 63–70.

Eccles, J. S., et al. (2000). Gender-role socialization in the family: A longitudinal approach. In T. Eckes & H. M. Trautner (Eds.), *The developmental social psychology of gender* (pp. 333–360). Hillsdale, NJ: Erlbaum.

Eckerman, C. O., Hsu, H.-C., Molitor, A., Leung, E. H. L., & Goldstein, R. F. (1999). Infant arousal in an en-face exchange with a new partner: Effects of prematurity and perinatal biological risk. *Developmental Psychology, 35*(1), 282–293.

Ecuyer-Dab, I., & Robert, M. (2004). Spatial ability and home-range size: Examining the relationship in Western men and women (*Homo sapiens*). *Journal of Comparative Psychology, 118*(2), 217–231.

Eddleston, M., Dissanayake, M., Sheriff, M. H. R., Warrell, D. A., & Gunnell, D. (2006). Physical vulnerability and fatal self-harm in the elderly. *British Journal of Psychiatry, 189*(3), 278–279.

Eder, R. A. (1989). The emergent personologist: The structure and content of 3½-, 5½-, and 7½-year-olds' concepts of themselves and other persons. *Child Development, 60*(5), 1218–1228.

Eder, R. A. (1990). Uncovering young children's psychological selves: Individual and developmental differences. *Child Development, 61*(3), 849–863.

Edler, C., Lipson, S. F., & Keel, P. K. (2007). Ovarian hormones and binge eating in bulimia nervosa. *Psychological Medicine, 37*(1), 131–141.

Edwards, V. J., Holden, G. W., Felitti, V. J., & Anda, R. F. (2003). Relationship between multiple forms of childhood maltreatment and adult mental health in community respondents: Results from the Adverse Childhood Experiences study. *American Journal of Psychiatry, 160*(8), 1453–1460.

Egerton, A., Allison, C., Brett, R. R., & Pratt, J. A. (2006). Cannabinoids and prefrontal cortical function: Insights from preclinical studies. *Neuroscience & Biobehavioral Reviews, 30*(5), 680–695.

Eimas, P. D., Sigueland, E. R., Juscyk, P., & Vigorito, J. (1971). Speech perception in infants. *Science, 171*(3968), 303–306.

Eisenberg, M. E., Neumark-Sztainer, D., & Paxton, S. J. (2006). Five-year change in body satisfaction among adolescents. *Journal of Psychosomatic Research, 61*(4), 521–527.

Eisner, E. W. (1990). The role of art and play in children's cognitive development. In E. Klugman & S. Smilansky (Eds.), *Children's play and learning: Perspectives and policy implications* (pp. 43–56). New York: Teachers College Press.

El-Sheikh, M. (2007). Children's skin conductance level and reactivity: Are these measures stable over time and across tasks? *Developmental Psychobiology, 49*(2), 180–186.

Elkind, D. (1967). Egocentrism in adolescence. *Child Development, 38*(4), 1025–1034.

Elkind, D. (1985). Egocentrism redux. *Developmental Review, 5*(3), 218–226.

Elkind, D. (2007). *The power of play: How spontaneous imaginative activities lead to happier, healthier children.* Cambridge, MA: Da Capo Press.

Ellis, A., & Dryden, W. (1996). *The practice of rational emotive behavior therapy.* New York: Springer.

Elliot, A. J., & Niesta, D. (2008). Romantic red: Red enhances men's attraction to women. *Journal of Personality and Social Psychology, 95*(5), 1150–1164.

Else-Quest, N. M., Hyde, J. S., Goldsmith, H. H., & Van Hulle, C. A. (2006). Gender differences in temperament: A meta-analysis. *Psychological Bulletin, 132*(1), 33–72.

Eltzschig, H., Lieberman, E., & Camann, W. (2003). Regional anesthesia and analgesia for labor and delivery. *New England Journal of Medicine, 348*(4), 319–332.

Emanuel, E. J., Fairclough, D. L., & Emanuel, L. L. (2000). Attitudes and desires related to euthanasia and physician-assisted suicide among terminally ill patients and their caregivers. *Journal of the American Medical Association, 284*(19), 2460–2468.

Emler, N., Tarry, H., & St. James, A. (2007). Postconventional moral reasoning and reputation. *Journal of Research in Personality, 41*(1), 76–89.

Epel, E. S., et al. (2006). Cell aging in relation to stress arousal and cardiovascular disease risk factors. *Psychoneuroendocrinology, 31*(3), 277–287.

Erikson, E. H. (1963). *Childhood and society.* New York: Norton.

Erikson, E. H. (1968). *Identity: Youth and crisis.* New York: Norton.

Erikson, E. H. (1975). *Life history and the historical moment.* New York: Norton.

Erikson, E. H. (1980). On the generational cycle—an address. In G. Junkers (Ed.). (2006). *Is it too late?: Key papers on psychoanalysis and ageing* (pp. 141–159). London: Karnac Books.

Eron, L. D. (1993). Cited in T. DeAngelis (1993), It's baaack: TV violence, concern for kid viewers. *APA Monitor, 24*(8), 16.

Eron, L. D., Huesmann, L. R., & Zelli, A. (1991). The role of parental variables in the learning of aggression. In D. J. Pepler & K. H. Rubin (Eds.), *The development and treatment of childhood aggression* (pp. 169–188). Hillsdale, NJ: Erlbaum.

Ersner-Hershfield, H., Mikels, J. A., Sullivan, S. J., & Carstensen, L. L. (2008). Poignancy: Mixed emotional experience in the face of meaningful endings. *Journal of Personality and Social Psychology, 94*(1) 158–167.

Escorial, S., et al. (2003). Abilities that explain the intelligence decline: Evidence from the WAIS-III. *Psicothema, 15*(1), 19–22.

Etaugh, C. A., & Bridges, J. S. (2006). Midlife transitions. In J. Worell & C. D. Goodheart (Eds.), *Handbook of girls' and women's psychological health: Gender and well-being across the lifespan* (pp. 359–367). Oxford series in clinical psychology. New York: Oxford University Press.

Eveland, B., Otto, S., & Caputo, J. (2006). Body mass index and activity level of parents and children. *Medicine and Science in Sports and Exercise, 37*(5), S21.

Facts about falling (2008, January 27). *Washington Post.* Available at http://www.washingtonpost.com/wp-dyn/content/article/2008/01/26/AR2008012601948.html

Facts about the Death With Dignity Act. (2007, September 22). Oregon Office of Disease Prevention and Epidemiology. Available at http://www.oregon.gov/DHS/ph/pas/faqs.shtml

Fagot, B. I. (1990). A longitudinal study of gender segregation: Infancy to preschool. In F. F. Strayer (Ed.), *Social interaction and behavioral development during early childhood* (pp. 73–76). Montreal: La Maison D'Ethologie de Montreal.

Fagot, B. I., & Hagan, R. (1991). Observations of parent reactions to sex-stereotyped behaviors:

Age and sex effects. *Child Development, 62*(3), 617–628.

Fagot, B. I., & Leinbach, M. D. (1993). Gender-role development in young children: From discrimination to labeling. *Developmental Review, 13*(2), 205–224.

Fagot, B. I., Rodgers, C. S., & Leinbach, M. D. (2000). Theories of gender socialization. In T. Eckes & H. M. Trautner (Eds.), *The developmental social psychology of gender* (pp. 65–89). Hillsdale, NJ: Erlbaum.

Fair, R. C. (2007). Estimated age effects in athletic events and chess. *Experimental Aging Research, 33*(1), 37–57.

Fan, C. S., & Lui, H.-K. (2008). Extramarital affairs, marital satisfaction, and divorce: Evidence from Hong Kong. *Contemporary Economic Policy, 22*(4), 442–452.

Fantz, R. L. (1961). The origin of form perception. *Scientific American, 204*(5), 66–72.

Fantz, R. L., Fagan, J. R., III, & Miranda, S. B. (1975). Early visual selectivity. In L. B. Cohen & P. Salapatek (Eds.), *Infant perception: From sensation to cognition, Volume 1* (pp. 249–346). New York: Academic Press.

Farmer, A., Elkin, A., & McGuffin, P. (2007). The genetics of bipolar affective disorder. *Current Opinion in Psychiatry, 20*(1), 8–12.

Fay, M. P. (2004). *Estimating age-conditional probability of developing cancer using a piecewise mid-age joinpoint model for the rates.* Technical Report # 2003-03-2004. Statistical Research and Applications Branch, NCI.

Federal Interagency Forum on Child and Family Statistics. (2005). *America's children: Key national indicators of well-being, 2005.* Washington, DC: U.S. Government Printing Office.

Federal Interagency Forum on Child and Family Statistics. (2007). *America's children: Key national indicators of well-being, 2007.* Washington, DC: U.S. Government Printing Office.

Feijó, L., et al. (2006). Mothers' depressed mood and anxiety levels are reduced after massaging their preterm infants. *Infant Behavior & Development, 29*(3), 476–480.

Feinberg, M. E., Neiderhiser, J. M., Howe, G., & Hetherington, E. M. (2001). Adolescent, parent, and observer perceptions of parenting: Genetic and environmental influences on shared and distinct perceptions. *Child Development, 72*(4), 1266–1284.

Feiring, C. (1993, March). *Developing concepts of romance from 15 to 18 years.* Paper presented at the meeting of the Society for Research in Child Development, New Orleans, LA.

Feiring, C., & Lewis, M. (1991). The transition from middle to early adolescence: Sex differences in the social network and perceived self-competence. *Sex Roles, 24*(7–8), 489–509.

Feldman, R., & Masalha, S. (2007). The role of culture in moderating the links between early ecological risk and young children's adaptation. *Development and Psychopathology, 19*(1), 1–21.

Fergusson, A. (2007). What successful teachers do in inclusive classrooms: Research-based teaching strategies that help special learners succeed. *European Journal of Special Needs Education, 22*(1), 108–110.

Fernandez-Twinn, D. S., & Ozanne, S. E. (2006). Mechanisms by which poor early growth programs type-2 diabetes, obesity and the metabolic syndrome. *Physiology & Behavior, 88*(3), 234–243.

Féron, J., Gentaz, E., & Streri, A. (2006). Evidence of amodal representation of small numbers across visuo-tactile modalities in 5-month-old infants. *Cognitive Development, 21*(2), 81–92.

Field, A. P. (2006). The behavioral inhibition system and the verbal information pathway to children's fears. *Journal of Abnormal Psychology, 115*(4), 742–752.

Field, T. (1999). Sucking and massage therapy reduce stress during infancy. In M. Lewis & D. Ramsay (Eds.), *Soothing and stress* (pp. 157–169). Hillsdale, NJ: Erlbaum.

Field, T., Hernandez-Reif, M., Feijó, L., & Freedman, J. (2006). Prenatal, perinatal and neonatal stimulation: A survey of neonatal nurseries. *Infant Behavior & Development, 29*(1), 24–31.

Filus, A. (2006). Being a grandparent in China, Greece and Poland. *Studia Psychologiczne, 44*(1), 35–46.

Finegan, J. K., Niccols, G. A., & Sitarenios, G. (1992). Relations between prenatal testosterone levels and cognitive abilities at 4 years. *Developmental Psychology, 28*(6), 1075–1089.

Finkelman, J. M. (2005). Sexual harassment. In A. Barnes (Ed.), *The handbook of women, psychology, and the law* (pp. 64–78). Hoboken, NJ: Wiley.

Fisch, S. M. (2004). *Children's learning from educational television: Sesame Street and beyond.* Hillsdale, NJ: Erlbaum.

Fisher, B. S., Daigle, L. E., Cullen, F. T., & Turner, M. G. (2003). Reporting sexual victimization to the police and others: Results from a national-level study of college women. *Criminal Justice & Behavior, 30*(1), 6–38.

Fiske, A. (2006). The nature of depression in later life. In S. H. Qualls & B. G. Knight (Eds.), *Psychotherapy for depression in older adults* (pp. 29–44). Hoboken, NJ: Wiley.

Fitzgerald, H. E., et al. (1991). The organization of lateralized behavior during infancy. In H. E. Fitzgerald, B. M. Lester, & M. W. Yogman (Eds.), *Theory and research in behavioral pediatrics* (pp. 155–184). New York: Plenum.

Fivush, R. (2002). Scripts, schemas, and memory of trauma. In N. L. Stein et al. (Eds.), *Representation, memory, and development: Essays in honor of Jean Mandler* (pp. 53–74). Hillsdale, NJ: Erlbaum.

Fivush, R., & Hammond, N. R. (1990). Autobiographical memory across the preschool years: Toward reconceptualizing childhood amnesia. In R. Fivush & J. A. Hudson (Eds.), *Knowing and remembering in young children.* Cambridge: Cambridge University Press.

Fivush, R., Kuebli, J., & Clubb, P. A. (1992). The structure of events and event representations: A developmental analysis. *Child Development, 63*(1), 188–201.

Fivush, R., Sales, J. M., Goldberg, A., Bahrick, L., & Parker, J. (2004). Weathering the storm: Children's long-term recall of Hurricane Andrew. *Memory, 12*(1), 104–118.

Flavell, J. H. (1993). Young children's understanding of thinking and consciousness. *Current Directions in Psychological Science, 2*(2), 40–43.

Flavell, J. H., Miller, P. H., & Miller, S. A. (2002). *Cognitive development* (4th ed.). Upper Saddle River, NJ: Prentice Hall.

Florsheim, P. (Ed.). (2003). *Adolescent romantic relations and sexual behavior: Theory, research, and practical implications.* Hillsdale, NJ: Erlbaum.

Flouri, E., & Buchanan, A. (2003). The role of father involvement and mother involvement in adolescents' psychological well-being. *British Journal of Social Work, 33*(3), 399–406.

Flynn, J. R. (2003). Movies about intelligence: The limitations of *g. Current Directions in Psychological Science, 12*(3), 95–99.

Foley, G. M. (2006). Self and social–emotional development in infancy: A descriptive synthesis. In G. M. Foley & J. D. Hochman (Eds.), *Mental health in early intervention: Achieving unity in principles and practice* (pp. 139–173). Baltimore: Paul H. Brookes.

Fontaine, A.-M. (2005). Écologie développementale des premières interactions entre enfants: Effet des matériels de jeu. *Enfance, 57*(2), 137–154.

Food and Drug Administration. (2004, July 20). *Decreasing the chance of birth defects.* Available at http://www.fda.gov/fdac/features/996_bd.html

Forbush, K., Heatherton, T. F., & Keel, P. K. (2007). Relationships between perfectionism and specific disordered eating behaviors. *International Journal of Eating Disorders, 40*(1), 37–41.

Ford, C. S., & Beach, F. A. (1951). *Patterns of sexual behavior.* New York: Harper & Row.

Forman-Hoffman, V. L., Ruffin, T., & Schultz, S. K. (2006). Basal metabolic rate in anorexia nervosa patients: Using appropriate predictive equations during the refeeding process. *Annals of Clinical Psychiatry, 18*(2), 123–127.

Foster-Clark, F. S., & Blyth, D. A. (1991). Peer relations and influences. In R. M. Lerner, A. C. Petersen, & J. Brooks-Gunn (Eds.), *Encyclopedia of adolescence* (pp. 767–771). New York: Garland.

Fozard, J. L., & Gordon-Salant, S. (2001). Changes in vision and hearing with aging. In J. E. Birren & K. W. Schaie (Eds.), *Handbook of psychology of aging* (5th ed., pp. 241–266). San Diego: Academic Press.

Franklin, A., Pilling, M., & Davies, I. (2005). The nature of infant color categorization: Evidence from eye movements on a target detection task. *Journal of Experimental Child Psychology, 91*(3), 227–248.

Frayser, S. (1985). *Varieties of sexual experience: An anthropological perspective on human sexuality.* New Haven, CT: Human Relations Area Files Press.

Frazier, L. D., Newman, F. L., & Jaccard, J. (2007). Psychosocial outcomes in later life. *Psychology and Aging, 22*(4), 676–689.

Freedenthal, S. (2007). Racial disparities in mental health service use by adolescents who thought about or attempted suicide. *Suicide and Life-Threatening Behavior, 37*(1), 22–34.

Freeman, M. S., Spence, M. J., and Oliphant, C. M. (1993, June). *Newborns prefer their mothers' low-pass filtered voices over other female filtered voices.* Paper presented at the meeting of the American Psychological Society, Chicago, IL.

Frerichs, L., Andsager, J. L., Campo, S., Aquilino, M., & Dyer, C. S. (2006). Framing breastfeeding and formula-feeding messages in popular U.S. magazines. *Women & Health, 44*(1), 95–118.

Freund, A. M., & Baltes, P. B. (2002). The adaptiveness of selection, optimization, and compensation as strategies of life management. *Journals of Gerontology: Series B: Psycholog-*

ical Sciences & Social Sciences, 57B(5), P426–P434.

Fried, P. A., & Smith, A. M. (2001). A literature review of the consequences of prenatal marijuana exposure: An emerging theme of a deficiency in aspects of executive function. *Neurotoxicology and Teratology, 23*(1), 1–11.

Frisch, R. E. (1994). The right weight: Body fat, menarche and fertility. *Proceedings of the Nutrition Society, 53*(1), 113–129.

Frodi, A. M. (1985). When empathy fails: Infant crying and child abuse. In B. M. Lester & C. F. Z. Boukydis (Eds.), *Infant crying* (pp. 1–27). New York: Plenum.

Fromkin, V., et al. (2004). *The development of language in Genie: A case of language acquisition beyond the "critical period."* New York: Psychology Press.

Fry, D. P. (2005). Rough-and-tumble social play in humans. In A. D. Pellegrini & P. K. Smith (Eds.), *The nature of play: Great apes and humans* (pp. 54–85). New York: Guilford.

Furman, W., & Buhrmester, D. (1992). Age and sex differences in perceptions of networks of personal relationships. *Child Development, 63*(1), 103–115.

Furnham, A. (2009). Sex differences in mate selection preferences. *Personality and Individual Differences, 47*(4), 262–267.

Ganesh, M. P., & Magdalin, S. (2007). Perceived problems and academic stress in children of disrupted and non-disrupted families. *Journal of the Indian Academy of Applied Psychology, 33*(1), 53–59.

Gans, D., & Silverstein, M. (2006). Norms of filial responsibility for aging parents across time and generations. *Journal of Marriage and Family, 68*(4), 961–976.

Garber, H. L. (1988). *The Milwaukee Project: Preventing mental retardation in children at risk.* Washington, DC: American Association on Mental Retardation.

Gardner, H. (1983). *Frames of mind: The theory of multiple intelligences.* New York: Basic Books.

Gardner, H. (2006). *The development and education of the mind: The selected works of Howard Gardner.* Philadelphia: Routledge/Taylor & Francis.

Gartstein, M. A., Slobodskaya, H. R., & Kinsht, I. A. (2003). Cross-cultural differences in temperament in the first year of life: United States of America (U.S.) and Russia. *International Journal of Behavioral Development, 27*(4), 316–328.

Garvey, C. (1990). *Developing child.* Cambridge, MA: Harvard University Press.

Gaser, C., & Schlaug, G. (2003). Brain structures differ between musicians and nonmusicians. *Journal of Neuroscience, 23*(27), 9240–9245.

Gathercole, S. E., Pickering, S. J., Ambridge, B., & Wearing, H. (2004). The structure of working memory from 4 to 15 years of age. *Developmental Psychology, 40*(2), 177–190.

Gathercole, S. E., Pickering, S. J., Knight, C., & Stegmann, Z. (2004). Working memory skills and educational attainment: Evidence from national curriculum assessments at 7 and 14 years of age. *Applied Cognitive Psychology, 18*(1), 1–16.

Gavin, L., et al. (2009). Sexual and reproductive health of persons aged 10–24 years—United States, 2002–2007. *Morbidity and Mortality Weekly Report, 58*(27), 1–58. Available at http://www.cdc.gov/mmwr/preview/mmwrhtml/ss5806a1.htm

Gavin, N. I., et al. (2005). Perinatal depression: A systematic review of prevalence and incidence. *Obstetrics & Gynecology, 106*(5), 1071–1083.

Ge, X., et al. (2003). It's about timing and change: Pubertal transition effects on symptoms of major depression among African American youths. *Developmental Psychology, 39*(3), 430–439.

Geary, D. C. (2006). Sex differences in social behavior and cognition: Utility of sexual selection for hypothesis generation. *Hormones and Behavior, 49*(3), 273–275.

Georges, J.-J., The, A. M., Onwuteaka-Philipsen, B. D., & van der Wal, G. (2008). Dealing with requests for euthanasia. *Journal of Medical Ethics, 34*(3), 150–155.

Georgiades, S., et al. (2007). Structure of the autism symptom phenotype: A proposed multidimensional model. *Journal of the American Academy of Child & Adolescent Psychiatry, 46*(2), 188–196.

Gerard, J. M., Landry-Meyer, L., & Roe, J. G. (2006). Grandparents raising grandchildren: The role of social support in coping with caregiving challenges. *International Journal of Ageing & Human Development, 62*(4), 359–383.

Geschwind, D. H. (2000). Interview cited in D. E. Rosenbaum (2000, May 16), On left-handedness, its causes and costs. *New York Times*, pp. F1, F6.

Gesell, A. (1928). *Infancy and human growth.* New York: Macmillan.

Gesell, A. (1929). Maturation and infant behavior pattern. *Psychological Review, 36*(4), 307–319.

Ghetti, S., & Alexander, K. W. (2004). "If it happened, I would remember it": Strategic use of event memorability in the rejection of false

autobiographical events. *Child Development, 75*(2), 542–561.

Gibson, E. J. (1969). *Principles of perceptual learning and development.* New York: Appleton-Century-Crofts.

Gibson, E. J. (1991). *An odyssey in learning and perception.* Cambridge, MA: MIT Press.

Gibson, E. J., & Walk, R. D. (1960). The "visual cliff." *Scientific American, 202*(4), 64–71.

Giedd, J. N., et al. (2009). Anatomical brain magnetic resonance imaging of typically developing children and adolescents. *Journal of the American Academy of Child & Adolescent Psychiatry, 48*(5), 465–470.

Gilhooly, M. L., et al. (2007). Real-world problem solving and quality of life in older people. *British Journal of Health Psychology, 12*(4), 587–600.

Gilligan, C. (1982). *In a different voice.* Cambridge, MA: Harvard University Press.

Gilligan, C. (1990). Remapping the moral domain: New images of the self in relationship. In C. Zanardi (Ed.), *Essential papers on the psychology of women. Essential papers in psychoanalysis* (pp. 480–495). New York: New York University Press.

Giussani, D. A. (2006). Prenatal hypoxia: Relevance to developmental origins of health and disease. In P. Gluckman & M. Hanson (Eds.), *Developmental origins of health and disease* (pp. 178–190). New York: Cambridge University Press.

Glaser, K., Tomassini, C., Racioppi, F., & Stuchbury, R. (2006). Marital disruptions and loss of support in later life. *European Journal of Ageing, 3*(4), 207–216

Glasser, C. L., Robnett, B., & Feliciano, C. (2009). Internet daters' body type preferences: Race–ethnic and gender differences. *Sex Roles, 61*(1–2), 14–33.

Gleason, T. R. (2002). Social provisions of real and imaginary relationships in early childhood. *Developmental Psychology, 38*(6), 979–992.

Gleason, T. R. (2004). Imaginary companions and peer acceptance. *International Journal of Behavioral Development, 28*(3), 204–209.

Gleason, T. R., Gower, A. L., Hohmann, L. M., & Gleason, T. C. (2005). Temperament and friendship in preschool-aged children. *International Journal of Behavioral Development, 29*(4), 336–344.

Gleason, T. R., & Hohmann, L. M. (2006). Concepts of real and imaginary friendships in early childhood. *Social Development, 15*(1), 128–144.

Gleason, T. R., Sebanc, A. M., & Hartup, W. W. (2003). Imaginary companions of preschool children. In M. E. Hertzig & E. A. Farber (Eds.), *Annual progress in child psychiatry and child development: 2000–2001* (pp. 101–121). New York: Brunner-Routledge.

Glück, J., & Bluck, S. (2007). Looking back across the life span: A life story account of the reminiscence bump. *Memory & Cognition, 35*(8), 1928–1939.

Gobet, F., & Simon, H. A. (2000). Five seconds or sixty? Presentation time in expert memory. *Cognitive Science, 24*(4), 651–682.

Goel, P., Radotra, A., Singh, I., Aggarwal, A., & Dua, D. (2004). Effects of passive smoking on outcome in pregnancy. *Journal of Postgraduate Medicine, 50*(1), 12–16.

Golan, H., & Huleihel, M. (2006). The effect of prenatal hypoxia on brain development: Short- and long-term consequences demonstrated in rodent models. *Developmental Science, 9*(4), 338–349.

Goldman, J. S., Adamson, J., Karydas, A., Miller, B. L., & Hutton, M. (2008). New genes, new dilemmas: FTLD genetics and its implications for families. *American Journal of Alzheimer's Disease and Other Dementias, 22*(6), 507–515.

Goldschmidt, L., Day, N. L., & Richardson, G. A. (2000). Effects of prenatal marijuana exposure on child behavior problems at age 10. *Neurotoxicology and Teratology, 22*(3), 325–336.

Goldsmith, H. H., et al. (2003). Part III: Genetics and development. In R. J. Davidson et al. (Eds.), *Handbook of affective sciences* (pp. 295–299). London: Oxford University Press.

Goldstein, E. B. (2005). *Cognitive psychology: Connecting mind, research, and everyday experience.* Belmont, CA: Wadsworth.

Goldstein, I. (1998). Cited in Kolata, G. (1998, April 4). Impotence pill: Would it also help women? *New York Times,* pp. A1, A6.

Goldstein, I. (2000). Modifiable risk factors and erectile dysfunction: Can lifestyle changes modify risk? *Urology, 56*(2), 302–306.

Goldstein, I., & Alexander, J. L. (2005). Practical aspects in the management of vaginal atrophy and sexual dysfunction in perimenopausal and postmenopausal women. *Journal of Sexual Medicine, 2*(Supp. 3), 154–165.

Goldstein, I., Meston, C., Davis, S., & Traish, A. (Eds.). (2006). *Female sexual dysfunction.* New York: Parthenon.

Goldstein, S., & Brooks, R. B. (2005). *Handbook of resilience in children.* New York: Kluwer Academic/Plenum.

Golombok, S., et al. (2008). Developmental trajectories of sex-typed behavior in boys and girls:

A longitudinal general population study of children aged 2.5–8 years. *Child Development, 79*(5), 1583–1593.

Gonzalez, V. (2006). Cultural, linguistic, and socioeconomic factors influencing monolingual and bilingual children's cognitive development. In V. Gonzalez & J. Tinajero (Eds.), *Review of research and practice, Volume 3* (pp. 67–104). Hillsdale, NJ: Erlbaum.

González, Y. S., Moreno, D. S., & Schneider, B. H. (2004). Friendship expectations of early adolescents in Cuba and Canada. *Journal of Cross-Cultural Psychology, 35*(4), 436–445.

Goodman, C. G. (2007a). Family dynamics in three-generation grandfamilies. *Journal of Family Issues, 28*(3), 355–379.

Goodman, C. G. (2007b). Intergenerational triads in skipped-generation grandfamilies. *International Journal of Ageing & Human Development, 65*(3), 231–258.

Goodman, G. A. S., Rudy, L., Bottoms, B. L., & Aman, C. (1990). Children's concerns and memory: Issues of ecological validity in the study of children's eyewitness testimony. In R. Fivush & J. A. Hudson (Eds.), *Knowing and remembering in young children* (pp. 249–284). Cambridge: Cambridge University Press.

Gopnik, A., & Meltzoff, A. N. (1992). Categorization and naming: Basic-level sorting in eighteen-month-olds and its relation to language. *Child Development, 63*(5), 1091–1103.

Gopnik, A., & Slaughter, V. (1991). Young children's understanding of changes in their mental states. *Child Development, 62*(1), 98–110.

Gordon-Salant, S., Fitzgibbons, P. J., & Friedman, S. A. (2007). Recognition of time-compressed and natural speech with selective temporal enhancements by young and elderly listeners. *Journal of Speech, Language, and Hearing Research, 50*(5), 1181–1193.

Gormally, S., et al. (2001). Contact and nutrient caregiving effects on newborn infant pain responses. *Developmental Medicine and Child Neurology, 43*(1), 28–38.

Gottfried, G. M., Hickling, A. K., Totten, L. R., Mkroyan, A., & Reisz, A. (2003). To be or not to be a galaprock: Preschoolers' intuitions about the importance of knowledge and action for pretending. *British Journal of Developmental Psychology, 21*(3), 397–414.

Gottlieb, B. H., Still, E., & Newby-Clark, I. R. (2007). Types and precipitants of growth and decline in emerging adulthood. *Journal of Adolescent Research, 22*(2), 132–155.

Gottman, J. M., Coan, J., Carrère, S. & Swanson, C. (1998). Predicting marital happiness and stability from newlywed interactions. *Journal of Marriage and the Family, 60*(1), 5–22.

Graber, J. A., Seeley, J. R., Brooks-Gunn, J., & Lewinsohn, P. M. (2004). Is pubertal timing associated with psychopathology in young adulthood? *Journal of the American Academy of Child & Adolescent Psychiatry, 43*(6), 718–726.

Grace, D. M., David, B. J., & Ryan, M. K. (2008). Investigating preschoolers' categorical thinking about gender through imitation, attention, and the use of self-categories. *Child Development, 79*(6), 1928–1941.

Grady, D. (2003a). Postmenopausal hormones: Therapy for symptoms only. *New England Journal of Medicine, 348*(19), 1835–1837.

Grady, D. (2003b, June 25). Study finds new risks in hormone therapy. *New York Times.* Available at http://www.nytimes.com

Grall, T. S. (2009, November). *Custodial mothers and fathers and their child support: 2007.* US Bureau of the Census: Current Population Reports. Available at http://www.census.gov/prod/2009pubs/p60-237.pdf

Gray, C., Koopman, E., & Hunt, J. (1991). The emotional phases of marital separation: An empirical investigation. *American Journal of Orthopsychiatry, 61*(1), 138–143.

Gray, S. L., et al. (2008). Antioxidant vitamin supplement use and risk of dementia or Alzheimer's disease in older adults. *Journal of the American Geriatrics Society, 56*(2), 291–295.

Greco, C., Rovee-Collier, C., Hayne, H., Griesler, P., & Early, L. (1986). Ontogeny of early event memory: I. Forgetting and retrieval by 2- and 3-month-olds. *Infant Behavior and Development, 9*(4), 441–460.

Green, R. (1978). Sexual identity of 37 children raised by homosexual or transsexual parents. *American Journal of Psychiatry, 135*(6), 692–697.

Greene, S. M., Anderson, E. R., Doyle, E. A., Riedelbach, H., & Bear, G. G. (2006). Divorce. In K. M. Minke (Ed.), *Children's needs III: Development, prevention, and intervention* (pp. 745–757). Bethesda, MD: National Association of School Psychologists.

Greenough, W. T., Black, J. E., & Wallace, C. S. (2002). Experience and brain development. In M. H. Johnson, Y. Munakata, & R. O. Gilmore (Eds.), *Brain development and cognition: A reader* (2nd ed., pp. 186–216). Malden, MA: Blackwell.

Greidanus, J. A. (2007). A narrative inquiry into the experiences of bereaved children [Abstract]. *Dissertation Abstracts International Section A: Humanities and Social Sciences, 67*(9-A), 3447.

Grigorenko, E. L. (2007). Triangulating developmental dyslexia: Behavior, brain, and genes. In D. Coch, G. Dawson, & K. W. Fischer (Eds.), *Human behavior, learning, and the developing brain: Atypical development* (pp. 117–144). New York: Guilford.

Grilo, C. M., Masheb, R. M., & Wilson, G. T. (2005). Efficacy of cognitive behavioral therapy and fluoxetine for the treatment of binge eating disorder: A randomized double-blind placebo-controlled comparison. *Biological Psychiatry, 57*(3), 301–309.

Grindrod, C. M., & Baum, S. R. (2005). Hemispheric contributions to lexical ambiguity resolution in a discourse context: Evidence from individuals with unilateral left and right hemisphere lesions. *Brain and Cognition, 57*(1), 70–83.

Grolnick, W. S., McMenamy, J. M., & Kurowski, C. O. (2006). Emotional self-regulation in infancy and toddlerhood. In L. Balter & C. S. Tamis-LeMonda (Eds.), *Child psychology: A handbook of contemporary issues* (2nd ed., pp. 3–25). New York: Psychology Press.

Grön, G., Wunderlich, A. P., Spitzer, M., Tomczak, R., & Riepe, M. W. (2000). Brain activation during human navigation: Gender-different neural networks as substrate of performance. *Nature Neuroscience, 3*(4), 404–408.

Grossman, A. H. (2006). Physical and mental health of older, lesbian, gay, and bisexual adults. In D. Kimmel, T. Rose, & S. David (Eds.), *Lesbian, gay, bisexual, and transgender aging: Research and clinical perspectives* (pp. 53–69). New York: Columbia University Press.

Grossmann, A. H., D'Augelli, A. R., & O'Connell, T. S. (2003). Being lesbian, gay, bisexual, and sixty or older in North America. In L. D. Garnets & D. C. Kimmel (Eds.), *Psychological perspectives on lesbian, gay, and bisexual experiences* (2nd ed., pp. 629–645). New York: Columbia University Press.

Grossmann, K., et al. (2002). The uniqueness of the child–father attachment relationship: Fathers' sensitive and challenging play as a pivotal variable in a 16-year longitudinal study. *Social Development, 11*(3), 307–331.

Gruhn, D., Gilet, A.-L., Studer, J., & Labouvie-Vief, G. (2011). Age-relevance of person characteristics: Persons' beliefs about developmental change across the lifespan. *Developmental Psychology, 47*(2), 376–387.

Grundy, E., & Henretta, J. C. (2006). Between elderly parents and adult children: A new look at the intergenerational care provided by the "sandwich generation." *Ageing & Society, 26*(5), 707–722.

Grusec, J. E. (2002). Parenting socialization and children's acquisition of values. In M. H. Bornstein (Ed.), *Handbook of parenting* (2nd ed.), *Volume 5: Practical issues in parenting* (pp. 143–167). Hillsdale, NJ: Erlbaum.

Grusec, J. E. (2006). The development of moral behavior and conscience from a socialization perspective. In M. Killen & J. G. Smetana (Eds.), *Handbook of moral development* (pp. 243–265). Hillsdale, NJ: Erlbaum.

Guerin, D. W., Gottfried, A. W., & Thomas, C. W. (1997). Difficult temperament and behaviour problems: A longitudinal study from 1.5 to 12 years. *International Journal of Behavioral Development, 21*(1), 71–90.

Guerrini, I., Thomson, A. D., & Gurling, H. D. (2007). The importance of alcohol misuse, malnutrition and genetic susceptibility on brain growth and plasticity. *Neuroscience & Biobehavioral Reviews, 31*(2), 212–220.

Guiaux, M., van Tilburg, T., & van Groenou, M. B. (2007). Changes in contact and support exchange in personal networks after widowhood. *Personal Relationships, 14*(3), 457–473.

Güntürkün, O. (2006). Letters on nature and nurture. In P. B. Baltes et al. (Eds.), *Lifespan development and the brain: The perspective of biocultural co-constructivism* (pp. 379–397). New York: Cambridge University Press.

Gurba, E. (2005). On the specific character of adult thought: Controversies over post-formal operations. *Polish Psychological Bulletin, 36*(3), 175–185.

Gutknecht, L. (2001). Full-genome scans with autistic disorder: A review. *Behavior Genetics, 31*(1), 113–123.

Guttmacher Institute. (2007, June 8). Available at http://www.guttmacher.org

Guzikowski, W. (2006). Doula—a new model of delivery (continuous, nonprofessional care during the delivery). *Ceska Gynekologie, 71*(2), 103–105.

Haapasalo, J., & Moilanen, J. (2004). Official and self-reported childhood abuse and adult crime of young offenders. *Criminal Justice and Behavior, 31*(2), 127–149.

Hagenauer, M. H., Perryman, J. I., Lee, T. M., & Carskadon, M. A. (2009). Adolescent changes in the homeostatic and circadian regulation of sleep. *Developmental Neuroscience, 31*(4), 276–284.

Haier, R. J., Karama, S., Leyba, L., & Jung, R. E. (2009). MRI assessment of cortical thickness and functional activity changes in adolescent girls following three months of practice on a visual-spatial task. *BMC Research Notes, 2*(174), 1–7.

Haith, M. M. (1979). Visual cognition in early infancy. In R. B. Kearsley & I. E. Sigel (Eds.), *Infants at risk: Assessment of cognitive functioning.* Hillsdale, NJ: Erlbaum.

Haith, M. M. (1990). Progress in the understanding of sensory and perceptual processes in early infancy. *Merrill–Palmer Quarterly, 36*(1), 1–26.

Halgin, R. P., & Whitbourne, S. K. (1993). *Abnormal psychology.* Fort Worth, TX: Harcourt Brace Jovanovich.

Hall, D. T. (2004). The protean career: A quarter-century journey. *Journal of Vocational Behavior, 65*(1), 1–13.

Hall, G. S. (1904). *Adolescence: Its psychology and its relations to physiology, anthropology, sociology, sex, crime, religion and education, Volume 2.* New York: D Appleton & Company.

Halliday, L. F., & Bishop, D. V. M. (2006). Auditory frequency discrimination in children with dyslexia. *Journal of Research in Reading, 29*(2), 213–228.

Halpern, D. F. (2003). Sex differences in cognitive abilities. *Applied Cognitive Psychology, 17*(3), 375–376.

Halpern, D. F. (2004). A cognitive-process taxonomy for sex differences in cognitive abilities. *Current Directions in Psychological Science, 13*(4), 135–139.

Hamm, J. V. (2000). Do birds of a feather flock together? The variable bases for African American, Asian American, and European American adolescents' selection of similar friends. *Developmental Psychology, 36*(2), 209–219.

Hangal, S., & Aminabhavi, V. A. (2007). Self-concept, emotional maturity, and achievement motivation of the adolescent children of employed mothers and homemakers. *Journal of the Indian Academy of Applied Psychology, 33*(1), 103–110.

Hanlon, T. E., Bateman, R. W., Simon, B. D., O'Grady, K. E., & Carswell, S. B. (2004). Antecedents and correlates of deviant activity in urban youth manifesting behavioral problems. *Journal of Primary Prevention, 24*(3), 285–309.

Hannon, P., Bowen, D. J., Moinpour, C. M., & McLerran, D. F. (2003). Correlations in perceived food use between the family food preparer and their spouses and children. *Appetite, 40*(1), 77–83.

Hansen, J. C., Dik, B. J., & Zhou, S. (2008). An examination of the structure of leisure interests of college students, working-age adults, and retirees. *Journal of Counseling Psychology, 55*(2), 133–145.

Harel, J., & Scher, A. (2003). Insufficient responsiveness in ambivalent mother–infant relationships: Contextual and affective aspects. *Infant Behavior and Development, 26*(3), 371–383.

Harlow, H. F., & Harlow, M. K. (1966). Learning to love. *American Scientist, 54*(3), 244–272.

Harlow, H. F., Harlow, M. K., & Suomi, S. J. (1971). From thought to therapy: Lessons from a primate laboratory. *American Scientist, 59*(5), 538–549.

Harris, G. (2004, September 14). *FDA links drugs to being suicidal. New York Times.* Available at http://www.nytimes.com

Harris, J. R. (2007, March 26). To the editor: Day care and a child's behavior. *New York Times.* Available at http://www.nytimes.com

Harris, S. R., Megens, A. M., Backman, C. L., & Hayes, V. E. (2005). Stability of the Bayley II Scales of Infant Development in a sample of low-risk and high-risk infants. *Developmental Medicine & Child Neurology, 47*(12), 820–823.

Hart, S. J., Davenport, M. L., Hooper, S. R., & Belger, A. (2006). Visuospatial executive function in Turner syndrome: Functional MRI and neurocognitive findings. *Brain: A Journal of Neurology, 129*(5), 1125–1136.

Harter, S. (1990). Self and identity development. In S. S. Feldman & G. R. Elliott (Eds.), *At the threshold: The developing adolescent* (pp. 352–387). Cambridge, MA: Harvard University Press.

Harter, S. (2006). The self. In K. A. Renninger, I. E. Sigel, W. Damon, & R. M. Lerner (Eds.), *Handbook of child psychology* (6th ed.), *Volume 4: Child psychology in practice* (pp. 505–570). Hoboken, NJ: Wiley.

Harter, S., & Monsour, A. (1992). Developmental analysis of conflict caused by opposing attributes in the adolescent self-portrait. *Developmental Psychology, 28*(2), 251–260.

Harter, S., & Pike, R. (1984). The pictorial scale of perceived competence and social acceptance for young children. *Child Development, 55*(6), 1969–1982.

Harter, S., & Whitesell, N. R. (2003). Beyond the debate: Why some adolescents report stable self-worth over time and situation, whereas others report changes in self-worth. *Journal of Personality, 71*(6), 1027–1058.

Hartley, A. (2006). Changing role of the speed of processing construct in the cognitive psychology of human aging. In J. E. Birren & K. W. Schaie (Eds.), *Handbook of the psychology of aging* (6th ed., pp. 183–207). Amsterdam, Netherlands: Elsevier.

Hartman, M., & Warren, L. H. (2005). Explaining age differences in temporal working memory. *Psychology and Aging, 20*(4), 645–656.

Hartup, W. W. (1983). The peer system. In P. H. Mussen (Ed.), *Handbook of child psychology, Volume 4: Socialization, personality, and social development.* Hoboken, NJ: Wiley.

Hartup, W. W. (1993). Adolescents and their friends. In D. Laursen (Ed.), *Close friendships in adolescence* (pp. 3–22). San Francisco: Jossey-Bass.

Hasher, L. (2008). Cited in Reistad-Long, S. (2008, May 20). Older brain, wiser brain. *New York Times.* Available at http://www.nytimes.com

Hasselhorn, M. (1992). Task dependency and the role of typicality and metamemory in the development of an organizational strategy. *Child Development, 63*(1), 202–214.

Hassing, L. B., & Johansson B. (2005). Aging and cognition. *Nordisk Psykologi, 57*(1), 4–20.

Hastings, P. D., Zahn-Waxler, C., Robinson, J., Usher, B., & Bridges, D. (2000). The development of concern for others in children with behavior problems. *Developmental Psychology, 36*(5), 531–546.

Hatch, L. R., & Bulcroft, K. (2004). Does long-term marriage bring less frequent disagreements? *Journal of Family Issues, 25*(4), 465–495.

Hatcher, R. A., et al. (Eds.). (2007). *Contraceptive technologies* (18th rev. ed.). New York: Ardent Media.

Hatfield, E., & Rapson, R. L. (2002). Passionate love and sexual desire: Cultural and historical perspectives. In A. L. Vangelisti, H. T. Reis, et al. (Eds.), *Stability and change in relationships: Advances in personal relationships* (pp. 306–324). New York: Cambridge University Press.

Havighurst, R. (1972). In Robert Havighurst: Developmental theorist. Developmental task theory. Available at http://faculty.mdc.edu/jmcnair/EDF3214.Topic.Outline/Robert.Havighurst.htm

Hawkley, L. C., Burleson, M. H., Berntson, G. G., & Cacioppo, J. T. (2003). Loneliness in everyday life: Cardiovascular activity, psychosocial context, and health behaviors. *Journal of Personality & Social Psychology, 85*(1), 105–120.

Hay, D. F., Payne, A., & Chadwick, A. (2004). Peer relations in childhood. *Journal of Child Psychology and Psychiatry, 45*(1), 84–108.

Hayes, R., & Dennerstein, L. (2005). The impact of aging on sexual function and sexual dysfunction in women: A review of population-based studies. *Journal of Sexual Medicine, 2*(3), 317–330.

Hayflick, L. (1996). *How and why we age.* New York: Ballantine Books.

Hayne, H., & Fagen, J. W. (Eds.). (2003). *Progress in infancy research, Volume 3.* Hillsdale, NJ: Erlbaum.

Hayslip, B., Jr., & Kaminski, P. L. (2006). Custodial grandchildren. In G. G. Bear & K. M. Minke (Eds.), *Children's needs III: Development, prevention, and intervention* (pp. 771–782). Washington, DC: National Association of School Psychologists.

Hayslip, B., Jr., Neumann, C. S., Louden, L., & Chapman, B. (2006). Developmental stage theories. In J. C. Thomas, D. L. Segal, & M. Hersen (Eds.), *Comprehensive handbook of personality and psychopathology, Volume 1: Personality and everyday functioning* (pp. 115–141). Hoboken, NJ: Wiley.

Healy, M. D., & Ellis, B. J. (2007). Birth order, conscientiousness, and openness to experience: Tests of the family-niche model of personality using a within-family methodology. *Evolution and Human Behavior, 28*(1), 55–59.

Heilman, K. M., Nadeau, S. E., & Beversdorf, D. O. (2003). Creative innovation: Possible brain mechanisms. *Neurocase, 9*(5), 369–379.

Heimann, M., et al. (2006). Exploring the relation between memory, gestural communication, and the emergence of language in infancy: A longitudinal study. *Infant and Child Development, 15*(3), 233–249.

Heindel, J. J., & Lawler, C. (2006) Role of exposure to environmental chemicals in developmental origins of health and disease. In P. Gluckman & M. Hanson (Eds.), *Developmental origins of health and disease* (pp. 82–97). New York: Cambridge University Press.

Helwig, C. C. (2006). Rights, civil liberties, and democracy across cultures. In M. Killen & J. G. Smetana (Eds.), *Handbook of moral development* (pp. 185–210). Hillsdale, NJ: Erlbaum.

Henry, D., et al. (2000). Normative influences on aggression in urban elementary school classrooms. *American Journal of Community Psychology, 28*(1) 59–81.

Henzi, S. P., et al. (2007). Look who's talking: Developmental trends in the size of conversational cliques. *Evolution and Human Behavior, 28*(1), 66–74.

Herbenick, D., Reece, M., Sanders, S. A., Schick, V., Dodge, B., & Fortenberry, J. D. (2010). Sexual behavior in the United States: Results from a national probability sample of males and females ages 14 to 94. *Journal of Sexual Medicine, 7*(Supp. 5), 255–265.

Herbenick, D., Reece, M., Schick, V., Sanders, S. A., Dodge, B., & Fortenberry, J. D. (2010a). An event-level analysis of the sexual characteristics and composition among adults ages 18 to 59: Results from a national probability sample in the United States. *Journal of Sexual Medicine, 7*(Supp. 5), 346–361.

Herbenick, D., Reece, M., Schick, V., Sanders, S. A., Dodge, B., & Fortenberry, J. D. (2010b). Sexual behaviors, relationships, and perceived health status among adult women in the United States: Results from a national probability sample. *Journal of Sexual Medicine, 7*(Supp. 5), 277–290.

Herbert, L. E., et al. (2003). Alzheimer's disease in the U.S. population: Prevalence estimates using the 2000 census. *Archives of Neurology, 60*(8), 1119–1122.

Heron, M. P. (2007). Deaths: Leading causes for 2004. *National Vital Statistics Reports, 56*(5). Available at http://www.cdc.gov/nchs/data/nvsr/nvsr56/nvsr56_05.pdf

Heron, M. P. (2010). Deaths: Leading causes for 2006. *National Vital Statistics Reports, 58*(14). Available at http://www.cdc.gov/nchs/data/nvsr/nvsr58/nvsr58_14.pdf

Hershberger, S. L., & D'Augelli, A. R. (2000). Issues in counseling lesbian, gay, and bisexual adolescents. In R. M. Perez, K. A. De-Bord, & K. J. Bieschke (Eds.), *Handbook of counseling and psychotherapy with lesbian, gay, and bisexual clients* (pp. 225–247). Washington, DC: American Psychological Association.

Hertenstein, M. J., & Campos, J. J. (2004). The retention effects of an adult's emotional displays on infant behavior. *Child Development, 75*(2), 595–613.

Hetherington, E. M. (1989). Coping with family transition: Winners, losers, and survivors. *Child Development, 60*(1), 1–14.

Hetherington, E. M. (2006a). The effects of marital discord, divorce, and parental psychopathology. *New Directions for Child and Adolescent Development, 1984*(24), 6-33.

Hetherington, E. M. (2006b). The influence of conflict, marital problem solving and parenting on children's adjustment in nondivorced, divorced and remarried families. In A. Clarke-Stewart &

J. Dunn (Eds.), *Families count: Effects on child and adolescent development* (pp. 203–237). The Jacobs Foundation series on adolescence. Cambridge, England: Cambridge University Press.

Hetherington, E. M., et al. (1992). Coping with marital transitions. *Monographs of the Society for Research in Child Development, 57*(2–3, ser. 227).

Hicks, B. M., et al. (2007). Genes mediate the association between P3 amplitude and externalizing disorders. *Psychophysiology, 44*(1), 98–105.

Hill, S. E., & Flom, R. (2007). 18- and 24-month-olds' discrimination of gender-consistent and inconsistent activities. *Infant Behavior & Development, 30*(1), 168–173.

Hill, S. Y., et al., (2007). Cerebellar volume in offspring from multiplex alcohol dependence families. *Biological Psychiatry, 61*(1), 41–47.

Hines, D. A., & Finkelhor, D. (2007). Statutory sex crime relationships between juveniles and adults: A review of social scientific research. *Aggression and Violent Behavior, 12*(3), 300–314.

Hinojosa, T., Sheu, C., & Michel, G. F. (2003). Infant hand-use preferences for grasping objects contributes to the development of a hand-use preference for manipulating objects. *Developmental Psychobiology, 43*(4), 328–334.

Hochwarter, W. A., Ferris, G. R., Perrewé, P. L., Witt, L. A., & Kiewitz, C. (2001). A note on the nonlinearity of the age–job-satisfaction relationship. *Journal of Applied Social Psychology, 31*(6), 1223–1237.

Hoegh, D. G., & Bourgeois, M. J. (2002). Prelude and postlude to the self: Correlates of achieved identity. *Youth and Society, 33*(4), 573–594.

Hoff, E. (2006). Language experience and language milestones during early childhood. In K. McCartney & D. Phillips (Eds.), *Blackwell handbook of early childhood development* (pp. 233–251). Blackwell handbooks of developmental psychology. Malden, MA: Blackwell.

Hoff, E. V. (2005). A friend living inside me: The forms and functions of imaginary companions. *Imagination, Cognition and Personality, 24*(2), 151–189.

Hogan, A. M., de Haan, M., Datta, A., & Kirkham, F. J. (2006). Hypoxia: An acute, intermittent and chronic challenge to cognitive development. *Developmental Science, 9*(4), 335–337.

Hogan, A. M., Kirkham, F. J., Isaacs, E. B., Wade, A. M., & Vargha-Khadem, F. (2005). Intellectual decline in children with moyamoya and sickle cell anaemia. *Developmental Medicine & Child Neurology, 47*(12), 824–829.

Holland, J. J. (2000, July 25). Groups link media to child violence. Associated Press. Available at http://www.ap.org

Holland, J. L. (1997). *Making vocational choices: A theory of vocational personalities and work environments* (3rd ed.). Odessa, FL: Psychological Assessment Resources.

Holloway, J. H. (2004). *Part-time work and student achievement.* Alexandria, VA: Association for Supervision and Curriculum Development. Available at http://www.ascd.org/publications/ed_lead/200104/holloway.html

Homer, B. D., & Nelson, K. (2005). Seeing objects as symbols and symbols as objects: Language and the development of dual representation. In B. D. Homer & C. S. Tamis- LeMonda (Eds.), *The development of social cognition and communication* (pp. 29–52). Hillsdale, NJ: Erlbaum.

Honzik, M. P., Macfarlane, J. W., & Allen, L. (1948). The stability of mental test performance between two and eighteen years. *Journal of Experimental Education, 17*, 309–324.

Höpflinger, F., & Hummel, C. (2006). Heranwachsende Enkelkinder und ihre Großeltern: Im Geschlechtervergleich. *Zeitschrift für Gerontologie und Geriatrie, 39*(1), 33–40.

Hoppmann, C., & Smith, J. (2007). Life-history related differences in possible selves in very old age. *International Journal of Aging & Human Development, 64*(2), 109–127.

Horn, J. L., & Noll, J. (1997). Human cognitive capabilities: Gf-Gc theory. In D. P. Flanagan, J. L. Genshaft, & P. L. Harrison (Eds.), *Contemporary intellectual assessment: Theories, tests, and issues* (pp. 53–91). New York: Guilford.

Horton, S. M. (2008). Aging stereotypes: Effects on the performance and health of seniors [Abstract]. *Dissertation Abstracts International Section A: Humanities and Social Sciences, 68*(8-A), 3540.

Hossain, M., Chetana, M., & Devi, P. U. (2005). Late effect of prenatal irradiation on the hippocampal histology and brain weight in adult mice. *International Journal of Developmental Neuroscience, 23*(4), 307–313.

Hostetler, A. J., Sweet, S., & Moen, P. (2007). Gendered career paths: A life course perspective on returning to school. *Sex Roles, 56*(1–2), 85–103.

Hough, M. S. (2007). Adult age differences in word fluency for common and goal-directed categories. *Advances in Speech Language Pathology, 9*(2), 154–161.

Howe, M. L. (2006). Developmentally invariant dissociations in children's true and false memories: Not all relatedness is created equal. *Child Development, 77*(4), 1112–1123.

Huang, J. (2007). Hormones and female sexuality. In A. F. Owens & M. S. Tepper (Eds.), *Sexual health, Volume 2: Physical foundations* (pp. 43–78). Praeger perspectives: Sex, love, and psychology. Westport, CT: Praeger/Greenwood.

Huesmann, L. R., Dubow, E. F., Eron, L. D., & Boxer, P. (2006). Middle childhood family contextual factors as predictors of adult outcomes. In A. C. Huston & M. N. Ripke (Eds.), *Middle childhood: Contexts of development* (pp. 62–86). Cambridge, England: Cambridge University Press.

Huestis, M. A., et al. (2002). Drug abuse's smallest victims: In utero drug exposure. *Forensic Science International, 128*(2), 20–30.

Huizink, A. C., & Mulder, E. J. H. (2006). Maternal smoking, drinking or cannabis use during pregnancy and neurobehavioral and cognitive functioning in human offspring. *Neuroscience & Biobehavioral Reviews, 30*(1), 24–41.

Hultsch, D. F., Hertzog, C., Dixon, R.A., & Small, B. J. (1998). *Memory change in the aged.* New York: Cambridge University Press.

Hunt, C. E., & Hauck, F. R. (2006). Sudden infant death syndrome. *Canadian Medical Association Journal, 174*(13), 1861–1869.

Hur, Y. (2005). Genetic and environmental influences on self-concept in female pre-adolescent twins: Comparison of Minnesota and Seoul data. *Twin Research and Human Genetics, 8*(4), 291–299.

Hurd, Y. L., et al. (2005). Marijuana impairs growth in mid–gestation fetuses. *Neurotoxicology and Teratology, 27*(2), 221–229.

Hursting, S. D., Lavigne, J. A., Berrigan, D., Perkins, S. N., & Barrett, J. C. (2003). Calorie restriction, aging, and cancer prevention: Mechanisms of action and applicability to humans. *Annual Review of Medicine, 54*, 131–152.

Hussain, A. (2002, June 26). It's official: Men really are afraid of commitment. Reuters.

Hyde, J. S., Fennema, E., & Lamon, S. J. (1990). Gender differences in mathematics performance: A meta-analysis. *Psychological Bulletin, 107*(2), 139–155.

Hyde, J. S., Lindberg, S. M., Linn, M. C., Ellis, A. B., & Williams, C. C. (2008). Gender similarities characterize math performance. *Science, 321*(5888), 494–495.

Hyde, J. S. & Mertz, J. E. (2009). Gender, culture, and mathematics performance. *Proceedings of the National Academy of Sciences, 106*(22), 8801–8807.

Hynes, M., Sheik, M., Wilson, H. G., & Spiegel, P. (2002). Reproductive health indicators and outcomes among refugee and internally displaced persons in postemergency phase camps. *Journal of the American Medical Association, 288*(5), 595–603.

Iacoboni, M. (2009a). Do adolescents simulate? Developmental studies of the human mirror neuron system. In T. Striano & V. Reid (Eds.), *Social cognition: Development, neuroscience and autism* (pp. 39–51). Hoboken, NJ: Wiley-Blackwell.

Iacoboni, M. (2009b). Imitation, empathy, and mirror neurons. *Annual Review of Psychology, 60*, 653–670.

Iemmola, F., & Ciani, A. C. (2009). New evidence of genetic factors influencing sexual orientation in men: Female fecundity increase in the maternal line. *Archives of Sexual Behavior, 38*(3), 393–399.

Infant and Newborn Nutrition. (2007, April 10). National Institutes of Health, Department of Health and Human Services. Available at http://www.nlm.nih.gov/medlineplus/infantandnewbornnutrition.html

International Human Genome Sequencing Consortium. (2006). A global map of p53 transcription-factor binding sites in the human genome. *Cell, 124*(1), 207–219.

Jacklin, C. N., Wilcox, K. T., & Maccoby, E. E. (1988). Neonatal sex-steroid hormones and cognitive abilities at six years. *Developmental Psychobiology, 21*(6), 567–574.

Jacobs, D. M., Levy, G., & Marder, K. (2006). Dementia in Parkinson's disease, Huntington's disease, and related disorders. In M. J. Farah & T. E. Feinberg (Eds.), *Patient-based approaches to cognitive neuroscience* (2nd ed., pp. 381–395). Cambridge, MA: MIT Press.

Jacobs, J. E., Davis-Kean, P., Bleeker, M., Eccles, J. S., & Malanchuk, O. (2005). "I can, but I don't want to": The impact of parents, interests, and activities on gender differences in math. In A. M. Gallagher & J. C. Kaufman (Eds.), *Gender differences in mathematics: An integrative psychological approach* (pp. 246–263). New York: Cambridge University Press.

Jacobs, S. (1993). *Pathologic grief: Maladaptation to loss.* Washington, DC: American Psychiatric Press.

Jacobsen, J. S., et al. (2006). Early-onset behavioral and synaptic deficits in a mouse model of Alzheimer's disease. *Proceedings of the National Academy of Sciences, 103*(13), 5161–5166.

Jacobson, J. L., Jacobson, S. W., Padgett, R. J., Brumitt, G. A., & Billings, R. L. (1992). Effects of prenatal PCB exposure on cognitive processing efficiency and sustained attention. *Developmental Psychology, 28*(2), 297–306.

Jacobson, P. F., & Schwartz, R. G. (2005). English past tense use in bilingual children with language impairment. *American Journal of Speech-Language Pathology, 14*(4), 313–323.

James, W. (2007). *The principles of psychology.* New York: Cosimo. (Original publication 1890: New York: Henry Holt).

Jang, Y., Kim, G., Chiriboga, D. A., & Cho, S. (2008). Willingness to use a nursing home. *Journal of Applied Gerontology, 27*(1), 110–117.

Janssen, E. (Ed). (2006). *The psychophysiology of sex.* Bloomington: Indiana University Press.

Jayson, S. (2008, June 8). More view cohabitation as acceptable choice. *USA Today.* Available at http://www.usatoday.com/news/nation/2008-06-08-cohabitation-study_N.htm

Jeng, S.-F., Yau, K.-I. T., Liao, H.-F., Chen, L.-C., & Chen, P.-S. (2000). Prognostic factors for walking attainment in very low birth weight preterm infants. *Early Human Development, 59*(3), 159–173.

Jepsen, D. A., & Choudhuri, E. (2001). Stability and change in 25-year occupational career patterns. *Career Development Quarterly, 50*(1), 3–19.

Johannes, C. B., et al. (2000). Incidence of erectile dysfunction in men 40 to 69 years old: Longitudinal results from the Massachusetts male aging study. *The Journal of Urology, 163*(2), 460–463.

Johnson, J. G., Zhang, B., & Prigerson, H. G. (2008). Investigation of a developmental model of risk for depression and suicidality following spousal bereavement. *Suicide and Life-Threatening Behavior, 38*(1), 1–12.

Johnson, W., & Bouchard, T. J., Jr., (2007). Sex differences in mental abilities: *g* masks the dimensions on which they lie. *Intelligence, 35*(1), 23–39.

Johnson, W., & Krueger, R. F. (2006). How money buys happiness: Genetic and environmental processes linking finances and life satisfaction. *Journal of Personality and Social Psychology, 90*(4), 680–691.

Johnson, W., McGue, M., Krueger, R. F., & Bouchard, T. J., Jr. (2004). Marriage and personality: A genetic analysis. *Journal of Personality and Social Psychology, 86*(2), 285–294.

Johnson-Greene, D., & Inscore, A. B. (2005). Substance abuse in older adults. In S. S. Bush, &

T. A. Martin (Eds.), *Geriatric neuropsychology: Practice essentials* (pp. 429–451). Studies on neuropsychology, neurology and cognition. Philadelphia: Taylor & Francis.

Jones, D. C., & Crawford, J. K. (2006). The peer appearance culture during adolescence: Gender and body mass variations. *Journal of Youth and Adolescence, 35*(2), 257–269.

Jones, S. S., & Hong, H.-W. (2005). How some infant smiles get made. *Infant Behavior & Development, 28*(2), 194–205.

Jonkman, S. (2006). Sensitization facilitates habit formation: Implications for addiction. *Journal of Neuroscience, 26*(28), 7319–7320.

Jordan, J. V., Kaplan, A. G., Miller, J. B., Stiver, I. P., & Surrey, J. L. (1991). *Women's growth in connection.* New York: Guilford.

Jorgensen, G. (2006). Kohlberg and Gilligan: Duet or duel? *Journal of Moral Education, 35*(2), 179–196.

Joshi, P. T., Salpekar, J. A., & Daniolos, P. T. (2006). Physical and sexual abuse of children. In M. K. Dulcan & J. M. Wiener (Eds.), *Essentials of child and adolescent psychiatry* (pp. 595–620). Washington, DC: American Psychiatric Publishing.

Joshi, R. M. (2003). Misconceptions about the assessment and diagnosis of reading disability. *Reading Psychology, 24*(3–4), 247–266.

Joung, H.-M., & Miller, N. J. (2007). Examining the effects of fashion activities on life satisfaction of older females: Activity theory revisited. *Family & Consumer Sciences Research Journal, 35*(4), 338–356.

Judge, T. A., & Klinger, R. (2008). Job satisfaction: Subjective well-being at work. In M. Eid, & R. J. Larsen (Eds.), *The science of subjective well-being* (pp. 393–413). New York: Guilford.

Kagan, J. (2009). Review of *Loneliness: Human nature and the need for social connection. The American Journal of Psychiatry, 166*(3), 375-376.

Kagan, J., & Klein, R. E. (1973). Cross-cultural perspectives on early development. *American Psychologist, 28*(11), 947–961.

Kagan, L. J., MacLeod, A. K., & Pote, H. L. (2004). Accessibility of causal explanations for future positive and negative events in adolescents with anxiety and depression. *Clinical Psychology and Psychotherapy, 11*(3), 177–186.

Kaiser Family Foundation, Holt, T., Greene, L., & Davis, J. (2003). *National survey of adolescents and young adults: Sexual health knowledge, attitudes, and experiences.* Menlo Park, CA: Henry J. Kaiser Family Foundation.

Kaminski, P. L., & Hayslip, B., Jr. (2006). Gender differences in body esteem among older adults. *Journal of Women & Aging, 18*(3), 19–35.

Kaminski, R. A., & Stormshak, E. A. (2007). Project STAR: Early intervention with preschool children and families for the prevention of substance abuse. In P. Tolan, J. Szapocznik, & S. Sambrano (Eds.), *Preventing youth substance abuse: Science-based programs for children and adolescents* (pp. 89–109). Washington, DC: American Psychological Association.

Kanevsky, L., & Geake, J. (2004). Inside the zone of proximal development: Validating a multi-factor model of learning potential with gifted students and their peers. *Journal for the Education of the Gifted, 28*(2), 182–217.

Karapetsas, A., & Kantas, A. (1991). Visuomotor organization in the child: A neuropsychological approach. *Perceptual and Motor Skills, 72*(1), 211–217.

Karatekin, C., Marcus, D. J., & White, T. (2007). Oculomotor and manual indexes of incidental and intentional spatial sequence learning during middle childhood and adolescence. *Journal of Experimental Child Psychology, 96*(2), 107–130.

Karavasilis, L., Doyle, A. B., & Markiewicz, D. (2003). Associations between parenting style and attachment to mother in middle childhood and adolescence. *International Journal of Behavioral Development, 27*(2), 153–164.

Katz, R., Lowenstein, A., Phillips, J., & Daatland, S. O. (2005). Theorizing inter-generational family relations: Solidarity, conflict, and ambivalence in cross-national contexts. In V. L. Bengtson et al. (Eds.), *Sourcebook of family theory & research* (pp. 393–420). Thousand Oaks, CA: Sage.

Katzman, D. K. (2005). Medical complications in adolescents with anorexia nervosa: A review of the literature. *International Journal of Eating Disorders, 37*(Supp.), S52–S59.

Kauff, N. D., & Offit, K. (2007). Modeling genetic risk of breast cancer. *Journal of the American Medical Association, 297*(23), 2637–2639.

Kavanagh, K., et al. (2007). Characterization and heritability of obesity and associated risk factors in vervet monkeys. *Obesity, 15*(7), 1666–1674.

Kavanaugh, R. D. (2006). Pretend play. In B. Spodek & O. N. Saracho (Eds.), *Handbook of research on the education of young children* (2nd ed., pp. 269–278). Hillsdale, NJ: Erlbaum.

Kavcic, T., & Zupancic, M. (2005). Sibling relationship in early/middle childhood: Trait- and dyad-centered approach. *Studia Psychologica, 47*(3), 179–197.

Kawas, C. H., & Brookmeyer, R. (2001). Aging and the public health effects of dementia. *New England Journal of Medicine, 344*(15), 1160–1161.

Kaye, W. H., et al. (2004). Genetic analysis of bulimia nervosa: Methods and sample description. *International Journal of Eating Disorders, 35*(4), 556–570.

Kazdin, A. E. (2000). Treatments for aggressive and antisocial children. *Child and Adolescent Psychiatric Clinics of North America, 9*(4), 841–858.

Kazui, H., et al. (2008). Association between quality of life of demented patients and professional knowledge of care workers. *Journal of Geriatric Psychiatry and Neurology, 21*(1), 72–78.

Kearney, C. A., & Bensaheb, A. (2007). Assessing anxiety disorders in children and adolescents. In S. R. Smith & L. Handler (Eds.), *The clinical assessment of children and adolescents: A practitioner's handbook* (pp. 467–483). Hillsdale, NJ: Erlbaum.

Keen, D., Rodger, S., Doussin, K., & Braithwaite, M. (2007). A pilot study of the effects of a social-pragmatic intervention on the communication and symbolic play of children with autism. *Autism, 11*(1), 63–71.

Keller, H., Kärtner, J., Borke, J., Yovsi, R., & Kleis, A. (2005). Parenting styles and the development of the categorical self: A longitudinal study on mirror self-recognition in Cameroonian Nso and German families. *International Journal of Behavioral Development, 29*(6), 496–504.

Kellman, P. J., & Arterberry, M. E. (2006). Infant visual perception. In D. Kuhn et al. (Eds.), *Handbook of child psychology, Volume 2: Cognition, perception, and language* (6th ed., pp. 109–160). Hoboken, NJ: Wiley.

Kellogg, R. (1959). *What children scribble and why.* Oxford: National Press.

Kellogg, R. (1970). Understanding children's art. In P. Cramer (Ed.), *Readings in developmental psychology today.* Del Mar, CA: CRM.

Kelly, L. et al. (2009). Palliative care of First Nations people. *Canadian Family Physician, 55*(4), 394–395.

Kemp, C. L. (2005). Dimensions of grandparent–adult grandchild relationships: From family ties to intergenerational friendships. *Canadian Journal on Aging, 24*(2), 161–178.

Kemp, E. A., & Kemp, J. E. (2002). *Older couples: New romances.* Berkeley, CA: Celestial Arts.

Kempes, M., Matthys, W., de Vries, H., & van Engeland, H. (2005). Reactive and proactive aggression in children: A review of theory, findings and the relevance for child and adolescent psychiatry. *European Child & Adolescent Psychiatry, 14*(1), 11–19.

Kendler, K. S., Gardner, C. O., Gatz, M., & Pedersen, N. L. (2007). The sources of comorbidity between major depression and generalized anxiety disorder in a Swedish national twin sample. *Psychological Medicine, 37*(3), 453–462.

Keogh, A. F., & Whyte, J. (2006). Exploring children's concepts of intelligence through ethnographic methods. *Irish Journal of Psychology, 27*(1–2), 69–78.

Kerns, K. A., Abraham, M. M., Schlegelmilch, A., & Morgan, T. A. (2007). Mother–child attachment in later middle childhood: Assessment approaches and associations with mood and emotion regulation. *Attachment & Human Development, 9*(1), 33–53.

Khurana, A., Cooksey, E. C., & Gavazzi, S. M. (2011). Juvenile delinquency and teenage pregnancy: A comparison of risk profiles among Midwestern European American and African American female juvenile offenders. *Psychology of Women Quarterly, 35*(1). DOI:10.1177/0361684310384103

Killen, M., & Smetana, J. G. (Eds.). (2006). *Handbook of moral development.* Hillsdale, NJ: Erlbaum.

Kim, J.-Y., McHale, S. M., Osgood, D. W., & Crouter, A. C. (2006). Longitudinal course and family correlates of sibling relationships from childhood through adolescence. *Child Development, 77*(6), 1746–1761.

King, P. M., & Kitchener, K. S. (2004). Reflective judgment. *Educational Psychologist, 39*(1), 5–18.

King, V., & Scott, M. E. (2005). A comparison of cohabiting relationships among older and younger adults. *Journal of Marriage and Family, 67*(2), 271–285.

Kinsbourne, M. (2003). The corpus callosum equilibrates the cerebral hemispheres. In E. Zaidel & M. Iacoboni (Eds.), *The parallel brain: The cognitive neuroscience of the corpus callosum* (pp. 271–281). Cambridge, MA: MIT Press.

Kinsey, A. C., Pomeroy, W. B., & Martin, C. E. (1948). *Sexual behavior in the human male.* Philadelphia: W. B. Saunders.

Kinsey, A. C., Pomeroy, W. B., Martin, C. E., & Gebhard, P. H. (1953). *Sexual behavior in the human female.* Philadelphia: W. B. Saunders.

Kirby, P. G., Biever, J. L., Martinez, I. G., & Gómez, J. P. (2004). Adults returning to school: The impact on family and work. *Journal of Psychology: Interdisciplinary and Applied, 138*(1), 65–76.

Kirchler, E., Pombeni, M. L., & Palmonari, A. (1991). Sweet sixteen… Adolescents' problems and the peer group as source of support. *European Journal of Psychology of Education, 6*(4), 393–410.

Kirkcaldy, B. D., Shephard, R. J., & Siefen, R. G. (2002). The relationship between physical activity and self-image and problem behaviour among adolescents. *Social Psychiatry and Psychiatric Epidemiology, 37*(11), 544–550.

Kirkpatrick, R. C. (2000). The evolution of human homosexual behavior. *Current Anthropology, 41*(3), 385–413.

Kistner, J. (2006). Children's peer acceptance, perceived acceptance, and risk for depression. In T. E. Joiner, J. S. Brown, & J. Kistner (Eds.), *The interpersonal, cognitive, and social nature of depression* (pp. 1–21). Hillsdale, NJ: Erlbaum.

Kjelsås, E., Bjornstrom, C., & Götestam, K. G. (2004). Prevalence of eating disorders in female and male adolescents (14–15 years). *Eating Behaviors, 5*(1), 13–25.

Klaus, M. H., & Kennell, J. H. (1978). Parent-to-infant attachment. In J. H. Stevens Jr. & M. Mathews (Eds.), *Mother/child, father/child relationships* (pp. 5–29). Washington, DC: National Association for the Education of Young Children.

Kleiber, D. A., & Kelly, J. R. (1980). Leisure, socialization, and the life cycle. In S. E. Iso-Ahola (Ed.), *Social psychological perspectives on leisure and recreation* (pp. 91–137). Springfield, IL: Charles C. Thomas.

Klein, P. J., & Meltzoff, A. N. (1999). Long-term memory, forgetting and deferred imitation in 12-month-old infants. *Developmental Science, 2*(1), 102–113.

Kliegel, M., Jäger, T., & Phillips, L. H. (2008). Adult age differences in event-based prospective memory: A meta-analysis on the role of focal versus nonfocal cues. *Psychology and Aging, 23*(1), 203–208.

Klier, C. M. (2006). Mother–infant bonding disorders in patients with postnatal depression: The Postpartum Bonding Questionnaire in clinical practice. *Archives of Women's Mental Health, 9*(5), 289–291.

Klintsova, A. Y., & Greenough, W. T. (1999). Synaptic plasticity in cortical systems. *Current Opinion in Neurobiology, 9*(2), 203–208.

Kloep, M., & Hendry, L. B. (2007). Retirement: A new beginning? *Psychologist, 20*(12), 742–745.

Klohnen, E. C., & Luo, S. (2003). Interpersonal attraction and personality: What is attractive—

self similarity, ideal similarity, complementarity or attachment security? *Journal of Personality and Social Psychology, 85*(4), 709–722.

Knaak, S. (2005). Breast-feeding, bottle-feeding and Dr. Spock: The shifting context of choice. *Canadian Review of Sociology and Anthropology, 42*(2), 197–216.

Knafo, A., & Plomin, R. (2006a). Parental discipline and affection and children's prosocial behavior: Genetic and environmental links. *Journal of Personality and Social Psychology, 90*(1), 147–164.

Knafo, A., & Plomin, R. (2006b). Prosocial behavior from early to middle childhood: Genetic and environmental influences on stability and change. *Developmental Psychology, 42*(5), 771–786.

Knickmeyer, R. C., Wheelwright, S., Taylor, K., Raggatt, P., Hackett, G., & Baron-Cohen, S. (2005). Gender-typed play and amniotic testosterone. *Developmental Psychology, 41*(3), 517–528.

Kniffin, K. M., & Wilson, D. S. (2004). The effect of nonphysical traits on the perception of physical attractiveness: Three naturalistic studies. *Evolution and Human Behavior, 25*(2), 88–101.

Kochanska, G. (2001). Emotional development in children with different attachment histories: The first three years. *Child Development, 72*(2), 474–490.

Kochanska, G., Coy, K. C., Murray, K. T. (2001). The development of self-regulation in the first four years of life. *Child Development, 72*(4), 1091–1111.

Kogan, M. D., et al. (2000). Trends in twin birth outcomes and prenatal care utilization in the United States, 1981–1997. *Journal of the American Medical Association, 284*(3), 335–341.

Kohl, C. (2004). Postpartum psychoses: Closer to schizophrenia or the affective spectrum? *Current Opinion in Psychiatry, 17*(2), 87–90.

Kohl, J. V. (2007). The mind's eyes: Human pheromones, neuroscience, and male sexual preferences. *Journal of Psychology & Human Sexuality, 18*(4), 313–369.

Kohlberg, L. (1963). Moral development and identification. In H. W. Stevenson (Ed.), *Child psychology: 62nd yearbook of the National Society for the Study of Education* (pp. 277–332). Chicago: University of Chicago Press.

Kohlberg, L. (1966). Cognitive stages and preschool education. *Human Development, 9*, 5–17.

Kohlberg, L. (1969). Stage and sequence: The cognitive-developmental approach to socialization. In D. A. Goslin (Ed.), *Handbook of social-*

ization theory and research (pp. 347–480). Chicago: Rand McNally.

Kohlberg, L. (1981). *The meaning and measurement of moral development.* Worcester, MA: Clark University Press.

Kohlberg, L. (1985). *The psychology of moral development.* San Francisco: Harper & Row.

Kohlberg, L., & Kramer, R. (1969). Continuities and discontinuities in childhood and adult moral development. *Human Development, 12*(2), 93–120.

Kohyama, J., Shiiki, T., Ohinata-Sugimoto, J., & Hasegawa, T. (2002). Potentially harmful sleep habits of 3-year-old children in Japan. *Journal of Developmental and Behavioral Pediatrics, 23*(2), 67–70.

Kolata, G. (2007, May 8). Genes take charge, and diets fall by the wayside. *New York Times.* Available at http://www.nytimes.com

Kolb, B., & Gibb, R. (2007). Brain plasticity and recovery from early cortical injury. *Developmental Psychobiology, 49*(2), 107–118.

Konijn, E. A., Bijvank, M. N., & Bushman, B. J. (2007). I wish I were a warrior: The role of wishful identification in the effects of violent video games on aggression in adolescent boys. *Developmental Psychology, 43*(4), 1038–1044.

Kopp, C. B. (1989). Regulation of distress and negative emotions: A developmental view. *Developmental Psychology, 25*(3), 343–354.

Korff, S. C. (2006). Religious orientation as a predictor of life satisfaction within the elderly population [Abstract]. *Dissertation Abstracts International: Section B: The Sciences and Engineering, 67*(1-B), 550.

Krackow, E., & Lynn, S. J. (2003). Is there touch in the game of Twister? The effects of innocuous touch and suggestive questions on children's eyewitness testimony. *Law and Human Behavior, 27*(6), 589–604.

Krebs, D. L., & Denton, K. (2005). Toward a more pragmatic approach to morality: A critical evaluation of Kohlberg's model. *Psychological Review, 112*(3), 629–649.

Kristensen, P., & Bjerkedal, T. (2007). Explaining the relation between birth order and intelligence. *Science, 313*(5832), 1717.

Kroeger, K. A., & Nelson, W. M., III. (2006). A language programme to increase the verbal production of a child dually diagnosed with Down syndrome and autism. *Journal of Intellectual Disability Research, 50*(2), 101–108.

Krojgaard, P. (2005). Continuity and discontinuity in developmental psychology. *Psyke & Logos, 26*(2), 377–394.

Krueger, C., Holditch-Davis, D., Quint, S., & DeCasper, A. (2004). Recurring auditory experience in the 28- to 34-week-old fetus. *Infant Behavior & Development, 27*(4), 537–543.

Kübler-Ross, E. (1969). *On death and dying.* New York: Macmillan.

Kuczaj, S. A., II (1982). On the nature of syntactic development. In S. A. Kuczaj II (Ed.), *Language development, Volume 1: Syntax and semantics.* Hillsdale, NJ: Erlbaum.

Kuczmarski, R. J., et al. (2000, December 4). CDC growth charts: United States. *Advance Data from Vital and Health Statistics*, No. 314. Hyattsville, MD: National Center for Health Statistics.

Kuhl, P. K., et al. (1997). Cross-language analysis of phonetic units in language addressed to infants. *Science, 277*(5326), 684–686.

Kuhl, P. K., et al. (2006). Infants show a facilitation effect for native language phonetic perception between 6 and 12 months. *Developmental Science, 9*(2), F13–F21.

Kuhn, D. (2007). Editorial. *Cognitive Development, 22*(1), 1–2.

Kulick, D. (2006). Regulating sex: The politics of intimacy and identity. *Sexualities, 9*(1), 122–124.

Kulik, L. (2000). Women face unemployment: A comparative analysis of age groups. *Journal of Career Development, 27*(1), 15–33.

Kulik, L. (2004). Perceived equality in spousal relations, martial quality, and life satisfaction. *Families in Society, 85*(2), 243–250.

Kunz, J. A. (2007). The life story matrix. In J. A. Kunz, & F. G. Soltys (Eds.), *Transformational reminiscence: Life story work* (pp. 1–16). New York: Springer.

Kunzmann, U., & Baltes, P. B. (2005). The psychology of wisdom: Theoretical and empirical challenges. In R. J. Sternberg & J. Jordan (Eds.), *A handbook of wisdom: Psychological perspectives* (pp. 110–135). New York: Cambridge University Press.

Kurdek, L. A. (2005). What do we know about gay and lesbian couples? *Current Directions in Psychological Science, 14*(5), 251–254.

Kurdek, L. A. (2006). Differences between partners from hetersosexual, gay, and lesbian cohabiting couples. *Journal of Marriage and the Family, 68*(2), 509–528.

Kurzban, R., & Weeden, J. (2005). HurryDate: Mate preferences in action. *Evolution and Human Behavior, 26*(3), 227–244.

Kushnir, J., & Sadeh, A. (2009). Childhood fears, neurobehavioral functioning, and behavior problems in school-age children. *Child Psychiatry & Human Development, 41*(1), 88–97.

Kvaal, K., et al. (2008). Co-occurrence of anxiety and depressive disorders in a community sample of older people. *International Journal of Geriatric Psychiatry, 23*(3), 229–237.

Kwok, H.-K. (2006). A study of the sandwich generation in Hong Kong. *Current Sociology, 54*(2), 257–272.

Kwok, H. W. M. (2003). Psychopharmacology in autism spectrum disorders. *Current Opinion in Psychiatry, 16*(5), 529–534.

Labouvie-Vief, G. (2006). Emerging structures of adult thought. In J. J. Arnett & J. L. Tanner (Eds.), *Emerging adults in America* (pp. 59–84). Washington, DC: American Psychological Association.

Labouvie-Vief, G., & González, M. M. (2004). Dynamic integration: Affect optimization and differentiation in development. In D. Y. Dai & R. J. Sternberg (Eds.), *Motivation, emotion, and cognition* (pp. 237–272). Hillsdale, NJ: Erlbaum.

Labrell, F., & Ubersfeld, G. (2004). Parental verbal strategies and children's capacities at 3 and 5 years during a memory task. *European Journal of Psychology of Education, 19*(2), 189–202.

Lachman, M. E. (2004). Development in midlife. *Annual Review of Psychology, 55*, 305–331.

Laflamme, D., Pomerleau, A., & Malcuit, G. (2002). A comparison of fathers' and mothers' involvement in childcare and stimulation behaviors during free-play with their infants at 9 and 15 months. *Sex Roles, 47*(11–12), 507–518.

Lai, H.-L., et al. (2006). Randomized controlled trial of music during kangaroo care on maternal state anxiety and preterm infants' responses. *International Journal of Nursing Studies, 43*(2), 139–146.

Lam, K. S. L., Aman, M. G., & Arnold, L. E. (2006). Neurochemical correlates of autistic disorder: A review of the literature. *Research in Developmental Disabilities, 27*(3), 254–289.

Lam, T. H., Shi, H. J., Ho, L. M., Stewart, S. M., & Fan, S. (2002). Timing of pubertal maturation and heterosexual behavior among Hong Kong Chinese adolescents. *Archives of Sexual Behavior, 31*(4), 359–366.

Lamb, M. E., & Ahnert, L. (2006). Nonparental child care: Context, concepts, correlates, and consequences. In K. A. Renninger, I. E. Sigel, W. Damon, & R. M. Lerner (Eds.), *Handbook of child psychology* (6th ed.), *Volume 4: Child psychology in practice* (pp. 950–1016). Hoboken, NJ: Wiley.

Lamers, C. T. J., Bechara, A., Rizzo, M., & Ramaekers, J. G. (2006). Cognitive function and mood in MDMA/THC users, THC users and non-drug using controls. *Journal of Psychopharmacology, 20*(2), 302–311.

Lampl, M., Veldhuis, J. D., & Johnson, M. L. (1992). Saltation and stasis: A model of human growth. *Science, 258*(5083), 801–803.

Lange, G., & Pierce, S. H. (1992). Memory-strategy learning and maintenance in preschool children. *Developmental Psychology, 28*(3), 453–462.

Langlois, J. H., et al. (2000). Maxims or myths of beauty? A meta-analytic and theoretical review. *Psychological Bulletin, 126*(3), 390–423.

Lansford, J. E., Malone, P. S., Castellino, D. R., Dodge, K. A., Pettit, G. S., & Bates, J. E. (2006). Trajectories of internalizing, externalizing, and grades for children who have and have not experienced their parents' divorce or separation. *Journal of Family Psychology, 20*(2), 292–301.

Lantolf, J. P., & Thorne, S. L. (2007). Sociocultural theory and second language learning. In B. VanPatten & J. Williams (Eds.), *Theories in second language acquisition: An introduction* (pp. 201–224). Hillsdale, NJ: Erlbaum.

LaPointe, L. L. (Ed.). (2005). Feral children. *Journal of Medical Speech-Language Pathology, 13*(1), vii–ix.

Lapsley, D. K. (2006). Moral stage theory. In K. Killen & J. G. Smetana (Eds.), *Handbook of moral development* (pp. 37–66). Hillsdale, NJ: Erlbaum.

Larroque, B., et al. (2005). Temperament at 9 months of very preterm infants born at less than 29 weeks' gestation: The Epipage study. *Journal of Developmental & Behavioral Pediatrics, 26*(1), 48–55.

Larson, R., & Richards, M. H. (1991). Daily companionship in late childhood and early adolescence: Changing developmental contexts. *Child Development, 62*(2), 284–300.

Larsson, I., & Svedin, C. (2002). Experiences in childhood: Young adults' recollections. *Archives of Sexual Behavior, 31*(3), 263–273.

Latham, G. P., & Budworth, M.-H. (2007). The study of work motivation in the 20th century. In L. L. Koppes (Ed.), *Historical perspectives in industrial and organizational psychology* (pp. 353–381). Hillsdale, NJ: Erlbaum.

Lattanzi-Licht, M. (2007). Religion, spirituality, and dying. In D. Balk et al. (Eds.), *Handbook of thanatology* (pp. 11–17). New York: Routledge/Taylor & Francis Group.

Lau, A. S., Litrownik, A. J., Newton, R. R., Black, M. M., & Everson, M. D. (2006). Factors affecting the link between physical discipline and child externalizing problems in Black and White families. *Journal of Community Psychology, 34*(1), 89–103.

Laumann, E. O., et al. (2006). Sexual activity, sexual disorders and associated help seeking behavior among mature adults in five Anglophone countries from the Global Survey of Sexual Attitudes and Behaviors. *Archives of Sexual Behavior, 35*(2), 145–161.

Laumann, E. O., Gagnon, J. H., Michael, R. T., & Michaels, S. (1994). *The social organization of sexuality.* Chicago: University of Chicago Press.

Laumann, E. O., Mahay, J., & Youm, Y. (2007). Sex, intimacy, and family life in the United States. In M. Kimmel (Ed.), *The sexual self: The construction of sexual scripts* (pp. 165–190). Nashville, TN: Vanderbilt University Press.

Laurendeau, M., & Pinard, A. (1970). *The development of the concept of space in the child.* New York: International Universities Press.

Lawrence, E., Nylen, K., & Cobb, R. J. (2007). Prenatal expectations and marital satisfaction over the transition to parenthood. *Journal of Family Psychology, 21*(2), 155–164.

Leaper, C. (2002). Parenting girls and boys. In M. H. Bornstein (Ed.), *Handbook of parenting* (2nd ed.), *Volume 1: Children and parenting* (pp. 189–225). Hillsdale, NJ: Erlbaum.

Lecanuet, J.-P., Granier-Deferre, C., & DeCasper, A. (2005). Are we expecting too much from prenatal sensory experiences? In B. Hopkins & S. P. Johnson (Eds.), *Prenatal development of postnatal functions: Advances in infancy research* (pp. 31–49). Westport, CT: Praeger/Greenwood.

Lecanuet, J.-P., Granier-Deferre, C., Jacquet, A.-Y., & DeCasper, A. J. (2000). Fetal discrimination of low-pitched musical notes. *Developmental Psychobiology, 36*(1), 29–39.

Leclerc, C. M., & Hess, T. M. (2007). Age differences in the bases for social judgments: Tests of a social expertise perspective. *Experimental Aging Research, 33*(1), 95–120.

Leder, S., Grinstead, L. N., & Torres, E. (2007). Grandparents raising grandchildren: Stressors, social support, and health outcomes. *Journal of Family Nursing, 13*(3), 333–352.

Leerkes, E. M., & Crockenberg, S. C. (2006). Antecedents of mothers' emotional and cognitive responses to infant distress: The role of family, mother, and infant characteristics. *Infant Mental Health Journal, 27*(4), 405–428.

Legro, R. S., et al. (2007). Clomiphene, metformin, or both for infertility in the polycystic ovary syndrome. *New England Journal of Medicine, 356*(6), 551–566.

Lejeune, C., et al. (2006). Prospective multicenter observational study of 260 infants born to 259 opiate-dependent mothers on methadone or high-dose buprenophine substitution. *Drug and Alcohol Dependence, 82*(3), 250–257.

Lemaire, P., & Arnaud, L. (2008). Young and older adults' strategies in complex arithmetic. *American Journal of Psychology, 121*(1), 1–16.

Lengua, L., J., Honorado, E., & Bush, N. R. (2007). Contextual risk and parenting as predictors of effortful control and social competence in preschool children. *Journal of Applied Developmental Psychology, 28*(1), 40–55.

Lenneberg, E. H. (1967). *Biological foundations of language.* Hoboken, NJ: Wiley.

Lenroot, R. K., et al. (2009). Differences in genetic and environmental influences on the human cerebral cortex associated with development during childhood and adolescence. *Human Brain Mapping, 30*(1), 163–173.

Leonard, S. P., & Archer, J. (1989). A naturalistic investigation of gender constancy in three- to four-year-old children. *British Journal of Developmental Psychology, 7*(4), 341–346.

Leonardo, E. D., & Hen, R. (2006). Genetics of affective and anxiety disorders. *Annual Review of Psychology, 57,* 117–137.

Leone, J. L. (2000). Psychosocial factors leading to harmony or disharmony in sibling relationships in mid-life when faced with caregiving responsibilities for aging parents [Abstract]. *Dissertation Abstracts International: Section B: The Sciences and Engineering, 61*(4-B), 2245.

Letourneau, E. J., Schoenwald, S. K., & Sheidow, A. J. (2004). Children and adolescents with sexual behavior problems. *Child Maltreatment: Journal of the American Professional Society on the Abuse of Children, 9*(1), 49–61.

Leung, C., McBride-Chang, C., & Lai, B. (2004). Relations among maternal parenting style, academic competence, and life satisfaction in Chinese early adolescents. *Journal of Early Adolescence, 24*(2), 113–143.

Lever, N., et al. (2004). A drop-out prevention program for high-risk inner-city youth. *Behavior Modification, 28*(4), 513–527.

Levine, D. (2000). Virtual attraction: What rocks your boat. *CyberPsychology & Behavior, 3*(4), 565–573.

Levinson, D. J. (1996). *The seasons of a woman's life.* New York: Knopf.

Levinson, D. J., Darrow, C. N, & Klein, E. B. (1978). *Seasons of a man's life.* New York: Knopf.

Levinthal, B. R., & Lleras, A. (2007). The unique contributions of retinal size and perceived size on change detection. *Visual Cognition, 15*(1), 101–105.

Levpušcek, M. P. (2006). Adolescent individuation in relation to parents and friends: Age and gender differences. *European Journal of Developmental Psychology, 3*(3), 238–264.

Lewinsohn, P. M., Rohde, P., Seeley, J. R., Klein, D. N., & Gotlib, I. H. (2000). Natural course of adolescent major depressive disorder in a community sample: Predictors of recurrence in young adults. *American Journal of Psychiatry, 157*(10), 1584–1591.

Lewis, B. A., et al. (2004). Four-year language outcomes of children exposed to cocaine in utero. *Neurotoxicology and Teratology, 26*(5), 617–627.

Lewis, H. L. (2003). Differences in ego identity among college students across age, ethnicity, and gender. *Identity, 3*(2), 159–189.

Lewis, M., & Feiring, C. (1989). Early predictors of childhood friendship. In T. J. Berndt & G. W. Ladd (Eds.), *Peer relationships in child development* (pp. 246–273) Hoboken, NJ: Wiley.

Li, Q. (2007). New bottle but old wine: A research of cyberbullying in schools. *Computers in Human Behavior, 23*(4), 1777–1791.

Lickliter, R. (2001). The dynamics of language development: From perception to comprehension. *Developmental Science, 4*(1), 21–23.

Light, L. L., Patterson, M. M., Chung, C., & Healy, M. R. (2004). Effects of repetition and response deadline on associative recognition in young and older adults. *Memory & Cognition, 32*(7), 1182–1193.

Lindau, S. T., Schumm, L. P., Laumann, E. O., Levinson, W., O'Muircheartaigh, C. A., & Waite, L. J. (2007). A study of sexuality and health among older adults in the United States. *New England Journal of Medicine, 357*(8), 762–775.

Lipman, E. L. et al. (2006). Testing effectiveness of a community-based aggression management program for children 7 to 11 years old and their families. *Journal of the American Academy of Child & Adolescent Psychiatry, 45*(9), 1085–1093.

Lippa, R. A. (2010). Gender differences in personality and interests: When, where, and why? *Social and Personality Psychology Compass, 4*(11), 1098–1110.

Lipsitt, L. P. (2002). Early experience and behavior in the baby of the twenty-first century. In J. Gomes-Pedro et al. (Eds.), *The infant and family in the twenty-first century* (pp. 55–78). London: Brunner-Routledge.

Lipsitt, L. P. (2003). Crib death: A biobehavioral phenomenon? *Current Directions in Psychological Science, 12*(5), 164–170.

Ll-qi, Z., & Fu-xi, F. (2006). Preschool children's understanding of death. *Chinese Journal of Clinical Psychology, 14*(1), 91–93.

Locke, B. D., & Mahalik, J. R. (2005). Examining masculinity norms, problem drinking, and athletic involvement as predictors of sexual aggression in college men. *Journal of Counseling Psychology, 52*(3), 279–283.

Löckenhoff, C. E., & Carstensen, L. L. (2004). Socioemotional selectivity theory, aging, and health: The increasingly delicate balance between regulating emotions and making tough choices. *Journal of Personality, 72*(6), 1395–1424.

Lorant, V., et al. (2005). A European comparative study of marital status and socio-economic inequalities in suicide. *Social Science & Medicine, 60*(11), 2431–2441.

Lorenz, F. O., Wickrama, K. A. S., Conger, R. D., & Elder, G. H., Jr. (2006). The short-term and decade-long effects of divorce on women's midlife health. *Journal of Health and Social Behavior, 47*(2), 111–125.

Lorenz, K. (1962). *King Solomon's ring.* London: Methuen.

Lorenz, K. (1981). *The foundations of ethology.* New York: Springer-Verlag.

Lovaas, O. I., Smith, T., & McEachin, J. J. (1989). Clarifying comments on the young autism study: Reply to Schapler, Short, and Mesibov. *Journal of Consulting and Clinical Psychology, 57*(1), 165–167.

Lubinski, D. (2004). Introduction to the Special Section on Cognitive Abilities: 100 years after Spearman's (1904) "'General intelligence,' objectively determined and measured." *Journal of Personality and Social Psychology, 86*(1), 96–111.

Lubinski, D., & Benbow, C. P. (2000). States of excellence. *American Psychologist, 55*(1), 137–150.

Lucariello, J. M., Hudson, J. A., Fivush, R., & Bauer, P. J. (Eds.). (2004). *The development of the mediated mind: Sociocultural context and cognitive development.* Hillsdale, NJ: Erlbaum.

Luciano, M., Kirk, K. M., Heath, A. C., & Martin, N. G. (2005). The genetics of tea and coffee drinking and preference for source of caffeine in a large community sample of Australian twins. *Addiction, 100*(10), 1510–1517.

Ludwick, R., & Silva, M. C. (2003, December 19). Ethical challenges in the care of elderly persons. *Online Journal of Issues in Nursing.* Available at http://nursingworld.org/ojin

Ludwig, F. M., Hattjar, B., Russell, R. L., & Winston, K. (2007). How caregiving for grandchildren affects grandmothers' meaningful occupations. *Journal of Occupational Science, 14*(1), 40–51.

Lund, D. A., & Caserta, M. S. (2001). When the unexpected happens: Husbands coping with the deaths of their wives. In D. A. Lund (Ed.), *Men coping with grief* (pp. 147–167). Amityville, NY: Baywood.

Lupien, S. J., Maheu, F., Tu, M., Fiocco, A., & Schramek, T. E. (2007). The effects of stress and stress hormones on human cognition: Implications for the field of brain and cognition. *Brain and Cognition, 65*(3), 209–237.

Lykken, D. T. (2006a). The mechanism of emergenesis. *Genes, Brain & Behavior, 5*(4), 306–310.

Lykken, D. T. (2006b). Psychopathic personality: The scope of the problem. In C. J. Patrick (Ed.), *Handbook of psychopathy* (pp. 3–13). New York: Guilford.

Lykken, D. T., & Csikszentmihalyi, M. (2001). Happiness—stuck with what you've got? *Psychologist, 14*(9), 470–472.

Lynam, D. R., Caspi, A., Moffitt, T. E., Loeber, R., & Stouthamer-Loeber, M. (2007). Longitudinal evidence that psychopathy scores in early adolescence predict adult psychopathy. *Journal of Abnormal Psychology, 116*(1), 155–165.

Lynne, S. D., Graber, J. A., Nichols, T. R., Brooks-Gunn, J., & Botvin, G. J. (2007). Links between pubertal timing, peer influences, and externalizing behaviors among urban students followed through middle school. *Journal of Adolescent Health, 40*(2), 181.e7–181.e13.

Lyon, G. R., Shaywitz, S. E., & Shaywitz, B. A. (2003). A definition of dyslexia. *Annals of Dyslexia, 53*(1), 1–14.

Maccoby, E. E. (1990). The role of gender identity and gender constancy in sex-differentiated development. In D. Schrader (Ed.), *New directions for child development, No. 47. The legacy of Lawrence Kohlberg.* San Francisco: Jossey-Bass.

Maccoby, E. E. (2000). Perspectives on gender development. *International Journal of Behavioral Development, 24*(4), 398–406.

Maccoby, E. E. (2002). Parenting effects: Issues and controversies. In J. G. Borkowski et al. (Eds.), *Parenting and the child's world: Influences on academic, intellectual, and social-emotional development* (pp. 35–46). Hillsdale, NJ: Erlbaum.

Maccoby, E. E., & Jacklin, C. N. (1974). *The psychology of sex differences.* Stanford, CA: Stanford University Press.

Macfarlane, A. (1975). Olfaction in the development of social preferences in the human neonate. In M. A. Hofer (Ed.), *Parent–infant interaction* (pp. 103–117). Amsterdam: Elsevier.

Macfarlane, A. (1977). *The psychology of childbirth.* Cambridge, MA: Harvard University Press.

Maciejewski, P. K., Zhang, B., Block, S. D., & Prigerson, H. G. (2007). An empirical examination of the stage theory of grief. *Journal of the American Medical Association, 297*(7), 716–723.

Mackie-Magyar, J., & McCracken, J. (2004). Review of autism spectrum disorders: A research review for practitioners. *Journal of Child and Adolescent Psychopharmacology, 14*(1), 17–18.

Maclean, A. M., Walker, L. J., & Matsuba, M. K. (2004). Transcendence and the moral self: Identity integration, religion, and moral life. *Journal for the Scientific Study of Religion, 43*(3), 429–437.

Madon, S., et al. (2001). Am I as you see me or do you see me as I am? Self-fulfilling prophecies and self-verification. *Personality and Social Psychology Bulletin, 27*(9), 1214–1224.

Magolda, M. B. B. (2004). Evolution of a constructivist conceptualization of epistemological reflection. *Educational Psychologist, 39*(1), 31–42.

Mahay, J., & Lewin, A. C. (2007). Age and the desire to marry. *Journal of Family Issues, 28*(5), 706–723.

Mahler, M. S., Pine, F., & Bergman, A. (1975). *The psychological birth of the human infant: Symbiosis and individuation.* New York: Basic Books.

Maimburg, R. D., & Væth, M. (2006). Perinatal risk factors and infantile autism. *Acta Psychiatrica Scandinavica, 114*(4), 257–264.

Major, G. C., Doucet, E., Trayhurn, P., Astrup, A., & Tremblay, A. (2007). Clinical significance of adaptive thermogenesis. *International Journal of Obesity, 31*(2), 204–212.

Malamuth, N. M., Huppin, M., & Paul, B. (2005). Sexual coercion. In D. M. Buss (Ed.), *The handbook of evolutionary psychology* (pp. 394–418). Hoboken, NJ: Wiley.

Malinosky-Rummell, R., & Hansen, D. H. (1993). Long-term consequences of childhood physical abuse. *Psychological Bulletin, 114*(1), 68–79.

Malone, P. S., et al. (2004). Divorce and child behavior problems: Applying latent change score models to life event data. *Structural Equation Modeling, 11*(3), 401–423.

Maluccio, A. N., & Ainsworth, F. (2003). Drug use by parents: A challenge for family reunification practice. *Children and Youth Services Review, 25*(7), 511–533.

Mandler, J. M. (1990). Recall and its verbal expression. In R. Fivush & J. A. Hudson (Eds.), *Knowing and remembering in young children* (pp. 317–330). Cambridge: Cambridge University Press.

Mangina, C. A., & Sokolov, E. N. (2006). Neuronal plasticity in memory and learning abilities: Theoretical position and selective review. *International Journal of Psychophysiology, 60*(3), 203–214.

Maratsos, M. P. (2007). Commentary. *Monographs of the Society for Research in Child Development, 72*(1), 121–126.

Marcia, J. E. (1991). Identity and self-development. In R. M. Lerner, A. C. Petersen, & J. Brooks-Gunn (Eds.), *Encyclopedia of adolescence* (pp. 527–531). New York: Garland.

Marean, G. C., Werner, L. A., & Kuhl, P. K. (1992). Vowel categorization by very young infants. *Developmental Psychology, 28*(3), 396–405.

Markham, B. (2006). Older women and security. In J. Worell & C. D. Goodheart (Eds.), *Handbook of girls' and women's psychological health: Gender and well-being across the lifespan* (pp. 388–396). Oxford series in clinical psychology. New York: Oxford University Press.

Marks, L., Nesteruk, O., Swanson, M., Garrison, B., & Davis, T. (2005). Religion and health among African Americans. *Research on Aging, 27*(4), 447–474.

Marquis, C. (2003, March 16). Living in sin. *New York Times,* p. WK2.

Marron, D. J., & Rayman, J. R. (2002). Addressing the career development needs of adult students in research university settings. In S. G. Niles (Ed.), *Adult career development: Concepts, issues and practices* (3rd ed., pp. 321–337). Columbus, OH: National Career Development Association.

Marsh, B. (2011, January 29). Timeline: Trying to whip us into shape. Available at http://www.nytimes.com/interactive/2011/01/30/weekinreview/30marsh.html

Marsiglio, W. (2004). When stepfathers claim stepchildren: A conceptual analysis. *Journal of Marriage and Family, 66*(1), 22–39.

Martin, C. L., & Ruble, D. N. (2004). Children's search for gender cues: Cognitive perspectives on gender development. *Current Directions in Psychological Science, 13*(2), 67–70.

Martin, C. L., Ruble, D. N., & Szkrybalo, J. (2002). Cognitive theories of early gender development. *Psychological Bulletin, 128*(6), 903–933.

Martin, J. A., et al. (2006). Births: Final data for 2004. *National Vital Statistics Report, 55*(1). Hyattsville, MD: National Center for Health Statistics.

Marushima, R. (2000). Relation of generativity to self-concept among middle-aged adults. *Japanese Journal of Educational Psychology, 48*(1), 52–62.

Marwick, C. (2000). Consensus panel considers osteoporosis. *Journal of the American Medical Association, 283*(16), 2093–2095.

Masi, G., Mucci, M., & Millepiedi, S. (2001). Separation anxiety disorder in children and adolescents: Epidemiology, diagnosis, and management. *CNS Drugs, 15*(2), 93–104.

Maternity Center Association. (2004, April). *What every pregnant woman needs to know about cesarean section.* New York: Author.

Mathews, T. J., & MacDorman, M. F. (2007). Infant mortality statistics from the 2004 period linked birth/infant death data set. *National Vital Statistics Reports, 55*(14).

Matlin, M. W. (2008). *The psychology of women* (8th ed.). Belmont, CA: Thomson/Wadsworth.

Matthews, A. K., Hughes, T. L., & Tartaro, J. (2006). Sexual behavior and sexual dysfunction in a community sample of lesbian and heterosexual women. In A. M. Omoto & H. S. Kurtzman (Eds.). *Sexual orientation and mental health.* (pp. 185–205). Washington, DC: American Psychological Association.

Matthews, J. (1990). Drawing and individual development. In R. M. Thomas (Ed.), *The encyclopedia of human development and education: Theory, research, and studies.* Oxford: Pergamon.

Matthews, R. A., Del Priore, R. E., Acitelli, L. K., & Barnes-Farrell, J. L. (2006). Work-to-relationship conflict: Crossover effects in dual-earner couples. *Journal of Occupational Health Psychology, 11*(3), 228–240.

Maxwell, C. D., Robinson, A. L., & Post, L. A. (2003). The nature and predictors of sexual victimization and offending among adolescents. *Journal of Youth & Adolescence, 32*(6), 465–477.

McCabe, M. P. (2005). The role of performance anxiety in the development and maintenance of sexual dysfunction in men and women. *International Journal of Stress Management, 12*(4), 379–388.

McCall, R. B., Applebaum, M. I., & Hogarty, P. S. (1973). Developmental changes in mental performance. *Monographs of the Society for Research in Child Development, 38*(3, ser. 150).

McCarthy, B. W., & Fucito, L. M. (2005). Integrating medication, realistic expectations, and therapeutic interventions in the treatment of male sexual dysfunction. *Journal of Sex & Marital Therapy, 31*(4), 319–328.

McCartney, K., Owen, M. T., Booth, C. L., Clarke-Stewart, K. A., & Vandell, D. L. (2004). Testing a maternal attachment model of behavior problems in early childhood. *Journal of Child Psychology and Psychiatry, 45*(4), 765–778.

McClellan, J. M., & Werry, J. S. (2003). Evidence-based treatments in child and adolescent psychiatry: An inventory. *Journal of the American Academy of Child & Adolescent Psychiatry, 42*(12), 1388–1400.

McCracken, M., Jiles, R., & Blanck, H. M. (2007). Health behaviors of the young adult U.S. population: Behavioral risk factor surveillance system, 2003. *Preventing Chronic Disease, 4*(2), A25. Available at http://www.ncbi.nlm.nih.gov/pmc/articles/PMC1893124/

McCrae, R. R., et al. (2000). Nature over nurture: Temperament, personality, and life span development. *Journal of Personality and Social Psychology, 78*(1), 173–186.

McCrae, R. R., & Costa, P. T., Jr. (1997). Personality trait structure as a human universal. *American Psychologist, 52*(5), 509–516.

McCrae, R. R., & Costa, P. T., Jr. (2006). Cross-cultural perspectives on adult personality trait development. In D. K. Mroczek & T. D Little (Eds.), *Handbook of personality development* (pp. 129–145). Hillsdale, NJ: Erlbaum.

McDevitt, T. M., & Ormrod, J. E. (2002). *Child development and education.* Upper Saddle River, NJ: Prentice Hall.

McDonough, L. (2002). Basic-level nouns: First learned but misunderstood. *Journal of Child Language, 29*(2), 357–377.

McEwan, M. H., Dihoff, R. E., & Brosvic, G. M. (1991). Early infant crawling experience is reflected in later motor skill development. *Perceptual and Motor Skills, 72*(1), 75–79.

McGlaughlin, A., & Grayson, A. (2001). Crying in the first year of infancy: Patterns and prevalence. *Journal of Reproductive and Infant Psychology, 19*(1), 47–59.

McGrath, M., et al. (2005). Early precursors of low attention and hyperactivity in a preterm sample at age four. *Issues in Comprehensive Pediatric Nursing, 28*(1), 1–15.

McHale, J. P., & Rotman, T. (2007). Is seeing believing? Expectant parents' outlooks on coparenting and later coparenting solidarity. *Infant Behavior & Development, 30*(1), 63–81.

McHale, S. M., Kim, J.-Y., & Whiteman, S. D. (2006). Sibling relationships in childhood and adolescence. In P. Noller & J. A. Feeney (Eds.), *Close relationships: Functions, forms and processes* (pp. 127–149). New York: Psychology Press/Taylor & Francis.

McIlvane, W. J., & Dube, W. V. (2003). Stimulus control topography coherence theory: Foundations and extensions. *Behavior Analyst, 26*(2), 195–213.

McKee-Ryan, F., Song, Z., Wanberg, C. R., & Kinicki, A. J. (2005). Psychological and physical well-being during unemployment: A meta-analytic study. *Journal of Applied Psychology, 90*(1), 53–76.

McManus, C. (2003). Right hand, left hand: The origins of asymmetry in brains, bodies, atoms and cultures. *Cortex, 39*(2), 348–350.

McManus, I. C., et al. (1988). The development of handedness in children. *British Journal of Developmental Psychology, 6*(3), 257–273.

Meaney, K. S., Dornier, L. A., & Owens, M. S. (2002). Sex-role stereotyping for selected sport and physical activities across age groups. *Perceptual and Motor Skills, 94*(3), 743–749.

Meier, B. P., Robinson, M. D., & Wilkowski, B. M. (2006). Turning the other cheek: Agreeableness and the regulation of aggression-related primes. *Psychological Science, 17*(2), 136–142.

Meijer, A. M., & van den Wittenboer, G. L. H. (2007). Contribution of infants' sleep and crying to marital relationship of first-time parent couples in the first year after childbirth. *Journal of Family Psychology, 21*(1), 49–57.

Meinert, C. L., & Breitner, J. C. S. (2008). Chronic disease long-term drug prevention trials: Lessons from the Alzheimer's Disease Anti-Inflammatory Prevention Trial (ADAPT). *Alzheimer's & Dementia, 4*(1, Supp. 1), S7–S14.

Melamed, S., Meir, E. I., & Samson, A. (1995). The benefits of personality-leisure congruence. *Journal of Leisure Research, 27*(1), 25–40.

Meldrum, M, L. (2003). A capsule history of pain management. *Journal of the American Medical Association, 290*(18), 2470–2475.

Mellon, M. W. (2006). Enuresis and encopresis. In G. G. Bea, & K. M. Minke (Eds.), *Children's needs III: Development, prevention, and intervention* (pp. 1041–1053). Washington, DC: National Association of School Psychologists.

Mellon, M. W., & Houts, A. C. (2006). Nocturnal enuresis. In J. E. Fisher & W. T. O'Donohue (Eds.), *Practitioner's guide to evidence-based psychotherapy* (pp. 432–441). New York: Springer Science + Business Media.

Meltzoff, A. N. (1988). Infant imitation and memory: Nine-month-olds in immediate and deferred tests. *Child Development, 59*(1), 217–225.

Meltzoff, A. N., & Prinz, W. (Eds.). (2002). *The imitative mind: Development, evolution, and brain bases.* New York: Cambridge University Press.

Mendle, J., et al. (2006). Family structure and age at menarche: A children-of-twins approach. *Developmental Psychology, 42*(3), 533–542.

Merrill, L. L., Crouch, J. L., Thomsen, C. J., & Guimond, J. M. (2004). Risk for intimate partner violence and child physical abuse: Psychosocial characteristics of multi-risk male and female Navy recruits. *Child Maltreatment: Journal of the American Professional Society on the Abuse of Children, 9*(1), 18–29.

Metcalfe, J. S., et al. (2005). Development of somatosensory-motor integration: An event-related analysis of infant posture in the first year of independent walking. *Developmental Psychobiology, 46*(1), 19–35.

Metzger, K. L., et al. (2007). Effects of nicotine vary across two auditory evoked potentials in the mouse. *Biological Psychiatry, 61*(1), 23–30.

Meyer, S., & Shore, C. (2001). Children's understanding of dreams as mental states. *Dreaming, 11*(4), 179–194.

Michael, R., Gagnon, J., Laumann, E., & Kolata, G. (1994). *Sex in America: A definitive survey.* Boston: Little Brown.

Milgram, R. M., & Livne, N. L. (2006). Research on creativity in Israel: A chronicle of theoretical and empirical development. In J. C. Kaufman & R. J. Sternberg (Eds.), *The international handbook of creativity* (pp. 307–336). New York: Cambridge University Press.

Millar, W. S. (1990). Span of integration for delayed-reward contingency learning in 6- to 8-month-old infants. In A. Diamond (Ed.), *The development and neural bases of higher cognitive functions* (pp. 239ff). New York: New York Academy of Sciences.

Miller, A. L., Wyman, S. E., Huppert, J. D., Glassman, S. L., & Rathus, J. H. (2000). Analysis of behavioral skills utilized by suicidal adolescents receiving dialectical behavior therapy. *Cognitive and Behavioral Practice, 7*(2), 183–187.

Miller, C. F., Trautner, H. M., & Ruble, D. N. (2006). The role of gender stereotypes in children's preferences and behavior. In L. Balter & C. S. Tamis-LeMonda (Eds.), *Child psychology: A handbook of contemporary issues* (2nd ed., pp. 293–323). New York: Psychology Press.

Miller, S. M., Boyer, B. A., & Rodoletz, M. (1990). Anxiety in children: Nature and development. In M. Lewis & S. M. Miller (Eds.), *Handbook of developmental psychopathology* (pp. 191–207). New York: Plenum.

Mills, B., Reyna, V. F., & Estrada, S. (2008). Explaining contradictory relations between risk perception and risk taking. *Psychological Science, 19*(5), 429–433.

Miniño, A. M., Heron, M. P., Murphy, S. L., & Kochanek, K. D. (2007). Deaths: Final data for 2004. *National Vital Statistics Reports, 55*(19). Available at http://www.cdc.gov/nchs/data/nvsr/nvsr55/nvsr55_19.pdf

Minkler, M., & Fuller-Thomson, E. (2005). African American grandparents raising grandchildren: A national study using the Census 2000 American Community Survey. *Journals of Gerontology: Series B: Psychological Sciences and Social Sciences, 60B*(2), S82–S92.

Miscarriage. (2007, January 11). Available at http://www.nlm.nih.gov/medlineplus/ency/article/001488.htm

Mischo, C. (2004). Fördert Gruppendiskussion die Perspektiven-Koordination? *Zeitschrift für Entwicklungspsychologie und Pädagogische Psychologie, 36*(1), 30–37.

Mitchell, A. L. (2006). Medical consequences of cocaine. *Journal of Addictions Nursing, 17*(4), 249.

Mitchell, D. D., & Bruss, P. J. (2003) Age differences in implicit memory: Conceptual, perceptual, or methodological? *Psychology and Aging, 18*(4), 807–822.

Mock, S. E., & Cornelius, S. W. (2007). Profiles of interdependence: The retirement planning of married, cohabiting, and lesbian couples. *Sex Roles, 56*(11–12), 793–800.

Mock, S. E., Taylor, C. J., & Savin-Williams, R. C. (2006). Aging together: The retirement plans of same-sex couples. In D. Kimmel, T. Rose, & S. David (Eds.), *Lesbian, gay, bisexual, and transgender aging: Research and clinical perspectives* (pp. 152–174). New York: Columbia University Press.

Moen, P., Huang, Q., Plassmann, V., & Dentinger, E. (2006). Deciding the future. *American Behavioral Scientist, 49*(10), 1422–1443.

Moen, P., Kim, J. E., & Hofmeister, H. (2001). Couples' work/retirement transitions, gender, and marital equality. *Social Psychology Quarterly, 64*(1), 55–71.

Moens, E., Braet, C., & Soetens, B. (2007). Observation of family functioning at mealtime: A comparison between families of children with and without overweight. *Journal of Pediatric Psychology, 32*(1), 52–63.

Mohan, R., & Bhugra, D. (2005). Literature update. *Sexual and Relationship Therapy, 20*(1), 115–122.

Molinari, L., & Corsaro, W. A. (2000). Le relazioni amicali nella scuola dell'infanzia e nella scuola elementare: Uno studio longitudinale. *Età Evolutiva, 67*, 40–51.

Monat, A., Lazarus, R. S., & Reevy, G. (Eds.). (2007). *The Praeger handbook on stress and coping, Volume 2.* Westport, CT: Praeger/Greenwood.

Montemayor, R., & Eisen, M. (1977). The development of self-conceptions from childhood to adolescence. *Developmental Psychology, 13*(4), 314–319.

Moore, D. R. & Heiman, J. R. (2006). Women's sexuality in context: Relationship factors and female sexual functioning. In I. Goldstein, C. Meston, S. Davis, & A. Traish (Eds.), *Female sexual dysfunction* (pp. 63–84). New York: Parthenon.

Morelli, G. A., Oppenheim, D., Rogoff, B., & Goldsmith, D. (1992). Cultural variation in infants' sleeping arrangements: Questions of independence. *Developmental Psychology, 28*(4), 604–613.

Morrell, J., & Steele, H. (2003). The role of attachment security, temperament, maternal perception, and care-giving behavior in persistent infant sleeping problems. *Infant Mental Health Journal, 24*(5), 447–468.

Morry, M. M., & Gaines, S. O. (2005). Relationship satisfaction as a predictor of similarity ratings: A test of the attraction-similarity hypothesis. *Journal of Social and Personal Relationships, 22*(4), 561–584.

Morton, S. M. B. (2006). Maternal nutrition and fetal growth and development. In P. Gluckman & M. Hanson (Eds.), *Developmental origins of health and disease.* (pp. 98–129). New York: Cambridge University Press.

Moses, L. J., & Flavell, J. H. (1990). Inferring false beliefs from actions and reactions. *Child Development, 61*(4), 929–945.

Mosher, W. D., Chandra, A., & Jones, J. (2005). *Sexual behavior and selected health measures: Men and women 1 B 44 years of age, United States, 2002. Advance data from vital and health statistics.* Centers for Disease Control and Prevention. National Center for Health Statistics, Number 362, Figures 2 and 3.

Moshman, D. (2005). *Adolescent psychological development* (2nd ed.). Hillsdale, NJ: Erlbaum.

Most, S. B., Sorber, A. V., & Cunningham, J. G. (2007). Auditory Stroop reveals implicit gender association in adults and children. *Journal of Experimental Social Psychology, 43*(2), 287–294.

Mueller, R., Pierce, K., Ambrose, J. B., Allen, G., & Courchesne, E. (2001). Atypical patterns of cerebral motor activation in autism: A functional magnetic resonance study. *Biological Psychiatry, 49*(8), 665–676.

Muhlbauer, V., & Chrisler, J. C. (Eds.). (2007). *Women over 50: Psychological perspectives.* New York: Springer Science + Business Media.

Munroe, R. H., Shimmin, H. S., & Munroe, R. L. (1984). Gender role understanding and sex role preference in four cultures. *Developmental Psychology, 20*(4), 673–682.

Muraco, A. (2006). Intentional families: Fictive kin ties between cross-gender, different sexual orientation friends. *Journal of Marriage and Family, 68*(5), 1313–1325.

Muris, P., Bodden, D., Merckelbach, H., Ollendick, T. H., & King, N. (2003). Fear of the beast: A prospective study on the effects of negative information on childhood fear. *Behaviour Research and Therapy, 41*(2), 195–208.

Myers, J. E., Madathil, J., & Tingle, L. R. (2005). Marriage satisfaction and wellness in India and the United States: A preliminary comparison of arranged marriages and marriages of choice. *Journal of Counseling & Development, 83*(2), 183–190.

Nadeau, L., et al. (2003). Extremely premature and very low birthweight infants: A double hazard population? *Social Development, 12*(2), 235–248.

Nagin, D. S., & Tremblay, R. E. (2001). Parental and early childhood predictors of persistent physical aggression in boys from kindergarten to high school. *Archives of General Psychiatry, 58*(4), 389–394.

National Center for Children in Poverty. (2004). Low-income children in the United States (2004). Available at http://cpmcnet.columbia.edu/dept/nccp

National Center for Education Statistics. (2005). *Projections of Education Statistics to 2014* (23rd ed.), Table 11. Available at http://nces.ed.gov/pubs2005/2005074.pdf

National Center for Education Statistics. (2007). *Dropout rates in the United States: 2005.* Washington, DC: Author. Available at http://nces.ed.gov/pubs2007/dropout05

National Center for Education Statistics. (2010). *The condition of education 2010.* Washington,

DC: Author. Available at http://nces.ed.gov/pubsearch/pubsinfo.asp?pubid=2010028

National Center for Health Statistics. (2010). *Health, United States, 2009: With special feature on medical technology.* Hyattsville, MD: Author. Available at http://www.cdc.gov/nchs/data/hus/hus09.pdf

National Center for Injury Prevention and Control, Office of Statistics and Programming, Centers for Disease Control and Prevention. (2007a, March 29). National Center for Health Statistics (NCHS), National Vital Statistics System. Available at http://webappa.cdc.gov/cgi-bin/broker.exe

National Center for Injury Prevention and Control. (2007b, July 11). Suicide: Fact sheet. Available at http://www.cdc.gov/ncipc/factsheets/suifacts.htm

National Guideline Clearinghouse. (2007). Use of clomiphene citrate in women. Available at http://www.guideline.gov/summary/summary.aspx?ss=15&doc_id=4843&nbr=3484. Last updated January 29, 2007

National Hospice and Palliative Care Organization (NHPCO). (2007). NHPCO facts and figures: Hospice care in America. Available at http://www.nhpco.org/files/public/Statistics_Research/NHPCO_facts-and-figures_Nov2007.pdf

National Institutes of Health. (2002). Available at http://cerhr.niehs.nih.gov/genpub/topics/vitamin_a-ccae.html.

National Sleep Foundation. (2007). Children's sleep habits. Available at http://www.sleepfoundation.org/article/hot-topics/backgrounder-later-school-start-times

National Sleep Foundation. (2009a). Backgrounder: Later school start times. Available at http://www.sleepfoundation.org/article/hot-topics/backgrounder-later-school-start-times

National Sleep Foundation. (2009b). Children and sleep. Available at http://www.sleepfoundation.org/site/c.huIXKjM0IxF/b.4809577/k.BA8B/Children_and_Sleep.htm

Natsopoulos, D., Kiosseoglou, G., & Xeromeritou, A. (1992). Handedness and spatial ability in children: Further support for Geschwind's hypothesis of "pathology of superiority" and for Annett's theory of intelligence. *Genetic, Social, and General Psychology Monographs, 118*(1), 103–126.

Nauta, M. M. (2007). Career interests, self-efficacy, and personality as antecedents of career exploration. *Journal of Career Assessment, 15*(2), 162–180.

Naveh-Benjamin, M., Brav, T. K., & Levy, O. (2007). The associative memory deficit of older adults: The role of strategy utilization. *Psychology and Aging, 22*(1), 202–208.

Naveh-Benjamin, M., Hussain, Z., Guez, J., & Bar-On, M. (2003). Adult age differences in episodic memory: Further support for an associative-deficit hypothesis. *Journal of Experimental Psychology: Learning, Memory, and Cognition, 29*(5), 826–837.

Nduati, R., et al. (2000). Effect of breastfeeding and formula feeding on transmission of HIV-1. *Journal of the American Medical Association, 283*(9), 1167–1174.

Neisser, U., et al. (1996). Intelligence: Knowns and unknowns. *American Psychologist, 51*(1), 77–101.

Nelson, C. A., de Haan, M., & Thomas, K. M. (2006). *Neuroscience of cognitive development: The role of experience and the developing brain.* Hoboken, NJ: Wiley.

Nelson, C. A., & Luciana, M. (Eds.). (2001). *Handbook of developmental cognitive neuroscience.* Cambridge, MA: MIT Press.

Nelson, C. A., & Ludemann, P. M. (1989). Past, current, and future trends in infant face perception research. *Canadian Journal of Psychology, 43*(2), 183–198.

Nelson, K. (1973). Structure and strategy in learning to talk. *Monographs of the Society for Research in Child Development, 38*(1–2, ser. 149).

Nelson, K. (1981). Individual differences in language development: Implications for development of language. *Developmental Psychology, 17*(2), 170–187.

Nelson, K. (1990). Remembering, forgetting, and childhood amnesia. In R. Fivush & J. A. Hudson (Eds.), *Knowing and remembering in young children* (pp. 301–316). Cambridge: Cambridge University Press.

Nelson, K. (1993). Events, narratives, memory: What develops? In C. A. Nelson (Ed.), *Minnesota symposia on child psychology, Volume 26: Memory and affect in development* (pp. 1–24) Hillsdale, NJ: Erlbaum.

Nelson, K. (2005). Cognitive functions of language in early childhood. In B. D. Homer & C. S. Tamis-LeMonda (Eds.), *The development of social cognition and communication* (pp. 7–28). Hillsdale, NJ: Erlbaum.

Nelson, K. (2006). Advances in pragmatic developmental theory: The case of language acquisition. *Human Development, 49*(3), 184–188.

Nelson, K., & Fivush, R. (2004). The emergence of autobiographical memory: A social cultural developmental theory. *Psychological Review, 111*(2), 486–511.

Nesdale, D., & Lambert, A. (2007). Effects of experimentally manipulated peer rejection on children's negative affect, self-esteem, and maladaptive social behavior. *International Journal of Behavioral Development, 31*(2), 115–122.

New York Times/CBS News Poll, April 22–26, 2009. (2009, April 27). Available at http://graphics8.nytimes.com/packages/images/nytint/docs/new-york-times-cbs-news-poll-obama-s-100th-day-in-office/original.pdf

Newburn-Cook, C. V., et al. (2002). Where and to what extent is prevention of low birth weight possible? *Western Journal of Nursing Research, 24*(8), 887–904.

Newman, R., Ratner, N. B., Jusczyk, A. M., Jusczyk, P. W., & Dow, K. A. (2006). Infants' early ability to segment the conversational speech signal predicts later language development: A retrospective analysis. *Developmental Psychology, 42*(4), 643–655.

Neyer, F. J. (2002). Twin relationships in old age. *Journal of Social and Personal Relationships, 19*(2), 155–177.

Nielsen, S. J., & Palmer, B. (2003). Diagnosing eating disorders: AN, BN, and the others. *Acta Psychiatrica Scandinavica, 108*(3), 161–162.

Nielsen, S. J., & Popkin, B. M. (2003). Patterns and trends in food portion sizes, 1977–1998. *Journal of the American Medical Association, 289*(4), 450–453.

Niemeier, H. M., Raynor, H. A., Lloyd-Richardson, E. E., Rogers, M. L., & Wing, R. R. (2006). Fast food consumption and breakfast skipping: Predictors of weight gain from adolescence to adulthood in a nationally representative sample. *Journal of Adolescent Health, 39*(6), 842–849.

Nigg, J. T., Goldsmith, H. H., & Sachek, J. (2004). Temperament and attention deficit hyperactivity disorder: The development of a multiple pathway model. *Journal of Clinical Child and Adolescent Psychology, 33*(1), 42–53.

Nigg, J. T., Hinshaw, S. P., & Huang-Pollock, C. (2006). Disorders of attention and impulse regulation. In D. Cicchetti & D. J. Cohen (Eds.), *Developmental psychopathology, Volume 3: Risk, disorder, and adaptation* (2nd ed., pp. 358–403). Hoboken, NJ: Wiley.

Nimrod, G. (2007). Retirees' leisure. *Leisure Studies, 26*(1), 65–80.

Nisbett, R. E. (2007, December 9). All brains are the same color. *New York Times.* Available at http://www.nytimes.com

Nisbett, R. E. (2009). *Intelligence and how to get it: Why schools and cultures count.* New York: Norton.

Njus, D. M., & Bane, C. M. H. (2009). Religious identification as a moderator of evolved sexual strategies of men and women. *Journal of Sex Research, 46*(6), 546–557.

Noblitt, L., Vance, D. E., & Smith, M. L. D. (2010). A comparison of case study and traditional teaching methods for improvement of oral communication and critical-thinking skills. *Journal of College Science Teaching, 39*(5), 26–32.

Nock, M. K., Kazdin, A. E., Hiripi, E., & Kessler, R. C. (2006). Prevalence, subtypes, and correlates of DSM-IV conduct disorder in the National Comorbidity Survey Replication. *Psychological Medicine, 36*(5), 699–710.

Nolen-Hoeksema, S., Stice, E., Wade, E., & Bohon, C. (2007). Reciprocal relations between rumination and bulimic, substance abuse, and depressive symptoms in female adolescents. *Journal of Abnormal Psychology, 116*(1), 198–207.

Nomaguchi, K. M. (2006). Maternal employment, nonparental care, mother–child interactions, and child outcomes during preschool years. *Journal of Marriage and Family, 68*(5), 1341–1369.

Nonnemaker, J. M., & Homsi, G. (2007). Measurement properties of the Fagerström Test for nicotine dependence adapted for use in an adolescent sample. *Addictive Behaviors, 32*(1), 181–186.

Noppe, I. C., & Noppe, L. D. (2004). Adolescent experiences with death: Letting go of immortality. *Journal of Mental Health Counseling, 26*(2), 146–167.

Norton, A., et al. (2005). Are there pre-existing neural, cognitive, or motoric markers for musical ability? *Brain and Cognition, 59*(2), 124–134.

Nurnberg, H. G., et al. (2008). Sildenafil treatment of women with antidepressant-associated sexual dysfunction. *Journal of the American Medical Association, 300*(4), 395–404.

Nuttman-Shwartz, O. (2007). Is there life without work? *International Journal of Aging & Human Development, 64*(2), 129–147.

Oates, J., & Messer, D. (2007). Growing up with TV. *Psychologist, 20*(1), 30–32.

O'Boyle, M. W., & Benbow, C. P. (1990). Handedness and its relationship to ability and talent. In S. Coren (Ed.), *Left-handedness: Behavior implications and anomalies. Advances in Psychology, 67* (pp. 343–372): Oxford, England: Amsterdam: North-Holland.

O'Dea, J. A. (2006). Self-concept, self-esteem and body weight in adolescent females: A three-year longitudinal study. *Journal of Health Psychology, 11*(4), 599–611.

O'Doherty, J., et al. (2003). Beauty in a smile: The role of medial orbitofrontal cortex in facial attractiveness. *Neuropsychologia, 41*(2), 147–155.

O'Donnell, L., et al. (2003). Long-term influence of sexual norms and attitudes on timing of sexual initiation among urban minority youth. *Journal of School Health, 23*(2), 68–75.

Ogunfowora, O. B., Olanrewaju, D. M., & Akenzua, G. I. (2005). A comparative study of academic achievement of children with sickle cell anemia and their healthy siblings. *Journal of the National Medical Association, 97*(3), 405–408.

Ohnishi, T., Matsuda, H., Hirakata, M., & Ugawa, Y. (2006). Navigation ability dependent neural activation in the human brain: An fMRI study. *Neuroscience Research, 55*(4), 361–369.

O'Keeffe, M. J., O'Callaghan, M., Williams, G. M., Najman, J. M., & Bor, W. (2003). Learning, cognitive, and attentional problems in adolescents born small for gestational age. *Pediatrics, 112*(2), 301–307.

Ollendick, T. H., & King, N. J. (1991). Origins of childhood fears: An evaluation of Rachman's theory of teen-acquisition. *Behavior Research and Therapy, 29*(2), 117–123.

Olson, S. L., Bates, J. E., Sandy, J. M., & Lanthier, R. (2000). Early developmental precursors of externalizing behavior in middle childhood and adolescence. *Journal of Abnormal Child Psychology, 28*(2), 119–133.

Oltjenbruns, K. A., & Balk, D. E. (2007). Life span issues and loss, grief, and mourning: Part 1. The importance of a developmental context: Childhood and adolescence as an example. In D. Balk et al. (Eds.), *Handbook of thanatology* (pp. 143–163). New York: Routledge/Taylor & Francis Group.

Omori, M., & Ingersoll, G. M. (2005). Health-endangering behaviours among Japanese college students: A test of psychosocial model of risk-taking behaviours. *Journal of Adolescence, 28*(1), 17–33.

O'Neill, D. K., & Chong, S. C. F. (2001). Preschool children's difficulty understanding the types of information obtained through the five senses. *Child Development, 72*(3), 803–815.

O'Neill, D. K., & Gopnik, A. (1991). Young children's ability to identify the sources of their beliefs. *Developmental Psychology, 27*(3), 390–397.

Orel, N. (2006). Lesbian and bisexual women as grandparents: The centrality of sexual orientation in the grandparent–grandchild relationship. In D. Kimmel, T. Rose, & S. David (Eds.), *Lesbian, gay, bisexual, and transgender aging: Research and clinical perspectives* (pp. 175–194). New York: Columbia University Press.

Örnkloo, H., & von Hofsten, C. (2007). Fitting objects into holes: On the development of spatial cognition skills. *Developmental Psychology, 43*(2), 404–416.

Orstavik, R. E., Kendler, K. S., Czajkowski, N., Tambs, K., & Reichborn-Kjennerud, T. (2007). Genetic and environmental contributions to depressive personality disorder in a population-based sample of Norwegian twins. *Journal of Affective Disorders, 99*(1–3), 181–189.

Ortega, V., Ojeda, P., Sutil, F., & Sierra, J. C. (2005). Culpabilidad sexual en adolescentes: Estudio de algunos factores relacionados. *Anales de Psicología, 21*(2), 268–275.

O'Shea, R. P., & Corballis, P. M. (2005). Binocular rivalry in the divided brain. In D. Alais & R. Blake (Eds.), *Binocular rivalry* (pp. 301–315). Cambridge, MA: MIT Press.

Oster, H. (2005). The repertoire of infant facial expressions: An ontogenetic perspective. In J. Nadel & D. Muir (Eds.), *Emotional development: Recent research advances* (pp. 261–292). New York: Oxford University Press.

Ouellette, G. P. (2006). What's meaning got to do with it: The role of vocabulary in word reading and reading comprehension. *Journal of Educational Psychology, 98*(3), 554–566.

Oztop, E., Kawato, M., & Arbib, M. (2006). Mirror neurons and imitation: A computationally guided review. *Neural Networks, 19*(3), 254–271.

Paavola, L., Kemppinen, K., Kumpulainen, K., Moilanen, I., & Ebeling, H. (2006). Maternal sensitivity, infant co-operation and early linguistic development: Some predictive relations. *European Journal of Developmental Psychology, 3*(1), 13–30.

Page, K. (1999, May 16). The graduate. *Washington Post Magazine, 152*, pp. 18, 20.

Palmer, E. L. (2003). Realities and challenges in the rapidly changing televisual media landscape. In E. L. Palmer & B. M. Young (Eds.), *The faces of televisual media: Teaching, violence, selling to children* (2nd ed., pp. 361–377). Hillsdale, NJ: Erlbaum.

Pancsofar, N., & Vernon-Feagans, L. (2006). Mother and father language input to young children: Contributions to later language development.

Journal of Applied Developmental Psychology, 27(6), 571–587.

Park, H.-O. H., & Greenberg, J. S. (2007). Parenting grandchildren. In J. Blackburn & C. N. Dulmus (Eds.), *Handbook of gerontology: Evidence-based approaches to theory, practice, and policy* (pp. 397–425). Hoboken, NJ: Wiley.

Park, N. S., et al. (2008). Religiousness and longitudinal trajectories in elders' functional status. *Research on Aging, 30*(3), 279–298.

Parke, R. D., & Buriel, R. (2006). Socialization in the family: Ethnic and ecological perspectives. In N. Eisenberg, W. Damon, & R. M. Lerner (Eds.), *Handbook of child psychology* (6th ed.), *Volume 3: Social, emotional, and personality development* (pp. 429–504). Hoboken, NJ: Wiley.

Parten, M. B. (1932). Social participation among preschool children. *Journal of Abnormal and Social Psychology, 27*(3), 243–269.

Patel, M. M., et al. (2009). Broadening the age restriction for initiating rotavirus vaccination in regions with high rotavirus mortality: Benefits of mortality reduction versus risk of fatal intussusception. *Vaccine, 27*(22), 2916–2922.

Patenaude, J., Niyonsenga, T., & Fafard, D. (2003). Changes in students' moral development during medical school: A cohort study. *Canadian Medical Association Journal, 168*(7), 840–844.

Paterson, D. S., et al. (2006). Multiple serotonergic brainstem abnormalities in sudden infant death syndrome. *Journal of the American Medical Association, 296*(17), 2124–2132.

Patrick, S., Sells, J. N., Giordano, F. G., & Tollerud, T. R. (2007). Intimacy, differentiation, and personality variables as predictors of marital satisfaction. *Family Journal, 15*(4), 359–367.

Patterson, C. J. (2006). Children of lesbian and gay parents. *Current Directions in Psychological Science, 15*(5), 241–244.

Patterson, G. R. (2005). The next generation of PMTO models. *Behavior Therapist, 28*(2), 27–33.

Patterson, M. M., & Bigler, R. S. (2006). Preschool children's attention to environmental messages about groups: Social categorization and the origins of intergroup bias. *Child Development, 77*(4), 847–860.

Pauli-Pott, U., Mertesacker, B., & Beckmann, D. (2003). Ein Fragebogen zur Erfassung des frühkindlichen Temperaments im Elternurteil. *Zeitschrift für Kinder- und Jugendpsychiatrie und Psychotherapie, 31*(2), 99–110.

Paulussen-Hoogeboom, M. C., Stams, G. J. J. M., Hermanns, J. M. A., & Peetsma, T. T. D. (2007). Child negative emotionality and parenting from

infancy to preschool: A meta-analytic review. *Developmental Psychology, 43*(2), 438–453.

Paus, T., et al. (1999). Structural maturation of neural pathways in children and adolescents: In vivo study. *Science, 283*(5409), 1908–1911.

Pawaskar, M. D., & Sansgiry, S. S. (2006). Over-the-counter medication labels: Problems and needs of the elderly population. *Journal of the American Geriatrics Society, 54*(12), 1955–1956.

Paxton, S. J., Neumark-Sztainer, D., Hannan, P. J., & Eisenberg, M. E. (2006). Body dissatisfaction prospectively predicts depressive mood and low self-esteem in adolescent girls and boys. *Journal of Clinical Child and Adolescent Psychology, 35*(4), 539–549.

Paxton, S. J., Norris, M., Wertheim, E. H., Durkin, S. J., & Anderson, J. (2005). Body dissatisfaction, dating, and importance of thinness to attractiveness in adolescent girls. *Sex Roles, 53*(9–10), 663–675.

Peck, R. C. (1968). Psychological developments in the second half of life. In B. L. Neugarten (Ed.), *Middle age and aging* (pp. 88–92). Chicago: University of Chicago Press.

Pelphrey, K. A., et al. (2004). Development of visuospatial short-term memory in the second half of the first year. *Developmental Psychology, 40*(5), 836–851.

Pemberton, E. F. (1990). Systematic errors in children's drawings. *Cognitive Development, 5*(4), 395–404.

Penn, H. E. (2006). Neurobiological correlates of autism: A review of recent research. *Child Neuropsychology, 12*(1), 57–79.

Pereira, B., Mendonça, D., Neto, C., Valente, L., & Smith, P. K. (2004). Bullying in Portuguese schools. *School Psychology International, 25*(2), 241–254.

Perls, T. T. (2005). The oldest old. *Scientific American, 272*(1), 70–75.

Perls, T. T., et al. (2002). Life-long sustained mortality advantage of siblings of centenarians. *Proceedings of the National Academy of Sciences, 99*, 8442–8447.

Perren, S., & Alsaker, F. D. (2006). Social behavior and peer relationships of victims, bully-victims, and bullies in kindergarten. *Journal of Child Psychology and Psychiatry, 47*(1), 45–57.

Perrig-Chiello, P., Perrig, W. J., Uebelbacher, A., & Stähelin, H. B. (2006). Impact of physical and psychological resources on functional autonomy in old age. *Psychology, Health & Medicine, 11*(4), 470–482.

Perrone, K. M., Webb, L. K., & Jackson, Z. V. (2007). Relationships between parental attachment,

work and family roles, and life satisfaction. *Career Development Quarterly, 55*(3), 237–248.

Perry, P. J., et al. (2001). Bioavailable testosterone as a correlate of cognition, psychological status, quality of life, and sexual function in aging males: Implications for testosterone replacement therapy. *Annals of Clinical Psychiatry, 13*(2), 75–80.

Perry, W. G. (1970/1998). *Forms of intellectual and ethical development in the college years: A scheme.* New York: Holt, Rinehart and Winston.

Perry, W. G. (1981). Cognitive and ethical growth: The making of meaning. In A. W. Chickering & Assoc. (Eds.), *The modern American college* (pp. 76–116). San Francisco: Jossey-Bass.

Perry-Jenkins, M., Goldberg, A. E., Pierce, C. P., & Sayer, A. G. (2007). Shift work, role overload, and the transition to parenthood. *Journal of Marriage and Family, 69*(1), 123–138.

Persson, G. E. B. (2005). Developmental perspectives on prosocial and aggressive motives in preschoolers' peer interactions. *International Journal of Behavioral Development, 29*(1), 80–91.

Philip, J., et al. (2004). Late first-trimester invasive prenatal diagnostic results of an international randomized trial. *Obstetrics & Gynecology, 103*(6), 1164–1173.

Phillips, D. A., & Styfco, S. J. (2007). Child development research and public policy: Triumphs and setbacks on the way to maturity. In J. L. Aber et al. (Eds.), *Child development and social policy: Knowledge for action* (pp. 11–27). APA Decade of Behavior volumes. Washington, DC: American Psychological Association.

Phipps, M. G., Blume, J. D., & DeMonner, S. M. (2002). Young maternal age associated with increased risk of postneonatal death. *Obstetrics and Gynecology, 100*, 481–486.

Physical Activity Fact Sheet. (2005). President's Council on Physical Fitness and Sports, Department of Human Services. Available at http://www.fitness.gov/resources_factsheet.htm

Piaget, J. (1932). *The moral judgment of the child.* London: Kegan Paul.

Piaget, J. (1936/1963). *The origins of intelligence in children.* New York: Norton.

Piaget, J. (1946/1962). *Play, dreams, and imitation in childhood.* New York: Norton.

Piaget, J. (1976). *The grasp of consciousness: Action and concept in the young child.* Cambridge, MA: Harvard University Press.

Piaget, J., & Inhelder, B. (1962). *Le développement des quantités physiques chez l'enfant* (2nd rev. ed.). Neuchâtel, Switzerland: Delachaux & Niestle.

Pichichero, M. E. (2006). Prevention of cervical cancer through vaccination of adolescents. *Clinical Pediatrics, 45*(5), 393–398.

Piek, J. P. (2006). *Infant motor development.* Champaign, IL: Human Kinetics.

Pierce, K. M., & Vandell, D. L. (2006). Child care. In G. G. Bear & K. M. Minke (Eds.), *Children's needs III: Development, prevention, and intervention* (pp. 721–732). Washington, DC: National Association of School Psychologists.

Pine, D. S., et al. (2001). Fluvoxamine for the treatment of anxiety disorders in children and adolescents. *New England Journal of Medicine, 344*(17), 1279–1285.

Pinker, S. (1994). *The language instinct.* New York: William Morrow.

Pinker, S., & Jackendoff, R. (2005). The faculty of language: What's special about it? *Cognition, 95*(2), 201–236.

Pinquart, M., & Schindler, I. (2007). Changes of life satisfaction in the transition to retirement. *Psychology and Aging, 22*(3), 442–455.

Plomin, R. (Ed.). (2002). *Behavioral genetics in the postgenomic era.* Washington, DC: American Psychological Association.

Plomin, R., Owen, M. J., & McGuffin, P. (1994). The genetic basis of complex human behaviors. *Science, 264*(5166), 1733–1739.

Plomin, R., & Walker, S. O. (2003). Genetics and educational psychology. *British Journal of Educational Psychology, 73*(1), 3–14.

Polivy, J., Herman, C. P., & Boivin, M. (2005). Eating disorders. In J. E. Maddux & B. A. Winstead (Eds.), *Psychopathology: Foundations for a contemporary understanding* (pp. 229–254). Hillsdale, NJ: Erlbaum.

Poltorak, D. Y., & Glazer, J. P. (2006). The development of children's understanding of death. *Child and Adolescent Psychiatric Clinics of North America, 15*(3), 567–573.

Popma, A., et al. (2007). Cortisol moderates the relationship between testosterone and aggression in delinquent male adolescents. *Biological Psychiatry, 61*(3), 405–411.

Porfeli, E. J. (2007). Work values system development during adolescence. *Journal of Vocational Behavior, 70*(1), 42–60.

Porter, R. H., Makin, J. W., Davis, L. B., & Christensen, K. M. (1992). Breast-fed infants respond to olfactory cues from their own mother and unfamiliar lactating females. *Infant Behavior and Development, 15*(1), 85–93.

Posey, D. J., et al. (2007). Positive effects of methylphenidate on inattention and hyperactivity in pervasive developmental disorders: An analysis of secondary measures. *Biological Psychiatry, 61*(4), 538–544.

Posner, M. I., & Rothbart, M. K. (2007). *Relating brain and mind: Educating the human brain.* Washington, DC: American Psychological Association.

Powlishta, K. K. (2004). Gender as a social category: Intergroup processes and gender-role development. In M. Bennett & F. Sani (Eds.), *The development of the social self* (pp. 103–133). New York: Psychology Press.

Powlishta, K. K., Sen, M. G., Serbin, L. A., Poulin-Dubois, D., & Eichstedt, J. A. (2001). From infancy through middle childhood: The role of cognitive and social factors in becoming gendered. In R. K. Unger (Ed.), *Handbook of the psychology of women and gender* (pp. 116–132). Hoboken, NJ: Wiley.

Pratt, C., & Bryant, P. (1990). Young children understand that looking leads to knowing (so long as they are looking into a single barrel). *Child Development, 61*(4), 973–982.

Pressley, M., & Hilden, K. (2006). Cognitive strategies. In D. Kuhn, R. S. Siegler, W. Damon, & R. M. Lerner (Eds.), *Handbook of child psychology* (6th ed.), *Volume 2: Cognition, perception, and language* (pp. 511–556). Hoboken, NJ: Wiley.

Pressman, S. D., et al. (2005). Loneliness, social network size, and immune response to influenza vaccination in college freshmen. *Health Psychology, 24*(3), 297–306.

Priner, R., Freeman, S., Perez, R., & Sohmer, H. (2003). The neonate has a temporary conductive hearing loss due to fluid in the middle ear. *Audiology & Neurotology, 8*(2), 100–110.

Provence, S., & Lipton, R. C. (1962). *Infants in institutions.* New York: International Universities Press.

Proverbio, A. M., Riva, F., & Zani, A. (2010). When neurons do not mirror the agent's intentions: Sex differences in neural coding of goal-directed actions. *Neuropsychologia, 48*(5), 1454–1463.

Prull, M. W., Gabrieli, J. D. E., & Bunge, S. A. (2000). In F. I. M. Craik & T. A. Salthouse (Eds.), *Age-related changes in memory: A cognitive neuroscience perspective. The handbook of aging and cognition* (2nd ed., pp. 91–153). Hillsdale, NJ:Erlbaum.

Puente, S., & Cohen, D. (2003). Jealousy and the meaning (or nonmeaning) of violence. *Personality & Social Psychology Bulletin, 29*(4), 449–460.

Pujol, J., et al. (2006). Myelination of language-related areas in the developing brain. *Neurology, 66*(3), 339–343.

Pulverman, R., Hirsh-Pasek, K., Golinkoff, R. M., Pruden, S., & Salkind, S. J. (2006). Conceptual foundations for verb learning: Celebrating the event. In K. Hirsh-Pasek & R. M. Golinkoff (Eds.), *Action meets word: How children learn verbs* (pp. 134–159). New York: Oxford University Press.

Qin, W., et al. (2006). Calorie restriction attenuates Alzheimer's disease type brain amyloidosis in squirrel monkeys (*Saimiri sciureus*). *Journal of Alzheimer's Disease, 10*(4), 417–422.

Quigley, N. R., & Tymon, W. G., Jr. (2006). Toward an integrated model of intrinsic motivation and career self management. *Career Development International, 11*(6), 522–543.

Quinsey, V. L., et al. (2006). Sex offenders. In V. L. Quinsey et al. (Eds.), *Violent offenders: Appraising and managing risk* (2nd ed., pp. 131–151). Washington, DC: American Psychological Association.

Rabin, R. C. (2007, August 28). For a low-dose hormone, take your pick. *New York Times.* Available at http://www.nytimes.com

Radvansky, G. A., Zacks, R. T., & Hasher, L. (2005). Age and inhibition: The retrieval of situation models. *Journals of Gerontology: Series B: Psychological Sciences and Social Sciences, 60B*(5), P276–P278.

Raikes, H., et al. (2006). Mother–child bookreading in low-income families: Correlates and outcomes during the first three years of life. *Child Development, 77*(4), 924–953.

Ramey, C. T., Campbell, F. A., & Ramey, S. L. (1999). Early intervention: Successful pathways to improving intellectual development. *Developmental Neuropsychology, 16*(3), 385–392.

Randel, B., Stevenson, H. W., & Witruk, E. (2000). Attitudes, beliefs, and mathematics achievement of German and Japanese high school students. *International Journal of Behavioral Development, 24*(2), 190–198.

Rapin, I. (1997). Autism. *New England Journal of Medicine, 337*(2), 97–104.

Rathus, J. H., & Miller, A. L. (2002). Dialectical Behavior Therapy adapted for suicidal adolescents. *Suicide and Life-Threatening Behavior, 32*(2), 146–157.

Rathus, S. A., Fichner-Rathus, L., & Nevid, J. S. (2011). *Human sexuality in a world of diversity* (8th ed.). Boston: Allyn & Bacon.

Rattan, S. I. S., Kristensen, P., & Clark, B. F. C. (Eds.). (2006). *Understanding and modulating aging.* Malden, MA: Blackwell.

Rebar, R. W., & DeCherney, A. H. (2004). Assisted reproductive technology in the United States. *New England Journal of Medicine, 350*(16), 1603–1604.

Reddy, H. & Burton, R. (1971). "I Am Woman". Copyright Irving Music, Inc., and Buggerlugs Music Co.

Reddy, L. A., & De Thomas, C. (2007). Assessment of attention-deficit/hyperactivity disorder with children. In S. R. Smith & L. Handler (Eds.), *The clinical assessment of children and adolescents: A practitioner's handbook* (pp. 365–387). Hillsdale, NJ: Erlbaum.

Redshaw, M., & van den Akker, O. (2007). Editorial. *Journal of Reproductive and Infant Psychology, 25*(2), 103–105.

Reece, M., Herbenick, D., Schick, V., Sanders, S. A., Dodge, B., & Fortenberry, J. D. (2010). Sexual behaviors, relationships, and perceived health among adult men in the United States: Results from a national probability sample. *Journal of Sexual Medicine, 7*(Supp. 5), 291–304.

Reef, S., Zimmerman-Swain, L., & Coronado, V. (2004). Disease description: Rubella is a viral illness caused by a togavirus of the genus *Rubivirus.* Available at http://www-r.gluetext.com/content/r/Rubella/Rubella_immunization.html

Rees, S., Harding, R., & Inder, T. (2006). The developmental environment and the origins of neurological disorders. In P. Gluckman & M. Hanson (Eds.), *Developmental origins of health and disease* (pp. 379–391). New York: Cambridge University Press.

Reif, L. V., Patton, M. J., & Gold, P. B. (1995). Bereavement, stress, and social support in members of a self-help group. *Journal of Community Psychology, 23*(4) 292-306.

Reijneveld, S. A., et al. (2004). Infant crying and abuse. *Lancet, 364*(9442), 1340–1342.

Reis, O., & Youniss, J. (2004). Patterns in identity change and development in relationships with mothers and friends. *Journal of Adolescent Research, 19*(1), 31–44.

Reitzes, D. C., & Mutran, E. J. (2004). The transition to retirement. *International Journal of Aging & Human Development, 59*(1), 63–84.

Reitzes, D. C., & Mutran, E. J. (2006). Lingering identities in retirement. *Sociological Quarterly, 47*(2), 333–359.

Rendell, P. G., Castel, A. D., & Craik, F. I. M. (2005). Memory for proper names in old age: A disproportionate impairment? *Quarterly Journal of Experimental Psychology A: Human Experimental Psychology, 58A*(1), 54–71.

Reschly, A., & Christenson, S. L. (2006). School completion. In G. G. Bear & K. M. Minke (Eds.), *Children's needs III: Development, prevention, and intervention* (pp. 103–113). Washington, DC: National Association of School Psychologists.

Rest, J. R. (1983). Morality. In P. H. Mussen (Ed.), *Handbook of child psychology, Volume 3: Cognitive development* (pp. 556–629). Hoboken, NJ: Wiley.

Retsinas, J. (1988). A theoretical reassessment of the applicability of Kübler-Ross's stages of dying. *Death Studies, 12*(3), 207–216.

Reynolds, C. A., Barlow, T., & Pedersen, N. L. (2006). Alcohol, tobacco and caffeine use: Spouse similarity processes. *Behavior Genetics, 36*(2), 201–215.

Rice, C. E., et al. (2007). A public health collaboration for the surveillance of autism spectrum disorders. *Paediatric and Perinatal Epidemiology, 21*(2), 179–190.

Richards, J. C., Hof, A., & Alvarenga, M. (2000). Serum lipids and their relationships with hostility and angry affect and behaviors in men. *Health Psychology, 19*(4), 393–398.

Rietjens, J., et al. (2008). Continuous deep sedation for patients nearing death in the Netherlands: Descriptive study. *British Medical Journal, 336*(7648), 810–813.

Riggio, R. E., & Woll, S. B. (1984). The role of nonverbal cues and physical attractiveness in the selection of dating partners. *Journal of Social and Personal Relationships, 1*(3), 347–357.

Rizzolatti, G., Fadiga, L., Fogassi, L., & Gallese, V. (2002). From mirror neurons to imitation: Facts and speculations. In A. N. Meltzoff & W. Prinz (Eds.), *The imitative mind: Development, evolution, and brain bases* (pp. 19–41). New York: Cambridge University Press.

Roberts, B. W., & DelVecchio, W. F. (2000). The rank-order consistency of personality traits from childhood to old age: A quantitative review of longitudinal studies. *Psychological Bulletin, 126*(1), 3–25.

Roberts, B. W., Walton, K. E., & Viechtbauer, W. (2006). Patterns of mean-level change in personality traits across the life course: A meta-analysis of longitudinal studies. *Psychological Bulletin, 132*(1), 1–25.

Roberts, R. E., Roberts, C. R., & Duong, H. T. (2009). Sleepless in adolescence: Prospective data on sleep deprivation, health and functioning. *Journal of Adolescence, 32*(5), 1045–1057.

Robins, R. W., & Trzesniewski, K. H. (2005). Self-esteem development across the lifespan. *Current Directions in Psychological Science, 14*(3), 158–162.

Robins, R. W., Trzesniewski, K. H., Tracy, J. L., Gosling, S. D., & Potter, J. (2002). Global self-esteem across the lifespan. *Psychology and Aging, 17*(3), 423–434.

Robins Wahlin, T., Lundin, A., & Dear, K. (2007). Early cognitive deficits in Swedish gene carriers of Huntington's disease. *Neuropsychology, 21*(1), 31–44.

Roebers, C. M., & Schneider, W. (2002). Stability and consistency of children's event recall. *Cognitive Development, 17*(1), 1085–1103.

Roeser, R. W., Peck, S. C., & Nasir, N. S. (2006). Self and identity processes in school motivation, learning, and achievement. In P. A. Alexander & P. H. Winne (Eds.), *Handbook of educational psychology* (pp. 391–424). Hillsdale, NJ: Erlbaum.

Roffwarg, H. P., Muzio, J. N., & Dement, W. C. (1966). Ontogenetic development of the human sleep–dream cycle. *Science, 152*(3722), 604–619.

Ronald, A., et al. (2006). Genetic heterogeneity between the three components of the autism spectrum: A twin study. *Journal of the American Academy of Child & Adolescent Psychiatry, 45*(6), 691–699.

Rondal, J. A., & Ling, L. (2006). Neurobehavioral specificity in Down's syndrome. *Revista de Logopedia, Foniatría y Audiología, 26*(1), 12–19.

Roopnarine, J. L., Krishnakumar, A., Metindogan, A., & Evans, M. (2006). Links between parenting styles, parent–child academic interaction, parent–school interaction, and early academic skills and social behaviors in young children of English-speaking Caribbean immigrants. *Early Childhood Research Quarterly, 21*(2), 238–252.

Rose, A. J., Swenson, L. P., & Carlson, W. (2004). Friendships of aggressive youth: Considering the influences of being disliked and of being perceived as popular. *Journal of Experimental Child Psychology, 88*(1), 25–45.

Rose, S. A., Feldman, J. F., & Jankowski, J. J. (2001). Visual short-term memory in the first year of life: Capacity and recency effects. *Developmental Psychology, 37*(4), 539–549.

Rose, S. A., Feldman, J. F., & Jankowski, J. J. (2004). Infant visual recognition memory. *Developmental Review, 24*(1), 74–100.

Rose, S. A., Feldman, J. F., & Jankowski, J. J. (2005). The structure of infant cognition at 1 year. *Intelligence, 33*(3), 231–250.

Rose, S. A., Feldman, J. F., & Wallace, I. F. (1992). Infant information processing in relation to six-year cognitive outcomes. *Child Development, 63*(5), 1126–1141.

Rosen, T., Pillemer, K., & Lachs, M. (2008). Resident-to-resident aggression in long-term care facilities. *Aggression and Violent Behavior, 13*(2), 77–87.

Rosenstein, D., & Oster, H. (1988). Differential facial responses to four basic tastes. *Child Development, 59*(6), 1555–1568.

Rosenthal, R., & Jacobson, L. (1968). *Pygmalion in the classroom.* New York: Holt, Rinehart & Winston.

Rospenda, K. M., et al. (2005). Is workplace harassment hazardous to your health? *Journal of Business and Psychology, 20*(1), 95–110.

Ross, H., Ross, M., Stein, N., & Trabasso, T. (2006). How siblings resolve their conflicts: The importance of first offers, planning, and limited opposition. *Child Development, 77*(6), 1730–1745.

Ross, J. L., Roeltgen, D., Feuillan, P., Kushner, H., & Cutler, W. B. (2000). Use of estrogen in young girls with Turner syndrome: Effects on memory. *Neurology, 54*(1), 164–170.

Rotenberg, K. J., et al. (2004). Cross-sectional and longitudinal relations among peer-reported trustworthiness, social relationships, and psychological adjustment in children and early adolescents from the United Kingdom and Canada. *Journal of Experimental Child Psychology, 88*(1), 46–67.

Roth, G. S., et al. (2004). Aging in rhesus monkeys: Relevance to human health interventions. *Science, 305*(5689), 1423–1426.

Rothbart, M. K., Ellis, L. K., & Posner, M. I. (2004). Temperament and self-regulation. In R. F. Baumeister & K. D. Vohs (Eds.), *Handbook of self-regulation: Research, theory, and applications* (pp. 357–370). New York: Guilford.

Rothbart, M. K., & Sheese, B. E. (2007). Temperament and emotion regulation. In J. J. Gross (Ed.), *Handbook of emotion regulation* (pp. 331–350). New York: Guilford.

Rottinghaus, P. J., Betz, N. E., & Borgen, F. H. (2003). Validity of parallel measures of vocational interests and confidence. *Journal of Career Assessment, 11*(4), 355–378.

Rottinghaus, P. J., Coon, K. L., Gaffey, A. R., & Zytowski, D. G. (2007). Thirty-year stability and predictive validity of vocational interests. *Journal of Career Assessment, 15*(1), 5–22.

Roulet-Perez, E., & Deonna, T. (2006). Autism, epilepsy, and EEG epileptiform activity. In R. Tuchman & I. Rapin (Eds.), *Autism: A neu-rological disorder of early brain development* (pp. 174–188). London: Mac Keith Press.

Rovee-Collier, C. (1993). The capacity for long-term memory in infancy. *Current Directions in Psychological Science, 2*(4), 130–135.

Rowen, B. (1973). *The children we see.* New York: Holt, Rinehart & Winston.

Rubia, K., et al. (2006). Progressive increase of frontostriatal brain activation from childhood to adulthood during event-related tasks of cognitive control. *Human Brain Mapping, 27*(12), 973–993.

Rubin, K. H., Bukowski, W. M., & Parker, J. G. (2006). Peer interactions, relationships, and groups. In N. Eisenberg, W. Damon, & R. M. Lerner (Eds.), *Handbook of child psychology* (6th ed.), *Volume 3: Social, emotional, and personality development* (pp. 571–645). Hoboken, NJ: Wiley.

Ruble, D. N., Martin, C. L., & Berenbaum, S. A. (2006). Gender development. In N. Eisenberg, W. Damon, & R. M. Lerner (Eds.), *Handbook of child psychology* (6th ed.), *Volume 3: Social, emotional, and personality development*. (pp. 858–932). Hoboken, NJ: Wiley.

Ruchkin, V., & Vermeiren, R. (2006). Juvenile justice. *Child and Adolescent Psychiatric Clinics of North America, 15*(2), xix–xxii.

Rudolph, K. D., & Flynn, M. (2007). Childhood adversity and youth depression: Influence of gender and pubertal status. *Development and Psychopathology, 19*(2), 497–521.

Rudolph, K. D., Lambert, S. F., Clark, A. G., & Kurlakowsky, K. D. (2001). Negotiating the transition to middle school: The role of self-regulatory processes. *Child Development, 72*(3), 929–946.

Rudy, D., & Grusec, J. E. (2006). Authoritarian parenting in individualist and collectivist groups: Associations with maternal emotion and cognition and children's self-esteem. *Journal of Family Psychology, 20*(1), 68–78.

Rumbold, A. R., et al. (2006). Vitamins C and E and the risks of preeclampsia and perinatal complications. *New England Journal of Medicine, 354*(17), 1796–1806.

Runyon, M. K., & Kenny, M. C. (2002). Relationship of attributional style, depression, and posttrauma distress among children who suffered physical or sexual abuse. *Child Maltreatment: Journal of the American Professional Society on the Abuse of Children, 7*(3), 254–264.

Rusconi, A. (2004). Different pathways out of the parental home: A comparison of West Germany and Italy. *Journal of Comparative Family Studies, 35*(4), 627–649.

Rushton, J. P., Skuy, M., & Fridjhon, P. (2003). Performance on Raven's Advanced Progressive Matrices by African, East Indian, and White engineering students in South Africa. *Intelligence, 31*(2), 123–137.

Russ, S. W. (2006). Pretend play, affect, and creativity. In P. Locher, C. Martindale, & L. Dorfman (Eds.), *New directions in aesthetics, creativity and the arts: Foundations and frontiers in aesthetics* (pp. 239–250). Amityville, NY: Baywood.

Russell, J. E. A. (2008). Promoting subjective well-being at work. *Journal of Career Assessment, 16*(1), 117–131.

Russell, S.T. (2006). Substance use and abuse and mental health among sexual-minority youths: Evidence from Add Health. In A. M. Omoto & H. S. Kurtzman (Eds.), *Sexual orientation and mental health: Examining identity and development in lesbian, gay, and bisexual people* (pp. 13–35). Washington, DC: American Psychological Association.

Rutter, M. (2006). The psychological effects of early institutional rearing. In P. J. Marshall & N. A. Fox (Eds.), *The development of social engagement: Neurobiological perspectives* (pp. 355–391). Series in affective science. New York: Oxford University Press.

Ryan, R. M., & Deci, E. L. (2000). Self-determination theory and the facilitation of intrinsic motivation, social development, and well-being. *American Psychologist, 55*(1), 68–78.

Rybash, J. M., & Hrubi-Bopp, K. L. (2000). Source monitoring and false recollection: A life span developmental perspective. *Experimental Aging Research, 26*(1), 75–87.

Ryff, C. D., Singer, B. H., & Seltzer, M. M. (2002). Pathways through challenge: Implications for well-being and health. In L. Pulkkinen & A. Caspi (Eds.), *Paths to successful development: Personality in the life course* (pp. 302–328). New York: Cambridge University Press.

Saaristo-Helin, K., Savinainen-Makkonen, T., & Kunnari, S. (2006). The phonological mean length of utterance: Methodological challenges from a crosslinguistic perspective. *Journal of Child Language, 33*(1), 179–190.

Sabattini, L., & Leaper, C. (2004). The relation between mothers' and fathers' parenting styles and their division of labor in the home: Young adults' retrospective reports. *Sex Roles, 50*(3–4), 217–225.

Sabia, J. J. (2008). There's no place like home: A hazard model analysis of aging in place among older homeowners in the PSID. *Research on Aging, 30*(1), 3–35.

Sadker, D. M., & Silber, E. S. (Eds.) (2007). *Gender in the classroom: Foundations, skills, methods, and strategies across the curriculum.* Hillsdale, NJ: Erlbaum.

Sadler, T. W. (Ed.). (2005). Abstracts of papers presented at the thirty-fifth annual meeting the Japanese Teratology Society, Tokyo, Japan. *Teratology, 52*(4), b1–b51.

Saffran, J. R., Werker, J. F., & Werner, L. A. (2006). The infant's auditory world: Hearing, speech, and the beginnings of language. In D. Kuhn, R. S. Siegler, W. Damon, & R. M. Lerner (Eds.), *Handbook of child psychology, Volume 2: Cognition, perception, and language* (6th ed., pp. 58–108). Hoboken, NJ: Wiley.

Saggino, A., Perfetti, B., Spitoni, G., & Galati, G. (2006). Fluid intelligence and executive functions: New perspectives. In L. V. Wesley (Ed.), *Intelligence: New research* (pp. 1–22). Hauppauge, NY: Nova Science Publishers.

Saigal, S., et al. (2006). Transition of extremely low-birth-weight infants from adolescence to young adulthood: Comparison with normal birth-weight controls. *Journal of the American Medical Association, 295*(6), 667–675.

Saiki, J., & Miyatsuji, H. (2007). Feature binding in visual working memory evaluated by type identification paradigm. *Cognition, 102*(1), 49–83.

Saito, S., & Miyake, A. (2004). On the nature of forgetting and the processing–storage relationship in reading span performance. *Journal of Memory and Language, 50*(4), 425–443.

Salapatek, P. (1975). Pattern perception in early infancy. In L. B. Cohen & P. Salapatek (Eds.), *Infant perception: From sensation to cognition, Volume 1: Basic visual processes* (pp. 133–248). New York: Academic Press.

Sales, J. M., Fivush, R., & Peterson, C. (2003). Parental reminiscing about positive and negative events. *Journal of Cognition and Development, 4*(2), 185–209.

Salmivalli, C., Ojanen, T., Haanpää, J., & Peets, K. (2005). "I'm OK but you're not" and other peer-relational schemas: Explaining individual differences in children's social goals. *Developmental Psychology, 41*(2), 363–375.

Salthouse, T. A. (2001). Structural models of the relations between age and measures of cognitive functioning. *Intelligence, 29*(2), 93–115.

Salthouse, T. A., & Babcock, R. L. (1991). Decomposing adult age differences in working memory. *Developmental Psychology, 27*(5), 763–776.

Salthouse, T. A., & Berish, D. E. (2005). Correlates of within-person (across-occasion) variability in reaction time. *Neuropsychology, 19*(1), 77–87.

Salthouse, T. A., & Davis, H. P. (2006). Organization of cognitive abilities and neuropsychological variables across the lifespan. *Developmental Review, 26*(1), 31–54.

Salthouse, T. A., & Siedlecki, K. L. (2007). Efficiency of route selection as a function of adult age. *Brain and Cognition, 63*(3), 279–286.

Salthouse, T. A., Siedlecki, K. L., & Krueger, L. E. (2006). An individual differences analysis of memory control. *Journal of Memory and Language, 55*(1), 102–125.

Salzarulo, P., & Ficca, G. (Eds.). (2002). *Awakening and sleep–wake cycle across development.* Amsterdam: John Benjamins.

Sandman, C., & Crinella, F. (1995). Cited in Margoshes, P. (1995). For many, old age is the prime of life. *APA Monitor, 26*(5), 36–37.

Santelli, J. S., et al. (2003). Reproductive health in school-based health centers: Findings from the 1998–99 census of school-based health centers. *Journal of Adolescent Health, 32*(6), 443–451.

Santelli, J. S., Lindberg, J. D., Abma, J., McNeely, C. S., & Resnick, M. (2000). Adolescent sexual behavior: Estimates and trends from four nationally representative surveys. *Family Planning Perspectives, 32*(4), 156–165, 194.

Santos, D. C. C., Gabbard, C., & Goncalves, V. M. G. (2000). Motor development during the first 6 months: The case of Brazilian infants. *Infant and Child Development, 9*(3), 161–166.

Saroglou, V., & Galand, P. (2004). Identities, values, and religion: A study among Muslim, other immigrant, and native Belgian young adults after the 9/11 attacks. *Identity, 4*(2), 97–132.

Sarrazin, P., Trouilloud, D., & Bois, J. (2005). Attentes du superviseur et performance sportive du pratiquant: Amplitude et fonctionnement de l'effet Pygmalion en contexte sportif. *Bulletin de Psychologie, 58*(1), 63–68.

Sarrazin, P., Trouilloud, D., Tessier, D., Chanal, J., & Bois, J. (2005). Attentes de motivation et comportements différenciés de l'enseignant d'éducation physique et sportive à l'égard de ses élèves: Une étude en contexte naturel d'enseignement. *Revue Européenne de Psychologie Appliquée, 55*(2), 111–120.

Sasaki, C. (2007). Grounded-theory study of therapists' perceptions of grieving process in bereaved children [Abstract]. *Dissertation Abstracts International: Section B: The Sciences and Engineering, 68*(1-B), 635.

Saudino, K. J., & Eaton, W. O. (1993, March). *Genetic influences on activity level, II. An analysis of continuity and change from infancy to early childhood.* Paper presented at the meeting of the Society for Research in Child Development, New Orleans, LA.

Sava, S., & Yurgelun-Todd, D. A. (2008). Functional magnetic resonance in psychiatry. *Topics in Magnetic Resonance Imaging, 19*(2), 71–79.

Save the Children. (2004). *State of the world's mothers 2004.* Available at http://www.savethechildren.org/atf/cf/{9def2ebe-10ae-432c-9bd0-df91d2eba74a}/SOWM_2004_final.pdf

Save the Children. (2008). *State of the world's mothers 2008.* Available at http://www.savethechildren.org/publications/mothers/2008/SOWM-2008-full-report.pdf

Savickas, M. L. (2005). The theory and practice of career construction. In S. D. Brown & R. W. Lent (Eds.), *Career development and counseling* (pp. 42–70). Hoboken, NJ: Wiley.

Savin-Williams, R. C. (2007). Girl-on-girl sexuality. In B. J. R. Leadbeater & N. Way (Eds.), *Urban girls revisited: Building strengths* (pp. 301–318). New York: New York University Press.

Savin-Williams, R. C., & Berndt, T. (1990). Friendship and peer relations. In S. S. Feldman & G. R. Elliott (Eds.), *At the threshold: The developing adolescent* (pp. 277–307). Cambridge, MA: Harvard University Press.

Savin-Williams, R. C., & Diamond, L. M. (2004). Sex. In R. M. Lerner & L. Steinberg (Eds.), *Handbook of adolescent psychology* (2nd ed., pp. 189–231). Hoboken, NJ: Wiley.

Sayegh, Y., & Dennis, W. (1965). The effect of supplementary experiences upon the behavioral development of infants in institutions. *Child Development, 36*(1), 81–90.

Scarr, S. (1993, March). *IQ correlations among members of transracial adoptive families.* Paper presented at the meeting of the Society for Research in Child Development, New Orleans, LA.

Schacter, D. I. (1992). Understanding implicit memory: A cognitive neuroscience approach. *American Psychologist, 47*(4), 559–569.

Schaffer, H. R., & Emerson, P. E. (1964). The development of social attachments in infancy. *Monographs of the Society for Research in Child Development, 29*(94).

Schaie, K. W. (1994). The course of adult intellectual development. *American Psychologist, 49*(4), 304–313.

Schaie, K. W. (2002). The impact of longitudinal studies on understanding development from young adulthood to old age. In W. W. Hartup & R. K. Silbereisen (Eds.), *Growing points in developmental science* (pp. 307–328). New York: Psychology Press.

Schaie, K. W. (2005). What can we learn from longitudinal studies of adult development? *Research in Human Development, 2*(3), 133–158.

Schaie, K. W., Willis, S. L., & Caskie, G. I. L. (2004). The Seattle longitudinal study: Relationship between personality and cognition. *Aging, Neuropsychology, and Cognition, 11*(2–3), 304–324.

Schaie, K. W., & Zanjani, F. A. K. (2006). Intellectual development across adulthood. In C. Hoare (Ed.), *Handbook of adult development and learning* (pp. 99–122). New York: Oxford University Press.

Scharf, M., Shulman, S., & Avigad-Spitz, L. (2005). Sibling relationships in emerging adulthood and in adolescence. *Journal of Adolescent Research, 20*(1), 64–90.

Scheithauer, H., Hayer, T., Petermann, F., & Jugert, G. (2006). Physical, verbal, and relational forms of bullying among German students: Age trends, gender differences, and correlates. *Aggressive Behavior, 32*(3), 261–275.

Scheres, A., & Castellanos, F. X. (2003). Assessment and treatment of childhood problems (2nd ed.): A clinician's guide. *Psychological Medicine, 33*(8), 1487–1488.

Schmidtke, A., Sell, R., & Lohr, C. (2008). Epidemiology of suicide in older persons. *Zeitschrift für Gerontologie und Geriatrie, 41*(1), 3–13.

Schmitt, D. P. (2008). An evolutionary perspective on mate choice and relationship initiation. In S. Sprecher, A. Wenzel, & J. H. Harvey (Eds.), *Handbook of relationship initiation* (pp. 55–74). New York: CRC Press.

Schneewind, K. A., & Kupsch, M. (2007). Patterns of neuroticism, work-family stress, and resources as determinants of personal distress: A cluster analysis of young, dual-earner families at the individual and couple level. *Journal of Individual Differences, 28*(3), 150–160.

Schonfeld, A. M., Mattson, S. N., & Riley, E. P. (2005). Moral maturity and delinquency after prenatal alcohol exposure. *Journal of Studies on Alcohol, 66*(4), 545–554.

Schoppe-Sullivan, S. J., Mangelsdorf, S. C., Brown, G. L., & Sokolowski, M. S. (2007). Goodness-of-fit in family context: Infant temperament, marital quality, and early coparenting behavior. *Infant Behavior & Development, 30*(1), 82–96.

Schraf, M., & Hertz-Lazarowitz, R. (2003). Social networks in the school context: Effects of culture and gender. *Journal of Social and Personal Relationships, 20*(6), 843–858.

Schuetze, P., Lawton, D., & Eiden, R. D. (2006). Prenatal cocaine exposure and infant sleep at 7 months of age: The influence of the caregiving environment. *Infant Mental Health Journal, 27*(4), 383–404.

Schuetze, P., Zeskind, P. S., & Eiden, R. D. (2003). The perceptions of infant distress signals varying in pitch by cocaine-using mothers. *Infancy, 4*(1), 65–83.

Schultz, D. P., & Schultz, S. E. (2008). *A history of modern psychology* (9th ed.). Belmont, CA: Thomson/Wadsworth.

Schultz, W. W., et al. (2005). Women's sexual pain and its management. *Journal of Sexual Medicine, 2*(3), 301–316.

Schumacher, D., & Queen, J. A. (2007). *Overcoming obesity in childhood and adolescence: A guide for school leaders.* Thousand Oaks, CA: Corwin Press.

Schuurmans, J., et al. (2006). A randomized, controlled trial of the effectiveness of cognitive-behavioral therapy and sertraline versus a wait-list control group for anxiety disorders in older adults. *American Journal of Geriatric Psychiatry, 14*(3), 255–263.

Schwartz, S. J. (2001). The evolution of Eriksonian and neo-Eriksonian identity theory and research: A review and integration. *Identity, 1*(1), 7–58.

Scott, J. R. (2006). Preventing eclampsia. *Obstetrics & Gynecology, 108*(4), 824–825.

Scourfield, J., Van den Bree, M., Martin, N., & McGuffin, P. (2004). Conduct problems in children and adolescents: A twin study. *Archives of General Psychiatry, 61*(5), 489–496.

Secker-Walker, R. H., & Vacek, P. M. (2003). Relationships between cigarette smoking during pregnancy, gestational age, maternal weight gain, and infant birthweight. *Addictive Behaviors, 28*(1), 55–66.

Sefcek, J. A., Brumbach, B. H., Vasquez, G., & Miller, G. F. (2007). The evolutionary psychology of human mate choice: How ecology, genes, fertility, and fashion influence mating strategies. *Journal of Psychology & Human Sexuality, 18*(2–3), 125–182.

Segrin, C., Powell, H. L., Givertz, M., & Brackin, A. (2003). Symptoms of depression, relational quality, and loneliness in dating relationships. *Personal Relationships, 10*(1), 25–36.

Seidah, A., & Bouffard, T. (2007). Being proud of oneself as a person or being proud of one's physical appearance: What matters for feeling well in adolescence? *Social Behavior and Personality, 35*(2), 255–268.

Selman, R. L. (1976). Social-cognitive understanding. In T. Lickona (Ed.), *Moral development and behavior: Theory, research, and social issues* (pp. 299–316). New York: Holt, Rinehart & Winston.

Selman, R. L. (1980). *The growth of interpersonal understanding: Developmental and clinical analysis.* New York: Academic Press.

Selman, R. L., & Dray, A. J. (2006). Risk and prevention. In K. A. Renninger, I. E. Sigel, W. Damon, & R. M. Lerner (Eds.), *Handbook of child psychology* (6th ed.), *Volume 4: Child psychology in practice* (pp. 378–419). Hoboken, NJ: Wiley.

Serbin, L. A., Poulin-Dubois, D., Colburne, K. A., Sen, M. G., & Eichstedt, J. A. (2001). Gender stereotyping in infancy: Visual preferences for and knowledge of gender-stereotyped toys in the second year. *International Journal of Behavioral Development, 25*(1), 7–15.

Sexton, S. A. (2008). The influence of social support systems on the degree of PTSD symptoms in the elderly [Abstract]. *Dissertation Abstracts International: Section B: The Sciences and Engineering, 68*(7-B), 4846.

Shafto, M. A., Burke, D. M., Stamatakis, E. A., Tam, P. P., & Tyler, L. K. (2007). On the tip-of-the-tongue: Neural correlates of increased word-finding failures in normal aging. *Journal of Cognitive Neuroscience, 19*(12), 2060–2070.

Shaywitz, B. A., Lyon, G. R., & Shaywitz, S. E. (2006). The role of functional magnetic resonance imaging in understanding reading and dyslexia. *Developmental Neuropsychology, 30*(1), 613–632.

Shaywitz, S. E. (1998). Dyslexia. *New England Journal of Medicine, 338*(5), 307–312.

Shaywitz, S. E., Mody, M., & Shaywitz, B. A. (2006). Neural mechanisms in dyslexia. *Current Directions in Psychological Science, 15*(6), 278–281.

Shear, K., Jin, R., Ruscio, A. M., Walters, E. E., & Kessler, R. C. (2006). Prevalence and correlates of estimated DSM-IV child and adult separation anxiety disorder in the National Comorbidity Survey Replication. *American Journal of Psychiatry, 163*(6), 1074–1083.

Sheeber, L. B., Davis, B., Leve, C., Hops, H., & Tildesley, E. (2007). Adolescents' relationships with their mothers and fathers: Associations with depressive disorder and subdiagnostic symptomatology. *Journal of Abnormal Psychology, 116*(1), 144–154.

Sherwin-White, S. (2006). The social toddler: Promoting positive behaviour. *Infant Observation, 9*(1), 95–97.

Shin, H. B., & Bruno, R. (2003). *Language use and English speaking ability: 2000*. Washington, DC: U.S. Bureau of the Census.

Shiota, M. N., & Levenson, R. W. (2007). Birds of a feather don't always fly farthest. *Psychology and Aging, 22*(4), 666–675.

Shirk, S., Burwell, R., & Harter, S. (2003). Strategies to modify low self-esteem in adolescents. In M. A. Reinecke et al. (Eds.), *Cognitive therapy with children and adolescents: A casebook for clinical practice* (2nd ed., pp. 189–213). New York: Guilford.

Shneidman, E. S. (1977). Aspects of the dying process. *Psychiatric Annals, 17*(8), 391–397.

Shonk, S. M., & Cicchetti, D. (2001). Maltreatment, competency deficits, and risk for academic and behavioral maladjustment. *Developmental Psychology, 37*(1), 3–17.

Shroff, H., et al. (2006). Features associated with excessive exercise in women with eating disorders. *International Journal of Eating Disorders, 39*(6), 454–461.

Shultz, K. S., & Adams, G. A. (Eds.). (2007). *Aging and work in the 21st century*. New York: Erlbaum.

SIDS Network. (2001, May 14). Available at http://www.sids-network.org

Siegel, L. S. (1992). Infant motor, cognitive, and language behaviors as predictors of achievement at school age. In C. Rovee-Collier & L. P. Lipsitt (Eds.), *Advances in infancy research, Volume 7* (pp. 275–298). Norwood, NJ: Ablex.

Siegel-Hinson, R. I., & McKeever, W. F. (2002). Hemispheric specialisation, spatial activity experience, and sex differences on tests of mental rotation ability. *Laterality: Asymmetries of Body, Brain and Cognition, 7*(1), 59–74.

Siegler, R. S., & Alibali, M. W. (2005). *Children's thinking* (4th ed.). Upper Saddle River, NJ: Prentice Hall.

Siegrist, J., Von Dem Knesebeck, O., & Pollack, C. E. (2004). Social productivity and well-being of older people. *Social Theory & Health, 2*(1), 1–17.

Sierra, F. (2006). Is (your cellular response to) stress killing you? *Journals of Gerontology: Series A: Biological Sciences and Medical Sciences, 61A*(6), 557–561.

Signorello, L. B., & McLaughlin, J. K. (2004). Maternal caffeine consumption and spontaneous abortion: A review of the epidemiologic evidence. *Epidemiology, 15*(2), 229–239.

Silbereisen, R. K. (2006). Development and ecological context: History of the psychological science in a personal view and experience—An interview with Urie Bronfenbrenner. *Psychologie in Erziehung und Unterricht, 53*(1), 241–249.

Silventoinen, K., et al. (2007). Genetic and environmental factors in relative weight from birth to age 18: The Swedish young male twins study. *International Journal of Obesity, 31*(4), 615–621.

Silver, R. C., & Wortman, C. B. (2007). The stage theory of grief. *Journal of the American Medical Association, 297*(24), 2692.

Simion, F., Cassia, V. M., Turati, C., & Valenza, E. (2001). The origins of face perception: Specific versus nonspecific mechanisms. *Infant and Child Development, 10*(1–2), 59–65.

Simonelli, A., Monti, F., & Magalotti, D. (2005). The complex phenomenon of failure to thrive: Medical, psychological and relational-affective aspects. *Psicologia Clinica dello Sviluppo, 9*(2), 183–212.

Simonelli, A., Vizziello, G. F., Bighin, M., De Palo, F., & Petech, E. (2007). Transition to triadic relationships between parenthood and dyadic adjustment. *Età Evolutiva, 86*, 92–99.

Simons, T., & O'Connell, M. (2003). *Married-couple and unmarried-partner households: 2000*. Washington, DC: U.S. Census Bureau. Available at http://www.census.gov/prod/2003pubs/censr-5.pdf

Simonton, D. K. (2006a). Creative genius, knowledge, and reason: The lives and works of eminent creators. In J. C. Kaufman & J. Baer (Eds.), *Creativity and reason in cognitive development* (pp. 43–59). New York: Cambridge University Press.

Simonton, D. K. (2006b). Creativity around the world in 80 ways ... but with one destination. In J. C. Kaufman & R. Sternberg (Eds.), *The international handbook of creativity* (pp. 490–496). New York: Cambridge University Press.

Simonton, D. K. (2007). Creative life cycles in literature: Poets versus novelists or conceptualists versus experimentalists? *Psychology of Aesthetics, Creativity, and the Arts, 1*(3), 133–139.

Simpkins, S. D., Fredricks, J. A., Davis-Kean, P. E., & Eccles, J. S. (2006). Healthy mind, healthy habits: The influence of activity involvement in middle childhood. In A. C. Huston & M. N. Ripke (Eds.), *Developmental contexts in middle childhood: Bridges to adolescence and adulthood* (pp. 283–302). Cambridge studies in social and emotional development. New York: Cambridge University Press.

Sims, C. S., Drasgow, F., & Fitzgerald, L. F. (2005). The effects of sexual harassment on turnover in the military. *Journal of Applied Psychology, 90*(6), 1141–1152.

Singer, L. T., et al. (2005). Prenatal cocaine exposure and infant cognition. *Infant Behavior & Development, 28*(4), 431–444.

Sirrs, S. M., et al. (2007). Normal-appearing white matter in patients with phenylketonuria: Water content, myelin water fraction, and metabolite concentrations. *Radiology, 242*(1), 236–243.

Skeels, H. M. (1966). Adult status of children with contrasting early life experiences: A follow-up study. *Monographs of the Society for Research in Child Development, 31*(3, ser. 105).

Skinner, B. F. (1957). *Verbal behavior*. New York: Appleton.

Skoczenski, A. M. (2002). Limitations on visual sensitivity during infancy: Contrast sensitivity, vernier acuity, and orientation processing. In J. W. Fagen & H. Hayne (Eds.), *Progress in infancy research, Volume 2* (pp 169–214). Hillsdale, NJ: Erlbaum.

Slater, A. (2000). Visual perception in the young infant: Early organization and rapid learning. In D. Muir & A. Slater (Eds.), *Infant development: The essential readings* (pp. 216–235). Malden, MA: Blackwell.

Slater, A., Mattock, A., & Brown, E. (1990). Size constancy at birth: Newborn infants' responses to retinal and real size. *Journal of Experimental Child Psychology, 49*(2), 314–322.

Slaughter, V., & Griffiths, M. (2007). Death understanding and fear of death in young children. *Clinical Child Psychology and Psychiatry, 12*(4), 525–535.

Slavin, R. E. (2006). *Educational psychology: Theory and practice* (8th ed.). Boston: Allyn & Bacon.

Sloan, S., Sneddon, H., Stewart, M., & Iwaniec, D. (2006). Breast is best? Reasons why mothers decide to breastfeed or bottlefeed their babies and factors influencing the duration of breast-feeding. *Child Care in Practice, 12*(3), 283–297.

Slobin, D. I. (2001). Form/function relations: How do children find out what they are? In M. Tomasello & E. Bates (Eds.), *Language development: The essential readings* (pp. 267–290). Malden, MA: Blackwell.

Smetana, J. G. (1990). Morality and conduct disorders. In M. Lewis & S. M. Miller (Eds.), *Handbook of developmental psychopathology*. New York: Plenum.

Smetana, J. G. (2005). Adolescent–parent conflict: Resistance and subversion as developmental process. In L. Nucci (Ed), *Conflict, contradiction, and contrarian elements in moral development and education* (pp. 69–91). Hillsdale, NJ: Erlbaum.

Smetana, J. G., Campione-Barr, N., & Metzger, A. (2006). Adolescent development in interpersonal and societal contexts. *Annual Review of Psychology, 57,* 255–284.

Smiley, P. A., & Johnson, R. S. (2006). Self-referring terms, event transitivity and development of self. *Cognitive Development, 21*(3), 266–284.

Smith, C. L., Calkins, S. D., Keane, S. P., Anastopoulos, A. D., & Shelton, T. L. (2004). Predicting stability and change in toddler behavior problems: Contributions of maternal behavior and child gender. *Developmental Psychology, 40*(1), 29–42.

Smith, P. K. (2005). Play: Types and functions in human development. In B. J. Ellis & D. F. Bjorklund (Eds.), *Origins of the social mind: Evolutionary psychology and child development* (pp. 271–291). New York: Guilford.

Smock, P. J. (2000). Annual review of sociology. Cited in Nagourney, E. (2000, February 15). Study finds families bypassing marriage. *New York Times,* p. 8.

Smolka, E., & Eviatar, Z. (2006). Phonological and orthographic visual word recognition in the two cerebral hemispheres: Evidence from Hebrew. *Cognitive Neuropsychology, 23*(6), 972–989.

Smoll, F. L., & Schultz, R. W. (1990). Quantifying gender differences in physical performance: A developmental perspective. *Developmental Psychology, 26*(3), 360–369.

Snarey, J. R. (1994). Cross-cultural universality of social-moral development: A critical review of Kohlbergian research. In B. Puka (Ed.), *New research in moral development* (pp. 268–298). New York: Garland.

Snarey, J. R., & Bell, D. (2003). Distinguishing structural and functional models of human development. *Identity, 3*(3), 221–230.

Snegovskikh, V., Park, J. S., & Norwitz, E. R. (2006). Endocrinology of parturition. *Endocrinology and Metabolism Clinics of North America, 35*(1), 173–191.

Snow, C. (2006). Cross-cutting themes and future research directions. In D. August & T. Shanahan (Eds.), *Developing literacy in second-language learners: Report of the National Literacy Panel on Language-Minority Children and Youth* (pp. 631–651). Hillsdale, NJ: Erlbaum.

Snyder, H. M., & Sickmund, M. (2006). *Juvenile offenders and victims: 2006 national report.* Washington, DC: U.S. Department of Justice, Office of Justice Programs, Office of Juvenile Justice and Delinquency Prevention.

Snyderman, M., & Rothman, S. (1990). *The IQ controversy.* New Brunswick, NJ: Transaction.

Solano, C. H., Batten, P. G., & Parish, E. A. (1982). Loneliness and patterns of self-disclosure. *Jour-nal of Personality and Social Psychology, 43*(3), 524–531.

Soliz, J. (2007). Communicative predictors of a shared family identity: Comparison of grandchildren's perceptions of family-of-origin grandparents and stepgrandparents. *Journal of Family Communication, 7*(3), 177–194.

Solomon, C. G., & Dluhy, R. G. (2003). Rethinking postmenopausal hormone therapy. *New England Journal of Medicine, 348*(7), 579–580.

Sommerfeld, J. (2003, April 3). Study: The pill can avoid periods without "spotting." *Seattle Times.* Available at http://community.seattletimes .nwsource.com/archive/?date=20030403&slug =period03m

Sommers, M. S. (2008). Age-related changes in spoken word recognition. In D. B. Pisoni & R. E. Remez (Eds.), *The handbook of speech perception* (pp. 469–493). Blackwell handbooks in linguistics. Malden, MA: Blackwell Publishing.

Sonnentag, S. (2003). Recovery, work engagement, and proactive behavior. *Journal of Applied Psychology, 88*(3), 518–528.

Sontag, L. W., & Richards, T. W. (1938). Studies in fetal behavior: Fetal heart rate as a behavioral indicator. *Child Development Monographs, 3*(4).

Soons, J. P. M., & Liefbroer, A. C. (2008). Together is better? Effects of relationship status and resources on young adults' well-being. *Journal of Social and Personal Relationships, 25*(4), 603–624.

Sorce, J., Emde, R. N., Campos, J, J., Klinnert, M. D. (2000). Maternal emotional signaling: Its effect on the visual cliff behavior of 1-year-olds. In D. Muir & A. Slater (Eds.), *Infant development: The essential readings* (pp. 282–292). Essential readings in developmental psychology. Malden, MA: Blackwell.

Sousa, L., & Figueiredo, D. (2002). Dependence and independence among old persons. *Reviews in Clinical Gerontology, 12*(3), 269–273.

Soussignan, R., & Schaal, B. (2005). Emotional processes in human newborns: A functionalist perspective. In J. Nadel & D. Muir (Eds.), *Emotional development: Recent research advances* (pp. 127–159). New York: Oxford University Press.

South, S. J., Haynie, D. L., & Bose, S. (2007). Student mobility and school dropout. *Social Science Research, 36*(1), 68–94.

Spelke, E. S., & Owsley, C. (1979). Inter-modal exploration and knowledge in infancy. *Infant Behavior and Development, 2*(1), 13–27.

Spieker, S. J., et al. (2003). Joint influence of child care and infant attachment security for cognitive and language outcomes of low-income toddlers. *Infant Behavior and Development, 26*(3), 326–344.

Spitz, R. A. (1965). *The first year of life: A psychoanalytic study of normal and deviant object relations.* New York: International Universities Press.

Spitzer, R. L., Gibbon, M., Skodol, A. E., Williams, J. B. W., & First, M. B. (2002). *DSM–IV–TR casebook.* Washington, DC: American Psychiatric Press.

Sprecher, S. (1998). Insiders' perspectives on reasons for attraction to a close other. *Social Psychology Quarterly, 61*(4), 287–300.

Sprecher, S., Sullivan, Q., & Hatfield, E., (1994). Mate selection preferences: Gender differences examined in a national sample. *Journal of Personality and Social Psychology, 66*(6), 1074–1080.

Sroufe, L. A. (1998). Cited in S. Blakeslee (1998, August 4). Re-evaluating significance of baby's bond with mother. *New York Times,* pp. F1, F2.

Sroufe, L. A., Waters, E., & Matas, L. (1974). Contextual determinants of infant affectional response. In M. Lewis & L. Rosenblum (Eds.), *The origins of fear* (pp. 49–72). Hoboken, NJ: Wiley.

Staff, J., Mortimer, J. T., & Uggen, C. (2004). Work and leisure in adolescence. In R. M. Lerner & L. Steinberg (Eds.), *Handbook of adolescent psychology* (2nd ed., pp. 429–450). Hoboken, NJ: Wiley.

Stagnitti, K., Unsworth, C., & Rodger, S. (2000). Development of an assessment to identify play behaviours that discriminate between the play of typical preschoolers and preschoolers with pre-academic problems. *Canadian Journal of Occupational Therapy, 67*(5), 291–303.

Stahmer, A. C., Ingersoll, B., & Koegel, R. L. (2004). Inclusive programming for toddlers autism spectrum disorders: Outcomes from the Children's Toddler School. *Journal of Positive Behavior Interventions, 6*(2), 67–82.

Stams, G. J. M., Juffer, F., & van IJzendoorn, M. H. (2002). Maternal sensitivity, infant attachment, and temperament in early childhood predict adjustment in middle childhood: The case of adopted children and their biologically unrelated parents. *Developmental Psychology, 38*(5), 806–821.

Stanford, J. N., & McCabe, M. P. (2005). Sociocultural influences on adolescent boys' body image and body change strategies. *Body Image, 2*(2), 105–113.

Stankoff, B., et al. (2006). Imaging of CNS myelin by positron-emission tomography. *Proceedings of the National Academy of Sciences, 103*(24), 9304–9309.

Stanley, M. A., & Beck, J. G. (2000). Anxiety disorders. *Clinical Psychology Review, 20*(6), 731–754.

Stauffacher, K., & DeHart, G. B. (2006). Crossing social contexts: Relational aggression between siblings and friends during early and middle childhood. *Journal of Applied Developmental Psychology, 27*(3), 228–240.

Stearns, V., Beebe, K. L., Iyengar, M., & Dube, E. (2003). Paroxetine controlled release in the treatment of menopausal hot flashes. *Journal of the American Medical Association, 289*(21), 2827–2834.

Steele, H. (2005a). Editorial. *Attachment & Human Development, 7*(4), 345.

Steele, H. (2005b). Editorial: Romance, marriage, adolescent motherhood, leaving for college, plus shyness and attachment in the preschool years. *Attachment & Human Development, 7*(2), 103–104.

Stein, D. J., Collins, M., Daniels, W., Noakes, T., & Zigmond, M. (2007). Mind and muscle: The cognitive–affective neuroscience of exercise. *CNS Spectrums, 12*(1), 19–22.

Steinberg, L. (1996). *Beyond the classroom: Why school reform has failed and what parents need to do.* New York: Simon & Schuster.

Stemberger, J. P. (2004). Phonological priming and irregular past. *Journal of Memory and Language, 50*(1), 82–95.

Sternberg, R. J. (1986). A triangular theory of love. *Psychological Review, 93*(2), 119–135.

Sternberg, R. J. (2000). In search of the zipperump-a-zoo. *Psychologist, 13*(5), 250–255.

Sternberg, R. J. (2006a). A duplex theory of love. In R. J. Sternberg, & K. Weis (Eds.), *The new psychology of love* (pp. 184–199). New Haven, CT: Yale University Press.

Sternberg, R. J. (2006b). The nature of creativity. *Creativity Research Journal, 18*(1), 87–98.

Sternberg, R. J. (2007). A systems model of leadership: WICS. *American Psychologist, 62*(1), 34–42.

Sternberg, R. J. (2011). The theory of successful intelligence. In R. J. Sternberg & S. B. Kaufman (Eds.). *The Cambridge handbook of intelligence* (pp. 504–527). Cambridge: Cambridge University Press.

Sternberg, R. J., & Williams, W. M. (1997). Does the Graduate Record Examination predict meaningful success in the graduate training of psychologists? *American Psychologist, 52*(6), 630–641.

Stevens, B., et al. (2005). Consistent management of repeated procedural pain with sucrose in preterm neonates: Is it effective and safe for repeated use over time? *Clinical Journal of Pain, 21*(6), 543–548.

Stevenson, H. W., Chen, C., & Lee, S. (1993). Mathematics achievement of Chinese, Japanese, and American children: Ten years later. *Science, 259*(5091), 53–58.

Stevenson, J. (1992). Evidence for a genetic etiology in hyperactivity in children. *Behavior Genetics, 22*(3), 337–344.

Stewart, A. J., Ostrove, J. M., & Helson, R. (2001). Middle aging in women: Patterns of personality change from the 30s to the 50s. *Journal of Adult Development, 8*(1), 23–37.

Stewart, J. Y., & Armet, E. (2000, April 3). Aging in America: Retirees reinvent the concept. *Los Angeles Times.* Available at http://articles .latimes.com/2000/apr/03/news/mn-15453

Stifter, C. A., & Wiggins, C. N. (2004). Assessment of disturbances in emotion regulation and temperament. In R. DelCarmen-Wiggins & A. Carter (Eds.), *Handbook of infant, toddler, and preschool mental health assessment* (pp. 79–103). New York: Oxford University Press.

Stipek, D., & Hakuta, K. (2007). Strategies to ensure that no child starts from behind. In J. L. Aber et al. (Eds.), *Child development and social policy: Knowledge for action* (pp. 129–145). APA Decade of Behavior volumes. Washington, DC: American Psychological Association.

Stipek, D., Recchia, S., & McClintic, S. (1992). Self-evaluation in young children. *Monographs of the Society for Research in Child Development, 57*(1, ser. 226).

Stoel-Gammon, C. (2002). Intervocalic consonants in the speech of typically developing children: Emergence and early use. *Clinical Linguistics and Phonetics, 16*(3), 155–168.

Storch, E. A., et al. (2007). Peer victimization, psychosocial adjustment, and physical activity in overweight and at-risk-for-overweight youth. *Journal of Pediatric Psychology, 32*(1), 80–89.

Stores, G., & Wiggs, L. (Eds.). (2001). *Sleep disturbance in children and adolescents with disorders of development: Its significance and management.* New York: Cambridge University Press.

Strassberg, D. S., & Holty, S. (2003). An experimental study of women's Internet personal ads. *Archives of Sexual Behavior, 32*(3), 253–260.

Stratton, T. D., et al. (2005). Does students' exposure to gender discrimination and sexual harassment in medical school affect specialty choice and residency program selection? *Academic Medicine, 80*(4), 400–408.

Straus, M. A., & Field, C. J. (2003). Psychological aggression by American parents: National data on prevalence, chronicity, and severity. *Journal of Marriage and Family, 65*(4), 795–808.

Strayer, J., & Roberts, W. (2004). Children's anger, emotional expressiveness, and empathy: Relations with parents' empathy, emotional expressiveness, and parenting practices. *Social Development, 13*(2), 229–254.

Streri, A. (2002). Hand preference in 4-month-old infants: Global or local processing of objects in the haptic mode. *Current Psychology Letters: Behaviour, Brain and Cognition, 7*(1), 39–50.

Striegel-Moore, R. H., et al. (2003). Eating disorders in White and Black women. *American Journal of Psychiatry, 160*(7), 1326–1331.

Stright, A. D., Neitzel, C., Sears, K. G., & Hoke-Sinex, L. (2001). Instruction begins in the home: Relations between parental instruction and children's self-regulation in the classroom. *Journal of Educational Psychology, 93*(3), 456–466.

Strock, M. (2004). *Autism spectrum disorders (pervasive developmental disorders).* NIH Publication NIH-04–5511. Bethesda, MD: National Institute of Mental Health, National Institutes of Health, U.S. Department of Health and Human Services. Available at http://www.nimh .nih.gov/publicat/autism.cfm

Strohner, H., & Nelson, K. E. (1974). The young child's development of sentence comprehension: Influence of event probability, nonverbal context, syntactic form, and strategies. *Child Development, 45*(3), 567–576.

Strutt, G. F., Anderson, D. R., & Well, A. D. (1975). A developmental study of the effects of irrelevant information on speeded classification. *Journal of Experimental Child Psychology, 20*(1), 127–135.

Sukhodolsky, D. G., Golub, A., Stone, E. C., & Orban, L. (2005). Dismantling anger control training for children: A randomized pilot study of social problem-solving versus social skills training components. *Behavior Therapy, 36*(1), 15–23.

Sullivan, S. E., Martin, D. F., Carden, W. A., & Mainiero, L. A. (2003). The road less traveled. *Journal of Leadership & Organizational Studies, 10*(2), 34–42.

Sulloway, F. J. (2007). Birth order and intelligence. *Science, 316*(5832), 1711–1712.

Sun, S. S., et al. (2005). Is sexual maturity occurring earlier among U.S. children? *Journal of Adolescent Health, 37*(5), 345–355.

Suomi, S. J., Harlow, H. F., & McKinney, W. T. (1972). Monkey psychiatrists. *American Journal of Psychiatry, 128*(8), 927–932.

Supple, A. J., & Small, S. A. (2006). The influence of parental support, knowledge, and authoritative parenting on Hmong and European American adolescent development. *Journal of Family Issues, 27*(9), 1214–1232.

Sylva, K., et al. (2007). Curricular quality and day-to-day learning activities in pre-school. *International Journal of Early Years Education, 15*(1), 49–65.

Szaflarski, J. P., et al. (2006). A longitudinal functional magnetic resonance imaging study of language development in children 5 to 11 years old. *Annals of Neurology, 59*(5), 796–807.

Takahashi, M., & Sugiyama, M. (2003). Improvement and prevention of misbehavior in a junior high school student: An analysis of behavioral contingency and change of stimulus function in a social setting. *Japanese Journal of Counseling Science, 36*(2), 165–174.

Talbot, L. A., Morrell, C. H., Fleg, J. L., & Metter, E. J. (2007). Changes in leisure time physical activity and risk of all-cause mortality in men and women. *Preventive Medicine: An International Journal Devoted to Practice and Theory, 45*(2–3), 169–176.

Tallandini, M. A., & Valentini, P. (1991). Symbolic prototypes in children's drawings of schools. *Journal of Genetic Psychology, 152*(2), 179–190.

Tamis-LeMonda, C. S., Cristofaro, T. N., Rodriguez, E. T., & Bornstein, M. H. (2006). Early language development: Social influences in the first years of life. In L. Balter & C. S. Tamis-LeMonda (Eds.), *Child psychology: A handbook of contemporary issues* (2nd ed., pp. 79–108). New York: Psychology Press.

Tan, R. S. (2002). Managing the andropause in aging men. *Clinical Geriatrics 7*(8), 63–67.

Tan, R. S., & Culberson, J. W. (2003). An integrative review on current evidence of testosterone replacement therapy for the andropause. *Maturitas, 45*(1), 15–27.

Tanner, J. L. (2006). Recentering during emerging adulthood: A critical turning point in life span human development. In J. J. Arnett & J. L. Tanner (Eds.), *Emerging adults in America: Coming of age in the 21st century* (pp. 21–55). Washington, DC: American Psychological Association.

Tanner, J. M. (1989). *Fetus into man: Physical growth from conception to maturity.* Cambridge, MA: Harvard University Press.

Tanner, J. M. (1991a). Adolescent growth spurt, I. In R. M. Lerner, A. C. Petersen, & J. Brooks-Gunn (Eds.), *Encyclopedia of adolescence* (pp. 277–303). New York: Garland.

Tanner, J. M. (1991b). Secular trend in age of menarche. In R. M. Lerner, A. C. Petersen, & J. Brooks-Gunn (Eds.), *Encyclopedia of adolescence* (pp. 637–641). New York: Garland.

Tapper, K., & Boulton, M. J. (2004). Sex differences in levels of physical, verbal, and indirect aggression amongst primary school children and their associations with beliefs about aggression. *Aggressive Behavior, 30*(2), 123–145.

Tashiro, T., Frazier, P., & Berman, M. (2006). Stress-related growth following divorce and relationship dissolution. In M. A. Fine & J. H. Harvey (Eds.), *Handbook of divorce and relationship dissolution* (pp. 361–384). Hillsdale, NJ: Erlbaum.

Task Force on SIDS (Sudden Infant Death Syndrome). (2005). The changing concept of Sudden Infant Death Syndrome: Diagnostic coding shifts, controversies regarding the sleeping environment, and new variables to consider in reducing risk. *Pediatrics, 116*(5), 1245–1255.

Tassi, F., Schneider, B. H., & Richard, J. F. (2001). Competitive behavior at school in relation to social competence and incompetence in middle childhood. *Revue Internationale de Psychologie Sociale, 14*(2), 165–184.

Taylor, C. (2007, March 26). To the editor: Day care and a child's behavior. *New York Times.* Available at http://www.nytimes.com

Taylor, M. (1999). *Imaginary companions and the children who create them.* London: Oxford University Press.

Taylor, M., & Hort, B. (1990). Can children be trained in making the distinction between appearance and reality? *Cognitive Development, 5*(1), 89–99.

Taylor, M. F., Clark, N., & Newton, E. (2008). Counselling Australian baby boomers. *British Journal of Guidance & Counselling, 36*(2), 189–204.

Tehrani, J. A., & Mednick, S. A. (2000). Genetic factors and criminal behavior. *Federal Probation, 64*(2), 24–27.

Tenenbaum, H. R., et al. (2010). "It's a boy because he's painting a picture." Age differences in children's conventional and unconventional gender schemas. *British Journal of Psychology, 101*(1), 137–154.

Terracciano, A., Costa, P. T., Jr., & McCrae, R. R. (2006). Personality plasticity after age 30. *Personality and Social Psychology Bulletin, 32*(8), 999–1009.

Thapar, A., Langley, K., Asherson, P., & Gill, M. (2007). Gene-environment interplay in attention-deficit hyperactivity disorder and the importance of a developmental perspective. *British Journal of Psychiatry, 190*(1), 1–3.

Thiele, D. M., & Whelan, T. A. (2006). The nature and dimensions of the grandparent role. *Marriage & Family Review, 40*(1), 93–108.

Thomas, A., & Chess, S. (1989). Temperament and personality. In G. A. Kohnstamm, J. E. Bates, & M. K. Rothbart (Eds.), *Temperament in childhood* (pp. 187–247). Chichester, England: Wiley.

Thompson, A. M., Baxter-Jones, A. D. G., Mirwald, R. L., & Bailey, D. A. (2003). Comparison of physical activity in male and female children: Does maturation matter? *Medicine and Science in Sports and Exercise, 35*(10), 1684–1690.

Thompson, I. M., et al. (2005). Erectile dysfunction and subsequent cardiovascular disease. *Journal of the American Medical Association, 294*(23), 2996–3002.

Thompson, R. A. (2006). The development of the person: Social understanding, relationships, conscience, self. In N. Eisenberg, W. Damon, & R. M. Lerner (Eds.), *Handbook of child psychology* (6th ed.), *Volume 3: Social, emotional, and personality development* (pp. 24–98). Hoboken, NJ: Wiley.

Thompson, R. A., Easterbrooks, M. A., & Padilla-Walker, L. M. (2003). Social and emotional development in infancy. In R. M. Lerner et al. (Eds.), *Handbook of psychology: Developmental psychology* (pp. 25–106). Hoboken, NJ: Wiley.

Thompson, R. A., & Limber, S. P. (1990). "Social anxiety" in infancy: Stranger and separation reactions. In H. Leitenberg (Ed.), *Handbook of social and evaluation anxiety* (pp. 85–137). New York: Plenum.

Thompson, R. A., & Meyer, S. (2007). Socialization of emotion regulation in the family. In J. J. Gross (Ed.), *Handbook of emotion regulation* (pp. 249–268). New York: Guilford.

Thornton, L. M., Andersen, B. L., Crespin, T. R., & Carson, W. E. (2007). Individual trajectories in stress covary with immunity during recovery from cancer diagnosis and treatments. *Brain, Behavior, and Immunity, 21*(2), 185–194.

Thurstone, L. L. (1938). Primary mental abilities. *Psychometric Monographs, 1.*

Timmerman, L. M. (2006). Family care versus day care: Effects on children. In B. M. Gayle et al. (Eds.), *Classroom communication and instructional processes: Advances through meta-analysis* (pp. 245–260). Hillsdale, NJ: Erlbaum.

Tobbell, J. (2003). Students' experiences of the transition from primary to secondary school. *Educational and Child Psychology, 20*(4), 4–14.

Togsverd, M., et al. (2008). Association of a dopa-mine beta-hydroxylase gene variant with depression in elderly women possibly reflecting noradrenergic dysfunction. *Journal of Affective Disorders, 106*(1–2), 169–172.

Tomiyama, T., et al. (2008). A new amyloid β variant favoring oligomerization in Alzheimer's-type dementia. *Annals of Neurology, 63*(3), 377–387.

Ton, M., & Hansen, J. C. (2001). Using a person-environment fit framework to predict satisfaction and motivation in work and marital roles. *Journal of Career Assessment, 9*(4), 315–331.

Towse, J. (2003). Lifespan development of human memory. *Quarterly Journal of Experimental Psychology: Human Experimental Psychology, 56A*(7), 1244–1246.

Towse, J., & Cowan, N. (2005). Working memory and its relevance for cognitive development. In W. Schneider, R. Schumann-Hengsteler, & B. Sodian (Eds.), *Young children's cognitive development: Interrelationships among executive functioning, working memory, verbal ability, and theory of mind* (pp. 9–37). Hillsdale, NJ: Erlbaum.

Trehub, S. E., & Hannon, E. E. (2006). Infant music perception: Domain-general or domain-specific mechanisms? *Cognition, 100*(1), 73–99.

Troxel, W. M., & Matthews, K. A. (2004). What are the costs of marital conflict and dissolution to children's physical health? *Clinical Child and Family Psychology Review, 7*(1), 29–57.

Trudel, G.A., Goldfarb, M.A., Préville, M., Boyer, R. (2007, August). The relationship between marital functioning and psychological distress in the elderly. Presentation to the meeting of the American Psychological Association, San Francisco, CA.

Tsuneishi, S., & Casaer, P. (2000). Effects of preterm extrauterine visual experience on the development of the human visual system: A flash VEP study. *Developmental Medicine and Child Neurology, 42*(10), 663–668.

Turkheimer, E. (1991). Individual and group differences in adoption studies of IQ. *Psychological Bulletin, 110*(3), 392–405.

Twist, M. (2005). Review of *Relationship therapy with same-sex couples*. *Journal of Marital & Family Therapy, 31*(4), 413–417.

U.S. Bureau of the Census. (2004). *Statistical abstract of the United States* (124th ed.). Washington, DC: U.S. Government Printing Office.

U.S. Bureau of the Census. (2006). *Statistical abstract of the United States* (126th ed.). Washington, DC: U.S. Government Printing Office.

U.S. Bureau of the Census. (2007). *Statistical abstract of the United States* (127th ed.). Washington, DC: U.S. Government Printing Office.

U.S. Bureau of the Census. (2008). *Statistical abstract of the United States* (128th ed.). Washington, DC: U.S. Government Printing Office.

U.S. Bureau of the Census. (2010, November 10). U.S. Census Bureau reports men and women wait longer to marry [Press release]. Available at http://www.census.gov/newsroom/releases/archives/families_households/cb10-174.html

U.S. Bureau of the Census. (2011, January 20). *The 2011 statistical abstract*, Population: Marital status and living arrangements. Available at http://www.census.gov/compendia/statab/cats/population/marital_status_and_living_arrangements.html

U.S. Department of Agriculture. (2005). *Adequate nutrients within calorie needs. Dietary guidelines for Americans*. Washington, DC: Author. Available at http://www.health.gov/dietaryguidelines/dga2005/document/html/chapter2.htm

U.S. Department of Health and Human Services. (2004a). *Bone health and osteoporosis: A report of the Surgeon General*. Available at http://www.surgeongeneral.gov/library/bonehealth

U.S. Department of Health and Human Services. (2004b). *Child abuse and neglect fatalities: Statistics and interventions—Child maltreatment 2002*. Available at http://dc.mandatedreporter.org/pages/docs/Child-Abuse-and-Neglect-Fatalities.pdf

U.S. Department of Justice. (Accessed 2006, February 15). Criminal victimization in the United States. Statistical Tables, 2003. Office of Justice Programs, Bureau of Justice Statistics. Available at http://www.ojp.usdoj.gov/bjs/abstract/cvus/rape_sexual_assault.htm

Umek, L. M., Podlesek, A., & Fekonja, U. (2005). Assessing the home literacy environment: Relationships to child language comprehension and expression. *European Journal of Psychological Assessment, 21*(4), 271–281.

UNAIDS. (2006). *Report on the global AIDS epidemic: Executive summary*. Geneva, Switzerland: Joint United Nations Programme on HIV/AIDS (UNAIDS). Available at http://data.unaids.org/pub/GlobalReport/2006/2006_gr-executivesummary_en.pdf

UNICEF. (2006). *The state of the world's children: 2007*. New York: United Nations.

United Nations Statistics Division. (2004, March). *UNESCO: World and Regional Trends*, Table 8. Available at http://unstats.un.org/unsd/mdg/Resources/Attach/Products/Progress2005/goal_8.pdf

Uylings, H. B. M. (2006). Development of the human cortex and the concept of "critical" or "sensitive" periods. *Language Learning, 56*(Supp. 1), 59–90.

van de Beek, C., van Goozen, S. H. M., Buitelaar, J. K., & Cohen-Kettenis, P. T. (2009). Prenatal sex hormones (maternal and amniotic fluid) and gender-related play behavior in 13-month-old infants. *Archives of Sexual Behavior, 38*(1), 6–15.

Vandello, J. A., & Cohen, D. (2003). Male honor and female fidelity: Implicit cultural scripts that perpetuate domestic violence. *Journal of Personality & Social Psychology, 84*(5), 997–1010.

van den Dries, L., Juffer, F., van IJzendoorn, M. H., & Bakermans-Kranenburg, M. J. (2009). Fostering security? A meta-analysis of attachment in adopted children. *Children and Youth Services Review, 31*(3), 410–421.

van der Sluis, S., Vinkhuyzen, A. A. E., Boomsma, D. I., & Posthuma, D. (2010). Sex differences in adults' motivation to achieve. *Intelligence, 38*(4), 433–446.

Vander Ven, T., & Cullen, F. T. (2004). The impact of maternal employment on serious youth crime: Does the quality of working conditions matter? *Crime & Delinquency, 50*(2), 272–291.

Van Hiel, A., Mervielde, I., & De Fruyt, F. (2006). Stagnation and generativity: Structure, validity, and differential relationships with adaptive and maladaptive personality. *Journal of Personality, 74*(2), 543–574.

van IJzendoorn, M. H., & Hubbard, F. O. A. (2000). Are infant crying and maternal responsiveness during the first year related to infant–mother attachment at 15 months? *Attachment and Human Development, 2*(3), 371–391.

van IJzendoorn, M. H., & Juffer, F. (2006). The Emanuel Miller Memorial Lecture 2006: Adoption as intervention. Meta-analytic evidence for massive catch-up and plasticity in physical, socio-emotional, and cognitive development. *Journal of Child Psychology and Psychiatry, 47*(12), 1228–1245.

van Rijn, S., Swaab, H., Aleman, A., & Kahn, R. S. (2006). X chromosomal effects on social cognitive processing and emotion regulation: A study with Klinefelter men (47,XXY). *Schizophrenia Research, 84*(2–3), 194–203.

van Solinge, H., & Henkens, K. (2005). Couples' adjustment to retirement: A multi-actor panel study. *Journals of Gerontology: Series B: Psychological Sciences and Social Sciences, 60B*(1), S11–S20.

Vares, T., Potts, A., Gavey, N., & Grace, V. M. (2007). Reconceptualizing cultural narratives of mature women's sexuality in the Viagra era. *Journal of Aging Studies, 21*(2), 153–164.

Vartanian, O., Martindale, C., & Kwiatkowski, J. (2003). Creativity and inductive reasoning: The relationship between divergent thinking and performance on Wason's 2-4-6 task. *Quarterly Journal of Experimental Psychology: Human Experimental Psychology, 56A*(4), 641–655.

Vastag, B. (2003). Many questions, few answers for testosterone replacement therapy. *Journal of the American Medical Association, 289*(8), 971–972.

Vellas, B., Gillette-Guyonnet, S., & Andrieu, S. (2008). Memory health clinics: A first step to prevention. *Alzheimer's & Dementia, 4*(1, Supp. 1), S144–S149.

Vellutino, F. R., Fletcher, J. M., Snowling, M. J., & Scanlon, D. M. (2004). Specific reading disability (dyslexia): What have we learned in the past four decades? *Journal of Child Psychology and Psychiatry, 45*(1), 2–40.

Veríssimo, M., & Salvaterra, F. (2006). Maternal secure-base scripts and children's attachment security in an adopted sample. *Attachment & Human Development, 8*(3), 261–273.

Vermeiren, R., Bogaerts, J., Ruchkin, V., Deboutte, D., & Schwab-Stone, M. (2004). Subtypes of self-esteem and self-concept in adolescent violent and property offenders. *Journal of Child Psychology and Psychiatry, 45*(2), 405–411.

Villani, S. (2001). Impact of media on children and adolescents: A 10-year review of the research. *Journal of the American Academy of Child & Adolescent Psychiatry, 40*(4), 392–401.

Virji-Babul, N., Kerns, K., Zhou, E., Kapur, A., & Shiffrar, M. (2006). Perceptual-motor deficits in children with Down syndrome: Implications for intervention. *Down Syndrome: Research & Practice, 10*(2), 74–82.

Visscher, W. A., Feder, M., Burns, A. M., Brady, T. M., & Bray, R. M. (2003). The impact of smoking and other substance use by urban women on the birthweight of their infants. *Substance Use and Misuse, 38*(8), 1063–1093.

Vitiello, B. (Ed.). (2006). Guest editorial: Selective serotonin reuptake inhibitors (SSRIs) in children and adolescents. *Journal of Child and Adolescent Psychopharmacology, 16*(1–2), 7–9.

Volkova, A., Trehub, S. E., & Schellenberg, E. G. (2006). Infants' memory for musical performances. *Developmental Science, 9*(6), 583–589.

Volling, B. L. (2003). Sibling relationships. In M. H. Bornstein et al. (Eds.), *Well-being: Positive development across the life course* (pp. 205–220). Hillsdale, NJ: Erlbaum.

Volterra, M. C., Caselli, O., Capirci, E., & Pizzuto, E. (2004). Gesture and the emergence and development of language. In M. Tomasello & D. I. Slobin (Eds.), *Beyond nature–nurture* (pp. 3–40). Hillsdale, NJ. Erlbaum.

Volz, J. (2000). Successful aging: The second 50. *Monitor on Psychology, 31*(1), 24–38.

VonDras, D. D., Powless, D. R., Olson, A. K., Wheeler, D., & Snudden, A. L. (2005). Differential effects of everyday stress on the episodic memory test performances of young, mid-life, and older adults. *Aging & Mental Health, 9*(1), 60–70.

von Gontard, A. (2006). Elimination disorders: Enuresis and encopresis. In C. Gillberg, R. Harrington, & H.-C.Steinhausen (Eds.), *A clinician's handbook of child and adolescent psychiatry* (pp. 625–654). New York: Cambridge University Press.

Vorauer, J. D., Cameron, J. J., Holmes, J. G., & Pearce, D. G. (2003). Invisible overtures: Fears of rejection and the signal amplification bias. *Journal of Personality & Social Psychology, 84*(4), 793–812.

Vukman, K. B. (2005). Developmental differences in metacognition and their connections with cognitive development in adulthood. *Journal of Adult Development, 12*(4), 211–221.

Vygotsky, L. S. (1962). *Thought and language.* Cambridge, MA: MIT Press.

Vygotsky, L. S. (1978). *Mind in society: The development of higher psychological processes.* Cambridge, MA: Harvard University Press.

Wachs, T. D. (2006). The nature, etiology, and consequences of individual differences in temperament. In L. Balter & C. S. Tamis-LeMonda (Eds.), *Child psychology: A handbook of contemporary issues* (2nd ed., pp. 27–52). New York: Psychology Press.

Wade, T. D., Bulik, C. M., Neale, M., & Kendler, K. S. (2000). Anorexia nervosa and major depression: Shared genetic and environmental risk factors. *American Journal of Psychiatry, 157*(3), 469–471.

Wahler, R. G., Herring, M., & Edwards, M. (2001). Coregulation of balance between children's prosocial approaches and acts of compliance: A pathway to mother–child cooperation? *Journal of Clinical Child Psychology, 30*(4), 473–478.

Wainright, J. L., Russell, S. T., & Patterson, C. J. (2004). Psychosocial adjustment, school outcomes, and romantic relationships of adolescents with same-sex parents. *Child Development, 75*(6), 1886–1898.

Wald, J., & Losen, D. J. (2007). Out of sight: The journey through the school-to-prison pipeline. In S. Books (Ed.), *Invisible children in the society and its schools* (3rd ed., pp. 23–37). Hillsdale, NJ: Erlbaum.

Walitza, S., et al. (2006). Genetic and neuro-imaging studies in attention deficit hyper-activity disorder. *Nervenheilkunde: Zeitschrift für interdisziplinaere Fortbildung, 25*(6), 421–429.

Walkup, J. T., et al. (2001). Fluvoxamine for the treatment of anxiety disorders in children and adolescents. *New England Journal of Medicine, 344*(17), 1279–1285.

Wall, A. (2007). Review of *Integrating gender and culture in parenting. Family Journal, 15*(2), 196–197.

Wall, G., & Arnold, S. (2007). How involved is involved fathering? *Gender & Society, 21*(4), 508–527.

Wallerstein, J., Lewis, J., Blakeslee, S., Hetherington, E. M., & Kelly, J. (2005). Issue 17: Is divorce always detrimental to children? In R. P. Halgin (Ed.), *Taking sides: Clashing views on controversial issues in abnormal psychology* (3rd ed., pp. 298–321). New York: McGraw-Hill.

Walsh, B. T., et al. (2006). Fluoxetine after weight restoration in anorexia nervosa: A randomized controlled trial. *Journal of the American Medical Association, 295*(22), 2605–2612.

Walter, J. L., & LaFreniere, P. J. (2000). A naturalistic study of affective expression, social competence, and sociometric status in preschoolers. *Early Education and Development, 11*(1), 109–122.

Walther, F. J., den Ouden, A. L., & Verloove-Vanhorick, S. P. (2000). Looking back in time: Outcome of a national cohort of very preterm infants born in the Netherlands in 1983. *Early Human Development, 59*(3), 175–191.

Wang, L. (2005). Correlations between self-esteem and life satisfaction in elementary school students. *Chinese Mental Health Journal, 19*(11), 745–749.

Wang, S.-H., Baillargeon, R., & Paterson, S. (2005). Detecting continuity violations in infancy: A new account and new evidence from covering and tube events. *Cognition, 95*(2), 129–173.

Watson, J. B. (1924). *Behaviorism.* New York: Norton.

Waxman, S. R., & Lidz, J. L. (2006). Early word learning. In D. Kuhn, R. S. Siegler, W. Damon, & R. M. Lerner (Eds.), *Handbook of child psy-*

chology (6th ed.), *Volume 2: Cognition, perception, and language* (pp. 299–335). Hoboken, NJ: Wiley.

Wechsler, D. (1975). Intelligence defined and undefined: A relativistic appraisal. *American Psychologist, 30*(2), 135–139.

Weckerly, J., Wulfeck, B., & Reilly, J. (2004). The development of morphosyntactic ability in atypical populations: The acquisition of tag questions in children with early focal lesions and children with specific-language impairment. *Brain and Language, 88*(2), 190–201.

Weinberg, R. A. (2004). The infant and the family in the twenty-first century. *Journal of the American Academy of Child & Adolescent Psychiatry, 43*(1), 115–116.

Weinshenker, M. N. (2006). Adolescents' expectations about mothers' employment: Life course patterns and parental influence. *Sex Roles, 54*(11–12), 845–857.

Weisler, R. H., & Sussman, N. (2007). Treatment of attention-deficit/hyperactivity disorder. *Primary Psychiatry, 14*(1), 39–42.

Welk, G. J., Wood, K., & Morss, G. (2003). Parental influences on physical activity in children. *Pediatric Exercise Science, 15*(1), 19–33.

Weller, E. B., & Weller, R. A. (1991). Mood disorders. In M. Lewis (Ed.), *Child and adolescent psychiatry: A comprehensive textbook* (pp. 646–664). Baltimore: Williams & Wilkins.

Wellman, H. M., Fang, F., Liu, D., Zhu, L., & Liu, G. (2006). Scaling of theory-of-mind understandings in Chinese children. *Psychological Science, 17*(12), 1075–1081.

Weng, X., Odouli, R., & Li, D.-K. (2008, January 25). Maternal caffeine consumption during pregnancy and the risk of miscarriage: a prospective cohort study. *American Journal of Obstetrics and Gynecology, 198*(3), 279, 279.e1–279.e8.

Wenger, G. C., Dykstra, P. A., Melkas, T., & Knipscheer, K. C. P. M. (2007). Social embeddedness and late-life parenthood: Community activity, close ties, and support. *Journal of Family Issues, 28*(11), 1419–1456.

Wenger, G. C., & Jerrome, D. (1999). Change and stability in confidant relationships. *Journal of Aging Studies, 13*(3), 269–294.

Wennergren, A.-C., & Rönnerman, K. (2006). The relation between tools used in action research and the zone of proximal development. *Educational Action Research, 14*(4), 547–568.

Wentworth, N., Benson, J. B., & Haith, M. M. (2000). The development of infants' reaches for stationary and moving targets. *Child Development, 71*(3), 576–601.

Wentzel, K. R., Barry, C. M., & Caldwell, K. A. (2004). Friendships in middle school: Influences on motivation and school adjustment. *Journal of Educational Psychology, 96*(2), 195–203.

Werker, J. F. (1989). Becoming a native listener. *American Scientist, 77*(1), 54–59.

Werker, J. F., et al. (2007). Infant-directed speech supports phonetic category learning in English and Japanese. *Cognition, 103*(1), 147–162.

Werker, J. F., & Tees, R. C. (2005). Speech perception as a window for understanding plasticity and commitment in language systems of the brain. *Developmental Psychobiology, 46*(3), 233–234.

Werner, E. E. (1988). A cross-cultural perspective on infancy. *Journal of Cross-Cultural Psychology, 19*(1), 96–113.

Werner, L. A., & Bernstein, I. L. (2001). Development of the auditory, gustatory, olfactory, and somatosensory systems. In E. B. Goldstein (Ed.), *Blackwell handbook of perception* (pp. 669–708). Handbook of experimental psychology series. Boston: Blackwell.

Wethington, E., Kessler, R. C., & Pixley, J. E. (2004). Turning points in adulthood. In O. G. Brim, C. D. Ryff, & R. C. Kessler (Eds.), *How healthy are we?: A national study of well-being at midlife* (pp. 586–613). The John D. and Catherine T. MacArthur Foundation series on mental health and development. Studies on successful midlife development. Chicago: University of Chicago Press.

Whitehead, B. D., & Popenoe, D. (2006). *The state of our unions: The social health of marriage in America.* New Brunswick, NJ: Rutgers University.

Whitehouse, E. M. (2006). Poverty. In G. G. Bear & K. M. Minke (Eds.), *Children's needs III: Development, prevention, and intervention* (pp. 835–845). Washington, DC: National Association of School Psychologists.

Wickwire, E. M., Jr., Roland, M. M. S., Elkin, T. D., & Schumacher, J. A. (2008). Sleep disorders. In M. Hersen & D. Michel (Eds.), *Handbook of psychological assessment, case conceptualization, and treatment, Volume 2: Children and adolescents* (pp. 622–651). Hoboken, NJ: Wiley.

Wierzalis, E. A., Barret, B., Pope, M., & Rankins, M. (2006). Gay men and aging: Sex and intimacy. In D. Kimmel, T. Rose, & S. David (Eds.), *Lesbian, gay, bisexual, and transgender aging: Research and clinical perspectives* (pp. 91–109). New York: Columbia University Press.

Willett, W. C. (2005). Diet and cancer. *Journal of the American Medical Association, 293*(2), 233–234.

Willetts, M. C. (2006). Union quality comparisons between long-term heterosexual cohabitation and legal marriage. *Journal of Family Issues, 27*(1), 110–127.

Williams, M. S. (2004). The psychology of eating. *Psychology and Health, 19*(4), 541–542.

Willis, S. L., & Schaie, K. W. (2006). Cognitive functioning in the baby boomers: Longitudinal and cohort effects. In S. K. Whitbourne & S. L. Willis (Eds.), *The baby boomers grow up: Contemporary perspectives on midlife* (pp. 205–234). Hillsdale, NJ: Erlbaum.

Wilson, E. O. (2004). *On Human Nature.* Cambridge, MA: Harvard University Press.

Wilson, H. W., & Widom, C. S. (2010). The role of youth problem behaviors in the path from child abuse and neglect to prostitution: A prospective examination. *Journal of Research on Adolescence, 20*(1), 210–236.

Wilson, J. M. B., Tripp, D. A., & Boland, F. J. (2005). The relative contributions of waist-to-hip ratio and body mass to judgments of attractiveness. *Sexualities, Evolution & Gender, 7*(3), 245–267.

Wilson, P. (2004). A preliminary investigation of an early intervention program: Examining the intervention effectiveness of the Bracken Concept Development Program and the Bracken Basic Concept Scale–Revised with Head Start students. *Psychology in the Schools, 41*(3), 301–311.

Windsor, T. D., Anstey, K. J., Butterworth, P., & Rodgers, B. (2008). Behavioral approach and behavioral inhibition as moderators of the association between negative life events and perceived control in midlife. *Personality and Individual Differences, 44*(5), 1080–1092.

Winner, E. (2000). The origins and ends of giftedness. *American Psychologist, 55*(1), 159–169.

Winzelberg, A. J., et al. (2000). Effectiveness of an Internet-based program for reducing risk factors for eating disorders. *Journal of Consulting and Clinical Psychology, 68*(2), 346–350.

Witherington, D. C., Campos, J. J., Anderson, D. I., Lejeune, L., & Seah, E. (2005). Avoidance of heights on the visual cliff in newly walking infants. *Infancy, 7*(3), 285–298.

Witkowska, E., & Gådin, K. G. (2005). What female high school students regard as harassment. *International Journal of Adolescent Medicine and Health, 17*(4), 391–406.

Wocadlo, C., & Rieger, I. (2006). Educational and therapeutic resource dependency at early school-age in children who were born very preterm. *Early Human Development, 82*(1), 29–37.

Wodrich, D. L. (2006). Sex chromosome anomalies. In L. Phelps (Ed.), *Chronic health-related dis-*

orders in children: Collaborative medical and psychoeducational interventions (pp. 253–270). Washington, DC: American Psychological Association.

Wojslawowicz Bowker, J. C., Rubin, K. H., Burgess, K. B., Booth-Laforce, C., & Rose-Krasnor, L. (2006). Behavioral characteristics associated with stable and fluid best friendship patterns in middle childhood. *Merrill-Palmer Quarterly, 52*(4), 671–693.

Wolfenden, L. E., & Holt, N. L. (2005). Talent development in elite junior tennis: Perceptions of players, parents, and coaches. *Journal of Applied Sport Psychology, 17*(2), 108–126.

Woolfolk, A. E. (2010). *Educational psychology.* Upper Saddle River, NJ: Pearson.

Worell, J., & Goodheart, C. D. (Eds.). (2006). *Handbook of girls' and women's psychological health: Gender and well-being across the lifespan.* New York: Oxford University Press.

Worrell, F. C. (1997). An exploratory factor analysis of Harter's Self-Perception Profile for Adolescents with academically talented students. *Educational and Psychological Measurement, 57*(6), 1016–1024.

Wozniak, J. R., & Lim, K. O. (2006). Advances in white matter imaging: A review of in vivo magnetic resonance methodologies and their applicability to the study of development and aging. *Neuroscience & Biobehavioral Reviews, 30*(6), 762–774.

Wright, C., & Birks, E. (2000). Risk factors for failure to thrive: A population-based survey. *Child: Care, Health, and Development, 26*(1), 5–16.

Wright, D. W., & Young, R. (1998). The effects of family structure and maternal employment on the development of gender-related attitudes among men and women. *Journal of Family Issues, 19*(3), 300–314.

Wulff, K., & Siegmund, R. (2001). Circadian and ultradian time patterns in human behaviour. Part 1: Activity monitoring of families from prepartum to postpartum. *Biological Rhythm Research, 31*(5), 581–602.

Xie, H. L., Yan, B., Signe M., Hutchins, B. C., & Cairns, B. D. (2006). What makes a girl (or a boy)

popular (or unpopular)? African American Children's perceptions and developmental differences. *Developmental Psychology, 42*(4), 599–612.

Xu, J. Q., Kochanek, K.D., Murphy, S.L., & Tejada-Vera, B. (2010). Deaths: Final data for 2007. *National Vital Statistics Reports, 58*(19). Available at http://www.cdc.gov/nchs/data/nvsr/nvsr58/nvsr58_19.pdf

Yaffe, K., Haan, M., Byers, A., Tangen, C., & Kuller, L. (2000). Estrogen use, APOE, and cognitive decline: Evidence of gene-environment interaction. *Neurology, 54*(10), 1949–1953.

Yamada, H., et al. (2000). A milestone for normal development of the infantile brain detected by functional MRI. *Neurology, 55*(2), 218–223.

Yamasue, H., et al. (2008). Sex-linked neuroanatomical basis of human altruistic cooperativeness. *Cerebral Cortex, 18*(10), 2331–2340.

Yarrow, L. J., & Goodwin, M. S. (1973). The immediate impact of separation: Reactions of infants to a change in mother figures. In L. J. Stone, H. T. Smith, & L. B. Murphy (Eds.), *The competent infant: Research and commentary* (pp. 1032–1040). New York: Basic Books.

Yarrow, L. J., Goodwin, M. S., Manheimer, H., & Milowe, I. D. (1971, March). *Infant experiences and cognitive and personality development at ten years.* Paper presented at the meeting of the American Orthopsychiatric Association, Washington, DC.

Yonelinas, A. P. (2002). The nature of recollection and familiarity: A review of 30 years of research. *Journal of Memory and Language, 46*(3), 441–517.

Yost, M. R., & Zurbriggen, E. L. (2006). Gender differences in the enactment of sociosexuality. *Journal of Sex Research, 43*(2), 163–173.

Youniss, J., & Haynie, D. L. (1992). Friendship in adolescence. *Developmental and Behavioral Pediatrics, 13*(1), 59–66.

Yurgelun-Todd, D. A. (2007). Emotional and cognitive changes during adolescence. *Current Opinion in Neurobiology, 17*(2), 251–257.

Zacks, R. T., Hasher, L., & Li, K. Z. H. (2000). Human memory. In F. I. M. Craik & T. A. Salthouse (Eds.), *Age-related changes in*

memory: A cognitive neuroscience perspective. *The handbook of aging and cognition* (2nd ed., pp. 293–357). Hillsdale, NJ: Erlbaum.

Zaidi, A. U., & Shyraydi, M. (2002). Perceptions of arranged marriages by young Pakistani Muslim women living in a Western society. *Journal of Comparative Family Studies, 33*(4), 495–514.

Zajonc, R. B. (2001). The family dynamics of intellectual development. *American Psychologist, 56*(6–7), 490–496.

Zan, B., & Hildebrandt, C. (2003). First graders' interpersonal understanding during cooperative and competitive games. *Early Education and Development, 14*(4), 397–410.

Zarbatany, L., McDougall, P., & Hymel, S. (2000). Gender-differentiated experience in the peer culture: Links to intimacy in preadolescence. *Social Development, 9*(1), 62–79.

Zeifman, D. M. (2004). Acoustic features of infant crying related to intended caregiving intervention. *Infant and Child Development, 13*(2), 111–122.

Zeintl, M., Kliegel, M., & Hofer, S. M. (2007). The role of processing resources in age-related prospective and retrospective memory within old age. *Psychology and Aging, 22*(4), 826–834.

Zelazo, P. R. (1998). McGraw and the development of unaided walking. *Developmental Review, 18*(4), 449–471.

Zheng, S., & Colombo, J. (1989). Sibling configuration and gender differences in preschool social participation. *Journal of Genetic Psychology, 150*(1), 45–50.

Zimmerman, B. J. (2000). Self-efficacy: An essential motive to learn. *Contemporary Educational Psychology, 25*(1), 82–91.

Zosuls, K. M., et al. (2009). The acquisition of gender labels in infancy: Implications for gender-typed play. *Developmental Psychology, 45*(3), 688–701.

Zweigenhaft, R. L., & Von Ammon, J. (2000). Birth order and civil disobedience: A test of Sulloway's "born to rebel" hypothesis. *Journal of Social Psychology, 140*(5), 624–627

Autism
   causes of, 170–171
   features of, 169–170
   risks by paternal age, 79
   treatment of, 171
   twins and, 56–57
Autism spectrum disorders (ASDs), 168–171
Autobiographical memory, 218
Autonomous morality, 280
Autosomes, 44, 45
Axon, 124

Babbling, 150
Babinski reflex, 108
Barbiturates, 413
Bargaining, 590
Bayley Scales of Infant Development, 147
Beauty, 441–442
Bed-wetting, 204–205
Behaviorism, 6, 13–16
Benign, 478
Bereavement, grief and, 604–607
Bias, 302
"Big five" personality traits, 507
Bilingualism, 290, 291
Biological perspective, 18–20
Biological theory, 18–20
Birth order, 233–234
Bisexuals, 382, 519, 564, 565
Blastocyst, 64, 65
Blood tests, 55
Blood-sugar tolerance, 476
Body fat, 474
Body imgae, 352
Bon Festival, 606
Bonding, 104, 105–106
Bone density, 475, 533–534
Brain
   development of, 125–128
   development in adolescence, 352–353
   development in early childhood, 193–194
   development in infancy, 127–128
   growth spurts of, 127
   in late adulthood, 550
   nature and nurture in development, 128
   plasticity of, 194
   role of prenatal brain organization in gender-
      typed behavior, 250–251
   structures of, 126
   structures involved in language, 158
Brain death, 588, 589
Braxton-Hicks contractions, 80, 81
Brazelton Neonatal Behavioral Assessment Scale,
   106, 107, 147
Breast cancer, 477
Breast-feeding, 123–124
Breech (bottom-first) presentaion, 86, 87
Broca's aphasia, 158

Bulimia nervosa, 356–357
Bullying, 329–330

CA. *See* Chronological age
Caffeine, 77
Calorie restriction, 539–540, 557
Canalization, 122
Cancer, 478–480
   deaths due to, 478
   in late adulthood, 542, 543, 600
   lifetime risk of being diagnosed with, 479
   role of exercise in reducing risk of, 272
Cannabis. *See* Marijuana
Cardiovascular fitness, 409
Career development
   for adolescents, 369–371
   choosing a career and stages of, 433–434
   developmental tasks in beginning a career,
      435
   Holland's career typology, 369, 370
Carrier, 48
Case study, 26, 27
Cat in the Hat, The (Seuss), 69
Cataracts, 532, 533, 542
Categorical self, 242
Causality, 209
Celibacy, 450, 451
Cellular-clock theory, 538
Cellular-damage theories of aging, 538, 539
Centers for Disease Control and Prevention
      (CDC), 91, 410
Centration, 210
Cephalocaudal, 66
Cephalocaudal development, 118–119
Cerebellum, 126
Cerebrum, 126
Cervical cancer, 479
Cervix, 80, 81
Cesarean section (C-section), 86–87
Child abuse, 167–168
Child development
   pioneers in, 5
   study of, 4–5
Child mortality, 90–91
Child rearing, 227–231
   effects of situation and child on parenting
      styles, 231
   enforcing restrictions, 228–229
   grandparenting role in, 517–519
   parenting styles, 229–230
Childbirth, 82–93
   last month of pregnancy and, 83
   maternal and child mortality, 90–91
   methods of, 85–87
   problems, 87–90
   stages of, 82–85
Childhood disintegrative disorder, 169
Children's Television Act, 214

Chorionic villus sampling (CVS), 52, 53
Chromosomes, 43, 45
Chronological age (CA), 296, 297
Chronosystem, 22, 23
Churchgoing, 569
Chuseok, 606
Cialis, 489
Cigarettes, 77–78
Civil unions, 456–457
Class inclusion, 210, 211–212, 279
Classical conditioning, 12, 13, 14
Clear-cut-attachment phase, 162
Climacteric, 484, 485
Cliques, 380
Clitoris, 349
Cocaine, 76
Cognitive development
   in adolescence, 358–371
   cognition and the sociocultural setting, 427
   college and, 430–432
   in early childhood, 206–225
   factors in, 212–215
   information-processing approach to, 144–146
   Labouvie-Vief's theory of pragmatic thought,
      428
   language development and, 149–159, 224–225
   measuring in infants, 146–149
   in middle childhood, 268–275
   Perry's theory of epistemic cognition,
      427–428
   Piaget's stages of, 18, 19
   Piaget's theory of, 140–144
   play and, 235–236
   postformal thinking, 428–429
   preoperational stage of, 207–212
   Vygotsky's sociocultural theory of, 23–24
Cognitive theory, 16–18
Cognitive–affective complexity, 428
Cognitive-developmental theory
   evaluation of Piaget's theory, 144
   of gender-typing, 253–254
   of personality development in middle
      childhood, 309
   Piaget's theory of, 17–18, 19
Cohabitation, 451–454, 570–571
Cohort effect, 30, 31, 491–492
College, 375, 430–432, 551
Colorectal cancer, 477, 479
Commitment, 373
Conception, 58–59, 65
Concrete operational stage, 276–279
Concrete operations, 276
   applications of Piaget's theory to education,
      279
   class inclusion, 279
   conservation, 277
   transitivity, 278–279
Conduct disorders, 312, 313–314

Levitra, 489
Life crisis, 8, 9
Life expectancy
    at birth by region, country, and gender, 531
    defined, 530
    gender differences in, 531–532
Life reviews, 560
Life span, 530
Life structure, 438, 439
Life-events approach, 505–506
Life-span perspective, 6
Literacy, development in middle childhood, 290
Living will, 596–597
Local anesthetic, 84, 85
Locomotion, 130–132
Loneliness, 448–449
Longevity, 530
Longitudinal research, 30
Long-term memory, 287–288, 550–552
Los Angeles Times, 579
Love
    as appraisal of arousal, 445
    jealousy and, 447–448
    Sternberg's triangular theory of, 446, 447
Low-birth-weight infants, 88–90
Lung capacity, 474

MA. *See* Mental age
Macrosystem, 20, 21
Malaria, 201
Males
    accidental injuries and, 202
    adolescent growth spurt, 345–348
    adolescent physical development, 348–349
    adults' behavior toward infant, 180–181
    attention deficit/hyperactivity disorder and,
        273
    autism and, 169
    average newborn weight, 69
    behavior of infant, 180
    causes of death, 543
    child sexual abuse, 167
    childhood depression, 314
    conduct disorders and, 313
    development of gender roles, 245
    dyslexia and, 274
    early versus late maturers, 351
    friendships, 326–327, 380
    gender differences, 245–248, 271–272
    gender differences in cognitive abilities,
        361–363
    gender differences in moral development,
        365
    gross motor skills in early childhood, 195
    growth patterns in early childhood, 193
    growth patterns in infancy, 120
    growth patterns in middle childhood,
        268–269

life expectancy of, 531–532
masturbation, 383
mathematical ability, 313, 363
mean level of self-esteem, 563–564
memory functioning in early childhood, 219
peer acceptance and rejection, 326
prevalence of adolescent employment, 371
primary sex characteristics, 345
rough-and-tumble play and, 196
self-esteem in, 312, 376
sex-linked chromosomal abnormalities, 49–50
sexual behavior in adolescence, 383–385
sperm cells and sex chromosomes, 60
theories of gender-typing, 248–257
types of play and, 236
Malignant, 478
Malnutrition, 71, 201
Mammary glands, 349
Marijuana (Cannabis), 76
Marriage
    arranged, 456
    in early adulthood, 454–459
    equality and civil unions, 456–457
    marital satisfaction, 455, 458–459
    married percentage of U.S. persons, 455
    purpose of, 455
    role in late adulthood, 569–570
    selection of mate, 457
    types of, 455–457
Masturbation, 382
Maternal depression, 103–105
Maternal employment, 322
Maternal mortality, 90–91
Mathematical ability, 313, 363
Maturation, 6, 7
Mature learners, 498–499
Mean length of utterance (MLU), 152–153
Measles, 201
Media, aggression and influences of, 240–242
Medicaid, 540
Medicare, 540
Medulla, 116–117
Meiosis, 44
Memory
    associative, 549–550
    for college grades, 1 to 50 years later, 551
    development in early childhood, 217–220
    development of recall, 288–289
    factors influencing, 218–219
    in late adulthood, 547–553
    long-term, 287–288, 550–552
    in middle adulthood, 496–497
    prospective, 552–553
    role in information-processing approach,
        144–145
    short-term, 286–287
    strategies, 220
    structure of, 286

Menarche, 348, 349–350
Menopause, 484, 485
Menstruation, 349–351
Mental age (MA), 296
Mercy killing, 593
Mesoderm, 66
Mesosystem, 20, 21
Metabolism, 475
Metacognition, 288, 289
Metamemory, 288, 289
Metastases, 478
Methadone, 75
Microsystem, 20, 21
Middle adulthood
    aerobic capacity, 476
    blood-sugar tolerance, 476
    bone density, 475
    cancer and, 478–480
    causes of death, 477
    changes in intellectual abilities, 490–494
    cognitive development, 490–499
    creativity and learning, 497–499
    deaths due to cancer and heart disease in, 478
    defined, 472
    entering midlife, 504–505
    evolving parent–child relationships, 514–515
    friendships, 520–521
    grandparenting, 515–521
    Havighurst's developmental tasks of, 500–501
    health, 476–481
    heart disease and, 480–481
    immune system, 481–483
    information processing, 495–497
    lean-body mass and body fat, 474
    life-events approach, 505–506
    lung capacity, 474
    metabolism, 475
    middle-aged children and aging parents,
        519–520
    muscle strength, 474
    personality development, 500–513
    physical development, 472–489
    reaction time, 474
    sensory functioning, 473
    sexuality, 483–489
    siblings, 520
    skin and hair, 473
    social development, 514–521
    stability and change in, 507–509
    theories of development in, 501–503
    work in, 510–513
Middle childhood
    behavioral problems that arise, 313–319
    children with disabilities, 272–275
    cognitive development, 276–291
    concrete operational stage, 276–279
    creativity and intellectual development,
        305–306

Middle childhood *(Continued)*
  development of intelligence and creativity, 292–307
  development of the self-concept in, 311–313
  differences in intellectual development, 303–305
  effects of divorce during, 324–325
  exercise and fitness, 272
  fine motor skills, 271
  gender differences in, 271–272
  gross motor skills, 271
  growth patterns, 268–271
  language development and literacy, 289–291
  moral development, 280–284
  motor development, 271–272
  nutrition and growth, 269
  overweight in children, 269–271
  patterns of intellectual development, 302–303
  peer relationships, 326–327
  personality development, 308–319
  physical development, 268–275
  role of family in, 321–323
  school, 328–333
  social development, 320–333
Middle-aged children, aging parents and, 519–520
Midlife crisis, 502, 503
Midlife transition, 502, 503
Midwife, 84, 85
Milwaukee Project, 214
Mind, theory of, 215–217
Mirror neurons, 146
Mirror technique, 178
Miscarriage, 52, 53
Mitosis, 44
Modeling, 230
Models, 154
Monogamy, 454
Monozygotic (MZ) twins, 46
Moral behavior, 365–366
Moral development, 280–284
  in adolescence, 363–366
  age and type of, 365
  evaluation of Kohlberg's theory on, 366
  gender differences in, 365
  Kohlberg's theory of, 281–284
  moral behavior and moral reasoning, 365–366
  Piaget's theory of, 280–281
Moral realism, 280
Moral reasoning, 365–366
Moratorium, 372, 374, 399
Moro reflex, 108
Morphemes, 152
Motility, 61
Motor development
  control of hands, 129
  in early childhood, 194–199
  in infancy, 128–132

lifting and holding torso and head, 129
  in middle childhood, 271–272
Mourning, 604
Multidirectionality, 490
Multifactorial problems, 48, 50
Multiple intelligences, 294–296
Multiple sclerosis, 124, 125
Muscle strength, 474
Muscular dystrophy, 52
Mutations, 44
Mutism, 169
Myelin sheaths, 124, 125
Myelination, 124, 125
MZ twins. *See* Monozygotic twins

Narcotics, 75
National Hospice and Palliative Care Organization (NHPCO), 591
Natural childbirth, 86
Naturalistic observation, 26, 27
Nature and nurture issue, 24
  perceptual development, 139
  role in language development, 154–157
Negative correlation, 26, 27
Negative reinforcers, 14, 15
Neglect, 167–168
Neonates. *See also* Infancy; Infants
  characteristics of, 106–112
  classical conditioning of, 112
  defined, 86
  operant conditioning of, 112
Nerves, 124
Nervous system, development of, 124–125
Neural tube, 66
Neurons, 124, 125
Neurotransmitters, 124
Newborns. *See* Neonates
NHPCO. *See* National Hospice and Palliative Care Organization
Nightmares, 203
Nocturnal emissions, 348
Nocturnal erections, 536
Non-rapid-eye-movement (non-REM) sleep, 112, 113–114
Non-REM sleep. *See* Non-rapid-eye-movement sleep
Nonsocial play, 236
Normal aging, 540
Nursing homes, 568
Nurture and nature issue, 24
  perceptual development, 139
  role in language development, 154–157
Nutrition
  in adolescence, 354
  guidelines for infants, 122–124
  in middle childhood, 269
  patterns of eating in early childhood, 200
  prenatal development and, 71

Obesity, 411
Object permanence, 142–144
Objective morality, 280
Observational learning, 240–241
Oedipus complex, 252–253
Operant conditioning, 12, 13
Operations, 207
Oral rehydration therapy, 201
Osteoarthritis, 542, 543
Osteoporosis, 354, 485–486, 532, 533–534, 545
Ova, 59, 409
Ovarian cycle, 65
Overextension, 152
Overregularization, 220, 221–223
Overweight, 411
  causes of, 270–271
  in children, 269–271
  children in America, 269–270
Ovulation, 46
Oxygen deprivation, 87
Oxytocin, 80, 81

Pacifier, 114, 115
Palliative care, 591
Panic disorder, 566
Parent–child relationships, 321, 514–515
Parenthood, 459–461
  in dual-earner families, 460–461
  role overload and, 460
  single, 461
Parents
  child rearing, 227–231
  effects of situation and child on parenting styles, 231
  enforcing restrictions, 228–229
  influences on adolescent sexual behavior, 385
  lesbian and gay, 322
  parenting styles in adolescence, 378
  parenting styles in early childhood, 229–230
  preterm newborn babies and, 89–90
  prosocial behavior and, 238
  relationships with adolescents, 377–378
  as role models for activity, 196
Parten's types of play, 236, 237
Passages (Sheehy), 504
Passive euthanasia, 596
Passive sentences, 223
Pathological aging, 540
Peer groups, 380
Peer influence, 381
Peer relationships
  in adolescence, 378–381
  influences on adolescent sexual behavior, 385
  in middle childhood, 326–327
Pelvic inflammatory disease (PID), 62
Perception
  active–passive controversy in perceptual development, 138–139

development in infancy, 132–139
development of object permanence, 142–144
fetal, 69
hearing, 110, 136–137
nature and nurture issue in perceptual
development, 139
smell, 110–111
taste, 111
touch, 111, 138
vision, 109, 132–136
Perceptual constancy, 135–136
Perceptual development
active–passive controversy in, 138–139
nature and nurture in, 139
Perimenopause, 484, 485
Peripheral vision, 133
Permissive–indulgent parents, 230
Personal fable, 360–361
Personality development
"big five" personality traits, 507
in early childhood, 242–243
in middle childhood, 308–319
personality themes among college-educated
women, 508, 509
shifts in, 508
theories of, 308–310
Person(s) of the Opposite Sex Sharing Living
Quarters (POSSLQ), 452
Perspective-taking skill levels, 310
Perspective-taking skills, 238
Petting, 383
Phenotypes, 56
Phenylketonuria (PKU), 50, 51
Phobias, 316, 317
Phobic disorder, 566
Phonetic method, 290, 291
Phonological processing, 275
Physical activity
in early adulthood, 412
in early childhood, 196
Physical development
in early childhood, 192–205
in infancy, 118–122
in middle childhood, 268–275
Physician-assisted suicide, 594, 595
PID. See Pelvic inflammatory disease
Pincer grasp, 128
Pitch, 110
PKU. See Phenylketonuria
Placenta, 64, 65, 68
Plaque, 480, 557
Plasticity, 194, 490, 491
Play
cognitive development and, 235–236
gender differences in, 246–247
kinds of, 235
Parten's types of, 236, 237
symbolic, 207–208, 235

PMDD. See Premenstrual dysphoric disorder
PMS. See Premenstrual syndrome
Pneumonia, 201
Polyandry, 456
Polygamy, 454
Polygenic, 43
Polygyny, 454
Positive correlation, 26, 27
Positive reinforcers, 14, 15
Possibilities, age of, 399
POSSLQ. See Person(s) of the Opposite Sex
Sharing Living Quarters
Postconventional level, 284, 362, 363–365
Postformal thinking, 428–429
Postpartum depression, 104–105
Postpartum period, 102
PPD. See Postpartum depression
Practical problem solving, 497
Pragmatic thought, 428
Pragmatics, 222, 223–224
Precausal, 208, 209
Preconventional level, 282
Preeclampsia, 73
Prelinguistic vocalizations, 148, 149
Premature babies, 73
Premenstrual dysphoric disorder (PMDD),
420, 421
Premenstrual syndrome (PMS), 420, 421
Prenatal, 52, 53
Prenatal development, 58–81
critical periods in, 71–72
drugs use by parents and, 74–78
embryonic stage, 66–68
environmental influences on, 70–78
fetal stage, 68–70
germinal stage, 64–66
nutrition and, 71
parents' age and, 78–79
Rh incompatibility, 74
sexually transmitted infections and,
72–73
teratogens and health problems of the
mother, 71
Prenatal testing, 52–55
Preoperational stage, 207–212
Prepared childbirth, 86
Presbycusis, 532, 533
Presbyopia, 472, 473
Pretend play, 207–208
Preterm infants
intervention programs, 90
low-birth-weight infants and, 88–90
risks associated with, 88
signs of, 89
treating, 89
Primary circular reactions, 140, 141
Primary mental abilities, 293
Primary sex characteristics, 344, 345

Problem solving, 553
Procedural memory, 496
Progesterone, 351
Progestin, 74, 75
Programmed theories of aging, 537–538
Prosocial behavior, 236–238
Prospective memory, 547, 552–553
Prostaglandins, 80, 81, 420
Prostate cancer, 477, 479
Proximodistal, 66
Proximodistal development, 118, 119
Psychoanalytic theory, 7–10, 11–12
Psychodynamic theory
of gender-typing, 252–253
of personality development in middle
childhood, 308–309
Psycholinguistic theory, 156, 157
Psychological development, in late adulthood,
562–567
Psychological moratorium, 372, 399
Psychosexual development
comparison of psychosocial development
theory and, 11–12
defined, 6
Freud's theory, 7–9
Psychosocial development
comparison of psychosexual development
and, 11–12
defined, 8
Erikson's theory, 9–10, 502–503, 559
Peck's developmental tasks, 559–560
Puberty, 344, 345–352, 384–385
Punishment, 14, 15
Pygmalion effect, 330, 331

Qing Ming Festival, 606
Questions, 223

Random assignment, 29
Rape, 422–424
Rapid-eye-movement (REM) sleep, 112, 113–114,
203
Reaction time, 270, 271, 474
Reading
children with Down syndrome and, 304
learning disorders and, 274–275
methods of teaching, 290–291
self-esteem and, 312
skills development in middle childhood, 290,
291
Recall memory, 288–289
Receptive vocabulary, 150
Recessive traits, 47–48
Reciprocity, 444, 445
Referential language style, 150, 151
Reflexes, 107–109
Regression, 232, 233
Rehearsal, 220

Rehearsing, 286, 287
Reinforcement, 12, 13, 230
Rejecting–neglecting parents, 230
Relativistic thinking, 428
Religion, 568–569, 595
Remarriage, 570–571
REM sleep. *See* Rapid-eye-movement sleep
Research methods, 26–33
   case studies, 27
   correlation, 27–28
   cross-sectional research, 30–31
   cross-sequential research, 31–32
   ethical considerations, 32–33
   example of cross-sequential research, 32
   experiment, 28–29
   gathering information, 26–27
   longitudinal research, 30
   naturalistic-observation studies, 27
Respiratory distress syndrome, 88, 89
Retirement
   adjustment to, 575–576
   factor analysis of leisure activities of retirees, 577
   leisure activities and, 576–577
   planning, 574–575
Retrospective memory, 547, 552
Rett's disorder, 169
Rh incompatibility, 74
Rhesus monkeys, 166, 540
Rheumatoid arthritis, 543, 544
Right-brained, 194
Ritalin, 274
Romantic love, 444, 445, 446
Romantic relationships, 380
Rooting reflex, 107
Rote rehearsal, 496
Rough-and-tumble play, 196
Rubella, 73

SAD. *See* Separation anxiety disorder
Same-sex marriage, 456–457
Sandwich generation, 520
SBIS. *See* Stanford-Binet Intelligence Scales
Scaffolding, 24, 212
Schemes, 16, 17
School. *See also* Education
   adolescent in, 366–368
   bullying, 329–330
   dropouts, 367, 368
   entry into, 328–329
   environment, 331
   teachers, 330–333
School phobia, 318
School refusal, 318–319
Scribbles, 197
Scripts, 218
Seasons, 439, 503

Seattle Longitudinal Study, 491
Secondary circular reactions, 140, 141
Secondary sex characteristics, 345
Secular trend, 346, 347–348
Selective attention, 284–285
Selective optimization with compensation, 578
Self-concept
   development in adolescence, 375–376
   development in middle childhood, 311
   in early childhood, 242
   in infancy, 176–178
   psychoanalytic views of, 177
Self-esteem
   development in adolescence, 376
   development in middle childhood, 312
   in late adulthood, 562–564
   mean level as a function of age, 563
Self-focus, 397
Self-fulfilling prophecy, 330, 331
Semen, 348
Sensitive period, 158–159
Sensorimotor stage
   defined, 140
   development of object permanence, 142–144
   substages of, 141–142
Sensory functioning
   in late adulthood, 533
   in middle adulthood, 473
Sensory memory, 284, 285–286
Sentence development, 152–154
Separation anxiety disorder (SAD), 316, 317
Separation and individuation, 437–438
Separation–individuation process, 176, 177
Serial monogamy, 450, 451
Seriation, 278
Serotonin, 316
Sesame Street, 215
Sex chromosomes, 44, 45
Sexism, 332–333
Sex-linked chromosomal abnormalities, 48, 49–50
Sex-linked genetic abnormalities, 52
Sexual differentiation, 67–68
Sexual dysfunctions, 487–489
Sexual harassment, 332, 424–425
Sexuality
   in adolescence, 382–387
   adolescent male–female sexual behavior, 383–385
   in early adulthood, 417–425
   frequency of sex by age, 417
   frequency of sex in the past 12 months according to age, 484
   gender differences in sex hormones and fertility, 486
   gender identity, 382–383

hormone replacement therapy, 486
   in late adulthood, 535–537
   masturbation, 383
   for men in late adulthood, 536–537
   menopause, perimenopause, and climacteric, 485–486
   in middle adulthood, 483–489
   patterns of sexual activity in late adulthood, 537
   rape, 422–424
   sexual dysfunctions, 487–489
   sexual orientation, 417–419
   sexually transmitted infections, 419–420, 422–423
   teenage pregnancy, 385–387
   for women in late adulthood, 536
Sexually transmitted infections (STIs), 72–73, 419–420, 422
Shaping, 154, 155
Short-term memory, 286–287
Siblings, 232–233, 520, 572–573
Sickle-cell anemia, 50, 51
SIDS. *See* Sudden infant death syndrome
Sight vocabulary, 290, 291
Single life, 450–451, 572
Single parenthood, 461
Sleep
   in adolescence, 355
   disorders, 203–204
   in early childhood, 202–204
   in infancy, 112–114
   in late adulthood, 534–535
Sleep apnea, 534
Sleep terrors, 202, 203
Sleepwalking, 203–204
Small for gestational age, 88
Smell, 110–111
Smoking. *See* Cigarettes
Social cognition, 309
Social cognitive theory
   defined, 16–17
   of gender-typing, 254–256
   of personality development in middle childhood, 308–309
Social deprivation, 165–167
Social development
   in late adulthood, 558–573
   in middle adulthood, 514–521
   in middle childhood, 320–333
Social play, 236
Social referencing, 174
Social smile, 164
Sociocultural perspective, 23–24
Sociocultural theory, 23–24
Socioemotional selectivity theory, 560, 561–562
Soiling, 205

Wear-and-tear theory, 538, 539
Wechsler scales of intelligence, 299–301
Wernicke's aphasia, 158
Whole brain death, 588, 589
Whole-object assumption, 220, 221
Widowhood, 571–572
Wisdom, 555
Word fluency, 492

Word-recognition method, 290
Work
    adolescents and, 371
    career change in middle adulthood, 511
    job satisfaction, 510–511
    in middle adulthood, 510–513
    unemployment, 511–513
Working memory, 286

XXX syndrome, 50
XYY sex chromosomal structure, 50

Zone of proximal development, 22, 23, 212

Diversity Index

Ethnicity and Race, Religion, Disability, Language, and World Cultures